THE CONDUCT OF JUST AND LIMITED WAR

THE CONDUCT OF JUST AND LIMITED WAR

WILLIAM V. O'BRIEN

PRAEGER

PRAEGER SPECIAL STUDIES • PRAEGER SCIENTIFIC

Library of Congress Cataloging in Publication Data

O'Brien, William Vincent.
    The conduct of just and limited war.

    1. War. 2. Just war doctrine. 3. Limited
war. I. Title.
U21.2.O25   172',42   81-11883
ISBN 0-03-059346-8   AACR2

Published in 1981 by Praeger Publishers
CBS Educational and Professional Publishing
A Division of CBS, Inc.
521 Fifth Avenue, New York, New York 10175 U.S.A.

© 1981 by Praeger Publishers

123456789   145   987654321

Printed in the United States of America

This book is dedicated to

my wife

Madge L. O'Brien

PREFACE

The initial research and writing for this book was accomplished during a sabbatical leave from Georgetown University, 1977-78. During this period I was Senior Fellow in Law, Morality, and War at Georgetown's Center for Strategic and International Studies (CSIS). I am grateful to David M. Abshire, chairman of CSIS, for his indispensable support and encouragement. I likewise recall with appreciation the collegial contributions to my work of the CSIS scholars and staff. Special thanks are due to Walter Laqueur, Jon Vondracek, and Jean Newsom for making possible the publication of a brief monograph entitled U.S. Military Intervention: Law and Morality, Washington Papers no. 68 (Beverly Hills, Calif.: Sage, 1979), which explores some of the central themes of this book.

During my residence at CSIS I conducted two sessions in which experts in the fields of law, morality, and military science reviewed the early chapters of this book. I acknowledge the comments and criticisms of this group, which included Prof. James T. Johnson, chairman of the Department of Religion at Rutgers University; Dr. Leroy Walters, director, Prof. James Childress, and Joseph P. Kennedy, Sr., professor of Christian Ethics, of the Kennedy Institute of Ethics; Prof. R. Bruce Douglass and Rev. James V. Schall, S.J., both of Georgetown's Department of Government; Robert Gessert, General Research Corporation; Rev. J. Bryan Hehir, United States Catholic Conference; and Waldemar Solf, chief of the International Law Branch, Office of the Judge Advocate General, Department of the Army. Professor Johnson led the initial discussion with a comprehensive critique, and I have had the benefit of his comments and criticisms throughout the period in which the book was completed.

Rev. J. Donald Freeze, S.J., executive vice-president for Academic Affairs and Provost, Georgetown University, helped me to complete the work by authorizing a lightened teaching assignment and providing support for secretarial assistance with the manuscript. The chairman of the Government Department, Karl Cerny, gave me every consideration and encouragement during the entire period. My colleagues in the Department of Government assisted me with their knowledge, advice, and interest. I have particularly profited from the assistance of Bruce Douglass and Father Schall, whose contributions continued after the CSIS sessions, as well as from the help of John Bailey and Stephen Gibert.

Professor Gibert added a significant dimension to my work by making possible the discussion of critical issues of the law of war and limited war in the weekend seminars he and I conducted for students in the Georgetown master's program in National Security Studies. Professor Gibert organized and now directs this program, which provides an opportunity to debate strategic and normative defense issues with professional men and women from the military services and the civilian agencies dealing with national security matters. Participants in the program provide an ideal source of realistic assessment of the just- and limited-war theories advanced in this book. My research was also enhanced by contributions of members of my Law of War seminars in the National Security Studies program.

Throughout the years in which I have been working on this book, I have had the good fortune to discuss issues relating to the Yom Kippur War of 1973 and the continuing problems of military intervention and possible conflict in the Middle East with visiting Israeli professors in the Department of Government. I thank Moshe Ma'oz, Oded Eran, Yaacov Ro'i, Michael Yizhar, Aaron Klieman, and Eytan Gilboa for their views on these issues.

In the summer of 1979, under a grant from the National Endowment for the Humanities, Prof. Guenter Lewy and I conducted a six-week institute at the University of Massachusetts-Amherst on the teaching of morality and war in college courses. Twenty professors, selected from institutions of all sizes and kinds from across the country, participated. They represented a wide spectrum of perspectives on politics, war, law, and morality and vigorously debated the central themes developed in this book as they were advanced in lectures and discussions. Suffice it to say that I am acutely aware that the views expressed in the institute and repeated in this book are both disputed and supported by knowledgeable and thoughtful scholars. Professor Lewy's advice and example as a scholar have sustained me throughout the writing of the book.

At a time when the positive international law of war is undergoing a revival in international conferences and in the armed services of the United States, I have been extremely fortunate in having the continuing assistance of the experts in the International Law Branch of the Office of the Judge Advocate General, Department of the Army. I have already mentioned Waldemar Solf's participation in the CSIS study group. However, his guidance and informed criticism of my work go back over many years and have been indispensable. I must thank him also for permitting me to read the advance manuscript of his forthcoming work (with M. Bothe and K. J. Partsch), New Rules for Victims of Armed Conflict: Commentary to the Additional Protocols to the Geneva Conventions (Leiden: Sijthoff, forthcoming). Wally Solf's successor, Hays Parks, has been equally helpful. Both men are conspicuous for their dedication to the task of developing the law of war in the context of realistic military policies as well as for

their technical legal expertise and diplomatic skill. While he was an
Army Judge Advocate General officer, Capt. Edward R. Cummings
also contributed to my understanding of recent developments in the
law of war. Mention must also be made of the influence of Col. James
Miles and Maj. Burrus Carnahan, whose participation in the Georgetown National Security Studies weekend seminars and personal assistance gave me a better understanding of the views of the United States
Air Force on the laws of war generally and of the new Air Force
pamphlet 110-31 in particular.

I am grateful to Maj. Gen. Robert L. Schweitzer, then director
of the Strategy, Plans, and Policy Directorate of the United States
Army staff, and his associates for reviewing and commenting on the
manuscript. General Schweitzer is now on the staff of the National
Security Council where his strategic vision and profound understanding
of the moral dilemmas of war should ensure his contribution to the
kind of enlightened national security policies discussed in Chapter 13.

This book has been written in a period when the intense passions
of the Vietnam era have subsided enough so that recognition can be
given to the basic fact of life that war is still with us as a human
problem that cannot be exorcised by moral condemnations or avoided
by wishful thinking. There is a renewed willingness to debate the
legitimacy and necessity of armed defense of fundamental rights.
Since September 1980, the initiative of Bishop John J. O'Connor,
vicar general of the Military Vicariate for the U.S. Armed Forces,
in organizing study groups to review the relevance of traditional just-
war doctrine to modern war and debates over military service and
national security policies has contributed importantly to the beginnings
of long overdue studies and discussions in which the author is privileged to participate.

A further manifestation of the renaissance in just-war/limited-
war thinking has been the recent scholarship of the English historian
Geoffrey Best. I was able to confirm many aspects of my understanding of the historical evolution of the modern law of war from Professor Best's presentations during his residence at the Woodrow Wilson
Center of the Smithsonian Institution in 1979 and from his book, Humanity in Warfare, which was the product of his research while in
Washington. Much of the discussion in my book of the policy processes that led to the Royal Air Force/United States Air Force bombing policies in World War II reflects the treatment of the subject in
Professor Best's work.

This book has greatly profited from the contributions of my
students, both in the regular undergraduate and graduate programs
at Georgetown and in the National Security Studies program already
mentioned. The contributions range from thoughtful and informative
term papers to class and seminar discussions to the collection of

elusive pieces of information and documentation. Those who have so contributed are too numerous to mention, but I should particularly like to acknowledge the insights and assistance of Lt. Col. George Jurkovitch, Lt. Col. Robert Linhard, Joshua Muravchick, Lt. Col. Ed Murphy, Capt. Robert Palmer, Hayden Peake, Sriral Perera, and Susan Shekmar. Many of my former students have also contributed to my work. I especially appreciated the help of Richard Parrino and Dr. Gary Wasserman.

As always, Joseph Jeffs and his staff at the Lauinger Library at Georgetown provided the best professional support for my research efforts.

When my friends, colleagues, and students read this book, they will recognize the places where their information and advice has been put to good use. They will also have no difficulty in finding the places where, having considered their views, I have persevered in positions different from those they recommended. I trust that they will grant me the presumption of having taken these positions with—to use a just-war term—right intention. If anything is needed in the perennial debates over just and limited war it is that spirit of charity that is the essence of just-war right intention.

CONTENTS

Page

PREFACE   vii

Chapter

1   THE PERENNIAL REQUIREMENT OF JUST AND
    LIMITED WAR   1

PART I

JUST WAR

2   <u>JUS AD BELLUM</u>: PERMISSIBLE RECOURSE TO
    WAR   13

3   <u>JUS IN BELLO</u>: THE JUST CONDUCT OF WAR   37

4   JUST WAR APPLIED: THE UNITED STATES IN
    WORLD WAR II AND KOREA   71

5   JUST WAR APPLIED: THE UNITED STATES IN
    VIETNAM   91

6   CRITICAL ISSUES OF JUST WAR: NUCLEAR DE-
    TERRENCE AND WAR AND CONVENTIONAL WAR   127

7   CRITICAL ISSUES OF JUST WAR: THE <u>JUS AD
    BELLUM</u> OF REVOLUTIONARY/COUNTERINSUR-
    GENCY WAR   154

8   CRITICAL ISSUES OF JUST WAR: THE <u>JUS IN
    BELLO</u> OF REVOLUTIONARY/COUNTERINSUR-
    GENCY WAR   175

PART II

LIMITED WAR

9   THE MEANING OF LIMITED WAR   207

Chapter   Page

10   KOREA: THE PRECEDENTAL LIMITED WAR   238

11   VIETNAM: LIMITED WAR ON TRIAL   257

12   THE YOM KIPPUR WAR: AN EXEMPLARY LIMITED
      WAR   277

PART III

IMPLEMENTATION OF JUST–WAR
AND LIMITED–WAR GUIDELINES

13   MODES AND CHANNELS FOR THE LIMITATION OF
      WAR   301

14   THE CONDUCT OF JUST AND LIMITED WAR:
      STATE OF THE QUESTION   329

NOTES   361

BIBLIOGRAPHY   447

INDEX
                                                        481

ABOUT THE AUTHOR   497

1

THE PERENNIAL REQUIREMENT OF JUST AND LIMITED WAR

It is almost 60 years since the post-World War I generation embarked on the great experiment of changing the fundamental nature of the international system. The war system was to be replaced with a new world order in which international law and organization ensured the peaceful settlements of international disputes and collective security enforcement action squelched the presumably rare challenges to the world public order. The wars, near wars, bitter disputes, and ever increasing defense preparations of nations since the days of the League of Nations testify to the failure of the great experiment. Today we face the fact that the second great world organization of this era, the United Nations, has only peripheral influence on international conflicts, and there is no possibility of collective security enforcement action brought by the UN Security Council—with the rare exception of the South African case.

Given the potential destructiveness of nuclear war, conventional war, and revolutionary subconventional war—each terrible in its own way—the failure of international law and organization and of collective security is a grim fact indeed. War in all of its contemporary forms is sufficiently destructive to warrant the exhaustion of all reasonable hopes of avoiding it. But, when those hopes are exhausted and the probability of war stretches out before us from the present to the distant future, there comes a point where the responsible person recognizes that the first priority problem in a war system is not the elimination of war but its limitation and containment.

That is the perspective of this book. I am profoundly conscious of the logical and moral weight of the injunction of Vatican II that we must have a completely fresh reappraisal of war.[1] This is usually taken to mean finding a way to eliminate armed coercion from the international system. Serious contemplation of such a reformed international system casts doubt on the possibility and desirability of

1

eliminating all armed coercion. Even one world under a world authority would have to be policed through measures of force, unless one
posits a fundamental transformation of human nature that even Pope
Paul VI found unlikely.[2] Even a very optimistic vision of one world,
without war, involves acceptance of war in different form: international police action by a world authority in defense of world law and
order. Such action would involve all of the normative and practical
issues of just and limited war discussed in this book. *

Moreover, proponents of a world without war have no way of
reconciling the right of revolution with the abolition of armed coercion.
One world may not be just to all, as has already been the case in historical regional worlds. In an era that produces more and more double
standards, contemporary internationalists tend to condemn war while
endorsing revolution. Again, regardless of the label, the use of
armed coercion by revolutionaries raises the issues discussed in this
book.

It is my position that the most original fresh reappraisal of war
will, if it deals with reality, conclude that recourse to armed coercion is a perennial feature of the human condition. The use of armed
force takes place, of necessity, at all levels of society from the local
level of domestic police to the national level of revolutionary war to
the international level of interstate conflict. If this is true, a fresh
reappraisal that would simply wish away war is irrelevant to the problem and irresponsible.

What are the alternatives? Aside from the outlawry-of-war approach, one finds two others. One is that war is a social phenomenon

---

*My references to Vatican II and contemporary popes reflects
my own perspectives as a Catholic scholar writing in the just-war tradition. These perspectives are maintained throughout the book for two
reasons. First, they are derived from a tradition with which I am
familiar, having devoted my scholarly life to its study and practical
application. Second, the principal authoritative literature on the
morality of war centers on the older just-war tradition and its more
recent interpretation within the Catholic church. As the references
and citations that follow throughout the book will demonstrate, the
focus on Catholic formulations of just-war issues persists regardless
of the religious or philosophical affiliations or positions of the leading
modern scholars dealing with the normative problems of war, most of
whom are not Catholic. Accordingly, when I begin the discussions of
the moral issues of modern war with references to Catholic sources,
I am not implying that there may not be equally good or superior formulations to be found in other sources. I am starting from the sources
that I know best and that are usually discussed in the contemporary
ecumenical analyses of the moral issues of war.

that has its own logic and course, which, once launched, moves inexorably, more or less beyond the control of those who started it, a kind of cosmic throwing of the dice. The other approach is that war is a continuation of politics by other means. (Ironically, Clausewitz is invoked in support of both approaches.) The first approach leads to total war. The second leads to limited war, and it can be made to lead to just war. For the advocate of total war, the challenge is to find the essence of war and exploit it without restraint until total victory has been gained. For those guided by just-war and limited-war doctrines, the problem is to set morally acceptable goals for and limits on war as an instrument of policy.[3]

Modern wars show a tendency toward total war. Indeed, this tendency is at the heart of the initiative to outlaw war as an unacceptable instrument of policy. Total war is not the only kind of war, and armed coercion in some form is a requirement of nations in the present international system. Given the unacceptability of total war on the one hand, and the virtually nonexistent hopes for a world without war on the other, some kind of just and limited war remains a necessity.

Accordingly, in this reappraisal of war, the focus will be on established approaches rather than futuristic speculation looking to a fundamental change in the international system based on fundamental changes in human nature. These are the just-war and limited-war approaches. The just-war tradition looks for the moral justification of war as well as its limitation. The limited-war tradition looks for the political justification of war as well as its limitation. They are in part complementary, in part overlapping.

Neither the just-war tradition nor contemporary limited-war approaches have been as extensively thought through and elaborated as they need to be if they are to guide responsible statesmen and commanders. Just-war theories existed for centuries but were seldom reflected in the behavior of would-be Christian nations. Limited-war theories have been developed in reaction to contemporary total war and the threat of nuclear war, but their application remains very uncertain. A serious, thoroughgoing examination of just-war and limited-war theories constitutes a fresh reappraisal. It is certainly something that has not been attempted. Beyond that, an attempt to apply the concepts and guidelines of just-war and limited-war theories to contemporary conflicts constitutes a practical exercise that is likewise unique. This reappraisal may very well fall short of what the Council Fathers of Vatican II had in mind, but it is the reappraisal that is needed immediately if we are to contain armed violence in the world long enough to permit more ambitious reappraisals.

This book shall attack the problem of war from the perspectives of just and limited war. Some clarification about the meaning of these terms is in order.

JUST WAR

The just-war tradition begins with the efforts of St. Augustine to justify Christian participation in Roman wars. From this foundation, St. Thomas Aquinas and other Scholastic thinkers developed the Scholastic just-war doctrine. This doctrine reached its mature form by the time of the writings of Vitoria and Suarez in the sixteenth and seventeenth centuries. Various Protestant moralists and secular writers dealt with just-war issues during the Reformation, but by the eighteenth century just-war doctrine was becoming a curiosity that was not taken seriously. It remained for the twentieth century reactions against total war to spark renewed studies in the just-war tradition. The Catholic church, through papal encyclicals and pronouncements and, most recently, through the documents of Vatican II, has built up a corpus of social teaching on war founded on just-war doctrine. [4]

Protestant moralists and secular humanists have increasingly used just-war doctrine as a starting point for their own analyses of modern war. Indeed, today some of the most respected interpreters of just-war doctrine are Protestants. It is fair to say that nonpacifist Christian moralists generally accept some form of just-war doctrine as the basis for their discussions of modern war. [5]

Accordingly, just-war doctrine today consists of traditional Scholastic just-war theory enriched by the contemporary social teaching of the Catholic church on war and the scholarship of Protestant and secular moralists and philosophers. To these components one must add the positive international law of war. Since the seventeenth century this law has been developing. For a long time it dealt almost exclusively with the legal regulation of the conduct of war; since World War I it has also addressed the question of the legal permissibility of recourse to force. This law should be considered part of the just-war doctrine.

It is worthwhile to consider the wider implications of this expansion of the just-war doctrine to include the positive international law of war. Since Roman times there has been a fruitful interrelation between jus naturale—natural law—and jus gentium—the law of peoples, the law of nations. As Heinrich Rommen explained so well in his classic works on natural law, the jus naturale is the law that is deduced from the nature of man and from a body of theological and philosophical first principles. The jus gentium, on the other hand, is inductively derived, based on observable consensus in human beliefs, attitudes, and behavior. Natural-law thinkers hope that the two will tend to coincide, to complement, and to reinforce each other. [6]

Just-war doctrine was originally jus naturale—natural law in character. Deductions were made from basic theological and philosophic concepts and applied to the decision to take human lives in war. The concern was not for what men did in war but what they ought to do and refrain from doing based on natural-law reasoning. As will be seen in the more extended discussions in Chapters 2 and 3, this jus naturale approach was incomplete, notably on the essential subject of the conduct of war. Even in the predominantly natural-law just war, therefore, there was introduced a jus gentium element that came to constitute virtually all of the just-war teaching on the just conduct of war. [7]

Meanwhile, beginning in the seventeenth century and culminating in the twentieth century, a positive international law of war developed, a jus gentium grounded in the customary practices of belligerents and formulated by an inductive process into legal prescriptions. Catholic social thought and modern just-war writers have assimilated this positive jus gentium into just-war doctrine, much as the Scholastics incorporated the customary jus gentium of the Age of Chivalry into their just-war doctrine. [8]

Thus, in this book, just-war doctrine means the traditional Scholastic doctrine as developed by the contemporary social teachings of the Catholic church on war, scholarly commentaries, and the positive international law of war.

An additional point must be added to this understanding of the content of just-war doctrine. Like Paul Ramsey, the foremost just-war scholar of our time, I view just-war doctrine as a practical body of moral guidelines applicable to real life, not a museum piece to be preserved for its own sake. [9] Just-war doctrine has been and remains a mere beginning, a set of questions to be considered by belligerents and those who judge their actions, and some indications of answers. John Courtney Murray, S.J., calls just war a <u>Grenzmoral</u>, observing that

> in desperate cases, in which conscience is perplexed, the wise moralist is chary of the explicit and the nice, especially when the issue, as here, is one of social not individual morality. In such cases hardly more than a <u>Grenzmoral</u> is to be looked for or counseled. In fact, the whole Catholic doctrine of war is hardly more than a <u>Grenzmoral</u>, an effort to establish on a minimal basis of reason a form of human action, the making of war, that remains always fundamentally irrational. [10]

I hope to expand and clarify the borders of this <u>Grenzmoral</u>. I shall attempt to remain faithful to the meaning of the great writers of the just-war tradition, but fidelity to them is not as important to me as responsiveness to the requirements of a conflict-ridden world for just-war guidelines.

LIMITED WAR

The theory and practice of limited war is probably as old as
the history of war. In our time the concept has connoted alternatives
to total war (World Wars I and II) and strategic nuclear war. Modern
limited-war theories developed particularly in the 1950s in reaction
to the policies of nuclear massive retaliation. Proponents of limited
war included scholars such as Kissinger, Osgood, Brodie, and Aron;
military men such as Generals Taylor and Gavin; public figures such
as Atomic Energy Commission commissioner Murray; and moralists
such as Father Murray who linked limited war to traditional just-war
doctrines. The intellectual context of this growth of limited-war
theory was the prevailing Realist orientation of international relations scholars such as Carr, Morgenthau, and Thompson and moralists
such as Niebuhr and Lefever. [11]

These limited-war thinkers and activists do not form a coherent
school as is the case with just-war thinkers. A good deal of their
thought is independent and unrelated to that of others interested in the
same issues. Today, however, we can synthesize limited-war thought
and see some common concerns and prescriptions. It is my intention
to propose a consensus of limited-war thinking as the equivalent of the
core doctrine of just war. This consensual core will be applied to
contemporary problems as limited-war theory.

OBSTACLES TO JUST AND LIMITED WAR

It must be acknowledged from the outset that there are formidable
obstacles to just-war and limited-war approaches. These include the
total-war legacy, the problem of nuclear deterrence and war, and the
contemporary record of and prospects for war and revolution.

Total war is a strong brew that continues to attract despite severe hangovers. Total war is psychologically appealing to fighting
men and supporting home fronts. It addresses the need to justify the
radical character of war by absolute ends supported with absolute conviction and the most absolute means available. It captures the familiar
jingoist mood, "We would rather not fight, but if they force us to,
we'll go all out and win." When the cause is ideological, perceived
to involve societal and/or physical survival, total war makes a lot of
sense.

It is, therefore, the task of the just-war theorist to advise the
advocates of total war that both their ends and means are subject to
moral limits; that there is no such thing as a moral, unlimited, total
war. It is the task of the limited-war proponent to point out the political contradictions of total war, its practical infeasibility, and the

realistic and more efficacious alternatives of limited war. These tasks are difficult and continuing for just-war and limited-war thinkers. If there is any war at all, the tendency is usually toward total war. Just-war limited-war restraints are needed from the beginning. Their maintenance becomes increasingly difficult if the war is not short and successful.

Since 1945 the already difficult problem of total war has been greatly exacerbated by the threat of nuclear war. Indeed, there is a widespread belief that the existence of nuclear war means that war has ceased to be a usable instrument of policy. This, of course, has not proved to be the case in the conflict-ridden history of the postwar world. Dulles's much-criticized concept of nuclear brinksmanship has proved to be valid. We live by brinksmanship. Nuclear nations set out their nuclear deterrent umbrellas. Beneath those protecting umbrellas they engage in considerable warlike activity. Even the nonnuclear powers, whose protection by a nuclear ally is always problematic, flirt with nuclear disaster as they deploy their own military instruments. Nevertheless, it is certainly true that every discussion of modern war is haunted by the possibility that the most just and limited war may escalate into a nuclear war that is morally and politically indefensible, ruinous to the belligerents and the world community alike. As a result, it can be accepted as a general caveat that no just-war/limited-war analysis is complete and acceptable without an estimate of the dangers of nuclear war and a concomitant recognition of those dangers in the calculus of permissibility. This caveat will be taken very seriously in this book.

Another obstacle to just and limited wars as realistic objectives is the conviction that there are few credible examples of such wars in history and little practical possibility of such wars in the future. A traditional source of embarrassment to just-war theorists has been the lack of evidence that statesmen and commanders have taken their prescriptions seriously. Worse, it is widely and reasonably believed that a great deal of cheating, hypocrisy, and propaganda is covered in just-war vestments. This is in part the fault of just-war scholars who have been delinquent in not studying seriously the actual practice of belligerents in terms of just-war guidelines. It is only fairly recently that scholars have seriously attempted to compare just-war precepts with the behavior of Christian nations in the Middle Ages and Renaissance when, presumably, their moral force was greatest. What research we have does not, on its face, encourage confidence about just behavior in war. Attempts to evaluate modern wars in just-war terms have been few, limited, and mainly focused since 1945 on the use of the atomic bombs at Hiroshima and Nagasaki and the projected use of nuclear weapons in future wars. It is hoped that this study will remedy this defect in just-war doctrine by dealing with recent wars in some detail and by addressing the practical issues facing belligerents in foreseeable future conflicts.[12]

The main body of the limited-war literature is tied to one historic war—the Korean conflict—and to hypothetical wars, principally in defense of the North Atlantic Treaty Organization (NATO).[13] The related revolutionary war/counterinsurgency literature has more historical referents (for example, the Indochina wars, the Malayan and Greek insurgencies, and the Algerian revolution).[14] It is notable that the Vietnam War has not produced a literature stressing its character as a limited war. There is, then, a very mixed record on the basis of which to assess modern limited-war theory. But, on balance, it can be said that this record presents as many obstacles to acceptance of limited-war theories as it does instances of limited-war success. Even Korea, the successful limited war, is not widely remembered with satisfaction. Most of the limited wars—conventional and subconventional—fought by western belligerents have been lost, often after long, bitter struggles resulting in intense internal discord. For Americans the whole experience is summed up in the slogan, "No More Vietnams." Thus, the contemporary record of limited wars discourages support for such wars in the future. Moreover, prospects are not good for altering this disposition in order to make possible necessary future limited wars. The limited wars of the 1950s and 1960s were begun at the high point in Western confidence both in the validity of the stated goals and in the capability to realize them. A new round of limited wars would be initiated in an atmosphere of pessimism both about the goals and the ability to achieve them. To be sure, a more sober attitude would be preferable to the unwarranted overconfidence of the past. Nonetheless, if a genuine requirement for recourse to limited wars in the future is determined, it must be acknowledged that the history of contemporary limited wars will engender skepticism and opposition to the very idea.

Given the perennial need for war as an instrument of policy and the dangers of nuclear war or of reversion to conventional total war, it is necessary to overcome the skepticism about just and limited war. To this end the record needs to be much more carefully reviewed and evaluated. It should always be borne in mind that just and limited war as concepts and as policies are always subject to attack from total-war advocates on the one hand and antiwar critics on the other. Would-be just and limited wars will usually fall far short of the expectations for victory of the total-war proponents whereas any war is anathema to the peace movement. One of the purposes of this book is to examine historical wars in terms of the standards of just and limited war and to indicate the extent to which such wars have met those standards, not the standards either of total war or of the proponents of peace at any price.

PURPOSE AND ORGANIZATION

The principal purpose of this book is to summarize modern just-war and limited-war concepts, doctrine, and guidelines and apply them to contemporary conflicts and to the continuing issues of defense, deterrence, and intervention. A second purpose is to explore the problems of implementing the prescriptions and guidelines of just-war and limited-war theories within the U.S. defense establishment. The focus of the book is on the security problems of the United States as seen by a U.S. citizen holding the values of U.S. tradition. However, in making this study it is believed that a contribution will be made to just-war doctrine and limited-war theories and policies of general application.

The book is organized in three parts. Part I will summarize the just-war doctrines concerning permissible recourse to war, jus ad bellum, and the just conduct of war, jus in bello. To meet the need for more concrete applications of just-war concepts, Chapters 4 and 5 will apply just-war criteria to U.S. participation in World War II and the Korean and Vietnam wars. Chapters 6, 7, and 8 will analyze nuclear war, deterrence, conventional war, and revolutionary/counterinsurgency war in terms of just-war criteria.

Part II will summarize the meaning of limited war as it has developed in contemporary theory and practice. Three limited wars —Korea, Vietnam, and Yom Kippur—will then be examined in the light of these limited-war concepts.

Part III will analyze the problems of implementation of just-war and limited-war policies. It will examine the existing modes of limitation and direction of war across a spectrum of political, political/military, military, and legal sources of authority. These include basic political and military policy directives, the definition and assignment of military missions, political and administrative control of strategic and tactical policies and their execution, control of the composition and support of the forces engaged in a conflict, the field commanders' basic directives, rules of engagement, and the rules of international law. The point of the inquiry will be to evaluate the potential for just-war and limited-war prescriptions and guidelines being translated into policy and military directives.

The second part of this inquiry will concern the channels of limitation and direction through which just-war and limited-war prescriptions and guidelines must pass. The roles of civilian decision makers, the Joint Chiefs of Staff, commanders in the field, and the chain of command will be investigated. The concept of command responsibility, controversial from the Yamashita case to the Calley case, will be explored. At this point, the role of public opinion and political activism as sources of limitation of belligerent freedom of action in a democracy such as the United States will be considered. A concluding chapter will attempt to summarize the substantive just-war and limited-war prescriptions and guidelines and the organizational and procedural requirements for implementing them.

This book addresses a number of tasks that have not hitherto been adequately undertaken. First, it provides a comprehensive restatement in policy-relevant terms of modern just-war doctrine and limited-war theories. Second, it applies this doctrine and these theories to recent armed conflicts, thereby demonstrating their practical meaning and significance. Third, it indicates preferred just-war/ limited-war policies with respect to future strategies, tactics, and weapons development relevant to conflicts that may break out in the future. Fourth, it analyzes the problems of implementing just-war and limited-war guidelines in the present U.S. defense establishment.

A good deal of the modern literature on just war is concerned with theoretical concepts and approaches. This book attempts to move beyond this literature to serious application of these concepts and approaches to the issues of modern war. The literature on limited war has been characterized by considerably more effort toward practical application, but this has usually taken the form of a discussion of selected problems rather than of a comprehensive limited-war analysis of a particular war. Most important, while just-war and limited-war theorists nod in passing and acknowledge the importance of each other's work, the interrelation between the normative tasks of prescribing just-war requirements for initiating and conducting war and the political-military policy tasks of enjoining limited-war guidelines that may make it possible for belligerents to meet just-war conditions has scarcely been explored. It is hoped that this book will contribute to the elaboration in practical terms of the content of just and limited war and to the clarification of their complementary relationship.

PART I

JUST WAR

2

JUS AD BELLUM:
PERMISSIBLE RECOURSE TO WAR

The original just-war doctrine of St. Augustine, St. Thomas, and other Scholastics emphasized the conditions for permissible recourse to war—the jus ad bellum. To this doctrine was added another branch of prescriptions regulating the conduct of war, the jus in bello. Before discussing the jus ad bellum in this chapter and the jus in bello in the next, a few observations on the components and characteristics of the modern just-war doctrine employed in this book are in order.

From its statement by St. Thomas and its mature elaboration by the seventeenth century at the hands of the Scholastics, just-war doctrine evolved from wholly religious sources to a mixture of religious and secular sources. Thus, two secular sources—the chivalric code and customary law (jus gentium)—were added to the basic doctrine as laid down by St. Thomas and other Scholastics. The result is called the Classic Just War Doctrine. After the decline of both Scholastic and secular just-war theories in the period from the seventeenth to the twentieth centuries, there has been a twentieth century revival of just-war thinking referred to as Modern Just War Doctrine. Its components are both religious and secular.[1]

Thus, in its long evolution, just-war doctrine has assumed an eclectic character. It spans several normative disciplines. In its origins just-war doctrine is heavily theological. As it developed in Scholastic thought it became more and more philosophical, an expression of natural law. At the same time, just-war theory was enriched by the chivalric code and by emerging jus gentium, the law of nations. In the twentieth century, just-war doctrine has been elaborated in a substantial body of Catholic social thought on war of mixed theological-philosophical character. The contemporary just-war literature by moral and legal publicists likewise reflects varied emphases from theological to philosophical to pragmatic political-military. The un-

13

certainty about the proper characterization of just-war doctrine is demonstrated by Fr. John Courtney Murray's famous article on the subject, which was reproduced in virtually identical form five times. Two versions are entitled "Theology and Modern War"; three are entitled "Morality and Modern War."[2]

In addition to uncertainty as to the place of just-war theory in normative disciplines, there is little clarity about its proper designation. The two most recurring terms used in connection with the just-war concept are doctrine and theory. Although a historian of ideas might make some sense out of the terms, there is little precision or consistency in usage. Doctrine sounds rather more theological; theory, more philosophical. However, contemporary usage does not seem to make any rigorous distinctions between the terms. Doctrine has a more prescriptive connotation; just-war doctrine is a body of prescriptions that must be obeyed if a war is to be just. Theory suggests a set of questions that ought to be asked by one desiring to wage a just war. If we combine the two terms and use them more or less interchangeably, we would define just-war doctrine/theory as a comprehensive set of guidelines for the initiation and waging of just war. In this book the term just-war doctrine will be used.

Other problems of terminology, rooted in underlying substantive issues, remain. In its early history just-war doctrine emphasized justice. He who had justice on his side was empowered to wage a just war. As the doctrine was developed and as the practical problems inherent in the just-unjust belligerent dichotomy became evident, more and more emphasis was placed on ensuring that recourse to war was a last resort and that the war would be waged justly. As we shall see, the theoretically severe limitations on recourse to war imposed by modern international law sharply restrict the pursuit of justice. The pluralistic, divided nature of the international system discourages emphasis on justice as the touchstone of justification for recourse to armed coercion. Today, therefore, just war is not an entirely descriptive term for the moral/legal guidelines for recourse to armed coercion and the conduct of armed conflict.[3] A more descriptive adjective would be permissible, a usage favored in the U.S. tradition of the law of war from Lieber's code for the Union armies of 1863 to the contemporary writings of Professor Myres S. McDougal and his associates.[4] Thus, permissible war would be more accurate than just war. Permissible war conveys the basic thought that recourse to war is an exceptional prerogative that has to be justified, not a right readily available to those who consider themselves just. It is also a general prerogative available exceptionally to all nations and other belligerent entities on grounds other than a subjective finding that they are just and their enemies are unjust.

I do not propose, however, to jettison the term just war. It has a long and honorable history and it has become a reasonably clear source of guidelines for and limitations on decisions to go to war and decisions about the conduct of war. Permissible war has already been labeled by some U.S. international lawyers as permissible violence, permissible force, and permissible armed coercion, but without making any serious inroads into the general tendency to use the term just war. [5] Just war will continue to be the term used in this book, but it will be qualified and elaborated on in terms of the more modern usage, permissible war—hence the subtitle of this chapter.

It was observed in Chapter 1 that just-war doctrine has two sources, natural law—jus naturale—and law of the people—jus gentium. Some might challenge this analysis, insisting that a third is the theological source, the teaching of Christ. While this discussion has acknowledged that there are theological elements in just-war doctrine, it remains the case that the church's just-war doctrine is mainly natural law, albeit natural law of a special kind. Theological approaches to just war are limited by the fact that Christ's teaching was almost exclusively directed to individuals, not nations and other corporate bodies. This teaching includes very few direct references to war. Christians have always disagreed on the import of these references. Interpretations range from pacifist to bellicist. It is, moreover, difficult to separate and distinguish the theological and philosophical natural-law elements in Scholastic thought generally. When it comes to scholastic just-war thinking, the task becomes particularly difficult. The best solution is to consider that St. Thomas and the Scholastics dealt with the morality of war in terms of grace-elevated natural law (grace-elevated in that it was written from the perspectives of Christians benefiting from Christ's teaching about human nature rather than from the perspectives of a pagan natural-law view of human nature). The just-war doctrine is essentially natural-law theory enriched by the perspectives of Christian theology on the one hand and the positive law jus gentium on the other. The theological acceptability of this theory has been demonstrated over the centuries by the fact that it has been acknowledged as the basis for the teaching of the church on war. [6]

The social teaching of the church on war is characterized by a familiar blend of theology and philosophic natural law. The force of this teaching is somewhat controverted. It is not viewed as part of the basic doctrine of the church, and in this connection use of the term doctrine with just war must be qualified. Nevertheless, just-war doctrine in the context of the broader treatment of the problem of war is the most authoritative guidance on the subject offered by the church. It must be taken seriously by Catholics, and it has recommended itself to moralists of other faiths, as well as to secular scholars, as a basis for normative analysis of war.

Indeed, just-war doctrine is intended for a wider audience. It remains primarily natural law in its content and expression, addressed to men qua men. In Pope John XXIII's words in <u>Pacem in Terris</u>, it speaks to all "men of good will." Moreover, the focus of the Catholic just-war doctrine finds parallels in other religious traditions (for example, Islam) and in secular international law theories of the age of Grotius and of the present UN system.[7] It is the aim of this book to explore the rich potential of just-war doctrine to provide analyses that are useful to all who are interested in finding normative limits to war.

The growth of Modern Just War Doctrine is an interesting subject that has been the object of increasing scholarly attention. However, the primary concern of this book is with the present doctrine and its applicability to present and future conflicts. I will undertake, therefore, to present the substance of the doctrine as it stands today, beginning first with the <u>jus ad bellum</u> and then proceeding in the next chapter to the <u>jus in bello</u>. As the discussion unfolds it will be seen that there is a constant interaction between the two parts of the just-war doctrine. The three major categories of <u>jus ad bellum</u> guidelines concern competent authority, just cause, and right intention. Competent authority determines belligerent status under the <u>jus in bello</u>. Just cause sets the underlying referent for determinations of the proportionality of the means used under <u>jus in bello</u>. Right intention controls the evolution of goals after the war has started and the substance and spirit of its termination, again important to the issue of proportionality of means. The <u>jus in bello</u> controls the conduct of the war and should be based on right intention.

OVERVIEW OF THE <u>JUS AD BELLUM</u>

The <u>jus ad bellum</u> lays down conditions that must be met in order to have permissible recourse to armed coercion. They are conditions that should be viewed in the light of the fundamental tenet of just-war doctrine: the presumption is always against war. The taking of human life is not permitted to man unless there are exceptional justifications. Just-war doctrine provides those justifications, but they are in the nature of special pleadings to overcome the presumption against killing.[8] The decision to invoke the exceptional rights of war must be based on the following criteria: there must be competent authority to order the war for a public purpose; there must be a just cause (it may be self-defense or the protection of rights by offensive war) and the means must be proportionate to the just cause and all peaceful alternatives must have been exhausted; and there must be right intention on the part of the just belligerent. Let us examine these criteria.

Competent Authority

St. Thomas held that

> for a war to be just three conditions are necessary. First,
> the authority of the ruler within whose competence it lies to
> declare war. A private individual may not declare war; for
> he can have recourse to the judgment of a superior to safe-
> guard his rights. Nor has he the right to mobilize the peo-
> ple, which is necessary in war. But since responsibility
> for public affairs is entrusted to the rules, it is they who
> are charged with the defence of the city, realm, or province,
> subject to them. . . . And St. Augustine says in his book
> Contra Faustum (XXIII, 73): "The natural order of men, to
> be peacefully disposed, requires that the power and decision
> to declare war should lie with the rulers."[9]

Insofar as large-scale, conventional war is concerned, the issue
of competent authority is different in modern times than it was in the
thirteenth century. The decentralized political system wherein public,
private, and criminal violence overlapped, as well as the state of
military art and science, permitted a variety of private wars. So it
was important to insist that war—in which individuals would be called
upon to take human lives—must be waged on the order of public authorities for public purposes. This is not a serious problem in most
parts of the world today. Only states have the material capacity to
wage large-scale, modern, conventional war. Two other problems
do, however, exist in connection with the condition of competent authority. First, there may be disputes as to the constitutional competence of a particular official or organ of state to initiate war. Second, civil war and revolutionary terrorism are frequently initiated
by persons and organizations claiming revolutionary rights.

Most states today, even totalitarian states, have specific constitutional provisions for the declaration and termination of war. If
an official or state organ violates these provisions, there may not be
a valid exercise of the sovereign right to declare and wage war. In
such a case the first condition of the just war might not be met. This
was the charge, implicitly or explicitly, against President Johnson
in the Vietnam War. Johnson never requested a declaration of war
from Congress with which he shared war-making powers. War critics
asserted that the undeclared war was illegal. A sufficient answer to
this charge is to be found in congressional cooperation in the war effort and in the refusal of the courts to declare the war unconstitutional.
This point will be raised again in this chapter in dealing specifically
with the Vietnam War.[10] At this point it is sufficient to raise the is-

sue as illustrative of the problem of competent authority within a constitutional state.

In this connection a word should be said about declaring wars. Any examination of modern wars will show that the importance of a declaration of war has diminished greatly in international practice. Because of the split-second timing of modern war, it is often undesirable to warn the enemy by way of a formal declaration. Defense measures are geared to react to hostile behavior, not declarations. When war is declared it is often an announcement confirming a condition that has already been established. Nevertheless, if a particular state's constitution does require a formal declaration of war and one is not forthcoming, the issue of competence is raised. If a public official exceeds his authority in mobilizing the people and conducting war, there is a lack of competent authority.

The second problem, however, is by far the greatest. Today, rights of revolution are frequently invoked by organizations and individuals. They clearly do not have the authority and capacity to wage war in the conventional sense. However, they do wage revolutionary war, often on an international scale. Indeed, international terrorism is one of the most pervasive and difficult problems facing the international community.

All major ideologies and blocs or alignments of states in the international system recognize the right of revolution. Usually their interpretations will emphasize the rights of revolution against others, not themselves. Catholic thought recognizes this right, too, although often in a most reluctant and tortured fashion.[11] Logically, there should be an elaborate jus ad bellum and jus in bello for revolutionary war, but development of such a doctrine has never been seriously attempted. As a result, the issues of revolutionary war tend to be treated on an ad hoc basis as special cases vaguely related to the regular categories of just war. Given this state of the doctrine, it will be necessary in this book to assimilate revolutionary warfare problems into the traditional just-war categories, but particular care will be taken to identify the special problems of this kind of war.

The differences between conventional war waged by states and revolutionary war waged by rebels against states are profound. Given the formidable power of most modern governments, particularly in regard to their comparative monopoly of armed force, revolutionary rights can be asserted mainly by covert organizations waging guerrilla warfare and terrorism. The option of organizing a portion of a state and fighting a conventional civil war in the manner of the American, Spanish, or Nigerian civil wars is seldom available.

The covert, secret character of modern revolutionary movements is such that it is often hard to judge their claims to qualify as the competent authority for oppressed people. There is a decided tendency to follow the Leninist model of revolutionary leadership wherein the self-selected revolutionary elite decides on the just revolutionary cause, the means, and the circumstances of taking the initiative, all done in the name of the people and revolutionary justice. As a revolution progresses, the task of certifying competent authority continues to be difficult. Support for the revolutionary leadership is often coerced or given under conditions where there is not popular acceptance of the revolutionary authority of that leadership or its ends and means. Recognition by foreign powers of belligerency—or even of putative governmental powers—is an unreliable guide given subjective, politicized recognition policies.

To complicate matters, individuals and small groups take up revolutionary war tactics, principally terrorism in the form of airplane hijacking, hostage kidnapping, assassination, and indiscriminate bombing attacks. These acts are performed in the name of greatly varying causes, some of which could not be considered revolutionary. Sometimes the alleged justifications are political or ideological, but, on investigation, the real motivation turns out to be personal and criminal. Since most revolutionary movements manifest themselves in behavior difficult to distinguish from that of cranks and criminals, the task of sorting out revolutionaries entitled to acceptance as competent authorities is excruciating.

Two issues need to be resolved concerning revolutionary activity. First, insofar as treating revolutionaries as belligerents in a war and not as common criminals is concerned, the ultimate answer lies in the character, magnitude, and degree of success of the revolutionaries. If they can organize a government that carries on their war in a controlled fashion (assuming a magnitude requiring countermeasures that more resemble war than ordinary police operations), and if the conflict continues for an appreciable time, the revolutionaries may have won their right to be considered a competent authority for purposes of just war. Beyond this enumeration of criteria it seems unprofitable to generalize.

Second, concerning the authority of rebel leaders to mobilize the people by ordering or coercing individuals to fight for the revolutionary cause, the conscience of the individual takes precedence. Lacking any color of authority to govern, the rebels cannot of right compel participation in their cause. Needless to say, they will very probably compel participation by intimidation.

Just Cause

St. Thomas continues his discussion of the conditions of a just war.

>Secondly, there is required a just cause: that is that those
>who are attacked for some offence merit such treatment.
>St. Augustine says (Book LXXXIII) q.: <u>Super Josue</u>, qu.
>X): "Those wars are generally defined as just which avenge
>some wrong, when a nation or a state is to be punished for
>having failed to make amends for the wrong done, or to re-
>store what has been taken unjustly."[12]

Over the years this brief and vague definition was expanded, amended,
and elaborated. Authorities vary in their presentation of just cause,
but it seems to break down into four subdivisions: the substance of
the just cause, the forms of pursuing just cause, the requirement of
proportionality of ends and means, and the requirement of exhaustion
of peaceful remedies.

The substance of the just cause must, in Childress's formulation,
be sufficiently "serious and weighty" to overcome the presumption
against killing in general and war in particular. In Childress's approach, with which I am in essential agreement, this means that
there must be a "competing prima facie duty or obligation" to "the
prima facie obligation not to injure and kill others."[13] Childress
mentions as "serious and weighty" prima facie obligations the following: (1) "to protect the innocent from unjust attack," (2) to restore rights wrongfully denied," (3) "to re-establish a just order."[14]

This is an adequate basis, reflective of the older just-war
literature, for discussing the substance of just cause. Indeed,
Childress is more explicit than many modern commentators who
simply state that there should be a just cause. Still, it is only a
beginning. It is unfortunate that modern moralists have generally
been so concerned with the issue of putatively disproportionate
means in modern war that they have neglected the prior question
of the ends for which these means might have to be used (that is,
just cause). In practical terms, this task of evaluating the substance of just cause leads inescapably to a comparative analysis
of the characteristics of the polities or political-social systems
posed in warlike confrontation. Specifically, one must ask
whether the political-social order of a country like the United
States is sufficiently valuable to warrant its defense in a war
against a country like the Soviet Union, which, if victorious,
would impose its political-social order on the United States.

Even more difficult for those who would answer in the affirmative is the question whether the United States should intervene to protect a manifestly imperfect political-social order (South Korea, South
Vietnam or, perhaps, that of a state such as Jordan, Saudi Arabia,

or Pakistan) in order to prevent its conquest by a totalitarian communist state like the Soviet Union, North Korea, or North Vietnam; or even by a puppet state of the Soviet Union as Syria may turn out to be.

In brief, in our time the substance of the just-cause condition of just war has been essentially the issue of being either Red or dead. Whether the negative goal of not being Red is sufficient to justify a war that may leave many dead and still not ensure a political-social order of very high quality (a continuing probability in most of the Third World) is a most difficult question that has divided many men of goodwill in the post-World War II era. Any just-war analysis that does not face the question of the comparative justice and character of contending political-social orders is not offering responsible answers to the just-war ends/means dilemmas of the modern world.

Moreover, there is a further inescapable issue in the relationship between a particular just cause and the general problem of deterring and defending against aggressions designed to impose by force different, often totalitarian and tyrannical regimes on target nations. One need not adhere to a deterministic domino theory to admit that such aggressions and forcible impositions of political-social orders can gain momentum and feed on themselves. In these circumstances, the just cause of defending a particular country against aggression and political-social coercion may merge into the broader regional or even global just cause of deterring and repulsing this use of force.

These "Red or dead" issues arise in all modern U.S. wars. They may or may not be critical in some local wars not involving the United States or other Western democracies, but comparable problems of the consequences of conquest are engendered by fundamental rifts such as those between Israel and the radical Arab states; India and Pakistan; and even between communist states such as Vietnam, Cambodia, and the People's Republic of China.

By comparison, the substantive just causes of the older just-war literature are almost insignificant. In the modern world the just cause often has to do with the survival of a way of life. Claims that this is so can be false or exaggerated, but they are often all too legitimate. They must be taken seriously in assessing the substance of just cause in modern just-war analyses. [15]

However, passing the test of just cause is not solely a matter of positing an end that is convincingly just, although that is the indispensable starting point. It is also necessary to meet the tests posed by the other three subdivisions of just cause.

The forms of pursuing just cause are defensive and offensive wars. The justice of self-defense is generally considered to be axiomatic. Just-war doctrine, following Aristotle and St. Thomas as well as the later Scholastics, places great importance on the state as a natural institution essential for man's development. Defense of the state is prima facie defense of an essential social institution. So strong is the presumption in favor of the right of self-defense that the requirement of probable success, to be discussed under proportion-ality, is usually waived. [16]

Offensive wars raise more complications. In classical just-war doctrine, offensive wars were permitted to protect vital rights unjustly threatened or injured. Moreover, in a form now archaic, offensive wars of vindictive justice against infidels and heretics were once permitted. Such wars disappeared with the decline of the re-ligious, holy-war element as a cause of and rationale for wars. Thus, the forms of permissible wars today are twofold: wars of self-de-fense and offensive wars to enforce justice for oneself. [17] As will be seen, even the second is now seemingly prohibited by positive inter-national law. But in terms of basic just-war theory it remains an option. A war of vindictive justice wherein the belligerent fights against error and evil as a matter of principle and not of necessity is no longer condoned by just-war doctrine. [18]

Applying these guidelines to the contemporary world, a U.S. war of self-defense against a Soviet attack is clearly just. Under modern just-war doctrine, without regard to positive international law, a U.S. offensive war to regain Alaska, lost in a previous war of ag-gression, would be just. Under the original concept of vindictive jus-tice, an offensive war to free the Soviet people from communist rule would be just. Under modern just-war theory, such an offensive war would not be permitted. Nor would it be permitted to launch an of-fensive war to save a part of the Soviet population from genocide. In-deed, once wars for vindictive justice are removed, the forms of just war amount essentially to an extended right of self-defense. The right of offensive war is tied to reasserting rights previously violated and to preventing recurrence of these and comparable injuries.

This understanding of the available forms of just war has been further modified by the jus ad bellum of modern international law. The United Nations Charter confirms a trend started by the League of Nations Covenant sharply curtailing the right of states to use armed force as an instrument of foreign policy. Article 2(4) of the charter lays down a general prohibition against the threat or use of force against the territorial integrity or political independence of any state. Chapter 7 of the charter provides for UN enforcement action to sup-press threats to the peace under the concept of collective security. Security Council enforcement action under Chapter 7 is recognized to be the only form of offensive war legally permissible. Aggression is to be deterred, suppressed, and punished by collective enforce-ment action, not by state self-help. The only form of legally permissible war now available to a state is a war of individual or collective self-defense, reiterated in Article 51 as a right to be exercised pending Security Council action under Chapter 7.[19] If there is any doubt about modern just-war guidelines regarding the hypothetical cases discussed above, there is none under international-law guidelines. The United States has no legal right to engage in an offensive war to save a people from communism or some other tyrannical form of government or even from genocide, unless it is part of a UN enforcement action, an unlikely possibility given Security Council divisions.[20] A minority of scholars argue for the permissibility of humanitarian intervention under the UN jus ad bellum. They argue that protection of human rights is as much a concern or value in the UN Charter as is avoidance of war. Hence, they contend, the charter should be interpreted so as to make possible sanctions by individual states on behalf of human rights in extreme cases (for example, genocide or massive violation of human rights) in the absence of effective UN sanctions. They further contend that it is possible to intervene to protect human rights without violating the essence of Article 2(4), since a truly disinterested, altruistic, humanitarian intervention would not be directed against the territorial integrity or political independence of the target state. Both arguments are difficult to accept, and the position of those who hold them is clearly a minority position among publicists. My greatest difficulty with this view, however, is that there are no examples extant to illustrate humanitarian intervention in contemporary practice.[21]

There were no humanitarian interventions to protect the Ibos in the Biafran Civil War, the Cambodians suffering under the Khmer Rouge regime (the conquest by Vietnam is neither disinterested nor altruistic), or the Ugandans under Idi Amin (again, the Tanzanian conquest was justified as necessary to remove illegal occupation of Tanzanian territory and threats to its security, not as humanitarian intervention). In the final analysis, it is clear that India's intervention in the 1971 Bangladesh War, held by Walzer to be justified on humanitarian grounds, was more fundamentally a war inspired by India's desire to cripple and perhaps destroy Pakistan.[22]

Thus, modern international law has sacrificed justice in its attempt virtually to eliminate the competence of the state to engage in war unilaterally.[23] The problem is that this decision to put peace, security, and stability above justice in the international hierarchy of values was based on the assumption that there would be both effective collective security to enforce the peace and the peaceful settlement of disputes. In the face of the manifest failure of collective security, it can be argued that a state suffering grave injustice would reasonably reclaim its sovereign right to wage just war. The UN system is now in a crisis in which states may be expected to think and act this way, thus putting the UN legal regime of force in question. In effect, the charter is a world social contract whereby individual sovereign competence to use the military instrument was severely restricted in favor of collective security. This social contract is now threatened with a wholesale return to the state of nature by the states of the world. The states, not having received security in exchange for conceding much of their competence to use armed force, would now reclaim that competence in full.[24]

For the moment no such explicit renunciation of the UN regime of force has occurred. On the contrary, the law of the charter continues to be reaffirmed by word, if not by deed. But the law of the charter is certainly not based on solid evidence of a disposition in state practice and expectations to view unilateral recourse to armed force as prohibited except in self-defense.

We have, then, in international law a ban on offensive war; in effect, a "no-first-strike" rule. The rule is precarious and often violated, but it represents the cumulative aspirations of men and nations in the twentieth century. It seems clear that contemporary just-war doctrine accepts this further limitation of international law on permissible recourse to armed coercion. The inclusion of the limitations of the UN regime into just-war teaching is effected notwithstanding the precarious nature of that regime and presumably in full cognizance of the many injustices in the present international system that might otherwise furnish just cause for just offensive wars. As evidence of this acceptance of the "self-defense-only" attitude, one notices in contemporary papal and conciliar documents references restricted to defense when security requirements are acknowledged. This means that the only way to come to the assistance of a nation suffering from grave injustice is through collective self-defense. The only way to assist a people not constituting a state who suffer injustice is to encourage them to create a state so that they can invite assistance under the justification of collective self-defense.[25]

There is an important implication of the restrictions on the first use of armed coercion imposed by contemporary international law. It is that the so-called measures short of war, which involved the threat or use of armed coercion, are no longer legally permissible. Prior to the League of Nations-United Nations period, a state could take so-called self-help measures, including the threat and use of armed coercion, to protect its rights and sanction international law. A number of different terms were used for these measures, but the generic term is reprisals. Indeed, reprisals formed part of both the jus ad bellum and the jus in bello. We must here address the problem of the status of jus ad bellum reprisals under modern international law.

The essence of the right of reprisal is that it permits the commission of otherwise illegal acts in retaliation for antecedent illegal acts injurious to the victim. The purpose of reprisals, as undertaken by the victim of illegal, injurious acts, is threefold: to correct the imbalance created by the illegal acts or aggressions against a law-abiding victim, to deter repetition of such acts, and to serve as a sanction for international laws that have been violated. [26]

The rules governing reprisals are vague and controverted. In the period prior to the UN regime—which prima facie eliminates any right of reprisal with armed coercion not justified as self-defense—there was little agreement over the law of armed reprisals. Some authorities required an unsatisfied demand for discontinuation of the illegal acts and reparation as a condition for recourse to reprisals. Everyone agreed that reprisals should be necessary and proportionate, but there was little agreement about the referent of proportionality. Given the three purposes, proportionality might be measured in terms of the need to correct the imbalance between agressor and victim, the need to deter repetition, or the need to provide effective sanctions for international law. The choice of a referent for judging the proportionality of reprisals makes a great deal of practical difference. Correction of the imbalance may mean essentially a tit for tat retaliation in kind. However, as the age of nuclear deterrence has shown, deterrence may justify acts disproportionate to the original delinquency if they are proportionate to the requirement of detering repetition. Sanctioning of international law as a rationale yields no self-evident guidance for measuring proportionality.

Moreover, dilemmas of defining and applying the right of reprisal confront an even more fundamental difficulty: namely, modern international law permits no use of armed coercion except as part of UN-authorized enforcement actions or, in Article 51, individual or collective self-defense. The prevailing view of authorities is that the right of self-defense is the sole right of armed self-help. [27] Armed reprisals are prima facie violations of international law unless they can be assimilated into the right of self-defense. This means that it is not always legally permissible to retaliate, even for an armed attack. For example, if a U.S. military aircraft is shot down by the Soviets over the high seas adjacent to the Soviet Union, the United States cannot invoke the right of reprisal and shoot down a Soviet aircraft picked at random unless such action could be shown to be part of a necessary policy of self-defense. It also means that armed coercion may be used by the victim of highly injurious, nonmilitary coercion as a matter of self-defense, not reprisal.

There is no reason, however, why the legitimate functions of traditional reprisals cannot adequately be carried out by self-defense measures. If we look to practical rather than doctrinal considerations, we find that of the two characteristics said to distinguish armed reprisals from self-defense (that is, deterrence or prevention, on the one hand, and punishment and sanctioning of the law on the other), only the first affects the content of the right. Both rights depend upon the occurrence of a prior illegal act; on reasonable efforts to obtain a peaceful, legal remedy; and on a consequent necessity to resort to normally forbidden means that must be proportionate to the necessity of self-help. The only practical difference between them is that self-defense, strictly construed, is limited to repelling aggression, whereas the right of reprisal is quite flexible and permissive in its rationales. As long as the reprisal measures are necessary and proportionate, their form, timing, and locus need not be closely related to the form, timing, and locus of the original illegal act.

The second distinction between the purposes of self-defense and reprisal is nebulous and not very helpful in the kind of international legal order that now exists. In any event, the allegation that an act is done both to uphold an injured party's rights and to uphold the law does not alter the requirements of necessity and proportionality. If we concentrate on these requirements, it is clear that the main point at issue is whether self-defense must be limited to repelling illegal armed coercion or whether it can include preventive measures as well. I take the latter view. It is clear that anticipatory self-defense is a legitimate form of self-defense if there is a clear and present danger of aggression. This was the case, for example, in the circumstances leading to the Israeli attack on its Arab enemies in the 1967 Six Day War. This position results in justification for greater latitude in self-help measures than is conceded by the restrictive interpretations of the right of self-defense. In my view, proper use of the right of anticipatory self-defense will meet most of the legitimate requirements for self-help in an era when the old reprisals "short of war" are illegal as such under the UN Charter. [28]

Taken out of the armed reprisal/self-defense dichotomy, self-help measures may be preventive, but they must be closely related to the proximate sources of illegal armed coercion. Under present international law, a state may not use self-help measures that, while possibly of such a character as to deter or prevent illegal coercion, are not closely related to such illegal coercion. Thus, military coercion may be employed not only to repel but also to prevent imminent illegal military coercion and, if necessary, to attack the proximate sources of recurring illegal military coercion. A good recent example is furnished by the Israeli limited attack on south Lebanon following a Palestine Liberation Organization (PLO) raid launched from that area. PLO announcements and the pattern of the raid against Israel indicated that this was the precursor of similar raids. The Israelis attacked the PLO strongholds from which the March 1978 raid had come and from which more such attacks could reasonably be expected.

There are several advantages to this position. First, it tends toward a rule of retaliation in kind. This is much preferable to the traditional, wide-ranging right of reprisal. The proportionality of reprisals is very hard to judge when they are not related to the proximate sources of illegal coercion. Second, it tends to lessen the likelihood that retaliation will fall upon the innocent, a perennial fault of reprisals. Third, by emphasizing the functional necessities of defense rather than the elusive requirements of sanctioning the international legal order, this formulation tends to reduce opportunities for pious, hypocritical justifications of acts, the true necessity and proportionality of which are dubious.

Turning from the forms of just war we come to the heart of just cause—proportionality between the just ends and the means. This concerns the relationship between raison d'état (the high interests of state) and the use of the military instrument in war as the means to achieve these interests. This concept of proportionality at the level of raison d'état is multidimensional. To begin with, the ends held out as the just cause must be sufficiently good and important to warrant the extreme means of war, the arbitrament of arms. Beyond that, a projection of the outcome of the war is required in which the probable good expected to result from success is weighed against the probable evil that the war will cause.[29]

The process of weighing probable good against probable evil is extremely complex. The balance sheet of good and evil must be estimated for each belligerent. Additionally, there should be a balancing of effects on individual third parties and on the international common good. International interdependence means that international conflicts are difficult to contain and that their shock waves affect third parties in a manner that must be accounted for in the calculus of probable good and evil. Moreover, the international community as such has its international common good, which is necessarily affected by any war. Manifestly, the task of performing this calculus effectively is an awesome one. But even its successful completion does not fully satisfy the demands of the just-war condition of just cause. Probing even further, the doctrine requires a responsible judgment that there is a probability of success for the just party. All of these calculations must be concluded convincingly to meet the multidimensional requirement of just cause.[30]

Moreover, the calculus of proportionality between probable good and evil in a war is a continuing one. It should be made before the decision to go to war. It must then be reviewed at critical points along the process of waging the war. The best informed estimates about wars are often in error. They may need revision or replacement by completely new estimates. The jus ad bellum requirement of proportionality, then, includes these requirements:

There must be a just cause of sufficient importance to warrant its defense by recourse to armed coercion.

The probable good to be achieved by successful recourse to armed coercion in pursuit of the just cause must outweigh the probable evil that the war will produce.

The calculation of proportionality between probable good and evil must be made with respect to all belligerents, affected neutrals, and the international community as a whole before initiating a war and periodically throughout a war to reevaluate the balance of good and evil that is actually produced by the war.

These calculations must be made in the light of realistic estimates of the probability of success.

If we always return to the starting point of just-war doctrine (the presumption against war), it will be clear that many extremely grave and important threats and injustices may not constitute sufficient just cause. For example, modern war is not an appropriate instrument for collecting defaulted debts. It may not be a permissible response to unjust treatment of a state's nationals. In a dangerous world there are many injustices that do not provide sufficient justification for recourse to armed force. Not even a clear case of self-defense may be enough for just cause. Thus, the United States would not be justified in going to war with the Soviet Union because the latter had shot down a U.S. aircraft in cold blood over international waters. At least, such an event would not constitute sufficient just cause without other contributing circumstances. Finally, it is quite clear that a state with a real and serious grievance ought not to precipitate a war in which it had no chance of success (for example, Israel against the Soviet Union).

Father Murray, in his authoritative interpretation of the modern just-war doctrine, principally as expounded by Pope Pius XII, emphasizes that the calculus of proportion must address a comparison "between realities of the moral order and not sheerly between the two sets of material damage and loss."[31] Murray further states that

> the standard is not a "eudaemonism and utilitarianism of materialist origin," which would avoid war merely because it is uncomfortable, or connive at injustice simply because its repression would be costly. The question of proportion must be evaluated in more tough-minded fashion, from the viewpoint of the hierarchy of strictly moral values. It is not enough simply to consider the "sorrows and evils that flow from war." There are greater evils than the physical death and destruction wrought in war. And there are human goods of so high an order that immense sacrifices may have to be borne in their defense. By these insistences Pius XII transcended the vulgar pacifism of sentimentalist and materialist inspiration that is so common today.[32]

Implicit in Father Murray's analysis of proportion is the conviction that there are just, or at least more tolerable, and unjust, or intolerable, polities. In a war between a just or tolerable polity and an unjust or intolerable polity, a victory of the unjust will probably result in the forcible imposition of an unjust social order on the defeated polity. This was the case in the countries conquered by Hitler. (One can make this judgment notwithstanding the fact that the character of many of the conquered polities would be best characterized as barely tolerable.) Certainly conquest by the Soviet Union has meant the forcible imposition of unjust, intolerable polities (save in the unique case of Finland). To argue that these imposed, unjust polities are tolerable in the sense that the generality of the population somehow survives or that they sometimes become less oppressive than they have been is not to alter the basic judgment an analyst holding the values reflected in the just-war tradition would apply.

Thus, the question of proportion between a putatively just cause and the costs of pursuing that cause cannot be addressed without an assessment of the fundamental character of the warring polities and the probable consequences of defeat for each. In the century of the total war, when major conflict usually pits one way of life against another, this means that the implications of defeat tend to be total in terms of the radical transformation of the defeated party. In the light of one's assessment of the relative justice or tolerability of the contending parties' polities, such a radical transformation may be for the better (for example, West Germany after 1945) or the worse (for example, East Germany after 1945).

It may be objected that this interpretation of just-war proportionality creates an unacceptable bias in favor of polities whose values the just-war analyst shares. This is an inevitable problem that must be acknowledged and that the analyst must constantly deal with in conscience. However, identification with a belligerent's values and the conviction that the belligerent's defeat would bring an intolerable imposition of an unjust polity need not and must not result in an automatic, blind endorsement of all wars and all belligerent conduct by polities whose values the analyst shares and/or deems just or tolerable. The whole point of the complex normative analyses that just-war doctrine requires is that it is not enough to have a just polity and it is not enough to be able to show that the enemy has an unjust polity that he will impose on you if he wins. This is only the foundation, albeit the indispensable starting point, in the just-war analysis. The just polity must have a just cause and that cause must be pursued in consonance with the just-war conditions if the war of the just is to be just.

In a trenchant critique of jus ad bellum concepts of proportionality, Tucker observes the following.

In bellum justum, it is true, the requirement of proportionality possesses a broader meaning than does the requirement of proportionality in international law. In the latter, the proportionality required is little more than what may be termed a proportionality of effectiveness. In the former, the proportionality required is both a proportionality of effectiveness and a proportionality of value. In bellum justum it is not enough that the use of force is proportionate, though no more than proportionate, to the effective protection of endangered interests or values. To this proportionality of effectiveness must be added a proportionality of value, requiring that the values preserved through force are proportionate to the values sacrificed through force. Indeed, it is the proportionality of value rather than of effectiveness upon which primary emphasis is placed in bellum justum. At the same time, the requirement of a proportionality of value can hardly be regarded as a meaningful restraint, however great the emphasis placed on it. Devoid entirely of the element of specificity, it is . . . a prescription that can readily be adjusted to the most varied of actions. It is not surprising that the requirement of a proportionality of value has been invoked with an apparent plausibility on all sides of the nuclear issue by Christian moralists. It illustrates that a prescription the converse of which is manifestly absurd can tell us very little about how men ought to behave. [33]

There is no easy way to answer Tucker's objection that the concept of proportion in just-war jus ad bellum lacks specificity and restraining force. This state of affairs is hardly surprising given the lack of serious effort to apply the concept to concrete situations. Only after such efforts have been made will it be possible to begin to become specific about the "hierarchy of strictly moral values" to which Father Murray alludes in the passage quoted. Whether, in such efforts to apply the jus ad bellum concept of proportion in concrete cases, there would be the element of permissiveness that Tucker seems to find characteristic of the notion of proportionality would depend on the integrity and seriousness of the decision makers and moralists dealing with the case. This, of course, is true of all of the concepts invoked in efforts to restrain warlike initiatives and conduct.

As concerns what Father Murray calls the second consideration of proportionality—probability of success—a similar call for inclusion of moral values is made. Murray observes the following:

Pius XII required an estimate of another proportion between the evils unleashed by war and what he called "the solid probability of success" in violent repression of unjust action. The specific attention he gave to this condition was immediately prompted by his awareness of the restiveness of the people who are presently captive under unjust rule and who are tempted to believe, not without reason, that their rescue will require the use of force. This condition of probable success is not, of course, simply the statesman's classical political calculus of success. It is the moral calculus that is enjoined in the traditional theory of rebellion against tyranny. [34]

There is an important qualification to the requirement of probability of success. A war of self-defense may be engaged in irrespective of the prospects for success, particularly if there is a great threat to continued existence and to fundamental values. The limits, if any, of this qualification are unclear. It seems to be conceded that a desperate, if not hopeless, defense is permitted if the moral values to which Father Murray refers are clearly threatened by the aggressor. Whether there are any limits to the right of self-defense is something that will be addressed in Chapter 4 when the general guidelines of just-war doctrine are applied to critical issues of modern war. [35]

The last component of the condition of just cause is that war be employed only as a last resort after the exhaustion of peaceful alternatives. To have legitimate recourse to war, it must be the ultima ratio, the arbitrament of arms. This requirement has taken on added significance in the League of Nations-United Nations period. It was the intention of the nations that founded these international organizations to create the machinery for peace that would replace self-help in the form of recourse to war and limit the need for collective security enforcement action to extreme cases of defiance of international law and order. There are certainly adequate institutions of international negotiations, mediation, arbitration, and adjudication to accommodate any nation willing to submit its international disputes to peaceful settlement. Indeed, the existence of this machinery for peaceful settlement has prompted international lawyers and statesmen to adopt a rough rule of thumb: the state that fails to exhaust the peaceful remedies available before resorting to war is prima facie an aggressor.

There are a number of difficulties with this presumption. First, it is an inescapable fact that states generally have not been willing to risk their most vital interests on the outcome of international processes beyond their control. While there have been some important exceptions, hopes for widespread, indeed, routine use of the institutions for peaceful settlement have been greatly disappointed. Comparatively minor matters may be turned over to international institutions, but the most vital interests are held closely by states who protect them with the threat or use of force. It is impossible to imagine the United States or the Soviet Union, for example, agreeing in the 1960s to settle the Berlin question on the basis of an arbitral award or a judicial decision by the International Court of Justice. Where peaceful settlements have been made on matters of vital interest, they have generally resulted from traditional diplomatic negotiations backed up by force.

The second difficulty with peaceful alternatives to war, which underlies the fact of state practice, is that disputes that are the mainsprings of conflict often have their origins in differences that are not themselves soluble except by force or abandonment of fundamental values. If communist and noncommunist factions resolve to rule all of Germany, Korea, or Vietnam and to impose their ideological systems on the whole of these nations, there can be no peaceful settlement except the peace of victor and vanquished. If the Arabs deny the right of Israel to exist in territory claimed to be rightly Arab and Israel declines to give up its national existence, there is no possible peaceful solution unless, again, it is the solution of final victory for one side or the other. Intermediate resolutions of these fundamental conflicts can be reached as in the cases of Germany and Korea. They will never be final and there will be no definitive peaceful solution unless the parties alter their intentions and compromise their values. The Vietnam experience shows how utterly ephemeral such peaceful solutions may be if one side has the power and will to take it all.

In such situations, where there are irreconcilable differences between states or other international actors, no permanent peaceful solution is possible. The only hope is for fundamental commitments to change or to view the matter in drastically different ways. If there is little or no evidence of such fundamental change, a state may reasonably exhaust the peaceful alternatives at a pretty brisk pace. To be sure, a state's international reputation must be protected by holding out a willingness to use the institutions of peaceful settlement. But, given the present status of these institutions in international politics, it could very well be the case that a nation comes to the legitimate conclusion that it has no prospects for peaceful solutions and that it should plan and launch its just war with emphasis on meeting the other just-war conditions.

Moreover, there is a third problem with the apparently attractive peaceful alternatives to war. The international system has not succeeded in establishing a clear center for the management of international institutions for pacific settlement.[36] The United Nations, keystone of the whole system of international law and organization, has always been a political organization to the extent that a state in the political minority could plausibly argue that it could not receive justice if it submitted to the jurisdiction of UN institutions. To the United States, now in the political minority in the United Nations, the problem of politization of the organization appears to be worsening. The Soviets, the Chinese, and other communist states have never consented to much UN interference in their affairs. Typically, where serious progress has been made on major problems, as in the case of arms control, it has taken place primarily outside UN organs.

The United Nations has occasionally been useful in providing peace-keeping forces, but its role as a source of peaceful solutions to international conflicts and disputes over vital interest has been modest. The International Court of Justice has proved to be a disappointing, almost irrelevant institution virtually boycotted by the communist states. The more traditional institutions of negotiation and mediation have played their part in alleviating some conflicts. But, on the whole, the machinery for peace has not lived up to expectations.

All this is not to deny that there is and ought to be a requirement of just-war doctrine that war be a last resort. Every reasonable peaceful alternative should be exhausted. It is the case, however, because of the difficulties here discussed, that this exhaustion of peaceful alternatives will more often take the form of a final confirmation of the limits than of a total submission of a state's vital interests to the uncertainties of peaceful settlement of disputes in its present state.

Right Intention

St. Thomas concludes his exposition of the conditions of just war with the following:

> Thirdly, there is required a right intention on the part of the belligerents: either of achieving some good object or of avoiding some evil. So St. Augustine says in the book De Verbis Domini: "For the true followers of God even wars are peaceful, not being made for greed or out of cruelty, but from desire of peace, to restrain the evil and assist the good." So it can happen that even when war is declared by legitimate authority and there is just cause, it is nevertheless made unjust through evil intention. St. Augustine says in Contra Faustum (LXXIV): "The desire to hurt, the cruelty of vendetta, the stern and implacable

spirit, arrogance in victory, the thirst for power, and all that is similar, all these are justly condemned in war."[37]

Among the elements of the concept of right intention, several points may be distinguished. First, right intention limits the belligerent to the pursuit of the avowed just cause. That pursuit may not be turned into an excuse to pursue other causes that might not meet the conditions of just cause. Thus, if the just cause is to defend a nation's borders and protect them from future aggressions, but the fortunes of war place the just belligerent in the position to conquer the unjust nation, such a conquest might show a lack of right intention and change the just war into an unjust war. The just cause would have been realized by a war of limited objectives rather than a war of total conquest.[38]

Second, right intention requires that the just belligerent have always in mind as the ultimate object of the war a just and lasting peace. There is an implicit requirement to prepare for reconciliation even as one wages war. This is a hard saying. It will often go against the grain of the belligerents' disposition, but pursuit of a just and lasting peace is an essential characteristic of the difference between just and unjust war. Accordingly, any belligerent acts that unnecessarily increase the destruction and bitterness of war and thereby endanger the prospects for true peace are liable to condemnation as violations of the condition of right intention.[39]

Third, underlying the other requirements, right intention insists that charity and love exist even among enemies. Enemies must be treated as human beings with rights. The thrust of this requirement is twofold. Externally, belligerents must act with charity toward their enemies. Internally, belligerents must suppress natural animosity and hatred, which can be sinful and injurious to the moral and psychological health of those who fail in charity. Gratuitous cruelty may be as harmful to those who indulge in it as to their victims.[40]

Right intention raises difficult moral and psychological problems. It may well be that its tenets set standards that will often be unattainable insofar as the thoughts and feelings of belligerents are concerned. War often treats individuals and nations so cruelly and unfairly that it is unrealistic to expect them to banish all hatred of those who have afflicted them. We can, however, more reasonably insist that just belligerents may not translate their strong feelings into behavior that is prohibited by the rule of right intention. A nation may feel tempted to impose a Carthaginian peace, but it may not exceed just cause by giving in to that temptation. A nation may have good reason for feeling that the enemy deserves the full force of all means available, but the requirement to build for a just and lasting peace prohibits this kind of vengeance. The enemy may have behaved abominably, engendering righteous indignation amounting to hatred, but the actions of the just belligerent must be based on charity.

Lest this appear to be so utterly idealistic as to warrant dismissal as irrelevant to the real world, let it be recalled that the greatest enemies of the modern era have often been brought around in the cyclical processes of international politics to become trusted allies against former friends who are now viewed with fear and distrust. If war is to be an instrument of policy and not, in St. Augustine's words, a "vendetta," right intention is a counsel of good policy as well as of morality.

THE JUDGMENTAL PROCESS

Having enumerated and discussed briefly the conditions for just war in the jus ad bellum, some discussion is in order concerning the judgmental process whereby the doctrine is applied. First, it should be remarked that the jus in bello requirements of just conduct of war, discussed separately in the next chapter, have to be included in the comprehensive judgment as to a war's moral permissibility. Jus in bello is an indispensable component of the mature just-war doctrine, even though St. Thomas addressed only what we now consider the jus ad bellum conditions. The inclusion of the jus in bello, then, is assumed in the discussion of the judgmental process.

An enumeration of the jus ad bellum conditions alone, however, is enough to indicate a problem of application of the doctrine. The problem arises out of the multiple character of the main conditions and complexities of their several elements. Do all conditions have to be met to have a just war? Must they all be met equally? If there is unevenness in the degree to which they are met, may their responsiveness to the criteria be, in effect, averaged out? One may take each of the three jus ad bellum conditions and hypothesize combinations of strong, average, and weak responses to their requirements. There is very little discussion of this basic problem in the just-war literature. In the comparatively rare cases where just-war conditions have been applied seriously, the tendency appears to have been to demand satisfactory responses to all three conditions, including all of their subordinate components distinguished above. [41]

There are strong reasons for asserting that all of the conditions must be met. Such a requirement is consonant with the presumption against war and the positing of the just-war conditions as necessary to overcoming this presumption. There is no evident hierarchy among the conditions. They form a comprehensive whole. However, different times and circumstances may make one or the other of the conditions more important and problematic. Moreover, a reasonable judgment that a condition is met or can be met may be altered or reversed by additional experience, information, and insights.

This last consideration raises the issue of continuing review discussed in relation to proportionality. It is clear that the conditions may be met by reasonable estimates of the situation before a war is initiated, but that either the situation or the belligerent's perception of it may change. When either occurs, the just belligerent is obliged to review the just-war conditions and decide whether they are still being met. The number of times that such a reassessment is indicated and the intervals between reassessments will depend on the fortunes of war.

There still remains the question whether a war can be just if a belligerent fails conspicuously to meet one of the conditions. One difficulty in addressing this question is the problem of defining conspicuous failure. It is difficult to make this determination with definitions and formulas. It may be better to try out the just-war categories on some recent wars and discover the problems of application before attempting to answer this question.

I propose to apply the just-war guidelines to some contemporary wars to demonstrate the judgmental process. First, however, it is necessary to turn to the second great part of the just-war doctrine, the jus in bello. It will be seen that the interplay between the jus ad bellum and the jus in bello is considerable, even though each has its independent jurisdiction. After an analysis of the basic components of the jus in bello, the two parts of the just-war doctrine will be combined in analyses of the U.S. participation in World War II, the Korean War, and the Vietnam War.

3

JUS IN BELLO:
THE JUST CONDUCT OF WAR

The contemporary jus in bello, viewed from the combined moral-legal perspectives of this book, includes principles and prescriptions drawn from modern just-war doctrine and contemporary positive international law of war. The positive law of war now includes lengthy conventional codes centering around the Hague Convention IV of 1907, the Geneva Conventions of 1949, and the two 1977 Geneva Protocols to those conventions. It will not be necessary to discuss all of these detailed international-law provisions of the jus in bello. Rather, this chapter will delineate the main principles and prescriptions of the just-war jus in bello supplemented by the principal corresponding and/or related rules of the positive law.

In the jus in bello that emerged rather late in the development of just-war doctrine, two basic limitations on the conduct of war were laid down. One was the principle of proportion requiring proportionality of military means to political and military ends. The other was the principle of discrimination prohibiting direct, intentional attacks on noncombatants and nonmilitary targets. These are the two categories of jus in bello limitations generally treated by modern works on just war. However, the history of attempts to limit the conduct of war reveals a third category of restrictions, namely, prohibited means (that is, means that by definition are considered disproportionate and cannot be used even if they can be discriminatory). This analysis shall consider this as a third category of basic jus in bello restrictions and will subdivide it into means mala in se and means mala prohibita.

In combining just-war and international-law jus in bello, one is confronted with a problem of fitting in the basic principles of the positive law with the just-war principles. These principles (namely, military necessity, humanity, and chivalry) are discussed and related to the jus in bello principles of just-war doctrine. Finally, my own concept of legitimate military necessity as embracing all of the elements of the just-war and international-law jus in bello will be advanced. Underlying all of the jus in bello is the concept of limited war as a normative prescription, a concept that overlaps with the political/military concept of limited war to be treated in Part II.

JUST WAR AS LIMITED WAR

The discussion of the jus ad bellum began with the presumption against recourse to war and the conditions that must be met in order to overcome that presumption. It was observed that even a war that begins as a just war may become unjust if the conditions are not met throughout its course. The single, underlying requirement for the conduct of just war is that such a war must be limited. Unlimited war is never just, no matter how important the just cause.

The basic concept of limited war as a legal imperative is expressed in Article 22 of the Hague Rules of 1907—which is the first article in Section 2, "Hostilities," chapter 1, "Means of Injuring the Enemy, Sieges and Bombardments": "The right of belligerents to adopt means of injuring the enemy is not unlimited."[1]

This provision is reiterated as one of three "Basic Rules" in Article 35(1) of the 1977 Geneva Protocol I to the 1949 Geneva Conventions in Section 1, "Methods and Means of Warfare": "In any armed conflict, the right of the Parties to the conflict to choose methods or means of warfare is not unlimited."[2] This basic principle means at least two things. First, a belligerent never has the open-ended right to use all means at his disposal and/or to use any means that will injure the enemy irrespective of their conformity to the rules of the jus in bello. Second, permissible armed coercion must be limited, that is to say, controlled. Means that tend to escape the control of the belligerent are prohibited.

In succeeding chapters concepts of limited war will be examined in the light of the requirements of enlightened political/military policy. Antecedent to that discussion, however, is the moral and legal requirement that all just and legally permissible war must be limited.

The Principle of Proportion

In the preceding chapter the principle of proportion was discussed at the level of raison d'état. One of the criteria of just-war jus ad bellum requires that the good to be achieved by the realization of the war aims be proportionate to the evil resulting from the war. When the principle of proportion is again raised in the jus in bello, the ques-

tion immediately arises as to the referent of proportionality in judging the means of war.[3] Are the means to be judged in relation to the
end of the war, the ends being formulated in the highest raison d'état
terms? Or are intermediate political/military goals, referred to in
the law-of-war literature as raison de guerre, the more appropriate
referents in the calculus of proportionality as regards the conduct of
a war?

There is no question that the ultimate justification for all means
in war lies in the just cause that is a political purpose, raison d'état.
But there are difficulties in making the ends of raison d'état the sole
referent in the jus in bello calculus of proportionality. First, relation of all means to the highest ends of the war gives little rationale
for or justification of discrete military means. If all means are
simply lumped together as allegedly necessary for the war effort,
one has to accept or reject them wholly in terms of the just cause,
leaving no morality of means. The calculus of proportionality in
just cause is the total good to be expected if the war is successful
balanced against the total evil the war is likely to cause.

Second, it is evident that a discrete military means could, when
viewed independently on the basis of its intermediary military end
(raison de guerre), be proportionate or disproportionate to that military end for which it was used, irrespective of the ultimate end of the
war at the level of raison d'état. If such a discrete military means
were proportionate in terms of its military end, it would be a legitimate belligerent act. If it were disproportionate to the military end,
it would be immoral and legally impermissible. Thus, an act could be
proportionate or disproportionate to a legitimate military end regardless of the legitimacy of the just-cause end of raison d'état.

Third, there is the need to be realistic and fair in evaluating
individual command responsibility for belligerent acts. The need to
distinguish higher political ends from intermediate military ends was
acute in the war-crimes trials after World War II. It is the law of
Nuremberg, generally accepted in international law, that the raison
d'état ends of Nazi Germany were illegal aggression. But the Nuremberg and other war-crimes tribunals rejected the argument that all
military actions taken by the German armed forces were war crimes
per se because they were carried out in pursuance of aggressive
war.[4] The legitimacy of discrete acts of the German forces was
judged, inter alia, in terms of their proportionality to intermediate
military goals, raison de guerre. This was a matter of justice to
military commanders accused of war crimes. It was also a reasonable way to evaluate the substance of the allegations that war crimes
had occurred.

The distinction is equally important when applied to a just belligerent. Assuming that in World War II the Allied forces were fighting

a just war, it is clear that some of the means they employed may have been unjust (for example, strategic bombing of cities and the two atomic bomb attacks). It is not difficult to assimilate these controversial means into the total Allied war effort and pronounce that total effort proportionate to the just cause of the war. It is much more difficult and quite a different calculation to justify these means as proportionate to discrete military ends. Even in the absence of war-crimes proceedings, a just belligerent ought to respect the jus in bello standards by meeting the requirement of proportionality of means to military ends.

To be sure, it is ultimately necessary to transcend concern for the responsibility of individual military commanders and look at the objective permissibility of a military means. Thus, it may be possible and necessary to absolve a commander from responsibility for an action taken that is judged to have been disproportionate but that appeared to him to be a proportionate, reasonable military action in the light of his imperfect estimate of the situation. This subject will be pursued in later chapters.[5]

It would appear that analyses of the proportionality of military means will have to take a twofold form. First, any military means must be proportionate to a discrete, legitimate military end. Second, military means proportionate to discrete, legitimate military ends must also be proportionate to the object of the war, the just cause. In judging the moral and legal responsibility of a military commander, emphasis should be placed on the proportionality of the means to a legitimate military end. In judging the ultimate normative permissibility, as well as the prudential advisability, of a means at the level of raison d'état, the calculation should emphasize proportionality to the just cause.

The focus of normative analysis with respect to a means of war will depend on the place of the means in the total pattern of belligerent interaction. Means may be divided roughly according to the traditional distinction between tactical and strategic levels of war. Tactical means will normally be judged in terms of their proportionality to tactical military ends (for example, the tactics of attacking or defending a fortified population center will normally be judged in terms of their proportionality to the military end of taking or holding the center). Strategic means will normally be judged in terms of their proportionality to the political/military goals of the war (for example, the strategy of attacking Japanese cities, first conventionally and then with atomic bombs, in order to force the surrender of Japan will be judged in terms of its proportionality to the just cause of the war).

It remains clear, however, that the two levels overlap. A number of tactical decisions regarding battles for population centers may produce an overall strategic pattern that ought to enter into the highest

calculation of the proportionality of a just war. The strategic decisions, on the other hand, have necessary tactical implications (for
example, strategic conventional and atomic bombing of Japan was an
alternative to an amphibious invasion) the conduct of which is essentially a tactical matter. The potential costs of such a tactical invasion strongly influenced the strategic choice to seek Japan's defeat by
strategic bombing rather than ground conquest.

Insofar as judgment of proportionality in terms of military ends
is concerned, there is a central concept appearing in all normative
analyses of human behavior—the norm of reasonableness. Reasonableness must always be defined in specific context.[6] However,
sometimes patterns of behavior recur so that there are typical situations for which common models of reasonable behavior may be prescribed. In domestic law this norm is concretized through the device
of the hypothetically reasonable man whose conduct sets the standard
to be emulated by law-abiding persons. The reasonable commander
is the counterpart of the reasonable man in the law of war. The construct of the reasonable commander is based upon the experience of
military men in dealing with basic military problems.[7]

Formulation of this experience into the kinds of working guidelines that domestic law provides, notably in the field of torts, has not
advanced very far. Its advancement is one of the purposes of this
book. We do, however, have some instances in which this approach
was followed. For example, the U.S. military tribunal in the Hostage
case found that certain retaliatory means used by the German military in occupied Europe in World War II were reasonable in view of
the threat to the belligerent occupant posed by guerrilla operations
and their support by the civilian population.[8] On the other hand, in
the Calley case a court comprised of experienced combat officers
found that Lieutenant Calley's response to the situation in My Lai was
altogether unreasonable, below the standard of reasonableness expected in combat in Vietnam.[9]

The difficulty with establishing the standards of reasonableness
lies in the absence of authoritative decisions that can be widely disseminated for mandatory emulation. In a domestic public order such
as the United States, the legislature and the courts set standards for
reasonable behavior. While the standards have supporting rationales,
their greatest strength lies in the fact that they are laid down by authority and must be obeyed. With the very rare exception of some of
the post-World War II war-crimes cases, authoritative standards for
belligerent conduct are found primarily in general conventional and
customary international-law prescriptions. These international-law
norms are often too general to provide the specific characterizations
of proportionate and disproportionate behavior that regularly issue
from domestic law in the form of reasonable man/reasonable conduct

cases. In these circumstances it is the task of the publicist to analyze historical and hypothetical cases and suggest the standards of reasonableness, of proportionality, that ought to apply. This is the purpose of the analyses of U.S. participation in and conduct of three contemporary wars (Chapters 4 and 5) and of the examination of some critical issues of just war in the different levels of modern conflict (Chapters 6, 7, and 8).

In summary, the principle of proportion deals with military means at two levels: (1) tactically, as proportionate to a legitimate military end, raison de guerre; and (2) strategically, as proportionate to the just-cause ends of the war, raison d'état. The definition of legitimate military end and the calculation of the proportionality of means to such an end is a matter of the preexisting standards set by the international law of war and of judgments of reasonableness in the light of accepted military practice. The definition of just cause and the calculation of proportionality of means employed in its pursuit are, as discussed in the previous chapter, matters of balancing the probable good and evil of a war in the light of the probability of success. The extent to which jus in bello analyses will focus on the tactical or the strategic, raison de guerre or raison d'état, will depend upon the importance and scope of a military means.

The Principle of Discrimination

The principle of discrimination prohibits direct intentional attacks on noncombatants and nonmilitary targets. [10] It holds out the potential for very great, specific limitations on the conduct of just war. Accordingly, debates over the meaning of the principle of discrimination have become increasingly complex and important as the character of war has become more total. It is in the nature of the principle of proportion to be elastic and to offer possibilities for justifications of means that are truly necessary for efficacious military action. However, it is in the nature of the principle of discrimination to remain rigidly opposed to various categories of means irrespective of their necessity to success in war. It is not surprising, then, that most debates about the morality of modern war have focused on the principle of discrimination.

Such debates are vastly complicated by the opportunities afforded in the definition of the principle of discrimination to expand or contract it by interpretations of its component elements. There are debates over the meaning of direct intentional attack, noncombatants, and nonmilitary targets.

In order to discuss the problem of interpreting the principle of discrimination, it is necessary to understand the origins of the principle. The most fundamental aspect of the principle of discrimination lies in its direct relation to the justification for killing in war. If the presumption against killing generally and war in particular is overcome (in the case of war by meeting the just-war conditions), the killing then permitted is limited to the enemy combatants, the aggressors. The exceptional right to take life in individual self-defense and in war is limited to the attacker in the individual case and the enemy's soldiers in the case of war. One may not attack innocent third parties as part of individual self-defense. In war the only permissible objects of direct attack are the enemy's soldiers. In both cases, the overriding moral prescription is that evil must not be done to obtain a good object. As will be seen, however, the literal application of the principle of discrimination tends to conflict with the characteristics of efficacious military action necessary to make the right of just war effective and meaningful.

However, it is important to recognize that the principle of discrimination did not find its historical origins solely or even primarily in the fundamental argument summarized above. As a matter of fact, the principle seems to have owed at least as much to codes of chivalry and to the subsequent development of positive customary laws of war. These chivalric codes and customary practices were grounded in the material characteristics of warfare during the medieval and Renaissance periods. During much of that time, the key to the conduct of war was combat between mounted knights and supporting infantry. Generally speaking, there was no military utility in attacking anyone other than the enemy knights and their armed retainers. Attacks on unarmed civilians, particularly women and children, would have been considered unchivalric, contrary to the customary law of war, and militarily gratuitous. [11]

These multiple bases for noncombatant immunity were fortified by the growth of positive international law after the seventeenth century. In what came to be known as the Rousseau-Portalis Doctrine, war was conceived as being limited to what we could call today "counterforce warfare." Armies fought each other like athletic teams designated to represent national banners. The noncombatants were spectators to these struggles and, unless they had the bad fortune to find themselves directly on the battlefield, immune in principle from military attack. Attacks on noncombatants and nonmilitary targets were now prohibited by a rule of positive international law. Here again, the principle of discrimination was grounded in material facts, the state of the art of war and the limited nature of the conflicts, that continued to make possible its application. Moreover, the political philosophy of the time encouraged a separation of public armed forces and the populations they represented. All of these military and political supports for discrimination were to change with the advent of modern total war. [12]

At this point it is necessary to clarify the status of the principle of discrimination in just-war doctrine as interpreted in this book. It is often contended that there is an absolute principle of discrimination prohibiting any use of means that kill noncombatants. It is further contended that this absolute principle constitutes the central limitation of just war and that it is based on an immutable moral imperative that may never be broken no matter how just the cause. This is the moral axiom mentioned above, that evil may never be done in order to produce a good result. In this formulation, killing noncombatants intentionally is always an inadmissible evil. [13]

These contentions have produced two principal reactions. The first is pacifism. Pacifists rightly argue that war inevitably involves violation of the absolute principle of discrimination. If that principle is unconditionally binding, a just war is difficult if not impossible to envisage. [14] The second reaction to the claims of an absolute principle of discrimination is to modify the principle by some form of the principle of double effect whereby the counterforce component of a military means is held to represent the intent of the belligerent, whereas the countervalue, indiscriminate component of that means is explained as a tolerable, concomitant, unintended effect—collateral damage in contemporary strategic terms. [15]

Paul Ramsey is unquestionably the most authoritative proponent of an absolute principle of discrimination as the cornerstone of just-war jus in bello. No one has tried more courageously to reconcile this absolute principle with the exigencies of modern war and deterrence. As will be discussed in Chapter 6, neither Ramsey nor anyone else can reconcile the principle of discrimination in an absolute sense with the strategic countervalue nuclear warfare that is threatened in contemporary deterrence. It is possible that Ramsey's version of discrimination could survive the pressures of military necessity at levels below that of strategic nuclear deterrence and war. But the fate of Ramsey's effort to reconcile an absolute moral principle of discrimination with the characteristics of modern war should indicate the grave difficulties inherent in this effort, difficulties that commentators such as Robert W. Tucker have termed intractable. [16]

The question then arises whether such heroic efforts to salvage an absolute principle of discrimination are necessary. As observed above, the principle of discrimination does not appear in the just-war jus in bello as a doctrinally established deduction from theological or philosophical first principles. Rather, it was historically the product of belligerent practice reflecting a mixture of moral and cultural values of earlier societies. Moreover, it is significant that in the considerable body of contemporary Catholic social teaching on war, embracing the pronouncements of Pope Pius XII and his successors and of Vatican II, the principle of discrimination is not prominent in any form, absolute or conditional. When weapons systems or forms of warfare are condemned, deplored, or reluctantly condoned, the rationales are so generalized that the judgments appear to be based on a mixed application of the principles of proportion and discrimination. If anything, these pronouncements seem more concerned with disproportionate rather than indiscriminate effects. [17]

It is a curious kind of supreme, absolute principle of the just-war doctrine that slips almost imperceptibly into the evolving formulations of the authoritative texts and then is omitted as an explicit controlling rationale in contemporary judgments by the church framed in just-war terms. Moreover, the persistent reiteration by the contemporary church that legitimate self-defense is still morally permissible should imply that such defense is practically feasible; otherwise the recognition of the right is meaningless. But, as the pacifists rightly observe, self-defense or any kind of war is incompatible with an absolute principle of discrimination.

It is my contention that the moral, just-war principle of discrimination is not an absolute limitation on belligerent conduct. There is no evidence that such a principle was ever seriously advanced by the church, and it is implicitly rejected when the church acknowledges the continued right of legitimate self-defense, a right that has always been incompatible with observance of an absolute principle of discrimination. Accordingly, I do not distinguish an absolute, moral, just-war principle of discrimination from a more flexible and variable international-law principle of discrimination. To be sure, the moral, just-war understanding of discrimination must remain independent of that of international law at any given time. But discrimination is best understood and most effectively applied in light of the interpretations of the principle in the practice of belligerents. This, after all, was the principal origin of this part of the jus in bello, and the need to check moral just-war formulations against contemporary international-law versions is perennial.

Such a position is in no sense a retreat from a position of maximizing normative limitations on the conduct of war. In the first place, as Ramsey's brave but ultimately unsuccessful efforts have demonstrated, attachment to an absolute principle of discrimination leads either to a finding that all war is immoral and the demise of the just-war doctrine or to tortured efforts to reconcile the irreconcilable. Neither serves the purposes of the jus in bello. Second, the rejection of an absolute principle of discrimination does not mean an abandonment of efforts to limit war on moral grounds. The principle of discrimination remains a critical source of both moral and legal limitations of belligerent behavior. As Tucker has observed, there are significant points of limitation between the position that no injury must ever be done to noncombatants and the position that there are no restraints on countervalue warfare.[18] The interpretations that follow here and in succeeding chapters will try to balance the need to protect noncombatants with the need to recognize the legitimate military necessities of modern forms of warfare. In this process one may err one way of the other, but at least some relevant, practical guidance may be offered belligerents. Adherence to an absolute principle of discrimination usually means irrelevance to the question of limiting the means of war or unconvincing casuistry.

In search of such practical guidance one may resume the examination of the principle of discrimination as interpreted both by moralists and international lawyers. Even before the principle of discrimination was challenged by the changing realities of total war, there were practical difficulties with the definition of <u>direct intentional attack</u>, <u>noncombatants</u>, and <u>nonmilitary targets</u>. It is useful, as a starting point for analysis, to recall a standard and authoritative exposition of the principle of discrimination by Fr. Richard McCormick.

> It is a fundamental moral principle [unanimously accepted by Catholic moralists] that it is immoral directly to take innocent human life except with divine authorization. "Direct" taking of human life implies that one performs a lethal action with the intention that death should result for himself or another. Death therefore is deliberately willed as the effect of one's action. "Indirect" killing refers to an action or omission that is designed and intended solely to achieve some other purpose(s) even though death is forseen as a concomitant effect. Death therefore is not positively willed, but is reluctantly permitted as an unavoidable by-product.[19]

An example that is frequently used in connection with this question is the use of catapults in medieval sieges of castles. The intention—indeed, the purpose—of catapulting projectiles over the castle wall was to kill enemy defenders and perhaps to break down the defenses. If noncombatants—innocents as they were called then—were killed or injured, this constituted a "concomitant effect," an "undesired by-product."[20]

The issues of intention, act, and multiple effects are often analyzed in terms of the principle of double effect, which Father McCormick's exposition employs without invoking the concept explicitly. After centuries of inconclusive efforts to apply the principle of double effect to the <u>jus in bello</u>, Michael Walzer has proposed his own version, which merits reflection and experimental application.

> The intention of the actor is good, that is, he aims narrowly at the acceptable effect; the evil effect is not one

of his ends, nor is it a means to his ends, and, aware of
the evil involved, he seeks to minimize it, accepting costs
to himself.[21]

It is probably not possible to reconcile observance of the principle of discrimination with the exigencies of genuine military necessity without employing the principle of double effect in one form or
another. However, this distinction between primary, desired effect
and secondary, concomitant, undesired by-product is often difficult
to accept.

It is not so hard to accept the distinction in a case where the
concomitant undesired effect was accidental (for example, a case
where the attacker did not know that noncombatants were present in
the target area). There would still remain, in such a case, a question as to whether the attacker ought to have known that noncombatants
might be present. Nor is it so hard to accept a double-effect justification in a situation where the attacker had reason to believe that
there might be noncombatants present but that this was a remote possibility. If, however, the attacker knows that there are noncombatants intermingled with combatants to the point that any attack on the
military target is highly likely to kill or injure noncombatants, then
the death or injury to those noncombatants is certainly "intended" or
"deliberately willed," in the common usage of those words.[22]

As will be seen in Chapters 6 and 8, this is an issue of interpretation that stands at the center of any effort to apply just-war
standards to the conduct of modern deterrence and war. But, at the
other end of the conflict spectrum, it also is a central issue in revo-
lutionary/counterinsurgency wars.

It is clear that insistence on an absolute principle of discrimination tends to put recourse to the principle of double effect into the
category of a kind of moral double-talk that appears unconvincing and
perhaps hypocritical. But if the principle of discrimination is viewed
as a relative principle enjoining the maximization of noncombatant
protection, it seems possible to employ double-effect explanations
for actions wherein the major intention is to effect counterforce injury on military objectives while acknowledging an inescapable intention of injuring countervalue targets and thereby predictably violating
the principle of discrimination to some extent. Ironically, a moral
evaluation of such a justification of mixed counterforce-countervalue
warfare would involve a calculus of proportion between the degree
and importance of the counterforce and countervalue injuries, respectively (ironically, because many strong proponents of the principle of discrimination are skeptical or scornful about the practical
utility of the principle of proportion as an effective source of limitations on belligerent conduct.)[23]

Turning to the object of the protection of the principle of discrimination—the innocents or noncombatants—another critical question of interpretation arises. How does one define noncombatants? How does one define nonmilitary targets? The assumption of separability of military forces and the populations they represented, found in medieval theory and continued by the Rousseau-Portalis Doctrine, became increasingly less valid after the wars of the French Revolution.

As nations engaged in total mobilization, one society or system against another, it was no longer possible to distinguish sharply between the military forces and the home fronts that rightly held themselves out as critical to the war effort. By the American Civil War this modern phenomenon had assumed critical importance. The material means of supporting the Confederate war effort were attacked directly and intentionally by Union forces. War in the age of the Industrial Revolution was waged against the sources of war production. Moreover, the nature of the attacks on noncombatants was psychological as well as material. Military forces have always attempted to break the will of the opposing forces as well as to destroy or scatter them. It now became the avowed purpose of military forces to break the will of the home front as well as to destroy its resources for supporting the war. This, of course, was to become a major purpose of modern strategic aerial bombardment.

To be sure, attacks on the bases of military forces have historically often been an effective strategy. But in the simpler world before the Industrial Revolution, this was not such a prominent option. When the huge conscript armies began to fight for profound ideological causes with the means provided by modern industrial mobilization and technology, the home front and consequently the noncombatants became a critical target for direct intentional attack.

The question then arose whether a civilian could be a participant in the overall war effort to such a degree as to lose his previous noncombatant immunity. Likewise, it became harder to distinguish targets that were clearly military from targets, such as factories or railroad facilities, that were of sufficient military importance to justify their direct intentional attack. It is important to note that this issue arose before the great increase in the range, areas of impact, and destructive effects of modern weaponry, conventional and nuclear. What we may term countervalue warfare was carried out in the American Civil War not because it was dictated by the weapons systems but because the civilian population and war-related industries and activities were considered to be critical and legitimate targets to be attacked.

In World War I this kind of attack was carried out primarily by the belligerents with their maritime blockades. Above all, these blockades caused the apparent demise of the principle of noncombatant immunity in the positive international law of war. Other factors in this demise were developments that revealed potentials not fully realized until World War II (for example, aerial bombardment of population centers and unrestricted submarine warfare). In World War II aerial bombardment of population centers was preeminent as a source of attacks on traditional noncombatants and nonmilitary targets. By this time the concept of total mobilization had advanced so far that a plausible argument could be made that vast segments of belligerent populations and complexes of industry and housing had become so integral to the war effort as to lose their noncombatant immunity.

In summary, well before the advent of weapons systems that are usually employed in ways that do not discriminate between traditional combatants and noncombatants, military and nonmilitary targets, the distinction had eroded. The wall of separation between combatants and noncombatants had been broken down by the practice of total societal mobilization in modern total war and the resulting practice of attacking directly and intentionally that mobilization base. Given these developments, it was difficult to maintain that the principle of discrimination was still a meaningful limit on war. Those who clung to the principle tended to reject modern war altogether as inherently immoral because it inherently violates the principle. In the international law of war, distinguished publicists were reduced to stating that terror bombing of noncombatants with no conceivable proximate military utility was prohibited, but that the rights of noncombatants to protection otherwise were unclear.[24]

One would not have expected this state of affairs to be improved by the passage of many years under the specter of the nuclear balance of terror. However, surprisingly enough, there has been a revival in positive international law of the principle of discrimination.

Article 48 of the 1977 Geneva Protocol I provides for the following:

> In order to ensure respect for and protection of the civilian population and civilian objects, the Parties to the conflict shall at all times distinguish between the civilian population and combatants and between civilian objects and military objectives and accordingly shall direct their operations only against military objectives.

In Protocol I the long-debated question of definition of combatants and noncombatants is resolved in such a way as to bring the law back to the pretotal-war practice. Combatants are defined in the sense of persons qualifying for belligerent status (Article 43). Civilians (that is, noncombatants) are defined as any persons not belonging

to the category of combatants as defined in the Third 1949 Geneva
Convention (Article 4) and Protocol I (Article 43). Article 50(3) of
Protocol I concludes that "the presence within the civilian population
of individuals who do not come within the definition of civilians does
not deprive the population of its civilian character."

Thus, the whole trend of the practice of belligerents from the
American Civil War to the present is disavowed in the new Geneva
Protocol I. Whether it will be ratified by a majority of states, including the great powers, and whether it will prove an effective source of
limitation rather than paper law remains to be seen. Having taken a
definite stand on the strict definition of noncombatant civilians and
civilian objects, the new code then deals with the details of their immunity from attack in Articles 51-56. These provisions will be quoted
or summarized in proportion to their relevance to the central concept
of discrimination.

Article 51 of Protocol I adheres to a strict definition of discrimination. Paragraph 1 provides that the "civilian population and individual civilians shall enjoy general protection against dangers arising from military operations." The rules that follow are to be observed, together with other applicable rules of international law,
"in all circumstances." The article then provides for the following:

> 2. The civilian population as such, as well as individual
> civilians, shall not be the object of attack. Acts or threats
> of violence the primary purpose of which is to spread ter-
> ror among the civilian population are prohibited.
> 3. Civilians shall enjoy the protection afforded by this
> Section, unless and for such time as they take a direct
> part in hostilities.
> 4. Indiscriminate attacks are prohibited. Indiscrimi-
> nate attacks are:
>
> (a) those which are not directed at a specific military ob-
> jective;
> (b) those which employ a method or means of combat which
> cannot be directed at a specific military objective; or
> (c) those which employ a method or means of combat the
> effects of which cannot be limited as required by this
> Protocol; and consequently, in each such case, are of a
> nature to strike military objectives and civilian objects
> without distinction.

Article 51(5) continues with a specification of the types of attacks that are to be considered as indiscriminate.

(a) an attack by bombardment by any methods or means
which treats as a single military objective a number of
clearly separated and distinct military objectives located
in a city, town, village or other area containing a similar
concentration of civilian objects; and
(b) an attack which may be expected to cause incidental
loss of civilian life, injury to civilians, damage to civilian
objects, or a combination thereof, which would be excessive
in relation to the concrete and direct military advantage
anticipated.

Article 51(6) prohibits "attacks against the civilian population or
civilians by way of reprisals." Article 51(7) seeks to prevent abuse
of noncombatant immunity by prohibiting the use of civilians "to shield
military objectives from attacks or to shield military operations."
Article 51(8) specifically provides that violations of these prohibitions
does not release the parties from the obligation to observe them.
Article 52 defines civilian objects as all objects that are not
military objectives. These latter are then defined.

2. Attacks shall be limited strictly to military objectives.
In so far as objects are concerned, military objectives are
limited to those objects which by their nature, location,
purpose or use make an effective contribution to military
action and whose total or partial destruction, capture or
neutralization, in the circumstances ruling at the time,
offers a definite military advantage.

Article 52(3) provides a presumption that such objects as places of
worship, dwellings, and schools are nonmilitary. Article 53 requires
protection of cultural objects and places of worship.
As will be discussed in Chapter 7, Article 54 of Protocol I, as
well as Article 14 of Protocol II, prohibits "starvation of civilians as
a method of warfare."[25] Article 55 of Protocol I deals with protection of the natural environment, and Article 56 provides for protection
of works and installations containing dangerous forces that, when attacked, might injure civilians.
In Article 57, "Precautions in attack," there is a rare example
of the conventional jus in bello undertaking to regulate the military
decision process with detailed prescriptions designed to maximize
protection of noncombatants. Also contained in this article is a provision in Section 3 that where a choice is possible, "between several
military objectives for obtaining a similar military advantage, the
objective to be selected shall be that the attack on which may be expected to cause the least danger to civilian lives and to civilian ob-

jects." Requirements for precautions to protect civilians are applied to military operations at sea or in the air in Section 4 of Article 57.

Article 58 of the protocol enjoins the target state to take all measures to remove civilians from the vicinity of military objectives, "avoid locating military objectives within or near densely populated areas," and take necessary measures to protect civilian persons and objectives "under their control against the dangers resulting from military operations." Article 59 prohibits attacks "by any means whatsoever" on "non-defended localities." This is elaborated on in Sections 2-7. A related provision is made in Article 60 for demilitarized zones.

The foregoing exposition demonstrates that the 1977 Geneva Protocol I undertakes to effect a drastic reform in international practice regarding the application of the principle of discrimination. The difficulties of implementing this new code, if and when it becomes conventional international law, will be discussed in succeeding chapters. Meanwhile, it is appropriate to compare the treatment of the revived principle of discrimination in the 1977 Geneva Protocol I with the recent United States Air Force manual, AFP 110-31, International Law—The Conduct of Armed Conflict and Air Operations. (This text is referred to as a manual even though it is technically not one in the sense of the Army Field Manual 27-10 on the law of land warfare. AFP 110-31 is a serious, authoritative, and authorized guide to U.S. belligerent behavior and will be treated as such.)[26]

AFP 110-31 provides important evidence of the practice and expectations of the United States. As a great power of primary military importance, the view of the United States on the law of war is critical. This is especially the case since AFP 110-31 is the first manual on the subject to be issued by the United States Air Force; it is held out as representative of standards of conduct to which the Air Force can and will adhere.

At the outset, in its treatment of the principle of humanity, the Air Force manual lays down the corollary principle of "the basic immunity of civilian populations and civilians from being objects of attack during armed conflict." Immediately thereafter the traditional distinction between "direct intentional" and "indirect concomitant" attack is invoked. (Note the congruence of the language with the provisions of the 1977 Protocol I, Article 57.)

> This immunity of the civilian population does not preclude unavoidable incidental civilian casualties which may occur during the course of attacks against military objectives, and which are not excessive in relation to the concrete and direct military advantage anticipated.[27]

The heart of the subject is treated in Chapter 5 of AFP 110-31 dealing with aerial bombardment. In addition to reasserting the principle of discrimination, Chapter 5 insists that provisions of the 1907 Hague Rules regulating bombardment (Articles 25-27) "are not historical curiosities but viable, active and enforceable standards for combatants."[28] Given the record of bombardments from land, sea, and air since World War I, this is a remarkable claim. However, the manual seeks to substantiate this claim by distinguishing U.S. bombing practices from those of the British and Germans in World War II. The United States, it is asserted, followed bombing practices consonant with the principle of discrimination and the prescriptions of the 1907 Hague Rules in World War II, as well as in the Korean and the Vietnam wars. It is contended that deviation from these standards—mainly by the other belligerents—was caused by three factors: the inaccuracy of bombing; "the escalating nature of reprisals and counterreprisals thereby demonstrating the importance of reciprocity in actual observance of the law"; and "the failure to separate effectively war industry and other vital targets from the population centers, thereby necessitating target area bombing."[29]

It appears to be the conviction of the Air Force authors of AFP 110-31 and their superiors who approved it that, with respect to conventional bombing, the Air Force can overcome these three factors (that is, bombing accuracy is now much improved, reprisals will be avoided, and belligerents are on notice to separate their military from their civilian targets or take upon themselves responsibility for civilian losses in military attacks).

These efforts by the Air Force to reconcile military considerations with the principle of discrimination are hampered by the manifest record of recent wars. For example, the manual acknowledges that "as a result of bombing, some major cities of Europe and Asia were substantially destroyed, including traditional military targets and areas of civilian housing and activity." But it is then claimed that "the Allies did not regard civilian populations and their housing as proper military targets and generally preferred to seek to destroy only the military aspects of the cities: their rail yards, war factories, communication facilities, military supply depots and the like."[30] These two statements compare the intention and/or preference of the Allies to attack only military targets with the fact that their practice resulted in substantial destruction of major cities. The key to the Air Force case that the principle of discrimination can be reconciled with the necessities of modern war is summed up in AFP 110-31 with the following claim:

> The U.S. 8th and 15th Air Force demonstrated to a skeptical world the military value of daylight precision bombing of

carefully selected military objectives, such as German submarine construction pens, aircraft industry, transportation and oil facilities.[31]

To this is added the claim that in conflicts since World War II,
the practices of the belligerents "indicate an increased interest in
avoiding civilian casualties from aerial bombardment." Thus, "the
earlier emphasis by the United States on precision bombing of military
objectives has been fully supported by other states."[32]
In pursuit of this position, AFP 110-31 lays down five general
restrictions on aerial bombardment: immunity of civilians, confinement of military operations to military objectives, precautions in attack, protection of works and installations containing dangerous forces,
and prohibition of attacks on undefended areas.[33] It will be seen that
these restrictions parallel relevant provisions of the 1977 Geneva
Protocol I. The four paragraphs of specific rules elaborating the
first restriction (immunity of civilians) constitute a summary of Articles 48-52 of the protocol.
The effort of the Air Force manual to incorporate the emerging
reiteration and elaboration of the principle of discrimination in the
1977 Geneva Protocol is commendable. However, the treatment of
some of the provisions found both in the protocol and the Air Force
manual reveals some of the problems of practical application that
ought to be borne in mind in appraising the probable effect of this revival and expansion of the principle of discrimination. For example,
Article 57(2)(c) of the protocol provides that "effective advance warning shall be given of attacks which may affect the civilian population,
unless circumstances do not permit." The identical language appears
in AFP 110-31. The manual admits that World War II practice "was
lax . . . because of the heavily defended nature of the targets attacked
as well as because of attempts to conceal targets."[34] Then, after
contending that "the practice of states recognizes that warning need
not always be given," AFP 110-31 asserts the following:

General warnings are more frequently given than specific
warnings, lest the attacking force or the success of its
mission be jeopardized. Warnings are relevant to the
protection of the civilian population and need not be given
when they are unlikely to be affected by the attack.[35]

This would seem to reduce the importance of warnings considerably.
It may well be a realistic and reasonable interpretation, but it results
in a much more modest prescription to belligerents than might be assumed from a reading of Article 57(2)(c) of the Geneva Protocol I and
the comparable provision of AFP 110-31.

There is another conspicuous example of a stern rule that is reduced to something rather innocuous. Article 59 of the 1977 Protocol I reiterates the rule of Article 25 of the 1907 Hague Convention IV that attacks on undefended localities are prohibited. The interpretation of this important restriction in AFP 110-31 is as follows:

> But cities behind enemy lines and not open to occupation may contain military objectives. The application of this undefended rule to aerial warfare, where the object of the attack was not to occupy the city but to achieve some specific military advantage by destroying a particular military objective, caused disagreements in the past. In the U.S. view, it has been recognized by the practice of nations that any place behind enemy lines is a defended place because it is not open to unopposed occupation. Thus, although such a city is incapable of defending itself against aircraft, nonetheless if it is in enemy held territory and not open to occupation, military objectives in the city can be attacked. [Emphasis added][36]

Again, the interpretation may be realistic and reasonable, but it reduces the immunity of undefended localities to the vanishing point. If this interpretation prevails, Article 59 of the 1977 Geneva Protocol I is as obsolete before the treaty enters into force as Hague Article 25 has been for over 60 years.

These two examples should serve as a caveat to those who assume that the new Geneva Protocol I will reform dramatically the disarray that modern deterrence and war have produced with respect to the principle of discrimination. Even if the treaty is ratified by a great majority of the world's military powers, it is subject to multiple interpretations. History teaches us that interpretations of the principle of discrimination tend to blunt its hard edge as a restraint on the conduct of just war.

It should be noted that the difficulties of interpreting the principle of discrimination continue to exist with respect to conventional means of warfare. Clearly the application of the principle to nuclear deterrence and war is even more problematic. This will be discussed, together with comparably difficult problems of applying the principle of discrimination in revolutionary war, in Chapters 6 and 8.

Prohibited Means

In addition to the restraints of the principles of proportion and discrimination, the just conduct of war is limited by a number of pro-

hibitions against the use of specific means of war. The rationales
for these prohibitions may overlap with either or both of the rationales
for the principles of proportion and discrimination. However, they
are independent limitations operating irrespective of whether a means
appears to meet the requirements of proportionality and/or discrimination.

Prohibited means may be mala in se and/or mala prohibita. A
means that is malum in se is inherently wrong and must never be used.
The source of this judgment may be found in morality, in traditional
natural law, or in the secular principle of humanity. Whatever its
normative source, a means that is recognized as being malum in se
is viewed as wrong, independent of any positive law prescriptions.
The absence of such legal prescriptions does not allow the use of
means mala in se.

Means mala prohibita need not necessarily be mala in se. Such
means may lend themselves to use that would be morally acceptable.
However, the merits and costs of such means have been weighed in a
lawmaking process and they have been prohibited. Thus a means
malum prohibitum may be capable of proportionate and discriminatory
application, but the law made by authoritative decision makers has
ruled out any use of this proscribed means.

Means Mala in Se

Genocide is malum in se. The origins of the concept of genocide are to be found in the Nuremberg charge of "crimes against humanity." Article 6(c) of the 1945 London Charter establishing the
Nuremberg International Military Tribunal and the Law of Nuremberg
defined as crimes against international law those

> crimes against humanity: namely, murder, extermina-
> tion, enslavement, deportation, and other inhumane acts
> committed against any civilian population, before or dur-
> ing the war, or persecutions on political, racial, or re-
> ligious grounds in execution of or in connection with any
> crimes within the jurisdiction of the tribunal. [37]

At the heart of the concept of crimes against humanity was the
crime to which the name genocide was given. The word genocide was
coined by Professor Raphael Lemkin by combining the Greek genos
("race," "nation," or "tribe") with the Latin suffix cide ("killing"). [38]
The word was adopted in the Nuremberg trial, notably by the British
prosecutor, Sir Hartley Shawcross. However, the category of
"crimes against humanity" was broader than genocide. Moreover,
the Nuremberg tribunal declined in its judgment to deal with crimes
against humanity, including genocide, that had occurred before the

outbreak of World War II. Furthermore, in its judgment the tribunal tended to assimilate crimes against humanity into war crimes. There were no cases where a defendant was found guilty of crimes against humanity but not of war crimes. The effect of this court at Nuremberg, then, was mainly symbolic. It constituted a reassertion of higher norms that nations and men are not free to violate, even in the absence of specific legal prohibitions.[39]

However, the Nuremberg trial provided the catalyst that produced the prohibition against genocide. Following unanimous adoption of a 1946 General Assembly resolution affirming that "genocide is a crime under international law," a Genocide Convention was adopted by the General Assembly in 1948 and came into force in 1951.[40] In the Genocide Convention the parties did "confirm that genocide, whether committed in time of peace or in time of war, is a crime under international law which they undertake to prevent and punish." Article 2 of the convention defines genocide as "any of the following acts committed with intent to destroy, in whole or in part, a national, ethnical, racial or religious group, as such." The specified acts include killing members of the group, causing serious bodily or mental harm to members of the group, deliberately inflicting on the group conditions of life calculated to bring about its physical destruction in whole or in part, imposing measures intended to prevent births within the group, and forcibly transferring children of the group to another group.

There is no provision in the Genocide Convention for international enforcement. The parties to the agreement "under take to enact, in accordance with their respective Constitutions, the necessary legislation to give effect to the . . . Convention and . . . to provide effective penalties." However, following the Nuremberg precedent, genocide is treated as a crime for which individuals may be tried by a competent tribunal of the state in the territory of which the act was committed, or by such international penal tribunal (there is none today) as may have jurisdiction with respect to those contracting parties that have accepted its jurisdiction.

In contemporary international and domestic politics, genocide has become an overused and abused term. It is important to clarify what is and is not rightly called genocide. The essence of the concept is expressed in the convention's definition of genocide as the commission of the specified acts "with intent to destroy, in whole or in part, a national, ethnical, racial, or religious group, as such." There must be intent to commit these acts against the target group. This means that the acts are carried out not in virtue of any legitimate public requirements of peace or war but purely for the sake of exterminating or degrading the target group. There is, in a case of genocide, no legitimate rationale of internal or international security or any other justification for the measures taken. The group is discriminated against and its destruction sought solely because it is what it is. Genocide is generally based on an ideology that places all persons within a group into an inferior category considered to be inherently undesirable and subversive to the state. This may be based on race, nationality, or ethnicity. Although the category is omitted from the convention, genocide may also be based on social class and, given communist practice, it would be proper to add this meaning to the concept of genocide.

The prototype for genocide is the Holocaust suffered by the Jews under the Nazi regime in Germany and occupied Europe. Jews were destroyed in numbers exceeding six million; millions more suffered extreme hardships of enslavement, imprisonment, torture, disruption of families, loss of property and livelihood, and other atrocities. None of this was remotely linked to any peacetime requirements of security or wartime exigencies.

It follows that wartime measures taken without genocidal intent that result in great loss of life, destruction, and social-political-economic dislocation are not genocide. The charge of genocide is frequently made in connection with recent wars and military preparations. Thus, there were charges of genocide against the United States in the Vietnam War and critics of nuclear deterrence frequently term nuclear war genocide. The conduct of the Vietnam War by the United States may or may not pass the tests imposed by the principles of proportion and discrimination and by specific law of war prohibitions, but it cannot properly be termed genocide. The United States did not have an intent to destroy either the nation of South or North Vietnam, as such. Indeed, its intent was to defend the former against the latter. Nor did the United States have the intent of destroying the Vietcong and their supporters, as such. Rather, there was the traditional intent of defeating an enemy and establishing peace. Most modern wars promise to be extremely costly to the belligerent populations, but that does not make them genocidal. Constant use of the charge of genocide in connection with wartime measures only confuses and dilutes its meaning so that a necessarily distinct category of limitation of belligerent behavior becomes hopelessly entangled with other, quite different limitations. Likewise, the task of analyzing the dreadful complexities of nuclear deterrence and nuclear war is only hindered by introducing the charge of genocide.

In conclusion, it must be reiterated that it is conceivable for a belligerent to employ genocidal policies as a means of war, but that such a means is malum in se. Genocide pursued for illicit, nonmilitary reasons under cover of war is likewise malum in se.

Means Mala Prohibita

The total number of means prohibited by the international law of war is great. They will not all be dealt with here. Instead, the most important prohibitions will be outlined and discussed briefly. These are: means causing superfluous suffering, chemical warfare, biological warfare, and grave offenses against the law of war as defined in the 1949 Geneva Conventions and the 1977 Geneva Protocol I to those conventions.

Means Causing Superfluous Suffering. The St. Petersburg Declaration of 1868 condemned "arms which uselessly aggravate the sufferings of disabled men, or render their death inevitable."[41] In the Hague Rules of 1907 this became Article 23(e), which provided that "in addition to the prohibitions provided by special Conventions it is especially forbidden . . . to employ arms, projectiles, or materials calculated to cause unnecessary suffering."

This general prohibition has proved difficult to apply. It has been invoked with respect to a variety of means including chemical warfare, nuclear warfare, and the use of napalm. Yet, the U.S. government has rightly maintained that means may be considered violative of the prohibition of superfluous suffering only in the case of specific international agreements certifying that a particular means does cause superfluous suffering. This has seldom happened. When it has, the means prohibited was usually thought to be of little or no military utility.[42]

The prohibition against means causing superfluous suffering is obviously a product of the principle of proportion. The problem has been that means that are very effective are seldom seriously considered as falling into the prohibited category. Means that are obsolete or of questionable effectiveness are sometimes banned under this category.

Chemical Warfare. Article 23(a) of the 1907 Hague Rules especially forbade the use of "poisoned weapons." In all likelihood, this rule did not anticipate the advent of gas warfare in World War I. Rather, it referred to poisoned weapons (for example, swords, spears, and arrows) and to the use of poison in food or water supplies, means condemned because of their uncontrollable character, the inevitability of death, and the fact that they were considered treacherous and dishonorable. Thus, the widespread use of gas warfare in World War I found belligerents without controlling international-law rules, and they took advantage of the situation by unlimited use of gas. Then, after unconvincing efforts to pretend that gas had been subject to legal regulation, the nations produced the Geneva Gas Protocol of June 17, 1925.

This convention outlaws the use of "asphyxiating, poisonous or other gases, and of all analagous liquids, materials or devices."[43]

Although two major powers—the United States and Japan—did not ratify the Geneva Gas Protocol, it appears to have been observed by the practice of states since 1925. Thus, in a period embracing World War II and many other wars, the only use of gas has been by Italy in the war with Ethiopia, Japan in the war with China, and the United States in the Vietnam War. However, it may also be said that the practice of belligerents establishes that the ban on gas warfare is a "no first use" arrangement. All militarily important powers reserve the right to retaliate in kind if chemical warfare is used against them, and they maintain elaborate chemical warfare establishments for that purpose. It should be noted that the Soviets are given to dire threats of use of chemical means in the event of a major conflict.[44]

The United States finally ratified the 1925 Geneva Gas Protocol, effective January 22, 1975, with a reservation permitting the retaliatory use of chemical weapons and agents.[45] In the Vietnam War the United States maintained that nonlethal chemical means such as antiplant agents and riot control agents were permissible. This is a very controversial subject. On the one hand, it is clear that these nonlethal agents have many reasonable uses in war and are probably preferable to other means of uncontested legality. On the other hand, admission of these exceptions to the general ban on chemical warfare erodes the wall around the prohibited category and threatens a Pandora's box effect that could break down the restraints on chemical warfare altogether. The United States has held out for these nonlethal means in an executive order by President Ford on April 8, 1975. Under this policy directive, the United States renounced first use of herbicides in war except for use under regulations applicable to their domestic use for U.S. bases and defense perimeters. Presumably this would mean such use mainly for stripping natural cover that was dangerous to the security of a base or force. Crop destruction would not seem to be implied. Under Ford's order the United States also renounced first use of riot control agents except in defensive military modes to save lives.[46]

Biological Warfare. For most of the years since World War I, biological warfare was lumped together with chemical warfare (CB or BC) and even with nuclear warfare (CBR). Biological warfare is now the object of the 1972 Convention on the Prohibition of the Development, Production, and Stockpiling of Bacteriological (Biological) and Toxin Weapons and on their Destruction.[47] The authoritative commentary of AFP 110-31 explains that biological weapons or methods of warfare are prohibited whether they are directed against persons, animals, or plants. The rationale for the ban lies in the "wholly in-

discriminate and uncontrollable nature of biological weapons." The
ban is said by the Air Force manual to be confirmed by "the practice
of states in refraining from their use in warfare."[48]

In order to focus on the most salient prohibitions of the positive
law of war, it is useful to consider the "grave breaches" singled out
in the 1949 Geneva Conventions and 1977 Geneva Protocol I. The 1949
Geneva Conventions for the Amelioration of the Conditions of the
Wounded and Sick in Armed Forces in the Field (GWS) in Article 50;
for the Amelioration of the Condition of the Wounded, Sick and Shipwrecked Members of Armed Forces at Sea (GWS-SEA) in Article 51;
Relative to Treatment of Prisoners of War (GPW) in Article 130;
and Relative to the Protection of Civilians in Time of War (GC) in
Article 147 cite as grave offenses willful killing; torture or inhuman
treatment, including biological experiments; and willful causing of
great suffering or serious injury to body or health.[49]

GWS, GSW-SEA, and GC in the same respective articles cite
as grave offenses extensive destruction and appropriation of property
not justified by military necessity and carried out unlawfully and wan-
tonly.

The 1949 Geneva PW Convention further cites as grave offenses
in Article 130 compelling a prisoner of war to serve in the forces of
the hostile power and willfully depriving a prisoner of war of the rights
of fair and regular trial prescribed in this convention.

Article 147 of the 1949 Geneva Civilians Convention adds to the
list of grave offenses unlawfully deporting a protected person to serve
in the forces of a hostile power, compelling a protected person to
serve in the forces of a hostile power, willfully depriving a protected
person of the rights of fair and regular trial prescribed in this convention, and taking hostages. These offenses are all established,
therefore, in conventional international law.

The 1977 Geneva Protocol I adds a large number of additional
grave offenses to be incorporated into new conventional law. Thus,
Article 11 makes detailed provisions for the protection of the physical
and mental health and integrity of persons in the power of the adverse
party. Article 85 of Protocol I deals with grave breaches. Article
85 refers to the grave breaches specified in the 1949 Geneva Conventions as well as to those enumerated in Article 11 of the protocol. In
addition, Article 85 condemns as "grave breaches of this Protocol,
when committed willfully, in violation of the relevant provisions of
this Protocol, and causing death or serious injury to body or health"
six prohibited acts. The first four of these have already been identified in the discussion of the principle of discrimination as developed
by the protocol.

To these prohibitions against violations of the principle of discrimination, the specification of grave offenses of Article 85 adds

making a person the object of attack in the knowledge that he is hors de combat and the perfidious use, in violation of Article 27, of the distinctive emblem of the red cross, red crescent, or red lion and sun, or of any other protection signs recognized by the conventions of Protocol I. Article 85 then continues to supplement grave offenses against civilians as already defined by the 1949 conventions with the following:

1. Transfer by the occupying power of parts of its own civilian population into the territory it occupies, or the deportation or transfer of all or parts of the population of the occupied territory within or outside this territory, in violation of Article 49 of the Civilians Convention;

2. Unjustifiable delay in the repatriation of prisoners of war or civilians;

3. Practices of apartheid and other inhuman degrading practices involving outrages upon personal dignity, based on racial discrimination;

4. Designation of the clearly recognized historical monuments, works of art, or places of worship that constitute the cultural or spiritual heritage of peoples as the object of attack, causing as a result extensive destruction thereof, when such places are not located in the immediate proximity of military objectives; and

5. Deprivation of a person protected by the conventions referred to in paragraph 2 of this article of the rights of fair and regular trial.

Article 85 of Protocol I concludes: "Without prejudice to the application of the Conventions and of this Protocol, grave breaches of these instruments shall be regarded as war crimes."

The 1977 Geneva Protocol II relating to the protection of victims of noninternational armed conflict does not have an article defining grave breaches, but its Article 4—"fundamental guarantees"—provides a number of specific prohibitions of acts violative of the protocol's norms for "Humane Treatment." These prohibitions reiterate in part those of common Article 3 of the 1949 Geneva Conventions relating to the "case of armed conflict not of an international character occurring in the territory of one of the High Contracting Parties." There are other prohibitions (for example, starvation as a method of warfare and forced displacement of civilians) in Protocol II, which will be discussed, together with those just enumerated, in Chapter 8.

It is difficult at this point to evaluate all of these conventional grave breaches of the positive jus in bello. They are surely not of equal weight or salience either in moral or military terms. But they are either established or in the process of being accepted in positive international law. As such they represent the most authoritative available inventory of acts mala prohibita in the jus in bello.

Duties of Belligerents:
Prisoners of War and Civilians

In addition to prohibiting the means and behavior banned by modern conventions, the positive law of war lays down elaborate duties for belligerents to perform with respect to prisoners of war and civilians under military occupation. It is unnecessary to mention all of these duties, but a summary will serve as a reference point for discussions of belligerent occupation in specific contexts.

Prisoners of war (PWs) and the wounded and sick are entitled to the following:

1. Quarter, the right to surrender and become PWs;
2. Protection, the right to be removed from dangerous areas as expeditiously and safely as the military situation permits;
3. Decent treatment, as defined by the Hague Convention IV of 1907 and other conventions, then by the 1949 Geneva Convention on Treatment of Prisoners of War, now supplemented by the 1977 Geneva Protocol I;
4. Verification of decent treatment by the International Committee of the Red Cross and/or a designated protecting power;
5. Immunity from reprisals, torture, and abuse from the detaining power's population and any other mistreatment not adequately justified by reasonable requirements of security and discipline.

The body of positive international law protecting prisoners of war is one of the most extensive and highly developed chapters of modern international law.[50] As will be seen, there are some major difficulties in applying and enforcing this law. They will be addressed in succeeding chapters, particularly in Chapter 8.

In cases of occupation of enemy territory, a belligerent is entitled to use such territory as a base of continuing operations. Generally speaking, the occupying power has the right to use the resources of the occupied area much as the original sovereign would. There is a price for this use, however, and there are definite duties placed upon the belligerent occupant by the 1907 Hague Convention IV, the 1949 Geneva Convention Relative to the Protection of Civilian Persons in Time of War, and supplemented by the 1977 Geneva Protocol I. Essentially, the belligerent occupant is obliged to provide the fundamental protection and governmental services that would have been made available by the displaced sovereign and respect the "precarious" character of belligerent occupation by refraining from attempting any fundamental alterations of the political, social, and economic institutions of the occupied areas.

Given its role as a temporary governing power, the belligerent occupant is entitled to obedience and cooperation as long as it remains faithful to the guidelines of the law of war. Like the regime of prisoners of war, the law of belligerent occupation is one of the most highly developed parts of modern international law. [51] However, it too is plagued with difficulties that will be explored in succeeding chapters.

RELATION OF JUST WAR TO THE
PRINCIPLES OF THE LAW OF WAR

In U.S. understanding of the positive law of war, there are three underlying and controlling principles: military necessity, humanity, and chivalry. It is appropriate to review them here and relate them to the basic principles of just-war jus in bello.

These three principles of the law of war appear in most U.S. military manuals. The latest, AFP 110-31, will be quoted here. Under the rubric "Determinants of the Law," the manual treats "basic principles," "custom," and "international agreements." The first of the basic principles is defined as follows:

> Military Necessity. Military necessity is the principle
> which justifies measures of regulated force not forbidden
> by international law which are indispensable for securing
> the prompt submission of the enemy, with the least pos-
> sible expenditure of economic and human resources.
> [Emphasis added][52]

AFP 110-31 distinguishes four basic elements of the definition of military necessity.

> (i) that the force used is capable of being and is in fact
> regulated by the user; (ii) that the use of force is neces-
> sary to achieve as quickly as possible the partial or com-
> plete submission of the adversary; (iii) that the force used
> is no greater in effect on the enemy's personnel or prop-
> erty than needed to achieve his prompt submission (econ-
> omy of force); and (iv) that the force used is not otherwise
> prohibited. [53]

It will be observed that the principle of military necessity is a normative principle as well as a political-military principle of utility. The principle "justifies measures of regulated force" (emphasis added). This corresponds to the just-war working assumption that armed coercion may be justifiable. [54] The first element of the definition—regulation—is likewise consonant with the essential just-war insistence that justifiable force must be regulated. The second element is that of true necessity or true utility. It means that no measure of war is justifiable if it cannot pass the political-military test of true utility, even if it does not violate any of the moral and legal limitations on war.[55] The third element is the just-war <u>jus in bello</u> principle of proportion. Note that it is also the military-science principle of economy of force, discussed under limited war in Chapter 9 and in succeeding chapters on limited war.[56] The fourth element limits the justifiable use of force to that permitted by positive international law.[57]

Turning to the second basic principle of the law of war, AFP 110-31 states the following:

> <u>Humanity</u>. Complementing the principle of necessity
> and implicitly contained within it is the principle of humanity which forbids the infliction of suffering, injury
> or destruction not actually necessary for the accomplishment of legitimate military purposes. This principle of
> humanity results in a specific prohibition against unnecessary suffering, a requirement of proportionality, and
> a variety of more specific rules examined later. The
> principle of humanity also confirms the basic immunity
> of civilian populations from being objects of attack during
> armed conflict. This immunity of the civilian population
> does not preclude unavoidable incidental civilian casualties which may occur during the course of attacks against
> military objectives, and which are not excessive in relation to the concrete and direct military advantage anticipated.[58]

It will be seen that this understanding of the principle of humanity holds it to be the source of the two basic limitations on the conduct of war; namely, the principles of proportion and discrimination. Whereas the source of these two principles in just war is a mixture of theology, natural law, and customary law, in the U.S. view the principles of proportion and discrimination are drawn from a secular principle of humanity. In both the just war and positive law of war, as traditionally viewed by the United States, the source of the basic principles of the <u>jus in bello</u> is not entirely in the consensual, conventional, or customary law but in some higher law. This is a logical development given the natural-law orientation of the United States from its inception.

Finally, the air force manual holds out chivalry as a basic principle and determinant of the law of war.

Chivalry. Although difficult to define, chivalry refers to the conduct of armed conflict in accord with well-recognized formalities and courtesies. During the Middle Ages, chivalry embraced the notion that combatants belonged to a caste, that their combat in arms was ceremonial, that the opponent was entitled to respect and honor, and that the enemy was a brother in the fraternity of knights in arms. Modern technological and industrialized conflict has made war less a gentlemanly contest. Nevertheless, the principle of chivalry remains in specific prohibitions such as those against poison, dishonorable or treacherous misconduct, misuse of enemy flags, uniforms, and flags of truce. The principle of chivalry makes armed conflict less savage and more civilized for the individual combatant. [59]

It will be recalled that the chivalric code made major contributions to the development of the just-war jus in bello, notably in connection with the development of the principle of discrimination. While the subjects linked to the principle of chivalry today are not the most critical of the law of war, they are important. In particular, the relation of chivalry to recognition of enemies as honorable adversaries is important to the just conduct of war. Moreover, the emphasis on good faith enjoined by the principle of chivalry is fundamental to meeting the just-war requirement of reasonable negotiations to terminate a war once it has begun.

This chapter has attempted to summarize the requirements of just-war jus in bello in the comprehensive principle of legitimate military necessity. Starting with the concept of military necessity as a normative principle that justifies as well as limits measures of armed coercion, it has included all of the three basic principles distinguished in the U.S. tradition, as well as the natural-law, just-war principles, in a definition of military necessity that also embraces its application. The definition of legitimate military necessity arrived at is summed up in the following:

Legitimate military necessity consists in all measures immediately indispensable and proportionate to a legitimate military end, provided that they are not prohibited by the laws of war or the natural law, when taken on the decision of a responsible commander, subject to review. [60]

This definition begins with the requirement of true military utility embodied in the law-of-war principle of military necessity as interpreted by the United States. It includes the principle of proportion as a part of that principle of military necessity, as a principle of humanity as understood by the United States, and as a principle of natural law as reflected in the traditional just-war doctrines. The definition includes the principle of discrimination as a subordinate principle of the principle of humanity and as a natural-law principle in just-war doctrine. The definition includes recognition of the positive law of war, whether as elaborations on the foregoing principles or as individual prescriptions with independent rationales. Finally, by holding military necessity subject to natural law, the definition reserves the question of means mala in se, which are not justified by military utility even in the absence of controlling principles, rules of just-war doctrine, and the positive international law of war.

The definition includes the procedural elements of decision by a responsible commander subject to review to emphasize that all permissible military actions must be controlled, public acts engendering responsibility on the part of the belligerent and his representative in the person of the responsible commander. An act of armed coercion that conforms to the requirements of this definition is a legitimate act of military necessity, justified under the just-war jus in bello and the positive international law of war. An action that does not meet all of the requirements of the definition of legitimate military necessity is not a justified, legitimate measure of war.

REPRISALS UNDER THE JUS IN BELLO

The primary hope for enforcement of the jus in bello rests in self-enforcement by responsible and enlightened belligerents. However, not all belligerents are responsible and enlightened all of the time. Important demands of military necessity, in the sense of raw military utility, often clash with the restrictions of the just-war and international-law jus in bello. Such clashes often occur in connection with the most frequently employed and potentially decisive means and methods of warfare. In these circumstances, violations may be expected, and the traditional remedy for the victim of such violations is that of reprisals.

Reprisals remain a somewhat reluctantly permitted institution in the jus in bello. The discussion of such reprisals will follow the treatment of the United States Army's FM 27-10 and the United States Air Force's AFP 110-31, the latter in particular since it is the most recent and the more elaborate. AFP 110-31 uses the definition of reprisal of the U.S. military tribunal in the war-crimes trial of U.S. v. Ohlendorf:

> Reprisals in war are commission of acts which, although illegal in themselves, may, under the specific circum-

stances of the given case, become justified because the
guilty adversary has himself behaved illegally, and the
action is taken in the last resort, in order to prevent the
adversary from behaving illegally in the future. [61]

Reprisals differ from rétorsion, another form of retaliation, in that
rétorsion responds to an injurious or objectionable, but legally permissible, act with an act that is likewise injurious or objectionable,
but legal.

AFP 110-31 lays down eight conditions for the use of reprisals.

1. They "must respond to grave and manifestly unlawful acts,
committed by an adversary government, its military commanders,
or combatants for whom the adversary is responsible."
2. They "must be for the purpose of compelling the adversary
to observe the law of armed conflict. Reprisals cannot be undertaken
for revenge, spite, or punishment. Rather they are directed against
an adversary in order to induce him to refrain from further violations
of the law of armed conflict."
3. "There must be reasonable notice that reprisals will be
taken."
4. "Other reasonable means to secure compliance must be attempted."
5. "A reprisal must be directed against the personnel or property of an adversary."
6. "A reprisal must be proportional to the original violation.
Although a reprisal need not conform in kind to the same type of acts
complained of (bombardment for bombardment, weapon for weapon),
it may not significantly exceed the adversary's violation either in violence or effect. Effective but disproportionate reprisals cannot be
justified by the argument that only an excessive response will fore-
stall further transgressions."
7. "It must be publicized."
8. "It must be authorized by national authorities at the highest
political level and entails full state responsibility."[62]

In the jus in bello for international conflict, there are a number
of specific prohibitions against reprisals against protected persons;
namely, prisoners of war, the wounded and sick, the shipwrecked,
medical personnel, and buildings or equipment. In the jus in bello for
both international and noninternational conflict, there are prohibitions
against reprisals related to collective penalties, all measures of intimidation or of terrorism directed at civilians, pillage, and the
taking of hostages. Finally, in the jus in bello for international conflicts, civilians under the enemy's control previously not protected

from reprisals are now protected against them by the provisions of
1977 Geneva Protocol I, Article 51(6).

AFP 110-31 suggests a number of practical considerations that
argue against recourse to reprisals. One that is particularly important is that reprisals and counterreprisals have historically eroded if
not collapsed the law of war. For example, the law of war at sea was
virtually obliterated by the reprisal spiral engaged in by the Allies and
Central Powers in World War I. A good bit of the rationalization for
city-busting air attacks in World War II was provided by the notion of
reprisals.[63]

Nevertheless, a generally law-abiding belligerent may find itself in a position where the enemy is systematically violating the rights
of its combatants and noncombatants under the law of war. What is
such a belligerent to do then? The recurring example of permissible
reprisals of U.S. law-of-war manuals is not too helpful. FM 27-10,
for example, advises that "the employment by a belligerent of a weapon
the use of which is normally precluded by the law of war would constitute a lawful reprisal for intentional mistreatment of prisoners of
war held by the enemy."[64] AFP 110-31 states that "if any enemy
employs illegal weapons against a state, the victim may resort to
the use of weapons which would otherwise be unlawful in order to
compel the enemy to cease its prior violation."[65] Apparently, in
both cases the illegal weapons would be chemical or biological warfare. No other weapon is presently illegal per se.

But suppose the enemy denies quarter, denies minimal standards
of PW treatment, denies the protection guaranteed by the jus ad bellum
to civilians, or engages in any combination of the prohibited practices
discussed above? The specific prohibitions of the law against reprisals now preclude retaliation in kind for most foreseeable illegal acts,
notably those concerning prisoners of war and civilians.[66] The vague
references in U.S. military manuals on the law of war to "illegal
weapons" for reprisal purposes seems marginal to irrelevant to many
foreseeable circumstances of victimization by a law-breaking belligerent. If one combines the present conventional jus in bello with the
doctrine of U.S. military manuals on the subject of reprisals, it develops that there is virtually no permissible option of reprisals left
to an injured belligerent. One may then seek comfort in the approach
of AFP 110-31 that reprisals are probably counterproductive and
harmful to the integrity of the law of war in any case.[67] Nevertheless, it appears that the contemporary jus in bello has left law-abiding belligerents very much at a disadvantage vis-à-vis law-breaking
belligerents.

The sad state of the institution of reprisals underscores the extent to which observance of the law of war is dependent on the moral
standards of the belligerents. Reciprocity and fear of reprisals are

not sufficient to enjoin compliance with the law where its requirements restrict critical military options. Only a principled commitment to the conduct of just and limited war will suffice to keep a belligerent steadfast in observance of the jus in bello.

Having surveyed the basic principles, most important specific legal prescriptions, and the possible exceptions to the jus in bello under the right of reprisal, Chapters 6 and 8 will explore in greater detail the implications of this body of law for nuclear and conventional warfare (Chapter 6) and revolutionary/counterinsurgency warfare (Chapter 8). First, however, it is necessary to demonstrate the application of the just-war and international-law jus ad bellum and jus in bello to specific contemporary wars. This will be done in Chapter 4 with respect to U.S. participation in World War II and the Korean conflict and in Chapter 5 in the case of U.S. intervention in Vietnam.

4

JUST WAR APPLIED:
THE UNITED STATES IN
WORLD WAR II AND KOREA

It is my intention to apply just-war doctrine in three ways.
First, in this chapter and the next I will analyze U.S. participation
in World War II, the Korean War, and the Vietnam War in terms of
the just-war conditions. Then just-war doctrine will be interpreted
with respect to some of the outstanding issue areas of modern conflict in Chapters 6, 7, and 8. Finally, in Part III, possible future
conflicts in which the United States might participate will be analyzed
in terms of the just-war conditions as well as the guidelines for limited
war developed in Part II.

In examining these three recent U.S. wars in just-war terms,
I do not attempt analyses that are or purport to be definitive in terms
of historical accuracy and completeness or normative rigor. Such
an undertaking would probably require separate books on each of the
three wars. Moreover, I am cognizant of the fact that most serious
observers have by now reached their own conclusions concerning the
moral and prudential acceptability of U.S. participation in these wars.
My purpose, accordingly, is not to justify or condemn the U.S. record.
Rather, it is to illustrate in terms of familiar historical examples the
application of just-war doctrine. This is an important task, particularly in view of the paucity of contemporary, extended, just-war analyses. In this chapter and the next, the just-war analyses will be limited to examinations of U.S. and Allied ends and means except where
consideration of enemy aims and behavior is necessary.

In the applications of just-war doctrine that follow, the difficulties of evaluating compliance with just-war requirements will be manifest. It will be seen that in the wars that are widely accepted as just
or condemned as unjust there is always a very mixed record of compliance with and deviation from the just-war conditions. The issue of
overall evaluation of the moral permissibility of a war is well illus-

trated in all three of the wars under scrutiny. It can be seen that a strict interpretation of just-war doctrine, requiring scrupulous adherence to each and every just-war condition, would probably disqualify all three of the wars. However, a more flexible interpretation, permitting a preponderance of favorable showings on most conditions to outweigh one or two apparent failures to meet just-war standards, will be seen to produce judgments that are within the reach of conscientious belligerents while still maintaining reasonable normative standards for the initiation and conduct of war.

THE UNITED STATES IN WORLD WAR II

The U.S. wars against Germany and Japan present different patterns of intentions and behavior. Each will be discussed in turn under the categories of the just-war doctrine except where the issues raised with respect to each are closely related (for example, in respect to strategic bombing).

Jus ad bellum

Competent Authority

The issue of competent authority was solved for the United States by the attack on Pearl Harbor and the subsequent German declaration of war against the United States. The United States began its participation in World War II with a prima facie case of just war in legitimate self-defense. The issue would be whether an initially just war would remain just by reason of U.S. compliance with the just-war conditions. But, by reason of the attacks and declarations of war by the Axis powers, the U.S. government had a self-evident, competent authority to wage a war of self-defense.

Had either the European or Pacific war begun with some form of offensive U.S. action, there would have been questions of competent authority. Prior to Pearl Harbor, Roosevelt's manuevering, including the involvement of the U.S. Navy in a shooting war with German submarines, was of questionable constitutionality and in defiance of the wishes of about half of the Congress and the people of the United States. Had the United States been drawn into the war through Roosevelt's provocative interventions on behalf of Britain, serious issues of competent authority would have been raised. Pearl Harbor and the German declaration of war left these issues moot.

Just Cause

For the United States the basic just causes were as follows:

1. Self-defense of the United States and collective self-defense of Britain;
2. Liberation of Europe from occupation by a totalitarian, repressive German regime and subsequent rescue of Jews and other victims of genocide;
3. Suppression, punishment, and deterrence of aggression in violation of the international law of the League of Nations; and
4. Reestablishment of the new international system based on international law and organization.

These goals were set at the highest political level (raison d'état). They formed the ends for which the means of the war are to be proportional under just-war jus ad bellum. As discussed in Chapter 3, there is also a critical consideration of proportionality in the jus in bello, addressed to the various specific belligerent actions pursued in the course of the war. The referent for that analysis is that of the military objective (raison de guerre). As discussed in Chapters 2 and 3, the two levels overlap in political, military, and normative analyses. However, the best course is to restrict reference to the goals of the war mainly to the jus ad bellum component of just-war analyses.

The just cause in the case of the war against Japan included the four elements of the war aims in the European war, with some differences. These were self-defense of the United States and collective self-defense of the victims of aggressions by Japan in the Pacific; liberation of areas overrun by the Japanese from a totalitarian and repressive, but not genocidal regime; suppression, punishment, and deterrence of aggression in violation of the international law of the League of Nations; and reestablishment of the new international system based on international law and organization.

These war aims must be appraised in terms of the components of the just-war category, namely, proportion, probability of success, and exhaustion of peaceful remedies.

In the calculus of proportionality in the European war, the good that was sought was the removal of the reality and the future threat of German aggression, repression, and genocide as well as the establishment of conditions wherein aggression would be deterred and a new international system based on peace, law, and order established. One other objective emerged important in the course of the war: the successful conclusion of the war before the Hitler regime developed effective atomic weapons.

The evil that was necessary in order to accomplish these good ends involved unparalleled destruction, loss of life, human suffering, social dislocation, social and political instability, and the upsetting of the European and world balance of power. The predictable result was that a totalitarian communist regime in the Soviet Union, in many ways as bad as that of the Nazis, was given the opportunity to take over much of Europe and to threaten all of it. The means involved the waging of total war to the fullest extent permitted by military capabilities. The costs were extremely high. Nevertheless, there is broad acceptance of the war against Germany as a proportionate response to the predicament produced by Hitler's conquests and policies.

Was there a solid probability of success? Despite the desperate situation in December 1941, the answer is affirmative. However, a much more difficult question would be whether the Americans and British alone would have had a sufficient probability of success if the Soviet Union had made a separate peace with the Germans. In that case, the cost of liberating Europe would have been tremendous. There would have been a sufficient probability of success to pass the just-war requirement, but only barely.

Two issues are raised by the last of the just-cause conditions, the requirement of exhaustion of peaceful remedies. One is the sufficiency of prewar efforts at peaceful settlement; the other concerns efforts to terminate the war. Before the war, it seems clear, adequate efforts were made to avoid war. They failed because of the apparently insatiable ambitions of Hitler's Germany. Indeed, the peace attempts of the Munich period seemed to teach a lesson that there could be excessive efforts to avoid war by attempts at peaceful settlement with an aggressor pursuing an open agenda. In any event, the United States had little to do with these efforts and confronted the fact of repeated acts of aggression by Hitler prior to being drawn into the conflict by enemy action.

The sufficiency of efforts to find ways to terminate the war, consonant with just cause but short of total war to the bitter end, are more questionable. It may be granted that there never were very good prospects for a satisfactory negotiated peace. But such a peace was apparently never seriously contemplated or sought. When Roosevelt and Churchill adopted the war goal of unconditional surrender and made it clear that they would not negotiate any kind of peace with the Hitler regime, they went a long way toward guaranteeing that this would be a total war fought for total ends. The very formulation—unconditional surrender—tends to violate the conditions and spirit of just war. [1]

One must be careful in pursuing this criticism. Surely the horrendous nature of Hitler's aggressions, repression, and genocide justified very extensive prosecution of the war to bring them to an end.

The prewar record of Nazi Germany did not entitle it to any benefit of the doubt with respect to terminating the war justly. Yet unconditional surrender as a goal went too far. Had Hitler been overthrown and responsible elements in Germany sought a negotiated peace, just-war doctrine would have counseled serious consideration of the offer. Moreover, hindsight might support such a development in view of the great advantages accruing to the USSR from the unconditional-surrender policy. No such occasion arose. The desperate attempts of Hitler's successors at the end of the war came too late to raise legitimately the issue of acceptance of reasonable terms short of unconditional surrender for ending the war.

In summary, the United States had an eminently just cause against Germany. The evil caused by the war was proportionate to the good of accomplishing the goals of the just cause; there was a good probability of success, but the justice of the war was to some extent imperiled by the demand for unconditional surrender.

Turning to the war against Japan, the calculus of proportionality parallels that involved in assessing the war with Germany but with some differences. The Japanese occupation regimes were repressive and imperialist but less objectionable than those of the Germans. In most cases they replaced similar, if more moderate, Western colonial regimes. The enormous difference was that there was no issue of genocide. The Japanese-occupied empire was not such an affront to basic moral values as was the German. Moreover, the costs of overcoming the Japanese (at least prior to the contemplated invasion of the homeland) was markedly less than in the war with Germany. Most of the fighting occurred in isolated, sparsely inhabited islands. The great destruction and dislocation of the European war was not matched. The Pacific war did, however, upset the Asian balance of power, increasing the power and opportunities of the USSR and paving the way for the emergence of the People's Republic of China. Overall, the good accomplished by the war against Japan outweighed the evil— up to the last days of the war. Anticipating jus in bello questions to follow, the conventional bombing of Japanese cities—particularly vulnerable to fire bombing—raised the same questions as city busting in Germany. Obviously, the use of the atomic bomb to destroy Hiroshima and Nagasaki involved evil results that would challenge any claim to proportionate good coming from the successful culmination of the war.

Indeed, the use of the atomic bombs raises two fundamental and difficult issues of just-war evaluation. First, it raises the issue of the effect on the judgment of a war as generally just when one major controversial feature of the conduct of the war threatens to outweigh an otherwise satisfactory compliance with the conditions of the jus ad bellum. Second, the use of the atomic bomb against Hiroshima and Nagasaki represents a clear example of means so potent that their use may only be justified in terms of the calculus of <u>jus ad bellum</u> proportionality at the highest level of <u>raison d'état</u> rather than at the normal level for assessment of the means of war, <u>raison de guerre</u> in the light of the <u>jus in bello</u>. To be sure, there are those who would argue that the use of the atomic bombs was proportionate to reasonable military necessities viewed from the perspectives of <u>raison de guerre</u> and the <u>jus in bello</u>. But most justifications of Hiroshima and Nagasaki tend to emphasize that these attacks served to bring the war to an end. [2]

There was never any real doubt about the probability of success against Japan if enough U.S. power could be mobilized and directed to the Pacific.

While U.S. negotiations with Japan prior to the war have been criticized as excessively inflexible, the issue of exhaustion of peaceful remedies by the United States was rendered moot by the Pearl Harbor attack. It appears that there was little if any disposition on the part of Japan to negotiate a termination of the war until the very end. At that point the United States did soften its demands for unconditional surrender and negotiated an armistice acceptable to the Japanese. Thus, the U.S. record on this score is better than in the war with Germany, although the character of the respective enemies undoubtedly played a critical role in determining these different approaches and outcomes. In summary, the United States met all of the just-war conditions of just cause if it can be concluded that the conventional and atomic attacks on Japanese cities did not reach such a level of disproportionate evil as to nullify or depreciate the otherwise sufficient balance of good over evil.

Right Intention

Finally, the just-war <u>jus ad bellum</u> requires right intention. Despite the enormity of the stakes, moral as well as material, the war of the United States and its Western Allies conformed to the condition of right intention. By forming the United Nations, the Western Allies did limit themselves to their original just cause. They made the most serious effort in history to establish a just and lasting peace through a world organization. They pursued enlightened occupation policies in Germany. Indeed, the performance of the Western Allies reveals the important difference between subjective desires and intentions and actual behavior. In their hearts the Western belligerents were understandably motivated by hatred and a desire for vengeance for German aggressions and war crimes. However, their behavior toward the Germans was remarkably restrained, with one exception—the conduct of strategic bombing.

The issue of strategic bombing will be considered in the analysis of the war with Germany in terms of the <u>jus in bello</u>. It was not

thought to be sufficiently decisive to raise initially under the rubric
of proportionality in just cause, as were the fire bombing and atomic
bombing of Japanese cities. This is a controversial point, and it may
well be that the strategic bombing of German cities was so indiscriminate and disproportionate as to depreciate from the good-evil calculus
of jus ad bellum proportionality. In any event, it seems clear that
the intention of the Western Allies, particularly (and understandably)
of the United Kingdom, was to avenge German war crimes by attacking German cities. This seems to be an important rationale over and
above arguments of military necessity. Accordingly, whatever proportionality the attacks on German cities by the Western Allies may
have had either in terms of highest raison d'état or of raison de guerre,
the record of what we would now call countervalue attacks on German
cities reflects defects in the right intention of the otherwise just victims of German aggression.

We have here a good example of the complexities and difficulties
of applying the just-war conditions. On two aspects of right intention
the United States and its Western Allies performed well. On the third
aspect, charity and avoidance of hatred and vengefulness, the just
belligerents risked their just-war credentials by aerial attacks that,
as will be seen in the next section, violated jus in bello limitations
and manifestly reflected uncharitable motivations. That this lack of
charity for the perpetrators of the aggression, the Blitz, widespread
war crimes, and genocide was understandable does not alter the fact
that, in this regard, the United States and its allies failed the test of
right intention.

In my view, the United States and its Western Allies overcame
their delinquencies in just cause (demand for unconditional surrender)
and right intention (vengeful attacks on German cities). Their treatment of occupied Germany belatedly corrected the unconditional-surrender policy, and their overall conduct of the war was sufficiently
good to balance the failures of charity and violations of jus in bello
limitations that marked the strategy of bombing cities. My view is
influenced by the conviction that the basic cause was about as just as
will be found in modern history. It is significant, however, that even
a war for such a manifestly just cause can leave doubt as to the performance of the just belligerent in meeting the just-war conditions.

It would not have been surprising had the United States failed
to meet the condition of right intention in the war with Japan. U.S.
attitudes were understandably conditioned by the shock of the Pearl
Harbor attack, the conquest of the Philippines, the Bataan Death March,
and other Japanese atrocities, as well as by racial prejudices that
prevailed within the armed services and throughout U.S. society.
Despite all of these factors, however, the U.S. record of right intention was good. The original purposes of the war were adhered to

and the United States did not take advantage of victory by unreasonable demands on Japan. Indeed, the rigor of unconditional surrender was relaxed in the peace terms. The United States did take over the Micronesian trust territory from Japan, which had abused its mandate over the islands by fortifying and exploiting them. Acquisition of a trust over Micronesia was arranged with the United Nations in conformity with the charter. The United States occupied the Ryukyu and Bonin islands, which had been Japanese territory, but relinquished them after years of gradual reversion. As remarked before, the United States took the lead in organizing the United Nations to create a new international system aimed at improving the record of the League of Nations. Certainly right intention was manifested in the conduct of the occupation of Japan. But, as remarked in the discussion of just-cause proportionality, right intention was jeopardized by the conventional and atomic countervalue attacks on Japanese cities at the end of the war. It is argueable that these attacks had a higher plausible military necessity than similar conventional attacks against German cities and were less conspicuously motivated by hatred and a desire for vengeance. Still, these attacks raise an issue of inadequate right intention as they do of proportionality.

Once again we have a case of a belligerent meeting most of the conditions of the jus ad bellum but engaging in conduct which is sufficiently controversial to cast doubt on the sufficiency of its response to the just-war conditions. Notwithstanding the questions raised by countervalue attacks on Japanese cities, especially the atomic attacks, the United States and the Western Allies demonstrated right intention in the war against Japan and so managed to meet all of the jus ad bellum conditions.

Jus in bello

It is not the purpose of this discussion to undertake a comprehensive critique of the conduct of World War II by the United States and its Western Allies. What is required for a just-war evaluation of the U.S. record is an examination of possible violations of just-war and positive international-law jus in bello so significant that they might affect critically the jus ad bellum analysis and render a prima facie just war unjust. This aspect of the interrelation of the jus ad bellum and the jus in bello has already been demonstrated in the jus ad bellum analysis. It appears to be unlikely that serious issues of the jus in bello will not be anticipated by the inquiries necessitated by the just-cause proportionality condition and the right-intention condition of the jus ad bellum. This is particularly the case with respect to the basic jus in bello principles of proportion and discrimination and to the category of acts mala in se, presently represented by the crime of genocide. It remains to be seen whether the detailed law of war comprising acta prohibita will yield cases of violations of such gravity and large scale as to affect critically the justice of a war. This is not to depreciate the importance of the acta prohibita but to suggest that they will not usually be central to the calculus of the just war.

Accordingly, it is appropriate to limit the jus in bello discussion of the conduct of the United States and its Western Allies in World War II to those issues where the gravity and scope of the issues is such as to question the legitimacy of the behavior of the putatively just belligerent. Those issues have already been identified in the jus ad bellum analysis as those raised by the conventional and atomic attacks on cities.

The conventional attacks raise the issues of proportion and discrimination. The atomic attacks raise these issues as well as issues of superfluous suffering and possible violation of prohibitions against chemical warfare.

Conventional Aerial Attacks on Cities

U.S. and Allied conventional attacks on German and Japanese cities challenged the limitations imposed by the basic jus in bello principles of proportion and discrimination. The raids caused high levels of death, destruction, and social dislocation over extended metropolitan areas. The objectives of the raids were mixed and, as indicated in the jus ad bellum analysis, controversial. Clearly the raids were directed in part against traditional military targets (for example, military installations, key transportation and communication facilities, factories producing and storage facilities containing material directly used in the prosecution of the war).

However, a second aspect of the raids was their attack on the total social environment in which the military targets were located. Not only was the destruction of those targets sought, it was also intended that the raids interfere with or destroy altogether the operation of the general society in which significant military production and activity took place. Thus, for example, destruction of the housing, transportation facilities, sources of food and water, and sources of energy for the general populace was barely justified as impairing or preventing the continuation of the war effort in the area. This objective was obviously a license to attempt the general destruction of whole metropolitan areas.

As noted in the jus ad bellum analysis, a third element in the bombing rationale was vengeance for the misery brought on victims of German and Japanese aggression and war crimes. In the case of the Germans there was a strong sense of retaliation in kind. However, it should be pointed out that U.S. and Allied raids were not reprisals of limited duration. They constituted a principal component of Allied strategy carried on to the end of the war irrespective of German conduct and capabilities. Finally, closely interrelated to the rationale of incapacitating the enemy war effort and the element of vengeance was the general desire to destroy the morale of the civilian population so that the will to continue the war would be eroded. Indeed, some air power proponents may still have dreamed of the collapse of the national will of the enemy as foreseen by Douhet. [3]

The results of these countervalue attacks were unparalleled death and destruction, as well as social dislocation, in German and Japanese metropolitan areas. The homefronts that made total war possible were made the victims of total war from the air (total, that is, in the preatomic age). The outcomes in terms of realization of the objectives of the attackers remain disputed. By and large, the attacks on traditional military targets were effective. The ultimate effectiveness of attacks on enemy war industries and activities remains controverted. There is one position frequently encountered in critiques of the war that interprets the U.S. Strategic Bombing Surveys as concluding that the German war industry, at least, survived all of the Allied attacks to a remarkable degree. If the justification for the city-busting attacks rested heavily on destruction of the German war industry, the case is a poor one. It appears that the verdict on the effects of bombing on Japanese war-making potential is more favorable to the bombing. However, assessment of the effects of bombing on the war-making capabilities of a belligerent is a complicated business, and it can be argued that Germany was sufficiently crippled in a number of critical ways so that occasional examples of war production surviving aerial attacks are comparatively irrelevant when compared with the overall issue of bombing effectiveness. There remains the extremely difficult question as to whether the degree of injury done to the German and Japanese war-making capabilities was proportionate to the harm done to the German and Japanese societies. Further, there is the issue of whether the military utility of those attacks was achieved at the expense of gross violations of the principle of discrimination. [4]

As indicated in the jus ad bellum analysis, to the extent that U.S. and Allied aerial attacks were motivated by a desire for vengeance and justified as retaliation in kind, they were violative of just-war principles of just-cause proportionality and right intention, as well as of the jus in bello principles of proportion and discrimination. This leaves the rationale of eroding and/or breaking the morale or will of the enemy population by aerial attacks on population centers. As a collateral effect of otherwise acceptable attacks on military targets, such a rationale would appear to be permissible. To the extent

that attacks would not be firmly grounded on the need to attack targets
as military objectives, the rationale of attacking the morale of the
enemy's population would seem to be hardly distinguishable from so-
called terror bombing. Terror bombing was abhorred during the war
and has recently been prohibited in the 1977 Geneva Protocol I. One
concludes that the only acceptable rationale for aerial attacks on cities
is the destruction of clearly military targets comprising facilities
and/or activities very closely related and critical to the war effort.

The upshot of the pattern of mixed rationales for conventional
strategic bombing in World War II is that most attacks raised a question of the proportionality between the bona fide military utility of
destroying military and quasi-military targets in the area and the
collateral damage done to noncombatants and nonmilitary targets.
Moreover, in all attacks on cities the issue was raised as to the extent to which the raids involved direct, intentional attacks on noncombatants and nonmilitary targets.

Analysis of U.S. and British strategic bombing practices is
complicated by a number of factors. Three appear to be particularly
relevant to this inquiry. First, as the recent United States Air Force
(USAF) manual on the law of international conflict points out, there
were different emphases in the USAF and Royal Air Force (RAF)
strategic bombing policies. Because of differences in estimated technical capabilities, the USAF preferred daylight precision bombing
whereas the RAF continued the nighttime area bombing that had been
initiated before the USAF was a major participant in the air war. It
also appears that there was a greater concern on the part of the USAF
to avoid civilian casualties and damage. The British seemed to have
assumed that German aggression and war crimes, particularly the
Blitz against England, had engendered a right of retaliation in kind,
with an open-ended program of countervalue attacks going far beyond
anything that could be justified as reprisals. [5]

However, one must be careful in these generalizations. Both
air forces cooperated in the other's raids. Indeed, multiphase attacks
on metropolitan areas, continuing for several days, in which day and
nighttime bombings succeeded each other, were common. [6] Nevertheless, for purposes of analysis, it is probably fair to distinguish
U.S. precision-bombing policies from British area-bombing policies.

Second, somewhat vitiating the distinction just made, the accuracy of all strategic bombing in World War II was not at best very
precise. Problems of navigation, weather, and enemy resistance
with fighter attacks and intense antiaircraft fire rendered accurate
bombing very difficult. Thus, a substantial margin for error had to
be assumed even in raids characterized as "precision" bombing.
This fact was grimly underlined for Allied ground forces on the numerous occasions when supporting air strikes fell on friendly troops.

Third, in analyzing the degree of compliance of U.S. and British aerial bombardment policies with the jus in bello, it is necessary to recognize the importance of fire-storm bombings in those policies. In the course of the war, the U.S. and British air forces learned how to create "fire storms" through the right combinations and sequences of regular explosives and fire bombs. Weather completed the job. In the case of Japan, the cities were, of course, terribly vulnerable. This practice, which culminated in the holocaust in Dresden, clearly presented a separate category of bombing policy to be judged in terms of the principles of proportion and discrimination. [7]

Thus, bombing military targets in metropolitan areas, with World War II margins for error in accuracy, necessarily involved the infliction of substantial collateral damage. But the deliberate creation of fire storms in such areas can hardly be characterized as causing collateral damage. The obvious intention is to burn out huge areas of cities.

Accordingly, three separate types of U.S. and British air attacks on German and Japanese cities can be identified. The first type is precision bombing of military targets with the likelihood of collateral damage owing to inaccuracy. The second type involves area attacks on military targets with generally greater collateral damage from blast and fire resulting both from inaccuracy and the greater area of the target. The third type—fire-storm bombing—involves the deliberate burning of large metropolitan areas not as collateral damage but as the primary target. In the third type the claim to be attacking military targets is mainly a peg on which to hang the true purpose, namely, to create a massive fire storm in a population center.

When applying the principles of proportion and discrimination to these three types, and in the light of the other factors previously mentioned, the following outlines of a normative analysis appear:

1. Precision bombing against military targets produced substantial collateral damage because of inaccuracy. Generally speaking, such bombing was proportionate if the military target was sufficiently vital to warrant the collateral damage. It would meet the requirements of discrimination, in most cases, only with the assistance of the principle of double effect.

2. Area bombing necessarily tended to produce greater collateral damage than precision bombing, so that there tended to be a disproportionate destruction of nonmilitary targets. Area bombing was considerably less discriminate than precision bombing, to the point where even the use of the principle of double effect probably could not bring such bombing within the limits required for compliance with the principle of discrimination.

3. Area fire-storm bombing, pegged to military targets, in most cases was grossly disproportionate to the value of those targets.

Such bombing was a flagrant violation of the principle of discrimination, since its primary purpose was intentionally to kill and render homeless tens of thousands of noncombatants.

4. Precision bombing linked to fire-storm bombing tended to take on the character of such disproportionate and indiscriminate attacks.

There were enough instances of all of the categories to make them significant variables in the calculus of proportion and the determination of compliance with the principle of discrimination as modified by the principle of double effect. Had the U.S. and British aerial attacks on German and Japanese cities been almost entirely confined to attempted precision bombings of military targets, the Allied strategic bombing policies would have met the requirements of the principle of proportion even if, in individual cases, disproportionate damage was done. Had Allied attacks been limited to precision bombing of military targets in metropolitan areas, they would have met the requirements of the principle of discrimination with, however, major indispensable assistance from the principle of double effect. Without double effect, most of the precision bombing in German and Japanese cities could be condemned as excessively violative of the principle of discrimination.

However, a very considerable part of Allied bombing was area bombing of Germany. It is possible that in some of that bombing the damage to nonmilitary targets was proportionate to the vital military targets destroyed. In other cases the damage was undoubtedly disproportionate. But in all cases, it would appear area bombing was indiscriminate to a degree difficult to defend, even with the help of the principle of double effect. [8]

Finally, it is clear that fire-storm bombing of German and Japanese cities was countervalue warfare, tending to be disproportionate per se in terms of normal military necessity. There is no doubt that fire bombing of population centers violated the principle of discrimination beyond any possible rescue from the principle of double effect.

Taken together, standard area bombing and fire bombing constituted a major, if not the major, part of U.S. and British strategic bombing. They were, and were intended to be, a salient, characteristic component of the total war effort against Germany and Japan. Their violation of the basic jus in bello principles of proportion and discrimination was, therefore, sufficiently significant to jeopardize the claim of the Western Allies to be conducting a just war.

The implications of these jus in bello violations for jus ad bellum proportionality and right intention have already been discussed. The question remains whether these violations are so serious that they should tip the balance in the evaluation of the extent to which a belligerent meets the just-war conditions. My conclusion is that the just cause in this case is so strong that even this major pattern of jus in bello violations is not sufficient to vitiate it.

It is, however, important to take notice of the deleterious consequences of U.S. and British countervalue bombing practices in World War II. These practices destroyed any attempt to contend that the principle of discrimination prevailed in the practice and expectations of belligerents as a matter of positive international law. This is dramatically reflected in the absence of any serious prosecution for illegal aerial bombing at the Nuremberg and other war-crimes trials. [9] In other words, the Blitz and other Axis excesses in aerial warfare were treated during the war as warrants for retaliation in kind with a vengeance but not for postwar war-crimes proceedings. Clearly the victors did not want their own record of aerial bombardment brought into court. The fall of the principle of discrimination is further reflected in the general consensus of postwar international-law publicists who despaired of the survival of the principle of discrimination, already badly eroded in World War I. [10]

Moreover, the virtual disappearance of the principle of discrimination as a viable international law-of-war prescription left the way open for a ready acceptance of the atomic bombings of Hiroshima and Nagasaki. It was plausibly argued that one atomic bomb was merely a more economic equivalent of a large-scale raid with conventional blast and fire bombs.

The Atomic Attacks on Japan

The atomic bomb attacks against Hiroshima and Nagasaki raised the basic jus in bello issues of proportionality and discrimination on an unprecedented scale. Additionally, the new phenomenon of destructive atomic radioactivity caused some to question whether atomic warfare violated the principle of humanity and the ancillary prescriptions against weapons causing superfluous suffering. Finally, radioactivity was likened to poison, and it was argued that the broad prohibitions of the Geneva Gas Protocol of 1925 were applicable to atomic weapons.

As remarked in the jus ad bellum analysis, the unique aspect of the issue of proportionality as applied to Hiroshima and Nagasaki was that the calculus involved both the raison de guerre calculation of proportion to a military goal and the raison d'état calculation of proportion to the successful conclusion of the war. At that stage of the war, the political goal and the military task were the same: complete the defeat of Japan and end the war. The two strategies for achieving this goal appeared to be to invade Japan and conquer it or intimidate the Japanese by the use of the atomic bombs. It was believed that the atomic destruction of Japanese cities would compel surrender. This belief seems to have been borne out by events. However, it remains important to assess the proportionality of the attacks in terms of military necessity.

Given the record of bitter and often suicidal resistance of the Japanese armed forces, it was reasonably anticipated that a campaign to invade and conquer the home islands would be extremely costly both to the U.S. and Allied invaders and the Japanese defenders. It was estimated that the invasion phase alone would cost several hundred thousand Allied casualties. Further, it is evident that a last ditch defense of Japan would cause huge losses in lives and damage within the Japanese society.

It was the contention of President Truman and Secretary of War Stimson that the losses and damage inflicted in the atomic attacks that compelled Japanese surrender were proportionate to the losses that the military on both sides and the Japanese society would have suffered had the atomic bombs not been used and Japan been attacked conventionally. [11] I find this argument persuasive and agree that the atomic attacks were proportionate in the sense that they accomplished a strategic task with less loss of life and damage to the Japanese society than would have occurred in a conventional campaign.

It is impossible, however, to reconcile the atomic attacks with the principle of discrimination, even with the utmost extension of the principle of double effect. No previous act of war involved intentional direct attacks on noncombatants and nonmilitary targets to the extent that the atomic destruction of Hiroshima and Nagasaki did. The cities had military targets within their confines and activities supportive of the war. But the vast majority of persons and targets in those cities were noncombatants and nonmilitary. The proportions were such that the destruction of the cities emerges as the primary purpose of the attacks while the incidental destruction of military targets appears to fall into the category of collateral damage, thus reversing the usual and prefered ratio. While the exact results of an atomic explosion were unknown, it was reasonable to expect destruction of the magnitude wrought by the attacks.

It is certainly the case that the deleterious and often long-term or permanent effects of radioactive contamination could be characterized as superfluous suffering. These effects presented a new dimension to the spectrum of death and suffering inflicted by modern weapons. However, if one follows the U.S. government's view that superfluous suffering must be defined in state practice, it develops that, since atomic/nuclear weapons causing radioactive contamination have not, as such, been subjected to international legal prohibitions or restrictions, the superfluous suffering category does not contribute to the evaluation of the atomic attacks on Japan. [12] Moreover, in the absence of authoritative decisions that nuclear weapons cause superfluous suffering, the subjective comparison of atomic radioactive fallout with the suffering caused by regular explosives and fire bombs is inconclusive. This underscores the fact that the critical variable in the superfluous suffering calculus has been the utility of the weapon. If it is decisive or highly useful, the pain and death it inflicts will not be considered superfluous. It is only when a weapon is ineffective or marginal that it is branded superfluous.

Finally, attempts have been made to include atomic/nuclear warfare either under the Hague Regulation 23 prohibitions against poison and poisoned weapons or the Geneva Gas Protocol of 1925, which prohibits "the use in war of asphyxiating, poisonous or other gases, and of all analagous liquids, materials or devices."

However, it is clear that the prohibition against poison and poisoned weapons is declaratory of historical prescriptions that predate modern chemical warfare, much less atomic war. The Geneva Gas Protocol of 1925 was designed to prohibit the repetition of the use of gas warfare of the kind employed in World War I. To argue that this convention should be applied to a means as new, unforeseen, and decisive as the atomic bomb is to argue that atomic bombs were proscribed before they were invented. Given the reluctance of belligerents to limit decisive means of war, evidenced by the failure since 1945 to outlaw nuclear weapons, the attempt to stretch the Geneva Gas Protocol to cover atomic war appears to be unwarranted. It has, in fact, not been taken very seriously in state practice or among international-law publicists. [13]

This still leaves the just-war analyst with the issue of nuclear radioactivity. The long-term or permanent consequences of nuclear radioactive contamination have to be included in the calculus of proportionality. Moreover, as will be discussed in chapters dealing with contemporary nuclear problems, the threat of nuclear fallout to vast regions of the world and mankind raise issues unknown to the prenuclear age.

I conclude that if the use of nuclear weapons can be justified in the context of World War II, the attacks on Hiroshima and Nagasaki are about as defensible as can be imagined, since they did foreseeably and in fact end the war quickly and preclude greater losses to the belligerents and the Japanese society. I think that this is the case even if full account is taken of the long-term and permanent effects of radioactive fallout. However, the case was an unusual one that may not often recur. Had Japan been a bit stronger, the attacks would not have forced surrender and the lack of decisive effect would detract from the proportionality of the atomic attacks. Had Japan been a bit weaker, it could be argued (as some do) that the use of the atomic bombs was unnecessary.

As to the gross violation of the principle of discrimination involved, there is little to do except admit it openly and accept the fact that, ever since, major powers operating in the nuclear age have been confronted with the fact that the principal means of deterrence and defense in existence is incompatible with the principle of discrimination. The nuclear age has created a whole new category of war conduct deterrence issues that simply do not fit into the traditional jus in bello.

In the foregoing analysis it has been concluded that the United States violated the jus in bello principle of proportion in a substantial number of the aerial attacks on Germany and Japan, particularly those that employed area bombing and most particularly those that constituted fire-storm bombing. It was also concluded that, while the atomic bombings of Hiroshima and Nagasaki were proportionate to the cost of terminating the war conventionally, they, like most of the area bombing of Germany, were violative of the principle of discrimination. Indeed, it was said after the war that the practice of the United States and its Western Allies had completed the elimination of the principle of discrimination as a viable rule of positive international law.

Yet I have found that the total-war efforts against Germany and Japan met the just-war conditions sufficiently to qualify these wars as just. This is possible primarily because of the justice of the cause and the general compliance of the United States and its Western Allies with the just-war conditions. But certification of U.S. participation in World War II as just should not obscure the fact that the price for victory in that war was substantial violation of the principle of proportion and even more extreme violation of the principle of discrimination. This left the United States at the outset of the nuclear age with concepts and practices contrary to just-war requirements, something that has concerned proponents of just and limited war ever since.

THE UNITED STATES IN THE KOREAN WAR

Jus ad bellum

Competent Authority

In the Korean War there was some doubt about President Truman's authority to engage the United States. These doubts grew as the war dragged on but did not reach the extent of the objections to Johnson's policies in the Vietnam War. These objections never reached the point where the issue of competent authority in just-war terms was serious.

Just Cause

The just cause claimed in the Korean War was unique in history. For the first time a state purported to be acting on behalf of a system of world public order rather than for its own political advantage. Clearly, there were strategic reasons for U.S. intervention (for example, containment of the Soviet Union and its communist allies in general and containment in Asia, especially for the protection of Japan). But the crux of the U.S. position was that the North Korean attack constituted a gross violation of the ban on the use of the military instrument in the UN Charter and a challenge to the new, international public order which could not be permitted to succeed. The United States attempted to channel its intervention through the United Nations and got as far as a Security Council finding that the North Korean attack constituted aggression and a threat to the peace before the Soviets returned to the body they had been boycotting over the exclusion of the People's Republic of China. The just cause in the Korean War may be expressed as collective self-defense on behalf of a victim of aggression; a substitute for UN enforcement action against an aggressor found to constitute a threat to the peace designed to surpress, punish, and deter aggression; and containment of Communist expansion by aggression and maintenance of the Free World strategic position in the Far East.

Liberation of North Korea and/or mainland China from Communist rule was not part of the original just cause. Liberation of North Korea and unification of Korea was, briefly, a cause during the height of General MacArthur's successes. [14]

In the calculation of proportionality of probable good and evil, it is necessary, as in reviewing World War II, to look beyond the material results and beyond the countries directly involved. The war brought great loss of life, destruction, social dislocation, and suffering to the Koreans. For the South Koreans the stakes involved their future, either as subjects of an oppressive communist regime or of an authoritarian, anticommunist regime. In view of later developments and current apprehensions about the quality of life in South Korea, it could be argued that, after all that suffering, the South Koreans are not markedly better off than they would have been under the Communists. On the whole, it would seem that the South Koreans are decidedly better off than their North Korean compatriots and have some prospects for improving their position. Had they been incorporated into Communist Korea, they would have suffered greater losses of fundamental freedoms, found a lower standard of living, and had no more prospect for real improvement than in other communist countries. North Korea is notoriously one of the most repressive of those countries. This raises the critical issue of reversibility. The anticommunist regime in South Korea is reversible. It is possible for the South Koreans to change it if they really want to. Communist regimes have historically been irreversible. Once in power they have not been displaced.

But the Korean War was not fought only for the South Koreans. The second dimension of the case requires us to transcend the issue of forcible reunification of Korea by a communist dictatorship. The United States acted reasonably in taking the view that this was a test of the willingness of the Free World nations to resist the kinds of aggression that had so recently been outlawed by the UN Charter. The defense of South Korea was proportionate to the need to resist such aggression and to deter other aggressions.

The issue of probability of success is complex in the case of the Korean War. Just-war doctrine would recognize South Korea's right to defend itself without insistence on a probability of success. No discussion has come to light on the extent to which an intervening collective defender can invoke the same open-ended rights of defense. The best view would seem to be that a party intervening in the defense of another ought to meet the requirement of probable success. Assuming this to be the case, what were the U.S. prospects? Initially they were not good. The United States had inadequate forces immediately available. The joint South Korean-U.S. defense just barely held on until U.S. reinforcements turned the tide. However, throughout there should have been no doubt that the United States and South Korea could defeat North Korea. All estimates turned on the prospects for intervention by either the Communist Chinese or the Soviets or both.

The U.S. decision to intervene was based on the assumption that by fighting a careful, limited war, the intervention of the Red Chinese or the Soviets could be avoided (see Chapter 10). Efforts were made to this end; unsuccessful as regarding the Communist Chinese, successful as concerning the Soviets. Given the serious character of the just cause—response to and deterrence of flagrant agression—the risk of a wider war with the Communist Chinese and/or Soviets was reasonable.

There remains another problem which is central to this book. How does one define success in the calculus of probable success? In traditional political-military terms, success means victory. However, in just-war terms success would mean accomplishment of the just ends. In this case the just ends were the successful defense of South Korea and deterrence of further aggression against South Korea or any other nation. These ends were accomplished despite the complications of Communist Chinese intervention. While such an outcome was by no means self-evident, it was a reasonable expectation. Had success been interpreted to mean the complete defeat, World War II fashion, of North Korea, it seems possible that there might have been a Soviet intervention on top of the Communist Chinese intervention. Had the United States taken the opportunity to "unleash" Chiang Kai-shek and to try to liberate mainland China, hopes for success through victory would have been so farfetched as to fail to meet the requirements of probable success.

There was little occasion for exhaustion of peaceful remedies before the North Korean attack, but the U.S. record was respectable. What is more important, the United States was open to initiatives for peaceful settlement during the course of hostilities, at times risking its military situation in order to pursue negotiations. The war ended through negotiations in a demonstration of U.S. willingness to terminate the conflict and avoid further risks of enlargement and escalation.

Right Intention

Responsiveness by the United States to the condition of right intention was uncommonly good in the Korean War. There is, however, the issue of revised objectives. The United States entered the war to defend South Korea, not liberate North Korea from Communist control. When the opportunity arose, the objectives were enlarged to include unification of Korea. The subjective intention was certainly altruistic. It did, however, trigger the very response from the Communist Chinese that had been discounted in the original calculus of proportionality by the resolve to keep the war limited to the defense of South Korea. Had the United States perpetuated the war in order to liberate North Korea, the effort would probably have been disproportionate and dangerous. Otherwise, the negotiations for a truce, including the exchange of prisoners of war, reveal attitudes and policies on the part of the United States that set a high standard for right intention. The behavior and attitudes of the Communist belligerents, particularly with regard to U.S. and UN prisoners of war, as well as their treatment of occupied South Korea, gave ample reason for hatred and a demand for vengeance. On the contrary, the U.S. attitude was charitable and restrained, and the emotions of the South Korean government under Rhee were kept in check, albeit with considerable difficulty.

Jus in bello

It is believed that no jus in bello issues raised by the U.S.-UN conduct of the war were sufficiently important to weigh heavily in just-war evaluations. Strategic bombing continued to tend toward disproportionate destruction, and the principle of discrimination was again violated, although not in the flagrant manner of World War II. Because of the less advanced nature of North Korea, this aspect of the war was not as critical and the bombing policies were certainly no worse than in World War II. All in all, U.S. participation in the Korean War clearly met the conditions for a just war.

5

JUST WAR APPLIED: THE UNITED STATES IN VIETNAM

If World War II is often viewed as the last good war and the Korean War a somewhat Quixotic police action, the American participation in the Vietnam War, 1965-73, is widely denounced as "illegal and immoral." This characterization has been the easier to sustain with respect to a long war that ended in frustration and defeat, leaving few supporters, either hawks or doves. But the Vietnam War has valid claims to legitimacy as a just war. Moreover, it is a war that should be studied carefully for its lessons rather than thrust under the rug, as is the present tendency. Many of the material and moral problems of the Vietnam War are problems that the United States may encounter again. Finally, as Guenter Lewy demonstrates at length and in authoritative detail in America in Vietnam, many of the impressions of fact and the resultant normative judgments made in the course of the war may not stand up in the light of a more dispassionate review of the emerging record of the conflict. [1]

JUS AD BELLUM

Competent Authority

As remarked in Chapter 2, U.S. entrance into the Vietnam War as a full belligerent in 1965 raised questions about the competent authority of President Johnson to commit the nation to war. But critics who deny the legality of this undeclared war face an overwhelming evidence of its legality in the fact of eight years of congressional supporting legislation and action, the refusal of the courts to challenge the war's legality, and the acceptance by the overwhelming majority of the population of the legitimacy of the war effort notwithstanding their regrets over its lack of success. This is not to deny that it would have been better constitutionally and prudentially to have gone to Congress for a proper declaration of war. Under the War Powers Resolution of 1973, this will have to be done within a short term in any future conflicts. But it bears repeating that as a matter of international practice formal declarations of war are not required and seldom given. [2]

Just Cause

The U.S. just cause in Vietnam was very similar to the goals in the Korean War. It was to defend a victim of aggression, South Vietnam, and thereby to deter further aggression in violation of world public order. Further, the United States sought to defend against and deter a particular form of aggression involving Communist expansion by armed force and intimidation. To the objection that the fighting in South Vietnam was nothing but a civil war, the United States answered that the conflict was directed and supported by North Vietnam in acts of "indirect aggression." Indirect aggression against South Vietnam was later supplemented critically by direct aggression from North Vietnamese troops. In terms of UN law, hostile acts were emanating from one international person and taking effect across an international boundary to threaten the territorial integrity and political independence of another international person (for example, aggression was taking place). South Vietnam, widely recognized as an independent, sovereign entity in international law and diplomacy, had the right of self-defense against such aggression. The United States, under Article 51 of the UN Charter, had the right of intervention in an act of collective self-defense. [3]

It should be noted that, in contrast to the Korean War, the United States steadfastly refused to consider liberating Communist North Vietnam. Linked to the primary just cause of collective self-defense and deterrence of aggression was the "domino theory" belief that the peace and security of the rest of Southeast Asia would be jeopardized by Communist success in South Vietnam. Beyond this, and by no means farfetched, it was believed that there was a need to resist a tide of indirect aggression linked to civil wars that appeared to be developing throughout the Third World. [4]

Opponents of the war never accepted these war aims. They continued to insist that the war was essentially a civil war, that the Saigon regimes deserved to be overthrown, and that it was both illegal and wrong for the United States to intervene. U.S. public opinion originally supported the Johnson administration's goals. Later, as the public became discouraged, support diminished. However, the decline in support appears to have been more a question of lessened belief in the feasibility of the U. S. goals than in their original validity. In any event, it remains disputed whether there was a just cause in the Vietnam War. I believe that there was. In my view, it was valid to analogize from the Korean experience and hold that major aggression, indirect as well as direct, must be resisted and deterred by collective self-defense whenever possible. It was, moreover, valid to consider the general regional security of Southeast Asia and adapt a forward strategy for the defense of that region.

Were the costs of the Vietnam War proportionate to the goals of the United States and of South Vietnam? The costs included great loss of life, material destruction, social dislocation, and political instability in South Vietnam. There was considerable loss of life and destruction in North Vietnam because of the U. S. bombing and further expansion of the war into Laos and Cambodia with devastating results for those countries. Finally, the war cost over 50,000 American lives, many times more than that in casualties, and a most severe disruption of U. S. polity. For the United States this went on for eight years; the fighting continued for the Vietnamese until the collapse of the Saigon regime in 1975. The psychological and social shock waves of the war spread throughout the world as it became a central rallying theme for the protest movements of the late 1960s and early 1970s.

The evaluation of proportionality is complicated by three factors. First, there was fundamental disagreement over the ends. Those rejecting the ends as either invalid or unrealistic automatically considered the means and costs disproportionate. Second, the war was finally lost, although it does not follow that all of the ends of the war were not achieved. [5] To ask retrospectively whether a lost war entailed disproportionate costs is to be virtually assured of the answer that it did. Third, the proportionality of the means was in considerable measure a function of the particular strategies and tactics pursued, notably search-and-destroy missions in the South and bombing in the North. The strategies and tactics will be discussed in some detail in the jus in bello section following.

With these factors in mind, and without prejudice to a separate assessment of U. S. strategies and tactics in Vietnam in terms of jus in bello principles and prescriptions, I conclude that means and costs of the Vietnam War were proportionate to the ends pursued. Assuming a degree of success comparable to that in the Korean conflict, the good achieved would have outweighed the evil caused by U. S. involvement in the war. This raises the question of the calculus of probable success.

Estimating the probability of success for South Vietnam and the United States proved to be the downfall of the American decision makers. Viewing the war with an excessive emphasis on purely military aspects, the United States calculated that it could save South Vietnam from the brink of defeat and collapse and then build it back to a point where the North Vietnamese and Vietcong would have no hope for victory and would have to desist. Two nonmilitary variables were badly underestimated in this evaluation. First, the United States underestimated the will and staying power of the North Vietnamese and Vietcong leadership and the loyalty and durability of their rank and file. Accordingly, estimates of the probable duration of the war were extremely inaccurate and overoptimistic. Second, given the actual prospects for protracted conflict against a determined Asian Communist enemy, U.S. leaders greatly overestimated the willingness of key American elites to support the war. In effect, the estimates of the battlefield results during the period of active U.S. belligerency were overoptimistic but not unreasonable. What was utterly in error were the estimates of the amount of time and support that Hanoi and Washington respectively had at their disposal. [6]

All of this is not to forget the primary defender, South Vietnam. It is true that the performance of the South Vietnamese leadership was disappointing. However, a barely adequate performance was all that could have been expected of South Vietnam at any point in the conflict. That was a given in the situation and a starting point in the calculus of probability of success. On the whole, the mere survival of this battered state until 1975 is remarkable. Certainly, if the people of South Vietnam had included a substantial number who were strongly attracted to the Communists, this survival would have been impossible. The spectacular failure of the South Vietnamese people to rise in support of the Vietcong in the 1968 Tet Offensive is but a characteristic indication of the failure of the Communists to attract adequate popular support.

The point is that the war was not justified primarily in terms of the virtues of the Saigon regimes and their right to continue to rule. It was fought on the proposition that these regimes, like any other in a world replete with weak and inept governments, have the right not to be victimized by external aggression, direct or indirect, when confronted by a civil war. Since it appears clear that the efforts of South Vietnam alone to deal with a civil war plus an attack by North Vietnam would not suffice, the essential point in calculating the prospects for the outcome of the war—given an assumption that South Vietnam would somehow hold on—was the comparative capabilities and will of North Vietnam and the Vietcong and that of the United States.

Thus, a prescient supporter of the war might still have had doubts in 1965 as to whether there was a solid probability of success. Such doubts obviously could be decisive in subsequent years, and indeed, many who had supported the war changed their views. Many who changed from proponents to opponents of the war did so not because they would not have preferred to achieve the administration's goals but because they thought that the probability of success was insufficient to warrant the continued costs of the war.

One might say, then, that there was a sufficient probability of success in 1965. It would be disputed as to the point between 1965 and 1973 when the probability of success reached a point too low to justify continuation of the war by the United States. But that point was reached, in the view of most Americans, well before the Paris peace settlement of 1973. The issue is somewhat blurred by the issue of "Vietnamization" of the war. The Nixon administration maintained that it would continue in the war until South Vietnam could safely be left to deal with its insurgency and the North Vietnamese invaders alone. It was asserted that this was the case by the time of the 1973 settlement. Thus, U.S. participation would no longer be necessary. This claim was in part substantiated when South Vietnam confounded its critics by dealing effectively with the 1972 Communist offensive. It must be remembered, however, that this South Vietnamese success was made possible in important measure by U.S. air support. Nevertheless, the performance of the Army of the Republic of Vietnam (ARVN) forces disproved the contention that South Vietnam had no viability or legitimacy. In 1975, with all direct U.S. support withdrawn, South Vietnam collapsed under a comprehensive attack by a North Vietnam whose allies continued to give her their full support.

Since the assumption in this analysis has been that South Vietnam was always a weak state with weak governments, its final defeat was not surprising. But that defeat could not have occurred without the failure of U.S. will to carry through on its commitment to suppress, punish, and deter aggression. It also could not have occurred if the will of the North Vietnamese and the Vietcong had been broken. Whether the war could have been fought in ways better calculated to break the will of the Communists is now the subject for critiques of the conduct of the war. This subject will be explored to some extent in the discussion of limited war in Chapter 11.

Obviously, the issue of balancing probable good and evil is most difficult as regards South Vietnam. It is reasonable to believe that the 1965 decision to continue the war with large-scale U.S. assistance in order to prevent the imminent fall of South Vietnam to the Communists was one in which the means were proportionate to the end. Of course, from the outset this calculus assumed that the forcible takeover of a nation in order to subject it to Communist rule should be prevented by all possible means, including a war that would certainly be very injurious to the threatened country. As the war progressed, it inflicted very severe damage on the material and societal fabric of South Vietnam.

Thus, it is widely believed that South Vietnam suffered far too much in the war—waged primarily by U.S. forces—fought in its defense. If it was not evident that this would become the case from the perspectives of 1965, it can be argued, the disproportionate damage likely to be suffered by South Vietnam became increasingly clear as the years of warfare passed. If, in fact, the evil resulting from defense of South Vietnam disproportionately outweighed the possible good of avoiding Communist conquest, just-war doctrine would require serious reconsideration by the intervening power (the United States) of the proportionality of the war to the just cause.

But ultimately the decision lay with the government and people of South Vietnam. Had South Vietnam insisted on coming to terms or surrendering outright, it would have been difficult for the intervening power to persist in the collective self-defense of a now unwilling defender. As it was, South Vietnam maintained a government that steadfastly refused to consider a negotiated peace that would imperil it, much less surrender. During the war, popular elections were held and the incumbent government sustained. All of this is discounted by critics who consider the South Vietnam government nothing more than a series of military dictatorships. But the fact remains that the South Vietnamese people supported their governments—minimally, to be sure—until the final collapse in 1975. As long as there was a South Vietnamese government in power, substantially supported by the people and willing to continue the war, it could not be said that the United States was imposing a disproportionately destructive war on Vietnam.

The last of the subcategories of just cause is exhaustion of peaceful remedies. The Vietnam War constitutes perhaps the best example of the point made earlier that many contemporary conflicts do not lend themselves to peaceful settlement, at least until a military decision is reached. In the Vietnam War there was never anything fundamental that was negotiable. Two rivals fought for the same land and people. Hanoi and the Vietcong wanted to unify all of Vietnam under a communist regime. The Communists might possibly have agreed at various points to the formation of a coalition government in which they would be included, permitting the familiar scenario in which coalition governments become communist governments. That was always unacceptable to the anticommunist regimes of South Vietnam and to the United States. The 1973 settlement that was finally reached turned out to be a face-saving device for the United States. It permitted continuation of the conflict and the conquest of South Vietnam by the Communists while the U.S. phased out of the war altogether. Nothing in the record of previous Communist behavior gave cause for surprise when this negotiated peace ended in renewed war and conquest. [7]

This predictable denouement renders all the more remarkable the insatiable quest of the United States for negotiations during the war. The virtually nonstop pleas for negotiations—anytime, anywhere

—interspersed with bombing halts, truces, and promises of development aid to the area certainly met and surpassed any reasonable requirement to seek a peaceful settlement. By any standard, there was exhaustion of peaceful remedies. [8]

Right Intention

Did the United States meet the requirements of the just-war condition of right intention in the Vietnam War? Despite accusations of imperialism and racism from the extreme left, the U.S. record of right intention in Vietnam was creditable. The goals of the original just cause were substantially adhered to. In its pronouncements and policies, the Johnson administration constantly reiterated that it sought no wider war. The Nixon administration did finally extend the war with the much condemned Cambodian incursion of 1970. However, as a sanctuary for the Communists, Cambodia had been an undeclared participant in the war in Vietnam for many years before 1970. Whether the extension of the war in the form of the 1970 incursion into Cambodia was a wise move or not, its rationale as part of the ongoing fight for Vietnam conformed to the original just cause.

The United States went so far in discouraging hatred and the desire for vengeance that it probably depreciated from popular support for the war. The contrast to the governmental propaganda policies and public opinion in World War II was extraordinary. The U.S. government openly disavowed the option of raising what Dean Rusk called a "war spirit." The U.S. government and people maintained a remarkably cool, detached view of the enemy who was attacking basic American values, killing U.S. soldiers, and engendering bitter domestic divisions. As the war dragged on it became popular for politicians and assorted celebrities to demonstrate their humanity by highly advertised contacts with enemy representatives and visits to Hanoi, all reluctantly tolerated by the U.S. government. Indeed, one of the questions left over from the Vietnam experience is whether one can maintain support for an extended war without arousing more war spirit than the U.S. government saw fit to elicit.

I conclude that in the Vietnam War the United States had competent authority and had a just cause, a collective defense of an ally victimized by aggression as authorized by Article 51 of the UN Charter. Assuming a degree of success comparable to that achieved in the defense of South Korea, a reasonable assumption, the probable good of a successful war was proportionate to the contemplated means and estimated costs. There was a probability of success sufficient to justify the war, particularly because it was one the South Vietnamese government pursued in self-defense, but U.S. decision makers

misjudged the probability of success. Peaceful remedies were essentially precluded by the nature of the enemy and the conflict, but
the United States more than met the requirement of exhausting chances
for such a settlement. Right intention was maintained to such an extent that popular support of the war was restricted.

Admittedly, this jus ad bellum evaluation of the U.S. participation in the Vietnam War is not shared by many today. At best it must
be conceded that the claims to a just cause by the United States in the
Vietnam War have been considerably less convincing than parallel
claims in World War II and the Korean War. This means that even
closer attention must be given to the second part of the just-war analysis, the jus in bello. In World War II, I have argued, an extremely
strong just cause outbalanced jus in bello violations of an important
character. In the Korean War, it has been my position, the jus ad
bellum requirements were met and there were no critical jus in bello
issues on the U.S.-UN side. However, in the Vietnam War both the
jus ad bellum and the jus in bello conditions raise critical and controversial issues. Given the dispute over the U.S. compliance with jus
ad bellum conditions, satisfactory compliance with the jus in bello
requirements becomes essential if the United States is to be judged to
have engaged in a just war in Vietnam.

JUS IN BELLO

The conduct of the war in Vietnam by the United States, South
Vietnam, and their allied forces raises jus in bello issues sufficient
to affect the total just-war evaluation under the following categories:

Use of firepower and bombing in South Vietnam,
Strategy and tactics of "search and destroy" missions,
Use of napalm,
Use of chemical warfare (nonlethal gases and herbicides),
Torture and mistreatment of prisoners of war,
Repressive measures with respect to the civilian population, and
Bombing of North Vietnam.

Use of Firepower and Bombing in South Vietnam

There seems to be broad agreement that U.S. and ARVN forces
in Vietnam used firepower in populated areas to an excessive degree.
The results were heavy civilian casualties and destruction and the
generation of large numbers of refugees. Generally speaking, the
overuse of firepower was a predictable result of increased capabilities available to ground forces and their potent components of tactical

air support including helicopter gunships. Any modern combat in populated areas can be expected to produce heavy casualties, destruction, and displacement in the civilian population. Moreover, it is characteristic of U.S. military tactics, copied by the South Vietnamese, to save the lives of U.S. servicemen by expending massive firepower. Finally, it must be pointed out that the Communist forces in Vietnam followed a pattern of fighting from within villages and hamlets so as to oblige U.S. and ARVN forces to use their firepower in ways that inevitably resulted in large scale civilian casualties and displacement as well as in the devastation of many small villages and hamlets. [9]

More specifically, excessive firepower was elicited by several recurring patterns of combat in Vietnam. First, there was the common sequence in which U.S./ARVN forces were fired on from villages or hamlets. Fire was returned. If a substantial fight ensued, Vietcong/North Vietnamese forces would then escape, leaving the inhabitants to suffer from continuing fire and assaults. Often the village or hamlet was devastated during or after the attack. It was rarely possible to determine whether the inhabitants had supported the enemy or been their victims. This pattern caused many civilian casualties and widespread displacement as well as the destruction of many villages and hamlets.

Second, it was often the case that the Communists held their ground in villages and hamlets and fought engagements from and in them, turning them into battlefields. Again, civilian relationships with the Communist forces ranged from virtual cobelligerency to support to victimization. [10]

Third, civilians often suffered from US/ARVN firepower in areas that had been designated free-fire or free-strike zones, later designated as specified strike zones. In theory, civilians had been cleared from such zones and/or given ample warning that they should stay clear of them. In practice, warnings and evacuations were ineffective and incomplete. Many could not be deterred from returning to these areas. Moreover, civilians who supported the Vietcong might be inclined to remain in them. The upshot was that many civilians were killed in such zones, particularly by tactical air attacks and by artillery bombardments that swept large areas with unobserved fire. [11]

Fourth, the institution of body counts undoubtedly contributed to the magnitude of civilian casualties in Vietnam. Body counts (casualty statistics) are a traditional feature of warfare and a major indicator of the fortunes of war. This is particularly the case in a war where success is not easily measured in terms of territory taken and held and where the effects of attrition on the enemy forces are critical to estimates of the progress of the war. However, it appears that excessive emphasis on body counts as proof of units' success in battle led to insensitivity with regard to distinguishing enemy military dead from civilian dead. This tendency was encouraged by the fact that Vietcong forces usually dressed in clothing that was almost indistinguishable from that of the rural population. Accordingly, it seems clear that very substantial numbers of civilian dead were included in U.S./ARVN body counts and that some units were willing to chance noncombatant casualties in part because those casualties would increase their body counts. [12]

These patterns of combat behavior raise issues of violation of the principles of proportion and discrimination. It is not necessary to do more than survey accounts of fighting in Vietnam to conclude that a very significant number of cases occurred in which firepower was grossly disproportionate to reasonable military necessity. Indeed, Military Assistance Command, Vietnam (MACV) directives warning against disproportionate reactions with firepower to minor attacks from hamlets and villages confirm that there was a major problem of overreaction. Moreover, such excessive use of firepower was violative of the principle of discrimination, since the collateral damage usually and predictably exceeded the injury to the enemy personnel and military targets. MACV directives also acknowledged this problem by demanding greater efforts to avoid noncombatant casualties. [13] In the case of the attacks on villages and hamlets from which sniping and hit-and-run attacks had emanated, the burden of violation of proportionality and discrimination must be attributed to the U.S./ARVN forces, notwithstanding the enemy's provocations.

However, in the cases where the enemy stood its ground and fought in and from population centers, responsibility must be shared, with most of it properly place on the Communist forces. In many cases the Communists left no alternative to the U.S./ARVN forces than the destruction of villages and hamlets used as military strongpoints, with attendant civilian casualties. Generally speaking, it seems fair to assign major responsibility to the Communist forces for the civilian losses, destruction, and displacement caused by turning population centers into battlefields.

The use of excessive firepower in free-fire/strike zones or specified strike zones, on the other hand, must be accepted as almost entirely a responsibility of the U.S. and South Vietnam. However, the permissibility of the operations conducted in those zones is difficult to assess. It was, on the whole, legitimate to clear civilians from areas in which enemy combat forces operated. This was a legitimate effort to simplify the task of the U.S./ARVN forces in locating and attacking the enemy forces. Indeed, such evacuations of civilians from active combat zones demonstrated an intention of protecting rather than attacking noncombatants. Moreover, in this mixed civil/international conflict, there was weight to the argument that the

South Vietnamese authorities had a right to order their own citizens out of portions of the national territory in a national emergency. These authorities also had the right to certify to their U.S. allies that such territory could be freely attacked on the assumption that all remaining occupants were enemy or enemy supporters.

Free-fire zones became one of the principal categories of alleged U.S. violations of the jus in bello in criticisms of the war. The modified and better controlled concept of selective strike zones does not seem to have been acknowledged by the war critics. Cutting through the image of free-fire zones as a monolithic category of practice that invariably produced disproportionate and indiscriminate use of firepower, it seems fair to say that the selective strike zones were often, but not invariably, abused. Some fault must be assigned to the South Vietnamese authorities who were often lax in certifying selective strike zones and in ensuring that the maximum possible number of noncombatants were in fact evacuated and prevented from returning to such zones. The U.S. forces were responsible for not sufficiently recognizing that selective strike zones were not wholly cleared of noncombatants and for operations therein that often were of marginal military utility with consequent violations of the principles of proportion and discrimination.

Finally, there is no question that the emphasis on body-count statistics as an indicator of military success contributed to an excessive, indiscriminate use of firepower in areas where enemy troops and noncombatants were intermixed. These excesses violated the principles of proportion and discrimination. There is general agreement on this among authoritative commentators on the war. [14]

All agree that the result of these combat practices was heavy loss of life and property as well as massive displacement in the South Vietnamese population. Critics of the war lay virtually all of the blame for these results on the United States and South Vietnam, ignoring enemy practices that contributed critically to the combat patterns that endangered the civilian population. It is widely asserted that the use of firepower generally and the practices of free-fire/free-strike zones and body counts constituted massive violations of the jus in bello. This appears to be an exaggerated and unwarranted charge. What remains clear is that excessive firepower was used so frequently, notably in connection with the situations and practices described, that it is a significant characteristic of the U.S./ARVN war effort. Part of this effort is justifiable in terms of military necessity, but much of it was disproportionate, unjustified by military necessity, and indiscriminate. It may be concluded that the principles of proportion and discrimination were violated sufficiently by the abuse of firepower so as to leave a record of violations of the basic principles of the jus in bello on a very large number of occasions.

In this connection it is necessary to distinguish violations of the jus in bello for which a belligerent is responsible from war crimes for which there is individual responsibility. It is well established that the proportionality of combat measures should be judged—for purposes of individual responsibility for war crimes—from the perspectives of the commanders in the field at the time of the acts in question. Thus, if a unit commander called for massive artillery and air support around his defense perimeter in the mistaken belief that his security was threatened, his action would be accepted if his estimate and actions were reasonable, even though there was no sufficient military necessity for that action. A great number of cases of disproportionate and indiscriminate abuse of firepower could no doubt be attributed to unfounded or exaggerated apprehensions and to the tendency to err on the side of one's own security.

However, the belligerents as legal and moral corporate entities are responsible for violations of the jus in bello, whatever the individual responsibility of commanders making good faith errors in judgment. The cumulative effects of thousands of command decisions to use more and more indiscriminate firepower than could be reasonably warranted by military necessity can add up to produce major jus in bello violations. Such major violations, when widely repeated, depreciate from a belligerent's claims to be conducting a just war. It appears that the U.S./ARVN forces in Vietnam did in fact use excessive firepower to the point where the just conduct of the war was placed in question.

Strategy and Tactics of Search-and-Destroy Missions

The general issue of excessive use of firepower would have arisen no matter where and how the Vietnam War was fought. Search-and-destroy missions brought the war to the countryside, but no alternative strategies could have avoided the necessity for combat operations in inhabited areas. Unlike war in the Sinai Desert, it is impossible to fight modern warfare with its greatly increased capabilities for firepower, even in areas as thinly populated as the Vietnam countryside, without inflicting civilian casualties and damage of a high magnitude.

However, some strategies and their indicated tactics were more likely than others to bring on combat that would be highly injurious to civilian lives and property. The search-and-destroy strategy and tactics followed by U.S. forces during most of the Vietnam War have been criticized as having been the source of the abuse of firepower and of many of the other practices that violated the jus in bello. This charge needs to be considered, but it should be made clear from the outset that a strategy of search-and-destroy as such is a perfectly legitimate military approach. Prudentially, it may not be the best approach in a war such as the Vietnam conflict; but, by military standards, it was a reasonable course to follow.

Moreover, a fundamental motivation in the choice of the search-and-destroy strategy was to avoid civilian casualties and damage. The idea was to keep the enemy away from the large population centers and force him to fight in rural and/or virtually uninhabited areas. It was the purpose of search-and-destroy missions to "seek out and destroy major Vietcong units, bases and other facilities." This, combined with aerial and other interdiction of enemy resupply and reinforcement routes, was expected to lead to "progressive destruction of the VC-DRV main force battalions." In brief, search and destroy was a traditional strategy of attrition.

The strategy did not produce the desired results. It developed that the capabilities of the enemy for reinforcing and resupplying his forces was underestimated consistently. Moreover, the enemy controlled the pace and level of intensity of the fighting, seldom being obliged to stand and fight unless he was willing. Accordingly, the war ground on inconclusively despite the severe casualties inflicted on the Communist forces by search-and-destroy missions. This meant that the military utility component in the calculus of military necessity tended not to be sufficiently decisive to justify as proportionate costs the casualties and damage inflicted on the civilian population in areas swept by search-and-destroy missions. [15]

As the war continued other deficiencies in the search-and-destroy strategy became apparent. While the strategy did succeed in keeping the Communists away from the larger population centers, it manifestly did not provide adequate security for large areas of rural Vietnam. The search-and-destroy missions would sweep an area clean of the enemy, but the Communists would return, often repeatedly, after these campaigns. Insufficient attention and resources were given to pacification and rural security until relatively late in the war. With the resources available, it was not possible to pursue search and destroy at the levels of 1965-69 and still mount the necessary positive programs of pacification and rural security. Thus, the search-and-destroy missions had the double disadvantage of failing to produce the desired military result and of diverting scarce resources from the efforts that were finally critical to the outcome of the war within the Vietnamese society.

U.S. forces tended toward an alternative strategy in the latter part of the war. This was to emphasize the holding of disputed areas with sufficient resources for pacification and security so that they could gradually develop some degree of capabilities for self-sufficiency and self-protection. This slower but more permanent approach of gradually expanding secured areas meant less sweeping over the countryside with large-unit operations. It also meant that military engagements were more likely to be fought under circumstances where combat practices could be kept proportionate and discriminate. Whether this approach would have ultimately won the war is hard to say, since the U.S. withdrawal and the subsequent Communist escalation to an all-out conventional assault on South Vietnam resulted in the collapse of the resistance of the South Vietnamese forces. [16]

It should be emphasized that the civilian casualties and damage caused by the search-and-destroy strategy and tactics were not limited to the immediate losses on the battlefield. Long-term devastation of villages and hamlets as well as of productive farming areas resulted from search-and-destroy missions. Population displacement and the generation of refugees in massive numbers was a major consequence of these missions. In summary, as the war went on, it appeared more and more difficult to justify the civilian casualties, damage, and displacement in terms of the military utility of search-and-destroy missions. Moreover, it was increasingly clear that the political consequences of the search-and-destroy strategy were cumulatively injurious to the positive mission of "winning the hearts and minds" of the Vietnamese people.

This verdict on search and destroy translates into a finding that this strategy produced disproportionate costs. Had the strategy been more successful, it would be more difficult to weigh its military utility against its injurious effects on the population. But, since the strategy produced disappointing military results, it is not so difficult to conclude that the results were disproportionate to the costs.

As described in the previous section, a great deal of indiscriminate use of firepower characterized search-and-destroy missions. This, of course, would be true of any combat fought in populated areas. However, the intention of the U.S./ARVN forces was to engage in counterforce operations. Civilian casualties and damage could fairly be considered collateral damage, allowable under the principle of double effect. Generally, it would appear that the search-and-destroy missions did not usually violate the principle of discrimination in the accepted sense of direct intentional attacks on noncombatants and nonmilitary targets.

Use of Napalm

Napalm is another of the focal points and symbols of opposition to the Vietnam War that came to convey a seemingly self-evident condemnation as being fundamentally illegal and immoral. There is no doubt that napalm burns cause intense suffering, and that the use of napalm properly raises the issue of possible violation of means that cause superfluous suffering.

However, as pointed out in Chapter 3, the application of the principle of superfluous suffering has tended to be difficult. The emphasis in early applications was on means that had little military utility, so that it was not difficult to pronounce the suffering they caused superfluous. But means of proved military utility have been condoned regardless of the suffering they cause. Napalm is an established, highly useful means. It is particularly effective against strong fortifications and jungle positions. Napalm has been used by belligerents during and since World War II and is part of the capabilities of most modern defense forces.

The United States would appear to be justified in its position that a weapon or means of war is not prohibited for causing superfluous suffering until it has been condemned by international law. In other words, there is no self-evident way of defining superfluous suffering except by the inductive approach of international practice. Despite the intense campaign against the use of napalm in the Vietnam War, international practice has still not produced a positive-law jus in bello prohibition against the use of napalm. It is difficult to go beyond this point in normative analysis. While it is a means that produces terrible suffering and is manifestly subject to disproportionate and indiscriminate use by belligerents, napalm is not as such a means that is disproportionate and indiscriminate. I conclude that the use of napalm generally by the United States in the Vietnam War was not a violation of the jus in bello.[17]

Use of Chemical Warfare (Nonlethal Gas and Herbicides)

As discussed in Chapter 3, a general prohibition of the 1925 Geneva Gas Protocol against the use of "asphyxiating, poisonous or other gases, and all analagous liquids, materials or devices" provides the most significant example of a specific jus in bello limitation on the conduct of hostilities. It is important to understand that the ban on chemical warfare is valuable not only on its own merits but as a rare example of successful arms limitation under international law. Accordingly, violations of the legal limitations on the use of chemical warfare (CW) take on a symbolic seriousness that should not be underestimated. This should be remembered when plausible arguments are made that various CW means are more humane than many that are permitted by the jus in bello.

When the Vietnam War began, the U.S. position on CW was somewhat ambiguous. The United States had never ratified the 1925 Geneva Gas Protocol and, accordingly, was not bound by it as a party.

In passing, it should be remarked that the protocol was and remains a fragile source of legal limitation on CW, since it really only prohibits the first use of gas by the parties to the convention. Its fragility is further increased by the broad reservations made by several of the great powers. A good argument could be made for the position that the 1925 Geneva Gas Protocol was not binding on the United States during the Vietnam War. However, under customary international law since World War I, it was clear that the use of CW was prohibited. The only use of gas during this period, by the Italians in Ethiopia and the Japanese in China, had been condemned by most states. The United States and its allies in World War II had declared that they would not use gas except in reprisal for prior use by the enemy. This position was held firmly at some cost. Requests from the U.S. military for permission to use gas against heavily fortified, Japanese-held islands were denied and heavy U.S. casualties were taken, in part because of this abstention from CW. [18]

Thus, when the Vietnam War began, the United States had, in effect, accepted and contributed to a customary rule of international law prohibiting the use of CW. It remained, of course, to define and apply the substance of that rule that would not necessarily be identical with the 1925 Geneva Gas Protocol, although the protocol was certainly the central reference point for decisions on the subject. This policy of abstention had survived the military necessities of World War II and the Korean War. It was to be changed in the Vietnam War.

Two categories of CW were in use by the United States in Vietnam. First, nonlethal, riot control gas was used. The primary justification for its use was that riot control gases such as tear gas and nausea gas provided a means to force fugitives from hiding in tunnels and bunkers where enemy troops often intermingled with noncombatants taking refuge during combat operations. The use of nonlethal gas could spare civilians from attacks with deadly means, and it could also reduce casualties of U.S. troops trying to dislodge mixed groups of enemy soldiers and noncombatants from their refuges.

The rationale was strengthened by the fact that the means used were considered humane in the context of riot control in countries all over the world. [19] Still, the use of nonlethal gas constituted a break in the policy of abstention from any use of gas. As such it raised a fundamental issue with respect to means of war that have been declared mala prohibita by the jus in bello. It may often be the case, as in the very broad category of chemical warfare prohibited by the 1925 Geneva Gas Protocol and complementary, customary international law, that some forms of a prohibited means may be eminently proportionate to reasonable military necessities, discriminate, and generally more humane than alternative permissible means. Still, to succumb to the argument that some forms of a prohibited category of means ought to be permitted is to break a critical threshold and open a Pandora's box of possible uses, some of which may not be proportionate, discriminate, and humane. Moreover, once the threshold is broken, it is difficult to prevent an uncontrolled spiral of reaction and counter-reaction until there is no limitation left at all.

A hint of the problems that arise once a threshold is broken was provided by the U.S. experience in Vietnam. The United States had started with the plausible rationale of forcing mixed combatant-noncombatant groups of fugitives from hiding with nonlethal gas, thereby tending to protect noncombatants from more deadly attack and save the lives of American soldiers. However, U.S. forces soon turned to dropping massive amounts of nonlethal gas on enemy troop positions to force the troops out of their protected entrenchments and into the open. The exposed enemy forces were then attacked with artillery and air strikes. If the humanitarian rationale provided justification for breaking a major jus in bello threshold and a U.S. policy that had survived two major wars, the rationale for using gas to force enemy troops out of their protected positions was surely not a convincing and proportionate one for expanding the use of CW.

It should be added that the term nonlethal is not entirely descriptive. In some cases, deaths, particularly of children and older people, may have resulted from intense doses of the gas in confined areas. Generally, however, the effects were not deadly. [20]

During the Vietnam War, the U.S. position was that nonlethal riot gases were not included in the international-law prohibition of CW. This position prevailed when the United States finally ratified the 1925 Geneva Gas Protocol, effective January 22, 1975. In President Ford's executive order of April 22, 1975, the United States renounced the first use of riot control, nonlethal agents except in defensive modes to save lives. Thus, the U.S. position has now narrowed the scope for use of nonlethal gas considerably. The United States continues, however, to interpret the 1925 Geneva Gas Protocol as not prohibiting the use of nonlethal gas. [21]

Determination of the legal permissibility of U.S. use of nonlethal gas in Vietnam is difficult. The position of the United States was not unreasonable, either as a matter of interpreting the jus in bello or of policy. In my view, however, the critical point is that, no matter how reasonable, the U.S. practice broke an important legal threshold as well as a U.S. policy that had been conserved through two wars at some cost. Too much was given up for justifications that were important but not decisive to the winning of the war and that were somewhat abused in practice. I conclude that U.S. use of nonlethal gas in Vietnam was an unjustified departure from the requirements of the jus in bello.

Herbicides were used in Vietnam for two purposes. First, they were used for defoliation to deny the enemy vital concealment along roads and trails, the defensive perimeters of U.S. and allied forces, and other combat and communications areas. Second, herbicides were used for crop destruction where it was believed that the crops were only or mainly for the use of enemy forces, their supporters, or those under enemy control. Destruction of crops was justified as the equivalent of denial to the enemy of stores of supplies or supply convoys. [22]

Each of these purposes was permissible under the jus in bello of the time, although the 1977 Geneva Protocols have now prohibited starvation as a means of warfare. The primary thrust of the objection to herbicides was that they were a form of forbidden CW. In addition, it was charged that the injury to the civilian population was disproportionate and indiscriminate. Finally, the use of herbicides was termed ecocide because of the alleged extensive and long-term ecological damage they caused.

It is not unreasonable to hold that herbicides are covered by the broad language of the 1925 Geneva Gas Protocol. However, it is less convincing to find that, like nonlethal gas, herbicides are also covered by a rule of customary international law. Whereas nonlethal gas can reasonably be assimilated into the pattern of belligerent abstention from gas warfare since World War I, the use of herbicides, as in Vietnam, is something quite different from familiar forms of chemical warfare.

There probably has not been sufficient practice to establish whether herbicides are included in the customary law prohibition of CW. The tenacity of the U.S. government in reserving the right to use herbicides reflected a strong conviction that they were not forbidden by the jus in bello. Moreover, just as it was argued in the case of nonlethal gas that the agents used were common in domestic police and antiriot arsenals, the argument was made that the herbicides were only weed killers, common in worldwide domestic use. I conclude that it is not established that the use of herbicides in war is per se a violation of the jus in bello.

The second charge, disproportionate and indiscriminate injury to civilians, is also difficult to analyze. In this discussion I will prescind from consideration of the 1977 Geneva Protocols' prohibition of starvation as a means of warfare. This is a new, rather unclear rule of an as yet unratified convention that may or may not prevail over immemorial belligerent practice. Historically, two military practices are analogous to the use of herbicides in Vietnam. First, there was never any limit on the prerogative of belligerent forces to clear a field of fire around their positions, a primary military necessity. Much of the defoliation program extended this practice over areas where friendly forces and supply convoys were subject to ambush because of the intense vegetation growing right up to the roads.

Second, crop destruction is related to historic starvation blockades that, however potentially disproportionate and indiscriminate, have flourished in belligerent practice and have been condoned by the jus in bello. Indeed, modern war has increased the scope of old-fashioned sieges involving a denial of access to the necessities of life for cities or castles to modern blockades of countries and even large parts of continents. In all of these cases the effect is felt heavily by noncombatants.

It may well be that review and curtailment of strategies of food denial and/or destruction are long overdue, hence the provisions prohibiting starvation as a means in the 1977 Geneva Protocols. It is quite possible that such strategies may, in individual cases, produce suffering, sickness, and death disproportionate to the military advantages achieved. But one cannot generalize about this subject readily. Often denial of sustenance to the enemy is an effective military strategy. It may save lives in the force employing it. Such a strategy of food denial and/or destruction is not self-evidently disproportionate.

Whether crop destruction with herbicides is violative of the principle of discrimination is also a matter for case-by-case analysis. In the first place, this analysis is complicated by the question of the relation of the putative noncombatants to the enemy forces. In some cases, crop destruction may be aimed at civilians whose support of the enemy forces is so direct and substantial that they can virtually be considered integral to them as auxiliaries. In other cases, the population may be supportive of the enemy while holding attitudes ranging from sympathy to indifference to intimidation. Civilians in these cases are increasingly distinguishable as noncombatants. In the first case, intentional use of crop destruction against both enemy military forces and their civilian auxiliaries is probably permissible. In the second broad range of cases, direct intentional use of crop destruction against the civilian population tends to violate the principle of discrimination. It should be observed, however, that in most of the cases of crop destruction, the civilian population does have the option of moving out of the area and escaping the effects of denial of food. In this sense a program such as the U.S. crop destruction effort in Vietnam is less destructive than the traditional siege of a city or the starvation blockade of a whole country where there is virtually no escape for the noncombatants.

It can probably be assumed that most of the Vietnamese civilians affected by U.S. crop destruction with herbicides were not so closely related to enemy activities as to make them legitimate targets for direct intentional attack. The issue, therefore, is whether such crop destruction can be justified under the principle of double effect as causing permissible collateral damage to noncombatants. My conclusion is that this is the case.

Arguments about the definition of ecocide, which is not an established jus in bello term, tend to be inconclusive. There is reason to believe that the charge of ecocide, coinciding as it did with the flourishing of the ecological movement in the context of the efforts of the peace movement to condemn the Vietnam War on all possible grounds, was exaggerated. The evidence available does not support the contention that permanent and irreparable ecological damage was done to Vietnam. Moreover, there is no basis in international law for the measuring of ecological damage and its characterization as permissible or impermissible except in the concept of wanton destruction. However, the defoliation programs in Vietnam were not wanton; they addressed legitimate military necessities. [23]

Nevertheless, the defoliation programs did tend to challenge one of the ancient strands in the jus in bello. Since very early times, there has been a presumption against means that cause permanent or disproportionate injury to the earth and the peoples it supports. The early history of the jus in bello reveals unwritten rules protecting wells, oases, fruit trees, and other vital sources of life in inhospitable regions. [24] I do not find that defoliation programs in Vietnam produced permanent ecological damage in violation of this ancient norm of the jus in bello. However, in light of the presumption against risking such damage, it is important to note that, in 1971, President Nixon ordered a rapid phase-out of herbicide operations in Vietnam over the objections of the military. It is also encouraging to recall that President Ford's presidential order of April 8, 1975, limits future use of herbicides to U.S. defense perimeters. [25]

I conclude that the herbicide defoliation programs as a whole were not violative of the restrictions on CW, did not generally result in disproportionate and indiscriminate injury to noncombatants, and did not cause impermissible damage to the ecology of Vietnam. I acknowledge that these conclusions are controversial, for this is a difficult subject to sort out normatively and in terms of military necessity. However, it seems clear that even a different finding, less favorable to the United States, does not produce a record of jus in bello violations so serious as to impair the American claims to have conducted a just war in Vietnam.

Torture and Mistreatment of Prisoners of War

Jus in bello issues concerning prisoners of war (PWs) by the U.S. and South Vietnamese forces include the applicability of the international law of war to the Vietnamese conflict, the responsibility of the United States for policies and practices of South Vietnam, the torture and mistreatment of PWs, and pressures to change sides in the conflict.

As will be discussed in Chapters 7 and 8, there has been and continues to be considerable difficulty and disagreement over the inclusion of participants in a civil war in the international-law regime protecting PWs. It is unclear whether, as a general proposition, the intervention of one or more outside parties settles the issue and makes the conflict international. However, this would seem to be the proper view. In the case of the Vietnam War, from the time of its full intervention in the conflict in 1965, the United States affirmed the applicability and binding character of the 1949 Geneva PW Convention. Unfortunately, the Communist belligerents were not so forthcoming. North Vietnam adhered to the convention but refused to accept supervision of a protecting power or the International Commission of the Red Cross (ICRC). The National Liberation Front was not a party to the convention and conspicuously failed to meet the standards set in common Article 3 of the 1949 Geneva Conventions, applicable to noninternational conflicts. Generally, the treatment by Communist belligerents of PWs in their custody was so bad as to constitute a major category of war crimes.[26] However, the concern of this analysis is for the conformity of U.S. and South Vietnamese forces to the requirements of the jus in bello protecting PWs.

Having said this, it must be pointed out that some of the considerations that have frustrated efforts to apply the PW regime to revolutionary/counterinsurgency wars made it difficult to ensure that the international-law jus in bello protecting PWs was observed in the Vietnam conflict. First, it was as difficult in Vietnam as it has been in other revolutionary/counterinsurgency wars to distinguish bona fide combatants from suspected subversives and both from the general population. Given the common lack of difference in dress between the Vietcong and the majority of the rural population and the Vietcong policy of fading into the ranks of that population, it was often difficult to separate combatants entitled to PW status from civilian detainees.

Second, although South Vietnam agreed to treat captured Vietcong as PWs, the fact still remained that such captives were viewed as South Vietnamese nationals. Accordingly, it was considered legitimate to attempt to persuade these captives to change sides and "rally" to the South Vietnamese government. The efforts to induce such changes in allegiance would not be permissible under the international-law PW regime as it applies to captured soldiers of an enemy state.[27]

These considerations affected the second issue to be treated here, U.S. responsibility for South Vietnamese PW policies and practices. Under Article 12 of the 1949 Geneva PW Convention, the United States was responsible for ensuring that PWs turned over to South Vietnam were treated according to the requirements of the convention.

There is no question about this U.S. responsibility, legally or morally. Moreover, as a matter of domestic and international politics, the United States was greatly concerned that South Vietnamese treatment of PWs be responsible to the requirements of the jus in bello. Charges of violations of the PW regime had a very detrimental effect on the war effort.

However, the fact that South Vietnamese authorities were dealing with their own domestic adversaries in a civil war when they held Vietcong PWs made it more difficult for the United States to control the treatment of such prisoners. This appears to have been particularly true with respect to torture and mistreatment of PWs in the initial stages of captivity. Here again, the character of the war as a revolutionary/counterinsurgency conflict contributed to the problem. As discussed in Chapter 8, the clandestine and terrorist characteristics of revolutionary warfare tend to engender rough treatment of captured revolutionaries. This should be prevented as far as possible, but an outside power is limited in its ability to do so.

These considerations provide perspective on U.S. problems concerning enemy PWs in Vietnam. However, they do not excuse, nor has the U.S. government claimed that they excuse, the United States from legal and moral responsibility for the treatment of PWs by South Vietnam. The question remains whether that treatment failed to meet the requirements of the jus in bello. If so, was the failure so significant as to affect the justice of the war effort?

Torture was a major issue in criticism of the conduct of the Vietnam War. The charges concerned torture by both U.S. and South Vietnamese personnel, although the bulk of the charges were directed at the latter. The charges claimed that torture and mistreatment (for further elaboration, see Chapter 8) accompanied interrogations seeking vital information about an elusive and dangerous enemy. There were also charges of completely gratuitous torture and mistreatment that did not even involve a plausible claim of military necessity.

It does not appear that critics have contended that torture was carried out in a routine manner, but it is claimed that it was sufficiently widespread to constitute a war-crime category. [28] As will be discussed in Chapter 8, although there are some military necessity arguments for torture in extreme cases, all the legal and moral presumptions are against torture. They are even more against mistreatment that lacks even a vestige of justification in military necessity. Certainly there was never any disposition on the part of the U.S. government to defend or condone torture and mistreatment of PWs.

Although self-appointed war-crimes trials and hearings produced confessions and testimony of torture of PWs by U.S. personnel, there does not seem to be a firm foundation for the charge that such torture and mistreatment was common, much less routine. It appears that instances of torture and mistreatment of PWs by Americans were neither authorized nor condoned by responsible U.S. commanders. When such torture did occur it was wrong and should have been the cause for remedial action by higher authority. However, it is hard to find an adequate basis in the available record of the war for a charge of torture and mistreatment of PWs by U.S. personnel so widespread as to affect significantly the evaluation of the just conduct of the war.[29]

The behavior of the South Vietnamese, on the other hand, appears to leave more serious questions. Most of the atrocity stories and pictures appearing in the media of Communist PWs being tortured involve South Vietnamese interrogation methods. Whatever the arguments for this kind of behavior in the early counterinsurgency stage of the war, the extreme case for torture to obtain vital information (discussed in Chapter 8) became irrelevant as the war evolved into a more conventional conflict. It is difficult to determine the actual extent of torture and mistreatment of Communist PWs by the South Vietnamese, but it seems clear that there was enough to raise a significant objection in terms of the just conduct of the war. I conclude that such torture, for which the United States, as original detaining power for a large portion of the PWs and as ally, shares responsibility with South Vietnam, depreciated from the jus in bello record of the United States in the Vietnam conflict.

Another prominent category of charges by the critics of the war was that South Vietnam failed to accord the protections of the 1949 Geneva PW Convention. This charge was usually focused on treatment of Vietcong rather than regular North Vietnamese PWs. The charges reflected the problems, referred to initially, of applying the jus in bello PW regime to civil wars.

Normally the prisoner of war has a right to be taken out of the conflict and held in a protected status until some settlement is reached. In a civil war such as that in Vietnam, however, each side claims all nationals of the country as potential subjects and undertakes to "educate" prisoners of war so that they will change sides. Such education may include coercive measures involving deprivation of the rights of prisoners of war. It may also include positive measures and rewards violative of the letter and spirit of the Hague and Geneva Conventions. Leaving aside the issue of forced labor, which has not figured prominently in debates on the conduct of the Vietnam War, the critical issue here is that of involuntary service in the armed forces of the detaining power.

Involuntary service in the armed forces of the detaining power is prohibited by several jus in bello conventions and violates the basic concept of PW status. It is, however, an understandable and widespread practice for opponents in a civil war to attempt to convert prisoners who appear to be genuine adherents of the other side's ideology and to recruit from the large numbers of PWs who appear to have no strong ideological convictions and who are willing to change sides and return to the war.

The key distinction between permissible conversion and recruitment in such circumstances and illegal violations of a basic right of the prisoner of war lies in the interpretation of "compelling a prisoner of war to serve in the forces of the hostile power." If the PW is persuaded by arguments and rewards, and if he does not consider the detaining power as hostile, it is permissible for him to rally to the side of a government that purports to be his own. But if measures involving violations of the PW regime are employed to compel prisoners to serve involuntarily in the forces of the detaining power, a grave breach has occurred. However, thus far the record of the war has not sustained a charge that there was a general deprivation of PW rights for the purpose of inducing involuntary service on the side of the South Vietnamese government.

If the foregoing analyses are correct, the contribution of the record of treatment of PWs in Vietnam by the United States and, more important, its South Vietnamese ally, is a mixed one. On the positive side, the applicability of the international-law PW regime was declared by the United States, and efforts were made to apply it to this mixed civil-international conflict. There seems to be no reason to doubt that, generally speaking, PW protections were adequately ensured for the Communist PWs. However, understandably, there were more evidences of violation of the PW regime with respect to indigenous Vietcong PWs than to regular North Vietnamese prisoners. With respect to the captured Vietcong, there were strenuous efforts at conversion, and these may have violated or stretched some of the rights of such prisoners under the jus in bello. If so, the effects do not seem so critical as to affect the evaluation of the just conduct of the war. What remains of deep concern is the evidence of torture and mistreatment of PWs. There does not seem to be an adequate basis for finding that this occurred on a large scale in the treatment of prisoners by U.S. troops, although there were deplorable violations of prisoners' rights. But it does appear that torture and mistreatment of PWs by South Vietnamese personnel were widespread, and this constitutes a black mark on the record of the conduct of the war. When the comprehensive calculus of jus ad bellum and jus in bello issues is made, the issue of torture and mistreatment of prisoners of the war must be included as depreciating from the just conduct of the war. The fact that this was the conduct of the ally of the United States and not of U.S. troops mitigates the moral responsibility somewhat, but it still must be taken into consideration in determining whether the United States fought a just war in Vietnam.

Repressive Measures with Respect to the Civilian Population

Consideration has already been given to the injuries suffered by Vietnamese civilians as a result of excessive use of firepower and of search-and-destroy missions, as well as from the effects of defoliation programs. Further consideration is required for other injuries to civilians caused by what are frequently termed the repressive measures of the United States and South Vietnam. The principal complaints concern murder, torture, mistreatment, and pillage; forcible population transfers; and the denial of due process to civilian detainees. Before dealing with these complaints, it should be noted that there does not appear to be a substantial body of charges of collective penalties and reprisals inflicted on civilians, although some of the overuse of firepower reflects a conviction that civilians in the target areas were supporting the enemy and, in effect, deserved to be fired on. However, it is remarkable that collective penalties and reprisals were not more in evidence, since they had been a prominent feature of earlier revolutionary/counterinsurgency types of war.

In dealing with the charges of repressive measures against civilians, it is important to distinguish between widespread patterns of behavior by individuals and individual units and the official policies and practices of the belligerents. Any attentive observer of the Vietnam War knows that repressive acts were committed against civilians and on a sufficiently large scale to draw widespread condemnation. The issue is whether these were primarily the unauthorized or even prohibited acts of soldiers and officers acting in disobedience to orders or the implementation of official policies. If the former, the belligerent is still responsible and inquiries will have to be made as to whether due diligence was exercised in preventing and punishing such violations of the jus in bello. If the latter, the policies will have to be reviewed. It is clear that murder, torture, mistreatment, and pillage concern unauthorized behavior. Forcible population transfers and the alleged denial of due process to civilian detainees concern official policies and their implementation.

There is a sufficient body of evidence to establish that, in the course of operations and sometimes even in quiet sectors, Vietnamese civilians were subjected to murder, torture, mistreatment, and pillage by U.S. and South Vietnamese troops. The treatment of the population of My Lai demonstrated what could happen to civilians in a search-and-destroy mission gone amok. The United States contends that the My Lai massacre was an aberration. Certainly, the U.S. rules of engagement and the exhortations to the troops from high commanders to observe the laws of war make it evident that My Lai and less notorious incidents of murder, torture, mistreatment, and pillage were committed in direct violation of orders and directives.[30]

Since there is no question that the U.S. command in Vietnam attempted to discourage, prevent, and punish these violations of the rights of civilians under the laws of war, the issue is whether the efforts by the command were reasonably diligent. A number of war-crimes trials, in the form of courts-martial, were conducted by the U.S. armed forces. Many more cases were investigated. Whatever the actual incidence of cases of murder, torture, mistreatment, and pillage in Vietnam, efforts were made to investigate and punish those guilty of such violations of the jus in bello. These U.S. war-crimes trials were conducted on a scale unprecedented in U.S. experience and far exceeding any such efforts in other countries during and following other wars. It remains difficult to evaluate this effort at bringing violators of the jus in bello to justice. Since one can only guess at the total number and notoriety of actual cases of criminal behavior by U.S. troops, much less by Vietnamese troops for whom the United States had no direct responsibility, it is hard to say whether the U.S. response was adequate. [31]

In these circumstances the best that can be done is to attempt to judge whether U.S. efforts at preventing and punishing perpetration of murder, torture, mistreatment, and pillage against Vietnamese civilians failed to reach a reasonable standard for belligerent conduct under the jus in bello. In view of the extraordinary record of the United States in issuing rules of engagement and directives designed to prevent this behavior and in view of the unprecedented volume of investigations and courts-martial conducted, it cannot be concluded that the U.S. performance fell below the standards of the jus in bello. Having said this, it must be emphasized that the gap between official policy and troop performance was so substantial as to permit entirely too many violations of civilian rights. These violations were wrong and depreciated from the just conduct of the war. Moreover, they had a very bad effect on the Vietnamese people whose allegiance was sought as the central object of the war. Such violations fueled criticism of the U.S. and South Vietnamese war effort throughout the world and contributed to the decline in support for that effort. It must be added that the record of convictions and severe sentences by the U.S. courts-martial was modest and left the impression that many guilty persons escaped virtually unscathed. Nevertheless, it cannot be concluded that murder, torture, mistreatment, and pillage was condoned by U.S. authorities on such a scale as to constitute a major element in the calculus of evaluating the just conduct of the war.

Forcible population transfers present very different considerations. Here, the overwhelming preponderance of activity resulted from official strategies and policies. At the heart of these strategies and policies was the determination to deny the Communist forces the protecting cover and resources of the population in areas under their

THE U.S. IN VIETNAM / 117

control. The Communists, following Mao, proclaimed the people the sea in which they, the revolutionary fish, swam. The United States and South Vietnam were determined to move the seas away from the fish.

The population was drained from areas where it was providing cover and support to the Communists, voluntarily or not, by a number of methods. Already discussed were search-and-destroy missions and the heavy use of firepower, as well as defoliation. These combat activities in areas where the Communists operated tended to drive the population away. This was a calculated U.S.-South Vietnamese refugee-generating strategy. In addition, there were policies of population relocation to secure areas (for example, the hamlet programs).[32]

As remarked previously, the status of population relocation in Vietnam under the jus in bello was not entirely clear because of the mixed civil-international character of the conflict. The South Vietnamese government purported to be clearing portions of its own nationals from its own territory in time of national emergency. However unclear it is whether the regular law of international conflict applied, it is warranted to hold out the general international-law standard of treatment accorded displaced persons as the norm by which to judge the relocation of Vietnamese.

Two issues arise in cases of population displacement: the necessity of displacement and the manner in which it is carried out. In an international conflict, the presumption is against forcible population transfers or evacuations of civilians to the territory of the occupying power (1949 Geneva Civilians Convention, Article 49). But even this presumption may be overcome when the evacuation is required by "the security of the population or imperative military reasons" (Article 49). If an alien invader may carry out forcible population transfers and evacuations under the 1949 Geneva Convention, an indigenous government engaged in a mixed civil-international conflict may certainly do as much under the circumstances specified in the Convention.[33]

It is true that, in considerable measure, the threat to the security of the population and the military necessities requiring their removal from various areas was engendered by U.S. and South Vietnamese strategies. Indeed, it is clear that refugee generation was part of those strategies. However, the counterinsurgency strategies in turn were developed in reaction to antecedent revolutionary strategies whereby the Communists solidified their hold on and increased their operations in the areas targeted by the U.S. and South Vietnam for refugee-generation activities and large-scale population transfers. Thus, even by the standards of the law of international conflict, the United States and South Vietnam were entitled to move the civilian population out of areas where they were endangered by and constituted an impediment to the conduct of operations.

The issue shifts, accordingly, to the treatment received by evacuees in strategic hamlets or refugee camps. Such places, of course, would house refugees generated by military operations as well as by officially organized population transfers. However, the overall strategy of denuding certain areas of their populations tended to produce similar treatment for all refugees. Discussions of this subject agree that the provisions for refugee housing and care were inadequate during much of the war. Planning and provision for refugees were overwhelmed by the influx. Finally the problem became so severe that refugee-generating strategies had to be revised to reduce the flow.[34]

To say that the provisions for refugees were unsatisfactory is not to say that they fell below the standards required by the jus in bello. It appears that the refugee camps provided the necessities of life and in some respects—for example, medical care—improved the lot of the refugees. Of course, it was impossible to make up for the shock of relocation and the more or less permanent loss for many of home, livelihood, and normal family and social life. The suffering and losses of the refugees, a considerable portion of the Vietnamese population, were great. They must be calculated in the cost of the war in terms of jus ad bellum proportionality. But the available evidence indicates that the treatment of displaced Vietnamese civilians by South Vietnam and the United States met the standards required by the law of international conflict.

The last category of alleged repressive measures against civilians to be considered is the denial of due process and decent treatment to civilian detainees. Large numbers of such persons were rounded up as suspected subversives, spies, or traitors. Charges that they were subject to inhumane treatment while in detention (for example, confined to barbarous "tiger cages") were widely circulated by critics of the war. The "tiger cage" and other charges of mistreatment of civilian detainees do not seem to have held up under examination. There is no strong evidence that civilian detainees were mistreated on a scale or to a degree that would seriously affect the record of the conduct of the war. Moreover, the statistics on civilian detainees show that there was a large and rather frequent turnover. Indeed, it appears that, rather than being too severe, the processing of civilian detainees was too lax, and that many dangerous subversives and enemy agents were released to resume their activities. Whatever the final verdict will be on this subject, it is already clear that the treatment accorded civilian detainees in Vietnam was at least equivalent to that normally dispensed in developing countries to suspected lawbreakers and subversives. Certainly no massive violations of human rights guaranteed by the jus in bello occurred. Given the nature of the conflict, the record was acceptable.[35]

Bombing of North Vietnam

The strategies and policies followed by the United States in the bombing of North Vietnam have been criticized from both ends of the spectrum of opinion about the Vietnam War. Opponents of the war would probably have objected to any bombing of North Vietnam, and lukewarm supporters of the war seized on bombing halts as the major path to the war's termination. Supporters of the war protested against the gradual and frequently interrupted strategic air campaigns as well as the exclusion of important targets from attack during most of the war. Neither extreme of opinion would be likely to endorse policies shaped in consonance with the principles of the just-war jus in bello.

The task of just-war analysis is to evaluate the bombing of North Vietnam in terms of the basic principles of proportion and discrimination. In so doing, a standard of reasonableness is likely to emerge that exceeds what would have been acceptable to the war's opponents or uneasy supporters but would have fallen far short of the demands of the war's more committed supporters. Thus, the just-war standard tends to share with the limited-war standard (discussed in Part II) the handicap of falling in between the preferred or even acceptable guidelines both of the doves and the hawks.

As has been the case in all recent U.S. wars, the proportionality of strategic bombing has to be judged in terms both of raison d'état, the purposes of the war, and raison de guerre, strategic and tactical necessities. At the level of raison d'état, the purposes of the bombing of North Vietnam were to compel the government of North Vietnam to desist in its support of the Vietcong and in its escalating direct aggression against South Vietnam, impair the effectiveness and lower the morale of the people of North Vietnam, raise the morale of the government and people of South Vietnam by bringing the war home to the North Vietnamese, and bring pressure on the North Vietnamese sufficient to force them to negotiate a settlement.

At the level of raison de guerre, the purposes of the bombing of the North were to interdict the flow of reinforcements and supplies to the Vietcong and regular North Vietnamese forces in the South and destroy North Vietnam's war-making potential. [36]

To these ends, extensive bombing campaigns were conducted in which the statistics in terms of sorties, as well as the number and weight of bombs dropped, far surpassed the totals of previous modern wars. This fact alone is often cited as proof that the bombing of North Vietnam was disproportionate. But the proportionality of means in war is determined by the relation between the ends and the means, not the means viewed independently.

The evaluation of the proportionality of the bombing of North Vietnam is particularly difficult because of its failure. In the case of the strategic bombing of Germany and Japan, the result was a complete victory, and the issue of proportionality was mainly a question of the extent to which that victory could fairly be credited to the strategic bombing component of the total-war effort. Once this is determined to an analyst's satisfaction, a judgment remains as to whether the costs of the bombing were proportionate to the contribution of the bombing to the successful achievement of the ends of the war. In the case of the Vietnam War, victory was not achieved, in part because the bombing of the North never achieved the results desired either in terms of raison d'état or raison de guerre. The North Vietnamese were not deterred from continuing and escalating the war. The effectiveness and morale of the North Vietnamese people, however shaken, was never reduced to the point where the war was decisively affected. Only the raison d'état objective of raising the morale of the South Vietnamese government and people, at the brink of defeat when the bombing started, was achieved. At the level of raison de guerre, the air attacks never managed to interdict the flow of reinforcements and supplies with decisive effect, although the effort no doubt greatly impaired the Communists' conduct of the war. North Vietnam's war-making potential was destroyed in large measure, but the key to the continuation of the war was the resupply from foreign communist powers whose points of entry were generally excluded from attack. [37]

Thus, whether or not the bombing was proportionate to the ends to which it was directed, it was not sufficient to achieve these ends. This fact permits opponents of the war to say that the destruction of the bombing was in vain and therefore disproportionate. It also permits supporters of the war to say that since the destruction was insufficient to produce the desired results, and since the ends or desired results were reasonable, the bombing of North Vietnam was not disproportionate but less-than-proportionate.

To a considerable extent, the failure of the strategic bombing of North Vietnam was the result of three factors. First, as a developing country, North Vietnam had only a limited number of targets vulnerable to and worthy of strategic bombing attacks. Second, the key targets in the Hanoi, Haiphong, and Chinese border areas where the main sources of Communist resupply from abroad were located were not attacked during most of the war for political and moral reasons. Third, once the main sources of Communist resupply were exempted, the effort at interdiction was doomed. As in previous wars, interdicting attacks on the supply lines were overcome quickly. So there were built-in limitations to the bombing strategies that tended to frustrate the attainment of U.S. objectives.

However, beyond these three important factors there was an even more important reason for the results of the bombing of North Vietnam. Unlike the strategic bombing of Germany and Japan in World

War II, the bombing of North Vietnam was not intended literally to break the will of the North Vietnamese government and people by the application of unlimited air power. General LeMay's prescription for winning the war by bombing the North Vietnamese back to the Stone Age was not followed. For, while North Vietnam was not an ideal target for strategic bombing of advanced industrial and communications complexes, it was as vulnerable as any other country to heavy countervalue attacks on population centers. To be sure, such attacks could not have been as readily camouflaged by intermixture with attacks on military targets in population centers as were many attacks on German and Japanese population centers in World War II. Nonetheless, had a disposition existed to punish the North Vietnamese people comparable to the determination to make the German and Japanese people suffer in World War II, both the efficiency and morale of the government and people of North Vietnam could have been much more severely lowered by strategic bombing.

However, it was never the U.S. policy to attempt to break the will of the North Vietnamese by air power, as emphatically recommended by the U.S. military and their congressional supporters. Instead, the United States remained committed to a policy of graduated deterrence and coercion that sought to discourage continuation of North Vietnamese policies without resorting to the kind of countervalue bombing that characterized the war against Germany and Japan.

In consequence, the bombing of North Vietnam produced a paradoxical result. It is possible that by eschewing the extreme means of massive countervalue air attacks, the United States lost its best chance to win the war, perhaps rather quickly. This is a possibility but, it must be insisted, not a certainty. In any event, the kind of bombing strategies actually followed proved to be ineffective in breaking the enemy's will or even in shaking it to the point where the war could be terminated on terms ensuring the security of South Vietnam. Had the war been so terminated, it seems likely that there would have been broad agreement that the bombing policies were proportionate to reasonable ends. I cannot accept the proposition that because the war did not end successfully, the bombing was disproportionate. I conclude that the bombing was proportionate, involving reasonable means to attempt to achieve reasonable ends.

Much of the foregoing discussion relates to the second basic jus in bello principle—discrimination. Again the key to the analysis is comparison with strategic bombing of Germany and Japan in World War II. Although the World War II bombing was primarily directed to military targets, it attacked metropolitan areas on a scale and in ways that were so clearly countervalue in nature as to render ludicrous justifications of indiscriminate attacks in terms of collateral damage. This was clearly not the case in the bombing of North Viet-

nam. In the first place, as just discussed, in Vietnam the United
States did not adopt the strategy of attempting to break the enemy's
will by air power. Accordingly, indiscriminate countervalue attacks
were neither intended nor required in the bombing of North Vietnam.
Second, during most of the war the United States either avoided or
restricted raids on population centers such as Hanoi and Haiphong.
This was in part due to a great concern to avoid confrontations with
the Soviet Union and the People's Republic of China. However, it
also reflected a reluctance to chance the inevitable collateral damage
that accompanies attacks on military targets in heavily populated areas.

Because of the limited nature of the U.S. bombing strategies in
North Vietnam, the issue of indiscriminate bombing never had significance sufficient to put in question the just conduct of the war. To
be sure, there were many charges of destruction of hospitals, schools,
and other nonmilitary and/or protected targets, and there was considerable loss of life among noncombatants as a result of U.S. air
raids. It may well be that in various cases bombing was so indiscriminate as to violate the jus in bello, although the evidence seems to
indicate that such cases were far fewer than contemporary debates
and propaganda claimed. But it is quite clear that there were no bombing campaigns against North Vietnam that emphasized indiscriminate,
countervalue warfare as was so widely practiced in the area attacks
on Germany and Japan in World War II. Even the much-condemned
Christmas bombing of 1972, whereby Nixon sought to compel North
Vietnam to agree to an acceptable settlement, was directed at legitimate military targets. Damage to noncombatants and nonmilitary
targets was clearly collateral and well within the bounds of what is
permitted by the principle of double effect.[38]

Other controversial issues concerning U.S. bombing practices
(for example, the "secret" bombing of Laos[39] and General Lavelle's
unauthorized and covert attacks on North Vietnam) do not concern
violations of the principles of proportion and discrimination. They
are, rather, issues of command control within the civilian and military chains of command, important to limited-war concepts but not
involving violations of the jus in bello.[40]

In summary, a review of the conduct of the Vietnam War by
the United States reveals serious violations of the conditions of the
just-war jus in bello. These violations fall far short of the extrava-
gant charges of war crimes by critics of the war. But even a supporter of the war cannot deny that just-war standards were not met
in a number of important categories. First, there is no question
that there was a widespread pattern of excessive use of firepower by
U.S. and ARVN troops throughout the war in violation of the principles of proportion and discrimination. Second, the search-and-destroy strategies and tactics, although in themselves generally permis-

sible as reasonable military conduct, in practice produced large-scale violations of the principles of proportion and discrimination. Third, the breaking of the chemical warfare threshold was unwarranted, although this was a more controversial and less significant departure from the standards of the jus in bello than the other violations. Last, the toleration of widespread torture and the mistreatment of Communist prisoners of war, mainly Vietcong, largely at the hands of the South Vietnamese, constituted a failure to live up to just-war jus in bello standards.

This means that even if one gives the United States satisfactory evaluations on the controversial issues of use of napalm, the treatment of civilians, and the bombing of North Vietnam, there remains a substantial body of conduct that falls short of the just-war jus in bello standards. How does this record affect the overall just-war evaluation of the U.S. war in Vietnam?

At this point it is necessary to narrow the issues even further to those that, if decided against the United States, would be sufficiently important to affect the just-war calculus critically. It cannot be said that possible violations of the ban on chemical warfare and the torture and mistreatment of Communist prisoners of war would have such a result. The U.S. record in Vietnam in jus in bello terms comes down to the importance accorded to the widespread violations of the basic principles of proportion and discrimination through abuse of firepower and the excesses of search-and-destroy missions. The key to making this evaluation would seem to be the fact that the U.S. command did not deliberately flout just-war standards. The violations of the principles of proportion and discrimination resulting from the interrelated practices of overuse of firepower and search-and-destroy strategies and tactics occurred despite the efforts of higher commanders to prevent them. The delinquencies arose as a consequence of inadequate command and control efforts, not, as in the case of strategic bombing in World War II, out of deliberate policies of using disproportionate and indiscriminate force. The distinct probability of abuse was inherent in modern firepower capabilities and in search-and-destroy strategies and tactics in populated areas, but more closely controlled use of both firepower and search-and-destroy techniques would have produced behavior compatible with just-war jus in bello standards.

Moreover, it must be reiterated that these U.S. violations of the jus in bello were in substantial measure the result of deliberate Communist policies of using the population as a shield. Often it was impossible to get at the enemy without risking disproportionate and indiscriminate actions.

At this point in the analysis it is necessary to point out that the very fact that these issues are discussed at all, much less discussed as critical to the evaluation of the U.S. war in Vietnam as just, is unique in contemporary critiques of war in terms of law, morality, and military science. The issue of disproportionate and/or indiscriminate damage to civilians in combat areas has not been discussed in political, military, or normative critiques of World War II or the Korean War. Indeed, this issue was not raised in the discussion of these wars in the preceding chapter because there is no sufficient basis in the existing literature for such a discussion. Yet, a general familiarity with the nature of the conduct of those wars is sufficient to support the proposition that disproportionate and indiscriminate use of firepower in ground operations in World War II and Korea was commonplace and probably produced civilian casualties and destruction quite comparable to, if not in excess of, that inflicted by the fighting in Vietnam.

To the extent that this impression is valid, it means that the conduct of the Vietnam War has been judged by a different, higher standard than that applied to the conduct of World War II and the Korean War. One reason for this higher standard may be the growing concern for concepts and policies of just and limited war that has developed in reaction to the excesses of modern total war and the threat of nuclear war. It would be encouraging to believe that this has been the case.

However, it also seems likely that there is either a conscious or unconscious elevation of jus in bello standards when there is serious disagreement over the legitimacy of war in jus ad bellum terms. This line of speculation leads in turn to the strong suspicion that a war that is lost may be difficult to justify retrospectively in jus ad bellum terms. Obviously the finding that a lost war was proportionate in terms of probable good and probable evil and that it met the condition of probability of success is problematical when the negative result is already known. Under these circumstances there is probably a natural tendency to be more stringent in jus in bello judgments about the conduct of a lost war.

The fact remains that in World War II the victorious United States and its Western Allies deliberately engaged in strategic countervalue attacks and in the atomic attacks that were by definition indiscriminate and of at least questionable proportionality. But the overwhelmingly just cause, in my view and that of the majority of observers, in effect carried the war to legitimacy despite major jus in bello violations. The Korean War was a reasonably clear case of a just war in jus ad bellum terms. Its conduct probably violated the principles of proportion and discrimination, but the Koreans did not complain and the world accepted these violations as the price for defending South Korea. But in the Vietnam War, divided opinions on the advisability and legitimacy of the defense of South Vietnam meant relentless scrutiny of the conduct of the war, a war in which civilian losses and destruction were both inevitable and harder to accept because of the way in which civilians were constantly intermixed into the combat environment.

In these circumstances it seems a harsh verdict indeed to hold that combat practices that violated the principles of proportion and discrimination should invalidate what I consider otherwise to be a just war conducted by the United States. This is particularly hard to accept given the substantial record of the U.S. command in attempting to prevent and alleviate these very practices. To condemn the Vietnam War on these jus in bello grounds means that the unintended use of disproportionate and indiscriminate means in Vietnam is weighed more heavily than the intended use of such means in a more clearly justified war against Germany and Japan. Such a judgment seems to imply a sliding scale whereby a more just war in terms of ends may use more questionable means, whereas a less just war in terms of ends is required to adhere more strictly to jus in bello standards.

This is a dangerous approach but difficult to avoid. I have found it necessary to take such an approach in evaluating World War II as a just U.S. war. It is perhaps inevitable that in the calculus of just war, the just ends are the most critical element. Clearly just ends do not justify any means. They do not justify very evil means used on a large scale in ways critical to the conduct of the war. But they may justify a war fought with a mixture of good and bad means in which the good predominates even though the bad is as significant as, say, the strategic countervalue bombing of Germany and Japan.

In this connection it is necessary to reiterate a point made in earlier chapters, namely, that the requirement of observance of the jus in bello falls equally on all belligerents, just defenders and aggressors alike. This is the position of positive international law emphatically endorsed by the United States. But to say that the requirement of observance of the jus in bello is equally applicable to all belligerents, and that violations of the jus in bello are an extremely important matter that affects the justice of a war, is not to say that it is improper to evaluate a war as just on the merits of its compliance with the jus ad bellum conditions if its jus in bello record is one of substantial compliance with just-war requirements.

I conclude that the U.S. jus in bello record in Vietnam, despite some major blemishes and many minor ones, is sufficiently good to qualify for just-war status if the jus ad bellum conditions are adequately met. As previously indicated, I believe that those conditions were met by the United States in Vietnam. The U.S. and allied violations of the jus in bello, most importantly in the matter of abuse of firepower and excesses in the implementation of search-and-destroy strategies and tactics, deserve condemnation and a resolve to reform. But they do not in themselves invalidate U.S. claims to having fought a just war in Vietnam.

However, to say that the U.S. violations of the <u>jus in bello</u> did not result in an unjust war is not to discount the consequences of these violations for the outcome of the war. As will be discussed in the discussions of counterinsurgency and limited war, combat strategies, tactics, and practices that produce such violations directly frustrate the positive policies that are essential to success in a war such as the Vietnam conflict. Thus, if violations of the <u>jus in bello</u> did not result in the United States fighting an unjust war in Vietnam, they contributed heavily to the loss of that war.

6

CRITICAL ISSUES OF JUST WAR: NUCLEAR DETERRENCE AND WAR AND CONVENTIONAL WAR

The principal forms of modern conflict are nuclear deterrence and war, conventional war, and revolutionary/counterinsurgency war. Common material and normative problems arise in all of these forms of conflict. Additionally, each form presents particular political, military, legal, and moral problems. In this chapter and the two that follow the three levels of conflict will be analyzed in terms of the critical just-war issues they raise. It is not intended to offer a comprehensive analysis of nuclear deterrence. However, the integral character of nuclear deterrence, the wars that would have to be fought when it failed to prevent them, and the ever-present danger of escalation to nuclear war in most contemporary conflicts requires that attention be given to the deterrent functions as well as to the war-fighting characteristics of nuclear warfare.

In this chapter I will deal with present issues of nuclear deterrence and war and of conventional war. To reiterate the orientation indicated at the beginning of this book, the problems will be viewed mainly as perceived by the United States. Following this chapter on nuclear and conventional levels of conflict, two chapters will be devoted to the issues of revolutionary/counterinsurgency war, a dominant form of modern conflict that has received less analysis in normative terms than have nuclear deterrence and war and conventional war.

NUCLEAR DETERRENCE AND WAR
AND THE JUS AD BELLUM

Nuclear deterrence is based on the credible threat of unacceptable damage to a potential aggressor. The threat consists of a sufficient nuclear-war potential and communication to an enemy of the intent and will to carry out the threat if certain eventualities occur. I take it as axiomatic that no threat can be credible unless there is the ability and will to carry it out if the deterrent fails. The eventualities that the deterrent is intended to deter cover a wide sprectrum. [1]

It is difficult to enumerate and/or categorize all of these eventualities. Once the nuclear potential to attack is present, it is conceivable that it might be used in response to comparatively minor attacks at what is called a low threshold. The problem is compounded by the fact that nuclear powers have an interest in ambiguity concerning the level of attacks that would elicit a nuclear response. It is useful, however, to distinguish the following eventualities that nuclear deterrence systems are designed to deter: conventional aggression, nuclear aggression, and first use of nuclear weapons in a conventional war.

These broad categories may also be broken down according to the identity of the target of the enemy threat, that is, self and an ally or other state.

The form and magnitude of the initial attack as well as the defensive response is particularly important in normative analyses. Attacks and counterattacks may be either counterforce, aimed at the enemy's military assets, or countervalue, deliberately aimed at his population, industry, and other nonmilitary targets. Attacks may be strategic, aimed at the principal enemy's homeland; theater, aimed at targets within an established area—such as that covered by the North Atlantic Treaty Organization (NATO) and Warsaw pacts; or tactical, limited to a tactical area of military operations.

Thus, nuclear deterrence deters against, inter alia, conventional aggression; nuclear aggression, including all-out strategic nuclear attack counterforce and countervalue, selective strategic nuclear attack counterforce and countervalue, strategic counterforce attack, theater counterforce and countervalue, theater counterforce, tactical counterforce and countervalue, and tactical counterforce; or conventional aggression escalated to nuclear aggression, involving any of the levels and forms distinguished (for example, strategic, theater, tactical, countervalue, or counterforce).

It is understood, of course, that the boundaries between the categories of this spectrum may be breached and that escalation to a more destructive level and form of nuclear war is always possible. This greatly complicates normative analysis. In the early literature on the subject, there was a tendency to choose a point in the spectrum that supported the analyst's bias. Thus, those who tended to condemn nuclear deterrence and war were prone to base their analyses on cases of the destruction of major cities. Those who wanted to demonstrate the feasibility of limited nuclear war might prefer to discuss nuclear battles at sea. Today we have reached the point where major nuclear powers such as the United States and the USSR have an extraordinary range of nuclear capabilities permitting uses that in themselves would pass all of the requirements of the jus in bello. However, these powers also have the capabilities to wage wars that clearly would violate all moral, legal, and prudential limits. The great problem is that once the more limited means are used it may be difficult to seal off the higher thresholds and to prevent escalation that is politically and militarily unjustified and contrary to the norms of just war.

In the analysis that follows, I assume that the nuclear deterrent has failed, aggression has occurred, and a nuclear response of some kind is under consideration. In addressing such situations, the just-war jus ad bellum is severely challenged by the awesome range of nuclear capabilities and possibilities. The requirement of competent authority raises issues far transcending the question of ordering defensive measures against an aggressor's attack. Which defensive measures shall be ordered? Which of the array of conventional and nuclear means available is appropriate? Since the decisions will usually have to be made very quickly, the complicated procedures of democratic war-declaring processes will ordinarily have to give way to the decision of a president or prime minister. To be sure, there will probably be relevant contingency plans and emergency procedures approved in some fashion by committees of the legislature. However, the decision to resist major aggression by a nuclear power will be mainly in the hands of the chief executive of the state attacked.[2]

The requirement of just cause is met prima facie in the case of aggression by virtue of the right of individual and collective self-defense. However, the requirement of proportionality between the just cause and the evil resulting from the means necessary to defend it is of major concern in the case of nuclear deterrence and war. To the extent that the destruction caused by just defense is suffered by third parties and/or the world community, it is possible that such a defense may be disproportionate in its evil effects. Certainly the requirement of jus ad bellum proportionality should create an obligation on the part of the just defender to use no more nuclear force than is necessary for a defense with a chance of success. Specifically, the just defender must limit his means so as to avoid, insofar as possible, injury to the rights of third parties and to the world community. In particular, the nuclear means used should not produce radioactive fallout that disproportionately threatens third parties and the world at large.

It is permitted to undertake self-defense without a probability of success. However, contemplation of nuclear defense raises the issue of a defense continued after little remained of the population, societal structure, and industry that was defended. There is the serious danger of destroying the defended state in the course of its defense. In addition to the decision to initiate defense against nuclear attack, there may have to be a decision whether to terminate the defense and offer some kind of surrender. Clearly, a just defense may lose its legitimacy if its object ceases to exist.

As in all just wars, a just defense must be preceded by exhaustion of peaceful alternatives to war. Since the focus here is on the case of defense against an aggressive attack, this requirement is of little relevance. It is conceivable that a state has earlier committed some grave injustices, refused peaceful settlement of ensuing claims, and thereby initiated an attack. The presumption is still against the permissibility of that attack, but the justice of the defender's cause and the calculation of proportionality would be affected by such circumstances.

There is another issue of exhaustion of peaceful remedies raised by nuclear deterrence and war. This is the adequacy of previous efforts to achieve arms control. Have the just defenders done everything they reasonably could to eliminate or limit those nuclear means that most challenge the requirements of proportionality and discrimination, including third parties and the world community as well as the enemy in the evaluation? The answer to this question goes beyond formal international arms control agreements. Essential to the meaning of arms control is the notion that a state may and should, by its own defense policies and strategies, mitigate the extreme dangers and destruction of modern war. Thus, a state that has been cooperative and forthcoming in formal arms control negotiations and has, at the same time, attempted to shape its nuclear strategies and weapons systems so as to minimize injury to potential enemy civilian populations and to the peoples of third countries, as well as to the world generally, has met the arms control requirement of exhaustion of peaceful alternatives to the worst kinds of nuclear war. A state may have refused to make serious attempts at formal arms control, and it may have fashioned nuclear deterrent and war policies and capabilities in ways that conspicuously threaten potential enemy populations, as well as the peoples of third countries and of the world at large. Such a state goes into a war without having met this part of the requirement of exhausting peaceful remedies in the age of obligatory arms control.[3]

Finally, just-war jus ad bellum requires right intention. With regard to the first component of right intention—that the war be limited to the pursuit of the just cause—it is possible to conceive of the issue developing in two quite different ways. On the one hand, it is likely that the destruction of nuclear war would be such that a just belligerent would be happy to end it as soon as its defense had proven successful. On the other hand, the losses entailed in a nuclear war might impel a successful defender to feel that the cost of the war justified, perhaps demanded, actions against the aggressors to ensure that such aggression would never again be possible. There could be a counterinvasion similar to that of North Korea in 1950 and possibly a conquest of the aggressor's territory.

Such a continuation of a just war might fail the test of right intention. All of the potential violations of the requirement of proportionality would continue to be risked. Still, right intention would permit repression of continuing threats to the security of the just belligerent. That, however, is different from the kind of ideological liberation dreamed of in the 1950s. In sum, it is possible to imagine a clear and present continuing danger of aggression sufficient to justify the continued risks of nuclear war involved in going beyond mere defense and embarking on a definitive campaign to conquer the aggressor. But all presumptions must be against continuation of nuclear war any longer than is truly necessary for legitimate, rather immediate, defense purposes.

As to the other two components of right intention, the goal of a just and lasting peace and avoidance of hatred for enemies, nuclear war would certainly produce conditions and feelings that would make these goals and qualities difficult to achieve. But they must be achieved if a war is to remain just. These requirements of right intention counsel limitation of a just war of defense with nuclear means to the minimal requirements of such a defense. They bar any continuation of an initially just defense in the form of a war of liberation, much less of revenge.

These are the general issues of just-war jus ad bellum raised by the possibility of nuclear war waged in defense against aggression. Two particular jus ad bellum issues require separate consideration. First, are there any general, normative considerations concerning the first use of nuclear means against a conventional attack? Second, if there is good reason to believe that nuclear aggression is about to be launched, is a preemptive nuclear attack permitted?

The issue of nuclear response to a conventional aggression obviously turns in part on the analysis of nuclear weapons systems under the jus in bello. However, the decision to begin with a nuclear defense is so fundamental as to require analysis in terms of raison d'état proportionality. If one assumes an illegal and immoral aggression in the form of a conventional attack, the means permitted to resist it may be judged in terms of proportionality to two just ends. First, the defense of the countries attacked should be considered prima facie just. Second, resistance to aggression as a contribution to the enforcement of international law and order is a just cause. Strong presumptions support the right of the victim of aggression and its allies to use whatever means are permitted by the jus in bello in their just defense. A nuclear defense against conventional aggression, then, may well meet the jus ad bellum requirement of proportionality. Whether it conforms to the limits of the jus in bello remains to be discussed. The specific determination as to whether a nuclear defense against conventional aggression is proportionate to the just ends of defending the victim and upholding international law and order can, finally, only be made in concrete cases. However, as a general proposition, there would appear to be no reason why recourse to nuclear defense against conventional aggression would not be potentially proportionate in jus ad bellum terms. The case for the military necessity of such a nuclear defense would have to be made in terms of the jus in bello principle of proportionality between military ends and requirements and military means.

The issue of preemptive nuclear attack is likewise dependent in part on jus in bello considerations. However, any preemptive attack violates the existing rule of international law against the first use of armed force. Indeed, there are interpretations of the rule against first use of armed force that require that an armed attack must actually have occurred across an international border before defensive measures may be taken. In my view such interpretations are excessively restrictive. The principle of effectiveness should guide interpretations of the right of self-defense. To be meaningful, the right of defense should be interpreted so as to maximize the chances for successful defense, within the basic framework of an aggression-defense situation. (Defense does not go so far as to justify preventive war.) Once the intent of the aggressor is manifest and he is taking measures to carry out that intent, the defender is justified in acting with armed force in anticipatory self-defense. [4]

Usually at this stage of the discussion, the Caroline case and Secretary of State Webster's dictum on it are introduced as the principal authority on anticipatory self-defense. Webster stated that

> respect for the inviolable character of the territory of
> independent states is the most essential foundation of
> civilization. . . . Undoubtedly it is just, that, while it
> is admitted that exceptions growing out of the great law
> of self-defence do exist, those exceptions should be con-
> fined to cases in which the "necessity of that self-defence
> is instant, overwhelming, and leaving no choice of means,
> and no moment of deliberation."[5]

The authority and relevance of this famous dictum have been exaggerated. It concerns a case of an "invasion" of Canada by a private group and their repulse by defensive measures of the Canadian government. The comic-opera character of the affair makes it a poor case on which to base the law of self-defense with respect to acts of armed coercion by governments. Moreover, the formula for the necessity of defense—instant, overwhelming, and leaving no choice of means and no moment of deliberation—is more rhetorical than substantive. Particularly unjustified is the implied requirement that there be no time for any other choice than the one taken. In the case of the Cuban missile crisis, the United States had weeks to formulate its case of the necessity to take measures deemed imperative to meet the threat. Some threats must be met instantly, but some may be met after protracted calculation.

A better formula for anticipatory self-defense should look to these criteria:

1. There must be a clear indication of an intent on the part of the alleged aggressor to attack.
2. There must be adequate evidence that preparations for the attack have advanced to the point where it is imminent.
3. The advantages of a preemptive attack must be proportionate to the risks of precipitating a war that might be avoided.

There is a model case for anticipatory self-defense in the Israeli preemptive attack on Egypt in 1967. In that case it was established that the Arab confrontation states and their fedayeen terrorist associates had the intention not only of invading Israel but of destroying it. This they had proclaimed vehemently, the volume and violence of their threats mounting to a crescendo in late May and early June of 1967. Preparations for an attack had taken the form of a massing of troops on Israel's borders, heightened air reconnaissance activity, and the forcible ejection of the UN peace-keeping forces that had been separating the enemies. The Gulf of Aqaba had been closed to Israel and international traffic bound for Israel in violation of general international law and the law particular to the settlement of the 1956 Middle East conflict. The results were calamitous for Israel's fragile economy. In these circumstances the Israelis concluded that there would inevitably be a war, that their own prospects were diminishing drastically, and that a first-strike war of anticipatory self-defense was the right course if the existence of Israel was to be preserved. [6]

Controversial as is the Israeli preemptive strike of 1967, it set a standard that is consonant with the criteria for anticipatory self-defense. Indeed, because of the precarious existence of the Israeli state, the 1967 war is an extreme case that may seldom be approximated. Not many threatened states would have both the vulnerability of Israel and the high degree of certainty of an imminent attack threatening national existence. Moreover, in the case of a possible nuclear aggression, it is probably unlikely that the aggressor would begin with the kinds of ancillary acts of aggression that marked Nasser's buildup against Israel in 1967. Accordingly, the risk that a perhaps avoidable war would be precipitated by a preemptive attack will usually be greater than in the Israeli case. Nevertheless, if these criteria can be met, anticipatory attack can be justified as an exception to the general proscription of first use of armed force that is central to the international law jus ad bellum and that must be considered incorporated into a modern just-war doctrine concerning recourse to armed force.

NUCLEAR DETERRENCE, WAR AND THE JUS IN BELLO

Proportion

If they are to be used, nuclear weapons must be proportionate to their military utility (raison de guerre) as well as to the overall requirements of just defense (raison d'état). Given the destructiveness, hazards of radioactivity, and dangers of escalation inherent in recourse to nuclear weapons, a general presumption exists against their proportionality if nonnuclear means of commensurate effectiveness are available. Thus, the calculus of proportionality for nuclear weapons differs from the same calculus for conventional means in two ways: the dangers of radiation and the dangers of escalation to higher levels of nuclear war. The reasonable belligerent will use conventional means when possible and will limit nuclear means as much as possible if their use becomes imperative. Under the concept of flexible response (a central component of limited war discussed in Part II), recourse to nuclear weapons should be curtailed, each threshold being held as long as possible.

In brief, the requirements of military necessity must be conservatively estimated and satisfied in the most limited way commensurate with a reasonable chance of success under flexible response strategies. Adherence to such strategies appears to be essential in the maximum effort to assure proportionality of defensive measures where a mixed conventional-nuclear capability exists. Nuclear weapons should not be used simply because they would have military utility but because there is no reasonable, alternative, conventional means. Thus, while the proportionality of a nuclear defense against conventional attack is conceivable, the presumption is against such a defense. This presumption must be overcome by a clear showing that conventional defense against conventional aggression is insufficient, and that the advantages of nuclear defense will be proportionate to the damage and dangers it entails.

The proportionality of nuclear weapons depends not only on their own characteristics, as viewed in the context of the environment in which they would be used, but on the nature of the military means employed by the enemy. Consider the various levels and forms of nuclear war. All-out nuclear war, counterforce and countervalue, is inherently disproportionate to any legitimate end. The only rational justification for a general nuclear war would be defense against a general nuclear attack. Given the present absence of serious defensive systems like ABM, the only defense in a nuclear war is preemptive destruction of the enemy's capability to devastate the just defender. That, however, does not call for an all-out countervalue attack, only counterforce. As a general proposition, an all-out strategic counterforce attack may be proportionate to the legitimate requirements of defense from strategic nuclear attack, dependent upon its collateral effects in the enemy state and worldwide.

The most likely occasion for a just defender to contemplate general countervalue attacks would be after having suffered such attacks. At that point the damage to be inflicted on the enemy would not be proportionate to the main political or military goals of the war, for they would have already been lost irrevocably. The main reason for launching general countervalue counterattacks in these circumstances would seem to be vengeance. It could be said that such counterattacks were in vindication of the failed deterrent that had been based on the threat of retaliation in kind for countervalue attacks. However, that exercise would have no practical point for the defeated and destroyed state.

Selective strategic attacks offer some possibility of proportionality. Selective strategic counterforce attacks could well be proportionate, depending on the circumstances. Selective strategic countervalue attacks carried on to deter a continuation of antecedent selective countervalue attacks by the aggressor could be justified. Unlike the case of retaliation for all-out countervalue attacks, there would still be cities and populations to defend and the retaliatory destruction of selected enemy population centers might be effective and proportionate as a means of defending them. [7]

Prescinding from the issue of escalation, it is not too difficult to make a case for the possibility of proportionate tactical use of nuclear weapons. As indicated, it is very difficult to make a case for the use of strategic nuclear weapons as proportionate to anything other than the counterforce requirements of protecting a belligerent's own cities and population. There is an important but elusive middle category currently called theater nuclear, which seems to be more acceptable than tactical nuclear in terms of potential proportionality as a means of defense. The definition of theater nuclear appears to be somewhat vague. It embraces weapons systems that have a greater range than tactical, battlefield weapons but less than what is necessary to reach from one nuclear superpower's homeland to the other's. Yet, in the case of theater nuclear weapons in Europe, their location allows such weapons the capability of attacking the homeland of one of the superpowers. One reason, apparently, for the imprecision of usage on this subject is that efforts to clarify it would greatly complicate arms control talks wherein there are agreed working definitions of strategic weapons systems. Those systems that are excluded from strategic arms limitation talks are provisionally considered to be, by definition, not strategic. [8]

The category of theater nuclear weapons is a critical one for a number of reasons. It has been said that nuclear weapons possess two inherent characteristics that distinguish them from conventional weapons: their radiation threat and their escalatory propensities. Certainly both of these distinguishing and dangerous features are conspicuously more prominent in the case of theater nuclear weapons than with battlefield tactical nuclear weapons. This fact should be borne in mind throughout the analysis of theater nuclear weapons in terms of the prospective proportionality that follows.

Generally, it appears that theater nuclear weapons are close to strategic nuclear weapons in their capabilities and in the issues they raise in terms of proportionality. Once deterrence, based in part on theater nuclear capabilities, has failed, it would be disproportionate for the victim of aggression to unleash a retaliatory general attack counterforce and countervalue, against a theater aggressor who had already devastated the nation or nations on whose behalf the defense was undertaken. Counterforce, theater nuclear war, keyed to defense against nuclear attack, would generally qualify as proportionate. Selective countervalue retaliation for selective, nuclear, countervalue attack at the theater level could very well be based on the fact that not all of the participants in the theater defense had been the victims of countervalue attacks, and that the need and right to deter such attacks continued.

In the case of coalition wars, the calculus of proportionality of recourse to nuclear weapons is different from that in the case of individual self-defense. In coalition wars the "self" that is defended is multiple. Virtual destruction of one or more of the members of the coalition may not end the war if the others fight on. The coalition has, accordingly, a greater basis for retaliation in kind against countervalue attacks, insofar as the principle of proportion is concerned. Indeed, it is possible to make a case for massive countervalue retaliation in kind even in a case of individual self-defense on the justification that this vindication of the deterrent threat would protect the population centers of other possible victims of aggression not then at war with the aggressor. The legitimacy of this would depend on the closeness of the existing connections between the belligerent victim of countervalue aggression and neutral states as well as the likelihood of either countervalue attack or blackmail directed against those neutrals by the aggressor.

The great difference between tactical and both strategic and theater nuclear war is the minimization of the problem of radioactive fallout in tactical nuclear war. The need to calculate the evil effects of widespread and long-lasting fallout on belligerents, neutrals, and the world community is comparatively minor or nonexistent. The calculus of proportionality is almost exclusively limited to the blast effects of the nuclear devices. To this calculus, however, must be incorporated recognition of the risks of escalation if recourse to limited nuclear means constitutes the first use of nuclear weapons in the conflict. [9]

These are some general considerations that must be addressed in any calculation of proportionality, jus ad bellum and jus in bello, when considering the use of nuclear weapons. There is no question that, aside from an all-out nuclear attack counterforce and countervalue, nuclear war may be waged in ways that would be proportionate to reasonable raison d'état ends, especially of self-defense, and to standard requirements of military necessity. A much more difficult test faces nuclear weapons, however, when the principle of discrimination is applied.

Discrimination

The principle of discrimination prohibits direct intentional attacks against noncombatants and civilian targets. In Chapter 3 it was pointed out that controversy exists with respect to the interpretation of direct, intentional, and noncombatants. However, there is no way of interpreting the principle of discrimination so as to reconcile it with countervalue nuclear attacks on population centers. Given the effects of the kinds of nuclear devices that would be used against population centers, it is clear that their use against such targets would involve the direct, not collateral, destruction of virtually everyone and everything within the target area. As to the intention and the possible refuge of the principle of double effect, in a countervalue attack on a population center it certainly cannot be maintained that the actor "aims narrowly at the acceptable effect," or that "the evil effect is not one of his ends," or that the evil effect is not "a means to his ends." Nor may it be contended that "aware of the evil involved," the actor "seeks to minimize it, accepting costs to himself." [10]

None of Walzer's useful refinements of the principle of double effect can be successfully satisfied in rationalizing a countervalue attack on population centers, no matter what the alleged combination of reasons for such an attack. Finally, it is certain that there are many persons and many civilian targets within the area of a countervalue attack that do not qualify as combatants or military targets by any criteria. Indeed, the essence of the threat of "unacceptable damage" on which mutual assured destruction (MAD) is based is that its implementation is unthinkable, therefore serious challenges to the threat are unthinkable, therefore the delicate balance of terror will continue to produce stability.

Ironically, it can be affirmed that the MAD threat of countervalue war is proportionate to the requirement for maintaining the nuclear balance of terror. It has in fact deterred superpower confrontations and nuclear war itself.[11] But MAD is patently based on the credible promise to carry out threats in flagrant violation of the principle of discrimination. As has been seen in Chapter 3, that principle is central to just-war doctrine and has now been revived in conventional international law, in the 1977 Geneva Protocols, and in the United States Air Force's manual on the law of international conflict.[12]

A dilemma exists. If the principle of discrimination is taken seriously and adhered to, the MAD threat of countervalue destruction must be abandoned. But if it were abandoned, the possibilities for aggressive war and nuclear blackmail would be grave and immediate. A one-sided abandonment of countervalue strategic deterrence would be vastly destabilizing. How does one deal with this dilemma? Basically, two approaches have been attempted by those who start with the assumption that there must be some kind of nuclear deterrent to maintain peace and stability. The first approach is to take advantage of the capability to inflict unacceptable countervalue damage and to use the threat of such damage as a deterrent while resolving never to use this capability to inflict such damage in the event that the deterrent failed. The second approach is to develop an avowed counterforce capability so substantial that it alone would be sufficient to deter both countervalue and counterforce attacks.

Overt advocacy of the first approach has been rare, and its foremost exponent, Paul Ramsey, has now disavowed it. Nevertheless, to the extent that the United States has not renounced MAD and replaced it with a counterforce deterrent congruent with the principle of discrimination, the United States either intends to violate that principle in the event that the deterrent fails, or it is risking reliance on the MAD countervalue deterrent even though it does not intend to engage in indiscriminate countervalue warfare. There is good reason to believe that Ramsey's notion of a secret resolve not to use indiscriminate countervalue warfare, which is not practical as a matter of formal official policy, still reflects a vague tendency in the thinking of decision makers and theorists who would stake everything on the effectiveness of a deterrent that threatened unthinkable damage in the belief and/or hope that the implementation of the threat would simply never become necessary.[13]

The second approach to resolving the conflict between the requirements of the principle of discrimination and the exigencies of strategic nuclear deterrence is to substitute a counterforce deterrent for MAD, sufficient to deter both counterforce and countervalue aggression. This approach involves grave technical difficulties subject to frequent change. The crux of the matter is development of means that could effectively destroy the enemy's nuclear weapons systems, even though they were protected by hardening and mobility. The efforts to accomplish this involve enhanced destructive power and accuracy. These efforts, problematic in themselves because of the technical complexities, are thwarted by some arms control proponents and by defense critics who oppose almost automatically any increase in nuclear weaponry. This state of affairs leaves the proponent of a sufficient counterforce deterrent very much at the mercy of the twists and turns of weapons research and development, the arms race, arms control negotiations and debates, and the unending political and bureaucratic battles over defense budgets. In brief, it is by no means certain that an adequate counterforce deterrent can be developed to replace the MAD countervalue deterrent. If such a deterrent were developed, it would be subject to technical obsolescence. In any event, a decisive effort to develop such a counterforce deterrent has not been made by the United States. [14]

If, notwithstanding these obstacles, a counterforce deterrent could be established that was sufficiently potent to replace the MAD countervalue deterrent, it would bring with it welcome prospects of conformity with the principle of discrimination. As already indicated, problems of proportionality would continue to exist, depending on the circumstances in which it might be necessary to execute the deterrent threat. The use of counterforce as a deterrent threat would raise the familiar questions of intent, of the degree of directness of the attack on noncombatants and civilian targets, and of the proportionality of collateral damage. But, by definition, a counterforce nuclear attack could be conducted in conformity with the requirements of the principle of discrimination.

It was considerations such as these, more critical today than in the late 1950s, that led Fr. John Courtney Murray and others to declare that the development of limited nuclear-war capabilities and strategies was a normative as well as political/military imperative. [15] Today, of course, the problem is enormously magnified. In the 1950s the issue was the possible necessary use of discriminate tactical nuclear weapons to deter and/or defend against conventional aggression. Today the issue is deterrence of and resistance to strategic nuclear attack, as well as conventional aggression to be discussed presently. The alternative to developing sufficient, counterforce, nuclear deterrence and defensive capabilities and strategies is arms control. This alternative is strongly urged by the church. However, it is clear that in the present era arms-control efforts are themselves based on nuclear deterrence—the worst, most indiscriminate, hence immoral, kind of nuclear deterrence. In these circumstances, the development of limited, nuclear-war, counterforce capabilities and strategies is the course most responsive to imperative political-military necessities, on the one hand, and the requirements of just-war doctrine and of arms-control goals, on the other.

One of the many obstacles to the effort to determine what might be morally permissible in nuclear deterrent threats and their possible enforcement has been the readiness of moral authorities to pronounce all nuclear weapons and nuclear warfare immoral. Treating nuclear weapons and war as an undifferentiated whole and basing their judgment on the effects of the extremes of all-out nuclear attack, the entire category of nuclear weapons and war has been condemned as though it were malum in se. There are good reasons for treating nuclear weapons and nuclear war as a single category and urging that they be renounced as an instrument of policy. However, given the variety of uses of nuclear weapons and of forms of nuclear war, their condemnation as malum in se is not warranted. [16]

Nevertheless, there are strong arguments supporting the contention that the first use of nuclear weapons is malum prohibitum. There is evidence of an unwritten rule of international conflict or rule of customary international law prohibiting the first use of nuclear weapons.

1. In an age of frequent and serious conflicts, often involving the nuclear powers and their allies, no nuclear weapons have been used and their use has seldom been seriously contemplated.

2. The often-repeated wish of the international community is to ban altogether the use of nuclear weapons or, failing that, limit their use to retaliation in kind.

3. The avowed rationale for nuclear deterrence is based on the belief that the stable deterrents will be effective and that no nuclear war will take place.

On the other hand, the following can be argued:

1. There is no conventional law prohibiting the use of nuclear weapons and none in prospect. The nuclear powers do not admit any legal limitation on the use of nuclear weapons as such.

2. The international system is presently based on the nuclear balance of terror that requires a credible readiness to use nuclear weapons. While nuclear deterrence of nuclear attack is possible under a no-first-use rule, superpower practice is to maintain the nuclear deterrent against conventional aggression as well, retaining the option of first use.

3. Clearly a nuclear power thinking itself in possession of certain knowledge of an impending nuclear first strike by an enemy would be likely to preempt.

4. The nonuse of nuclear weapons has increasingly been the result of the operation of the nuclear deterrent, not the convictions of nuclear powers that first use was legally or morally impermissible.

5. Nonnuclear powers with the present or potential capability of developing nuclear weapons have not felt legally or morally inhibited from doing so, notwithstanding the Treaty on the Non-Proliferation of Nuclear Weapons of 1968. [17]

From these arguments, pro and con, it is not possible to conclude with certainty that the first use of nuclear weapons is malum prohibitum. The most that seems warranted is the statement that there is a heavy presumption against the first use of nuclear weapons, as indicated in the discussion of their restriction by the principle of proportion.

There is a further dimension to this subject, that of proposed rules of conflict that might be developed before and during a conflict by nuclear enemies. Schelling and others have suggested that a belligerent might bargain through conflict patterns, indicating by what was done and not done various limits that it wished to place on the conduct of hostilities. [18] This subject will be pursued in the chapters on limited war. However, its pertinence to the just-war limits on nuclear war is considerable. If, by restricting defense against conventional aggression to conventional means, nuclear war would be excluded from a war between nuclear powers, a rule of the conflict might be established that should be honored even at considerable risk and loss to an individual belligerent.

Thus, if the level of a nuclear war, should it become unavoidable, could be limited to tactical or theater means and targets; and if nuclear attacks were strictly limited to counterforce attacks; and if nuclear operations were conducted so as not to threaten neutrals and the world with dangerous amounts of radiation—such rules of conflict could be more effective than all of the formal paper declarations, condemnations, and promises made by statesmen since Hiroshima. A note of pessimism and caution is in order, however. The Soviets have gone out of their way to denounce and deprecate the idea of such rules of conflict in a general war between the superpowers. There is no assurance that they would cooperate in developing and observing such rules of conflict. Moreover, the recent U.S. experience of trying to send "signals" to North Vietnam does not encourage confidence in the tacit bargaining approach to making customary jus in bello. [19]

CONVENTIONAL WAR AND THE
JUS AD BELLUM

The conventional-war category is vast. It covers all wars that do not involve the use of nuclear weapons and do not primarily take the form of guerrilla or other subconventional war. The scope, intensity, duration, and weapons characteristic of conventional wars vary with the belligerents, their war goals, and the means available to them. Analysis of conventional war is free from the more difficult dilemmas of proportion and discrimination raised by nuclear deterrence and war. It is not, however, free from the issue of escalation to nuclear war when the belligerents have nuclear capabilities. Moreover, the very terms under which conventional war may be made possible may be determined by nuclear deterrence (for example, the so-called nuclear umbrella). In this analysis an effort will be made to focus on some issues particularly associated with conventional war. In the process it will be necessary to generalize about this broad category and these generalizations should be understood as being subject to exceptions.

There is a general tendency to assume that nuclear wars will be short and that conventional wars will be long. Fortunately we do not have experience confirming the former assumption, and wars such as the 1967 Six-Day War or the 1973 Yom Kippur War show that conventional wars can be short. The pace of a conventional war will normally be slower to develop, although experience in the Middle East shows that such wars can come suddenly and develop with dizzying speed. On the whole, however, the problem of assuring competent authority in conventional war is different than it is in nuclear war. Initial decisions to go to war and to adopt the various strategies are more subject to the full scrutiny of the war-making process than in nuclear war. There will usually be more time for reflection on alternative options with respect to initiation, continuation, and termination of a conventional war. Accordingly, as in the U.S. wars in Korea and Vietnam, disputes over the sufficiency of the powers of the executive to pursue his course in war are likely to arise. Such disputes must be resolved on the basis of the constitutional law of the state in view of the circumstances of the war.

Conventional war is preeminently the instrument of coalition cooperation. While nuclear operations are integral to the capabilities and strategies of coalitions including the nuclear powers, the primary focus, even in NATO and the Warsaw Pact, is on conventional forces. This raises a form of just cause that has not been discussed thus far. It has been shown that the just cause of self-defense may be invoked by a belligerent for itself or for an ally or other state to whose assistance it comes (for example, Korea). It has also been recognized that a state may claim to be fighting for the principle of resistance to aggression (for example, Korea and Vietnam). Such a war for principle is fought in vindication of the concepts of collective security and the indivisibility of peace, in the absence of effective international organization enforcement action. In this principled rationale of collective security, there is also mixed a prudential judgment that a nation's own security is involved in resistance to aggression generally and, particularly, in areas of strategic importance to the intervening state.

There remains a form of collective self-defense (distinct from collective security), as in the case of NATO, where a number of states form a permanent defensive alliance in which they base their efforts at security on the principle that an attack against one is an attack against all. Although the participant in such a collective defensive alliance is not obligated to go to war automatically, it does have a sufficient reason and justification for doing so under the concept of the indivisibility of the peace within the defensive alliance vis-à-vis external aggressors.

Accordingly, when the proportionality of the just cause of self-defense is assessed in a case of collective self-defense, one has to weigh the importance not only of the defense of individual victims of aggression, but also of the corporate interests of the whole defense organization in its collective defense.

This aspect of the proportionality of collective defense is akin to the problem of nuclear deterrence. The strength of a collective defense system is the promise that any threat or aggression against any of its members may bring the united force of the alliance into play with a collective defense. If such an alliance is successfully challenged and "nibbled" at, much of the deterrent force of the arrangement is lost.

While conventional war generally does not threaten the devastation of the upper levels of nuclear war, it is sufficiently destructive, particularly when fought in advanced industrial countries, to raise serious issues of proportionality between just ends and probable evil in most foreseeable conventional wars. Aside from the question of radiation, a conventional war in an industrialized area might well rival nuclear war in destruction and social dislocation. Nevertheless, if the just cause is self-defense, there is a right of the victim of aggression and its allies to resist, even at great loss and at great risk. Unlike nuclear war, conventional war does not raise critical issues with respect to the rights of third parties and the world community. Most of the evil to be discounted in the calculus of proportion will befall the belligerents themselves.

As in the discussion of nuclear defense, the focus here is on conventional wars justified as defensive wars. Accordingly, the obligation to exhaust peaceful remedies is not particularly significant unless the war has somehow resulted from unjust and provocative behavior by the state attacked. It is, however, important for just defenders to be open to the possibilities of reasonable negotiations for the termination of the war.

Conventional war has its own typical problems of right intention. Conventional war is typically characterized by military rearrangement of the political map. As the occasion arises for termination of the conflict, states may be inclined to covet territory won at heavy cost. Whether such aspirations are consonant with right-intention requirements that a belligerent stick to its original war aims and work for a just and lasting peace is a difficult question that has most recently plagued the debates over the future of Israel's military conquests in the Middle East wars. The key to answering that question lies in the relation of additional goals and claims pursued to the original just cause. If the new goals and claims, born of success in battle, can be legitimately incorporated into the original just-war aims, they may be acceptable. If the new goals and claims evidence an effort to go beyond the just cause, they depreciate the right intention of the belligerent and prejudice the justice of the war.

CONVENTIONAL WAR AND THE
JUS IN BELLO

Of the many aspects of conventional war that warrant normative regulation and limitation, the most important include massive firepower and tactical air support, conventional strategic bombing, naval and air blockades, scorched-earth defense, chemical and biological warfare, and prisoners of war. The means of warfare represented in the first four categories will be analyzed primarily in terms of the principles of proportion and discrimination. Chemical and biological warfare is, of course, subject to these principles but is dealt with primarily in the jus in bello in terms of means mala prohibita. As will be seen, prisoners of war should be entirely a matter of humanitarian amelioration of the suffering of war, but the subject has been made in part a question of using PWs as a political-military means. This problem will be analyzed.

The destructive capacities of modern firepower from small arms and artillery had already been demonstrated in World Wars I and II. With the experience of the Korean War, the Vietnam War, and the Yom Kippur War, awareness has grown that even tactical conventional weapons, now routinely supplemented by tactical air support, may pose a threat to the limitations imposed by the principles of proportion and discrimination. In discrete tactical situations it is quite possible that conventional firepower may raise the same issues of proportion and discrimination as the blast effects of nuclear weapons. Such firepower may be disproportionate in its overall destructive effects to legitimate military requirements. It also may be indiscriminate in many contexts.

As brought out in the discussion of excessive use of firepower in the Vietnam War, there may be mitigating circumstances explaining, in part, violations of the principles of proportion and discrimination. But the fundamental and ever-increasing propensity of modern military technology and belligerent practice is toward almost routine excessive use of firepower. When, as in Vietnam, these excesses can be so conspicuous and pervasive as to threaten the just-war legitimacy of the entire war, it is clear that the problem is the first of the critical issues of modern jus in bello in conventional war.

The clear lesson of Vietnam is that extraordinary efforts will have to be made by a just belligerent to limit use of ground and tactical-air firepower in combat in populated areas. The lesson is underscored by the example of the magnitude of firepower in the Yom Kippur War—which, fortunately, was fought mainly in unpopulated areas. Such efforts at self-limitation will be difficult to maintain given the understandable propensity of commanders to err on the side of too much rather than too little firepower to achieve their objectives at the minimum loss of life to their troops. But, unless extraordinary— one could say heroic—efforts are made to hold the use of conventional firepower to uses and levels consonant with the principles of proportion and discrimination, the overwhelming propensity of modern conventional war to violate those principles will produce, at best, the results deplored in Vietnam and, at worst, a level of civilian losses and destruction that will raise the danger of whole countries being destroyed in the name of their own defense in the course of conventional combat.

Conventional strategic bombing in World War II undoubtedly violated the principle of proportion. Particularly in the last months of the war, there was little military necessity for massive raids on German population centers. The raid on Dresden is rightly considered to have had little military justification, and its destructive effects were grossly disproportionate to whatever genuine military necessity existed for the raid. The specific lesson to be learned from this experience is that the proportionality element of legitimate military necessity must be judged in terms of specific military utility. The idea that any injury may be inflicted upon an enemy, particularly in a just war against an aggressor, is contrary to just-war and international law-of-war standards. The related objective of destroying the morale of the enemy population by countervalue air attacks is also demonstrated by the World War II experience and is rightly condemned by the jus in bello. There must be a specific and sufficient military necessity to justify every military operation. This is the heart of the requirement of proportion. [20]

The practice of the United States in conventional strategic bombing in the Korean and Vietnam wars appears to have been considerably improved over the Allied performance in World War II. Although there is controversy over the proportionality of some missions, there was usually enough of a serious military objective to make U.S. air attacks potentially proportionate. This is something that could not be said about a substantial number of the attacks on Germany and Japan in World War II. Nevertheless, the task of keeping conventional strategic bombing within the bounds of reasonable proportion remains a major one.

Respect for the principle of discrimination has also seemed to increase in U.S. strategic bombing since World War II. While "precision" or "pinpoint" bombing claims may still be exaggerated, extraordinary advances have been made in bombing accuracy and the capability of discrimination is much enhanced. Still, in the Vietnam War, evidence was offered of U.S. attacks on hospitals, schools, and other protected targets. Collateral damage resulted from attacks in and near population centers. As indicated in Chapter 5, much of this civilian damage resulted from the intermixture of military and nonmilitary targets, in some cases undoubtedly by design. Another explanation lay in the greatly improved antiaircraft weapons systems that make bombing more hazardous and difficult, with resultant errors in accuracy. Both of these factors may be expected to continue to contribute to losses of civilians and civilian targets in strategic conventional bombing attacks. However, the advances made in accuracy should serve as the basis for an improved standard of reasonableness with respect to discrimination in air attacks on populated areas. The upshot is that, unlike nuclear strategic war, conventional strategic air war is technically capable of respecting the principle of discrimination and should be held to that basic jus in bello requirement. [21]

Well before there was a serious conventional-bombing capability and long before nuclear war, naval blockades were employed in what amounted to countervalue warfare. The Allied surface and German submarine blockades of World War I probably violated the principle of proportion, and they certainly violated the principle of discrimination. Whole populations were the targets of what were avowedly starvation blockades. While it was not possible literally to starve large numbers of people, the malnutrition and disease directly resulting from the blockades caused many deaths and much suffering. [22]

In World War II, air power greatly enhanced sea blockades. In the Vietnam War, air power was used to interdict supply routes and destroy crops with a view to starving the populations of areas believed to be supporting the enemy. The interdiction part of these efforts belongs to this discussion of conventional-war issues of the jus in bello. However, the destruction of food sources has thus far been a phenomenon of counterinsurgency war and will, accordingly, be treated in the next chapter. The continued practice of naval and air blockades presents just-war doctrine and the positive law of war with a generally unnoticed and/or underestimated challenge. Such blockades can easily produce disproportionate death, disease, and suffering, and they are intrinsically indiscriminate.

On the other hand, blockade is a perennial instrument of conventional-war strategy and tactics. While there have been movements to ban or limit various weapons, there has never been a serious effort to outlaw blockades, strategic or tactical. As will be seen in the next chapter, the 1977 Geneva Protocols I and II have provisions limiting the use of starvation as a means of warfare, but the emphasis seems to be on destruction of food and crops, not interdiction.[23] Moreover, the important military necessities justifying the use of blockades render this means of war almost immune from regulation. It may well be that the only solution to the dilemma of blockades is partial. In some conflicts it may prove possible to ensure that basic food, medical, and other requirements of life reach noncombatants through humanitarian arrangements, while the strategic or tactical blockade continues. For such arrangements to be acceptable to belligerents, adequate precautions would be necessary to prevent diversion and misuse of such supplies.[24]

Another perennial strategy and tactic that clashes with jus in bello principles is the so-called scorched-earth defense, generally associated with measures taken in a defender's own territory but sometimes used by a belligerent occupant when retreating. Scorched-earth measures take the form of massive devastation of an area from which a belligerent is retreating. The purpose is to deny the attacker provisions, shelter, and the assistance of the population as it advances. Sometimes scorched-earth withdrawals are conducted under no particular pressure as a routine measure to cover a regrouping of defenses (for example, the German forces on the western front in 1918).[25] More often, scorched-earth measures are taken by a defender under intense pressure as a means of buying time and breathing space as in the case of the German General Rendulic's withdrawal from Finmark in 1944, Van Manstein's withdrawal from the southern front in Russia after the collapse of the Stalingrad front in 1942-43, or the German retreat in the Vosges in the fall of 1944.[26] In war-crimes trials, such practices were charged to be violations of Article 23(g) of the 1907 Hague Regulations, which forbids belligerents "to destroy or seize the enemy's property, unless such destruction or seizure be imperatively demanded by the necessities of war." A broader formulation was provided by the enumeration of war crimes by the London Charter of the Nuremberg International Military Tribunal as "wanton destruction of cities, towns or villages, or devastation not justified by military necessity."[27]

The war-crimes cases on this subject are among the best existing, authoritative precedents on the principle of proportion. What Hague Article 23(g) and the war crimes provisions of the London Charter condemn is disproportionate destruction of an area. Several interesting issues arose in these cases. The most important is the treatment of Rendulic's use of scorched earth in the Hostage case, U.S. v. List et al. There the tribunal held that the commander's estimate of the situation at the time of the acts in question could be considered an acceptable basis for his claim of military necessity, even though the estimate proved to be overpessimistic and the actions taken were not, in retrospect, justified. In other words, the referent of necessity and proportionality is not the retrospective, objective fact of historical developments but the subjective appreciation of the situation by the commander, if it was reasonable, even though events proved it mistaken.[28]

Another interesting issue raised by the scorched-earth cases was the charge of defendants, all ground-force officers, that it was unfair to treat scorched-earth measures taken under duress as illegal, when aerial bombardment resulting in comparable damage was not treated as illegal. There were no war-crimes proceedings based on disproportionate and indiscriminate aerial bombardment. The ground-force officers claimed that their military necessities in such cases were immediate, whereas the military necessity for aerial bombardment was often less clear-cut and urgent. Moreover, while scorched-earth strategies make noncombatants suffer cruelly, they are usually limited in their direct effects on civilians to mass evacuations, not involving outright killing as in the case of aerial bombardments or ground assaults on populated areas.[29]

If scorched-earth policies are employed as a desperate measure by a retreating army in order to save itself, it is conceivable that such measures might meet the requirements of proportionality, as the tribunal decided in Rendulic's case. Since scorched-earth measures do not necessarily require the killing of noncombatants, they do not automatically violate the principle of discrimination. It could be argued that scorched-earth devastation may not be fundamentally different from that destruction of populated areas that occurs during protracted combat maneuvering and fighting. Much would depend on the manner in which the population was evacuated and the efforts made to sustain them. If scorched-earth measures are not always self-evidently violative of the principles of proportion and discrimination, all presumptions are against them. These presumptions would have to be overriden by a very substantial showing of military necessity and a serious effort to protect the lives of the noncombatants involved.

Chemical warfare (CW), used as a counterforce weapon, would pass the tests of proportionality and discrimination in many situations, but its use is prohibited by positive international law. However, the possibility of chemical warfare being used in conventional war remains prominent. The formulation of the rule against CW has always been that of no-first-use, leaving the question of the fate of the restriction once it has been broken. This question must be seriously contemplated. The Soviets, notwithstanding the international-law prohibitions against CW and their own condemnations of the United States for its CW policies, have consistently predicted that CW would be used in a general war. The Soviet Union, moreover, is by all odds the most prepared of the military powers of the world in terms of doctrine, equipment, and training in the realm of chemical warfare. [30]

If the rule prohibiting use of chemical means were thought to be declaratory of a fundamental, normative judgment that such means are mala in se, the problem of responding to first use of CW would be very difficult indeed. However, since CW is not malum in se and since it is capable of proportionate and discriminate use, there is no reason why its first use, in violation of the positive law of war, should not engender at least a right of reprisal on the part of the victim of such use. Retaliation in kind might deter continuation of the enemy's use of CW, and it would at least redress the unfair advantage he had gained by using it. Use of CW in reprisal must, of course, conform to the conditions mentioned in Chapter 3. [31]

The more difficult question, one of political/military policy as well as morality and law, is whether to consider that the first use of CW by the enemy has released all parties to the conflict from further limitation by the legal prohibition against its use. This is a complex issue. There have always been respectable arguments in favor of using CW, the most modest of which asserts that it is no worse and may sometimes be better than presently accepted means of war. On balance, however, most military experts have considered CW an unreliable and nondecisive means that was as well dispensed with. The banning of CW is as much a function of that judgment of limited utility as it is of condemnation of CW on normative grounds. The rationale for the ban is further buttressed by the threshold concept: CW represents a category of means that have been banned; it is better to hold the threshold than to experiment with exceptions. In brief, tolerable, even more humane, CW could easily become evil CW; therefore, it is best to have no CW.

If these rationales were to hold up under the challenge of the breach of the ban on CW by one side, the proper response would be carefully limited reprisals designed to bring the violations to a halt rather than a decision to cross the CW threshold and abandon the legal ban altogether.

This discussion has been predicated on the assumption that the CW use in question would be strictly counterforce in character. However, it is clear that in heavily populated areas the collateral effects of CW could be devastating, even if there were substantial civil defense measures. The victim of first-use CW would probably be concerned with the effects of chemical warfare on noncombatants on both sides of the front. This would further support the presumption against opening up a general CW war. If, of course, the enemy persists in using CW, there may not be any alternative.

It appears that biological warfare (BW), which is malum prohibitum under positive international law, is not considered a practical and decisive instrument of war. It appears likely that the jus in bello prohibition against BW will be respected. [32]

Finally, among the critical issues of conventional warfare is that of the protection of prisoners of war (PWs). Many of the jus in bello issues concerned with this subject arise both in conventional and revolutionary/counterinsurgency war. This is well demonstrated by the Korean and Vietnam wars which differed in military characteristics (the first was conventional for the most part, the second a mixture of conventional and subconventional) but raised common issues as well as problems particular to the respective conflicts. In conventional war some of the most critical issues concerning PWs are the proper notification of captivity and accounting for PWs; proper treatment (immunity from mistreatment and torture); inspection by the (ICRC) and/or the protecting power; and control and disciplining of PWs not truly hors de combat. Article 70 of the 1949 Geneva PW Convention prescribes that

> immediately upon capture, or not more than one week
> after arrival at a camp, even if it is a transit camp,
> likewise in case of sickness or transfer to hospital or
> to another camp, every prisoner of war shall be enabled
> to write direct to his family, on the one hand, and to the
> Central Prisoner of War agency provided for in Article
> 123, on the other hand, a card similar, if possible, to
> the model annexed to the present Convention, informing
> his relatives of his capture, address and state of health.
> The said cards shall be forwarded as rapidly as possible
> and may not be delayed in any manner.

If this requirement is complied with, the PW's government and his family should know that he is a prisoner of war and entitled to the benefits of that status, including the right of correspondence. If compliance with this requirement is effective, there should be no question of not knowing the number and identity of the PWs held by the enemy with reasonable accuracy.[33] While compliance may be difficult for revolutionary forces, as will be discussed in the next chapter, there is no excuse for the failure of conventional belligerents to permit notification of captivity of their PWs and for their failure to account for them. However, this was a problem in the Korean War where the Communist belligerents refused to accept the regulations of the 1949 Geneva PW Convention.[34] There were also difficulties in implementing this requirement in the Vietnam War because of the unsatisfactory performance of North Vietnam, especially with regard to United States Air Force personnel.[35] This basic and reasonable requirement of lawful belligerents was also the subject of bitter controversy at the end of the 1973 Yom Kippur War when Syria refused to turn over lists of the Israeli PWs it held, having denied them the rights of Article 70 of the Geneva PW Convention. Turning over the lists of Israeli PWs held by Syria became a bargaining chip in negotiations, a practice that is utterly contrary to the requirements of positive international law.[36]

All of the other issue areas discussed in this chapter have dealt with means and practices that are sometimes employed or may be employed by most belligerents, including the United States. The area of concern here, however, is one in which the matter is one-sided. The United States and its allies in modern conflicts have good records of compliance with the jus in bello requirements for permitting PWs to notify family and home country of their captivity as well as for accounting for the PWs in their hands. The underlying problem is that some belligerents, including prominent former and potential enemies of the United States and its allies, consider both their own and the enemy's PWs as pawns in a chess game. Other law-abiding belligerents are intensely solicitous of the welfare of each and every one of its own military personnel who becomes a PW and treat enemy PWs as they would like their own to be treated.

This well-known fact encourages some belligerents to bargain over the most fundamental rights of PWs, rights they are entitled to without concessions from their government under international law and the dictates of humanity. Thus, the accounting for and protection of PWs becomes a war aim of the just belligerent who may be forced to continue the conflict, inter alia, to secure that aim. Unfortunately, the record of prospective enemies of the United States and its allies suggests the strong likelihood that this fundamental breach of the prisoner-of-war regime will be encountered again.

The experience of the Korean War, as well as that with North Vietnamese behavior in the Vietnam War, proved that substandard treatment, mistreatment, and torture of PWs is a problem of conventional war wherein the belligerents have the capability of affording proper treatment. The somewhat different problems of assuring proper treatment in revolutionary war and counterinsurgency will be dealt with in the next chapter. To be sure, even in conventional war there may be practical difficulties in providing the treatment required by the PW regime. But in the Korean and Vietnam conflicts, there was overwhelming evidence that the substandard treatment, mistreatment, and torture of UN and U.S. PWs, respectively, was deliberately calculated to weaken them to prepare the way for coercive "reeducation" and, in some cases, attempted brainwashing. The purposes of such programs ranged from conversion to the captor's ideology, to incitement to disloyal and subversive attitudes, to the short-term intimidation requisite to elicit propaganda statements. Such programs violated all of the provisions of the Hague and Geneva conventions requiring good treatment and prohibiting torture, mistreatment, and forced participation in the war effort against the PW's own side. Nevertheless, reeducation programs have been a constant feature of communist belligerents' treatment of PWs in World War II, the Korean War, and the Vietnam War. [37]

The most obvious remedy for law-abiding belligerents would be reprisals in the form of some kind of retaliation in kind against the PWs of the lawbreaking belligerent. This is explicitly prohibited by the 1949 Geneva PW Convention, as brought out in Chapter 3, and is violative of the basic principle of humanity. [38] Moreover, as also remarked in Chapter 3, the effectiveness of reprisals as a remedy is questionable at best. If recourse to a previously unused weapon or means was thought to have the potential of altering an enemy's disposition to violate the PW regime, such a course might be necessary. However, this would have to be worked out in terms of the probable effects of the escalation, however justified, in the total calculus of a just and limited war. The rock-bottom problem underlying these dilemmas is that belligerents who notoriously violate the rights of others' PWs appear to be perfectly prepared to sacrifice their own PWs to reprisals in the unlikely event that their more scrupulous enemies would follow such a course.

There is little possibility of ascertaining the quality of treatment of PWs without close and thorough inspection by the ICRC and/ or protecting powers. Communist belligerents have consistently denied the neutral quality of the ICRC and have barred third-party inspections. Even if this is explained by nonadherence to and/or reservations about the principal relevant international conventions, such attitudes are in blatant violation of customary international law and the principle of humanity. There is no apparent remedy for law-abiding powers. Moreover, the law-abiding powers must not alter their commitment to cooperation with the ICRC and other third parties, even when the investigations of such bodies may be the cause of embarrassment. [39]

Finally, there is the problem of belligerents who fight the war with their PWs. The cornerstone of the PW regime is the concept that the prisoner is hors de combat (removed from the conflict). He is protected because he has surrendered and is no longer fighting. In the Korean War, many thousands of Communist PWs continued the conflict in the PW compounds. They were under the direct control and discipline of the Communist armed forces, staged riots and demonstrations on order, murdured and intimidated fellow PWs who desired to remain hors de combat, and generally served as a substantial instrument of the Communist powers in their fight-and-negotiate strategy. [40]

The task of controlling and disciplining such PWs while maintaining the rights of those who are not continuing the conflict is monumental, as the Korean experience demonstrated. At the very least, severe restrictive measures against recalcitrant PWs who are not living up to their part of the PW regime are in order. [41]

The discussion of critical issues relative to PWs will resume in Chapter 8 when particular problems occurring in revolutionary and counterinsurgency war will be examined.

In concluding this survey of critical issues of just war as they appear in nuclear deterrence, nuclear war, and conventional war, it must be observed that, although some of the issues are obviously of more importance (for example, recourse to nuclear war), all of them, including issues like the proper treatment of prisoners of war, are sufficiently important that failure to comply with the requirements of the jus ad bellum and jus in bello as they become concretized in these forms of war can jeopardize the claims of a belligerent with a basically just cause to be fighting a just war.

7

CRITICAL ISSUES OF JUST WAR: THE JUS AD BELLUM OF REVOLUTIONARY/ COUNTERINSURGENCY WAR

Much of contemporary armed conflict has taken the form of revolutionary war. Until recently many of these conflicts were wars of national liberation against colonial powers. Today, these wars are usually civil wars or mixed civil-international conflicts in which foreign powers and transnational parties intervene overtly or covertly. Revolutionary wars are generally fought over issues of domestic political, economic, and social justice, often complemented by nationalistic reactions to colonialism or so-called neocolonialism. The causes and forms of such conflicts are heterogeneous and do not fit neatly into Marxist-Leninist-Maoist or other revolutionary theories. However, in our time such wars have been heavily influenced by Marxist-Leninist-Maoist doctrine on how to make a revolution. Even when adherence to the teachings of such doctrines is loose and erratic, the rhetoric and style of modern revolutionary war tends to reflect them. To varying degrees, the strategies and tactics of revolutionary wars follow the Marxist-Leninist-Maoist doctrines. Finally, it is often the case that contemporary revolutionaries are aided and advised by communist states and transnational organizations to such a degree that their behavior and attitudes reflect the approach of their sponsors.[1]

Accordingly, the term revolutionary war is used there rather than guerrilla war or subconventional war. As Laqueur has shown, guerrilla war is an old form that can be used by political actors of all persuasions and that varies greatly according to the historical and geographical context.[2] Revolutionary war today may be limited to guerrilla warfare, but it also ranges from terroristic campaigns that would not constitute guerrilla war to full-fledged conventional warfare. As important, the far-reaching political and ideological aims of revolutionary war lend it a character that tends to clash with the limitations of the just war as well as of positive international law. In this discussion I will use the term revolutionary war to mean a revolutionary struggle to change or maintain a national political-economic-social system where the revolutionaries and their allies use unconventional means of warfare, principally guerrilla warfare. [3]

Counterinsurgency is a term with an unhappy history. It was widely used in the 1960s to describe the comprehensive counterrevolutionary strategies necessary for an incumbent regime and its allies to defeat modern revolutionary war. Although it never had a doctrinal basis comparable to the Marxist-Leninist-Maoist revolutionary war doctrines, the term counterinsurgency vaguely implied that there were proved ways of defeating revolutionary war. The fate of U.S. counterinsurgency efforts in Vietnam, blurred though they were by the escalation of the war to a largely conventional level, has discredited the term, as have the failures of French, Portuguese, and other colonial powers. Counterinsurgency remains, however, the best available term to describe counterrevolutionary warfare. [4]

Both revolutionary and counterinsurgency warfare rely heavily on the military instrument to gain their objectives. However, this kind of warfare is extremely political. In the 1960s it was commonly said that both sides in such conflicts sought above all to "win the hearts and minds of the people." This aspiration is now viewed with bitterness and cynicism, but the concept remains important. Although political power may, as Mao held, come first from the barrel of a gun, there is an unusually important role for the political, psychological, and economic instruments of policy on both sides in a revolutionary war. Whichever dominates, the military and nonmilitary elements must be complementary. [5]

The combination of military and nonmilitary means of coercion and persuasion in revolutionary war results in difficulties as well as opportunities when it comes to implementing just-war principles and the more detailed prescriptions of the positive law of international conflict. If the positive strategies of persuasion and reform can be emphasized, observance of the laws of war can be held out to a belligerent as a logical and beneficial dimension of its positive strategies. If, however, the belligerent feels constrained to emphasize military coercion it will often find itself at odds with just-war conditions and the positive law. It should be emphasized that this discussion addresses only the issue of the observance of just-war principles and the international law of armed conflict. Belligerents on both sides may, in following their positive policies of persuasion and reform, violate domestic law, including constitutional law and civil rights. Such violations, as well as those arising from military operations, may be considered as breaches of the emerging international law of human rights. That, however, is not of concern to this analysis unless the violations constitute a breach of the just-war conditions and the international law of armed conflict. [6]

Discussions of the typical revolutionary belligerent and its strategies and tactics continue to be based on Marxist-Leninist-Maoist theory and practice that has evolved into what could be better described as the Maoist-Ho Chi Minh approach. In this approach the revolutionaries are organized along classical Leninist lines in a clandestine political organization. It is firmly controlled by an executive central committee and characterized by extraordinary discipline. All policies are dictated by ideological imperatives applied by the leadership to the practical situations of the revolution. The high degree of centralization of decision making and control throughout the revolutionary organization makes possible a nuanced blending of the coercive military as well as persuasive or reformist nonmilitary elements of the total war effort. [7]

Usually the revolutionary belligerent will start with rather primitive bases in remote and inaccessible areas and/or in sanctuaries in adjacent foreign countries. Unlike the belligerents of conventional civil wars (such as the American Civil War), the revolutionary belligerent normally does not control large areas of territory including large populated areas and their resources and facilities. This fact greatly influences the character of the war the revolutionaries wage and, consequently, their ability and willingness to observe the law of war. [8]

From its remote bases and foreign sanctuaries, the revolutionaries launch their war. From both doctrinal attachment and necessity, they generally follow some variant of the basic Maoist-Ho Chi Minh three-phase strategy:

Phase 1: Recruitment and organization of the revolutionary party and armed forces; propaganda, subversion, political education of the masses; whatever political activity is feasible; selective terrorism (for example, assassinations, bombings, hijackings, and kidnappings);

Phase 2: Widespread guerrilla warfare (for example, hit-and-run attacks on government police and military formations and installations, attacks on governmental operations of all kinds); escalation of terror, emphasizing assassination, intimidation, and discrediting of key incumbent elites; deliberately provocative attacks designed to induce the counterinsurgents to engage in countermeasures producing a reprisal spiral effect that will injure and alienate innocent people;

Phase 3: Conventional mobile warfare accompanied by pressures for creation of a "national unity" popular front to create a coalition government the revolutionaries will first cooperate with and ultimately displace. [9]

To the extent that the counterinsurgent's weakness and their own military power permit, the revolutionaries will seek, area by area, to oust the regime's governmental apparatus from effective control and replace it with the revolutionary apparatus. This effort involves strategies designed to destroy the regime, often employing means that violate all standards of the law of war and of human rights. But it also is characterized by positive measures of reform and good government in the areas taken over, generally consonant with the standards of civilized nations. Some of the typical violations of the law of war resulting from this effort to tear down and replace an incumbent regime will be discussed presently.

The typical counterinsurgent belligerent is an incumbent government in a new and developing nation. It will often have connections with an earlier colonial power. Indeed, a good bit of the theory and practice of revolutionary/counterinsurgency war concerns the efforts of colonial powers to hold on to their dependencies. The typical counterinsurgent regime is faced with all of the notorious problems of developing nations. Its political, economic, and social systems are weak and struggling. It badly needs time to put its house in order, and it requires a great deal of external assistance. The challenge of revolutionary war catches such a regime at a grave disadvantage. Struggling just to mount the necessary societal base for development, it sees the society torn apart by civil strife and the destruction of war. The reactions of such a regime to revolutionary war are often marked by exasperation and foolish efforts to solve all problems by repression, a reaction that tends to play into the hands of the revolutionaries.

Like the revolutionaries, the counterinsurgents' approach to the conflict is twofold. There are nation-building or development programs to improve the condition of the polity and win the hearts and minds of the people. [10] At the same time, there are paramilitary and military "pacification" campaigns to restore law and order and security. Many of the law enforcement and counterinsurgency methods used in these campaigns raise questions of due process and individual rights, but they do not fall within the purview of the law of war. Thus, onerous curfews, restrictions on travel, searches, and other activities may violate civil liberties but not the requirements of the law of war. However, it is clear that any serious contemporary revolutionary war is likely to produce recourse to means prohibited or limited by the jus in bello. The main categories of such limits concern the use of disproportionate and/or indiscriminate firepower against targets with a heavily civilian character and measures of population control that challenge the standards set for belligerent occupation by the laws of war. Admittedly, these standards have not been accepted in conventional law as binding on belligerents in civil wars, but in my view they should be the basis for evaluation of the treatment of civilians in such conflicts.

It should be emphasized that revolutionary/counterinsurgency war treated as a noninternational conflict is only covered by a modest and precarious body of positive international law. It is possible to stretch that law a bit, and this should be done when possible, even within positive legal analyses. However, this book is concerned with the just-war limitations on the conduct of war. It assumes just-war limits irrespective of positive-law gaps or ambiguities. Where there are questions as to the technical applicability of positive, international, legal prescriptions they will be acknowledged. However, writing from a just-war perspective, it is possible to apply existing positive, international-law prescriptions to the conduct of revolutionary/counterinsurgency conflict on the basis that they ought to be obeyed as a matter of natural law if not of positive law.

REVOLUTIONARY WAR, COUNTERINSURGENCY, AND THE JUS AD BELLUM

Competent Authority

In revolutionary wars the jus ad bellum requirement of competent authority produces great controversy. The point of the conflict is a challenge to the incumbent regime. Yet it would seem that, at least in the initial period of a revolutionary war, the authority of the regime to take measures for the enforcement of law and order is self-evident. It may be, as Walzer argues, that at some point in the conflict there is such a drastic transfer of political and military support from the regime to the rebels as to warrant a conclusion that the regime no longer has authority to govern and to wage the war. [11] I would argue that the regime has competent authority until it is defeated altogether and the war ended. Suffice it to say that the incumbent regime has competent authority to wage counterinsurgency war at the outset of a civil war. That authority may be eroded and finally overthrown in the course of the war. It is also possible that the incumbent regime may somehow have acted unconstitutionally so that it has lost its mandate to govern. This would have to be determined by the constitutional law of the state.

It is common for interested states to intervene in civil wars, and the issue arises of their competence to be parties to the conflict. A good deal of legal argumentation has condemned such intervention in general, if not sweeping, terms. Such intervention is declared to be contrary to the general principle of nonintervention in the internal affairs of another sovereign state and contrary to the UN Charter prohibitions against the use of armed coercion. [12]

The difficulty that usually arises is that there are multiple interventions invited by both sides in the civil war. Each side alleges that the other has received illegal interventionary support from a foreign power. Accordingly, each side justifies its invitation to its foreign allies to enter what is supposed to be a civil war but has become a mixed civil-international conflict. In any event, it is clear from the most casual investigation of modern international practice that the more publicists and international bodies condemn intervention in civil strife as a violation of international law, the more such intervention abounds. Two issues of competent authority are raised by such interventions. First, there must be competent authority in the incumbent regime to invite and accept the foreign intervention. This leads one back to the issue of the duration of the regime's authority. My position, contrary to what seems to be the prevailing view recently, is that a regime may invite intervention at any time in the course of a civil war. I acknowledge that my view is contrary to the current authoritative legal opinion, but it coincides with international practice.

The second issue of competent authority for intervening powers is that of the constitutionality of the recourse to armed force if that is involved in the intervention by the foreign state. This differs from the same issue in nuclear and conventional war mainly in the degree to which intervention in revolutionary war is often gradual and ambiguous, as in the U.S. intervention in the Vietnam conflict. Often intervention on the counterinsurgent side grows incrementally from aid and technical assistance to extensive military advisory programs that often produce direct involvement in hostilities and full-fledged cobelligerency. However, notwithstanding its more complex and unclear character, military intervention to the extent of de facto cobelligerency must face the same constitutional and political hurdles as are required to certify competent authority in conventional war.

I do not presently foresee the likelihood of U.S. intervention on the side of revolutionaries, although such an eventuality is conceivable. If such intervention were desired, there would be considerable difficulties in justifying the action under international law. The international legal jus ad bellum does not turn on the justice or representative character of existing regimes. All regimes, no matter how unjust or unrepresentative, benefit from the UN Charter rule of Article 2(4) prohibiting the threat or use of force against the territorial integrity or political independence of another sovereign state. An armed intervention on behalf of rebels would violate Article 2(4).[13] Article 51 permits collective self-defense, thereby permitting intervention on behalf of an established regime when its civil war is linked with direct or indirect foreign intervention amounting to aggression. But in the case of a revolutionary force there is, at least at the outset of the war, no juridical "self" to profit from collective self-defense and, therefore, no mandate for intervention to defend the rebels.

To be sure, it has been argued that the right of self-defense resides in the people or nation. But, except in colonial wars, it is rarely possible to equate the people or nation with revolutionary movements and forces, notwithstanding their claims to be the sole representatives of the people or nation. No matter what the degree of plausibility to claims of competent authority by revolutionaries based on their alleged representative character, the rebels must acquire a degree of legal international personality before they can be treated as a belligerent.

The form that this issue takes in international law is that of belligerent status. Traditionally, the rights and duties of the laws of war were limited to states at war and to revolutionary organizations whose belligerency had been recognized by their civil adversary, the incumbent government, and by third parties. The system of recognition of belligerency did not work very well. The basic interest of a government combating revolutionaries is usually best served by denying them belligerency and treating them as criminals and disturbers of the peace. Accordance of belligerent status by third parties was largely a matter of convenience and selfish political advantage, not necessarily based on the actual political and military capabilities displayed by the revolutionaries. [14]

Even after the experience of resistance and independence movements in World War II, the 1949 Geneva Conventions were oriented toward interstate war. The only explicit allocation of rights and duties to participants in a civil war was in common Article 3 of the conventions, which applied to cases of "armed conflict not of an international character occurring in the territory of one of the High Contracting Parties." [15] This led to a state of affairs where it could be considered that the regular international law of war did not bind the parties to a civil war. This view, which still seems to prevail, is excessively narrow and convention-oriented. Notwithstanding the limits of conventional international law, the basic principles of the jus in bello should govern wherever the material conditions of war exist. This is a view that can be defended within positive international law and is clearly enjoined by just-war doctrine. Nevertheless, reluctance to acknowledge the applicability of the laws of war to civil war has left a normative gap in a most critical area of modern conflict.

Some efforts have been made to deal with this problem. It was considered so important by the 1974-77 Geneva Conference on the Reaffirmation and Development of International Humanitarian Law Applicable in Armed Conflicts that a separate convention, Protocol II, was devoted to the subject, namely, "the protection of victims of noninternational armed conflicts." Article I states that the protocol develops and supplements common Article 3 of the 1949 Geneva Conventions. Article 1 provides that the protocol shall apply

to all armed conflicts which are not covered by Article 1
of . . . Protocol I and which take place in the territory
of a High Contracting Party between its armed forces and
dissident armed forces or other organized armed groups
which, under responsible command, exercise such control
over a part of its territory as to enable them to carry out
sustained and concerted military operations and to implement this Protocol. [16]

The beneficiaries, then, of this conventional extension of the
law of war to civil war are "dissident armed forces or other organized
armed groups which" are under "responsible command." It is specified that they are expected to "exercise such control over a part of
[the disputed] territory as to enable them to carry out sustained and
concerted military operations and to implement this Protocol." It is
difficult, if not impossible, to devise a definition of revolutionary belligerents subject to the rights and duties of the laws of war that will
satisfactorily cover all the cases that arise. However, this is not a
bad beginning. It emphasizes that revolutionary belligerents should
display a public purpose and character; to be treated as belligerents,
revolutionaries must achieve a significant degree of political-military
success; and revolutionary belligerents must abide by their duties under the law of war.
    These qualities distinguish a revolutionary force worthy of rec-
ognition as a lawful belligerent from miscellaneous individuals and
groups that engage in violence, often claiming political, ideological,
social, racial, or other goals. When such individuals and groups
lack the clear public purpose, organization, control, willingness,
and ability to obey the laws of war as well as the actual power of revolutionary belligerents, they are not deserving of recognition as belligerents under the law of war. In an age where common criminals
are termed political prisoners by their sympathizers who want to
"liberate" them and where terrorism has become a major concern
throughout the world, it is important to be clear about these belligerent qualities. Accordingly, one may welcome Article 1(2) of Protocol II, which specifies that

this Protocol shall not apply to situations of internal disturbances and tensions, such as riots, isolated and spor-
adic acts of violence and other acts of similar nature, as
not being armed conflicts.

It is believed that this emerging positive international law blends
well into the just-war category of competent authority. Revolutionary-
war-competent authority is not a function of the alleged justice of the

revolutionary cause held out by revolutionary leaders. It is a product of organization, the exercise of control by responsible commanders, political and military success, and a credible willingness to accept the duties as well as the rights of belligerency under the law of war.

The line of analysis adopted here on the basis of the treatment of belligerent status in noninternational conflicts in 1977 Geneva Protocol II is, admittedly, blurred by the unfortunate Article 1(4) of 1977 Geneva Protocol I that purports to give privileged belligerent status to national liberation movements engaged in wars of national liberation against "colonial" and "racist" regimes and "alien" occupying powers. This provision, specifically aimed at South Africa and Israel, qualifies such national liberation movements as per se belligerents under the protocol designed for international conflicts without any requirement that they meet the substantial conditions for belligerency required for noninternational conflicts in Protocol II. It is clear that this provision is an aberration from the development of the positive law on the subject of belligerency reflected in 1977 Geneva Protocol II, Article 1. I treat it as an aberration and hold to the line of analysis adopted in this chapter and supported by the terms of Protocol II's Article 1.[17]

Just Cause

In the Scholastic, natural-law tradition from which most of just-war doctrine is derived, there are basically two causes for armed resistance against an incumbent regime: self-defense and reaffirmation of the sovereignty of the people.[18] If a regime is so oppressive that it threatens the fundamental rights of the members of the community and the common good it may be resisted by force. Or, if the government acts in ways contrary to the conditions established for the legitimate exercise of power, the people, as the original repository of political authority, have a right to reclaim that authority and vest it in a new government.

These just causes are integrally related to the issue of competent authority just discussed. That authority must be derived from the people whose rights are defended and whose sovereign prerogatives are reasserted. But it is easy to claim to speak for the people and their rights and difficult to determine whose voice should be heeded as the true revolutionary competent authority. As we have seen, the solution of the 1977 Geneva Protocol II is to accord revolutionary warfare the status of belligerency when those who conduct it are able to do so in a "sustained and concerted fashion." When they have done so, they may represent one or both of the two basic just causes for revolutionary war in the eyes of international law. Whether they in fact represent the people is another matter.

However, it will be recalled that, in addition to an essentially just cause, the just belligerent must meet the requirement of proportionality between the probable good and evil of the war. The Scholastic, natural-law literature is grudging in its acceptance of the right of armed resistance and uncomfortable with the word revolution. There is a decided inclination to place a presumption against the probable good resulting from a violent armed revolution outweighing the probable evil.[19] Still, it is conceded that, in extreme cases, revolutionary war may be justified. Such an attitude is, of course, in great contrast to modern revolutionary theories that assume the a priori "scientific" requirement of revolutionary change to produce an entirely new social system. Since such revolutionary theories and the ideological and political goals they produce are essentially utopian and open-ended, it becomes virtually impossible to assess the jus ad bellum proportionality of revolutionary action taken in their name. Indeed, viewed from most contemporary revolutionary perspectives, there is no such thing as a requirement of proportion either in the jus ad bellum or jus in bello.[20]

Modern revolutionary wars seem to place a particularly heavy emphasis on the principle that the ends justify the means. This is the essential characteristic of revolutionary just-war doctrine. The most destructive and cruel wars of attrition are fought as protracted conflicts until the revolution succeeds. No cost is considered too high for revolutionary success. Accordingly, there is no question of proportionality of means to ends; all means deemed necessary for the ends are acceptable and, indeed, mandatory.

Thus, most practitioners of revolutionary war today would reject, if they would even momentarily consider, traditional just-war restraints and adhere to their own teleological just war. This tends to be true even when the revolutionaries and their sympathizers are Christians. Moreover, it must be confessed that the modern church has been almost totally reluctant to proffer guidance on the just initiation and conduct of revolutionary war.[21] Yet, revolutionary war remains war, with material characteristics essentially identical to international conflict. All war is subject to the conditions of just-war doctrine as well as the increasingly developed principles and prescriptions of the positive law of war. Particularly in view of the importance of revolutionary/counterinsurgency war in the contemporary international system, it is important to persist in the attempt to find reasonable just-war guidelines for this kind of conflict.

If just-war doctrine is applied to revolutionary/counterinsurgency wars, instead of avoiding the issue of limitations on the conduct of such conflicts, the revolutionaries may be more disposed to consider just-war guidelines. Thus, there may be a possibility of raising the issue of the proportion of probable good to probable evil with revolutionaries who have been left to entrench the end-justifies-the-means approach, in part because of the reluctance of the church and of moralists to grapple with the issue of proportion in revolutionary war. Finally, counterinsurgents have a right to an accounting regarding their adversaries' ends and means. Those who oppose revolutionaries should have some basis for analyzing and countering their claims. This basis remains the jus ad bellum requirement of just cause and its central injunction that the probable evil to result from a war—any war—be proportionate to the probable good.

It would be a major success for traditional just-war doctrine if revolutionaries could be induced to relinquish their unlimited claims to use whatever means appear to be necessary for the attainment of the revolutionary ends. However, a serious problem would still remain. Revolutionaries often have as their end referent an open-ended utopia. Even if they conceded in principle that the utopia did not justify all and any means, it would still serve as the justification for means that would be very hard to define and limit. The counter-insurgents, on the other hand, are at an inherent disadvantage. The best that they can usually offer as the just cause is the continuation of the status quo, perhaps substantially reformed. Even a reformed status quo, in the typical revolutionary situation, will usually look unattractive and unworthy of the costs of war compared with the vague but idyllic utopia promised by the revolutionaries.

It would seem that the counterinsurgents could remedy this state of affairs and honestly improve the calculus of probable good and evil by increasing their reforms, thus making the society more attractive without revolutionary change, and by submitting their means to the limitations of just-war doctrine. Moreover, there is a further element that the counterinsurgents have both a right and duty to address. This is the projection of the probable outcome of the war in the event that the revolutionaries are victorious. We have adequate experience with the successes of contemporary revolutionaries to be able to predict the probable characteristics of the societies they will establish. Obviously these societies bear little resemblance to the utopias for which the revolutionary wars were fought. It may be expecting too much to demand that revolutionaries face reality and measure the proportionality of a civil war in terms of establishing a modern socialist or progressive society rather than in terms of a utopia. But it is not unwarranted to expect that counterinsurgents evaluate the costs of a revolutionary war in terms of its proportion to preventing the appearance of more Cubas, Algerias, Democratic Republics of Vietnam, and Cambodias where such are the prospects. On the other hand, a fair evaluation might project a more attractive new society after the revolution. But, if the just-war condition of proportion of probable good to evil is to be applied, the revolutionaries must not be permitted to justify otherwise disproportionate means on the argument that the utopia to be established will make everything worthwhile.

The prevailing pattern of revolutionary attitudes and conflicts also raises problems of asymmetry with regard to the just-war requirement that there be a solid probability of success. To the extent that the revolutionaries can legitimately claim self-defense, they profit from exemption from the requirement of probable success that goes with that claim. Moreover, following their "scientific" analysis of the situation, they can claim with confidence that they must succeed because they are in consonance with the tide of history. In case history needs a little prodding, they will also proclaim a willingness to persist in the protracted conflict for as long as is necessary to topple the incumbent regime. Such an essentially negative goal can be pursued, if necessary, with very modest means, indefinitely. So the revolutionaries will be able in good conscience to claim not the probability but the certainty of success.

On the other hand, the counterinusrgent belligerent may have difficulties in holding out an honest prospect for success. If Marxist claims to evaluate an "objective revolutionary situation" are exaggerated, there is still such a thing as a polity ripe for revolution. If this is the case, it may be assumed that the incumbent government is not dealing very effectively with the normal problems of the country. If, on top of normal difficulties, the incumbent government has to fight a bitter civil war of indeterminate duration, it will not usually be possible to give assurances of a solid probability of success.

Furthermore, in contemporary revolutionary wars it is standard practice for socialist states to intervene in varying important ways on the side of the rebels. Such intervention has often proved to be more effective and prolonged than intervention on the counterinsurgent's side. As a result, the probability of counterinsurgent success declines. One could virtually lay down a general presumption that where communist states can intervene in a revolutionary war (and today that is almost anywhere), they will. Accordingly, the counterinsurgent's calculus of probability of success will, in most cases, have to include the high probability of intervention on the side of the revolutionaries. Thus, uncertainty as to the prospective outcome of a revolutionary war is exacerbated by the virtual certainty of foreign intervention in the conflict. Sometimes a revolutionary war is decided as much by the effectiveness and staying power of the foreign allies of the parties as by their own success and persistence. All in all, the just-war requirement of probability of success is difficult to apply to a revolutionary war, particularly for the counterinsurgent.

We may assume that the just-war requirement of exhaustion of peaceful remedies has little relevance to a revolutionary war. However, conspicuous refusal to permit the people to settle issues peacefully by expressing their preferences may be evidence of the illegitimacy of either party's claim to represent the people. Given the manifest difficulties of ascertaining the will of the people in much of the world, this is an aspect of just war that should be approached with caution and skepticism.

Additionally, the requirement of exhaustion of peaceful remedies would require reasonable responses to bids for a negotiated settlement from either side and/or third parties. This too, however, is a subject that must be dealt with cautiously and realistically, since initiatives for negotiations and peaceful settlement may be spurious and injurious to the security of a party entering them in good faith with an adversary seeking unfair political and military advantages.

Right Intention

Right intention has historically been difficult to achieve in revolutionary/counterinsurgency wars. The first component of the concept requires that a belligerent limit itself to pursuit of the avowed just cause. However, in revolutionary/counterinsurgency war, each party seeks the same thing—complete control of the country's political-economic-social system. There is usually a total commitment on each side to control the same things. Limitation to pursuit of this total commitment is no limitation. Accordingly, the best remedy for excessive zeal in pursuing the rival just causes in civil strife is emphasis on the second component of the requirement of right intention. This is the goal of reconciliation leading to a just and lasting peace. Conscientious adherence to this goal will mitigate the pursuit of total control of the society. If each side sees its enemies as people it wants to live with in peace and cooperation rather than as conqueror ruling defeated enemies, right intention may be realized.

Emphasis on reconciliation will also reinforce the third component of right intention—freedom from hatred and the desire for vengeance, the historic legacy of revolutionary/counterinsurgency wars. Charity toward the enemy in civil war will mitigate the destruction and cruelty of the war and enhance the prospects for domestic peace and cooperation once the war is over. Unfortunately, the character of modern revolutionary/counterinsurgency war is often quite the opposite of a conflict in which right intention would prevail.

All of these difficulties may in part explain the reticence of just-war moralists and of the official church teachings to grapple with the problems of revolutionary/counterinsurgency war. But this kind of war, as war, must necessarily be subject to the same normative conditions as international war. Whether viewed from the perspectives of revolutionaries and counterinsurgents or of intervening allies on either side, a serious effort has to be made to evaluate revolutionary/counterinsurgency war by the traditional jus ad bellum categories.

FOREIGN INTERVENTION IN CIVIL WARS
AND THE JUS AD BELLUM

Discussion of foreign intervention on both sides of a civil war has been unavoidable in the foregoing analysis of the jus ad bellum and revolutionary/counterinsurgency war. It has been contended that the relationship of foreign interveners to contemporary civil-war adversaries is usually so integral and significant that it is impossible to discuss the jus ad bellum conditions without including the probable effects of foreign intervention in the calculus of proportion of ends and means, especially as concerns the probability of success. The subject of intervention in civil wars is sufficiently important to warrant a separate treatment of the jus ad bellum for foreign states undertaking such interventions.

The subject is notoriously difficult because of the great problems involved in defining intervention and determining what normative guidelines should be applied to the subject. It will be necessary first to propose a working definition of intervention and then attempt to clarify the confused state of normative doctrine intended to regulate it. Only then will it be possible to apply the just-war jus ad bellum conditions to the case of the foreign intervener in a civil revolutionary/counterinsurgency war.

It is by now well-recognized that the term intervention is used by statesmen, the media, and the public with such imprecision as to render it next to meaningless in the description and characterization of international interaction. As Rosenau has pointed out, the term should not be synonymous with influence, nor should it be used to describe any action directed toward another nation; yet diplomatic, media, and popular usage all tend in these directions. [22] The commonsense meaning of intervention carries the implication of something extraordinary and presumptively self-serving, yet the trend of usage is to apply intervention to such a spectrum of relationships and behavior as to embrace large areas of perfectly normal efforts at influencing the policies of other states, many of them friendly and/or directed toward altruistic purposes. Thus, the tendency of official and popular usage is to paint intervention as abnormal and presumptively wrong, whereas that usage extends to behavior that is not abnormal but common and often arguably beneficial.

A working definition is needed that will narrow the meaning of the term to behavior that is significantly different from the general patterns of international interaction. For the purposes of this discussion, I define intervention as the extraordinary interference of one sovereign state in the internal or external affairs of another. As two important guidelines in applying this definition, I take Rosenau's formulation of intervention as behavior toward another state that is

"convention-breaking" and addressed to its authority structure.[23]
That is to say, for purposes of the analyses in this book, intervention
involves behavior toward another that is unconventional in terms of
established relationships and practice (that is, "conventions"), and
that is intended to support, alter, or overthrow its authority structure. Whatever the inadequacies of my simple definition as amended
with Rosenau's two specifications, it is sufficient for a discussion of
intervention in civil wars.

In positive international law intervention is considered prima
facie illegal. The principle of nonintervention is supposed to be a
fundamental precept of the contemporary international legal order.
This principle is based on two even more fundamental, underlying
principles of international law, namely, the principles of equality of
sovereign states and of self-determination of peoples.[24]

The principle of equality of sovereign states is central to both
the international political and legal systems and is reiterated in Article 2(1) of the UN Charter. It may be traced back at least as far as
the efforts of Emerich de Vattel to assert for states something like
the rights and duties that Rousseau asserted for individual men.
Whatever the necessity for the principle of equality of states, it has
always suffered from the obvious fact that grave differences in power
make states unequal, and these power differences are necessarily reflected in their interactions in normal as well as extraordinary circumstances. Thus, the principle of equality of states aims at an ar-
tificial, unnatural state of affairs where the real inequality of states
is resisted in the name of a legal principle. Whatever the rationale
of the principle and the arguments for making it supreme in the hierarchy of international legal principles, it is manifestly a principle that
will frequently be violated; this certainly has been the case with the
derivative principle of nonintervention.[25]

The principle of self-determination of peoples, reiterated in
Article 1(2) of the UN Charter, is of more recent vintage as a supposed principle of positive international law.[26] As will be maintained
in the discussion of civil wars, international law has traditionally
stressed the fact of control of a people and territory rather than of
representation of a people. However, the principle of self-determination is usually cited as the underlying basis for the alleged rule of
nonintervention in civil wars.

It should be observed that the tendency among contemporary
publicists, diplomats, and political propagandists to treat the principles of equality of sovereign states and of self-determination and the
derivative principle of nonintervention as self-evidently the highest
principles in international law is not usually challenged formally as
a matter of international-law doctrine. Yet, the fact of frequent violation in practice of the principle of nonintervention suggests that, in

at least some cases, the states violating this principle are not callous lawbreakers, but actors pursuing some other fundamental values that they believe to be of greater normative weight and relevance than the principles of equality of sovereign states and self-determination. It surely is conceivable that there may be circumstances where nonintervention may mean failure to uphold justice. For example, there may be a situation in which a minority is being subjected to a denial of fundamental human rights behind the protective facade of the sovereignty exercised in virtue of the enjoyment of self-determination by a majority. Surely it cannot be the case that no matter how repugnant to law and morality the behavior of the majority toward the minority may become, there is no warrant for foreign intervention on behalf of the victims of inhuman, perhaps genocidal, treatment.[27]

In any event, the supposed fundamental principle of nonintervention is applied in chaotic fashion in international practice because of the failure of endless attempts in international conventions, resolutions of international organizations, and of publicists to define the term intervention. The result is an absurdity. Using the diplomatic, media, and popular meanings of the term, so broad as to embrace a substantial part of the total interaction of states, international legalists attempt to characterize an unmanageable mass of state behavior as intervention and then struggle to frame normative prescriptions to govern it. When such efforts combine the hopeless looseness of diplomatic, media, and popular usage with the rigidity of the nonintervention principle, they produce ludicrous results aptly condemned by Myres McDougal and his followers as "normatively ambiguous." It is merely confusing when, in discussing international politics, the term intervention is used to describe such a spectrum of relationships and interactions that it loses distinctive meaning.[28] It is, however, mischievous to apply these vague usages to judgments about the normative permissibility of state actions. Since there is a built-in implication in the term intervention that the act is not only unusual but presumptively self-serving and wrong, it is disquieting to be told that, for example, beneficent foreign aid or emergency relief, given without political strings and gratefully accepted, is intervention and, accordingly, a violation of the principle of nonintervention.

Of course, this confused state of affairs is ideal for propagandists and practitioners of domestic partisan politics who can cheerfully dispense accusations of intervention in the certainty that the characterization will be taken by many as self-evidently damning. But the state of usage in diplomatic, media, and popular circles is not such as to recommend its acceptance by the just-war analyst. It is with these considerations in mind that I accept the twofold definition of Rosenau as a starting point for political and normative analysis.

It would appear that two approaches to the issue of intervention in international law predominate. First, there is support for a flat rule of nonintervention without exceptions. This is the position of the Charter of the Organization of American States (OAS), Article 15, and of the UN General Assembly Resolutions on Intervention of 1965 and 1970. [29] Moreover, the formulation of these provisions is so broad as to suffer from all of the faults of exaggerated definitions of intervention just discussed. Second, however, there is the position, grounded in most of the traditional literature on the subject and a substantial record of state practice, that although the presumption is always against intervention, that presumption may be overridden by invocation of a limited number of exceptional justifications.

If proper weight is accorded the actual practice and expectations of states, the first approach—total nonintervention—is so divorced from reality as to discredit the pretensions of international law. Given the widespread patterns of intervention in most parts of the world (excepting relations between the advanced states of the Free World), it certainly cannot be maintained that total nonintervention is the norm of state practice in the present international system.

On the contrary, states not only intervene in the affairs of others, they often do so with an evident sense of rectitude. Whatever conclusions will be derived from a just-war analysis of the subject, it is evident that a sense of just intervention is widely enjoyed by a variety of international actors from all blocs and persuasions within the international system. As a matter of positive international law, the most that can be said for the principle of nonintervention is that it creates a presumption against some forms of intervention, the definition of which must be derived inductively from state practice. This presumption may be overridden by states invoking exceptional justifying causes acceptable to the international legal system.

Among the justifications for intervention that have been considered as exceptions to the general nonintervention principle are intervention by invitation of the incumbent regime, intervention by treaty right, humanitarian intervention, and intervention as collective self-defense and counterintervention. [30] Although extended discussion of all of these exceptional justifications for intervention is not necessary to the analysis of just-war jus ad bellum for revolutionary/counterinsurgency wars, it is necessary to mention some of the problems that confront those who would invoke any of these exceptions. It should be noted that these problems may arise with respect to intervention with the nonmilitary instruments of policy (political/diplomatic, psychological, and economic) and in situations not constituting civil war. However, the analysis that follows assumes a substantial use of the military instrument by the intervening power in the context of a civil-war situation.

Intervention by invitation is often criticized because of the alleged unjust and/or unrepresentative character of the regime issuing

the invitation. This criticism usually takes the particular form of the
charge that the incumbent government would not be able to hold power
without the support of the intervening power; that, accordingly, the
incumbent regime does not deserve to remain in power; and, that the
intervening power is denying the people of the country the right to determine who will rule them.[31]

There does not seem to be a very clear or firm consensus among
international-law authorities on the validity of this objection, although
the tendency is to sustain it if the invitation to intervene is not based
on the claim that there was an antecedent intervention on behalf of the
antigovernment forces. Thus, if a government is faced with a purely
internal war, with little or no significant foreign intervention on behalf of the rebels, the better opinion appears to be that a foreign
power ought not to intervene to sustain the threatened regime.[32]

Having said this, it should be pointed out that the contemporary
tendency to give the benefit of doubt to revolutionaries and credit
their claims to be the true representatives of the people is unwarranted. A government may be unrepresentative and unjust—probably
a substantial number of the world's governments are—but revolutionaries are not automatically representative and just. Indeed, in many
revolutionary/counterinsurgency wars neither side appears to persuade the people that they are superior either with respect to their
representative character or their justice.

In any event, it is clear that positive international law is not particularly concerned with the representative character or justice of governments. If such governments in fact control a sovereign state, they
take on the rights and duties of the representatives of international
persons. The principle of nonintervention, indeed, is based on the
assumption that sovereign equals should be generally immune from
interference with respect to their exercise of power, regardless of
their representative character, justice, or any other consideration.[33]

It is certainly true that just-war jus ad bellum emphasizing representation and justice might well justify intervention on the side of
a civil war that appeared to hold out the greater promise of realizing
these goals. It is not impossible that this could be the side of the incumbent regime. In such cases, a just-war approach would reject
the blanket nonintervention principle and sympathize with intervention
by invitation. Still, I would conclude that it would be better for just-
war jus ad bellum to follow the general lead of positive international
law and discourage intervention by invitation of the incumbent regime
where there is no evidence of prior intervention on the side of the
rebels. If this approach is followed, intervention by invitation would
be permissible only in the case of counterintervention for collective
self-defense. This, of course, was the essence of the U.S. position
with regard to intervention in Vietnam in the late 1950s and at the
point of escalation in 1965.

A further point should be mentioned. It has been suggested that a regime that has invited intervention to sustain it in a civil war may lose its claims to legitimacy and the right to invite foreign intervention if it is apparently losing that war. The implication is that a regime losing such an internal conflict proves itself unrepresentative and unjust by the fact it is doing poorly in the revolutionary war.[34] As previously pointed out, revolutionaries seldom have a self-evident superiority in their ability to represent the people or in putative justice; they may or they may not. Often they are a small, effective minority using the forms of revolutionary war that can often topple a regime without proving the credentials of the revolutionaries as superior representatives of the people. I would judge that an incumbent regime should retain whatever rights it has to invite foreign assistance as long as a civil war continues. As indicated, its case for inviting assistance is more credible if the intervention is needed to counter intervention on behalf of the rebels.

The next exceptional right to intervention that is sometimes recognized is that based on treaty. Despite the legal fiction of sovereign equality, the disparity in actual power between states is a perennial fact of life. Sometimes this fact is recognized by a special relationship between a strong and a weak power, often the historical product of an earlier colonial or hegemonial relationship. Such special relationships may be maintained informally, but they may also be the subject of specific treaty rights and duties. U.S. treaty obligations under the 1977 Panama Canal Treaties and Agreements may provide for such intervention in their provisions regarding U.S. responsibilities for the defense of the canal. These responsibilities probably take precedence over the formal reiteration in the treaties of the principle of nonintervention.[35]

Thus, intervention by treaty right may constitute an extraordinary involvement by one state in the internal and/or external affairs of another by the standards of current, normal state interaction. However, the fact that this extraordinary degree of involvement is contemplated by both parties in a treaty would mean that, in Rosenau's sense, it is not even intervention since it is not "convention breaking." In any event, however characterized, intervention by treaty right is presumptively legitimate as a matter of international law and the just-war jus ad bellum. To be sure, one could once again raise the issue of the representative character and justice of the government that made and invoked the treaty to invite foreign intervention. But this would seem to open an inquiry into the legitimacy and credentials of all of the states of the world. In particular cases, it may be proper to question the treaty base for intervention, but, as a general category, it would seem to form a plausible exception to the nonintervention principle. This subject will be pursued in discussing possible U.S. intervention in Panama.

Humanitarian intervention is a justification for violating the presumption of nonintervention that survives despite the fact that it was undoubtedly severely abused during the colonial period of the last several hundred years. Humanitarian intervention is an emergency action to protect the lives of a state's own nationals resident in a foreign country and/or the lives of aliens generally who are threatened by conditions there.[36] It is also conceivable that humanitarian intervention could be undertaken to protect nationals of the target state subjected to policies of extreme repression or genocidal extermination.[37] One could well imagine humanitarian intervention in states such as Uganda and Cambodia, both to protect aliens and to save nationals of those countries from genocide. Certainly a just-war jus ad bellum would be even more inclined to accept this justification for military intervention than positive international law, wherein the subject is somewhat controverted.

Finally, there is the justification that, when combined with intervention by invitation, most concerns the just-war jus ad bellum in revolutionary/counterinsurgency wars. This is intervention justified as counterintervention in response to an antecedent intervention on the rebel side in a civil war. Such counterintervention takes on the character of collective self-defense, since, if the previous intervention on the rebel side is significant and includes a conspicuous use of the military instrument, the incumbent regime is fighting not only a civil war but also an international war against a direct or indirect aggressor.[38] The spectrum of degrees of intervention on behalf of rebels is amply demonstrated by the course of the Vietnam War that was instigated, directed, and crucially supported by North Vietnam. To be sure, there was a bona fide element of internal civil war at all times, and, had the war been substantially limited to the internal conflict, no right of counterintervention would have arisen. However, the degree and importance of North Vietnamese participation in the civil war on the rebel side made that country a cobelligerent well before there was any comparable, direct U.S. military intervention, as well as prior to the point where both of the principal foreign interveners committed forces for direct engagement in the emerging international conflict.

In terms of positive international-law jus ad bellum, then, the key to the permissibility of military intervention is its justification as participation in collective self-defense measures warranted by antecedent intervention/aggression of another state making a significant military contribution to the rebel side in a revolutionary/counterinsurgency war. It should once again be emphasized that such intervention in support of revolutionary forces is commonplace and perhaps the greatest source of contemporary conflict.

There is a wide spectrum of nonmilitary and military assistance that a foreign power can provide to a rebel force, and the self-defense measures of a counterintervening power should be proportionate and appropriate to the necessity to counter the effects of such assistance. What is essential is that the antecedent intervention on behalf of the rebels frees both the incumbent regime and friendly states from the presumption against intervention in civil wars and permits military intervention into what has become a mixed civil-international conflict. With these considerations in mind, it is possible to pierce the confusion surrounding the broad subject of intervention and reduce the focus of military intervention to its permissibility in terms of the positive international law governing recourse to armed coercion under collective self-defense (UN Charter, Article 51) and the just-war jus ad bellum conditions applied in the analysis of the Vietnam War in Chapter 5.

It must be admitted that the need for evidence of antecedent intervention on behalf of rebels in a civil war is sometimes a source of severe controversy. Thus, in the case of the U.S.-OAS intervention into the 1965 Dominican Civil War, the United States was embarrassed in its efforts to establish an antecedent intervention by Cuba and other communist powers, because the links to such states on the rebel side were not sufficiently clear and substantial. This was in contrast to the contemporaneous Vietnamese situation where the role of North Vietnam was clear and crucial.[39]

The jus ad bellum of revolutionary/counterinsurgency war, then, remains in a confused and controverted state. The individual analyses that must be made regarding the just-war and international-law requirements for belligerent status and the moral and legal justifications for intervention in civil wars are all extremely difficult. These analyses require reexamination of the most fundamental issues of political, legal, and moral theory and their application in real situations that are usually complex and unclear. What exacerbates the problem of analysis is the fact that political, legal, and moral analyses and concepts are all intermixed in a normative mélange that becomes almost impossible to sort out. To this must be added the obvious fact that all perspectives—political, legal, and moral—are challenged by the contrary realities of actual revolutionary activity, regime responses, and multiple competing interventions in state practice as opposed to the rhetoric of nonintervention.

The only thing that is clear is that no simple prescriptions, (for example, flat nonintervention in a civil war) are normative or practically valid today. Some kind of just-war jus ad bellum calculus, applied on a case-by-case basis, remains the most promising approach to the continuing dilemmas of revolutionary/counterinsurgency wars and foreign interventions therein.

8

CRITICAL ISSUES OF JUST WAR: THE JUS IN BELLO OF REVOLUTIONARY/ COUNTERINSURGENCY WAR

As observed in Chapter 2, a modern just-war approach is obliged to take cognizance of and adopt, insofar as reasonable, the positive international law of war. In Chapter 6, the positive law provisions regarding critical issues have been integrated with the basic just-war jus in bello categories. It is my intention to continue this approach in the present chapter. Before doing so, however, several points should be made concerning the problem of legal regulation of revolutionary/counterinsurgency war.

First, legal regulation of revolutionary/counterinsurgency war is in a primitive state compared with the developed jus in bello for international conflict. The Hague Rules of Hague Convention IV of 1907 deal with the subject only in the establishment of the conditions for belligerent status under Article 1. Historically, the Hague Conventions were concerned with interstate war, and the problems of unconventional war, even as part of conventional international conflict, were not seriously addressed. The 1949 Geneva Conventions surprisingly tended to perpetuate this interstate conventional-war bias despite the importance of a variety of kinds of unconventional war in World War II and the numerous postwar conflicts of a civil or mixed civil-international nature. Only common Article 3 of the conventions dealt in rudimentary fashion with "the case of armed conflict not of an international character." The 1960s and 1970s were characterized by a proliferation of revolutionary/civil/unconventional wars and by calls for their regulation under the international law of war.

The 1977 Geneva Protocol II is a response to those appeals. Yet, it appears, a substantial opposition to or lack of enthusiasm for a comprehensive convention for civil wars on the part of the Third World and other states resulted in a rather brief and incomplete convention. This convention was not thoroughly analyzed and debated before it was accepted by the Geneva Conference as, in effect, the best version possible under the circumstances. [1] When, therefore, one assesses the progress made in the 1977 Geneva Protocol II in the light of existing provisions of earlier conventions and of the 1977 Geneva Protocol I regulating international conflict, it is important to be aware that the object of analysis is probably quite vulnerable to criticisms of incompleteness and superficiality. Faced with the prospect of restricting means typically employed in revolutionary/counter-insurgency wars, the majority of the participants in the Geneva Diplomatic Conference avoided the issue in part by not treating many of the standard jus in bello subjects in Protocol II. However, in this analysis I attempt to show some of the implications for revolutionary/counterinsurgency war when applying at least the basic principles and concepts of the regular international jus in bello to such conflicts.

Second, it should be emphasized that the difficulties of upholding the jus in bello in revolutionary/counterinsurgency warfare are, if anything, greater than those that occur in an international conflict of a primarily conventional character because of the tendency of the parties to take the approach that the superior justice of their ends justifies almost any means.

Third, it should be borne in mind that revolutionary belligerents, in particular, are often very limited as to what strategic and tactical options they may adopt if they are to have any chance of success. If a jus in bello prescription decisively interferes with one of these few options, it may mean a choice between no revolutionary war for a cause believed to be just or a war openly fought in defiance of the laws of war.

Fourth, given the great difficulty in practice of establishing the threshold between widespread criminal behavior and/or the terrorism of marginal political factions, on the one hand, and an activity whose political purpose, military success, magnitude, and duration warrants treatment as armed conflict, on the other, there is the perennial problem of determining when the jus in bello for noninternational conflicts ought to be applied. (See Article 1 of the 1977 Geneva Protocol II quoted and discussed below.)

With these points in mind, attention may be turned to the task of applying a modern jus in bello to the conduct of revolutionary/counterinsurgency war. The jus in bello that will be applied will be a combination of the basic jus in bello principles of just war, the positive international-law jus in bello designed primarily for conventional international conflict to the extent that it can be adapted to the problems of revolutionary/counterinsurgency war, and the emerging positive-law jus in bello for noninternational conflicts. It should be observed that this eclectic approach is justified, first, by the fact that the revolutionary/counterinsurgency wars are frequently mixed civil-international conflicts and often include substantial conventional as well as subconventional or guerrilla operations. Second, a just-war approach is free to seek the maximum normative restraint on the conduct of war and ought not to be constrained by the lawyer's natural conservatism when it comes to extending the law of international conflict to wars of a primarily civil nature. Having said this, it is necessary to acknowledge that some of the provisions of the jus in bello governing international conflicts are either inapplicable to or of questionable relevance to revolutionary/counterinsurgency wars. This will be recognized where appropriate.

PROPORTION AND MILITARY NECESSITY

It has already been pointed out that the jus ad bellum proportionality of revolutionary/counterinsurgency war is difficult to evaluate because of the propensity of the revolutionaries to admit no limit to the means that may be necessary to achieve their utopian end. In these circumstances, the more proximate evaluation of claims of proportionality and military necessity in the conduct of a revolutionary war will obviously be difficult. Moreover, the problem of proportionality is compounded by the fact that on both sides in a revolutionary/counterinsurgency war there will often be serious differences of opinion as to what constitutes true military necessity or utility.

In such conflicts both sides tend to develop internal debates over basic strategy. There is a recurring "hard-line/soft-line" dichotomy. The hard-liners want to solve most problems with military solutions, regardless of the impact on the society. The soft-liners insist that military solutions do not work and that they ruin the prospects for success in nonmilitary programs of persuasion and reform. Generally there are enough setbacks for both approaches to give support to arguments on both sides. The upshot is that military necessity/ utility tends to be measured in two quite conflicting ways. To the hard-liners, it is little exaggeration to say, the body count is the principal criterion of military utility on the counterinsurgent side. Other criteria are areas secured, roads kept open, and decline in the frequency and magnitude of enemy attacks. On the revolutionary side the same indicators are of interest to the hard-liners, although revolutionaries tend to place greater emphasis on psychological factors, such as rate of desertion in the government forces and state of morale in the military and civilian populations.

To the soft-liners on both sides, social statistics (for example, number of villages operating in a more or less normal fashion; number of hospitals, clinics, schools, and social services centers functioning; improvements in the agricultural and food distribution system) are indicators of the success of the revolutionary or counterinsurgency effort. The soft-liners have to concede the need for security to carry out their efforts, but they want that security with a minimum of destructive combat in populated areas and with firm restraints on police or security force activity.[2]

Military necessity, the first principle of the positive <u>jus in bello</u>, permits the use of only such force as is truly necessary for military success (that is, what is permitted by the just-war and positive-law principles of proportion). This principle becomes difficult to apply in revolutionary/counterinsurgency war because purely military success may not be congruent with the political, economic, and social successes that are equally, if not more important in such conflicts.

The temptation is to side with the soft-liners and endorse the proposition that true necessity usually coincides with observance of the law. However, if the military side of the conflict is lost, the positive side goes with it. This is true, of course, of both sides in the conflict. Moreover, it has been a recurring strategy of revolutionaries to single out the most positive programs, their key personnel, and the beneficiaries of those programs for violent attack. It is, after all, detrimental to the revolutionaries' interests and propaganda line for the counterinsurgents to be seen as making positive, successful efforts on behalf of the people. When this happens, the soft-liners must go back to the hard-liners for protection at the risk of unleashing more military actions that have military utility but may undermine the positive programs they are intended to protect.

An apparent line of resolution of such dilemmas would appear to be the maintenance of an extremely delicate balance between the military and nonmilitary components of the war effort on both sides. The practical dilemmas for those anxious to extend the operation of the <u>jus in bello</u> to such conflicts is that the whole concept of allying reasonable conduct of the conflict with respect for the law is frustrated by uncertainty as to what is the most reasonable conduct. In these circumstances it is necessary to exercise particular care in the interpretation of the principle of proportion.

The principle of proportion at the level of the <u>jus in bello</u> requires that in addition to having true military utility war measures must be proportionate to the specific military end in view. Having seen that the measurement of true utility in revolutionary/counterinsurgency war is already a major problem, the <u>jus in bello</u> analyst immediately confronts another problem. Usually revolutionary/counterinsurgency war turns on the initiatives of the rebels and the reaction of the regime to those initiatives. Particularly in phases 1 and 2 of such a conflict this is the case. As the war goes on, the regime, if it is sufficiently strong, will mount operations designed to seize the initiative. But at first the pace is generally set by the revolutionaries. However, the timing and character of revolutionary attacks are frequently fortuitous in character. Rebel attacks occur when an opportunity is found and exploited. There need not be much coherence in the attacks, and the end in view is an extremely broad one of weakening the enemy and destroying the confidence of the people in the regime.

Accordingly, it is often difficult to posit the clear military purpose that is the basis for a judgment of military necessity and proportionality. Revolutionary strategies and tactics are often rationalized only in the loosest, most permissive manner, ultimately to be absorbed into the pervasive revolutionary raison d'état of the destruction of the old order and its replacement with a utopian new order.

Thus, if the overall goal of subverting and destroying the incumbent order is a sufficient referent for revolutionary proportionality, then nothing will be disproportionate and revolutionaries will be freed from the restraints imposed by the principle of proportion on all belligerents. This surely cannot be accepted. Moreover, such an approach puts the counterinsurgent side at a great disadvantage. There is no question about the applicability of the requirement of proportionality to the counterinsurgent side. The referent of its claims of proportionate measures is the utility of the act in defeating the revolutionary forces against a broader goal of maintaining the status quo. No resolution of this emerging imbalance between the assumed standards of proportionality for revolutionary and counterinsurgent belligerents appears to be at hand. Some specific examples of this problem will arise in connection with specific jus in bello issues to be considered in the hypothetical case of a revolutionary/counterinsurgency war in Panama, discussed in Chapter 14.

DISCRIMINATION

Efforts to apply the principle of discrimination to revolutionary/counterinsurgency war are likewise frustrating. Basically, both sides tend to deny that there are any noncombatants. On the revolutionaries' side, the war is waged on behalf of "the people." All right-thinking persons are on the side of the people. Those who disagree, oppose, or even hesitate are "enemies of the people" and lackeys of the corrupt, fascist, puppet regime. So, no one not clearly supporting the revolution has the right to immunity from direct, intentional attack as required by the principle of discrimination. Moreover, revolutionary war is usually class war, and persons who, by their position under the existing regime and social order, belong to the "exploiter class" and are class enemies especially merit direct, intentional attack whether they carry arms or not (for example, the family of a government official or businessman may be more guilty

and worthy of attack than a drafted soldier). So whole categories of
persons who are clearly noncombatants under the traditional jus in
bello are held to be proper targets for attacks under the logic of revolutionary war. [3]

Similar considerations tend to incline incumbent regimes to
parallel attitudes and policies. All, or most, of the population is
supposed to be made up of loyal, law-abiding citizens. All of them
have a legal duty to assist in the repression of crime and insurrection.
If, by commission or omission, they fail in this duty, or if they actually appear to support the rebels, they will tend to be treated as
rebels (that is, proper objects of counterinsurgent attack). Moreover, in a guerrilla war it is often impossible to distinguish combatants from noncombatants. It is not unknown for women and children
to take a direct part in the hostilities. Indeed, it can be dangerous to
assume that a child will not throw a grenade or an old woman will
not set a booby trap. In areas where the rebels are permanently or
intermittently in control, all may be suspect with reason.

In addition to this tendency of both sides to deny noncombatant
status and immunity to large segments of the population, the typical
strategies and tactics of the belligerents in revolutionary/counterin-
surgency war render discrimination difficult in practice. Particularly
in phases 1 and 2 of revolutionary war, the insurgents use terror tactics designed to subvert the confidence of the population in the regime
and its prospects. The message implied in these tactics is that no
one is safe anywhere as long as the regime remains in power. In order to convey this message, the revolutionaries set off bombs in
crowded public places, engage in hit-and-run attacks that imperil
noncombatants in the area, engage in indiscriminate acts of reprisal
or intimidation against locales and areas guilty of supporting the government, and the like. As previously indicated, one purpose of these
attacks is to elicit a violent response from the regime's forces that
will involve more innocent people and thereby engender fear and bitterness toward the counterinsurgents. [4] A rebel force that knows its
business can literally create more resistance by provoking disproportionate and indiscriminate reprisals by the counterinsurgents, thereby
alienating the people and enhancing their disposition to support the
rebels, even though the latter's activity is actually the proximate
source of their suffering.

The counterinsurgents are likewise inclined to use indiscriminate strategies and tactics. Whole classes of persons or areas of the
country are submitted to pacification measures that do not discriminate beyond the loyal and the disloyal, with all presumptions that those
in the target classes and/or areas are disloyal. A typical form of
such action is the reprisal against a locale or area charged with having supported and/or condoned rebel activity that has caused serious

government losses. Such an area may be destroyed; the population may be evacuated en masse, perhaps confined to strategic hamlets or refugee camps. Indiscriminate firepower may be used by counterinsurgent land and air forces against "rebel strongholds" with population concentrations.

The earlier discussion of military necessity recognized the contradictions and ambiguities that exist with respect to the question of true utility in revolutionary/counterinsurgency war. Having acknowledged this point, however, it must likewise be acknowledged that the general tendency of belligerent practice in such wars is for the parties to believe that success requires their use of the disporportionate and indiscriminate strategies and tactics described. Particularly in the case of revolutionaries, it seems fair to say that the means that have most often succeeded have violated the principles of proportion and discrimination. To the extent that this interpretation is valid, major problems confront recent efforts to extend the international law of war to noninternational conflicts. Potential participants in such wars confirmed this fundamental difficulty in opposing provisions in the 1977 Geneva Protocol II that would have laid down some of the standard jus in bello restrictions, emanating from the principles of proportion and discrimination, on the conduct of hostilities. [5]

However, the situation is not so clear on the counterinsurgent side. Indeed, a strong case can be made that conformity to the principles of proportion and discrimination plus an effective development program is the most utilitarian as well as the normatively required policy for counterinsurgency. [6] Still, it is difficult to propose that there be a double standard under which the revolutionaries are free to violate the basic principles of the laws of war and the counterinsurgents must be faithful to them, no matter how their chances of success may be affected. This would seem to be particularly unjust where the most positive development strategies of the regime are wrecked by the disporportionate and indiscriminate attacks of the revolutionaries. [7] On the other hand, it may be argued that counterinsurgents are being held to the same fundamental precepts of humane law enforcement expected of a government in dealing with criminals where there is no question of reciprocity.

GENOCIDE

Both sides in revolutionary/counterinsurgency wars are inclined toward genocidal policies. Certain racial, ethnic, tribal, or religious groups or social classes may be particularly identified with one side or the other. In the context of typical revolutionary/counterinsurgency wars it is important to reiterate the earlier position taken in this book on the inclusion of repression and extermination of political and social groups and classes in the concept of genocide. Political and ideological considerations undoubtedly prevented inclusion of these critical categories in the Genocide Convention. However, it is well known that revolutionary/counterinsurgency wars involve discriminatory mistreatment of such groups and classes. Such disproportionate and indiscriminate treatment and attacks often achieve near-genocidal and genocidal effects. Moreover, given the hatreds engendered by such conflicts, there may be rather clear genocidal intention on either or both sides.

However, the question remains as to the proper characterization of measures that have near-genocidal effects but are carried out without genocidal intent. This was the issue in Vietnam, discussed in Chapters 3 and 5. Either or both of the sides in a revolutionary/counterinsurgency war may destroy a substantial part of the population and its characteristic culture in the process of fighting each other through the population. Both sides claim to be fighting for the people and their rights. They certainly have no intent to destroy the nation for whose leadership they are contending. Neither has an overwhelmingly clear mandate from the people in typical modern revolutionary wars. In these circumstances it seems clear to me that there is no question of genocide. There may well be a gross disporportion between the good for which either or both sides is fighting and the effects of the war on the nation. Moreover, when there is external intervention, as in Vietnam, the outside forces may escalate the conflict to levels that are too much for the indigenous society to bear. Again, this may be characterized as a violation of the principle of proportion. But, unless there is evidence that either the indigenous belligerents or their respective intervening allies have the intent of destroying the society over which they are fighting, the charge of genocide is inaccurate and unjustified. [8]

MEANS MALA PROHIBITA

Finally, there are some specific activities, often encountered in revolutionary/counterinsurgency wars, that are mala prohibita under the 1949 Geneva Conventions and the 1977 Geneva Protocols I and II. I will, as previously noted, interpret the substance and applicability of those conventions liberally, in consonance with a just-war approach to the jus in bello.

The most important categories of means mala prohibita are listed here:

1. attacks on the civilian population, as such;
2. denial of prisoner of war (PW) status and treatment;

3. torture and mistreatment, collective punishment, taking of
hostages, terrorism, outrages against personal dignity, slavery,
pillage, and threats to do any of these things;
4. denial to internees and detainees of reasonable treatment
and due process of law;
5. starvation of civilians as a method of combat; and
6. forced movement of civilians.

There are important differences between some of the categories.
First, the category concerning prisoners of war is not covered by the
conventional law for noninternational conflict except for the right of
quarter. However, in accordance with my contention that essential
PW rights of protection are derived from general principles of the
jus in bello applicable to all conflicts with the material characteristics of war, I include this category among the activities mala prohibita. Second, it should be noted that the prohibitions in the first
four categories are not subject to elastic clauses leaving open exceptions for extreme military necessity or other reasons. However,
the last two categories are subject to such exceptions, as will be explained.

Attacks on the Civilian Population as Such

Given the propensity of modern wars of all kinds to violate the
principle of discrimination and the particular problems of revolution-
ary/counterinsurgency wars in this regard, it is significant that
Article 13 of the 1977 Geneva Protocol II on noninternational conflicts
replicates Article 51 of Protocol I, discussed in Chapter 3. Article
13 of Protocol II, in language identical to that of Article 51 of Protocol I, provides for the following:

1. The civilian population and individual civilians shall
enjoy general protection against the dangers arising from
military operations. To give effect to this protection, the
following rules shall be observed in all circumstances.
2. The civilian population as such, as well as individual
civilians, shall not be the object of attack. Acts or threats
of violence the primary purpose of which is to spread terror among the civilian population are prohibited.
3. Civilians shall enjoy the protection afforded by this
Article, unless and for such time as they take a direct
part in hostilities.

As has been discussed with respect to the general principles of
proportion and discrimination, both sides in revolutionary/counter-

insurgency war tend to violate this rule and the principles underlying it. If it is to be respected and reconciled with the typical strategies and tactics of belligerents in such conflicts, two forms of justification will have to be advanced. First, belligerents will have to shape their operations so as to support the contention that their intent is to limit attacks to truly military objectives. The collateral effects on civilians will be said to be unintended and limited as much as possible. Thus, the now familiar debates of the morality and legality of strategic bombing and nuclear war and deterrence will spread to revolutionary/counterinsurgency war. Indeed, such debates have been in order all along, but the countervalue emphases of revolutionary/counterinsurgency war have not been recognized to the extent that corresponding strategies in nuclear war and conventional war have been.[9] Both the elements of intent and direct attack are subject to interpretation and debate. It may be hoped that the appearance of Article 13 elicits such debate.

Second, following the guidelines of Article 13(3), belligerents will have to have proof in hand that in some cases civilians have taken "a direct part in hostilities." This issue, too, parallels the conventional-war issue of participation in the war effort and consequent qualification as a proper target for direct attack. Finally, as to the prohibition of terror, also contained in common Article 3 of the 1949 Geneva Conventions and Article 4(2) of the 1977 Geneva Protocol II, Article 13 reiterates a clear-cut rule of the jus in bello that is frequently violated in revolutionary/counterinsurgency wars. This problem will be discussed below as a separate issue.

The question might be raised whether it would not have been sufficient to assimilate this discussion of new Article 13 of Geneva Protocol II of 1977 into the earlier discussion of the principle of discrimination. This could have been done, as the relevant articles of Protocol I were discussed together with the principle of discrimination in Chapter 3. However, it is important to give separate acknowledgment that the principle of discrimination, always applicable but often ignored, has been specifically recognized in an international convention (1977 Geneva Protocol II on noninternational conflicts) addressed primarily to revolutionary/counterinsurgency wars. The importance of this acknowledgment by states that had shown themselves to be reluctant to accept too many limitations on the conduct of such wars is striking.

Denial of Prisoner-of-War Status and Treatment

To repeat an earlier observation, there is not yet any conventional law incorporation of the regular jus in bello protecting PWs into the modest emerging law regulating noninternational conflicts. Nevertheless, it is my contention that the basic concepts of quarter—the right to surrender as a PW and to receive security and reasonable treatment—should be binding on belligerents in all wars. This section proceeds on that assumption.

One of the most intractable issues of revolutionary/counterinsurgency war has been that of belligerent status for revolutionary forces. Historically, incumbent regimes have sought to characterize and treat rebels as criminals, brigands, and traitors. To accord them the right to regular PW treatment is to recognize them as lawful belligerents, something that the regime wants to avoid if at all possible. Moreover, the guerrilla and sometimes terror tactics of the revolutionary forces do not dispose the counterinsurgents to treat captured revolutionaries as bona fide belligerents entitled to PW status and treatment. The relevant international law, laid down in the 1970 Hague Rules and reiterated to the present—even as unconventional war has become the rule rather than the exception in contemporary conflicts—is still tied to the assumption that conventional forces are the norm. Thus, the familiar four conditions of the Hague Rules are reiterated in the 1949 Geneva Conventions. To qualify for belligerent status and treatment, the revolutionaries had to

> meet certain requirements customarily required of all combatants, including:
>
> (a) being commanded by a person responsible for his subordinates,
> (b) having a fixed distinctive sign recognizable at a distance,
> (c) carrying arms openly, and
> (d) conducting their operations in accordance with the law of armed conflict. [10]

Moreover, it must again be pointed out that in order to be treated as belligerents, individuals and groups who meet the four requirements must be engaged in hostilities that may properly be termed armed conflicts in the sense of Article 1 of 1977 Geneva Protocol II, discussed below.

Each of these requirements for belligerent status poses problems for both sides in revolutionary/counterinsurgency war. There are built-in tendencies for the revolutionaries to fall short of all of the standards prescribed except that requiring command responsibility. It may often be the case that adherence to requirements (b), (c), and (d) would decisively lessen the revolutionaries' chances for success.

The 1977 Geneva Protocol I, applicable to international conflicts and a promising source of guidelines for noninternational revolutionary/counterinsurgency war conflicts, has somewhat lightened the re-

quirements for belligerent status. The first and fourth requirements
are reiterated in Article 43.

> The armed forces of a Party to a conflict consist of all
> organized armed forces, groups and units which are under
> a command responsible to that Party for the conduct of its
> subordinates, even if that Party is represented by a gov-
> ernment or an authority not recognized by an adverse Party.
> Such armed forces shall be subject to an internal disci-
> plinary system which, inter alia, shall enforce compliance
> with the rules of international law applicable in armed
> conflict.

The second and third conditions are addressed in Article 44,
wherein lightening of the requirements for combatant status is effected. Article 44(3) provides for the following:

> In order to promote the protection of the civilian popula-
> tion from the effects of hostilities, combatants are obliged
> to distinguish themselves from the civilian population while
> they are engaged in an attack or in a military operation
> preparatory to an attack. Recognizing, however, that there
> are situations in armed conflicts where, owing to the nature
> of the hostilities, an armed combatant cannot so distinguish
> himself, he shall retain his status as a combatant, provided
> that, in such situations, he carries his arms openly:
>
> (a) during each military engagement, and
> (b) during such time as he is visible to the adversary while
> he is engaged in a military deployment preceding the launch-
> ing of an attack in which he is to participate.
>
> Acts which comply with the requirements of this paragraph
> shall not be considered as perfidious within the meaning of
> Article 37, paragraph 1(c).

It should be noted that two declarations of understanding were
made by the United States when it signed the 1977 Geneva Protocols
I and II on December 12, 1977. The United States stated the following in the second of these:

> 2. It is the understanding of the United States of America
> that the phrase "military deployment preceding the launch-
> ing of an attack" in Article 44, paragraph 3, means any
> movement towards a place from which an attack is to be
> launched. [11]

Clearly these guidelines were intended for international conflicts only. As a matter of law, they cannot be assumed to apply in the noninternational conflicts regulated by Protocol II, which make up the bulk of revolutionary/counterinsurgency wars. Nonetheless, in keeping with my contention that the basic principles and concepts of the jus in bello ought to be applied to civil wars of the material scope and intensity of international wars, I suggest that the Protocol I provisions qualifying individual belligerent status be used as a working standard in noninternational conflicts.

It is, of course, quite difficult to formulate a definition of material war that will serve as a basis for the proposition that the jus in bello should apply when there is a material war even if it is not an international conflict. The old system of belligerency and insurgency being recognized by other states is archaic and irrelevant. [12] States, particularly those vulnerable to civil war, are anxious to keep a high threshold for the introduction of the international law of war. As discussed above, Article 1 of the 1977 Geneva Protocol II lays down the material conditions required for the coming into effect of the Protocol. [13]

It will be recalled that these requirements for belligerent status of revolutionary forces are quite demanding. Such forces often do not control much territory for any length of time. This depends very much on the geographical and social characteristics of the country involved. "Sustained and concerted military operations," as required by Article 1 of the 1977 Geneva Protocol II, may, indeed, be maintained without long-term control of territory, another requirement of Article 1. Long-term control of territory may not even be an objective of the revolutionaries until phases 2 or 3 of the Maoist revolutionary cycle. Nevertheless, it is believed that Article 1 of Protocol II represents progress in obtaining status for revolutionary forces under the jus in bello; consequently, it may help in assuring some chance that revolutionary soldiers will be granted prisoner-of-war status when captured.

Understanding that the new provisions of Articles 43 and 44 of the 1977 Geneva Protocol I are not directed to noninternational wars, I would nonetheless propose that belligerent status in such wars be determined in two ways: first, with respect to the belligerent status of the revolutionary government and forces, Article 1 of the 1977 Geneva Protocol II governs; and second, in the absence of specific provisions on the subject in Protocol II, the status of individual revolutionaries and their military formations should be guided by Articles 43 and 44 of the 1977 Geneva Protocol I. [14]

The problem of ensuring PW status and protection for bona fide revolutionary combatants is, of course, compounded by the fact that large numbers of suspected subversives are rounded up and detained

in a revolutionary war. In the absence of substantial uniforms or distinguishing insignia, it is hard to tell a guerrilla combatant from a
noncombatant supporter of the revolutionaries. With the best of intentions, it is often very difficult to sort out the persons who ought
to be PWs and those who are properly civilian detainees. Once PW
camps are operational, there are further problems that typically
plague counterinsurgency campaigns. Given the inherent tendency to
view the PWs as disloyal and criminal citizens, there is a natural
propensity to treat them in a manner more in keeping with the standards of domestic jails than of the international law regime for prisoners of war. Often domestic jails do not attain the levels of treatment required for PWs. If the counterinsurgent regime has active
foreign allies as cobelligerents, they share responsibility for enforcement of the law protecting PWs. Such allies also have a strong political interest in avoiding scandals over the treatment of captured
revolutionaries.

There are also problems of ensuring PW status and treatment
with respect to soldiers of the regime and foreign interventionary
forces. In the first place, revolutionary forces frequently disclaim
any obligation to abide by the international legal regulations governing PWs. If they do abide by these regulations they usually characterize the observance as voluntary, a matter of their own "enlightened
policy." Accordingly, observance by revolutionaries of the PW regime is usually selective and quite inadequate. Moreover, the revolutionaries typically reserve special treatment for the various categories of PWs in their hands. In a manner that parallels the regime's
tendency to treat rebels as criminals and traitors, the revolutionaries
are inclined to treat government troops as "enemies of the people"
subject to revolutionary justice. As to the personnel of foreign interveners, the revolutionaries will often activate the "war criminals"
approach of the North Koreans and Chinese Communists in the Korean
War and the North Vietnamese and Vietcong in the Vietnam War. [15]

These two positions combine to produce the conclusion that both
captured regime troops and foreign "aggressor" forces are ipso facto
war criminals, and that, as such, they do not have the right to normal
treatment as PWs. The practice of the communist belligerents in the
Indo-Chinese conflicts has been to then claim great credit for a lenient
policy that takes whatever form they desire. The result has not been
compliance with the standards of the jus in bello for the protection of
the PWs. Moreover, this basic posture has been combined with programs of "reeducation" of PWs wherein the PW must earn minimally
decent treatment by collaboration with the enemy in ways prohibited
by the laws of war. This will be discussed further in light of the
analysis of the practice of torture and mistreatment that, unfortunately, forms the backdrop for most "reeducation" programs.

It is to be hoped that the communist practice of denying PW status and protection to alleged war criminals (that is, all participants in alleged wars of aggression) will be discontinued now that such discrimination is expressly prohibited by the Preamble to the 1977 Geneva Protocol I. However, given the absence of separate provisions for PWs in Geneva Protocol II, it is, of course, still quite possible that denial of jus in bello standards of PW protection linked to allegations of aggression and criminality will persist. But the new provisions of the Preamble to Protocol I should improve an ambiguous situation that has been exploited by communist belligerents both in conventional and revolutionary/counterinsurgency wars.

Finally, there is a fundamental problem regarding the typical capacity of revolutionary forces to provide PW facilities commensurate with the standards of treatment enjoined by the jus in bello. Such forces often live in very primitive, difficult circumstances. They may have to move about through inhospitable terrain. Their supplies of food and medicine will usually be modest. Their own standard of living is low and the standard provided for their prisoners will tend to be lower. Even if there is a desire to comply with the legal obligations of a detaining power, it may not be possible for revolutionary forces to do so. Indeed, although the counterinsurgents are usually more advantaged, in a developing country the regime's capability to maintain adequate PW facilities may also be minimal.[16]

Torture and Mistreatment

Common Article 3 of the 1949 Geneva Conventions, in a provision repeated in Article 4(a) of the 1977 Geneva Protocol I, prohibits "at any time and in any place whatsoever: . . . violence to life and person, in particular murder of all kinds, mutilation, cruel treatment and torture."[17] One could take this provision point by point and discuss the tendency of belligerents in revolutionary/counterinsurgency wars to violate it. As previously discussed, the revolutionaries in particular would be severely constrained if they abstained from acts of terror and intimidation that involve the kinds of behavior specified. But, from this provision one kind of behavior stands out as so central to revolutionary/counterinsurgency wars that it warrants detailed consideration, namely, torture.

The prohibition against torture raises one of the central and most anguishing issues of reconciling military necessities with the jus in bello. Torture may be employed against captured enemy personnel or civilians. It is distinguishable from mistreatment, also prohibited. Mistreatment involves injury to protected persons for which there is no military necessity and little if any excuse. Unfortunately, deliberate mistreatment becomes a kind of torture. It is the basis for intimidation that results in coerced collaboration and illegal practices wherein PWs and other protected persons must earn the decent treatment to which they are legally entitled.

Torture is different from mistreatment in that it may have a plausible military utility. Torture is employed to obtain vital information for which there is an imperative military necessity. A belligerent, counterinsurgent or revolutionary, may have in hand a leader or other highly informed member of the enemy forces. This prisoner may have information that, if it becomes known to the captor, would save lives and change the course of the conflict in important ways. As a matter of proportionality, of utilitarian calculation unaffected by specific prohibitory rules, one can easily imagine circumstances where a case for torture could be made. An ephemeral period of pain and anxiety for the prisoner might produce information that could save the lives of hundreds and thousands of noncombatants and assist the putatively just belligerent in winning the war.

To be sure, the same case might be made for torture in conventional international conflicts. However, the magnitude and character both of conventional operations and of the intelligence functions therein make it much less likely that torture to obtain information could be justified. Generally, torture is not an indispensable means of acquiring intelligence in conventional war, and its use for that purpose does not have a utility proportionate to the evil of torture and the consequences of violating a clear and unqualified rule of the jus in bello.

However, the clandestine character of most revolutionary movements, as well as of the counterinsurgents' countermeasures, the emphasis on surprise hit-and-run operations, and the great dependency of both sides on types of operations that endanger innocent people all render more credible the argument that some torture for intelligence purposes is both inevitable and justified in revolutionary/counterinsurgency war. Certainly practice shows that torture is commonplace in such conflicts. This practice notoriously flouts the clear rules of the 1949 and 1977 Geneva Conventions and Protocols.[18]

Indeed, torture raises an issue that is almost as important as that of measures endangering the noncombatant population. It may be questioned whether revolutionary or counterinsurgency war can be waged with a reasonable chance of success without employing torture. Obviously, this is a most difficult proposition to argue. The subject is repulsive to the morally sensitive. Moreover, the subject is undefined in the law of war, including the conventions that prohibit torture.

The project on torture of the Comité des Experts sur la Torture now being considered by the United Nations, along with other studies, gives this definition of torture, which, in Article 1 of its "Draft Con-

vention for the Prevention and Suppression of Torture," is termed
a crime under international law.

ARTICLE II
(Definition of torture)

For the purposes of this Convention, torture is any conduct by which severe pain or suffering, whether physical
or mental, is intentionally inflicted on a person by or at
the instigation of a public official or for which a public
official is responsible under Article III, in order:

a) to obtain from that person or another person information or a statement or confession; or
b) to intimidate, discredit or humiliate that person or
another person; or
c) to inflict punishment on that person or another person,
save where such conduct is in a proper execution of a lawful sanction not constituting cruel, inhuman or degrading
treatment or punishment. [19]

This definition is sufficient to indicate at least two aspects of
torture. First, it may be done for a public purpose. Second, torture
is a highly subjective thing, a matter of mind as well as body. Accordingly, it is not easy to distinguish severe interrogation ("third
degree" methods) from inadmissibly cruel and degrading coercion.
One would not, for example, be confident that torture is never employed by police in the United States in their interrogation of suspected
criminals or otherwise. Indeed, in the absence of an accepted definition, such a statement could not be made. If the concept of torture
includes subjective fears and apprehensions of a detained person,
there is no such thing as detention without a degree of torture.
Thus, the prohibition of torture stands as the prohibition of
something that as yet is undefined in conventions of the jus in bello
that declare torture malum prohibitum. Yet torture, by any definition,
is notoriously practiced by revolutionary/counterinsurgency belligerents. There is no warrant in positive international law for recognizing this state of affairs by providing for some kinds of limited exceptions to the prohibitions against torture, or guidelines to control
such limited exceptions, as I attempted to do in War and/or Survival. [20] Moreover, it appears that torture rarely obtains reliable,
useful information that could not be obtained by skilled interrogators
operating with other information sources with which to confront the
prisoner. Still, in extreme cases, particularly in revolutionary/
counterinsurgency conflicts, torture to obtain vital information may
appear necessary, even to a generally just and law-abiding belligerent.

The subject will undoubtedly continue to frustrate efforts to prescribe and enforce realistic but humane regulations for the conduct of international and noninternational conflicts.[21]

I have argued that torture differs from mistreatment of PWs and detainees in that it could possibly have the purpose of obtaining vital information. This at least raises the problem of the evil means to a good and important end. Unhappily, torture is also imposed for other ends that are not defensible. The most common purpose both of mistreatment and torture in communist belligerent practice is to "reeducate" the captives to a view sympathetic to that of the captors. A related practice is to force the PWs and detainees to collaborate in imposing the will of the captors throughout the camps, down to the last prisoner and the last small matter of attitudes and behavior. These violations of the jus in bello protecting PWs have already been mentioned in the preceding chapter dealing with conventional war.[22] If anything, the tendency of communist revolutionary forces in revolutionary/counterinsurgency conflicts is to exercise even greater coercion on prisoners of war, both of the incumbent regime and of the regime's intervening allies.

Most of the mistreatment and even the torture that is carried out for illicit purposes does not qualify as brainwashing, wherein the whole orientation and value system of the prisoner is negated and replaced with a puppetlike adherence to that of the captor. But, to varying degrees, torture and mistreatment wreck the physical health and moral will of prisoners so that they become pliable tools of their captors. The most significant result of this process is coerced statements to be used for propaganda purposes. Given the important, if not decisive, role of domestic and international public opinion in determining the outcome of contemporary revolutionary wars, such propaganda, the fruits of flagrant violations of the jus in bello and the human rights of the captives, is one of the most outrageous weapons of modern revolutionary/counterinsurgency war. Torture and mistreatment to "reeducate" and to elicit cooperation for propaganda purposes is prohibited by the just-war doctrine and the positive law of war to all belligerents in all wars, and it should be considered a matter of special concern to prevent such behavior by forces of the United States and its allies.

Collective Punishment

Another practice prohibited by the jus in bello but flourishing in revolutionary/counterinsurgency wars is the infliction of collective punishments. This practice is prohibited by the 1949 Geneva Civilians Convention, Article 33, and the 1977 Geneva Protocol II, Article

4(2)(b). Both sides in such wars attempt to maintain control of the population through the threat and imposition of such collective punishments as fines, forced contributions, destruction of whole locales or areas allegedly used by the enemy, and the like. Such practices are not without credible rationales. If there is a conspicuous degree of cooperation and support for a party to the conflict in a locale or area, whether this collaboration be voluntary or coerced, the course of such a war may be decisively affected. Revolutionaries, in particular, require base areas that are supportive. Without them their operations become difficult or impossible. Discouraging such support through collective penalties imposed on the support locales or areas is a plausible strategy. On the other hand, such practices are indiscriminate, tend to be disproportionate, and are clearly prohibited by the jus in bello. Moreover, the effectiveness of collective punishment is highly questionable. There is good reason to believe that its negative repercussions outweigh its deterrent and utilitarian effects. The rule against collective punishment being unequivocal, proposed exceptions would have to manifest clear military necessity, high prospects of effectiveness of the measures, and serious efforts to limit the deleterious effects of the measures on protected persons.

Hostages

Taking hostages is a perennial practice in revolutionary/counterinsurgency war. The usual form is to take individuals who are highly thought of in the community and/or persons suspected of collaboration with the enemy and to hold them as hostages to ensure the cooperation of the general population or the inhabitants of a particular area. Although also employed by revolutionaries, particularly in contemporary hijackings and kidnappings, the historic practice of taking hostages is associated primarily with counterinsurgents (including belligerent occupation forces). Typically, at the occurrence of an attack against the counterinsurgents (for example, a bridge is blown up, sentries are murdered, a convoy is ambushed) a demand will be made to the population and their representatives to turn over those responsible for the attacks or assist in their apprehension. If the cooperation demanded is not forthcoming, there is the certainty that a certain number of the hostages will be executed. Often a drastic ratio will be set such as 100 hostages executed for every government or occupying-power soldier killed by the revolutionaries or resistance groups.[23]

The development of the jus in bello on this subject has been somewhat belated. The practice was well known at the time of the drafting of the 1899 and 1907 Hague Conventions, but the question was not covered by them. Accordingly, when, after World War II, Germany commanders were accused of taking and executing hostages as a war crime, they could respond with justification that there was no rule of international law against the practice. In the Nuremberg trial of U.S. v. List et al., the issue was so central that the case was termed the Hostage case. [24] In that case the tribunal ruled that an occupied population had minimal responsibilities of cooperation with the belligerent occupant and the duty to respect the occupant's security requirements. Additionally, the tribunal concluded that many of the anti-German partisan bands did not comply with the requirements of the law of war and were not entitled to the rights of lawful belligerents. The court rules that extreme enforcement measures were justified in cases where the occupied population did not fulfill their minimal obligations to the occupying power and the nature and conduct of resistance groups violated the law of war. As a last resort, the taking and execution of hostages was condoned by the tribunal. [25]

However, the taking of hostages is flatly prohibited by common Article 3 of the 1949 Geneva Conventions and Article 4(2)(c) of the 1977 Geneva Protocol II. Notwithstanding the arguments of the tribunal in the Hostage case, it would appear that the taking and execution of hostages is a cruel and provocative practice that often causes the belligerent employing it to lose more than it gains. The practice is an obvious source of alienation from the side that employs it.

However, the same practical conclusions may not apply to revolutionaries and resistance groups as they do counterinsurgents and occupying powers. The essence of contemporary terrorist hijacking and kidnapping is the taking and threatened execution of hostages. This is sometimes an effective way to secure recognition as a belligerent, to obtain release of fellow revolutionaries or terrorists, to obtain large sums of needed funds, and to spread the fear and apprehension that are important components in the revolutionaries' strategies. It seems unlikely that revolutionaries will forego this means. This may mean yet another instance in which the counterinsurgent is expected to obey the law while the revolutionaries are excused from compliance. Of course, the counterinsurgents may reject this one-sided proposition and continue to use the hostage as a weapon. [26]

Terrorism

The jus in bello prohibition of terrorism combines some of the problems of the prohibition of torture and of taking hostages. As in the case of torture, we have a prohibition without an authoritative definition. Since terrorism is an even broader and less self-evident term than torture, it is difficult to know what to make of its inclusion in common Article 3 of the 1949 Geneva Conventions and Article 4(2)(d) and Article 13 (discussed in the preceding chapter) of the 1977 Geneva Protocol II. The concept of terrorism seems to be directed at belligerent acts neither justified by military necessity nor permitted by the laws of war; its purpose is to spread terror in the target society and break the morale of the civilian population. Terrorism would generally involve violations of the principle of discrimination by attacking noncombatants and nonmilitary targets. Some acts are solely terroristic (for example, strafing refugee columns that are clearly separate from military targets). Other acts have military utility as well as a terrorist effect (for example, terror bombing of cities in which there are military targets [discussed in Chapter 4]). The key elements of the concept would seem to be the intent to use terror, the effect of terror, and the relative absence of proportionate military necessity for the measures taken.

Terrorism, unfortunately, shares with the taking of hostages the quality of prospective effectiveness, particularly for revolutionaries. The explicit, intentional use of terror as a standard strategy and tactic in the Maoist forms of revolutionary war has been recalled above.[27] There is little reason to expect that established revolutionary doctrine and past success will be repudiated by revolutionaries in order to respect the international law of war. In the case of counterinsurgents, terrorism, like the taking of hostages, is probably not a useful means for the belligerent supposedly fighting for law and order. Counterinsurgents tempted to fight terrorist fire with fire should be deterred by respect for the law of war and by enlightened self-interest.

Outrages against Personal Dignity

Outrages against personal dignity, prohibited by common Article 3 of the 1949 Geneva Conventions and Article 4(2)(e) of the 1977 Geneva Protocol II, are common in revolutionary/counterinsurgency war. Even if ordinary citizens escape direct attacks, collective punishments, arrest as hostages, and the direct effects of terrorism, the endless probing and counterprobing of this kind of war will usually reach the citizens and violate their personal dignity. To the extent that either side is interested in the long-range cooperation of such citizens, rude, undignified, and degrading treatment is counterproductive as well as illegal. Indeed, the positive elements in both revolutionary and counterinsurgency doctrine and practice specifically enjoin the forces in the field to prevent outrages against personal dignity. Nevertheless, the harsh practices of these wars seem to render inevitable frequent violation of this rule.

Slavery

One is tempted to pass by the prohibition against slavery in the 1977 Geneva Protocol II, Article 4(2)(f) as remote from the practice of belligerents. However, Nazi, Soviet, Red Chinese, and other totalitarian practice has developed the institution of slave labor and slave-labor camps wherein the inmates are held indefinitely and/or worked to death. [28] Usually such slavery will be explained as punishment for enemies of the people and/or "reeducation" of persons whose social antecedents, orientation, and conduct are incompatible with the regime or revolutionary belligerent. No excuse is to be found in legitimate military necessity for this kind of exploitation, degradation, and extermination of human beings, so there is no question of reconciling such necessity with the laws of war. The practice is illegal and immoral, although, unfortunately, not uncommon in revolutionary/counterinsurgency wars.

Pillage

Pillage is looting by individual soldiers. Long prohibited by custom, it has been contrary to conventional international law since the Hague Convention II of 1899 and is generally considered incompatible with necessary military discipline. Nevertheless, armies and revolutionary forces are sometimes permitted or even encouraged to engage in pillage. It has a terroristic effect, if that is desired. Pillage is also sometimes justified by military commanders as a reward for the hazards of combat, an attitude that is as old as history. However, it must be emphasized that the best doctrine and practice for revolutionary/counterinsurgency wars, on both sides, stands strongly in opposition to the condoning, much less the encouragement, of pillage. Troop excesses in this regard have proved to be one of the most damaging sources of opposition and resentment on the part of civilians. Here is a case where political and military necessity reinforce the jus in bello.

Denial to Internees and Detainees of
Reasonable Treatment and Due Process of Law

The 1977 Geneva Protocol II, Articles 4-6, requires that internees and detainees be accorded reasonable treatment and due process of law. [30] These requirements will usually affect the counterinsurgents more than the revolutionaries, since the former normally have much greater power and facilities to round up and detain suspects.

It is characteristic of revolutionary war that both sides must deal with subversive infiltrators and spies. Typically, the counterinsurgent side finds this more of a problem because the government organization is large, often disorganized and inefficient, and easily penetrated, whereas the revolutionaries are commanded by a small, tight, secret, highly disciplined organization. As a result, any accumulation of detainees in government custody is almost certain to include a very mixed bag of innocent people, enemy sympathizers, and dangerous subversives and spies. It is difficult at best to balance their rights to reasonable treatment and due process with the right of the regime to deal with truly dangerous persons who may be buried in this heterogeneous collection. Nevertheless, the counterinsurgent side must make every effort to accord reasonable treatment and due process in substantiation of its own domestic claims of legitimacy and in deference to the requirements of the jus in bello. The difficulties of South Vietnam and the United States in dealing with charges of mistreatment of detainees, discussed in Chapter 5, are illustrative of the problem and its seriousness for counterinsurgents.

Although the revolutionaries are unlikely to accumulate large numbers of captives, they have detainees of their own. Their problem, as with military PWs, is to meet reasonable standards of care and due process in primitive and precarious circumstances.

Starvation of Civilians as a Method of Combat

Starvation as both a strategic and tactical method of combat is well established in conventional war. It has been carried out historically by land armies, naval blockade, and, more recently, by aerial interdiction. Now the 1977 Geneva Protocol II has prohibited, in Article 14, "starvation of civilians as a method of combat." This prohibition should be interpreted in the light of the parallel provision of 1977 Geneva Protocol I, Article 54, mentioned in Chapter 3 as well as of Article 70 of relief actions in Protocol I.

While the intention of this rule is undoubtedly good, its interpretation and application will be difficult. The rule prohibits comprehensive interdiction of food supplies leading to starvation within an area as well as the systematic destruction of food supplies. But starvation by interdiction will be difficult to disentangle from the normal maneuvering of forces. If such maneuvers result in large numbers of civilians being trapped in areas where there are insufficient food supplies, we confront the ancient problem of the siege. Traditionally, international law has supported the right of the siege force to refuse to permit the evacuation of noncombatants through its lines to escape the dangers of combat and starvation. This traditional

right obviously enhanced the besieging force's chances for victory.
Indeed, in periods where defensive works were virtually invulnerable,
this was the main weapon available to siege forces. It would appear
that the rule against starvation as a method undertakes to remove this
historic right.[31]

While starvation blockades of large areas, whole countries, and
even continents may be strategic in scope, the description of starvation in Article 14 as a "method of combat" suggests a tactical use,
albeit such use might be part of a strategic pattern. As a method of
combat, it seems most likely that starvation would be employed by
counterinsurgents against areas supporting the revolutionaries, as in
the Biafran War.[32] However, it is possible that revolutionary forces
might develop sufficient interdictory capabilities to use starvation as
either a strategic or tactical method. In both cases, respect for the
new rule would entail relinquishing a proved, effective, and militarily
economical means of war. Whether this will occur is uncertain. The
alternative strategies and tactics may involve substantial losses on
the part of the belligerent foregoing starvation as a method of combat.
Such belligerents may not think that they should be compelled to make
such sacrifices to protect populations supportive of the enemy.

Where the method of combat prohibited by the 1977 Geneva Protocols I and II is interpreted to mean destruction of crops and food
stocks, it could apply to both sides in a revolutionary/counterinsur-
gency war. Here the limitation is more direct and stark. I assume
that such destruction could be separated from ordinary combat maneuvering. The presumably more technologically advanced counterinsurgent forces might emulate U.S. practices in Vietnam and destroy
crops intended for insurgent use by air attacks with herbicides. They
might also destroy crops and food stocks on the ground during sweep-
ings through areas considered to be permanently committed to the
revolutionaries.[33] The revolutionaries might do the same against
areas thought to be loyal to the regime. The effectiveness of such
measures would vary with the particular circumstances. The new
rule represents a humanitarian attempt to remove a cruel but time-
honored method of war. Whether this attempt will be successful in
light of the possible costs in terms of losses from alternative means
and strategies remains to be seen.

Forced Displacement of Civilians

The last specific prohibition of the positive international-law
jus in bello to be considered is that against forced displacement of
civilians. With respect to international conflict, Article 49 of the
1949 Geneva Civilians Conventions flatly prohibits massed forcible

transfers or deportations of protected persons to the territory of the occupying power or to any other country, "regardless of their motive." Article 49 then provides that "the Occupying Power may undertake total or partial evacuation of a given area if the security of the population or imperative military reasons so demand." Conditions for such a transfer are to be limited to what is unavoidable. The conditions provide for the care and protection of such protected persons during their displacement. This article governing international conflict provides the background for the new provision, Article 17 in the 1977 Geneva Protocol II for noninternational conflicts.

> 1. The displacement of the civilian population shall not be ordered for reasons related to that conflict unless the security of the civilians involved or imperative military reasons so demand. Should such displacements have to be carried out, all possible measures shall be taken in order that the civilian population may be received under satisfactory conditions of shelter, hygiene, health and nutrition.
> 2. Civilians shall not be compelled to leave their own territory for reasons connected with the conflict.

Article 17 addresses a serious problem. Whether it will prove sufficient to deal with it is problematic. Displacement of civilian populations is a common strategy in counterinsurgency war. It accomplishes several things. First, it removes portions of the population from vulnerability to attack, intimidation, and exploitation by the revel forces. Second, it takes civilians out of areas of likely combat, thus protecting them. Third and related to the second objective, it leaves behind areas that become eligible for designation as free-fire zones, or the more restricted specified strike zones, in which it can be assumed that everything that moves has an enemy character and is a legitimate target. This simplifies greatly tactical and ground attack procedures. Mass population displacements are akin to scorched-earth policies in that they leave the enemy in a zone depleted of human resources and subject to uninhibited attack.[34]

Such displacements in counterinsurgency war are common, not exceptional; strategic more often than tactical. If it can be managed satisfactorily, there is much to be said for denuding large areas (from which revolutionary forces operate) of their normal populations for extended periods of time. Thus, the conditions of the elastic clause of Article 17 that such displacements "shall not be ordered for reasons related to the conflict unless the security of the civilians involved or imperative military reasons so demand" are rather easily met. The counterinsurgents, through their own strategies and tactics, create, together with the revolutionary forces, a threat to the security of the civilians and the imperative military reasons for evacuating them. In order to violate this prohibition, the counterinsurgents would have to be guilty of displacement of persons in areas little affected by the conflict. Usually they would have no reason to do this, and it does not loom as a great problem. In most situations of population displacement, there will be a plausible security threat and military necessity. The exception to this evaluation would be in the case of ideological, political, even genocidal, motivations for massive population transfers as in the case of Nazi practices in World War II.

I am cognizant of the bitter denunciations of U.S. and South Vietnamese evacuations and population transfers in the Vietnam War, as discussed in Chapter 5. [35] Although the search-and-destroy strategies and tactics that generated refugees and provided the military necessity basis for many evacuations have been severely criticized, there is no particular prohibition against them in the positive law of war, and their conformity to the principles of proportion and discrimination is a matter of case-by-case judgment in context. Moreover, as observed in Chapter 5, the revolutionaries, by using the people as the sea in which the Maoist fishes swim, invite strategies of population displacement by the counterinsurgents. Thus, the issues of the "security of the civilians" and the "imperative military reasons" are created by the belligerent interaction of the conflict. It seems to me difficult to challenge the prudential decisions of the counterinsurgents to deal with the problem of the enemy's use of the population by removing the population in enemy-controlled areas.

To the extent, then, that the conditions laid down by the positive law of war for population displacement are not very restrictive, the crux of the matter is implementation of the rules protecting displaced persons. It appears, for example, that the government of South Vietnam did not provide adequately for the refugees produced either by mass population displacements or by the tide of battle. As discussed in Chapter 5, this finally required new strategies of deliberately reducing operations that generated displaced persons. The lesson is that a counterinsurgent power, using its competence to remove the population from insecure and/or combat areas, must either provide the satisfactory treatment demanded by Article 17 or shape its strategies so as to abate the flow of new refugees to crowded and inadequate camps, as was ultimately done in Vietnam.

The combination of massive population displacement with heavy use of firepower is the essence of the threat to the population prohibited in the 1977 Geneva Protocol II, Article 13, discussed at the beginning of this section. While there is no doubt that population displacement, like the use of massive firepower, can be violative of both the principles of proportion and discrimination, there is equally no doubt that each means used properly is indispensable to the fighting of counterinsurgent warfare. It is likewise clear that the use and abuse of the population as a shield, cover, and resource by revolutionary forces may be violative of the principles of proportion and discrimination because it predictably invites the destructive and disruptive counterinsurgency strategies that have been discussed. At the same time, such use of the population is indispensable to the success of the revolutionaries. It is for these reasons that I say that it is problematic whether Article 17 will provide sufficient guidance for the resolution of the profound and perhaps intractable problems of revolutionary/counterinsurgency war.

The direction to follow in resolving these dilemmas is clear. The counterinsurgents must improve their capacity to protect the security of the population and find more discriminating means of attacking the revolutionaries. But this prescription calls for great resources and for substantial and continuing success in battle, neither of which are easily come by in revolutionary/counterinsurgency wars. Like so many of the dilemmas of such conflicts, the line is very thin between tolerable voluntary relinquishment in the name of the law of needed means and imposition of restraints so great as to materially risk reasonable chances for success.

REPRISALS IN REVOLUTIONARY/ COUNTERINSURGENCY WAR

The basic analysis of the role of reprisals and their legal limits under the jus in bello, submitted in Chapter 3, ought, in my view, to apply essentially to revolutionary/counterinsurgency war.[36] There is a technical legal difficulty with this position, however. Although some revolutionary/counterinsurgency wars are mixed civil-international wars and, therefore, rather clearly governed by the regular law of international conflicts, many are only civil wars and are governed explicitly only by common Article 3 of the 1949 Geneva Conventions and the 1977 Geneva Protocol II for noninternational conflict.

A strict interpretation of the law governing noninternational conflict would hold that, since the provisions of the 1949 Geneva Conventions, with the exception of common Article 3, as well as of the 1977 Geneva Protocol I, do not apply to noninternational conflicts, their respective prohibitions against particular reprisals do not apply to such conflicts. Thus, many of the specific and far-reaching limits on the use of reprisals noted in Chapter 3 would not apply in noninternational conflicts. I have taken the position that, as much as possible, the regular international-law jus in bello should be applied and adapted to noninternational conflicts.

Thus, for example, I would want PWs in noninternational conflicts to have the same immunity from reprisals enjoyed by PWs in international conflicts. While protection of the wounded, sick, medical personnel, and medical buildings have not been discussed here, I would want the same protection against reprisals for them in noninternational conflicts. Finally, it would seem important to extend the protection of objects indispensable to the survival of the civilian population to include the same protection against reprisals as is provided by Article 54 of Protocol I for international conflicts.

Two general comments may be made with respect to reprisals in revolutionary/counterinsurgency war. First, such conflicts are notorious for reprisal spirals in which a constantly escalating and expanding chain of reprisals and counterreprisals collapse any pretense of conducting the war in accordance with the jus in bello. This is wrong in itself and should be prevented. Second, most of the evidence would support the position that these reprisal spirals produce results clearly contrary to the political goals of the war on both sides. It is hard enough to win the hearts and minds of the people and conduct successful revolutionary or counterinsurgency operations. When the viciousness of reprisals, generally against the innocent, is added to such a war, all hope of achieving a just and lasting settlement is removed.

Having said this, the point made in Chapter 3 about reprisals must be reiterated.[37] Abstention from reprisals may very well place the more law-abiding belligerent at a serious disadvantage vis-à-vis an enemy who consistently violates the jus in bello. In revolutionary/counterinsurgency war, this state of affairs could affect either side and could seriously influence the outcome of the conflict.

At this point a few summary reflections are in order on the material and normative dilemmas of revolutionary/counterinsurgency war, the most common form of modern conflict. While it is true that the circumstances of the belligerents in revolutionary/counterinsurgency war vary greatly, recurring characteristics typify the parties to such conflicts, and these belligerents tend to employ typical strategies and tactics. The strategies and tactics of revolutionary belligerents have repeatedly taken forms involving violations of the principles of proportion, discrimination, the prohibition of genocide, and a number of specific prohibitions of the 1949 Geneva Conventions and the 1977 Geneva Protocols I and II to those Conventions. These violations do not necessarily reflect a wanton disregard for the law. Rather, they often represent an example of the classic clash between the demands of true military necessity and the limitations of the just-war and positive international-law jus in bello.

While the usual circumstances of revolutionary/counterinsurgency wars do not often place counterinsurgents in the position of having to

violate the jus in bello in order to be successful, counterinsurgency
also has its military necessities that clash with the restrictions of
the jus in bello. Two interrelated approaches have been suggested to
reconcile military necessity and the jus in bello in revolutionary/
counterinsurgency wars. One is the theory that the framers of the
laws of war have taken into consideration the reasonable limits of
military necessity and that belligerents should be able to fight effectively and have a chance for success without violating the laws. There
is considerable reason to question the credibility of this claim insofar
as revolutionary/counterinsurgency wars are concerned.

The second approach to reconciling military necessity in revo-
lutionary/counterinsurgency wars with the jus in bello emphasizes
the political nature of such conflicts. Such wars are as often won politically in the contested country and in the arena of international politics and opinion as on the battlefield. It can be argued persuasively
that it is good strategy to abide by the limitations of the law of war
and do the right thing as a matter of good policy, if not of legal and
moral obligation. This second approach deserves endorsement with
reservations. The first reservation concerns the real possibility of
revolutionary forces not having the capability of fighting effectively
without some of the means proscribed by the jus in bello and of meeting the requirements of the law regarding prisoners of war, detainees,
and civilian noncombatants.

The second reservation concerns the willingness of counterinsurgents to accept to their detriment a double standard under which
they are expected to respect the full measure of the jus in bello applicable to revolutionary/counterinsurgency wars while accepting the
prospects of serious and widespread violations of that law by the revolutionary belligerent. Despite its unfairness, acceptance of the
double standard may be the best policy for counterinsurgents. However, the temptation of taking retaliatory actions will persist, despite
the virtual elimination of reprisals as a legally permissible option
under the present conventional law of war.

With these reservations, it is possible to conclude that adherence to the jus in bello is the best course for a belligerent in a revo-
lutionary/counterinsurgency war. Even an imperfect record of compliance with the law of war will tend to advance a revolutionary or
counterinsurgent belligerent's claims to legitimacy, internally and
internationally. It will continue to be difficult to reconcile the present
jus in bello with the military necessities of revolutionary/counterin-
surgency warfare. Nevertheless, the jus in bello holds out a standard
of conduct that good policy as well as international law enjoin on revolutionaries and counterinsurgents alike.[38]

PART II

LIMITED WAR

9

THE MEANING OF LIMITED WAR

The meaning of limited war today is a result of trends in the contemporary international system since its establishment in the seventeenth century. The present so-called Westphalian system of multiple sovereign state actors emerged from a period of religious wars. These wars had tended in many ways to become total war. However, the period from 1648 to 1789 was marked by the ascendency of limited wars for limited political purposes. With the French revolutionary and Napoleonic wars, the seeds of modern total war were sowed. The profound ideological rifts opened between the revolutionary and counterrevolutionary societies tended to make the ends and consequences of war in Europe more total. At the time, however, the means available were still comparatively limited, although the great increase in the size of armies produced greater effects than had been the case in limited wars fought by small professional armies.

It remained for the American Civil War to begin to link the greatly enhanced means being produced by modern science and technology in the age of the Industrial Revolution with the far-reaching ideological ends that increasingly characterized modern conflicts. The result in the American Civil War was the first modern total war. By the time of World War I, the means available to belligerents had become so devastating that there was an imbalance between them and the ends actually pursued. Indeed, as Aron has said, exaggerated ends had to be made up to justify the far-reaching effects of the means.[1]

World War II completed the evolution of modern total war. In this conflict the stakes were profound, involving quite different ways of life that had proved to be incompatible. Moreover, advances in military science and technology provided means that were sufficiently destructive to be termed <u>total</u> in the preatomic age. Those who viewed Germany in the summer of 1945 would not complain that the term <u>total</u>

war was exaggerated. Yet, on August 6, 1945, the concept of total war took a quantum jump with the advent at Hiroshima of atomic war. It then became necessary to distinguish between conventional total war and nuclear total war. Given the open-ended character of competing ideological and political causes and of military technology, the characterization total will always remain relative. Still, it is an important historical fact that all-out total wars have been fought in which there were virtually no restraints, with effects that are morally unacceptable and politically unjustified. The modern effort to revive the concept of limited war seeks to ensure that future conflicts will be both morally acceptable and politically justified; that they will be both just and limited.

In this chapter I will review briefly the antecedents of contemporary limited-war theory and practice. Then I will offer some guidelines for limited war in lieu of a definition. The substantial literature on the subject and the history of recent limited wars reveal some recurring themes that may be combined in a broad outline or checklist of components of limited war. Unlike the just-war conditions, they have not been formed into a coherent whole. The extent to which these limited-war concepts are considered obligatory for one professing to hold a limited-war position is not as great as that to which just-war proponents may be held to just-war precepts. Nonetheless, there are some basic propositions that are generally agreed upon by limited-war theorists and practitioners. I will undertake to summarize and analyze these basic propositions in this chapter. In Chapters 9, 10, and 11 I will investigate the application of these limited-war guidelines in terms of the experience in three contemporary wars.

THE ANTECEDENTS OF
CONTEMPORARY LIMITED WAR

Contemporary limited war has a number of sources. The most important appear to be modern political realism and the development of national security studies, the U.S. containment policy, the evolution of efforts at collective security and collective defense, the reaction against the variety of total war characterized by World War II, the search for strategic alternatives to nuclear war and massive retaliation, the experience of the Korean War, the United States Army's search for a role in the nuclear age, the rise of counterinsurgency, and revived just-war doctrine.

Political Realism and National Security Studies

The dominant approach to international politics in the interwar period was political idealism. As remarked in the opening pages

of this book, the age of Wilson and the League of Nations sought to replace the discredited political system that had brought on World War I
with a new system based on international law and organization. This
idealist approach expected that nations could be persuaded to renounce
the war system in exchange for new international institutions for settlement of disputes, backed up by collective security.

World War II proved that these hopes had been in vain. Accordingly, the most significant difference between the new United Nations
and the League lay in the provisions for collective security, epitomized in the creation of a powerful Security Council. Although stress
was still placed on peaceful settlement of disputes, there was a new
emphasis on putting "teeth" into international institutions through enforcement action by the Security Council. Although the hopes for collective security were, in their turn, to die, it is important to note
this fundamental alteration in the outlook within the international system with respect to war and peace. The principal organizers of the
1945 San Francisco Conference were moving the nations from an
idealistic faith in peaceful change and disarmament to a realistic emphasis on force to maintain international order.

Meanwhile, in the growing discipline of international relations,
the post-World War II period was one of great realistic ascendency.
Hans Morgenthau led a new wave of scholars concerned with the realities of power politics rather than aspirations for changing the international system.[2] The realists, whether political practitioners
or scholars, held to basically pessimistic concepts of human nature,
political society, and politics that emphasized the balancing of competing interests rather than the replacement of competitive power
politics with institutions based on mutual trust and devotion to the
common good.

For these realists, military coercion was not the unnatural, inherently evil, potentially uncontrollable force of nature that it was
thought to be by many of the idealists. Coercion, including armed
coercion, was considered to be a normal, if dangerous, instrument
of politics. Realists followed the Clausewitzian dictum that war is a
continuation of politics by other means. Accordingly, the problem of
war was not its elimination, but its subordination to reasonable political purposes and limitations.[3]

The realists were, of course, decisively reinforced in their
views by the events of the late 1940s and the 1950s. Idealist solutions
were manifestly victims of the cold war.

It must be observed that the triumph of realism in the cold war
era was not a victory for amorality over morality. The realists, who
included thinkers such as Morgenthau, Niebuhr, Thompson, and
Lefever with serious normative concerns, were insistent that law,
order, and justice not be abandoned in the futile pursuit of idealist

goals. [4] The fatal weakness of idealism in the post-World War II period was that it did not distinguish between the justice, however imperfect, of the so-called Free World and the totalitarian injustice of the communist world. The concepts and institutions of the idealists were addressed to a system made up of actors of approximately equal character in terms of the justice of their regimes. The differences between these actors were seen as amenable to peaceful solution through international law and organization. The possibility that there might be differences between international actors so fundamental that they should be beyond peaceful settlement was not contemplated in the idealist approach. The problem of seeking and defending justice through recourse to armed force was, however, recognized in the realist approach; it is not surprising, therefore, that the post-World War II era of conflict became the Age of Realism par excellence. In brief, political realism reiterated the proposition that armed coercion within the international system is natural and at times necessary, and that the problem of war is that of controlling such armed coercion through intelligent political direction rather than outlaw it or wish it away in exhortations to establish a new international system based on mutual trust.

As a result of the realist approach in politics and in the study of international relations, as well as of the implications of contemporary events, a new scholarly discipline emerged—the national security field. The emphases varied from traditional military history, arts, and science to military technology to behavioral studies of deterrence and conflict management. Gradually, these studies produced a new subfield of arms control wherein traditional disarmament concepts were related to the requirements of national security. In academia and in the new defense studies, "think tanks," defense scholars, and analysts addressed the complex problems of defense and arms control and thereby formed a solid and influential base for the development of limited-war concepts and policies. [5]

The development of national-security studies, however, did not mean that limited-war theories would necessarily become the source of all subsequent limited-war policies. As will be seen in the ensuing discussion, limited-war postures and conduct may be the result of antecedent limited-war theories, or they may result spontaneously from various other sources and influences. Indeed, one must be careful not to assume that limited-war postures and conduct are caused by limited-war theories simply because the link seems logical or plausible. Nevertheless, it is certainly true that the development of limited-war theories created a general atmosphere in which decision makers were more likely to think in limited-war terms, granted that other influences also caused them to think that way.

U.S. Containment Policy

The policy of containment adopted by the U.S. government under Truman and more or less acquiesced in by the Western Allies provided the requirement for defense of the so-called Free World, which, in turn, almost inevitably demanded limited-war policies and capabilities. Containment confronted the communist threat to the noncommunist world. The containment policy assumed several things about the Communist threat. First, it assumed that communist regimes violated basic human rights and values. Wherever possible, therefore, alternatives to communist domination must be provided and defended. Communism was unequivocably considered an evil to be avoided and, if necessary, fought. Second, it was taken as given that communist strategy, particularly that of the Soviet Union, was dynamic and would move to fill power vacuums and probe weak areas in the noncommunist world. There is, in brief, a communist threat. This threat is worldwide and must be contained wherever it constitutes a clear and present danger to states seeking freedom to choose noncommunist alternatives.

In the years since the late 1940s, the character and imminence of this threat has been downgraded, if not discredited. Today there is much less certainty about the evil character of communist regimes and their imperialist propensities. There is a tendency to believe that communist regimes become more liberal over time and that they are more likely to be conservative than adventuresome in their foreign policies as they mature. The debate over these interpretations continues. In recent times, the renewed interest in human rights has once again brought out the extent to which the treatment of their own people by communist regimes is incompatible with fundamental human values reiterated in the West and in international law. The varying disappointments of détente underscore the dangers of deprecating communist expansionism. Although the cold war has been declared dead repeatedly by proponents of détente, the fact remains that the Soviet Union and other communist regimes still operate repressive societies of an irreversible nature, and that they continue to seek to export their ideology and political systems and impose them by intimidation and force when persuasion and subversion fail.[6]

Thus, limited war was a reaction to a specific threat—the communist threat in the 20 years following World War II. Over time the threat ceased to be monolithic, a fact constantly recited by those who then conclude that no serious threat remains. But, in fact, the communist threat became the communist threats. While the Soviet rift with the People's Republic of China (PRC) broke up the main communist partnership, the resultant breakup of the communist world into power blocs and alliances left the noncommunist world facing a number of continuing threats throughout the world (for example, from the Soviet Union, Cuba, the PRC, North Korea, Vietnam, and Cambodia). These threats of external direct and indirect aggression remain, of course, linked to internal threats to security ranging from revolution and subversion to acquisition of power by legal means, as in the case of so-called Eurocommunism.

The original containment policy was committed to the general proposition that communist regimes should be prevented from expansion through subversion and aggression. Despite revisionist views of the nature of communist states and their expansionist tendencies, this is still U.S. policy.[7] The United States remains opposed to the forcible imposition of communist regimes by direct or indirect aggression. Admittedly, this opposition has more recently been rather ineffectual in the cases of direct Soviet and Cuban military intervention in Africa and the Soviet invasion of Afghanistan. The continuation of the containment policy means that limited-war policies and capabilities are still necessary for the defense of the noncommunist world.

The containment policy was based on further assumptions beyond those concerning the communist threat. It assumed a theory of international momentum. Drawing on the sad experiences with expansionist totalitarian regimes of the 1930s, the practitioners of containment were deeply convinced that successful aggression breeds more aggression. An aggressor, such as Hitler or the Japanese warlords, who remains unopposed tends to proliferate and accelerate his aggressions. Munichs lead to world wars. Accordingly, containment tended toward forward policies, even in areas of secondary importance where defense would be difficult, on the theory that aggression must be stopped at the earliest possible moment. Otherwise, it was believed, aggression will gather momentum and continue at ever more dangerous levels.

The theory of momentum has been absorbed in the domino theory, first articulated as such by President Eisenhower on April 8, 1954.[8] This absorption of the concept of international momentum into the domino theory is unfortunate in that Eisenhower's version is more narrow and particularistic. In this instance, the broader concept has been subsumed and in part obscured by a more narrow corollary. Eisenhower seemed to be arguing that if one country in Southeast Asia fell to aggression, adjacent countries would be prone to aggression in a geographic progression of conquests. Given the fact that each victim of aggression furnishes bases for both direct and indirect attacks against its neighbors, there is considerable validity to Eisenhower's domino theory. Moreover, the domino theory assumed that successive, successful aggressions would take on a momentum characteristic of international power relations. But, of course, each actor in a potential domino situation has its own strengths and weaknesses. If Vietnam falls to the Communists, Thailand is more vulnerable to communist direct and/or indirect aggression. It is not, however, inevitable that Thailand will be the next to fall, as suggested by the domino theory.

The broader concept of momentum transcends the geographical character of the domino theory. The concept of momentum addresses a worldwide arena when the potential aggressor has worldwide aspirations, which is true of the Soviet Union and, to varying degrees, of other communist regimes (for example, the PRC and Cuba). Thus, the links were seen by the practitioners of containment between the recurring Berlin crises and other threats to the North Atlantic Treaty Organization (NATO), the Korean War, the Vietnam War, the Cuban missile crisis, and the threat of exported revolution and indirect aggression in the Third World in the 1960s.

President Johnson, Dean Rusk, and the other principal architects of the Vietnam War were firm believers in the concept of momentum and acted in reliance on it. That conviction on their part received the more narrow label of the domino theory. Accordingly, in the post-Vietnam War era, the rationale for early resistance to aggression in order to stop its momentum has been in good measure discredited. Indeed, any rationale for the Vietnam War or anything like it is widely rejected and the domino theory has become one of the symbols of the supposedly disastrous Vietnam policy. This is unfortunate because the momentum concept remains valid, and it is an important foundation for the concept of limited war.

In summary, the containment policy was based both on the general concept of momentum and on the more particular corollary domino theory. One further point should be reiterated and emphasized. As remarked above, it is assumed in the containment policy that if resistance to aggression is postponed there is a serious danger that an ultimately inevitable confrontation will take the form of a catastrophic, central, total war rather than a local, limited war.

Collective Security and Collective Defense

Limited war is a natural policy for states dedicated to the concepts of collective security and collective defense. The two concepts are frequently confused and the usage seems to have become imprecise. Collective security is a total system within which individual recourse to force is prohibited and a central authority enforces this prohibition by sanctions. In principle, this central authority possesses a monopoly of legitimate force, as in a national public order. Both the League of Nations and the United Nations established collective security systems. The basic concept requires that all law-abiding participants in the system combine to suppress violations of the ban on individual recourse to armed coercion through enforcement action directed by a central authority. In the case of the United Nations, this is the Security Council. The underlying concept is that of the indivisibility of peace. Aggression anywhere within the system is a threat to all members of the system and to the security of the system as a whole.

Collective defense is the term for a defensive system against a potential aggression originating outside the system. It is a quasi-permanent alliance wherein all of the allies pledge that they will consider an attack against any of them to be an attack against all of them. The prototype is NATO. The collective defense efforts are coordinated by the NATO command structure.

It will be recalled that contemporary international law permits two forms of legal recourse to armed coercion. The first, enforcement action as a sanction of the United Nations or its regional agent, must be authorized by the UN Security Council. It is conceivable that a collective defense organization such as NATO might be ordered or authorized to take such enforcement action, but, given the identity of potential aggressors and their positions on the Security Council, this is unlikely. What is more likely is that members in a collective defense organization would justify their actions as collective self-defense under Article 51 of the UN Charter. This is the second permissible form of armed coercion under the UN system.

It is inherent in the concept of UN enforcement action as a sanction for collective security that the armed coercion take the form of limited war. The popular characterization of such coercion as a "police action" underscores its requirement of a limited, controlled effort to force an aggressor to desist. This is not to say that the appropriate ends and means of a limited war as a police action may not become controversial. The Korean police action was not a true enforcement action, but it is the closest thing we have to such an action. The changing goals of that war and the debates over the various self-imposed limits observed by the UN side reveal some of the problems that might be encountered in defining the limits of a bona fide UN enforcement. However, logically, each enforcement action is inherently limited by the goal of repressing aggression and removing the threat to the peace it represents.

There is a further, practical reason for enforcement action under collective security being limited. The essence of participation in such actions is willingness to put the good of the whole community above the particularistic interests of the various members. An individual aggression may not seem to threaten various members of the collective security system. Thus, France was not too interested in resisting Japanese aggression in the Far East in the 1930s. Many members of the United Nations might not want to become involved in resisting aggression in the contemporary Middle East. For collective security to work, the participating states in the system must remain faithful to the underlying concept of the indivisibility of peace. They must act as though a threat to peace and security anywhere within the system ultimately threatens their own peace and security.

This principled commitment to collective security proved impossible to maintain under the League of Nations. Great Power rivalries have blocked Security Council enforcement orders that might test such commitments under the UN collective security system. Again, the Korean War demonstrates the difficulties of police actions. The contributing participants to the UN force showed themselves to be very concerned that the ends and means of the operation be as limited as possible and that the action be terminated as soon as possible.

Basically the same problem confronts collective defense systems. Theoretically, it might be expected that participants in such a system would have more definite interests in the defense of other members and of the designated defense area generally. However, even the NATO basic treaty leaves room for avoiding participation in common defense against aggression. While the treaty provides that an attack on one shall be considered as an attack against all, all members are not automatically obliged to go to war when an aggression occurs. They are only obligated to consult in order to consider an appropriate response. In the event of aggression, it might well develop that Italy did not want to participate in the defense of Norway nor Denmark in the defense of Turkey. To the extent that there is likely to be reluctance to go to war for the integrity of the total defense system and the specific protection of the victim of aggression, participants in an arrangement such as NATO will certainly want the joint defense to be as limited in ends, means, and duration as possible. [9]

While the abstract indivisibility-of-peace concept (global or regional, as the case may be) tends to produce limited war, it also adds an important dimension to the ends of such wars and thereby, potentially, to the means and duration of police actions and collective defenses. In addition to the particular end of stopping the aggression and making the victim whole again, there is the goal of upholding the credibility of the collective security or collective defense system itself. An important feature of the UN action in Korea was the concern to demonstrate that the UN system had "teeth" in it and that aggression could be and would be repelled.

Reaction against Total War

The limited-war concepts and policies of the post-World War II era have been strongly influenced by the reaction against conventional total war of the kind waged in the two world wars. The reaction includes a rejection of the total-war understanding of war itself as well as of twentieth century total-war ends and means. Modern total war seems to owe a great deal of its misguided character to the no-war/total-war syndrome that has been particularly prevalent in the Western democracies and, above all, in the United States. This syndrome begins with the idea that war is unnatural—an uncontrollable force once released. Sherman's characterization of war as hell, most recently recalled by Walzer,[10] well describes this understanding of war. The no-war/total-war position tends to advocate avoidance of war at almost any cost. This position often includes disregard for defense needs and preparedness. Then, having said that war is a hell to be avoided at all costs, and having fallen victim to aggression, the proponents of this view justify total war as a crusade of the righteous against the wicked. Crusaders, in principle, need heed no restraints, and the wicked deserve punishment and have no rights, a dangerous attitude engendering total-war attitudes and practices.[11]

The total-war crusades of the righteous victims of aggressions are notable for open-ended goals (epitomized by the demand for the Axis's unconditional surrender in World War II) and unrestricted means. In such wars the means tended to develop their own independent logic uncurtailed by adequate political ends and guidelines. The enemy was evil and must be punished. Bombing was a good form of punishment and thus was encouraged to the end of World War II, beyond military necessity. Interestingly, while the totalitarian participants in World War II also had ideological, open-ended goals, their means tended to be more controlled, in consonance with the principles of political supremacy over the military instrument and the military principle of economy of force to be discussed below.

Other characteristics of modern total wars center in the belligerent societies. Total mobilization of all resources, human and material, is the hallmark of such wars. As has been observed in discussing the just-war principle of discrimination, this invites attack on traditional noncombatants and on the very fabric of society itself. It has been thought necessary to sustain this total mobilization by virtually unlimited use of the psychological instrument at home and abroad. The enemy is depicted in terms calculated to elicit hate and fear and to support the war effort at the highest and most sustained level. In total war, the whole society is mobilized to give its all in the fight for survival against a feared and hated enemy. Naturally, this material and psychological mobilization produces attitudes and behavior incompatible with the resumption of peaceful relations with the enemy after the war.

It is gratifying that total mobilization and all-out psychological warfare have not succeeded in blocking for long reconciliation and un-

derstanding between former enemy peoples. The experience of the
Western Allies in World War II and their principal enemies, Germany
and Japan, is evidence of that. But we should not forget that the total-
war policies obtained during the world wars resulted in the conduct of
war in ways that violated basic principles of politics, military science,
law, and morality.

All of these facets of total war were reviewed and criticized
after World War II. There was particular concern about the relationship between the no-war/total-war syndrome and the political power
and public opinion of the masses. It was feared that popular support
could only be obtained and sustained for total wars with grand, pre-
tentious goals. Moreover, critics suggested that the policies most
reflective of the crusade attitudes of victims of aggression were the
most counterproductive. Thus, strategic bombing policies of countervalue attacks on population centers were seen as typical of total
war. The critics of these policies contended that it was the traditional
counterforce strategies of the ground and naval forces, with tactical
air support, that defeated Germany and reduced Japan to a hopeless
position before Hiroshima.

World War II, then, provided a poignant example of total war
against which a variety of critics reacted. Given the apparent continuing need for defense, these critics attacked underlying no-war/
total-war assumptions of total war as well as its propensity to encourage unlimited ends and means.

Alternatives to Nuclear War and Massive Retaliation

With the advent of the atomic age, it became clear that alternatives to nuclear war must be sought as a matter of the highest priority.
Some, of course, argued that nuclear war precluded the further utility
of armed coercion as an instrument of policy. Proposals for world
government and the rule of international law abounded. However, the
cold war, as well as the turbulence in the emerging Third World,
made clear that war in some form would continue to be a feature of
the international system. The question was, What kind of war?

Confronted with the possession of nuclear weapons by the United
States and, soon thereafter, the Soviet Union, strategists tended to
follow one of the two lines of approach to security requirements. One
was massive retaliation and the other limited war. Massive retaliation attempted to convert what turned out to be an ephemeral U.S. nuclear superiority into an all-purpose deterrent of all forms of aggression, anywhere. It soon became evident, however, that massive retaliation was not an adequate or comprehensive defense strategy. Massive
retaliation did not provide a credible deterrent to the infinite variety
of potential aggressions, direct and indirect, that confronted the Free

World. Moreover, as Soviet nuclear strength grew, the sufficiency of U.S. threats of massive retaliation even against major nuclear attack was put more and more into question. By the early 1960s, there were increasing indications of European concern about the ability of the United States to deter attacks on Europe by massive retaliations. In another few years the issue of the sufficiency of the U.S. nuclear deterrent was even being questioned in terms of its ability to ensure that the United States would not be directly attacked. Long before this point was reached, however, there was grave concern over the issue of whether the U.S. strategic nuclear deterrent was of any use except to deter strategic nuclear attack and whether it could, in fact, deter conventional attacks in Europe or other areas of prime U.S. interest. [12]

Some of the reaction against nuclear massive retaliation was based on attitudes that were to become outmoded. There was a tendency to consider nuclear war—often referred to as "the atomic bomb" or "the bomb"—as a monolithic means. There was great concern that "it" (that is, nuclear war) escapes control and, therefore, "it" is not a usable instrument of policy. This attitude was soon challenged by the development of tactical nuclear weapons and the adoption of tactical nuclear policies, strategies, and tactics in defense preparations. It should be observed, however, that the appearance of tactical nuclear weapons did not preclude a continued opposition to reliance on any nuclear weapons on the theory that the whole nuclear category should be held behind a firebreak or threshold.

In any event, massive retaliation was increasingly seen as an inflexible, partially irrelevant, unusable strategy. Accordingly, limited war in the broadest sense (that is, anything short of general nuclear war) became an inevitable defense option for any contingency other than the direct threat of nuclear aggression. Thus was born the dual posture of nuclear deterrence to deter nuclear aggression and, perhaps, a central conventional war between the superpowers and their allies and unlimited war to deal with all of the other threats. [13]

The Korean War

The experience of the Korean War substantially increased the importance of limited-war options as well as raising many difficult issues concerning their implementation. The Korean experience confirmed the analysis of the realists that international conflict would continue to be a major problem notwithstanding hopes for peace in the UN age. The nature of the Communist aggression in this war confirmed the need for containment as the policy for the United States and its allies. The conflict likewise confirmed the need for collective security where possible and, alternatively, collective defense.

Above all, the Korean conflict demonstrated both the need for and the feasibility of limited war in a local conflict where one superpower was a belligerent and the other the principal instigator and supporter of the opposing belligerents. It was clear that there would be wars serious enough to warrant limited defense but not sufficiently important to justify either full-scale conventional war or nuclear war. Although nuclear options were still severely limited because of the comparatively small number of atomic bombs then available, the Korean War nevertheless provided evidence that nuclear war may not be an appropriate strategic option. [14]

The Korean War also revealed quite clearly the difficulties that limited-war policies would encounter. Above all, the Korean experience showed the breadth and depth of the no-war/total-war attitude. General MacArthur articulated this attitude perfectly when he contrasted his preference for a world without war with the proposition that once war is waged, there is no substitute for victory. [15] Despite this deep-rooted opposition from the most famous U.S. general and a sizable portion of the Congress and public, the Korean War was kept limited. It is true that the war finally was brought to its stalemate end under Eisenhower's threat of nuclear attack and conventional bombing of China. However, the import of those threats remains speculative. The fact is that the Korean War was kept limited to the end, and that it did succeed in its purpose of resisting aggression and demonstrating the general efficacy of the Free World's ability to resist aggression.

The United States Army's Search for a Role in the Nuclear Age

The emphasis of the Eisenhower administration on massive retaliation, nuclear defense policies, popularly described as "more bang for the buck," had the effect of cutting funds and resources for the limited-war capabilities of the army and navy. While United States Navy leaders voiced their disagreement, it was a succession of army leaders such as Generals Ridgway, Taylor, and Gavin whose arguments within the government and in nongovernment publications and pronouncements contributed most effectively to the growing debate over massive retaliation versus limited war. [16] The Korean War had shown that conventional limited wars were still possible, even probable. In addition, recurring crises from Berlin to Quemoy were threatening in a period that promised to produce a new wave of revolutionary wars mixed with indirect forms of aggression. The army leaders saw a requirement for their limited-war capabilities, augmented by better budgets and policies, in meeting the spectrum of threats that could not be deterred or dealt with by any form of massive retaliation. Moreover, it was clear that it was in their interest to call attention to these missions and their requirements to address them.

There was a substantial element of self-interest in the army's efforts to develop limited-war doctrine and capabilities. Massive retaliation threatened to reduce the army and the navy to token forces whose main function would be to provide the casus belli for massive retaliation when they were attacked and destroyed—the "trip wire" mission. This was not a mission that the army or navy could accept with equanimity. In brief, army leaders opposed defense policies that they conceived to be wrong strategically and bad for their service. They espoused policies that they believed would be more appropriate and relevant to existing threats to security as well as more favorable to their service insofar as a distribution of defense missions and resources was concerned.

The Rise of Counterinsurgency

In the years following the Korean War the model for limited-war defense against aggression was a conventional war such as that fought in Korea or a mixed conventional/limited nuclear war in the NATO region. The development of successful revolutionary war strongly supported by indirect aggression in the Greek, first Indo-Chinese, Algerian, and other conflicts posed a new problem. Aggression might take the form of mixed civil or revolutionary war and indirect aggression. As developments in South Vietnam after 1954 were to reveal, establishment of a conventional defense force on the model of that of South Korea was not sufficient to deal with this potent combined threat to the security of weak nations.

In response to this new threat, the United States developed doctrine, strategies, and tactics as well as new capabilities to wage counterinsurgency war. Military advisers and technical assistance were provided to indigenous counterinsurgency forces in friendly countries. Thus, limited war was divided into two forms: conventional and/or tactical nuclear limited war on the Korean and NATO models and unconventional counterinsurgency limited war on the model of the second Indo-Chinese War, 1954-65. In both models, the most critical feature was the superiority of the political over the military elements.[17] Subsequently, the U.S. war in Vietnam was fought in ways that sometimes appeared to violate the principle of political superiority in limited war; therein lies some of the explanation for the U.S. failure in that war.

Revived Just-War Doctrine

It must be admitted that most of the interest in limited war as
an alternative to conventional total war and to general nuclear war is
based on utilitarian rather than normative considerations. The quest
has been for defense policies that make political and military sense;
a quest, however, that is always the first positive step toward policies
that might meet the requirements of the just war. But there was, for
example, no great concern over the kinds of limits on the conduct of
war that have been discussed in the preceding section of this book on
the just war. As the defense debates of the 1950s developed, however, there was a revival of interest in just-war approaches, and
they became linked with the concept of limited war. These contemporary just-war approaches progressed through the same array of issues that other limited-war proponents had addressed and came to
similar conclusions. The realist assumption of the perennial need
for defense against aggression was accepted. The need to resist the
expansion of communism was, if anything, more decisively urged.
The denial of fundamental human values by communism was particularly the concern of proponents of revived just war. The background
for this concern was the growing evidence of repression and inhuman-
ity behind the Iron and Bamboo curtains (for example, the brutal subjugation of Hungary in 1956, evidence of repression in China, and the
atrocities in North Vietnam after 1954). So it was held that there was
a right and duty to resist communist aggression.

The development of nuclear weapons engendered a new interest
in the jus in bello and efforts to judge this new absolute weapon by the
traditional standards that had been neglected and ignored in recent
conventional wars. These efforts encountered the same issue described previously of deciding whether to treat nuclear weapons as
one category or to distinguish between potentially permissible and
impermissible nuclear weapons and uses. This interest coincided
with the renewed emphasis on limited war, in general, and limited
nuclear war, in particular, that characterized the late 1950s.

The result of this just-war revival was a substantial moral support for resistance to communist and other aggression through limited-war theories and policies. Just war also was held out to be the
basis for an urgently needed rethinking of the moral implication of
modern weapons systems and defense policies. [18]

THE NEED FOR LIMITED WAR TODAY

The sources just discussed contributed to the development of
limited-war theories and policies from the 1950s to the present. It

will be observed that all of these sources continue to exert an influence and to require and justify limited-war strategies. Indeed, they quite suffice as rationales for such strategies even though the significance and meaning of each of the sources has been seen somewhat differently at different times over the last 20 or more years. However, in addition to the sources of limited-war strategies that have existed since World War II, new challenges have appeared that provide further bases for limited-war requirements. The great expansion of Soviet naval power and of Soviet naval bases has created a new threat on the seas and in regions such as the Red Sea/Horn of Africa, the Indian Ocean, and even the Mediterranean Sea. This calls for enhanced U.S. naval—and perhaps ground force and air—limited-war capabilities. The perennially unstable conditions in the Middle East and Persian Gulf combined with the ever-present threat of Soviet intervention in that area creates a need for limited-war forces. The threat of revolutionary war and indirect aggression continues to be widespread in the Third World. There is a post-Vietnam reluctance to contemplate intervention in revolutionary conflicts, but such interventions may be unavoidable if truly vital U.S. interests are involved. I will now outline the principal guidelines of limited war that strategists and policy makers have developed in response to the challenges that have been discussed.

GUIDELINES FOR LIMITED WAR

There is no generally accepted definition of limited war. In practice, the term is used for all forms of war short of strategic nuclear war. Analysis of some of the principal works on the subject (for example, those of Osgood, Kissinger, Brodie, Halperin, and Deitchman) produces a number of principles and themes that recur sufficiently to provide a consensus outline of limited-war guidelines.[19] This heterogeneous list embraces many different aspects of the initiation, conduct and termination of international conflicts and is in no way the result of a systematic and comprehensive effort to build a theoretical model of limited war. Nevertheless, these guidelines suggested by strategists and defense thinkers have been sufficiently reflected in defense policies to warrant treating them cumulatively as the working definition of limited war.

The limited-war guidelines may be summarized as follows:

1. Political primacy and control over the military instrument
2. Limited objectives
3. Economy of force; proportionality of means to limited objectives
4. Voluntary, self-imposed rules of conflict; the most prominent categories are:

   a. Communication between belligerents and the development of
      explicit and implicit rules of the conflict
   b. Avoidance of direct superpower confrontation
   c. No nuclear weapons; or, tactical and/or theater nuclear weap-
      ons only
   d. Geographical confinement of the conflict
   e. Invocation of claims that the conflict is legally permissible
      and collectivization of the war
   f. Limited mobilization
   g. Restraint in the use of the psychological instrument
   h. Fight and negotiate strategies
   i. Introduction of third-party mediators and inspectors; involve-
      ment of international organizations
5. Flexible response based on a broad spectrum of capabilities and
   a will to avoid escalation

   These guidelines will be explained in the remainder of this chapter. The extent of their observance of the Korean, Vietnam, and Yom
Kippur wars will be appraised in Chapters 10, 11, and 12.

Political Primacy and Control
over the Military Instrument

   War is not an end in itself; it is an instrument of policy. This
is a basic maxim of politics, military science, and morality. It is
reflected in the distribution of power and formulations of the U.S.
Constitution relative to the use of military power. The application
of armed coercion is permissible only insofar as it advances the political purposes of war. This teleological view that the military instrument finds its justification, tasks, and limits in the political
goals and policies of a belligerent seems self-evident. However, it
is notorious that the military instrument tends to escape control and
to pursue its own ends. These ends may not be justified by the political ends. They may even be contradictory to those ends. All
war that is consonant with sound political and military principles is
limited war in that the military means are subordinate and necessary
to the political ends.
   The corollary of the principle of political primacy is the control
of the military instrument by the civilian leadership of a country. In
the Western democracies, literal civilian supremacy is mandated by
the fundamental law of the country. However, the principle of political primacy should be followed in a country in which the military exercise supreme authority. Civil supremacy as the reflection of political primacy is a requirement of statecraft.[20]

The issue of political primacy and civil superiority arises in many forms. It may become a problem when a military commander attempts to usurp his political superior's definition of war aims and strategic decisions, as was the case with MacArthur in the Korean War. However, political primacy and civil superiority may also fall by default. Many of the decisions critically affecting the future of Europe at the end of World War II were made by the military primarily with military considerations in mind in the absence of adequate higher civilian direction. Indeed, the whole unconditional surrender policy was an invitation to leave the termination of the war to the military, subject to the fortuitous course of events on the battlefield.

A limited war, then, is a war in which political ends always determine military means. This is the first and foremost guideline of limited war. Where there is a supreme civilian authority, the corollary of the principle of political primacy is that the civilian authority controls the use of the military instrument. Where the military rule the state, they should still apply the principle of primacy of political ends over military means.

Limited Objectives

Objectives in war, particularly in modern times, may become unlimited or open-ended. Proponents of an ideology may make the realization of the ideological goals the objectives of the war. This is usually the pursuit of a distant utopia. Thus, there was no apparent limit to Hitler's quest for the Thousand Year Reich. The revolutionary objectives of communist states and other communist international actors are potentially so sweeping as to defy limitation. The drastic transformation of Germany and Japan and their Axis allies, implicit in the UN demand of unconditional surrender in World War II, constituted an extraordinarily ambitious war objective. Indeed, states with democratic ideologies can sometimes pursue open-ended, virtually utopian objectives. Wilson's proposal that World War I be fought to make the world safe for democracy, if taken seriously, might have kept the nations at war indefinitely.

In the twentieth century wars have been fought for total ends—ideological, religious, racial, national—that transcended the acceptable limits of raison d'état. Such holy wars have been condemned by the just-war doctrine and by contemporary international law. Still, the temptation remains for those who conceive themselves to be righteous to defeat and destroy the wicked. International law, with its contemporary emphasis on peace and order, may be overridden by those claiming to speak for a superior order of justice. To such claims, modern limited-war thinking responds that modern war is too dangerous and destructive an instrument to be permitted unlimited play, even in the pursuit of a putatively just cause. Limited-war guidelines, in effect, concretize the just-war concept of proportionality between probable good and probable evil resulting from war. The limited-war theories and policies conclude that no probable good is proportionate to the evil of unlimited total war. Some examples of the problem of limiting war by limiting its objectives will be provided in the three chapters following on the Korean, Vietnam, and Yom Kippur wars.[21]

Economy of Force and Proportionality

Economy of force is one of the basic principles of war recognized by military science. The United States Army has varied the content, order, and priorities of its official lists of these principles, which currently include inter alia, the objective, offensive, mass, economy of force, maneuver, unity of command, security, surprise, and simplicity. Economy of force is clearly related to the principle of the objective, which ordains that each military action must contribute to the ultimate objective of defeating the enemy's armed forces. Economy of force is closely related to the principle of mass, which requires that superior military power be concentrated at the critical times and places to obtain a decisive result. Economy of force precludes diversion of assets from the main effort, which is pursued in consonance with the principles of objective and mass.[22]

The principle of economy of force reflects the fact that a belligerent's resources are not unlimited. They must be directed to achievement of the main objective (the defeat of the enemy's forces) and they must be used as sparingly as is consistent with success.

The principle of economy of force bears some relation to the normative principle of proportion of ends and means. To be sure, not all means consistent with the principle of economy of force would necessarily pass the normative test of proportionality. Indeed, there is a lack of clarity and/or agreement in some of the sources on the relation of the military principle of economy of force and the normative principle of proportion. Osgood states the following:

> An important corollary of the principle of political primacy may be called the economy of force. It prescribes that in the use of armed force as an instrument of national policy no greater force should be employed than is necessary to achieve the objectives toward which it is directed; or, stated another way, the dimensions of military force should be proportionate to the value of the objectives at stake.

Clearly, this is an expedient rule; for unless a nation has a large surplus of available military power in relation to its policy objectives, one can hardly conceive of the effective use of power without the efficient use as well. Moreover, as an examination of the interaction between military means and political ends will show, the proportionate use of force is a necessary condition for the limitation and effective control of war.

The moral implications of an economy of force are no less significant. For, as we have acknowledged, the violence and destructive that accompany the use of force are an obvious, though sometimes necessary, evil. Therefore, it is morally incumbent to use force deliberately and scrupulously and as sparingly as is consistent with the attainment of the national objectives at stake.[23]

McDougal and Feliciano observe the following:

To the student of history, the coincidence of "economy of force" as an underlying principle of the rational application of coercion with "military necessity" as a basic principle of the law of war will be apparent.[24]

AFT 110-31 holds that economy of force is one of the four components of the law-of-war principle of military necessity.[25] The United States Air Force pamphlet is at pains to persuade its readers of the convergence of legal requirements with the economy-of-force principle.[26] However, the army's FM 100-1 defines economy of force in a way that does not emphasize the disporportionate means not to be used.

MASS. Superior combat power must be concentrated at the critical time and place for decisive results. Superiority results from the proper combination of the elements of combat power. Proper application of this principle, in conjunction with other principles of war, may permit numerically inferior forces to achieve decisive combat superiority at the point of decision.

ECONOMY OF FORCE. This principle is the reciprocal of the principle of mass. Minimum essential means must be employed at points other than that of the main effort. Economy of force requires the acceptance of prudent risks in selected areas to achieve superiority at the point of decision. Economy of force missions may require limited attack, defense, cover and deception, or retrograde action.[27]

The foregoing quotation from FM 100-1 includes the principle of mass, since the manual states that economy of force is the "reciprocal" of mass. It is interesting to note that in parallel treatment in the now replaced FM 100-5 of 1968, it is observed that "economy of force does not imply husbanding, but the measured allocation of available combat power to the primary task as well as to supporting tasks."[28] The upshot seems to be that the reason "minimum essential means must be employed at points other than that of the main effort" (FM 100-1) is to permit application of the principle of mass. This is considerably more modest by way of limitation than Osgood's formulation that "no greater force should be employed than is necessary to achieve the objectives toward which it is directed."

Further study and analysis of the relationship between the normative principle of proportion and the political/military principle of economy of force is clearly needed. One cannot be sure of the state of the question even within U.S. military service publications. One is disconcerted, for example, to have the principles of war omitted from the 1976 FM 100-5 of the army, leaving the authority of the 1968 FM 110-5, which does discuss the principles, somewhat unclear. Moreover, differences have developed between the presentation of the question in different services. It was earlier remarked that AFP 110-31 emphasized the congruence of the legal principle of proportion and the military principle of economy of force.[29] It is, accordingly, interesting to find a recent and highly authoritative air force source —AFM 1-1, Functions and Basic Doctrine of the United States Air Force, 14 February 1979—that defines economy of force as follows:

> ECONOMY OF FORCE No more—or no less—effort should be devoted to a task than is necessary to achieve the objective. This is called economy of force. This phrase implies the correct selection and use of weapon systems, maximum productivity from available flying effort, and careful balance in the allocation of tasks. The nature of aerospace forces and our exploitation of technology has given us weapons that can be employed throughout the spectrum of conflict. Therefore, the destructive power and flexibility of aerospace forces can be tailored to fit any operational situation.[30]

This formulation of economy of force by the air force would seem to bring us full circle back to Osgood's definition. Perhaps the most prudent view of the matter is that of Howard, who concludes that

> the military principle of "economy of force" may sometimes conveniently coincide with the dictates of transcendent moral values, but there is little historical justification for assuming that this will always be the case.[31]

What is clear is that a military action must conform to the principle of economy of force in order to qualify for the normative test of proportionality. Thus, in the case of Allied strategic-bombing policies in World War II, a military critique might conclude that the allocation of resources to the air force was disporportionate to the contribution of strategic bombing to the war effort, hence a violation of the principle of economy of force. A normative critique might conclude that the means used to achieve the ends were, in this case, disproportionate.

Limited war emphasizes the principle of economy of force. Under limited war, the open-ended objective of doing all possible injury to the enemy is ruled out. Each application of military power must be tailored to a specific military objective based, in turn, on specific political objectives.

Voluntary Rules of Conflict

Communication between Belligerents—
Rules of Conflict

If limited war is to be fought for limited objectives with limited means, some relationship between the belligerents is necessary whereby such limits may be explicitly or implicitly proposed. Since war is a continuation of politics by other means, a political relationship exists between the belligerents. If both sides are committed to limited war, there are reciprocal needs to express preferences about the forms of limitation to be observed. [32]

As indicated, the communication necessary to propose and accept limits may be direct and explicit or indirect and implicit. As Schelling has suggested, "bargaining" over the limits of the conflict may be engaged in between belligerents. A state may propose limits by openly announcing them and/or by following policies of abstention that indicate that certain means will not be employed. The enemy may reciprocate with open acceptance of the limits or acquiesce through abstentions on its own part. Whether the agreement is formal or informal, explicit or tacit, there may be a bargain over the rules of conflict. [33]

On the other hand, as Halperin has brought out, limits may be entirely self-imposed and unilateral. They may even involve means or options not available to the enemy. Moreover, as indicated earlier, limits may be imposed for a number of reasons not having much to do with a conscious effort to develop rules of the conflict. Even in this case, however, the conspicuous character of unilateral self-imposed limits tends to confirm the overall limited nature of the war and to discourage escalatory tendencies. [34]

Avoidance of Direct Superpower Confrontation

It is difficult to imagine a serious direct confrontation between the superpowers that would not produce an unacceptable risk of strategic nuclear war. Accordingly, the record of limited war since World War II has been characterized by strenuous and continuing efforts by both superpowers to avoid such a confrontation. These efforts have taken the form of employment of surrogates or clients; avoidance of the appearance of direct threats to superpower territory; concealment of the participation of superpower personnel in shooting wars; abstention from interdiction of superpower supply routes to local wars; and formal, express pronouncements proclaiming the desire to avoid confrontation. [35]

This rule of contemporary conflict does not preclude a superpower direct confrontation leading to a limited war, but it makes the prospects for limiting such a war, should it occur, more difficult. The confrontation-avoidance rule deters superpower conflicts because of the threat that they would almost inevitably lead to strategic nuclear war. It may be necessary to revise that rule to hold out the prospect of superpower limited conflicts, but the price for such a revision would be, presumably, the lessening of the deterrent effect of the presumption that superpower war would mean strategic nuclear war. An extremely limited war of sorts was carried out by the United States in enforcing the Cuban Quarantine in 1962. Otherwise, there are no precedents. No one would, in effect, encourage the revision of this unwritten rule to encourage more frequent superpower confrontations. On the other hand, the U.S. policies of graduated deterrence and flexible response deny the inevitability of strategic nuclear war if and when the United States and the Soviet Union come head-to-head in direct hostile confrontation.

Limits on Nuclear Weapons

The most obvious rule of conflict in contemporary limited war is no first use of nuclear weapons. It is widely agreed that the nuclear threshold is the most clear and serious source of limitation on modern war. The temptation to cross this threshold has been resisted in both the Korean and Vietnam conflicts. [36]

However, the apparent insufficiency of massive retaliation threats and conventional defenses forced the West into a limited nuclear war posture in NATO starting in the late 1950s. Since then, the desire for limited-war options and rules of conflict has produced an ongoing search for limited nuclear thresholds that could be sufficiently delineated so as to avoid undue risk of escalation to strategic nuclear war. These efforts, on the other hand, have been blunted somewhat by the simultaneous encouragement of salutory ambiguity about the likely response to aggression against NATO, South Korea, and other areas whose defense is guaranteed.

Moreover, it is fair to say that the consensus of thinkers who have addressed the problem of limited nuclear war is decidedly pessimistic about the feasibility of maintaining viable thresholds once nuclear weapons have been used. This is not to say that such limits could not hold up but that the odds are decidedly against successful limitation of nuclear war.[37]

Geographical Confinement of Conflict

Placing geographic limits on conflicts ranks second only to avoidance of direct superpower confrontation and of nuclear war as a guideline for modern limited war. This is understandable. One of the most deplored characteristics of World Wars I and II was the epidemic manner in which they spread. The unending race for new allies and new theaters in order to unlock the prospects of stalemate or defeat resulted in a great extension of the destructiveness and misery of wars that would have been quite bad enough if limited to the countries with the main stakes in the conflict.

Moreover, while extension of a war into additional theaters may seem to offer new strategic opportunities, it can also stretch limited resources too thin, violating the principles of objective and mass. Accordingly, modern limited war has been guided by the principle that the conflict should be geographically limited to the immediate overt belligerents.

There has been a considerable price for fidelity to this guideline. By definition, it means that states and territories closely supporting a belligerent will be "sanctuaries" wherein its logistical support operations and even elements of its combat forces find a safe haven. Each limited war has had its protests against such sanctuaries, sometimes leading to geographical extension of the conflict (for example, the 1970 Cambodian attacks by the United States and South Vietnam). Indeed, the immunity of sanctuaries runs quite counter to the well-established, total-war practices of the twentieth century, which have sought to close off all avenues of support to the enemy through blockades that brought the demise of historic neutral rights. Thus, the geographic limitations of modern conflicts represent a decided success for limited-war efforts.

Explanations for this respect for geographic limits and sanctuaries may lie beyond the simple desire to limit the suffering of war and the expenditure of limited military assets. Geographic confinement is one of the most explicit signals of the intention to wage limited war. It can become a kind of symbol, along with the abstention from nuclear war, of an overall desire to keep a conflict limited.

This is important in respect to at least three different audiences: the enemy, the world at large, and the home front. The 1970 Cambodian incursion by the United States and ARVN forces provides a good example of the uproar that may ensue within all three of these audiences when a geographic limit is breached and a sanctuary invaded. Finally, it may be suggested that the highest civilian and military decision makers tend to be skeptical about the proposition that a war that cannot be terminated successfully within the limits of the rules of conflict will become decisively more capable of a successful conclusion once its geographic limits are extended and sanctuaries attacked. It is difficult to believe that the highest decision makers would forego success resulting from a geographic extension if they were really convinced that such extension would guarantee success. [38]

Legal Justification and Collectivization

Even though the UN collective security system has not been successful or even operational, the law limiting recourse to armed coercion has had its impact on the legal claims and war policies of contemporary belligerents. Usually, justification for recourse to force will take the form of claims of individual and collective self-defense, supplemented by invocations of regional security pacts. To lend credibility to such claims, strenuous efforts are often made to involve a number of allies who make contributions of varying degrees to the common war effort. The model is the UN police action in Korea.

The United States, in particular, has seemed to be greatly concerned with bringing an additional dimension of legitimacy to its participation in a conflict by introducing allies in a collective war effort. It seems to be believed by the U.S. government, presumably in the conviction that this belief is widely shared, that there is a basic political, legal, and moral superiority to collective recourse to armed coercion over individual, unilateral recourse to force (for example, the effort to bring more "flags" into the defense of South Vietnam). [39]

Limited Mobilization

Most students of limited war contrast the general mobilization of military personnel and of the whole society characteristic of total war with the limited mobilization of limited war. This is in part a function of the limited objectives of the limited war. Moreover, limited mobilization is usually a necessary policy in order to keep the support of a public that perceives that a war is not the ultimate test of national survival and/or vital interests that it has come to think of as the justification for war. Limited mobilization is, moreover, enjoined by economic necessities that may, perhaps, be ignored in an all-out, total war, but which cannot be disregarded in limited war.

One aspect of limited mobilization that has been particularly troublesome is the central problem of military personnel. As a general proposition, it is preferable to be able to fight a limited war with the most professional military force possible. The less the military have to contend with restless draftees, their anxious loved ones, and congressmen, the more possible it is to carry out the difficult and controversial tasks of fighting a limited war. The problems of conscript armies, ironically, are compounded by the fact that the war is limited and not total. In total war, virtually all are called to serve. If there is a draft, a limited war creates a deadly lottery in which the odds are usually stacked against the less affluent classes. These are inescapable dilemmas unless a country has produced a professional military force sufficiently large to conduct the limited war. Such limited wars, quite in contrast to the appellation brushfire, which has sometimes been accorded them, are often extended wars of attrition. The preferred solution of a mainly professional army is not always feasible.[40]

Restraint with the Psychological Instrument

The psychological instrument of policy embraces the total policies and resources of a government for reporting, explaining, and justifying its actions domestically and to the world at large. In modern total wars, the psychological instrument has been mobilized to support a belligerent's war aims and conduct and to paint the enemy as the embodiment of evil and depravity. The communist states have perfected this usage in the "hate campaigns." Within the limits of democratic tolerance and constitutional rights, sometimes stretched, the United States and its Western allies have engaged in comparable exercises in officially organized animosity toward the enemy and solidarity with the war effort.

Such excesses make it very difficult to maintain limits on the ends and means of war and to terminate a conflict without victory. The kind of clinical rationale that underlies limited war is ultimately unsatisfactory to populations grown accustomed to total wars against total enemies. Yet such rationales are necessary both in that they are honest and that they seek to keep a balanced perspective even with regard to a bitter enemy. As with the other rules of conflict, moreover, the fact of curbing the psychological instrument signals the intention to keep the war limited to the enemy, the world at large, and the home front.[41]

Fight and Negotiate

A concrete evidence of the general disposition of enemies in limited war to communicate is the practice of negotiating while the fighting continues. Sometimes truces are arranged during which negotiations proceed. More often, in large, modern, limited wars the fighting continues as the negotiating parties seek to bolster their bargaining positions. A not uncommon middle ground between these two versions of "fight and negotiate" is a reduced level of activity on active fronts.

This strategy, originally associated primarily with communist belligerents, can be very hard on the party in the conflict that has an open and critical society. Troops naturally do not like to fight when the war may be terminated without victory at any time. It is hard for commanders to order extremely limited operations and take casualties simply to reinforce the negotiators. Home fronts become intolerant of protracted, exasperating negotiations conducted simultaneously with seemingly meaningless combat activity that kills loved ones.

Nevertheless, the practice of fight and negotiate is surely a hallmark of modern limited war. It must be considered superior to exchanging signals through unilateral pronouncements and behavior patterns. Whatever the cost in terms of time and frustration (it can be excruciating, as the Korean negotiations proved), direct negotiations while the fighting continues are a characteristic and worthwhile feature of modern limited war. [42]

Third Parties—International Organizations

As often happens in cases of domestic conflict, parties to a limited war frequently turn to more or less neutral third parties, including international organizations, to help limit and terminate the conflict. However, it has proved difficult to find third parties acceptable to all sides. In the Korean War, the United Nations was formally one of the belligerents. Unfortunately, the communist states have questioned the objectivity of the International Committee of the Red Cross. Experiments with ad hoc commissions have, on the whole, failed.

Still, the quest for third-party intermediaries has continued in recent limited wars. Aside from whatever practical assistance such intermediaries can furnish, there is, once again, a symbolic importance to the introduction of third parties as an indication of a desire to keep the conflict limited and to terminate it as soon as possible. [43]

Flexible Response

Flexible response based on a broad spectrum of capabilities and the will to avoid escalation is the summary operational foundation of limited war. Since any variation of massive retaliation is unacceptable as a basic defense posture, the United States must be prepared to meet a great variety of challenges at whatever level of intensity is appropriate within the limited-war guidelines that have been discussed.[44]

This means that the major contingencies must be identified and planned for, that the capabilities to deal with them must be developed within the military, and that political and military strategies appropriate to the spectrum of threats be thought through. This is all acknowledged by recent U.S. administrations and by the military. The hopes for limited war and adequate defense rest on the successful implementation of the flexible-response concept by the United States.

APPLICATION OF THE LIMITED-WAR GUIDELINES

Having outlined the general limited-war guidelines suggested by limited-war theorists and practitioners, it is necessary to address the question of their application. Here is encountered a problem similar to that confronting application of the just-war doctrine. Should all of the principal guidelines be followed in order to qualify a conflict for a limited war? Are some guidelines more important than others? In any event, if a limited war is anything short of a general nuclear war, what differences does it make how we qualify putatively limited wars?

To take the last issue first, it is not enough to distinguish only between nuclear wars and all other forms of war. As the appellation total war suggests, a nonnuclear war may be total. It has been observed that total is a relative, expanding, but meaningful term for wars that are approaching the outer limits of violence and destruction and have exceeded the political limits that are the sole justification for war. I contend that a war must meet at least the main limited-war guidelines to qualify as a limited war, whether it is nuclear or conventional, a central superpower war or a local conflict, an international or a civil war.

What, then, are the indispensable limited-war requirements that must be met if war is to be considered politically acceptable and therefore potentially acceptable in just-war terms. In my view the first three limited-war guidelines (political primacy, limited objectives, and economy of force) are indispensable and mandatory, and the policies and capabilities of the fifth category of guidelines (flexible response) are indispensable to the realization of the goals of the first three guidelines. A limited war must constitute a controlled political exercise of the military instrument. The war must be fought for limited political objectives. The conduct of the war must conform to the

principle of economy of force. Such a war will usually require policies and capabilities of flexible response.

As to the fourth category of guidelines (voluntary rules of conflict), it is my contention that there should be such rules at work in
any limited war, but that the choices among the eight subcategories
of kinds of rules and procedures may rightly vary according to the
circumstances. There may, of course, be additional subcategories.
I think that it is axiomatic that there must be some kind of communication between belligerents, even if only very indirect, and that, if
the war is to be kept limited, some kinds of bargaining will take
place, even among the most bitter enemies.

The limited-war guideline discouraging direct confrontation
of the nuclear superpowers is important but not absolute. Exaggerated
concern for its observance would tend to penalize the side that observed
it faithfully while rewarding the side that took advantage of it to play
brinksmanship. Moreover, it is certainly in no one's interest to encourage the belief that if superpower confrontation does occur, strategic nuclear war is inevitable. (Actually, there are those who rely
entirely on countervalue deterrence for all defense who do take this
position, which I reject.) On the contrary, the infinite diversity of
possible circumstances in which the superpowers might confront one
another requires that the superpowers, at least, must maintain flexible-
response capabilities and policies.

I do not think that the no-first-use-of-nuclear-weapons rule is
absolute. Of course, it will be irrelevant when no nuclear powers
are directly involved in a conflict. Where nuclear powers are involved, I think that there are enough arguments for limited nuclear
war to provide persuasive rebuttals to arguments for an absolute ban
on nuclear weapons. However, every presumption is against introduction of nuclear weapons; the burden of proof on the would-be first
users of such weapons is extremely heavy.

As I have indicated, I think that geographic limits on war are
often justified on their own merits as well as being extremely useful
signals and symbols of the intention to keep a conflict limited. Having said this, I do not consider the geographic-limit guideline absolute.

The practice of justifying war initiatives in legal and moral
terms is essential to limited war. It is an appropriate corollary of
the first guideline (political primacy). There should be a good and
sufficient political purpose for the war, and that purpose should be
justifiable in legal and moral terms. Having said this, it must be admitted that the normative claims made by belligerents may sometimes be more permissive than restrictive in their implications and,
accordingly, may or may not be conducive to the conduct of limited
war. The related practice of legitimizing wars by collectivizing
them must likewise be viewed with some reserve. The fact that a

belligerent can convince a number of other states to join it in a collective action may provide important evidence of the prudence and normative permissibility of the action. It may not, however. In some instances belligerents may be able to collect allies regardless of the legitimacy of the cause. All in all, my impression is that the U.S. government has exaggerated the proposition that collective action is always superior to and preferable to unilateral action.

The guideline prescribing limited mobilization is really directed primarily at the great powers. Small states may have to mobilize totally even to fight limited wars. Moreover, the degree and need for mobilization by any state in any war depends upon the circumstances. What matters is the effect of mobilization on the character of the war. If the effect is to make the war an open-ended, protracted struggle with no holds barred and no quarter to the enemy, the war has obviously ceased to be limited. In this connection, we must always remember Aron's comments on World War I in which the belligerents, in his view, found it necessary to invent extreme war aims to justify the magnitude of the mobilization and the kind of war it had produced. Moreover, total mobilization is a signal to the enemy, the world at large, and the home front of the kind of war that is intended. Accordingly, restraint is essential in mobilization policies if a war is to be kept limited.

Closely related is the issue of use of the psychological instrument. Despite its tendency to distort, the psychological instrument conveys the intentions of the belligerent. If the intentions conveyed are for a bitter, total war, there is a very good chance that there will be such a war. Of all of the subcategories of rules of conflict, perhaps the rule of restraint with the psychological instrument comes closest to being mandatory for the belligerent determined to conduct a limited war.

Although the phenomenon of fight and negotiate is typical of limited war, it is not an absolute condition for such wars. It is always possible simply to stop fighting and to negotiate. Or, it is possible to fight to a stalemate or point of equilibrium wherein there is an imminent conclusion to the conflict without negotiations and truces or peace agreements. However, whatever the form, limited war must be brought to a conclusion. The pernicious results of Arab avoidance of this principle have plagued the Middle East. A war, particularly a limited war, should not be a vendetta that is perpetuated indefinitely.

There is support for an unwritten rule that limited wars should always be submitted to third-party mediation, particularly on the part of the United Nations and other relevant international organizations. Given the wavering effectiveness and objectivity of the United Nations and other international organizations, this rule ought not to be treated as absolute. It will be a matter for individual decision in context whether a third-party mediator and/or international organization should be brought into the process of terminating a limited war.

Finally, it is clear that policies and capabilities of flexible response based on a will to avoid escalation are prerequisites of limited war, essential prerequisites for the great powers. In summary the first, second, third, and fifth guidelines are mandatory for the belligerent attempting to qualify a war as limited. Some serious efforts to develop the fourth category of limits in the form of self-imposed rules of conflict are also necessary for a limited war; the form of these rules varies with the circumstances. Of the rules of conflict, probably the rule requiring restrained use of the psychological instrument is the most mandatory.

In the next three chapters these guidelines will be applied retrospectively to three contemporary limited wars in which the United States was either a direct participant or a close ally: the Korean War, the Vietnam War, and the Yom Kippur War.

10

KOREA:
THE PRECEDENTAL LIMITED WAR

The concept of limited war may be more or less acceptable to statesmen, military leaders, and ordinary citizens according to the formulation of that concept. If it is proposed to limit war on the grounds that the military instrument must always be the servant of politics and never an end in itself, the concept is acceptable enough. However, if the proposition is that a belligerent, pursuing ends held to be morally just and politically vital, will voluntarily withhold some of its military power for the sake of avoiding all-out war, the concept becomes more controversial. If it appears that the military power withheld could have contributed decisively to the attainment of the just and vital objects of the war, the dangers of all-out war will have to be clear, present, and substantial. Thus, the perennial dilemma of limited war is that of determining just how far one can push the limits in order to maximize achievement of just and vital ends without disproportionately risking an all-out war. In this sense, Dulles's much-decried term "brinksmanship" is not without some validity.

If the rationale for limited war is extended beyond avoidance of total war and/or nuclear war to include observance of the normative just-war prescriptions and guidelines discussed in Part I, then greater resistance to the concept may be expected. In any event, it clearly is not possible to reduce the complex maze of just and vital war goals and occasions for the imposition of limits into a universal model of limited war. In each conflict a just and reasonable belligerent will balance the probable gains likely to result from various strategies against the risk that important limits will be broken and all-out war risked.

In addition to this fundamental issue of avoidance of all-out, total war, there is a second calculation that must be made by the practitioner of limited war. Related to the principle of economy of force, this is the decision as to how much of his military assets the belligerent should invest in a particular conflict, given his other security requirements. In the case studies that follow, it will be remarked that limits in limited war often arise out of scarcity of military resources for multiple security responsibilities rather than from some principled determination to place limits on a conflict.

There have been no general wars of the magnitude of World Wars I and II since 1945, but there have been many so-called local wars. [1] Some of them were comparatively all-out or total in terms of the resources and commitment of the belligerents. Most, however, have been limited wars. There is, then a considerable base of experience on which to apply the limited-war categories distinguished in the previous chapter. However, this book is concerned primarily with the problem of limited war as it confronts the United States and its principal allies. Its focus is upon wars in which the United States and/or its allies have been principal belligerents. Accordingly, in this and the succeeding two chapters, the limited-war categories of Chapter 9 will be applied to three such wars. Two involved the United States as a major belligerent, the Korean and Vietnam wars. In the third, the Yom Kippur War, the United States played a major role in imposing limits on the conflict and in resupplying the Israeli forces. By recalling the extent to which the categories of limited war were relevant to each of these three wars, their meaning and possible relevance to future conflicts may be illuminated. The first conflict to be considered, then, is the Korean War, which was to become a precedental model in many respects for succeeding limited wars.

POLITICAL PRIMACY

The Korean experience has been the foundation for most contemporary analyses of limited war. [2] In that war, notably in the Truman-MacArthur controversy and the subsequent Great Debate in the United States, both the issues of the primacy of politics over the military instrument and of the civilian authority over the military were raised. [3] MacArthur's position appeared to be based on a concept of pure war as a last resort after politics had failed to find a peaceful solution. War was not a continuation of politics but an extreme alternative to politics. MacArthur contended that, once politics had failed and war took over, the sole function of politics was to set goals for the military. Once the goals were set (for example, defense of South Korea, reunification of Korea) the military instrument took over. Military commanders should, at this point, follow the logic of war and be guided by military science alone, unhampered by political limits on the military means they choose to seek the politically established ends. The military instrument was depicted by MacArthur as a profound force that could be turned on or off, but which, once turned on, should be used to the full extent of its capacity until victory was secured. [4]

The Truman administration, including the Joint Chiefs of Staff, rejected this concept of no war or total war. [5] In the first place, President Truman and his principal political and military advisers refused to accept MacArthur's concept as true and compelling. Moreover, the Truman administration had a number of reasons for seeking limited-war alternatives to total war. First, there was an underlying concern about the possibility of a third world war with the Soviet Union and efforts were made to avoid this possibility. [6] Second, Truman refused to risk a war with the People's Republic of China (PRC) on its own territory. [7] Third, the U.S. leaders insisted on husbanding resources for the defense of Western Europe, fearing that the whole Korean venture was a massive feint by the Soviets to set up European aggressions. [8]

Thus, the Truman administration rejected MacArthur's claim that, once the shooting starts, raison de guerre (military necessity) always must prevail over raison d'état. This rejection of MacArthur's position cost the Truman adminstration dearly. It was made clear that MacArthur's no-war-or-total-war view was shared by many Americans. Indeed, concern over this fact of U.S. political life pervades the post-Korean War literature on limited war. This concern continues to be central to the problem of limited war. [9]

It should be emphasized that foremost among the specific reasons for limiting the Korean War was the desire to avoid a third world war with the Soviet Union and, to a lesser degree, a full-scale war with the PRC on the Asian mainland. The resolution to avoid these wars predated development by the Soviet Union of a major nuclear capability and existed long before such a capacity was to be achieved by the Red Chinese. Today the first reason for limiting war is to avoid a strategic nuclear war. But it is important to remember that the Truman administration, whose willingness to face tough security decisions was considerable, balked at risking World War II-type total war and, instead, chose the difficult path of limited-war resistance to aggression.

Whereas MacArthur's challenge to the basic limited-war principle of continuing primacy of the political over the military components in wartime policy was clear, his challenge to civilian supremacy over the military within the U.S. government was more masked. MacArthur insisted that he was a most "subordinate" officer, that he always carried out his orders faithfully and respected his civilian superiors. So his challenge to these superiors was not completely open and explicit. However, by his actions (for example, his encouragement of Chiang Kai-shek; his unauthorized unilateral demand for the Communists to surrender, which preempted a Truman negotiation initiative; and his letters to the Veterans of Foreign Wars and to Congressman Martin urging different strategies), MacArthur competed with the Truman administration in the international as well as the domestic political realm. This flagrant and effective political competition did violate the principle of civilian supremacy and bring about MacArthur's relief. [10]

Moreover, the Korean War added a new dimension to the concept of civilian supremacy. This concept had already taken a plural form in the alliances of World Wars I and II. Now civilian supremacy included the United Nations, particularly the General Assembly, as well as those UN members who were participating in the joint defense of South Korea. The clashes between MacArthur and the Truman administration were rendered more difficult by the fact that Truman had to coordinate the policies of his UN allies and of the United Nations itself. MacArthur's initiatives and suggestions all took forms that drove the United States away from the central UN consensus on the limits of the war and in the direction of going it alone. In the post-World War II period, it has been and probably will continue to be the case that U.S. belligerency will often occur in conjunction with international organizations and with other states. Wherever this is so, civilian supremacy extends to the total allied/international organization political network. [11]

For the proponents of limited war, the Korean War remains the prime example of how such wars must be fought in the contemporary era. For the many opponents of limited war (professional military men, politicians, and ordinary citizens), the Korean War was the beginning of a wrong direction in U.S. policy and strategy. In my view the Truman administration's conduct of the war was generally exemplary. However, Truman may have made one major error in judgment, which requires review and reflection. If it was an error, it reflected a problem that came up again in the Vietnam War and will undoubtedly recur in other limited wars. This was the error of easing up military pressures too quickly in order to appear to be serious about negotiations for a termination of the conflict.

When peace negotiations began in June 1951, the Communist forces were defeated and in considerable disarray. Van Fleet's limited offensive (June through November 1951) provided an admirable "fight" component in a "fight and negotiate" situation. In November 1951 Truman laid down rules of engagement limiting the UN forces to active defense and forbidding any attack over battalion level without UN command permission. General Ridgway and Admiral Joy, chief UN negotiator, objected to the loss of military pressure. However, they were obliged to accept Truman's de facto 30-day ceasefire during which it was hoped that an armistice would be signed with the current contact line constituting the demarcation line. In fact, the Communists pocketed this reprieve and dragged on the negotiations for 20 months until July 1953. The UN forces were never again to have the ascendancy and initiative that they had had in the summer and fall of 1951. In this instance, the application of the principle of political supremacy over the military and of civilian authority over the military resulted in substantial reduction of the power and effectiveness of the military instrument with resultant losses in terms of the duration and political outcomes of the war. Above all, the loss of military momentum permitted the Communists to stall negotiations with consequent losses of life and resources. [12]

It is clearly contrary to basic political and military principles to view war as an either/or instrument that can be only turned off or on with no intermediate calibrations. But it is also contrary to the nature both of political and military power to ignore the phenomenon of momentum enjoyed by a successful military force. There are tides in the fortunes of war. When the tide is running for you, it is well to take full advantage of it; for when the tide has stopped or turned, whether by the enemy or politically motivated interruptions, it may well be impossible to start the tide running so decisively in your favor again. The problem remains to confront practitioners of limited war. The political hand on the levers of military power must be sensitive to the nature of that power and extract from it the full political leverage it can provide.

LIMITED OBJECTIVES

Had Truman and his UN allies taken a total-war approach to the Korean War, its objectives would have been the defeat of the sources of communist aggression and its scope would have been World War III. However, Truman and the UN renounced any such notion from the outset. The war aims were, initially, the defense and restoration of South Korea and the sanctioning of the UN Charter prohibition against aggression. [13] When the Communists were routed in the South after the Inchon landing, the possibility of "liberating" North Korea opened up. MacArthur's proposal to effect such a liberation was promptly accepted by Truman and by the UN General Assembly. Accordingly, a third war aim was proclaimed—the unification of Korea. [14] While there was some warrant for a UN-sponsored effort to unify Korea, albeit in a peaceful rather than wartime context, the implementation of this third aim expanded the original goals of the war and breached one of the most important limits voluntarily imposed by the UN side —geographic confinement of the conflict. The result was that the PRC entered and decisively expanded the war.

The entrance of Communist China into the conflict elicited a number of suggested new goals from MacArthur, all pointed at pursuing aggression to its source in true total-war fashion. These were all rejected by Truman and the United Nations, and MacArthur's efforts to promote them politically led directly to his relief. Moreover, as the stalemated military situation hardened and the United States and its UN allies tired of the war, the objective of unifying Korea was dropped. In the end, then, the Korean War was fought for the inter-related objectives of defending South Korea and sanctioning the UN prohibition against aggression.[15] These were objectives that are fully consonant with the just-war and international-law jus ad bellum, and they were eminently reasonable in terms of the contemporary requirement of defeating aggression without recourse either to conventional total war or nuclear war.

ECONOMY OF FORCE

The application of the principle of economy of force by Truman and the U.S. Joint Chiefs strongly complemented the a priori commitment to keep the Korean War limited. The outbreak of the war found the United States short of military assets to deal with the situation in Korea. Unwilling to demand a major mobilization of the American people, the Truman administration was able to marshal adequate forces for the war but nothing approaching the U.S. military potential. At the same time, the administration was faced with the urgent need to protect Western Europe and, accordingly, was raising forces for the North Atlantic Treaty Organization (NATO) that could otherwise have been used in Korea. Successful defense of South Korea was seen as important but less vital than defense of Western Europe, where, it was feared, the Soviets might strike if the United States were overextended in the Far East. In these circumstances, the operation of the principle of economy of force foreclosed extension of the rock-bottom objectives of securing South Korea and limited pursuit of that objective to approximately the minimum necessary to achieve it.

Economy of force also influenced the abstention from recourse to nuclear weapons in the Korean conflict. At the time the atomic stock was limited. That limited capability was reserved for Europe, although nuclear threats were made to bring the fight-and-negotiate period to a close, as will be discussed. In brief, the Truman administration and its allies saw the threat to the security of the Free World as considerably broader than that posed by the Korean War, even after the entrance of Red China. Accordingly, the principle of economy of force required that there be limits to the military resources committed to dealing with this threat. In terms of the principle, what it would have taken to "win" or to "win more" would have been disproportionate in terms of diversion of needed military resources from other theaters. [16]

The Korean War, then, was limited because the UN side was committed to a general concept of limited war as an instrument of politics, because this concept was honored in the limitation of objectives, and because the requirements of the military principle of economy of force dictated limits in the allocation of military resources to the conflict. Against this background, it is possible to examine the voluntary rules of the conflict the belligerents developed.

RULES OF CONFLICT

Communication between Belligerents

The limits in the Korean War seem to have been mainly unilaterally established without either explicit or implicit acceptance or proffer of reciprocity by the other side. Very little bargaining was done with the North Koreans. The initial announced objective of restoring the sovereignty and territorial integrity of South Korea could be taken as a signal that invasion and conquest of North Korea was not contemplated. During the period when this was the UN policy, North Korea was prevailing on the battlefield. In the circumstances this signal was, presumably, of little interest to them. Abruptly, with the change of the tide after the Inchon landing, the UN objective of unification of Korea was proclaimed, changing the scope of the war. After the Red Chinese intervention, the key actor on the Communist side was the PRC. The policies, whether unilateral or reciprocal, that kept the war limited thereafter were basically a function of U.S./UN and PRC interaction.

The first efforts to limit the scope of the war by assurances to the PRC manifestly ended in failure. The United States/United Nations were at great pains to assure the Red Chinese that the invasion and conquest of North Korea were not intended to threaten them. The Red Chinese were unimpressed. For their part, the Red Chinese tried to signal to the United States/United Nations through their own pronouncements and through intermediaries that invasion of North Korea would bring the PRC into the war. The United States/United Nations did not heed the warnings. As a result, the United States/United Nations ended up in a war with Red China that they definitely had wanted to avoid. [17]

Once Red China entered the war, attacks on its bases in Manchuria were an obvious option. The United States/United Nations voluntarily denied themselves this option. The rules of engagement prohibiting attacks beyond the Yalu became a controversial feature of the Korean War, one of the best known and most criticized of the limits of that limited war. This rule of the conflict was communicated by the fact of abstention from such attacks. It was underlined, as time went on, by public discussions in the United States and allied countries over the policy of abstention. There was never any acknowledgment of this voluntary restriction by the Communist side. It is believed that the Communist policy of not attempting serious air attacks on UN communications and logistical areas constituted a kind of reciprocity. However, this Communist policy may perhaps be better explained by the formidable air superiority of the UN side. [18]

A related rule of conflict developed out of a voluntary U.S. abstention from air raids on the Suiho Dam hydroelectric complex on the North Korean side of the Yalu River. This abstention reflected a reluctance to destroy a major target close to the Yalu. It also held back destruction of a facility vitally needed for industry and that serviced parts of Manchuria as well as Korea. Viewed in terms of maintaining escalatory options, it left an important target to be attacked if the time came when extra military pressure was desired. This time did come on June 24, 1952, when the Suiho complex was attacked by 500 UN aircraft. This would appear to have been an example of bargaining, first by abstention from attacks on a vital target and then by its destruction when the enemy proved adamant in negotiations. [19]

To keep the war limited, above all, the Soviet Union had to be kept out of direct participation in the conflict. Accordingly, the United States tried to reassure the Soviet Union by diplomatic communications and by a policy of partial abstention from bombing the North Korean port of Rashin, close to the Soviet border. [20]

In summary, then, communication of rules of the conflict in the Korean War took the form of diplomatic communications and public announcements directed at enemies and potential enemies and policies of self-limitation and abstention, acknowledged and debated in the free societies on the UN side. Further illustrations of rules of conflict will appear in the following discussions of specific rules.

Avoidance of Superpower Confrontation

The central role of the Soviet Union in the Korean War is well established. Premier Kim Il Sung of North Korea was a Soviet-trained product put into power and sustained by the Soviet Union. It is reasonable to believe that North Korea attacked South Korea either at the urging or with the encouragement and support of the Soviet Union. Soviet advisers were intermingled in the North Korean government and military. Word of willingness of the Communist side to negotiate peace came from the Soviet UN representative, Malik. Although the North Koreans certainly had their independent and sufficient casus belli, it is most likely that they served in the Korean War as a proxy force for the Soviets and the then more or less united Communist bloc. [21] In these circumstances, limitation of the war to avoid direct Soviet involvement in combat was difficult and went against the grain of nations accustomed to the logic of total war.

Nevertheless, Truman established from the outset and maintained throughout the war the basic rule that confrontation with the Soviet Union would be avoided if at all possible. This was communicated to the world at large in U.S. policy pronouncements that justified the war, inter alia, as a necessary alternative to World War III. It was communicated through the abstention from attacks against the port of Rashin near the Soviet border. It was communicated by public pronouncements and through diplomatic channels when the 38th parallel was crossed and the U.S./UN side was seeking to assure the Red Chinese and the Soviets that unification of Korea was not intended to be a threat to their security. Thus, this most important limit on the Korean War was established from the beginning and successfully maintained. [22]

Limits on Nuclear Weapons

When the Korean War broke out there was little political or military consensus on the extent to which nuclear weapons should be used. It was generally assumed that they would be used against the Soviet Union in the case of World War III. The role of nuclear weapons in more limited, local wars was unclear. The Korean War was a critically important occasion for setting precedents and trends with respect to nuclear weapons policy in less-than-total local wars. The rule of the conflict set by the U.S./UN side was that nuclear weapons were not to be used.

It appears that there were a number of practical reasons for the abstention from the use of nuclear weapons in Korea. First, there was a limited stock of atomic bombs and they had to be reserved for the most important and appropriate situations. In particular, at a time when U.S./NATO conventional defenses in Europe were dangerously weak, the atomic bombs were needed for deterrence and defense there. Holding back the limited supply of atomic weapons was required by the principle of economy of force in the light of strategic priorities.

Second, the Korean War, as fought within the geographic confines of Korea, offered insufficient targets to justify the use of nuclear weapons. The greatly superior U.S./UN air forces were able to destroy the limited industrial centers of North Korea. Interdiction of communication and supply lines would not have been a sufficient mission for nuclear attacks. Only if MacArthur's policies of attacking Red Chinese industrial and population centers had been adopted would there have been proper missions for nuclear forces. [23]

However, the Korean War was not to produce a clear precedent for abstention from nuclear warfare in local wars. Once Eisenhower was elected president and had visited Korea, he concluded that the impasse in the long-stalled, fight-and-negotiate quagmire had to be broken. It was his conviction that the Communists, particularly the Red Chinese, saw themselves as profiting from the impasse, partially in terms of solidifying their hold on their own people by constant appeals to wartime solidarity. With the military initiative at the front long since lost and with no prospects of bringing to bear sufficient conventional military power to regain the initiative, nuclear coercion appeared to be the only alternative to acceptance of a stalemate. Accordingly, Eisenhower determined that his administration would threaten the Red Chinese with nuclear attacks on their homeland if they did not come to terms in a timely and satisfactory fashion.

The nuclear threat was communicated to the Communist belligerents during the spring of 1953. During this time, the Communists launched a spring offensive that failed. By May 23, 1953, the UN commander, General Mark Clark, was able to make a last offer to the Communists, an offer they had to accept or expect the discontinuation of the talks and the resumption of the war in new ways (that is, with nuclear weapons). [24] On June 4, 1953, the UN prisoner-of-war propositions were accepted, and on July 27, 1953, the truce ending the war was signed. But one more nuclear threat remained to be made. On the same day that the truce was signed, the UN belligerents made a pledge, the Declaration of Sixteen, to defend South Korea against any further aggression. The pledge specified that any future defense of South Korea as would become necessary would not be confined to Korea. [25]

On balance it would seem wise to regard the abstention from use of nuclear weapons in the Korean War as a very modest precedent contributing to what is now a de facto no-first-use rule. The nonuse of nuclear weapons by the Truman administration appears to have been primarily a matter of reluctance to use scarce decisive weapons against less-than-vital targets. If we can believe that there was an Eisenhower threat conveyed to the Communists, there would have been nuclear attacks on the PRC had the truce talks not been resumed and successfully completed.

Geographical Confinement of the Conflict

As discussed above, the original war objectives of the United States/United Nations were restoration of full South Korean sovereignty and territorial integrity up to the 38th parallel. After the North Korean invasion collapsed, the northern border of North Korea was respected as the limit for combat, the most important segment of the boundary being that along the Yalu River. The decision not to attack Manchuria meant that logistical bases, communications lines, staging combat troops, and the Red Chinese air force all had a "sanctuary" beyond the Yalu. Thus, even after the PRC was a fighting cobelligerent, its territory was still excluded from attack. Respect for this sanctuary became a hallmark of the limited war in Korea.

The point has also been made earlier that MacArthur's proposals to attack Red Chinese territory were summarily rejected, inter alia, because of the determination of the U.S./UN side to confine the conflict geographically. It is interesting to see that this geographical confinement was considered vital even though the beneficiary of the self-imposed limitations, Red China, was the major enemy belligerent, not a potential belligerent. The war was already drastically expanded with the entrance of Red China, but the scope of the expansion was circumscribed by the U.S./UN confinement policies. [26]

Legal Justification and Collectivization

The Korean War is an interesting case study of legal claims and counterclaims. To the Western observer the North Korean attack appears to have come out of the blue without provocation or justification. The North Koreans, in a typical aggressor's ploy, felt constrained to argue that the South Koreans actually attacked them first, and that they counterattacked. Given the unfolding of the early events of the war, this was a ludicrous claim.

Because of the fortuitous fact that the Soviet delegate was boycotting the UN Security Council over the issue of representation of the PRC, the United States was able to obtain from the Security Council a finding of aggression by North Korea and an authorization for assistance to South Korea. This, plus the subsequent cooperation of the General Assembly, gave the United States a UN blanket to cover what at bottom was a U.S. policy of participating in the collective self-defense of South Korea.

The combined authority of the resolutions passed by the Security Council before the Soviet Union returned to contain the damage and of the General Assembly resolutions (notably the Uniting for Peace Resolution of November 3, 1950) made the war a UN "police action." However, it should be quite clear that this police action was not an enforcement action by the Security Council as contemplated by the UN Charter (see Chapter 7). It was essentially a collective defense as authorized by Article 51 of the charter, strengthened by the Security Council finding of North Korean aggression and the support of the General Assembly resolutions enjoining participation in the joint defense. As a result of these resolutions, the credibility of the U.S. claims of aggression, and the need for collective defense, some 16 nations contributed to the UN fighting force and many others provided assistance.[27]

In some respects the Korean case as a legal precedent may have been too much of a good thing insofar as U.S. policies and attitudes were concerned. The United States became accustomed to the idea that, when the United States resisted aggression, it could depend upon the United Nations—and, perhaps, on other international organizations—to weigh in with political and legal approval and support for the U.S. action. Within a few years after the end of the Korean War, the international system was greatly expanded by new nations of the Third World. The character of the General Assembly changed markedly. Today the assembly tends to be the instrument of the Third World blocs rather than either the United States, the Soviet Union, or other Great Powers. It is not inconceivable that a contemporary Uniting for Peace Resolution might brand Israel or South Africa as an aggressor and call upon members of the United Nations to participate in a "police action" against the condemned state. The United States, for its part, having long since ceased to be in a position where it can control the assembly as it did in 1950, would no longer accept the majority votes of the assembly as right and/or binding if it disagreed with them.

It may well be that the United States has accepted the fact of life that authority and allies are no longer readily available at the United Nations to support U.S. limited wars that are justified on their own merits in U.S. eyes. Legal justification comes essentially from the merits of the case, irrespective of the agreement or disagreement of international organizations. One could be wrong and still receive international-organization support, just as one could be right and receive international-organization condemnation or nonsupport. Further, the participation of other states in a collective defense certainly lends credence to the legal claims and justifications of the principal belligerents, but many nations could be collectively wrong, just as one nation alone could be right. In the end, the experience of the Korean "police action" may have spoiled U.S. policy makers. They felt that the United States was right and that the Free World agreed that it was right. This was a satisfying but, apparently, ephemeral experience. Today, on most difficult security issues, the United States stands alone or nearly alone. If it has allies, it can seldom expect them to be a majority of the United Nations. There is very little expectation that the United Nations as an organization will be helpful in establishing and supporting the legitimacy of U.S. claims to the right and duty to resist aggression. Accordingly, the emphasis in the Korean experience on UN authority and collective action may tend to point U.S. aspirations in the direction of unattainable searches for legitimacy in future conflicts.

Limited Mobilization

It has been observed that one of the fundamental sources of limitation in the Korean War was the unwillingness of the United States to embark on a full-scale war mobilization. The country was only five years beyond World War II. There was a substantial military establishment and significant stocks of military material. It proved possible to reactivate selective service fairly promptly. Under these conditions the United States was able to strengthen the forces committed to Korea and build up forces for Europe. But the mobilization base was insufficient to produce the large forces that would have been necessary to break the military stalemate in Korea, much less extend the war significantly to the PRC.

The Truman administration did not have a sufficient political base to obtain the necessary sacrifices to mobilize more fully. The country was badly divided, and the politics of the time were vicious. What came to be known in later crises and wars as the hawk faction existed, but it was, for the most part, violently opposed to Truman's conduct of the war as a limited war. The hawks alternated between MacArthuresque solutions based on bombing beyond the Yalu, dropping atomic bombs on Red Chinese cities, and "unleashing" Chiang Kai-shek against the mainland. More dovish elements respected the UN character of this resistance against aggression but favored a negotiated settlement, not an expanded war.

Thus, because Truman fought a limited war, he could not demand full mobilization for war or anything close to it. Because he could not have full mobilization, he was condemned to fight no more than a limited war.[28] I have listed limited mobilization among the guides for limited war. Perhaps it would be more accurate to call limited mobilization a necessary result and characteristic of limited war. However, it is conceivable that a government will sometime find itself with the opportunity to expand defense mobilization greatly, beyond the requirements of a limited war it is waging. In such circumstances I would argue for restrictions on defense mobilization, confining it to the levels necessary for the existing limited war and other outstanding security needs. It may be as well that a limited war is kept limited in part by the phenomenon that tends to limit the acceptable levels of mobilization because the public does not see a major war threat and commensurate requirements.

Restraint in the Psychological Instrument

The issue of full or partial mobilization is closely linked to that of use of the psychological instrument by the government waging limited war. In total war the psychological instrument is used to the utmost, domestically and internationally. The enemy is depicted in the worst possible light to the point that any amount of suffering and sacrifice appear to be justified in order that he may be defeated. To be sure, the public's perception of the enemy is essentially a function of the nature of the enemy and of the war as deduced from reasonably well-established, objective facts (for example, what was known about the Hitler regime and German conquests in World War II). However, the propaganda and psychological warfare of the twentieth century have embellished the evil character and threat of the enemy where they were substantial and created spurious evil and threats where there was little basis in fact.

The fear, destruction, and sacrifice of modern war are so great that extreme justifications are necessary to sustain the society that is suffering through a major war. Sometimes the manifest character of the enemy and the war are sufficient in themselves to sustain the war effort. But all governments seek to buttress the natural sentiments of the nation with propaganda excoriating the enemy and soliciting an all-out effort to defeat him.

If this is the case in total war, wherein the threat is usually sufficiently clear to move the least informed and perceptive citizens, the need for adept use of the psychological instrument is the more important in limited wars where the issues are often matters of principle and long-range policy rather than immediate, self-evident survival. It may be persuasive to one or more of the small foreign policy elites to say that if aggression is not stopped in Berlin or Korea, it is probable that aggression will be faced closer to home. This, however, is not such a compelling argument to the man in the street. Ideally, the ordinary citizen needs the equivalent of the kind of threat that sustains him through a total war.

It is at this point, however, that the dilemma of limited war with respect to use of the psychological instrument occurs. The citizen who is not strongly motivated against the enemy and is relatively unmoved by the issues for which the war is being fought may, for a time, accept the limited-war measures of his government. But if he is subjected to total-war variety propaganda, he will soon begin to wonder why the hated enemy is being spared the fullest force of his nation's armed might. If the war is one of aggression and the enemy are benighted totalitarians, why not bomb sanctuaries? Why not use nuclear weapons? Why not mobilize the full might of the nation and fight all out?

Knowing the strength of propaganda and the powerful impact it has had in the twentieth century, a responsible government is careful in its use of the psychological instrument. It attempts to justify the war but to avoid a crusade mentality that may stampede public opinion. This seems to have been the case in the Korean War policies of the Truman administration. In 1950 the administration was faced with a public view of communism, the Soviet Union and its satellites that could hardly have been more negative and antagonistic. Everything that Americans had come to learn about the communists since the end of the Great Alliance in 1945 was bad and frightening. The seizure of Eastern Europe and the reduction of its populations to subservience under the communists engendered the foundation for a near-universal anticommunism in the United States. The problem of the Truman administration was not to whip up anticommunist feeling. It was to control that feeling so as to produce support for a limited war against aggression by a junior partner in the Communist bloc.

A domestic propaganda effort comparable with those of World Wars I and II could have had the U.S. people straining to finish off the communists once and for all. Of course, the administration knew that this would not be a reasonable objective. So the United States fought a war against communist belligerents while its wartime government continued to be under constant and effective domestic attack for being "soft on communism" and riddled with spies and fellow travelers. Under these circumstances, it was exceedingly difficult for the Truman administration to find a nice point in wartime propaganda that would be just sufficient to sustain a lagging limited war and not so strong as to incite even greater demands for total war. And, indeed, the U.S. government did not succeed in selling its limited war to the people. Public opinion, originally strongly behind the U.S. intervention, became confused and discouraged. Denied encouragement for an anticommunist crusade and unwilling to accept the uninspiring rationales of limited war, the public concluded that the war had no sufficiently clear purpose and ought to be ended as soon as possible and in whatever way this could be accomplished.

The Korean War, then, is not a good example of a government holding the lid on the psychological instrument. It is, rather, an example of the difficulties of fighting a limited war when, as is usually going to be the case, it is neither desirable nor feasible to provide the public with the kind of wartime propaganda to which it has become accustomed in modern total wars. Moreover, the declining enthusiasm of the other nations participating in the "police action" indicated that their publics were not sufficiently inspired by the rationale of principled limited war to stop aggression. Thus, the problem of sustaining limited wars at home and in international opinion was shown to be formidable in the Korean War.[29]

Fight and Negotiate

The earlier discussion of the clash between the political decision to cease fighting and negotiate or to reduce the level of fighting
and negotiate with military momentum addressed a problem that
seems to recur in limited wars. In the Korean War a policy of fight
and negotiate was adopted in June 1951 and continued until the Panmunjom truce was signed in July 1953. There was never any agreement to a complete ceasefire. During the 20 months between November 1951 and July 1953, there was a pattern of reduced level of combat with intermittent local offensives. These offensives confirmed
that there was a military stalemate that could not be broken without
a major increase in military assets on one side or the other. Thus,
each side had to hold the military balance and, if possible, inch ahead
here or there in order to maintain a position of equality in the negotiations. There was no prospect of either party gaining enough military ascendancy to force political concessions at Panmunjom unless
one of the parties weakened its military strength and its national
will. [30]

This stalemate, however, was confined to the regular military
front. The Communists opened another front, that of the prisoner
of war (PW). Through infiltrated agents and previously indoctrinated
personnel who had become prisoners of the UN command, they dominated and organized large segments of the PW compounds. The ac-
tivist Communist PWs and those following their commands through
conviction or intimidation were able to carry out full-scale revolutionary operations within the PW camps. Riots, strikes, agitation,
even the capture of a U.S. general who was forced to make outrageous
admissions and concessions, all proved to be extremely effective
forms of de facto combat by personnel who were supposed to be hors
de combat. This PW combat contributed to the political-military
balance at Panmunjom. The Communist side cited the PW compound
outbreaks and their suppression as war crimes and atrocities. Given
the great propensity of the Free World elites to believe the worst
about their own side and the latent hostility and skepticism in countries like India, the Communist propaganda about mistreatment of
PWs influenced the political climate in which negotiations were conducted. [31]

The synchronization of PW outbreaks and Communist recriminations about them was so good as to indicate that the Communist
leadership was directing and orchestrating the war within the PW
camps and coordinating it with the Panmunjom negotiations. Thus,
a new dimension was added to the concept of fight and negotiate. As
remarked in the jus in bello discussions of Chapter 3, this abuse of
the protected status of PWs jeopardized the whole PW regime under

international law. [32] The Communist leaders, however, treated their own personnel who had become PWs as pawns in the fight-and-negotiate game, and they remained apparently unconcerned about the consequences of their policy either for the protection of their own people or for the maintenance of the international-law regime for PWs.

On the other hand, the Communist leaders recognized that the UN side was extremely concerned about the protection and timely return of their own personnel who were PWs under Communist control. The UN PWs became hostages, bargaining chips in the negotiations. As has been explained in Chapter 3, [33] the Communists denied any binding legal obligation to return the UN "war criminals"; hence any release of them was held out as an act of altruism. This exploitation of the Free World, humanitarian concern for its PWs has been an ugly feature of contemporary wars involving communist states and presents a continuing problem to their adversaries.

In the Korean War the issue of PW rights took an unusual turn because of the manifest unwillingness of large numbers of PWs from the Communist side to return to totalitarian societies. Traditional international-law provisions for prompt repatriation had assumed the normal desire of PWs to return to their homelands. However, experience with prisoners of war after World War II revealed that sending Soviet and Eastern European PWs home was often assurance of their death, imprisonment, or subjugation in a totalitarian society. The issue of giving PWs a fair choice about repatriation held up the Korean truce negotiations for long, bitter months. A struggle ensued between those on the UN side and the neutral Indian commissioners, who sought to give every PW such a choice, and the Communist PW leaders and enforcers, who attempted to persuade or intimidate every PW to return to the Communist homeland. This prolonged the fight-and-negotiate period and provided the Communist side with another category of hostages to be treated as pawns. The upshot was that, notwithstanding battlefield parity, political leverage existed on the Communist side by virtue of the two categories of PW hostages whose fate they controlled. [34]

This state of affairs compelled Eisenhower to threaten nuclear war against the Chinese homeland. This threat to escalate the fighting element of the situation appears to have been critical in bringing the negotiation element to a conclusion. [35]

Third Parties—International Organizations

A major hope and expectation of the international community since 1945 has been that international organizations would play a greater role in the alleviation and termination of international conflicts.

Where this would not be possible, it was expected that the traditional role of the neutral third-party mediator would be accepted by parties to conflict. In Korea, the most important limited war of the post-World War II era, heavy responsibilities were placed on third parties in a situation where no international organization was able to operate as a neutral party. The United Nations was a party to the conflict and the International Committee of the Red Cross was rejected as an acceptable neutral party by the Communist side. When the problem arose of conducting screening operations to allow prisoners of war to accept or reject repatriation, it was necessary to constitute an ad hoc Neutral Nations Repatriation Commission.

This commission originated in a plan proposed to the United Nations by India and adopted by the UN Political Committee on December 1, 1952. After having been violently opposed by the communist states, it was included in part in a Communist initiative at Panmunjom on May 7, 1953, and agreed to by the parties on July 8, 1953. The Neutral Nations Repatriation Commission constituted Sweden and Switzerland as members nominated by the UN side and Poland and Czechoslovakia as members nominated by the Communist side. The fifth member, India, was umpire and "sole provider of troops for the custodial force."

In October, after two months of prisoner-of-war exchanges, approximately 22,000 PWs remained. They were taken to the Demilitarized Zone for "explanations" by "explainers" who would encourage them to return home or go elsewhere. Despite many difficulties, the process was sufficiently effective so that 21,805 PWs from North Korea and the PRC still refused repatriation. Thus, the principle of voluntary repatriation was upheld, justifying the lives and months lost because of the prolongation of the war over this principle. It seems highly unlikely that this screening of PWs could have been accomplished without the work of the Neutral Nations Repatriation Commission. On the other hand, the commission would not have been successful had the communist states not decided to accept the outcome in order to bring the war to an end. This acceptance was manifest when they accepted, despite their violent protests, Syngman Rhee's unilateral release of 27,000 North Korean PWs on June 18, 1953, and their absorption into the South Korean society.

Predictably, the Neutral Nations Supervisory Commission (same members as the Repatriation Commission) was quite unsuccessful. The provisions prohibiting force buildups were consistently violated by the Communists and never acknowledged by the communist members of the commission. The commission's utility lay solely in its limited ability to record violations of the truce agreement. Maintenance of the truce over the years has been accomplished by the political-military balance of power established by the two sides. [36]

FLEXIBLE RESPONSE

The need for policies and requisite capabilities for a flexible response to aggression was painfully demonstrated in the Korean War. This need was one of the principal lessons learned by the United States, and it is frequently underscored in the limited-war literature of the ensuing period. It was largely a matter of luck that the United States had the forces available to commit to Korea. When they had to be reinforced, a series of ad hoc improvisations was necessary. It is not enough to be committed to policies and strategies of limited war. The means necessary to implement limited-war policies and strategies must be planned for and provided in time so that a spectrum of controlled, appropriate responses is available when aggression threatens or occurs.[37]

11

VIETNAM:
LIMITED WAR ON TRIAL

The Korean War was a limited war that provided a basis for development of the limited-war theories of the 1950s and 1960s. Notwithstanding considerable dissatisfaction with the conduct and results
of the Korean War, it was widely accepted as a preferable alternative
to the contemporary alternatives of total war and acquiescence in aggression. As discussed in the just-war analysis in Chapter 5, however, the Vietnam War was not accorded even the grudging acceptance of the Korean War either in terms of its necessity or its conduct.[1] But it remains a central example of limited war. The lesson
of Vietnam in the minds of many is that the United States either cannot or ought not undertake to fight a limited war. Since it is the position of this book that limited wars have been and predictably will be
necessary for a Great Power with the values and commitments of the
United States, it is important to analyze the Vietnam War in terms of
the limited-war guidelines that have been herein proposed.

POLITICAL PRIMACY

The context of strategic thought and policy in which the Vietnam
War unfolded was quite different from that of the Korean War. The
earlier vague working assumption that World War III with the Soviet
Union should be avoided had become the sophisticated concept of mutual deterrence through the nuclear balance of terror. The idea of
limited war under the strategic nuclear umbrella was widely accepted
and discussed. Counterinsurgency in revolutionary war was a prime
subject of political-military analysis. The ascendancy of the political
instrument in such wars was generally acknowledged. All in all, it
was well established that war must be a limited instrument of politics

and that the unfettered pursuit of military victory espoused by Mac-Arthur was an archaic and unacceptable objective. Consensus on these points had recently been confirmed in the 1964 presidential election when Senator Goldwater's version of the MacArthur victory concept was thoroughly rejected by the U.S. electorate.

This consensus was reflected in the conduct of the Vietnam War by the United States. Victory over North Vietnam was not sought, only discontinuance of aggression by that country in South Vietnam. A political settlement, even a very precarious one, remained the goal. There was no equivalent of the post-Inchon Korean War debate about crushing the Communist armies. To be sure, no decisive military victories comparable to the Pusan breakout and Inchon landing occurred, in large measure because of the nature of the war. But there is every indication that a comparable series of Communist defeats would not have led to the invasion, conquest, and forcible incorporation of North Vietnam into a unified Vietnam under southern control. MacArthur, backed by the Joint Chiefs of Staff, had insisted that the complete defeat of the Communist forces was the necessary response to aggression, and that this required invasion of North Korea. If the U.S. military believed that the same was true with respect to the Communist Vietnamese forces, they never were permitted a public debate over invasion of North Vietnam.

Besides eschewing land invasion of North Vietnam, the United States demonstrated its commitment to political primacy by the numerous bombing pauses and holiday truces that marked the war. These were invariably resisted by the military but insisted upon by the civilian leaders as politically necessary.

Political considerations consistently outweighed military requests with respect to bombing targets in North Vietnam. The rules of the conflict regarding abstention from attacks on various sanctuaries and off-limits targets were all developed on the basis of political objectives in the face of strong military objections. When some of these rules were discarded by the Nixon administration, it was directly in support of political objectives, not as part of a plan to achieve anything like military victory.[2] Generally speaking, political primacy characterized the Vietnam War even more than the Korean War.

There was no MacArthur of the Vietnam War and no great debate over civilian supremacy over the military. General Westmoreland and his successor, General Abrams, played the game by the rules laid down by the civilians. Although there has been postwar criticisms by many military figures of the political controls that hampered their military conduct of the war, the military backlash seems to have been less powerful than after the Korean War. While the Korean War was at least a partial success and the Vietnam War a defeat, there appears to be considerably more uncertainty as to what would have brought success in Vietnam than there was about the path to victory in Korea. Indeed, no one is very confident in discussing how the Vietnam War could have been successfully conducted, and there are many who flatly conclude that, given the limits imposed, it was an impossible assignment for the U.S. military.[3]

Nonetheless, the issue of political interference with the military conduct of the war at key points in the development of military momentum arose in the Vietnam War just as it did in the Korean War. This issue takes two forms, one general and one particular. In general, the rather frequent bombing pauses and holiday truces resulted in relaxation of the military pressures on the enemy, notably on his logistical centers and supply lines. These interruptions of bombing permitted resumption of Communist resupply operations that often had the effect of undoing a good deal of what was accomplished during attacks on the supply system.[4]

In particular, General Westmoreland has criticized substantial limits placed on the bombing of North Vietnam by President Johnson in his March 31, 1968, address to the nation. The Communist Tet Offensive had gained by objectives primarily in the hearts and minds of the U.S. people. But it had failed to accomplish its political and military objectives in Vietnam and had resulted in crushing defeats that, inter alia, apparently destroyed the core of the Vietcong forces and badly mauled the regular North Vietnamese forces. In these circumstances the indicated strategy was to put maximum military pressure on the Communists across the board. Instead, the whole tone of the Johnson administration's policies after Johnson's March 31 speech was one of acceptance of stalemate and pursuance of some kind of political settlement.[5]

It was unfortunate enough that the United States broke off its military momentum in the Korean War at a time of U.S./UN ascendancy and settled down to the fight-and-negotiate phase. But in the Vietnam War, the denial to Westmoreland of the initiative to press his counterattacks to the utmost before pressing for negotiations, perhaps partially replacing the image of U.S./South Vietnamese defeat in the Tet Offensive, led to a U.S. negotiating posture that was decidedly weaker than that held during the Korean negotiations.[6]

It is far from clear, of course, that greater support for a Westmoreland counteroffensive, complemented by the material and psychological effects of more intensive bombing, would have brought about decisively different results. The point is that it was the opinion of the responsible military commander in the field that such a vigorous general counteroffensive should be attempted. The political decision to restrict further U.S. military operations and to emphasize political negotiations with an enemy that had at that point displayed virtually no interest in negotiations was an example of civilian primacy over the military. But this decision resulted in the loss of military leverage in support of the political instrument at a time when that leverage was badly needed. This judgment, of course, was shared by President Nixon when he later used intensive bombing to pressure the Communists into concluding the peace negotiations at the end of 1972.

LIMITED OBJECTIVES

The objective of the United States in the Vietnam War from first to last was to defend South Vietnam from external aggression linked to internal Communist insurgency. The objective was not even to guarantee a government without communist participants or influence. The United States undertook to protect South Vietnam so that its people could have a free choice about their political future. However, the United States sought to prevent the imposition of a communist or communist-front government on South Vietnam by a combination of internal civil war and external armed aggression. As earlier observed, there was never any serious consideration of uniting Vietnam by a conquest of North Vietnam or even of an extension of the land war into North Vietnam in order to defeat the Communist armies. [7] As will be discussed under other limited-war categories, the United States repeatedly emphasized that it sought "no wider war," notably with the People's Republic of China (PRC) or the Soviet Union. [8]

On the other hand, over the course of the war, the United States extended its objectives to include the replacement of the Sihanouk regime in Cambodia with a military government allied to the United States. The war was also waged in part in Laos, although there the objectives were more subordinate to the exigencies of carrying out the war in Vietnam than to the liberation of the Laotians. These extensions were understandable given the fact that the communist effort to take over all of Indochina threatened the independence and integrity of these countries prior to the U.S./South Vietnamese actions that brought them squarely and overtly into the war. These developments will be discussed further in connection with the rule of conflict enjoining geographic limitation of the war. [9]

In addition to the particular objective of protecting South Vietnam from aggression, the Vietnam War was fought, as was the Korean War, as a practical sanction to the international-law prohibitions against aggression. Initially, the aggression was indirect, later direct. Both forms were properly considered aggression in the sense of the UN Charter and the post-World War II efforts to restrict the use of armed coercion. It was the reasonable belief of the U.S. leaders that acceptance of the lethal combination of indirect aggression and civil war constituted as much of a danger to the peace and international legal order of the 1960s as the conventional aggression of North Korea and the PRC had been in the 1950s. The Vietnam War, then, was fought to demonstrate the credibility of the U.S. commitment to resist aggression, direct or indirect, wherever possible.[10]

ECONOMY OF FORCE

There was little problem in observing the principle of economy of force in the Korean War because the forces available were less than adequate to fight the war and address the other security requirements of the United States and the Free World. There may have been a problem in the Vietnam War of disproportionate use of some available military assets. The extraordinary expenditure of ammunition of all kinds reflected a devastating use, perhaps abuse, of firepower on land and from the air. The large U.S. military establishment in Vietnam caused economic and social dislocation, which might have been avoided had the U.S. forces been leaner. The availability of a large combat ground force permitted search-and-destroy strategies and tactics that might have been more modestly carried out by lighter forces with less deleterious effects on the Vietnamese society.

These speculations are advanced only because of the mixed conventional-counterinsurgency character of the war. It was difficult to judge just what mix of traditional military power and of more subtle forms of political-military actions was proper to the Vietnam conflict. The war was fought at a high point of U.S. preparedness and in a context of comparative absence of other serious military threats. In these circumstances, the military principle of economy of force may have been stretched if not violated to the detriment of the political struggle that remained the ultimate arena of conflict.

Moreover, as the war dragged on, it became necessary to strip resources in Europe and the continental United States to the point that the United States would have been seriously embarrassed by a major threat on another front. This was briefly demonstrated before and during the 1967 June War in the Middle East when the United States would have been hard pressed to vindicate its position on keeping open the Straits of Tiran had the Israelis not solved the problem with their rapid and complete triumph.[11]

RULES OF CONFLICT

Communication between Belligerents

U.S. leaders in the Korean War had virtually no theoretical or practical background for the notion of communication between belligerents in the sense of Schelling's concept of bargaining.[12] They were accustomed to total war wherein one kept pounding against the enemy until unconditional surrender was forced. Negotiation for anything less was spurned as was the notion of limits on the means used in pursuit of the achievement of complete victory. Interestingly, these leaders in the Korean War quickly developed their own pragmatic concepts of communications and tried in a number of ways to signal the enemy and establish rules of the conflict.

By the time of the Vietnam War the whole idea of belligerent communication, signaling, and bargaining was well established in the study of international relations. Indeed, it was rather an "in" subject that was tossed about with some abandon by the national security specialists in government, academia, and the think tanks. Accordingly, one would assume that the Vietnam War would have been the conflict par excellence of belligerent communication and bargaining, resulting in rules of the conflict and fruitful negotiations leading to its termination. But this was not to be the case.[13]

The first major instance of bargaining by behavioral patterns appears to have developed with respect to the activities of U.S. advisers. From the early 1960s, U.S. combat advisers in growing numbers were operating so closely with the South Vietnamese forces that it was not uncommon for them to be involved in combat. However, neither the increasingly elaborate and conspicuous camps and facilities of the Green Berets and other U.S. advisory forces nor U.S. support facilities were subject to Vietcong attack. For its part, the United States refrained from overt escalation to the status of declared cobelligerency and denied or downplayed active participation in the conflict by U.S. personnel. The Tonkin Gulf incidents represented the first time that there was a direct attack on U.S. forces in the area. The circumstances, related to naval and amphibious operations, were somewhat particularistic. However, it was the series of attacks on U.S. bases and personnel in Pleiku and elsewhere, beginning on February 6, 1965, that marked the end of the immunity of U.S. forces and installations in South Vietnam from Vietcong attack.[14]

The U.S. reaction to this change of Communist signals and policies, of course, was to escalate the war and to involve the United States fully and overtly. To be sure, there were political and strategic reasons for this escalation that many felt to be essential to prevent the fall of South Vietnam, a cause that was considered legitimate on its own merits. However, it remains interesting that this escalation was only embarked on following a change in signals by the Communists, however needed increased U.S. participation in the conflict may have been then or earlier.[15]

Once the conflict had become a full-scale war for the United States, a number of policies were adopted that appear to have been intended as signals of a desire to keep the war limited. These included abstention from bombing attacks on Hanoi, Haiphong, and key dams and power plants, as well as other designated areas, at various times; establishment of truces during Vietnamese holidays; and abstention from a land invasion of North Vietnam.

Over the course of the war the unilateral rules of conflict observed by the United States and South Vietnam with respect to bombing attacks were suspended and reinstated according to the progress of the fighting and negotiating. The truces were generally observed subject to numerous local violations and the massive violation that was the Tet Offensive of 1968. The third rule of conflict was observed substantially throughout the conflict by the United States and South Vietnam.

There is little indication that these self-imposed restraints elicited any kind of reciprocal restraints on the part of the Communist parties to the conflict. However, it may well be that the main thrust of these signals was to convey to Peking and Moscow the U.S. determination to keep the war limited. This aspect of U.S.-initiated rules of the conflict will be discussed in connection with the subcategories of avoidance of superpower confrontation and geographic confinement of the conflict.

The process of turning bombing raids on and off, of expanding and contracting the target areas, was apparently more directed to the objective of compelling and/or encouraging peace negotiations than of eliciting reciprocity in the development of rules of the conflict. The truces in South Vietnam had the dual purpose of observing Vietnamese holidays and of offering opportunities to pursue negotiations. The effectiveness of these efforts will be considered under the subcategory of fight and negotiate. However, as in the Korean War, there was virtually no sign of acknowledgment of the signals by the Communist side much less of reciprocity either with respect to the conduct of the war or the initiation of negotiations. From the viewpoint of the military commanders, the restraints imposed unilaterally by the United States, as well as those few that took the form of reciprocal truces, presented the Communist side with gift "time outs" from the attrition of war without producing any tangible benefits to the U.S./South Vietnamese side. [16]

As in the Korean War, the communication of rules of the conflict took the twofold form of diplomatic communications and public pronouncements directed at enemies and of policies of self-limitation and abstention. These communications seem to have been supplemented by rather more secret and indirect diplomacy than was the case in the Korean War. In addition to the rules of conflict already discussed, there were other important rules and procedures that require individual treatment in terms of the subcategories distinguished in the general analysis of limited-war guidelines.

Avoidance of Superpower Confrontation

The superpower confrontation danger in the case of the Vietnam War was quite different than it had been in the Korean conflict. In the first place, while only the United States and the Soviet Union could be considered nuclear superpowers, the PRC was sufficiently formidable to warrant its inclusion in the efforts to avoid superpower confrontations. Moreover, Red China's proximity to Vietnam, the ideological and political links between the governments of Mao Tsetung and Ho Chi Minh, as well as the memory of the PRC's intervention in the Korean War all made it a more likely if less powerful additional belligerent. This perception was increased by Red China's rhetoric and beginning efforts with respect to the exportation of revolution. If the Soviet Union was a less likely participant in a war over Southeast Asia, the threat of direct confrontation leading to hostilities with the Soviets was sufficient to enjoin considerable caution on the part of the United States.

Clearly the repeated pronouncements by the Johnson administration concerning its determination to avoid a wider war were as much addressed to the Soviet Union and PRC as to the local communist belligerents and their Indo-Chinese neighbors. The limits on bombing North Vietnam clearly reflected this determination. The lifelines of the North Vietnamese/Vietcong war effort came overland from the PRC and by sea from the Soviet Union and the rest of the world. In particular the more sophisticated weaponry that was used by the Communists in the 1970s and ultimately contributed critically to the defeat of the Army of the Republic of Vietnam (ARVN) forces in a conventional war had to come from the Soviet Union and the PRC. Interdiction of these vital sources of military and other supplies would have been the most obvious strategy for containing the Communist war effort. However, the general desire to keep the war limited and the specific concern to avoid confrontations with the two great communist superpowers led the United States to impose restraints on its bombing that left these supply lines completely free for the better part of the war. The principal limits were the abstention from bombing North Vietnam within a strip adjacent to the Red Chinese border; abstention from mining and bombing Haiphong Harbor; and abstention from inteference on the high seas with vessels carrying supplies to North Vietnam.

These policies of abstention cost the United States and South Vietnam dearly. To be sure, the Korean and other wartime experiences had shown the difficulties of cutting off supply routes by air interdiction. However, an uninhibited policy of air interdiction of the supply routes from Red China would have cut back the North Vietnamese war-making capability substantially. Moreover, had the United States been willing to risk employment of the naval blockade practices of the two world wars against the Soviet Union and other powers who, by any definition, were supplying critical contraband of war to the North Vietnamese, a very significant reduction in the Communist side's war potential could have been effected. Such policies of interdiction and blockade might not have terminated a long war of attrition held to a low level of intensity. But it is difficult to imagine the Communist side developing and maintaining the capability of waging large-unit warfare in a protracted war if their supply routes from the PRC and USSR had been effectively cut.[17]

It remains extremely difficult to speculate about the extent to which the U.S. efforts to avoid superpower confrontations were necessary. As the war developed, and in the postwar years, the threat of PRC intervention, once thought serious, appears always to have been modest. There is no reason to believe that the Soviet Union would have risked a major war with the United States over the blockade of Southeast Asia. On the other hand, it is difficult for superpowers to back down when their freedom of action is challenged. A confrontation over attacks on Soviet shipping in North Vietnamese waters and/or interception of Soviet shipping on the high seas might have produced World War III as readily as other imaginable scenarios. The United States chose not to flirt with any such eventuality until the very end of the war when the general international situation, characterized by U.S.-Soviet détente and improved relations with the PRC, held out little danger of a superpower confrontation resulting from U.S. involvement in the Vietnam War.[18]

Limits on Nuclear Weapons

The Vietnam War offered a different kind of challenge to the policy of abstention from first use of nuclear weapons than did the Korean War. Certainly there were ample nuclear weapons available in a variety of forms and sizes, unlike the days of nuclear scarcity in the Korean War. On the other hand, thanks in part to the Korean precedent of abstention from nuclear war, the presumption against use of nuclear weapons had grown considerably by 1965.

Against this background, the firm U.S. policy of abstaining from nuclear war may be considered. As in the Korean War, a major particularistic consideration was the lack of industrial targets warranting nuclear attack. Indeed, the conventional bombing languished for lack of significant targets, given the special status of Hanoi and Haiphong.

However, given the inability to close or even substantially curtail the Ho Chi Minh trail and other supply routes into South Vietnam by conventional bombing, it is quite conceivable that nuclear bombings of those vital supply lines in a manner to produce protracted radiation could have decisively barred the Communist forces from maintaining their war potential. There would have been little fear of nuclear retaliation against South Vietnam. Voluntary abstention from such a policy was a major concession to the presumption against introduction of nuclear weapons.

Moreover, as the war progressed, Communist troop concentration became sufficiently dense so that tactical nuclear weapons would have had significant targets. In the 1968 battle at Khe Sanh, General Westmoreland considered the use of tactical nuclear weapons, a possibility discouraged by President Johnson. Writing in retrospect, General Westmoreland observes that

> there was another possibility at Khe Sanh: tactical nuclear weapons. Early in the fight President Johnson telephoned General Wheeler to ask if there might be a chance he would have to make such a decision, for he had no wish to be faced with it. Although I recognized the controversial nature of the subject and that employing tactical nuclear weapons would be a political decision, I nevertheless considered that I would be imprudent if I failed to acquaint myself with the possibilities in detail. Because the region around Khe Sanh was virtually uninhabited, civilian casualties would be minimal. If Washington officials were so intent on "sending a message" to Hanoi, surely small tactical nuclear weapons would be a way to tell Hanoi something, just as two atomic bombs had spoken convincingly to Japanese officials during World War II and the threat of atomic bombs induced the North Koreans to accept meaningful negotiations during the Korean War. It could be that use of a few small tactical nuclear weapons in Vietnam—or even the threat of them—might have quickly brought the war there to an end. No one could say so with certainty, of course, but surely a detailed consideration of the possibility was warranted. Although I established a small secret group to study the subject, Washington so feared that some word of it might reach the press that I was told to desist. I felt at the time and even more so now that to fail to consider this alternative was a mistake. [19]

However, given the presumption against first use of nuclear weapons, the U.S. policy of nuclear abstention cannot be considered a mistake but, rather, a reasonable policy of just and limited war.

Geographical Confinement of the Conflict

As observed in discussing the limited objectives of the Vietnam War, the typical guidelines regarding geographical confinement of the conflict were only partially maintained over the eight years of full U.S. involvement. The policy against extending the war on the ground into North Vietnam survived all temptations. For many years the United States held back from attacking Communist forces, installations, and activities in Laos and Cambodia. During the years when the Communists enjoyed the immunity of these sanctuaries, recriminations similar to those heard concerning the trans-Yalu sanctuaries of the Korean War were common among the U.S. military and their supporters. A substantial price was paid in terms of U.S./ARVN vulnerability to operations launched from would-be neutral territory.

In 1970 the Nixon administration determined to end this Communist advantage. The Cambodian incursion resulted not only in the full extension of the war into that country but in a change in regimes from the Sihanouk procommunist neutralist regime to that of a military government willing to become a cobelligerent with the United States. Whether the immediate strategic gains in terms of South Vietnamese security and a consequent improvement of conditions for a U.S. withdrawal from the war were sufficient to justify this extension remains somewhat unclear and controverted. The great domestic and international furor over the incursion can be substantially ignored in this calculation. These objections appear to have been the product of exasperation and outrage on the part of opponents of the war who wanted it simply ended when Nixon chose to protect an orderly U.S. exit by maximizing the strategic prospects of the South Vietnamese. More pertinent to the calculation of the prudence of the Cambodian incursion is the assessment of the extent to which it really improved the strategic situation and the price of that improvement in terms of the opening up of a new conflict in Cambodia. I suspect that the Cambodian venture will be found to have yielded insufficient gains to give retrospective warrant to the decision to involve Cambodia directly in the conflict, given the ultimately catastrophic course of events in Cambodia. If one further adds the domestic and international public opinion effects of the Cambodian incursion, one concludes that it was in itself a not unreasonable extention of the conflict, but that the negative effects were disproportionate to the strategic outcomes actually achieved.[20]

Legal Justification and Collectivization

The basic U.S. legal justification for its participation in the Vietnam War was at bottom the same as for the Korean War. The

United States contended that South Vietnam was the victim of indirect —and then direct—aggression from North Vietnam. Under Article 51 of the UN Charter, the United States was entitled to go to the assistance of South Vietnam in a collective self-defense. The great differences from the Korean War were that there was no UN finding of communist aggression, the alleged aggression was in the first instance indirect rather than direct, and there was no UN General Assembly Uniting for Peace Resolution and similar support for the U.S. action.[21]

It was observed earlier that the United States may have been spoiled by the experience of operating in Korea under UN auspices. Concerned that its action in Vietnam resemble as closely as possible the police action in Korea, the United States sought to clothe its participation in the war in the cloak of the Southeast Asian Treaty Organization (SEATO). This effort followed the lines of recent efforts to justify the U.S. actions in the Cuban Missile Crisis and the 1965 Dominican civil war as actions of the Organization of American States (OAS). In my view the OAS rationales for these two U.S. actions are quite strained and unpersuasive.[22] But they are pillars of legal argumentation compared with the SEATO justifications for the Vietnam War.

At least in the OAS cases the United States managed to obtain authorization for the regional organization to engage in actions that it had determined to take in any event. In the case of the Vietnam War there was, in effect, no SEATO to authorize anything. The organization as such did not act on the war. Individual members such as France and Pakistan disavowed the U.S. claims to be acting in virtue of the SEATO agreement. In my view, to the extent that the Johnson administration claimed to be acting on behalf of SEATO, it only impaired the credibility of its basic argument of collective self-defense, which was valid on its own merits.

Nevertheless, the Johnson administration sought to justify its SEATO rationale and to replicate in some measure the Korean phenomenon of an international police force by adding "flags" to the collective defense (for example, South Korea, Australia, New Zealand, and Thailand in combat roles; the Philippines and others in primarily humanitarian roles). The result was, at best, only an alleviation of the general image of a war in which the United States was the senior partner, the South Vietnamese the junior partner. The other states represented in Vietnam had the appearance of stage extras added for effect. It is difficult to find evidence that the addition of more "flags" really gave the U.S. claims to be fighting for international order more credibility.[23]

Limited Mobilization

As observed earlier, limited mobilization is as much a characteristic of as a guideline for limited war. Often the reasons for limited mobilization are extraneous to the principled determination to keep a war limited by restricting mobilization. In the case of the Vietnam War the reasons for limited mobilization were, once again, varied. In the first place, mobilization could be limited because, unlike the Korean situation, the war found the United States well prepared militarily with sizable ready forces and an ongoing draft. The war could be fought with the military assets in hand. Second, however, the war began at a time of great social and economic turbulence. Domestic problems were being addressed under the cloak of Lyndon Johnson's ambitious Great Society programs that would increasingly take money and resources. Johnson was equally dedicated to the achievement of the Great Society objectives and to the successful pursuit of the Vietnam War. This twofold commitment meant that major mobilization was not possible because it would deprecate from the Great Society programs already suffering from the competition of the war effort.

To complicate matters, Johnson chose to fight the war on the basis of the Tonkin Gulf resolution and subsequent congressional legislation supportive of the war rather than on the foundation of a formal declaration of war. It was probably impossible to elicit fuller mobilization for war without such a declaration. As the war attracted more critics, it became the Johnson policy to insist that it would be substantially terminated before long, and that it would be possible to accomplish the war's limited objectives with the military assets available.

In these circumstances, there were limits to the mobilization base for the war, albeit limits far broader and more permissive than war critics and proponents of reallocation of priorities and resources would have preferred. Accordingly, the question of whether the mobilization base should be held down to keep the war limited became academic. The fact is that Johnson succeeded to a remarkable degree for a considerable time in fighting the war and pressing the Great Society simultaneously. It was Nixon who had to pay a good deal of the price of this policy in dealing with the economic consequences of Johnson's guns-and-butter policies.

Finally, it must be observed that there is little evidence that the United States was disadvantaged in the Vietnam War because of its limited mobilization base. If anything, the U.S. forces in Vietnam had more purely military power at their disposal than was appropriate to the conflict, given the limited-war guidelines adopted.

Restraint in the Psychological Instrument

One of the greatest, perhaps the greatest, conscious restraints placed by the U.S. government on itself in the Vietnam War was in its use of the psychological instrument. The Korean War had demonstrated that the lack of a full-scale psychological campaign in the manner of the two world wars is detrimental to the war effort in a democracy such as the United States. In the Korean War the atmosphere had been so supercharged that the Truman administration, partly out of good judgment and partly out of self-preservation, chose to limit rather than stoke the flames of antipathy toward the enemy. Support for the war declined not only because it was protracted and inconclusive but also because there was, by World War II standards, no sufficiently persuasive image of a dangerous enemy whose defeat was vital to U.S. security.

The Vietnam War period in the United States provided a different set of problems for the Johnson administration. The anticommunist temper of the early 1950s had subsided, although the country continued to be generally disposed to a policy of containment of communist aggression. There was a vague apprehension that there was a communist threat in Southeast Asia, but it did not provoke the violent reactions that similar threats in more familiar areas (for example, Eastern Europe and China) had elicited in the 1940s and 1950s. In brief, the Vietnam War would be sustained by a solid base of anticommunist sentiment, but this base required nurturing.

However, it was the judgment of the Johnson administration that popular sentiment should not be permitted to get out of hand. The dangers of expansion and escalation of the war were foremost in the minds of the administration. The concern for the risk of nuclear war, if Vietnam policies led to superpower confrontations, was far greater for the Johnson administration than had been the parallel concerns of the Truman administration in the Korean War, great as the latter were. By the mid-1960s the United States was subject to strategic nuclear attack, a new and awesomely frightening circumstance. A wide margin had to be left between limited local war and the possibility of strategic nuclear war. Restraint in the use of the psychological instrument was one of the primary results of this new necessity of contemporary nuclear superpowers.

Because of its intense concern over the possibility that a heating up of public opinion might precipitate pressures for policies that would risk expansion and escalation, perhaps even nuclear war, the U.S. government deliberately withheld its hand in the matter of psychological warfare. It did not promote what Dean Rusk often referred to as a "war spirit." Limited war was to be fought as a cold, rational proposition, supported by reasonable and cooperative citizens who were expected to understand and accept this proposition.

It is still difficult to assess this policy of restraint with the psychological instrument. It is certainly true that by deliberately restraining prowar sentiment the administration left more play to antiwar sentiment. Over time the intensity of convictions on the antiwar side was shown to be markedly greater than the intensity of convictions among the war's supporters. Indeed, as the war dragged on, its supporters were often motivated as much by disagreement with and disdain for the opponents of the war as by positive convictions that the war itself was right, necessary, and properly conducted. On the other hand, there is the basic fact that residual grass-roots support for the war appears to justify U.S. government policies under Johnson, Nixon, and Ford. Despite all of the successes of the antiwar factions, the generality of U.S. people supported the war for eight years. This same support was never conditioned on demands for escalation of the kinds that the U.S. government was determined to avoid. In the end, the U.S. population supported the Vietnam War, and they supported it as a limited war without any serious demand for abandonment of the limited-war restraints adopted by their government.

The feat of holding the American people to their government's commitment to limited war in Vietnam is the more impressive because it was accomplished notwithstanding the enormous and generally antiwar impact of the media. Media coverage of the war and the opposition to it, as well as of the social turbulence in the country that affected wartime policies and attitudes, increased over time to produce a decidedly antiwar—indeed, antimilitary—sentiment. In World War II the media had cooperated with the government's efforts to sell the justice of the war and the duty to contribute to its successful conclusion at any cost. In the Korean War television had not yet taken hold and the press was somewhat divided, as was the country, between the moderates who supported the war and the hard-liners who wanted total war or no war. There was no prominent peace movement for the media to play up. In the Vietnam War the media soon discovered the endless potential of antiwar and antimilitary reporting. The resultant coverage of the war and related social developments raise a serious question about the feasibility of conducting limited war for a country like the United States. The record would seem to indicate that media support or evenhandedness will not be forthcoming unless the issues of the war are so overwhelmingly clear and/or the war so clearly a product of enemy initiatives and actions that there is no alternative to accepting its necessity.[24]

Fight and Negotiate

In the Korean War the U.S. intention was to fight and destroy the North Korean armed forces and then address the question of a political settlement. When the PRC intervened and the war became a stalemate, the United States fell into a fight-and-negotiate approach as a matter of practical necessity. In the Vietnam War the United States did not aspire to military victory over the North Vietnamese forces, something that would have led to an invasion of that country and a wider conflict. From the outset the U.S. strategy was to fight just enough to force the Communists in South and North Vietnam to negotiate.

The United States communicated this strategy verbally by endless calls for negotiations. These calls were underscored by bombing pauses and ground truces. The frequency and poignancy of these calls for negotiations became so great that the United States seemed to be pleading with the Communists to extricate it from the war. Not surprisingly, the communist factions in South Vietnam and the controlling North Vietnamese government turned a deaf ear to these pleas for negotiations. Neither increases nor reductions in the intensity of the conflict brought serious Communist inquiries about negotiations.[25]

As the war progressed the strong antiwar factions in the United States and the world community put heavy pressure on the United States to negotiate, including pressure to prepare the way for negotiations by stopping the bombing of the North and other unilateral restrictions. It may well be that the frequency and nervous quality of the U.S. bids for negotiations may be traced to these pressures. Whatever the reason, the United States did not profit from a fight-and-negotiate strategy—perhaps better described as a fight-and-plead-for-negotiations strategy. Despite the very substantial successes of the U.S./ARVN forces, the United States could not even obtain the equivalent of the Panmunjom talks of the Korean War until very late in the conflict.

When, at last, the Paris peace talks began, the situation was likewise quite different from the parallel case of the Korean War. In the Korean War military initiative and momentum were sacrificed, but there was still a full-scale U.S./UN military capability of impressive significance. The Paris peace talks occurred in the context of a gradual U.S. phasing-out of the Vietnam War. Not only were the numbers of troops being decreased, but the general context was such that the morale and effectiveness of the U.S. forces declined markedly. The United States, therefore, had little of the "fight" element left with which to conduct a fight-and-negotiate strategy. All hopes were being placed in Vietnamization. Given domestic trends in the United States, it was not even clear how long Vietnamization would receive adequate support in the form of military assistance from the United States. Time, generally, was on the side of the Communists. Nixon clearly had McGovern beaten before Kissinger's "peace is at hand" announcement. However, Nixon and Kissinger completed the negotiations with the Communists in the shadow of congressional restrictions on continued U.S. involvement in Vietnam, which placed severe limits on the time and assets available to complete the fight-and-negotiate process.[26]

In these circumstances, it is not surprising that the 1973 Paris Peace Agreement was not to prove durable. The upshot of the experience was that the United States could not find ways of fighting that were sufficiently effective to force negotiations even while a serious U.S. war effort was being exerted. When the United States phased out as a serious belligerent in the war, the Communists deigned to negotiate and were in a position to obtain the kind of peace that they could soon overturn in the process of complete conquest of South Vietnam.

There were two major and instructive exceptions to this general line of developments. The first was the effective "fight" of the ARVN forces, decisively assisted by U.S. air support, against the Communist's spring offensive in 1972. Kissinger's experience clearly shows that, as the expected Communist military victory failed to materialize, the Communist negotiating posture changed dramatically from arrogance and demands for capitulation to astonishing accommodation.[27]

The second exception to the U.S. failure to support negotiations with the coercive diplomacy of effective armed force was in the case of the so-called Christmas bombings of North Vietnamese targets in 1972, notably in Hanoi and Haiphong. The United States felt that the Communists had drawn back from earlier agreements reflected in Kissinger's "peace is at hand" statement of October 26, 1972. To force them to conclude the negotiations within the framework of the earlier agreement as the United States had understood it, the United States applied the only "fight" element remaining, strategic air power. The cause-and-effect relationships are not definitively established, but it is certainly the case that after the Linebacker II Christmas bombing, the Communists came back to negotiations ready to conclude the peace agreement more or less as the United States had undertaken it in November 1972.[28]

If the general record of fight and negotiate, then, is one of very little fighting accompanied by negotiations favorable to the Communists, the defeat of the Communist 1972 spring offensive and the Christmas bombings provide rare and critical examples of the fight element being used, apparently with favorable results insofar as the outcome of negotiations was concerned. However, the overall circumstances of the Vietnam negotiations were such that the final peace proclaimed in January 1973 did not survive further Communist aggression beyond 1975. By that time there were no available U.S. "fight" elements in the picture, and the Communist side was being reinforced by Communist allies whose involvement continued after the United States disengaged itself.

Third Parties—International Organizations

Attempts to negotiate a settlement in the Vietnam War were made almost entirely outside of the United Nations. The most numerous and significant occasions wherein third-party help was sought involved communist governments as intermediaries. At no time was the United Nations, through any of its organs, a focal point of peace initiatives. It appears that the North Vietnamese refused to operate under UN auspices because they claimed the war was an internal matter for Vietnam of which they were the sole legitimate representative. North Vietnam had not been accepted into UN membership.

The United States, for its part, was unwilling to entrust the matter to the Security Council, where the Soviets could control developments with their veto. As the war progressed, the temper of the General Assembly was more and more unfavorable to the United States and its goals in Vietnam. No Uniting for Peace Resolution for Vietnam was remotely conceivable, and the United Nations generally was not an institution from which the United States could any longer expect fair, much less sympathetic treatment.

There was one neutral body to turn to for some assistance. This was the International Control Commission (ICC) for Vietnam, established by the Geneva Accords of 1954 and consisting of personnel provided by India, Canada, and Poland. Some thought was given to involving the states participating in the ICC in peace negotiations, but nothing came of this. When the direct talks between the two sides produced the Paris Agreement of 1973, the ICC states, augmented by Hungary and Indonesia, were persuaded to reactivate this moribund commission and undertake to supervise the peace settlement with the new designation of the International Commission for Control and Supervision (ICCS). This undertaking proved to be as hopeless, because of noncooperation and cheating by the various Vietnamese belligerents, as had been the ICC's earlier efforts to implement the 1954 Geneva Accords. [29]

In summary, recourse to third parties in ending the Vietnam War was mainly confined to traditional diplomacy involving communist states. The United Nations remained irrelevant and the International Control Commission for Vietnam and its successor, the International Commission for Control and Supervision, only succeeded in adding another chapter to the record of international peacekeeping missions that fail because the parties have no intention of permitting them to succeed.

FLEXIBLE RESPONSE

As was the case with regard to the issue of political primacy, the strategic and policy context of the Vietnam War differed greatly from that of the Korean War with regard to the need for flexible response to aggression. From the Korean War the United States began to learn the need for flexible response capabilities and policies. The concept had been particularly emphasized under the Kennedy and Johnson administrations. The Vietnam War came at a time when flexible response was the hallmark of U.S. defense policy, and when considerable effort and resources had been devoted to implementing this policy. It could, accordingly, be expected that the U.S. military effort in Vietnam was handcrafted to fit the situation. However, this proved not to be the case.

The United States had developed counterinsurgency doctrine, policies, and forces. However, neither the strategies nor the forces —United States and South Vietnamese combined—were ever shown to be sufficient to win the Vietnam War as a primarily counterinsurgency war. This statement is made with the awareness that to this day we are not at all sure what would have constituted the most effective doctrine and capabilities for winning such a war. However, certain general problems can be identified. First, on the military side, the elite Special Forces units and other advisory groups intermingled with the South Vietnamese forces were probably not sufficiently large to transform the entire South Vietnamese military force into an effective instrument of counterinsurgency. What would have been required would be a considerable additional number of U.S. light counterinsurgency units working jointly with the South Vietnamese. The Marines achieved this kind of relationship, but this appears to have been exceptional among U.S. combat units.[30]

On the civil affairs side, the United States required from the outset personnel comparable in numbers and competence to those needed for the military missions of counterinsurgency. Civil affairs teams were needed along the line of those eventually developed in the Civil Operations and Revolutionary (Rural) Development Support (CORDS) program. The necessary technical skills and human qualities should have been found both among the military and U.S. civilian government resources to deal on a massive and continuing scale with the great problems of revolutionary development. In this regard the U.S. performance failed to meet the objective requirements of effective counterinsurgency. This failure, then, must be interpreted to mean that the flexible-response capabilities that had been promised were lacking in precisely the area of greatest known danger.

To be sure, counterinsurgency in Vietnam was dependent, ultimately, on the South Vietnamese. But the U.S. government had at hand unique resources for counterinsurgency. It had studied the problems of development as well as of revolutionary war at some length. It had developed doctrines and policies to address these problems. The U.S. government had engaged many of its civilian agencies in dealing with these problems and had developed a reservoir of experience. If all this knowledge, experience, and technical competence had been marshaled and applied in time in Vietnam, the chances for success would have been much greater. The failure to accomplish this on the civil affairs side should be taken to heart as a critical lesson learned. Flexible response in the future should always include the civil affairs component of doctrine and capabilities integrally with the military component of counterinsurgency.

There is a further criticism to be made of the performance of the United States in Vietnam in terms of flexible response. It is a major one. Having failed to provide the mix of military counterinsurgency and civil-affairs revolutionary-development forces and resources appropriate for the war, the United States conducted an essentially conventional war of attrition with conventional forces. To be sure, the massive use of helicopters and the development of air-mobile units addressed some of the particular problems of the Vietnam War. But the basic characteristics of the combat units and their strategies and tactics now appear to have been, to a considerable degree, inappropriate for this kind of war. Here was the source of the widespread destruction and dislocation that undermined the Vietnamese society and fueled antiwar criticism at home.

It is difficult to believe that planners controlling the organization and training of the divisions that fought the war would, in the years prior to 1965, have given them the same orientation if they could have foreseen the effects of their operations on the military counterinsurgency and civil affairs revolutionary-development aspects of the war. If the United States has to fight another war comparable to that in Vietnam, it will need extensive counterinsurgency forces and advisory teams working closely at all times with skilled civil-affairs teams to conduct the war in ways congruent with the preservation of the society that U.S. intervention is supposed to protect. [31]

12

THE YOM KIPPUR WAR:
AN EXEMPLARY LIMITED WAR

Application of the limited-war guidelines developed by the United
States to the wars of less powerful belligerents involves some adjustments. Most belligerents do not possess a nuclear capability. This
does not mean, however, that the threat of nuclear escalation may
not be part of the limited-war calculus of such belligerents. Nonnuclear belligerents may have superpower or other nuclear allies
who could be drawn into the conflict at the risk of nuclear escalation.
Limited-war guidelines should be shaped by such belligerents so as
to minimize the dangers of interventions leading to nuclear escalation. Also, guidelines for limited mobilization as an imminent restraint directed at great powers do not always apply to smaller
powers.

Otherwise, the basic rationale for limited war as waged by
nonnuclear belligerents is the traditional one—that war should be
used as an instrument of political policy and should not be allowed to
escape control either by reason of military technology, military adventurism, or the uncontrolled passions of a society and its leadership in the grip of a total-war psychology. Finally, although different
states, reflecting different religious and cultural heritages, develop
their own distinctive approaches to the problems raised by the Christian just-war tradition, the moral imperative to keep war as limited
as possible should be universal.

It is my intention to apply the limited-war guidelines discussed
thus far with respect to recent U.S. wars to the Yom Kippur War of
1973. I will assess briefly the record of Egypt and Israel in terms
of these guidelines. While Syria was a major participant and other
Arab cobelligerents played lesser roles, the basic concept of the
Arab attacks came from Egypt, and the two dominant actors in the
interaction between the belligerents during and since the war have
been Egypt and Israel.

POLITICAL PRIMACY

In 1973 Anwar Sadat was well in control of the Egyptian government. He commanded substantial support and loyalty in both the civilian and military branches of that government. The Egyptian military had a long history of defeats and frustrations and, apparently, was willing to follow Sadat's leadership in reviving Egypt's military power and prestige. One may speculate that the conservative strategic and tactical doctrines recently preached to the Egyptian military by Soviet advisers further discouraged military adventurism.

On the Israeli side there was no dearth of successful, ambitious, and daring military commanders. However, the democratic tradition of civilian control over the military was and remained well established. This primacy of civilians over military commanders and of political over military considerations was well demonstrated in the hours before the war began. Finally recognizing that the Arab attack was certain and imminent, the Israeli leadership was confronted with an air force proposal to strike first with a preemptive air attack. This proposal was firmly rejected. The political consequences of Israel once again striking the first blow in a Middle East conflict were judged by the civilian leadership to outweigh the military advantages of a preemptive first strike against an attack that was certain to inflict grave injury on Israel.[1]

It is more difficult to judge some later developments. General "Arik" Sharon seems to have exceeded and/or changed his orders when he moved out to exploit his small crossing of the Suez Canal instead of holding in place to permit General Adan to cross and go on the offensive. Later, the efforts to capture Suez City appear to have been pressed by tactical commanders without the full approval of the higher military commands and the civilian government. Sharon's unauthorized initiatives resulted in a brilliant strategic breakthrough and, at most, raised issues of fidelity to military orders and plans rather than to civilian control. The last minute efforts to capture Suez City cost many lives and much destruction and were militarily unsuccessful. All in all, these are relatively modest instances of subordinate commanders seizing the initiative and proceeding in unauthorized fashion. They probably represent an acceptable degree of individual military initiative reflective of a military establishment with a strong tradition of encouraging such initiative. Indeed, one would not even raise these instances of military independence except for the tight and delicate political constraints existing in Middle East wars. In sum, the Yom Kippur War saw no real challenge to civil supremacy and the primacy of the political over the military on either the Egyptian or Israeli side.[2]

LIMITED OBJECTIVES

The Yom Kippur War may have been the best example of a war fought for definite political, limited objectives in recent history. Egypt's goals, apparently acquiesced in by Syria and the other Arab cobelligerents to the extent that they were consulted, were partial reconquest of the territory lost in 1967 (in effect, establishment of a lodgment in that area); achievement of sufficient military success to provide a position of strength for negotiations; and realization, through a limited military success, of the goals of self-respect and unity within the Arab world and enhanced attention and respect in the international community, particularly on the part of the Great Powers.

Egypt does not seem to have thought that the defeat of the Israeli Defense Forces and the conquest and/or destruction of Israel was within the capabilities of the Arab forces. Whether these goals, affirmed as recently as 1967 and even after, would have been set had they seemed possible of achievement is difficult to say.[3] Syria, on the other hand, probably had intentions and aspirations rather more like the total-war goals of the Arabs in 1967 and in earlier wars. Syria, however, did not conceive or direct the Yom Kippur War. The principal Arab actor, Egypt, appears to have had very clear and very limited political objectives in mind from start to finish.[4]

Israel also had limited goals. It did not aspire to the total defeat and/or destruction of its Arab enemies. It did not really look to the acquisition of any more territory except in the sensitive Golan sector. Israel's objectives, then, were comparable to those of Egypt. It wanted to defend and hold as much of the occupied territories as possible, defend Israel proper, and win a limited military victory to provide a position of strength for negotiations. Politically and psychologically, the Israeli objective was to maintain the power and prestige gained in earlier victories.[5]

ECONOMY OF FORCE

Egypt deployed and engaged the bulk of its ground forces in Sinai. The Egyptian Air Force was held back to some extent, apparently for several reasons. Given past, disastrous encounters with the Israeli Air Force, there seems to have been some hesitation about engaging in a full-fledged battle for aerial supremacy. However, the conservative strategies and tactics used by the Egyptians, as well as their reliance on sophisticated missile defense systems, may have reduced the need for aggressive air support. In any event, the Egyptians do not seem to have envisaged using their air force for a knockout blow. This decision, of course, was consistent with their limited political and military objectives.[6]

Economy of force was practiced of necessity by Israel. Particularly in the early days of the war, before mobilization was completed, Israel was hard pressed to scrape up adequate forces for all threatened fronts. At their peak, the Israeli forces were able to defend all corners of the country only by highly efficient and rapid campaigns, moving successively from one area to another. Economy of force is not so much a prescribed option as a necessity for a belligerent with barely sufficient forces for the task at hand.

RULES OF CONFLICT

Communication between Belligerents

Direct communication, explicit or implicit, between the adversaries in the Yom Kippur War was minimal. A case can be made that Israeli reactions to Syrian missile attacks on population centers (for example, Kiryat Smonah), in the form of intensive attacks on Syrian home-front targets, constituted a case of signaling that continuation of Syrian countervalue attacks would result in devastating retaliation in kind. Sachar states:

> As early as the second day of hostilities, in fact, after
> the Syrians began launching SCUD missiles at Israeli
> towns and villages, Elazar won the cabinet's approval for
> an air offensive against the Syrian civilian economy. Immediately, then, Peled's fliers set about their assignment
> with deliberation and relentless thoroughness. The Syrian
> defense ministry, the radio station in Damascus, the Homs
> power station and fuel reservoir, the key oil terminal outlets at Banias, the major Syrian electric grids—all were
> destroyed or crippled. [7]

Whether the subsequent Syrian abstention from countervalue attacks was the direct result of this campaign or whether it was simply a function of the generally deteriorating Syrian military situation, the attacks on Israeli population centers did stop.

In any event, in the 1973 war the unwritten rule of Middle East conflicts prohibiting countervalue attacks on population centers held up. The rule seems to be firmly rooted in reciprocal fears of what such attacks would do to the populations of the warring nations. One could interpret the Syrian-Israeli interaction described above as a painful reminder to Syria of the existence of this rule and of the consequences of breaking it. (It should be remarked that tactical attacks on small Israeli population centers both during wars and in periods of undeclared hostilities has been a feature of the Middle East conflict from the beginning, but that serious attacks on larger Israeli cities have not occurred.)

It is, of course, not surprising that there was no explicit direct communication between the belligerents in the Yom Kippur War, since the Arabs did not recognize Israel and had had no diplomatic relations whatever with it. However, both sides were dependent upon the assistance of superpowers. The superpowers were supposed to be entwined in the embrace of détente. It was not difficult for the enemies to communicate with each other through their superpower allies. Moreover, all parties were UN members and it was possible to communicate indirectly by statements in UN organs and, through intermediaries, in quiet diplomacy at the United Nations. Finally, the International Committee of the Red Cross (ICRC) was able to function to some extent as an intermediary on the critical issues of identification, protection, and repatriation of prisoners of war.

As a result of the indirect belligerent communication, principally through U.S. Secretary of State Kissinger, the unprecedented direct communication of Kilometer 101 took place. There Egyptian General Abd al-Ghani al-Gamzi, commander of the Suez front, and Israeli General Aharon Yariv, former intelligence chief, negotiated an agreement permitting supply columns for the encircled Egyptian Third Army to be driven through Israeli lines by UN personnel. All in all, communication, both by signaling through behavior and by exchanges through intermediaries, proved to be sufficient to keep the war limited and to terminate it.

Avoidance of Superpower Confrontation

Since at least 1956 the Soviet Union had been playing brinksmanship in the Middle East with the unwritten rule of avoidance of superpower confrontation. During the 1956 Suez War, Khrushchev threatened England and France with the specter of nuclear attack if they did not withdraw. There was no counterreaction from the United States, which was at that time also insisting on the withdrawal of its two oldest allies. The Soviet Union subsequently exercised its influence to incite the Arab behavior that led to the 1967 war. Following that war, the Soviet Union increased its direct involvement in the area with massive programs of military aid and technical assistance. During the War of Attrition, the Soviets furnished active personnel for missile defense of Egypt and, in the latter stages of the conflict, active combat pilots. Since confrontation will usually arise out of the aggressive or provocative acts of one or the other of the superpowers, the escalation of direct Soviet military involvement in the War of Attrition can be said to have risked such confrontation. Had

Israeli-Soviet clashes escalated to a serious war, it would seem that the United States would have had little alternative to counterintervention against the Soviets.

In the 1973 war the Soviets started out with different postures in the two principal Arab belligerent states. They were only in Egypt on a limited basis as determined by Sadat who had shown his independence by expelling them in 1972. In Syria, however, the Soviets were heavily entrenched. Syria's resupply operations were integral to the Soviet military system. Soviet military advisers were widely dispersed throughout the Syrian armed forces and were highly influential.[8]

This is the background for the brush with superpower confrontation that featured the last phase of the Yom Kippur War. This limited confrontation came about roughly as the cumulative result of the following buildup of Soviet actions:

1. Soviet incitements to the Arabs to invade pre-1967 Israel, expand the number of Arab-state belligerents, use the oil and petrodollar weapons—all coupled with inflamatory denunciations of Israel;[9]

2. Against the background of supplying and training the Egyptian and Syrian armed forces, a massive Soviet sealift, started before hostilities, and airlift beginning October 9 to Syria and Egypt;[10]

3. The Soviet alerting of two or more airborne divisions, October 12, supposedly to intervene to protect Damascus—announced to Kissinger by Dobrynin;[11]

4. A major buildup of the Soviet fleet in the Mediterranean;[12]

5. Kosygin's trip to Cairo, October 15, and the resultant ceasefire proposal of October 18, which was prima facie unacceptable to Israel and the United States;[13]

6. The Soviet invitation to Kissinger to come to Moscow, October 19, in the context of what Kissinger termed "murderously dangerous" threats;[14]

7. Soviet charges that Israel was responsible for the breakdown of the ceasefire, followed by Dobrynin's threat to Kissinger, October 22, of Soviet intervention if the Israelis did not retreat to the ceasefire line of October 22;[15]

8. Following Kissinger's rejection of Sadat's proposal for a joint U.S.-Soviet peace-keeping force, the Soviet threat of unilateral intervention with its own troops, involving, inter alia, an attempted Soviet rescue of the Egyptian Third Army.

The last event took the form of Brezhnev's threat to Nixon in an urgent message of October 24 in which he stated the following:

I will say it straight, that if you find it impossible to act together with us in this matter, we should be faced with the necessity urgently to consider the question of taking appropriate steps unilaterally. Israel cannot be allowed to get away with the violations.[16]

On the other hand, the background to the U.S. reaction to Soviet activism and threats provides a striking contrast. The United States adamantly warned Israel that it must never, under any circumstances, strike the first blow in any new Middle East conflict. Moreover, when Israel withheld its preemptive first-strike option, it got no particular credit for doing so, despite the costs. Further, there was no apparent U.S. disposition to condemn the Arab attack on Israel, the United States attempting to treat the belligerents equally.[17] When Israel experienced problems in replacing the weapons and material eaten up by this highly intensive war, the United States was very slow and ambivalent in its reactions to urgent Israeli appeals for the kind of instant resupply being routinely furnished the Arabs by the Soviets.[18]

With this record, the United States took action, all in reaction to Soviet policies and initiatives. Nixon ordered a U.S. airlift to Israel on October 12, three days after the massive Soviet airlift began. In reaction to the Soviet threat of unilateral armed intervention on October 24, Nixon placed U.S. military commands throughout the world on "Defcom B," just below acute alert.[19]

At this point, the United States sent an additional aircraft carrier to the Mediterranean, transferred 60 heavy bombers from Guam to the continental United States, and alerted the 82nd Airborne Division for departure. It appears that the United States deliberately did not report these moves to the Soviet Union but was confident that they would be picked up by Soviet intelligence.[20] They were, and the Soviets got the message. On October 25, Brezhnev instructed his UN representative, Malik, to drop the insistence on a joint U.S.-Soviet peace-keeping force. Instead, a UN force of Austrian, Finnish, and Swedish units was dispatched to Egypt. On October 27, following the unsuccessful attempt on October 26 of the Egyptian Third Army to escape from its trap, the Kilometer 101 discussions were begun and a permanent ceasefire was assured.

Several observations may be made about this near miss between the superpowers. First, it is clear that the Soviet Union was willing to go to the brink and risk superpower confrontation as long as there was no firm U.S. reaction. Second, the U.S. alert and related countermoves seem to have forced a Soviet backdown. Without the U.S. alert, it seems quite possible that the Israelis would have been facing Soviet troops in Egypt. Third, had the Israelis refused to abide by the second ceasefire and, following the fondest desires of their military leaders, proceeded to finish off the Egyptians, the gauntlet would have been thrown down to the Soviets to come to the aid of the Egyptians or back off. It seems quite possible that, in those circumstances, the Soviet Union would have intervened with troops in Egypt, notwithstanding the strong possibility of direct confrontation with the United States.[21]

The avoidance of superpower confrontation seems to be attributable to the following factors, in this order: the willingness of Israel to relinquish a hard-won opportunity to inflict the greatest military defeat on the Arabs of any Middle East war; the willingness of the United States to challenge Soviet escalation and threats by serious preparations for counterintervention; and the willingness of the Soviet Union to back down and accept a solution not involving its own presence with troops in Egypt.

There was much debate at the time of the Nixon alert about the implications of the crisis for détente. Without essaying a comprehensive review of that debate, it may be said that détente considerations did not deter the Soviet Union from inciting, supporting, and escalating the Arab attack on Israel, nor did they deter the credible threat of direct Soviet military intervention in the conflict. It seems unlikely that concern over détente caused the Soviets to back away from the superpower confrontation. Rather, Israeli willingness to remove the principal excuse for Soviet intervention, continued entrapment of the Egyptian Third Army, and the U.S. display of resolve in the alert deterred the Soviets from continued escalations and increased direct involvement. The lesson to be learned may well be that, while avoidance of superpower confrontation is one of the most important guidelines of limited war, willingness to confront an aggressive superpower may be the best way to avoid an even more dangerous confrontation.

Limits on Nuclear Weapons

Egypt had no nuclear capability in 1973. It is widely believed that Israel had such a capability, but, if that was the case, there was no occasion to hint at its existence much less its possible use in the 1973 conflict. Since 1973 there has been increasing speculation that, as Israel faces the long-term prospects of a declining comparative military advantage over the Arab states, nuclear deterrence will become the core of Israel's defense. If and when that occurs, the same kinds of fundamental dilemmas will face Israel as have been faced by the North Atlantic Treaty Organization (NATO) alliance as to the appropriate and proportionate thresholds of nuclear deterrence and defense. These dilemmas will be infinitely more intractable and portentious, given the extremely fragile character of the Israeli state.[22]

Geographic Confinement of the Conflict

For a number of reasons, the general limited-war guideline prescribing geographical confinement of conflicts does not seem to be applied in the Middle East. The Arabs, for their part, proclaim a vague Arab unity of the Arab "nation." Needless to say, the Arab unity of the Arab nation is quickly abandoned when the sovereign rights and national goals of the individual Arab states clash. But, in principle, all Arab states are united against Israel—a proposition to which Egypt now furnishes an exception. There is, moreover, a trend toward expanding this galaxy to a union of all Muslim states against Israel.

Accordingly, when war breaks out with Israel, it can be expected that a large number of states not directly involved in the conflict will send expeditionary forces and other assistance. In some cases there is little that Israel can or is inclined to do to bring the war to these more remote cobelligerents (for example, Iraq, Libya, Tunisia, Algeria, and Morocco). If the interventions of such states became sufficiently important, and Israel was willing to divert the resources necessary, there is no reason why Israeli counterattacks, in the form, for example, of air attacks, might not be made against these Arab states.

In the 1973 war, Israel was very careful in its reaction to the active participation in battle areas of Arab forces other than those from Egypt and Syria. Jordan was permitted to contribute a force to the Syrian southern flank that saw some action without any direct Israeli counterattack on Jordan's forces in their own territory. In view of the demands on Israel's forces, this was a prudent policy.

Given the curious double standards presently prevailing in world politics and opinion concerning Israel and the Arabs, it seems likely that Israeli attacks on the other participating Arab cobelligerents such as Iraq, Libya, and Algeria would have brought sharp negative reactions. Very likely Israel would have been condemned for widening the conflict. The same double standard seems to continue to accept the blanket rationale of Arab unity to justify all degrees of cobelligerency by Arab states whenever some Arab states are at war with Israel.

Legal Justification and Collectivization

Both Egypt and Israel have developed traditions of international legal advocacy integral to their conduct of foreign relations and defense policy. Egypt basically justified its attacks as a liberation of its own territory that it claimed had been unjustly and illegally conquered and occupied by the Israelis.[23] Israel took the position that its 1967 preemptive attack had been a measure of justified anticipatory self-defense. The conquests and occupation that followed were the fruits of success in that war of self-defense. The purpose of the occupation was to force Arab recognition of the state of Israel and an acceptable settlement, particularly a settlement that would give Israel reasonably secure borders. To be sure, there was and continues to be disagreement within Israel as to whether all or most of the territories occupied since the 1967 war should be incorporated into Israel proper. Nevertheless, all Israelis agreed that the post-1967 war border was an internationally recognized and protected demarcation line reflecting the ceasefire and truce at the end of the war. An attack across that line was a breach of the 1967 agreements and tantamount to an attack across an international border, an act of aggression forbidden by international law.

Israel's 1967 attack on the Arabs was undertaken as a measure of anticipatory self-defense in the face of a clear and present danger of strangulation by the blockade of Aqaba and the imminent threat of invasion by the Arab forces poised on Israel's border.[24] The 1973 Arab attack, on the other hand, was planned and carried out not as a defense measure against an imminent Israeli attack but as a war to regain lost territories. Indeed, it must be noted that, given the failure of the parties to negotiate after the 1967 war, it remained unclear just how lost the occupied territories were. Recent negotiations clearly show that at least the Egyptian territories were not permanently lost. In any event, there are many lost and disputed territories around the world, and it is clear that the international legal prohibition of the use of armed coercion does not include a general exemption for the nations that aspire to reclaim such lost or disputed territories.

The reaction of the international community once again followed the familiar double standard for the Middle East. While Israel could hardly be condemned for fighting a defensive war, the Arab attackers were not condemned for violating the prohibition against the initiation of war. There was a general tendency in the United States and Europe to, in effect, suspend the operation of the legal jus ad bellum and treat the war as a kind of large-scale trial by knightly combat. The communist and Third World states tended to justify the Arab attack as a war of national liberation, self-evidently just and legally permissible.

Egypt and Syria were able to invoke the auspices and support of the Arab League. This was not done in the technical legal sense that the United States invoked the United Nations in the Korean War and the Southeast Asian Treaty Organization (SEATO) in the Vietnam War, but there was a general claim of legitimacy based on the authority of a regional international organization. To substantiate this claim, the Arab states contributed direct military support in many cases (as mentioned above) and indirect support politically and economically. The unleashing of the Arab oil "weapon" against states that supported Israel even modestly was an impressive act of collective coercion.[25]

In the combat zones, Egypt and Syria were able to add more "flags" to their order of battle with the arrival of sundry Arab contingents. It must be said, however, that the additional flags did not represent significant gains in effective military power. At the least, though, these additional Arab contingents increased the responsibilities of the tightly stretched Israeli forces and gave an aura of Arab solidarity to the war effort that substantially collectivized it.

Israel has no international organizational ties that can be invoked to justify and collectivize its war efforts. Its only ally, the United States, must play a complicated role of simultaneously being an ally of Israel and the principal mediator in Middle Eastern conflicts. Given trends in the United Nations and its agencies, Israel has virtually no hope, even in defensive wars, of obtaining legitimacy and support for its efforts except from the United States.

Limited Mobilization

Limited mobilization as a component of limited war has not been characteristic of the Middle East wars. Egypt's mobilization, like Syria's and that of other Arab cobelligerents, is limited by its degree of development rather than choice. Even so, it appears that these states have mobilized beyond the modest limits of their own state of development. If the Arab states could carry out total mobilization of effective manpower alone, they would confront Israel with extremely difficult problems in combat. As it is, although Arab armed forces greatly outnumber those of Israel, the quantitative differential is not sufficient to offset superior Israeli qualitative skills and capabilities. Otherwise, the Arab states are not sufficiently industrialized to make the concept of mobilizing the home front very relevant.

Israel, on the other hand, stands close to total mobilization at all times by reason of the substantial demands made on all able-bodied persons for military and related service and the maintenance of an everincreasing domestic defense industry. Even this high state of mobilization is insufficient, however, when war breaks out. When that happens, Israel mobilizes the whole society to an unprecedented degree.

Restraint in the Use of the Psychological Instrument

The hallmark of Arab behavior from 1948 through the period of the War of Attrition was the constant and violent use of the psychological instrument at home and abroad. It may very well be the case that reckless Arab propaganda and threats brought about the Israeli preemptive attack of 1967 as much as the serious material threats posed implicitly by the closing of the Gulf of Aqaba and the massing of troops on Israel's border.[26]

By the extreme standards of this experience, the use of the psychological instrument by Egypt in the 1973 war was comparatively reasonable. The goal of the utter destruction of Israel was not proclaimed with the prominence and insistence characteristic of Arab utterances both in war and peace up to that time. To be sure, the Egyptians increasingly misrepresented the results of the war as their fortunes faded. This, however, is not a critical issue insofar as limited war is concerned. Limited-war guidelines prescribe restraint in the use of the psychological instrument so that uncontrollable passions will not be built up, resulting in irresistible pressures for total war. The proof of Egyptian restraint in the use of the psychological instrument is that there were no such popular pressures—at least not in Egypt. The Egyptian population was able to accept with equanimity the ultimate result of the war as no better than a stalemate in which Egyptian forces had obviously ended up in a desperate situation. This evaluation would seem to be confirmed by Sadat's success in concluding the two Sinai agreements and, later, in his peace initiatives and 1977 visit to Israel.

The Israeli use of the psychological instrument on the home front was initially characterized by overconfident and perhaps misleading reports and statements. This was remedied and the country was given objective and at times sobering evaluations of the situation.[27] The acceptance by the Israeli society of the limits and the terms of termination of the war proves the restrained nature of Israeli use of the psychological instrument.

It should be remarked that appraisal of the Israeli psychological instrument is complicated by the fact that there is a very close relationship between the official agencies and activities of the Israeli government and the many private Jewish agencies and activities around the world. Given the present state of Israel's international relations (that is, relative isolation and great dependence on U.S. friendship), the activities of U.S. Jewish organizations and of individuals acting in a private capacity are a most important resource for the state of Israel in the field of political and psychological action.

While the commitment and dedication to Israel of these private organizations and individuals is never in question, they are inclined to display a certain independence in their approaches to supporting Israel. There is, in U.S. Jewry and elsewhere, a strong dove element that is inclined to look for ways of mitigating and terminating wars when they occur. Even the more hawkish Jewish elements tend to limit their position to firm support of a strong and independent Israel, eschewing advocacy of Israeli expansion by force. Their representations are not usually characterized by the extreme passions characteristic of pro-Arab propaganda and threats.

The balance sheet for the 1973 war with respect, at least, to the use by Egypt and Israel of the psychological instrument, is decidedly weighted on the side of restraint with a resultant moderation in popular attitudes and behavior that has been reflected in the conduct and termination of the war as well as in subsequent peace initiatives.

Fight and Negotiate

The limited objectives of both Egypt and Israel fit logically into the fight-and-negotiate method. The basic Egyptian problem was to judge the point at which it had gained as much by fighting as it was likely to achieve and then consider negotiation. Israel undoubtedly expected to do rather more ambitious fighting with more conclusive results before agreeing to negotiate. However, Israel knew from past experience that as soon as it would clearly appear to be winning the war in the field, the superpowers and the United Nations would intervene to force a ceasefire. All Israeli fighting had to be planned on the assumption that there would only be a few days in which to exploit major military successes.[28]

For purposes of analysis of the fight-and-negotiate patterns in the Yom Kippur War, the fighting may be broken down into three major time periods. First, there is the period from the first Arab attacks on October 6 until the entering into effect of the first ceasefire on October 22. Second, there is the period of fighting between the breakdown of the first ceasefire on October 22 and the establishment of the second ceasefire on October 24. Third, there is the period from October 24 to October 27 during which Egypt broke the second ceasefire, was subdued by the Israelis, and the parties were induced to negotiate the agreement of October 27 at Kilometer 101.

It is also necessary in such an analysis to recognize that the actual fighting of Egypt and its allies against Israel was supplemented by the threatened fighting of the United States and the Soviet Union. As a result, the analysis must deal with the fight-and-negotiate interaction of the two principal Middle East antagonists as well as with the prepare-and-threaten-to-fight interaction of the superpowers.

In terms of the fighting between Egypt and Israel, the period from October 6 to October 22 can be subdivided into the periods of

October 6 to October 15 and October 15 to October 22. Up until October 14 Egypt had succeeded substantially in achieving its desired goals. It was well established on the East Bank of the Suez in Sinai and ready to move to the offensive again in a second phase of the war. It is true that the war was going badly in Syria where the Israelis were pushing forward toward Damascus, eliciting urgent calls for help from Syria and threats of Soviet intervention. But the Egyptians' position looked good. Up to this point Egypt had shown no interest whatever in U.S. calls for a ceasefire and little more in the Soviet demand that an Israeli withdrawal to the 1967 border accompany a ceasefire. The latter demand, of course, was unacceptable to Israel.[29]

Then the military situation changed decisively. On October 14 the Egyptian attack, starting the second phase of the war in the south, resulted in a great tank battle in which the Egyptians were overwhelmingly defeated. On the morning of October 15, Sharon's forces established a small but comparatively undetected and unopposed bridgehead on the West Bank of the canal. By October 18, the battles to clear the corridor to the canal crossing area had been won by Israel and Sharon's forces were joined by Adan's. The Israelis proceeded to exploit the breakthrough north, south, and west of the crossing point so as to threaten the communications of the Egyptian armies in Sinai as well as major Egyptian cities. It should be emphasized that these events were in no small measure influenced by the keen awareness of the Israeli commanders that ceasefire negotiations would be starting very soon, their urgency accelerating to the extent that the Israeli gains became known.[30]

Thus, in the second period of the war, pressures for a negotiated ceasefire increased sharply. Interestingly, the pressures did not come in the first instance from Egypt, the belligerent suffering serious military reversals on the battlefield. Rather, they came from the Soviet Union, who was confronted by the defeat of both Syria and Egypt with staggering losses of Soviet-supplied weaponry and equipment as well as a catastrophic blow to Soviet prestige. Pressures for a ceasefire also came from the United States, who, while supplying Israel, was opposed to an overwhelming Israeli victory. The United States wanted a rough stalemate wherein the Arabs retained their honor as a foundation for renewed efforts to negotiate a comprehensive Middle East peace. This U.S. attitude had already manifested itself in warnings from Kissinger to Israeli Ambassador Dinitz that Israel must not continue to advance toward Damascus on the Syrian front. (Israel had independently decided to desist and had diverted forces to the Egyptian front.)[31]

The focal point, then, of the ceasefire pressures during the period October 15-22 involved the superpowers. First, Kosygin's visit to Cairo on October 18 resulted in a Soviet demand for a ceasefire. Second, it also produced the Sadat suggestion of a superpower peace-keeping force to enforce the ceasefire. This proposal, unacceptable to the United States, was pressed in terms of Soviet threats to establish and police a ceasefire unilaterally, if necessary, as discussed above apropos the superpower confrontation. It appears that the entire Cairo initiative of this period was the work primarily of Kosygin, since Sadat seems to have been slow to accept the realities of the battlefield situation, changing so drastically to his detriment.[32]

The denouement of the Kosygin-Sadat Cairo initiatives was the urgent invitation to Kissinger to go to Moscow where the ceasefire agreement of October 21, adopted by the UN Security Council as Resolution 338 on October 22, was agreed to by the superpowers. Egypt as well as Israel accepted the ceasefire; Syria ignored it, but her front was stabilized. It should be noted that the Moscow Agreement was congruent with the current military situation.[33] In summary, during the period October 6-22,

1. Egypt showed no interest in negotiations until it belatedly began to comprehend the extent of its defeat and continuing danger to its homeland, recognition of these facts having been registered under the urgent prodding of the Soviet Union. Egypt promptly accepted the first ceasefire on October 22.

2. Israel was uninterested in negotiations when it was suffering defeats and stalemate on the battlefield. Once the momentum of victory was achieved, Israel tried to extend its military gains to the utmost before time ran out and a ceasefire began. However, Israel, too, accepted the ceasefire promptly.

3. The Soviet Union, at first, sought a ceasefire that would give the Arabs all the territorial gains that they sought in the war, namely, complete withdrawal of Israel to the borders prior to the 1967 war. While Arab fortunes looked promising, the Soviet Union did not support U.S. ceasefire initiatives. As soon as the Syrians began to be defeated and especially after the Egyptian reverses of October 14-15, the Soviet Union, in effect, insisted on a ceasefire under threat of establishing and policing one unilaterally if the United States and Israel did not cooperate.

4. The United States sought a ceasefire and return to the October 6 lines from the outset of the conflict. No U.S. ceasefire initiatives seem to have had any effect except to spur the Israelis to move to the offensive (October 14-15). The U.S. role was that of intermediary to Israel in the successful conclusion of the effort at Moscow and at the United Nations, culminating in Resolution 338 and the ceasefire of October 22. The United States did obtain a ceasefire reflective of the military situation (that is, of Israel's battlefield successes).

In the period from October 22 to October 24, the first ceasefire was quickly broken and hostilities resumed full-scale. The main cause of the renewal of hostilities was the effort of the Egyptian Third Army to break out of the Israeli encirclement. However, it is clear that the Israeli commanders in Egyptian territory were anxious to have a further chance to complete the isolation of the Third Army and to take Suez City. They were not reluctant to resume the fighting. It is unclear to what extent the commanders on either side acted with the approval of their respective top civilian superiors. In any event, the immediate aim of the Egyptian resumption of hostilities was not so much to improve Egypt's negotiating position as to enable the Third Army to survive. Naturally, the fate of the Third Army would be an important element in the calculus of military gains and diplomatic gains.[34] But the fighting by Egyptian forces from October 22 to October 24 was more motivated by the impulse of survival than a desire to improve Egypt's negotiating position.

The motivation on the side of the Israeli military is also somewhat complex. It appears that the primary motivation was to deal Egypt the most decisive defeat in the history of Arab-Israeli wars. The lure of the purely military victory was strong. The fact that such a victory might actually be detrimental to the long-term prospects for stable peace between Israel and the Arabs does not seem to have dampened the enthusiasm of the Israeli military. They pressed desperately to take Suez City, with heavy losses, not to improve Israel's negotiating position, which was already as strong as it could be, but to win a proper military victory.[35] And, indeed, such successes as were registered between October 22 and October 24 did not improve Israel's position. On the contrary, these successes triggered the threat of direct Soviet intervention and the superpower confrontation.

This confrontation led to the Soviet withdrawal of its threats and the second ceasefire agreement negotiated by the superpowers and resulting in Security Council Resolution 339 of October 23, providing for a UN peace-keeping force. In summary, during the period October 22-24,

1. Egypt violated the first ceasefire and thereby incurred further military defeats, confirming the isolation of the Third Army.

2. Israel responded to the Egyptian violations with an all-out effort to gain a more complete military victory on the battlefield, fighting up to the last minute before the second ceasefire went into effect.

3. The Soviet Union attempted to prevent the further defeat of Egypt with a threat of direct intervention, thereby producing a superpower confrontation with the United States. Following this confronta-

tion, the Soviet Union became more reasonable and, with the United States, managed the second ceasefire through the United Nations.

4. The United States tried to restrain the Israelis but countered Soviet threats of direct intervention. By its firm stand the United States obliged the Soviet Union to revert to negotiations with the result that a second ceasefire went into effect. [36]

The third period of fight and negotiate in the Yom Kippur War, from October 24 to October 27, centered around a final Egyptian Third Army effort to break out, which was promptly squelched by the Israelis on October 26. However, the results of the Israeli military success were conditioned by U.S. insistence on resupply of the Third Army. Resupply was first effected by a single Red Cross convoy. Regular resupply in convoys operated by the United Nations was agreed to at the Kilometer 101 Agreement of October 27. So ended the fight-and-negotiate phase of the conflict. Subsequent negotiations were not carried out in the context of recent and/or imminent hostilities or of threats and emergency preparations by the superpowers.

The major lesson to be learned from the fight-and-negotiate aspects of the Yom Kippur War appears to be that there is a law of diminishing returns with respect to translating battlefield victories into political advantage. At least that is the case in Arab-Israeli wars. In this war it was shown that Israeli victories could go only so far before the war would be stopped by a ceasefire in the context of extreme superpower pressures. The Soviets could and did threaten direct intervention. The United States could have threatened cutoff of necessary military resupply had the Israelis not cooperated. Moreover, even those Israeli victories permitted by the constraints of superpower intervention were subject to a political ceiling imposed not only by the superpowers but by the United Nations and world opinion.

The Israeli military had the natural inclination to win a complete military victory. They came very close. But well before the completion of the victories they did achieve, they passed the point at which military success could be translated into political advantage for Israel. After that point was passed, further military successes, if anything, depreciated from Israel's negotiating position.

Egypt had a different problem. Its problem was an overestimation of the prospects for further military successes after October 14. Had Egypt indicated to the Soviet Union and to the United States a willingness to accept a ceasefire before October 14, it would have substantially achieved its war goals. Egypt would have won the first round of the war, established a firm lodgment in the Sinai, and been in a position of strength for negotiations. Instead, its military ambitions ruined a remarkable example of success in limited war. That is to say, Egypt's limited war should have been a complete failure, given the final outcome by October 27. However, because of the interaction of superpower influences and the general lack of sympathy for Israel in the United Nations and in world opinion, Sadat was able to salvage the essentials of his limited-war venture despite the debacles from October 14 to October 27. That this was the case, however, was the result of external forces, not Sadat's own use of the military instrument.

As remarked above, the lesson to be learned from the Soviet-U.S. interaction seems to be that willingness to face a superpower confrontation may result in the abatement of the confrontation and the peaceful resolution of the problems that brought on the confrontation. Throughout the Yom Kippur War, the U.S. role was one of mediator, seeking a ceasefire and negotiations leading toward a fair and lasting settlement between the Arabs and Israel. U.S. recourse to force, indirectly, in the form of arms resupply of Israel, was only reluctantly effected in response to massive Soviet resupply of the Arab belligerents. Further U.S. recourse to force came in the form of the alert of October 24 and the movement of air and sea forces toward the conflict area. In terms of keeping the war limited, terminating the conflict, and laying the basis for more lasting peace negotiations, U.S. positions and actions based on a posture of ready military strength were critical to the outcome of the Yom Kippur War.

Third Parties—International Organizations

The Middle East wars have been characterized by superpower mediation and by a great deal of UN involvement. UN Security Council resolutions have been treated as the bases for ceasefires, truces, and negotiations for a permanent peace. UN peace-keeping forces were introduced after the 1956 war. Their eviction by Nasser helped spark the 1967 war. Since the 1967 war, however, the increasing bias against Israel manifested in all organs of the United Nations has impaired the usefulness of that international organization as a fair and disinterested third party in Middle East conflicts. To be sure, the policies and diplomacy of the United Nations usually reflect the political power situation within the organization. But the image of the United Nations as a more or less neutral international organization permitted to play a number of useful roles in limiting, terminating, and preventing Middle East war has declined. With the virtual disappearance of that image of neutrality, a vacuum was left insofar as third-party mediation was concerned.[37]

Curiously, the United States, an avowed and active ally of Israel, has been able to step into the mediation vacuum and has had more success than the United Nations ever had in this role. The general pattern of third-party mediation during and following the Yom Kippur War is one in which the United States first acted more or less in concert with and then displaced the Soviet Union as the principal third-party element in the conflict. In the process, the United States was able to elicit UN mandates and to bring in UN participation as needed. But the initiative, particularly after October 24, was almost entirely in the hands of the United States.

In reviewing the events forming this pattern it should be borne in mind constantly that Israel and the Arabs had no diplomatic relations, the Kilometer 101 talks being the first direct Arab-Israeli talks in history. Moreover, the Soviet Union had no diplomatic relations with Israel since 1967. The principal events illustrating the unparalleled mediation effort of the United States appear to have been the two ceasefires; the agreement arranged by Assistant Secretary of State Sisco of November 11, 1973; the Geneva Conference of December 22, 1973; the First Sinai Agreement of January 18, 1974; and the Second Sinai Agreement of September 1975.

As has been described above in the discussion of fight-and-negotiate strategies, the ceasefires were arranged essentially by the Soviet Union and the United States, with the United States handling all negotiations with Israel. At this point the United States was also negotiating with the Arab belligerents, but they were to varying degrees still influenced by the Soviet Union. This was certainly the case with Egypt, which, notwithstanding its previous effort to shake free of the Soviets, was desperately dependent upon them during the Yom Kippur War. The two Security Council Resolutions, 338 and 339, were the result of Soviet-U.S. collaboration. Given the importance of past UN Security Council resolutions and the continuing importance of Resolution 242 of 1967, the role of the United Nations in arranging the ceasefire was secondary, formal but useful. Its contribution of peace-keeping forces was certainly essential, particularly as an alternative to the highly controversial joint Soviet-U.S. peace-keeping scheme. [38]

Following the successful establishment of the second ceasefire, there were still serious problems to be solved in order to prevent resumption of hostilities and to give some hope of progress toward the process of peace negotiations. Some of these problems were those of disengagement and separation of forces, provision for convoys to supply the Egyptian Third Army and Suez City, and the exchange of prisoners of war and lifting of the Arab blockade at Bab el Mandeb. Following Kissinger's successful meeting with Sadat in early November 1973, a mission by Assistant Secretary of State Sisco succeeded in obtaining an agreement between Egypt and Israel settling these difficult issues sufficiently so that they agreed to begin talks "in the framework of the agreement on the disengagement and separation of forces under the auspices of the United Nations." As a result, the Kilometer 101 talks—the first direct communication and negotiation between Egypt and Israel—were begun.[39] The way was paved for the Geneva Conference of December 22, 1973, under UN auspices. Although the Soviet Union would participate in the Geneva Conference, the entire process of negotiating with Egypt, Jordan, and Israel was carried out by the United States.

Another series of Kissinger "shuttle diplomacy" missions in December 1973 concluded the process of arranging for the Geneva Conference. Kissinger succeeded in obtaining agreement from Sadat and Hussein to sit in the same room and negotiate directly with the Israelis. Following the Kilometer 101 face-to-face military talks, this was an unprecedented event in the history of Israel and its conflicts with the Arab states. All of this was done through U.S. mediation with no direct UN or, for that matter, Soviet role involved. Indeed, Israel agreed to go to Geneva only under the understanding that the UN role would be purely formal. The conference, under the nominal chairmanship of UN Secretary General Waldheim, was brief and acrimonious. However, its very occurrence was a landmark in Arab-Israeli relations and a major achievement for U.S. diplomacy.[40]

Nevertheless, the format of Geneva presented serious problems. The USSR participation was an obvious problem for Israel and, to a growing extent, for Egypt and Jordan, who were interested in exploring the possibilities for serious peace negotiations. If and when the hard-line Arab cobelligerents, led by Syria, joined the conference, it could be expected that serious progress would be either extremely difficult or impossible. On the other hand, the indirect diplomacy of Kissinger's shuttle had led to the maintenance, improvement, and implementation of ceasefire agreements and to the unprecedented Geneva Conference. Kissinger, in a new shuttle exercise in January 1974, proposed to institutionalize his indirect approach as an alternative to the hazardous course of sole reliance on the Geneva Conference and/or the approach from the military level at Kilometer 101. The result was agreement of both Egypt and Israel to the Sinai Separation of Forces Agreement of January 18, 1974. The agreement divided the forces with a buffer zone manned by UN peace-keeping troops and limited the number and composition of troops each side could maintain in zones flanking the buffer zone. The UN force, then, was in a familiar posture certainly essential to the agreement. However, the U.S. involvement was extraordinary for Middle East peace-keeping arrangements. U.S. aerial reconnaissance of the disengagement areas was provided. Additionally, and critically, the United States agreed to "be fully responsive on a continuing and long-term basis to Israel's military equipment requirements."[41]

However, this extraordinary U.S. involvement in the First Sinai Agreement was further extended by the fact that the parties countersigned letters from Nixon to Sadat and Meir, respectively, acknowledging their commitment to the United States on issues such as the clearance and reopening of the Suez Canal and passage of non-military cargoes destined for Israel through the canal. In this way the agreement was, in effect, a triangular Egyptian-Israeli-U.S. agreement. [42] Finally, to reiterate, the whole agreement was negotiated by the United States with the parties, without Soviet or UN participation.

The Second Sinai Agreement resulted from developments set in motion by another Kissinger shuttle mission, starting in March 1975. When this attempt at first proved unsuccessful, Kissinger deemed the Israelis unreasonable. Pressure was applied through President Ford's warning to Israel of a U.S. reappraisal of its Middle Eastern policies and through a slowdown in delivery of promised arms shipments to Israel. A meeting in Bonn between Rabin, Ford, and Kissinger was productive. Subsequently, indirect diplomacy under U.S. leadership resumed in Washington through exchanges between Kissinger and the Egyptian and Israeli ambassadors. By late August 1975 Kissinger was able to go again to the Middle East and negotiate the Second Sinai Agreement, initialed by Sadat and Rabin on September 1, 1975. [43]

Once again there was an Israeli pullback, this time to behind the key Mitla and Gidi passes. Again there was a buffer zone manned by UN peace-keeping troops. In this second agreement, the U.S. surveillance early-warning role was increased to a critical extent. A U.S. civilian-operated electronic surveillance system was established, reporting to Egypt, Israel, and the United Nations. It is significant that both Egypt and Israel accepted this vital U.S. role, whereas they would not have accepted the same system operated by UN personnel. This was hardly surprising in the case of Israel, but Egypt's preference for a U.S., rather than a UN, surveillance-warning force reflects the extent to which the United States had come to be accepted as the reliable third-party mediator in the conflict. [44]

The Second Sinai Agreement was also notable for the continuation of the practice of supplementing the bilateral agreement between the parties with private communications between them and the United States. Finally, as in the First Sinai Agreement, the United States contributed directly to the total agreement by promising compensation to Israel for its withdrawal and its relinquishment of the Abu Rudeis and Ras Sudr oil fields in the form of U.S. financial aid for a period of five years as well as by a guaranteed oil supply to Israel should its other sources fail. [45]

It is clear that the record of the United States in terminating the Yom Kippur War, in preventing it from breaking out anew, in arranging for disengagement and other essential matters relating to a return to more or less peacetime conditions, and in establishing the basis for long-term Egyptian-Israeli peace negotiations is one of extraordinarily successful mediation. Credit for keeping the Yom Kippur War limited must go to the principal belligerents, Egypt and Israel, but equal credit is due the United States, without whose efforts from October 6 through September 1, 1975, the war could very well have turned into another open-ended conflict, which constantly risked both expansion and escalation, including direct superpower confrontations. Whatever success may ultimately be achieved through the continuing Egyptian-Israeli-U.S. negotiations rests on these achievements and finds its foundation in the limited war of 1973.

The Yom Kippur War confirmed that the United Nations can play an important role in providing peace-keeping forces, once the superpowers and the belligerent can agree on the terms of their introduction. But the war also confirmed that, where Israel is concerned, the United Nations by itself is not considered an acceptable third-party mediator by either Israel or the United States. In these circumstances the U.S. role in limiting the Yom Kippur War was decisive.

FLEXIBLE RESPONSE

Flexible response, central to U.S. strategic theory and practice, is not very relevant to the Egyptian and Israeli defense establishments and their conduct of the Yom Kippur War. Neither relies upon a nuclear capability, and their recent conflicts have not required a major unconventional capability. Both fight conventionally, and their forces seem to be well suited to the missions dictated by the general political and strategic situation. Both Egypt and Israel should be given credit for developing counterforce capabilities to implement their counterforce strategies. Their wars have been marked by a unique immunity of population centers from aerial attack. It should be noted, however, that both Egypt and Israel maintain their conventional counterforce capabilities at heavy economic and social costs. That they do so is to their credit. In summary, Egypt and Israel prepared for limited war and fought a limited war, despite their deep-rooted differences and their mutual fears for their survival. In fighting the Yom Kippur War, these two old enemies presented a model for other belligerents who, once they are at war, are enjoined by morality and common sense to fight a limited war. It is to be hoped that this example of restraint in the heat of war will be followed by an equally inspiring performance of the two enemies in their search for a lasting peace.

PART III

IMPLEMENTATION OF JUST-WAR AND LIMITED-WAR GUIDELINES

13

MODES AND CHANNELS FOR THE LIMITATION OF WAR

Any serious attempt to influence the conduct of war so as to maximize observance of moral and legal prescriptions, as well as limited-war guidelines, must address the process of decision and action in war. These processes must be analyzed in terms of modes or forms for the limitation of conduct. Such efforts should also be examined from the standpoint of the channels of limitation (that is, the elements in the chain of command that prescribe and execute war policies).

Among the modes of direction for military action that may be sources of limitation are the following:

Basic political/strategic directives and guidance from civilian decision makers;

Basic military/strategic directives and guidance from military decision makers implementing the political/strategic directives;

Orders defining and assigning military missions;

Political/military planning and policies determining the composition and support of the forces assigned to missions;

Political and administrative initiatives to monitor and control strategic and even tactical policies and their execution;

The field commanders' basic directives on strategy, tactics, and civil affairs policies;

The rules of engagement promulgated by theater and/or field commanders;

The international law of war as interpreted and enforced by decision makers throughout the chain of command; and

The international law of war as interpreted by the international community.

Contemplation of this rough overview of the most important modes for the limitation of belligerent behavior readily indicates the modest role of explicitly legal prescriptions and guidelines in eliciting such limitation. The character of belligerent behavior is mainly a function of the key political/military policies and decisions underlying that behavior and the characteristics of the forces deployed to carry out these policies and decisions. Once the military tasks have been set and the forces needed to accomplish them determined, certain typical results may be expected. If these results violate moral or legal prescriptions or limited-war guidelines, a conflict of military necessity with just-war/limited-war norms will have been virtually predetermined. Once the policies are set and the forces set in motion, there is little that the spokesmen for international law, much less morality or limited war, can do but protest with a view to marginal amelioration of the situation or discouragement of its perpetuation.

To be sure, in many situations policies and strategies may be carried out by forces that are sufficiently flexible to allow them to choose means that are responsive to the prescriptions of morality, law, and limited-war guidelines. In such cases, introduction of normative and limited-war restraints throughout the course of hostilities may be possible. But the experience of contemporary war inclines the observer not to expect this to be the case. In modern wars most of the military actions criticized as immoral, illegal, or violative of limited-war guidelines were clearly foreseeable consequences of basic decisions made concerning military ends and means. This is the heart of the problem of making just and limited war possible.

The foregoing outline of modes for the limitation of war suggests the channels of limitation. If war is to be controlled so as to be just and limited, initiatives are necessary through the following channels: civilian decision makers; military decision makers (for example, at the joint-chiefs level, theater commanders, field commanders); throughout the subordinate chain of command; and externally by public opinion, media commentaries, and political action.

One concept pervades the study of the channels of limitation of war; namely, command responsibility. If, at last, the war policies, strategies, and tactics followed result in violations of the prescriptions and guidelines of just-war doctrine, international law, and limited-war guidelines, responsibility must be assigned for these delinquencies and mistakes. In a general sense, of course, the belligerent as an international person is responsible. But both international and domestic law require individual responsibility for legal violations. Just-war and limited-war doctrines likewise require command responsibility as an indispensable prerequisite to the implementation of their prescriptions and guidelines. [1]

The preceding discussion of modes and channels for the limitation of war indicates the complexity of political/military processes and, accordingly, the care with which responsibility should be assigned to individuals who, however important, are only part of these processes that may produce immoral, illegal, or unrestrained belligerent behavior. Nevertheless, the general corporate responsibility of the state as an international person for its belligerent actions is not enough to satisfy the requirements of just war, international law, and limited war. Key decision makers and commanders must be held accountable for their policies and actions if just-war/limited-war restraints are to be made operational and meaningful.

I propose in this chapter to explore these modes and channels for the limitation of war, with emphasis on the issue of command responsibility. The point of the discussion will be to indicate, on the one hand, the positive opportunities for the limitation of war that are available if timely consideration is given to the requirements of just and limited war. However, the examples cited will often be negative, showing what can happen when open-ended or permissive rather than limited policies, strategies, and tactics are enjoined or condoned.

THE MODES FOR THE LIMITATION OF WAR

In this discussion of limitation of war, reference will be made to examples of directives that, in fact, impelled the violation of just-war/limited-war prescriptions and guidelines. The purpose of such examples is to show the critical formative effect of policy directives on wartime conduct. In some instances it will be possible to give more positive examples of restraint resulting from high policy directives. In either case, the point is the determinative effect of political/military directives on the conduct of war.

To begin at the top, with basic political/strategic directives and guidance, it is useful to trace the sources of British strategic bombing policy in World War II. This is a subject on which there is ample documentation and a distinguished critical literature.[2] It is also one of the most important subjects for critical review both in terms of just-war and limited-war standards, as observed in Chapter 4. British strategic-bombing policy is generally traced back to the seminal influences of General Hugh Trenchard, Royal Air Force (RAF) Chief of Staff during and following World War I. The central concept of this strategy, firmly established before World War II, was that of countervalue warfare. It was believed by the leaders of the RAF that the defeat of the enemy would result from direct attacks on his society that would have the effect not only of inflicting vast material destruction but also, most critically, of crushing civilian morale. This concept appears to have dominated pre-World War II RAF thinking and preparations. Needless to say, this strategic concept, albeit military in origin, had necessarily to be endorsed by the highest civilian decision makers and was, particularly after 1935.

Accordingly, the RAF was prepared for countervalue area bombing, mainly nighttime bombing, of a kind calculated to violate the normative and limited-war prescriptions and guidelines with respect to proportionality and discrimination. Such bombing was initiated in the period between May 1940 and the fall of 1942. However, it appears that during this period the RAF continued to describe its strategy as one of attacks on military targets with, of course, the usual collateral damage to civilians when the targets were in cities. By the end of 1942, however, area bombing of German cities was well advanced. [3]

The specific illustration of a key political/strategic directive appeared at the Casablanca Conference of January 1943. The Casablanca Directive issued by Roosevelt and Churchill gave the following orders with respect to strategic bombing:

> Your primary objective will be the progressive destruc-
> tion and dislocation of the German military, industrial
> and economic system, and the undermining of the morale
> of the German people to the point where their capacity
> for armed resistance is fatally weakened. [4]

The interpretation of this directive was to be disputed between the British and U.S. air forces, but, in the end, the British countervalue strategy continued and to a considerable extent dominated, notwithstanding the persistent and costly efforts of the U.S. Air Force to prove the efficacy of daylight precision bombing of military targets. The Casablanca Directive was reiterated from time to time throughout the war by similar policy directives.

There is a direct causal relationship between the Casablanca Directive on strategic bombing and the subsequent Allied bombing practice, including the area firebombing of German cities culminating in the destruction of Dresden in violent contravention of the principles of proportion and discrimination, contrary to the just-war condition of right intention, and obviously in contradiction to the restraining guidelines of limited war. [5] No intervention by experts on the law of war within the Allied high command and air forces, no amount of education or indoctrination within those forces in international law, just-war, or limited-war concepts, could have made more than a minor impact on the basic countervalue strategy confirmed and decreed by the Casablanca Directive. Given the already existing predispositions and capabilities of the RAF, disproportionate and indiscriminate countervalue bombing as the inevitable consequence of that green light to area bombing.

It should be made clear that the heart of the problem lay in the preexisting British strategic intention and operational capabilities, exacerbated by the course of the war. The lesson in this regard was, of course, that the nature of the conduct of the war is often predetermined by prewar planning and preparations. But the United States Air Force had different strategic concepts and was developing different operational capabilities, both of which could have been shared with the British. However, the Casablanca Directive seems to have given sufficient sanction to countervalue area bombing to ensure its triumph. A different directive, with avoidance of civilian losses enjoined rather than the crushing of civilian morale, emphasizing selective discriminate attacks on vital enemy war production facilities and traditional military targets, would have produced a different strategic-bombing record and could possibly have resulted in a much greater observance of the limits of just and limited war.

Basic strategic directives and guidance may also originate with military decision makers and be ratified by their civilian superiors. This appears to have been the case in one of the most critical strategic decisions of modern warfare, the commitment of U.S. forces in Vietnam to a big-unit, search-and-destroy war of attrition in addition to the ongoing counterinsurgency war. Available accounts are not entirely clear as to the sequence and import of initiatives and responses in this decision process. However, the authorization for U.S. forces to fight an offensive, big-unit war of attrition in Vietnam seems to have come about in the subsequent manner. [6]

General Westmoreland perceived that the enclave policy of maintaining U.S. troops in defensive postures around air and supply bases would prove insufficient to meet the threat from Vietcong (VC) and North Vietnamese forces in South Vietnam in the spring of 1965. Westmoreland, as early as March 1965, proposed that he be given major reinforcements enabling him to move in three phases from the defensive to the offensive.

President Johnson delayed giving a clear response pending evaluations of the effects of bombing North Vietnam on the enemy's will to continue the war while he pondered for the last time the decision to commit the United States wholly to the conflict. The evaluations of the early effects of the air war in the North, ranging from inconclusive to pessimistic, showed that there was no alternative to full-fledged U.S. involvement on the ground in South Vietnam. On the other hand, Johnson remained firm in his pledge to seek no wider war (for example, invading North Vietnam and risking involvement with the Red Chinese and Soviets). In these circumstances the alternatives seem to have been either to accept Westmoreland's strategic proposals or withdraw.

Gradually, Johnson, in the course of an agonized and secret decision process, approved Westmoreland's strategic concept and request for reinforcements. This decision process stretched from the approval of the National Security Council's National Security Action Memorandum (NSAM) 328 on April 1, 1965, to a nationally televised presidential press conference announcement on July 28, 1965. Meanwhile, the Joint Chiefs of Staff (JCS) directives and reports were supporting Westmoreland, and Secretary of Defense McNamara was accepting the Westmoreland-JCS line. Thus, a JCS study-group report given to McNamara on July 14, 1965, stated that the U.S. and allied forces would "seek out and destroy major Viet Cong units, bases and other facilities."[7]

In this case, then, the total complex of decisions and guidance came down essentially to a confirmation of the field commander's strategic concept and a pledge—often to be termed open-ended or a blank check—to provide the assets necessary to pursue that concept. The consequences have been discussed in Chapters 5 and 6.[8] Whatever the military arguments for the big-unit, search-and-destroy attrition strategy (and they remain substantial, given the political constraints on Westmoreland), most of the major just-war/limited-war dilemmas previously discussed in Chapters 5 and 11 were engendered by that strategy. Once again, as in the case of Allied strategic bombing in World War II, one could initiate all kinds of checks on belligerent behavior within the workings of Westmoreland's forces, but the general character of the war and the normative and limited-war problems it would encounter were established from the outset by the adoption of the Westmoreland strategy.

A commander's orders defining and assigning his mission may serve as a determinant of the kind of war he will wage. In the course of his stormy tenure in Korea, General MacArthur was given several specific directives defining his mission and laying down ground rules for his conduct of the war. For example, a major limited-war issue was raised twice, that of conducting operations north of the 38th parallel. MacArthur's original mission was to defend South Korea. His successes after the September 1950 Inchon landing made possible the invasion of North Korea. The mission was changed, not without considerable debate within the United States and the United Nations, to authorize forcible reunification of Korea. However, MacArthur was restricted in a number of ways, especially with regard to operations near and beyond the Yalu River boundary with Manchuria.[9]

Again, in March 1951 the success of General Ridgway's offensive brought about a second invasion of North Korea. Once again it was necessary to elicit the approval of higher civilian and military decision makers, and once again conditions limiting the invasion were established.[10] In both cases the dependence of MacArthur on his superiors for redefinition and/or modification of his mission had important results for the character of the war. Had MacArthur ultimately been given an open-ended mission of reunification of Korea by force, it would have been very hard to confine him with restrictions on attacks near and north of the Yalu, blockades of and air attacks against Red China, and other escalatory actions for which he demanded authorization.

In brief, a permanent change in MacArthur's mission would have meant a comparatively open-ended war in Korea rather than the limited war that took place. Such a war would inevitably have challenged the limits of just war and international law as well as overriding the guidelines of limited war. This is not to say that there is no argument for the MacArthur strategy, but it is clear that, by limiting MacArthur's mission in Korea, President Truman and the Joint Chiefs of Staff ensured that this war would conform to the basic presumptions and guidelines of just and limited war.

Political and military planning and policies determining the composition and support of the forces assigned to missions will go far to determine the character of the war and the degree to which it is possible for the commander to be responsive to just-war prescriptions and limited-war guidelines. The forces allocated to General Westmoreland in Vietnam were sufficient to carry out the search-and-destroy strategy he proposed, at least until 1968 when the decision was made to wind down the war and make an all-out diplomatic effort to end it. But the combat forces given to Westmoreland were not sufficiently large to permit a substantial diversion of U.S. combat units to quasi-permanent security duty in fixed localities. Moreover, the paucity of civil affairs units and personnel, both military and civilian, greatly hampered the conduct of the "other war" for the confidence and loyalty of the Vietnamese people.

It can, of course, be countered that it should have been within the capacity of the South Vietnamese army and government to perform these security and civil affairs tasks. But the fact was that they were as unable to perform them adequately as they were to defeat the main enemy forces in the field. The mission was to defend Vietnam from aggression and exported civil war. Westmoreland's response to the mission was limited, both with respect to military strategy and civil affairs, by the limited size and capabilities of the forces given him. Had he possessed more numerous combat units, permitting their division into offensive and defensive task forces, plus a strong civil affairs capability, he might well have prosecuted the war more successfully while being able to avoid some of the excesses growing out of his heavy emphasis on the search-and-destroy war of attrition. [11]

When a war is anticipated as a serious contingency, the issue of sufficiency of forces goes back to prewar planning and policies.

It is widely feared that existing forces committed to the defense of the North Atlantic Treaty Organization (NATO) are clearly insufficient to wage a successful conventional defense against a major Warsaw Pact attack. [12] If NATO is forced to escalate to nuclear war by the collapse of its conventional defenses, the responsibility will rest primarily on the civilian and military decision makers who placed NATO field commanders in an impossible position by limiting the forces available to them. However, there may still be time to shape the character of a NATO defense to conform more closely to just-war and limited-war standards by improving NATO's conventional capabilities.

Higher decision makers also shape the character of a war in their administrative initiatives to monitor and/or control strategic and sometimes even tactical policies and their execution. Not content merely to lay down broad policy and strategy, high decision makers may inquire into the detailed implementation of their directives or even retain direct control. This was the case with respect to the conduct of the strategic bombing of North Vietnam. The Johnson administration literally controlled bombing missions from the White House and inquired relentlessly into their results. Although the U.S. strategic bombing of North Vietnam has been criticized by both hawks and doves, it stands out as a unique example of a belligerent attempting to conform to just-war/limited-war standards not only by prescriptive policy decrees but by active engagement in the implementation process by the highest policy makers. Surely this is a landmark precedent of incalculable importance in the nuclear age. [13]

Moving down to the level of field commanders, basic directives on strategy, tactics, as well as civil affairs policies obviously have a determining effect on the character of a war. In the Vietnam War, General Westmoreland's big-unit, search-and-destroy, attrition strategy was explicitly directed at engaging the enemy in sparsely populated areas. Thus, Westmoreland commendably sought to remove major combat operations from the majority of the population. However, given the limits in his assets in combat troops and civil affairs personnel discussed above, the price of his strategy was to concede many populated areas to intermittent or permanent enemy control. Indeed, the corollary of Westmoreland's strategic directives was that efforts to ensure sustained control over populated areas subject to recurring enemy domination were to be subordinated to the pursuit of search-and-destroy missions.

Thus, in one sense Westmoreland's strategic directives to fight the enemy in the "boondocks" could be regarded as a salutory effort to increase the likelihood of combat operations being conducted in accordance with the principles of proportion and discrimination. Arguably, however, they discouraged tactical experiments in seizing and maintaining control of areas so that they would be more secure for the kind of civil-affairs activities essential to winning the war. [14]

Thus far the various modes of limitation discussed have been directives and actions tending to determine the nature of wartime operations. The point has been that such basic sources of strategy, tactics, and civil affairs activities have a decisive potential either for limiting war or for increasing the likelihood of violations of the prescriptions and guidelines of just and limited war. It remains to address the explicit prescriptions designed to limit belligerent behavior. These prescriptions take two forms. They may appear as rules of engagement (ROEs) or as rules of the international law of war.

It is difficult to determine the order in which these two forms of explicit limitation should be discussed. The international law of war (jus in bello) is, of course, antecedent to any particular rules of engagement. On the other hand, in any war the rules of engagement are the link between the basic policy directives and actions discussed above and the belligerent's efforts to interpret and apply the international law of war, to integrate moral considerations into policy guidance, and to develop limited-war guidelines for the conflict. The sequence in which the responsible commanders address sources of guidance and restraint is basic policy directives, rules of engagement, and application of the law of war. The rules of engagement are integral to the policy process, whereas the law of war is an external source of limitation. Accordingly, rules of engagement will be discussed first, then the international law of war.

Rules of engagement are ground rules laid down by responsible commanders throughout the chain of command. They may come from the level of the JCS. The usual source of ROEs is the theater and/or field commander (for example, General Westmoreland as commander, MACV in Vietnam). The ROEs span the spectrum of issues discussed in this book as prescriptions and guidelines of just and limited war. Thus, the ROEs frequently concern normative restrictions having their source in the international law of war and/or the moral values held by the commander and his superiors in the chain of command. The ROEs may very well go beyond the strict letter of the international law of war in their thrust. However, the normative emphasis in ROEs is on the obligations of the positive-law jus in bello. ROEs may also be directed to some of the policy objectives enjoined by limited-war guidelines. In such cases they are prescribing limits that derive more from policy determinations to keep the conflict limited than from legal or moral imperatives.

Rules of engagement are the most explicit operational prescriptions and guidelines for the limitation of war (with the exception of the rare case where the law of war flatly prohibits a specific means

or practice [for example, use of biological warfare or pillage]).
Commanders in the field will not normally be consulting manuals and
monographs on the international law of war, much less learned treatises on just war. While their general political orientation may set
the background for limited-war guidelines, they need specific ROEs
to apply general policy directives. Commanders in the field should
be expected to know and consult frequently the rules of engagement
pertinent to their operations. The ROEs, then, are the closest thing
that we have to an operational code for the conduct of just and limited
war in a particular conflict. [15]

General William R. Peers's report on the My Lai massacre
gives the following explanation of a critical ROE governing the use
of firepower in the Vietnam War.

> Early in the conflict, the magnitude of the firepower avail-
> able for employment was recognized. The individual
> soldier's rifle fire was supplemented by huge quantities of
> direct and indirect firepower from a large variety of
> sources. All means of firepower had to be carefully con-
> trolled and coordinated to insure successful, yet proper
> employment. Fire control and coordinating elements
> were organized at each level of command down to and in-
> cluding rifle companies. These elements had the capa-
> bility to coordinate and control all available means and
> sources of supporting firepower. However, because the
> varied sources of firepower had different delivery means
> and accuracy, the rules of employment for each varied.
> It was clear at an early date that the means of control
> and the rules that governed the employment of the dif-
> ferent types and sizes of ordinance were extremely im-
> portant.
>
> MACV Directives 95-4 and 525-18 were in effect in
> early 1968. These regulations dealt with combat opera-
> tions and, more particularly, with the control of fire-
> power delivered by artillery, mortar, air, and naval
> means.
>
> MACV Directive 95-4 stipulated that airpower should
> be employed with the objective of eliminating "incidents
> involving friendly forces, noncombatants, and damage to
> civilian property." In operational planning of battalion-
> level operations, it was required that representatives of
> aviation units participate in the tactical ground planning
> to provide for the necessary coordination and control of
> the firepower available within the aviation units. [16]

It will be seen that MACV Directive 95-4 sought to enforce the moral and legal principles of proportion and discrimination as well as the military principle of economy of force. It likewise sought to further the political ends of the war by minimizing attacks on civilians and their property. This ROE went far beyond the proclamation of a general admonition to avoid disproportionate and indiscriminate use of firepower. It prescribed, in addition, specific procedures to maximize the chances of the ROE being observed in the course of tactical air support, one of the most important sources of possible excess in the use of firepower.

It is not too much to say that an ROE such as MACV Directive 95-4 is more important as a limitation on belligerent conduct than most provisions of the positive international law of war. As remarked throughout this book, the international-law jus in bello is weakest with respect to the means of war and must rely mainly on the reiteration of the basic principles of proportion and discrimination. An ROE such as MACV Directive 95-4 concretizes these principles in a way that no rule of international law purporting to govern the means and methods of war is likely to do.

It must be acknowledged that observance of such ROEs in the Vietnam War was imperfect. As suggested in the earlier portions of this chapter, this was partly the result of the broad tendencies unleashed when the search-and-destroy attrition strategy was adopted and when limitations on the forces available inclined commanders to use firepower to replace manpower. [17] As will be discussed presently, the unsatisfactory record with respect to observance of this and other ROEs is also a matter of failures of command responsibility. However, if one is serious about applying just-war and international-law standards in war, ROEs such as MACV Directive 95-4 are obviously the necessary mode of explicit limitation.

A particularly impressive example of the imposition of rules of engagement is provided in the case of the U.S. "Christmas bombing," Linebacker II, of Hanoi in December 1972. It will be recalled that this was the "fight" element in Nixon's strategy to bring Hanoi back to a reasonable negotiating stance. [18] During the initial phase of the Linebacker II attacks on the most strongly defended target any air force had ever bombed, a strict rule of engagement sacrificed protective maneuvering for bombing accuracy. This is explained in a United States Air Force publication.

> Tactically, SAC Headquarters had directed that no maneuvering to avoid SAMS or fighters would be allowed by the bombers from the initial point (IP) on the bomb run to the target. Such maneuvers, called the "TTR" for their effect against target tracking radars, were a part of ARC Light operations. The order not to maneuver, which puzzled

the crew force, was predicated on a number of factors, one of which was concern over mid-air collisions—either among the bombers or the bombers and support forces. Of more importance was the need for mutual ECM [electronic countermeasures] support, which required cell integrity [a planned formation of three aircraft]. Most important of all, in this first stab at the enemy's vitals, was the political-military concern over the proximity of many strategic targets to population centers. This required the flight crews to be doubly sure they were on the planned course and in a trail formation, so that the train of bombs from each aircraft would impact along the desired path on the ground. The stabilization systems for the bombing computers aboard the aircraft required a certain amount of straight and level flight to properly solve the bombing problem; otherwise the bombs might be scattered outside the target zone. As the mission progressed, and analyses of accuracies could be made, this amount of straight and level flight might be reduced, if circumstances dictated. <u>However, accuracy and assured destruction were overriding considerations. Bombers on the first raids were required to stabilize flight for approximately four minutes prior to bomb release. It was a long four minutes. Unfortunately for some, it lasted less than that.</u>[19] [Emphasis added]

Here is an extraordinary example of a rule of engagement that aimed at discriminate bombing on both normative and political grounds at the expense of the greater vulnerability of the attacking aircraft and crews.

While rules of engagement are the most significant source of explicit normative and policy limitations on belligerent conduct, the international law of war is often interpreted and enforced directly by decision makers in the chain of command. The U.S. armed forces require training in the law of war, particularly that of the 1949 Geneva Conventions. In the Vietnam War troops were issued information cards (for example, "The Enemy in Your Hands," "Nine Rules of Conduct," and "Geneva Convention"). The Peers Report states that "these cards stressed humanitarian treatment and respect for the Vietnamese people and stipulated that each individual would comply with the Geneva Conventions of 1949. Individual methods of capture, care and treatment were specifically included in the cards." Moreover, in Vietnam all commissioned officers received a card entitled "Guidance for Commanders in Vietnam."[20]

Thus, the law of war, particularly its humanitarian chapters, is directly interjected into the training and operations of military personnel and units. It should also be noted that in the United States there is now in operation a review by international-law experts of weapons whose adoption is contemplated in order to assure their conformity with the law of war.[21]

The law of war may also become a source of limitation in the process of review of operations. Responsible commanders and staff officers must review operations to evaluate their compliance with mission policy directives, ROEs, and, when appropriate, the law of war. If law-of-war issues are raised, commanders will usually consult their Judge Advocate General (JAG) officers and reach conclusions about the legal permissibility of the actions taken.

Should these reviews identify clear or possible law-of-war violations, several courses of action are available. At the least, the responsible commander would call attention to the violations and warn against their continuation. If the violations are sufficiently serious, they would have to be reported as war crimes and courts-martial or disciplinary action taken. The point to be made here is that in the course of command review of operations, the international law of war may be a direct source of limitation of belligerent conduct.[22]

The last source of limitation of belligerent conduct is the international law of war as interpreted by foreign powers and by domestic and international opinion. The enemy, of course, interprets the law of war and makes claims that some of our actions are legally impermissible. No matter how farfetched such allegations may be, they have the effect of reminding us that real or apparent violations of the law of war may damage our reputation for rectitude. For a nation such as the United States, which holds out its wars as morally and legally justified to its own people and to the world, this is a serious concern.[23]

Third-party foreign governments may also intervene in the belligerents' process of claims and counterclaims. This was the case, for example, in the protests and criticisms of Sweden and other states regarding U.S. use of napalm in the Vietnam War.[24]

International organizations may play a role in bringing attention to law-of-war issues. The principal organs of the United Nations (the Security Council, the General Assembly, and the Secretary-General) may question, investigate, and pass judgment on belligerent behavior. The legal and practical effect of such interventions is generally problematic in the contemporary world because of the highly ideological, partisan character of so much UN activity. The International Court of Justice has generally not been involved with law-of-war questions. Much more serious, indeed central, is the role of the International Committee of the Red Cross (ICRC). The ICRC is directly mandated by conventional international law to continue its established customary role as protector and intermediary, mainly with respect to the enforcement of the humanitarian law of war. Unlike the organs of the United Nations, the ICRC is an important source of international legal and humanitarian limitation on war. It must be added, however, that, whereas the United States accords the ICRC the respect that law and tradition have enjoined, many belligerents, notably communist parties to the Korean and Vietnam conflicts, have not accepted the ICRC as a truly neutral party and have not cooperated with its important functions.[25]

The media, both domestic and foreign, have shown a propensity to play up allegations of violations of the law of war. Such allegations often complement various domestic and foreign private political action groups such as "Clergy Concerned" and various other groups concerned over U.S. conduct of the Vietnam War.[26] Such speculation and charges can result in a major buildup of world opinion. To be sure, the substance and importance of world opinion is usually hard to determine. Despite its elusive character, however, world opinion is a reality and may be a major factor in shaping the behavior of a belligerent concerned over its reputation for rectitude.

In the Korean War the communists invented out of whole cloth the charge that the U.S./UN forces were engaged in biological warfare. Before these utterly groundless charges were laid to rest, a worldwide movement condemning this alleged U.S. war crime had enjoyed considerable success, and the United Nations was obliged to conduct a major investigation into the charges.[27]

In the course of the Vietnam War a formidable body of world opinion had been developed condemning U.S. conduct of the war on numerous grounds. Some of the allegations involved were explored in Chapter 5 and elsewhere in this book and were properly raised, if often pursued in unfair and exaggerated fashion. Indeed, what Guenter Lewy has characterized as a "war crimes industry" developed to catalog and condemn U.S. conduct of the war.[28] Much of this criticism was rebuttable or the subject of honest disagreement among reasonable persons. Still, as unfair as the domestic and world debate over U.S. conduct of the war became, it did have the salutory effect of providing a source of limitation on U.S. behavior. Again and again, U.S. commanders admonished their troops to observe the law of war and rules of engagement, not only because it was the required and right thing to do but because failure to do so would fuel harmful criticism.[29]

CHANNELS OF LIMITATION

The principal channels of limitation of war are civilian decision makers (in the United States, the president and his designated representatives and advisers; the highest military staff (in the United States, the Joint Chiefs of Staff); theater commanders; field commanders; subordinate commanders in the chain of command; and in the cases of international forces or coalition warfare, executive civilian councils, military committees, and designated military commanders.

Policy directives, strategic and tactical orders, rules of engagement, and international legal prescriptions and guidelines are applied by responsible decision makers throughout a belligerent's civil and military chain of command. If just-war and limited-war prescriptions and guidelines are to be applied in practice, it must be done as the result of the efforts of these responsible decision makers.

The civilian decision makers, particularly the president, must lay down clear political and strategic guidelines reflecting just-war and limited-war standards if such standards are to be applied in the difficult wartime context outlined in this book. Moreover, the chief executive and other high civilian decision makers must inquire periodically into the extent to which just-war and limited-war standards are being met. This may not be easily accomplished.

In the first place, a prudent civilian superior will be conservative when it comes to intervening in the details of the field commander's efforts to carry out his mission. Excessive civilian interference in the conduct of a war cannot be accepted by a self-respecting commander and, in any event, will often lead to a loss of coherence in the military effort. In U.S. national security processes, inquiries into the conduct of a war will generally be channeled through the Joint Chiefs of Staff. Thus, the direction of war is effectively held in military hands and the JCS, as well as a theater commander such as the Commander in Chief, Pacific Command (CINCPAC) in the Vietnam War, will be the highest channel for the limitation of belligerent conduct.[30]

While the foregoing remarks are generally true, it must be recalled that in the Vietnam War the White House was a direct source of guidance and limitation on strategic bombing of North Vietnam. Moreover, the critical issues of escalation from conventional to nuclear war and of passing thresholds within nuclear war (for example, tactical battlefield nuclear to theater nuclear) will remain in the president's hands. So we must consider the president and his chosen advisers as the highest channels of limitation within the U.S. national security system.[31]

The JCS will, however, usually be the highest source of limitation followed by the theater commander. At both levels there is a responsibility to shape broad strategic and civil affairs policy so as to conform to the moral, legal, and political/military requirements of just and limited war.

There are, moreover, international channels of limitation. In a NATO war the highest source of decision would be the Supreme Allied Commander of Europe (SACEUR), subject to the policy directions of the Defense Planning Committee. One hesitates to elaborate since inquiries into the decision processes of NATO tend to be met with a response wherein reluctance to reveal classified information seems to be mixed with genuine uncertainty. [32] In a regional police action or peace-keeping action under an organization such as the Organization of American States (OAS), there would be international civilian committees and a designated OAS military field commander. [33] In a coalition war (for example, in an intervention in a Middle East conflict), there might be some kind of allied joint staff arrangement.

This international dimension of higher political and military direction is an important aspect of the problem of securing compliance with just-war and limited-war prescriptions and guidelines. Internationalization of a war effort may raise problems either in the direction of excessive concern with observance of political and normative limitations, as tended to be the case with some of the participating members of the UN force in Korea, or of deviation from just-war/limited-war standards that may have occurred in the treatment of prisoners of war (PWs) and civilians by the Saigon government in the Vietnam War. In either case, U.S. responsibility for compliance with moral, legal, and limited-war prescriptions and guidelines is essentially unaltered, but the problems of meeting those responsibilities are more complicated.

The most critical channel of limitation of war remains the field commander. He makes strategic and sometimes even tactical decisions and directs civil-affairs policies that go a long way toward determining the character of the war. The field commander's character and personality as a commander and as a man will be reflected in the substance and style of his command's performance. In the confusion of war, things that the field commander emphasizes as important will tend to be emphasized throughout his command in matters ranging from procedures to safeguard the civilian population in combat situations to the symbolic issues of military courtesy and discipline that often set the tone for a command's attitudes and behavior. On the other hand, those things the field commander neglects or downplays will receive little attention from subordinate commanders and troops already overtaxed in their efforts to deal with top-priority requirements. Moreover, the field commander will usually be the most direct source of authoritative rules of engagement, the critical bridge between policy and the law of war.

To be sure, despite the formidable presumptions of command responsibility to be addressed below, the field commander's intentions and admonitions are not always predestined to be carried out in practice. Responsible subordinate commanders as well as disciplined, obedient troops throughout the chain of command are necessary if just-war/limited-war standards are to be met. If, as in the case of the My Lai massacre, a field commander is betrayed by incompetent or immoral commanders and ill-trained, poorly disciplined troops, the good intentions and command emphases of that commander are of no avail. [34]

So implementation of just-war, international law-of-war, and limited-war prescriptions and guidelines requires the cooperation of responsible field commanders, faithful subordinates, and disciplined troops combining to produce a controlled military instrument of policy. International law has developed a schema of responsibility for state behavior in war as well as peace. It extends from state responsibility to command responsibility to individual responsibility. Sometimes an additional category of group or organizational responsibility is added as in the case of the criminal organizations condemned in the Nuremberg Trial of Major War Criminals. [35] The central concept in this schema is that of command responsibility, and it is mainly in terms of this concept that the channels for the limitation of war operate.

COMMAND RESPONSIBILITY

Responsibility for observance and enforcement of the law of war ultimately rests with sovereign states and other subjects of international law (for example, those who qualify as belligerents and international organizations with recognized rights and duties, such as the International Committee of the Red Cross). Responsibility may also be attributed directly to individuals, because of their critical role in the conduct of a war. Today, the law of state responsibility is in transition as a result of the quantitative and qualitative changes in the international political and legal system that have occurred since World War II. The confidence in the existence of a universal, objective international standard of responsibility and of a comprehensive body of law elaborating that standard and its application to a variety of international claims that previously existed is now replaced with uncertainty on all sides. In particular, the prospects for either acknowledgment of or obtaining satisfaction for international delinquencies for which another state is responsibile are more uncertain than ever, particularly in East-West and North-South disputes.

Nevertheless, the traditional law of international responsibility is instructive to those interested in developing the concept of individual command responsibility so critical to the enforcement of the prescriptions of morality and law as well as the guidelines of limited war. The basic principles of the traditional law of international responsibility relevant to command responsibility appear to be in four parts.

1. There is an international standard of behavior with respect to all the rights and duties of international persons. Failure to live up to this standard is a violation of international law, an international delinquency.[36]

2. State responsibility generally increases proportionately with the extent to which the violation was an official act of state. State responsibility exists, but to a lesser degree, for actions of state officials that were beyond their legal competence, contrary to or independent of general public policies and practices, or simply illegal under domestic law.[37]

3. International delinquencies are not judged in terms of absolute responsibility but are assessed in the light of a moderately demanding obligation to prevent acts violative of international law, supplemented by a more demanding obligation to repress and punish such acts.[38]

4. Both state and individual responsibility must be judged in the context of the facts of a particular situation and due regard should be given to extraordinary circumstances. Accordingly, the standard of state and individual responsibility is one of reasonableness in context.[39]

The foregoing principles of the international law of state responsibility may be applied more broadly to embrace responsibility for moral as well as legal prescriptions and for the political/military guidelines of limited war. Given the fact that observance of just-war and limited-war standards for a country such as the United States is above all a matter of self-enforcement of legal and policy prescriptions and guidelines, it is appropriate to broaden the strictly legal concept of international responsibility to include moral and political/military components. The intention is not to impose an unduly demanding set of standards on the United States through the interpretation of the international law of state responsibility, but rather to assist responsible U.S. decision makers in breaking down the broad concept of command responsibility into a cohesive set of manageable concepts.

Early discussions in this book have demonstrated that the basic just-war jus in bello is the foundation of the positive international-law jus in bello, and that they coincide in their insistence on the principles of proportion and discrimination. For the rest, in this book the detailed international-law jus in bello has been treated as a part of any modern just-war jus in bello. Accordingly, it is appropriate to utilize traditional, positive, international-law concepts of legal responsibility in developing a broader legal-moral just-war concept of responsibility.

It is perhaps an innovation to apply the concepts of individual responsibility to the responsibility of decision makers and commanders for violating limited-war guidelines that, of course, may not even be normative in nature. Nevertheless, as the discussion of modes and channels for the limitation has shown, there is a fundamental unity to the efforts of law, morality, and policy directives to control the use of the military instrument so as to produce results that are normatively permissible and in consonance with the basic political purposes of the war. Violation of limited-war guidelines by crossing into a proscribed geographic area or employing a weapons system or strategy that has been denied the commander as a matter of limited-war policies may not be illegal or immoral per se, but such acts may change the character of a war, wrench control away from superior authority, and create a new kind of conflict in which the propensity to violate law and morality as well as limited-war guidelines is dangerously increased.

In any event, at the level of domestic U. S. military law, the concept of individual command responsibility exists independently of international law. [40] It is the cornerstone of the controlled military instrument as a means responsive to the ends of the highest decision makers. Accordingly, the discussion of command responsibility that follows, while drawn from the international law of war as interpreted by the United States, will address the issue of responsibility for observing moral as well as legal prescriptions. Additionally, it will consider responsibility for complying with the limited-war guidelines of a particular conflict or military situation.

Applying the general principles developed in international law of state responsibility to individual command responsibility, we encounter a number of difficult issues. The first principle is that there is an international standard of belligerent behavior, and that failure to meet this standard is a violation of international law, an international delinquency. This principle applies almost exclusively to the normative just-war limits on war rather than to limited-war guidelines, although it could be applied to the latter. For example, if a commander proclaimed and acted as though the military instrument under his control was superior to political policy and above the control of his civilian superiors, he could be in prima facie violation of a universal precept of political primacy that is the heart of defense policies of most, if not all, nations. Aside from this eventuality, however, the issue of the international standard is an important one for those seeking to wage just war. Throughout this book the central importance but elusive character of the principle of proportion has been stressed. The principle of proportion implies that there is a standard whereby proportionate means may be distinguished from disproportionate means, by the belligerents as well as by third-party observers. This is perhaps the most important application of the principle of responsibility to meet an international standard in the conduct of war.

Moreover, the principle of discrimination also implies an international standard. Neither just war nor positive international law requires that means be totally discriminate, but there is a standard somewhere that must be defined and met if condemnation for indiscriminate means is to be avoided. As brought out in Chapter 3, perpetration of genocide is per se a violation of the international standard enjoined by morality and law alike. Many of the specific prohibitions of the positive-law jus in bello (for example, against torture and taking hostages) are held out as reflecting the international standard of belligerent conduct.

But how is the international standard ascertained by the responsible state and the responsible commander? The difficulty of determining what the standard is varies with the subject, but the technique of establishing the standard is clear. The state and the responsible commander should look to the explicit prescriptions of just war and the positive international law of war. Beyond that, they should look at precedental cases, war crimes proceedings, and causes célèbres in military history to see what kinds of actions were widely condemned as having violated the international standard regarding proportion, discrimination, genocide, or the other various means prohibited or limited by the law of war. Such material should be made known to all commanders as an integral part of their training in the law of war, and, indeed, it is increasingly reflected in the training materials of the U.S. armed forces.[41] There will still remain a difficult normative and practical judgment as to how the available evidence of the international standard relates to the particular case at hand. But the beginning of restraint may well rest simply in the recognition that there is an international standard of conduct, that it ought to be sought out by conscientious analysis of the particular case at hand, and that this standard should be observed in the belligerent's decisions and their implementation.

The second principle of state responsibility that may be applied to individuals is that the degree of responsibility is related to the extent to which behavior reflects official policies and acts of state. If it is the official policy of a belligerent to engage in indiscriminate, countervalue bombing of cities, there is direct, full responsibility for an act of state in violation of just-war and international-law prescriptions. Accordingly, those high decision makers who enjoin such policies are directly responsible for them. The degree of individual responsibility will be determined by the office and/or role of the individual and the extent of his consent to or acquiescence in the policies and his freedom of choice in the decision process.

At the other end of the spectrum both of state and individual responsibility are acts not ordained by or even in contravention of official policy. Thus, if a unit runs amok and massacres prisoners of war or civilian detainees in violation of prescribed policies, rules of engagement, and law-of-war instructions, there is still both state and individual responsibility. However, this responsibility is indirect and lesser in degree than in the case of violations of the jus in bello resulting from state-ordained policies.

In the middle of the spectrum are cases of violations that result from insufficient efforts of the high decision makers to control the implementation of policies that are themselves permissible by just-war/limited-war standards but that have a high potential for abuse. For example, relocation of the population of combat areas is permissible and sometimes even required, but the right to relocate may be abused. Moral and legal standards may be violated in the implementation of civilian relocation operations, and the political goals of a limited war may be prejudiced by actions taken solely for reasons of military necessity.

Within this spectrum of degrees of direct and indirect responsibility, two variables interact: the extent to which the wrongful behavior was or was not ordered by official decision makers and the degree of control exercised by responsible commanders down through the chain of command. The latter point is expressed in the third principle of state responsibility, namely, that neither state nor individual responsibility are absolute. They are, rather, assessed under a standard of reasonableness applied in the context of individual cases. This is established in the principal precedental war-crimes decisions: Yamashita,[42] von Leeb, and von List.[43]

In the Yamashita case, a U.S. military commission in Manila found that Yamashita, the commanding general of Japanese forces in the Philippines at the time of MacArthur's successful return, was guilty of failing to attempt to discover, prevent, and punish widespread war crimes perpetrated throughout his command. The commission did not attempt to charge or prove that Yamashita had ordered most of these violations or that he had knowledge of them in fact. (However, some of his orders were shown to have led to some of the war crimes, perhaps an example of the middle range of responsibility suggested above.) The commission did, however, hold Yamashita guilty under the concept of reasonable command responsibility, noting "that the crimes were so extensive and widespread, both as to the time and area, that they must either have been willfully permitted by the accused, or secretly ordered by the accused."[44]

It should be emphasized that, contrary to some interpretations, the Yamashita decision did not condemn the Japanese general on the basis of a concept of absolute liability or absolute command responsibility. It decided that, under a reasonable standard of command responsibility, Yamashita had a duty to discover, prevent, and punish war crimes carried out on a massive scale and with recurring patterns within his command. [45]

In the von Leeb case (the High Command case), a U.S. Military Tribunal at Nuremberg likewise applied a reasonable rather than absolute concept of command responsibility to General von Leeb and other high German officers. [46] Here the issue was responsibility for participating in the passing on and implementation of state policies violative of the jus in bello, notably the Commissar Order aimed at communist officials on the Eastern Front and the Commando Order (requiring summary execution without trial after interrogation) directed at spies, saboteurs, special forces raiders, and the like. Both orders violated the positive law of war as well as the minimal standards of humanity. Other violations of the jus in bello were also charged, but it will suffice here to focus on one patently illegal and immoral practice, that of executing so-called commandos without due process as required by the Commando Order.

In assessing individual responsibility for implementation of the Commando Order and other illegal orders, the tribunal required that the following conditions be met: that the commander passed an order in the chain of command, that the order was criminal in and of itself, and that the commander knew it was criminal. [47] The defendants were found to have acted in a variety of circumstances, and there were resultant differences in findings of guilt or innocence by reason of command responsibility. From the High Command case there emerged three basic rules with respect to the responsibility of commanders and staff officers. There is responsibility for issuing illegal orders, even if promulgated by the highest state authorities; implementing illegal orders; and acquiescing in the implementation of illegal orders.

The von Leeb case did not hold all officers and men within the chain of command responsible for illegal policies promulgated and implemented through the chain of command. Judgments were made as to the salient point in the chain of command, and those found to hold the power of command, as well as key staff officers, at those points were held responsible for the issuing and implementation of illegal orders. [48]

In the von List case (the Hostage case), the most important issue was responsibility for repressive antiguerrilla policies carried out within territorial jurisdictions over which General von List and others exercised command in a belligerent occupation context. Once again, the standard of responsibility was not absolute but reasonable. It was held that the commander was responsible for everything that he knew or should have known about. In this regard it was ruled that reports to a headquarters must be assumed to have been read by those to whom they were addressed, thus informing them of the practices of their subordinates. [49]

At this point the third principle of responsibility overlaps the first, that there is a standard of belligerent conduct to be observed. As previously noted, the standard is sometimes made explicit in the positive-law jus in bello. Where there is no explicit rule or standard, recourse must be had to professional military norms of behavior, judged in the light of moral and legal prescriptions. Having said in both the first and third principles of responsibility that there is a standard of reasonableness, one must posit something like the domestic-law concept of the "reasonable man." This reasonable military man is, of course, a construct, but he symbolizes the proposition that a responsible commander should address his military problems in a manner consonant with sound military doctrine as well as with the prescriptions and guidelines of just and limited war.

A nuance of disagreement exists between the author and Hays Parks, who has written the most comprehensive and thoughtful study of command responsibility. [50] I would simply hold out the proposition that there is such a thing as a reasonable commander whose hypothetical response to a particular military problem should set the standard for actual commanders addressing the same problem. Parks would break the concept down into a number of subjective factors (for example, rank, experience, and resources of the officer in a particular case) and evaluate performances in the light of these factors. But in both Parks's approach and my own, it is necessary to construct a reasonable standard of behavior by which an individual commander may be judged in a particular case. To do this fairly means bringing to bear a knowledge and understanding of the conduct of war, in general, and of the kind of conflict in question, in particular.

Finally, the fourth principle of responsibility requires that both state and individual be judged in the context of the particular situation with due regard given to extraordinary circumstances. This has already been anticipated to some extent in the discussions of the standard of reasonableness. A good example of an extraordinary situation would be that faced by General Rendulic of Germany when he faced pursuit and possible annihilation by the Soviet forces after Finland dropped out of World War II. His scorched-earth policies, deemed unnecessary in retrospect, were nevertheless accepted by a U.S. military tribunal as a reasonable response, given his perception of his predicament at the time he faced it. [51]

In summary, it will be seen that all four of the established principles of state responsibility identified apply to individual responsibility, notably command responsibility, and that they center on a concept of reasonable belligerent behavior to be ensured by reasonable command responsibility.

REPORTING AND PUNISHING
VIOLATIONS OF THE LAW OF WAR

The law-of-war conventions require adhering states to train their armed forces so as to understand and apply the law of war. If such efforts fail and the law of war is seriously violated, there is a duty under the conventions for the responsible state to prevent further violations and to punish those responsible for past violations. In order to carry out these duties, the state must have an effective system within the chain of command for the detection, reporting, and punishment of violations of the law of war. In principle, faithful performance of this duty would meet most of the moral requirements of just-war jus in bello as well as of the international law of war.

It will be remarked that this discussion will eschew insofar as possible the term war crimes. The dictum of Army Field Manual 27-10, reflecting the law of Nuremberg, to the effect that every violation of the law of war is a war crime is exaggerated and unhelpful. [52] The conventional law itself distinguishes violations generally from grave breaches. Violations may range from disputed technicalities to the most immoral behavior. To lump all violations in the category war crimes may be unfair in many cases and may tend to trivialize the concept of war crimes.

Moreover, the U.S. formulation that all violations of the law of war are war crimes runs counter to the practice of U.S. military law under which U.S. military personnel are never tried as war criminals but only for violations of the Unified Code of Military Justice under courts-martial proceedings. [53] This policy apparently results in a great emphasis on establishing the elements of the offense as a common crime rather than as a violation of the law of war (for example, the trials of Calley and Medina). One major consequence in the My Lai case was the virtual elimination of the principle of command responsibility, since the cases were keyed to the concept of direct participation of the accused rather than to his responsibility deriving from command and the circumstances of the violations. [54]

Added to this is the grave jurisdictional difficulty that U.S. service personnel cannot be tried by courts-martial after their discharge, and there is presently no adequate system providing jurisdiction over violations of the law of war by regular civilian courts or special military commissions. [55] At present, therefore, in light of the legal actions under the courts-martial system arising out of the Vietnam War, the idea of a self-imposed, domestic, military-law substitute for war-crimes proceedings has been established in the United States. However, this provision of a trial for violations of the law of war has not been sufficiently extensive or effective to be considered the main means whereby the United States enforces the law of war within its own armed forces. This may well be a healthy state of affairs rather than a failing on the part of the United States. A disciplined armed force should not be obliged to rely heavily on military criminal-law penalties in order to ensure observance of the law of war. The law of war should be enforced throughout the chain of command as a matter of the political-primacy and civilian-control elements of limited-war practice as well as of command responsibility for eliciting loyal and disciplined behavior in the implementation of basic policies and strategies.

The crux of the matter of ensuring compliance with the law of war is command responsibility, as discussed above. But a commander, even if diligent in his efforts to train his troops properly and to oversee their performance, cannot ensure proper conduct without broad assistance throughout the chain of command. This assistance should come, in the first place, from the normal performance of duties by the commander's subordinates. But, additionally, U.S. military directives prescribe special efforts on the part of all personnel in the chain of command to prevent, detect, repress, punish, and report violations of the law of war. To this duty should be added explicitly and with emphasis the requirement to prevent, detect, repress, punish, and report violations of the rules of engagement that, as discussed above, are frequently the most critical sources of limitation on belligerent conduct.

However, anyone familiar with the sociological realities of military service knows that the tasks enjoined on the chain of command with regard to violations of the law of war and rules of engagement are very difficult to carry out. There exists a class of people who are natural-born "whistle blowers." Such people can be relied upon to criticize, oppose, report, or to otherwise publicize seemingly wrongful or inappropriate conduct within an organization. Often they are ineffective, ignored, or written off as eccentrics. Occasionally such people are mean and vindictive troublemakers. Sometimes they are true men of conscience, and they become martyrs or honored saviors of the common good, depending on their fortune.

But, whatever their motivations and prospects, such whistle blowers are rare. The generality of the people in an organization, especially a military organization, avoid involvement with suspected wrongdoing or controversies. They fear that they may suffer reprisals from the suspects and some degree of ostracization from others in the organization. Moreover, in the case of enforcing the law of war and rules of engagement, a substantial number, perhaps the majority, of those in a military organization may tend to oppose or accept only reluctantly the very norms of behavior they are expected to uphold by cooperation in combating violations of those norms.

If these generalizations are substantially valid, the impressive mandate to everyone in the U.S. military chain of command to help enforce just-war and limited-war prescriptions and guidelines must be considered a good start that needs strengthening through further constructive thought and action. The central focus of this effort should be on the duty of responsible commanders throughout the chain of command to make possible the conditions under which their subordinate may be able to bring to their attention the information required to enforce the law of war and rules of engagement. As a general proposition, it is not enough to rely on spontaneous whistle blowing against unlawful or inappropriate behavior. The odds are too great against such individual initiatives making a serious impact on a broad pattern of belligerent behavior. Rather, the responsible commanders must diligently draw out from their commands the information they need and are required by law and morality to have about the conduct of their troops.

Specifically, responsible commanders must make it known that those who report violations of the law of war and rules of engagement will be protected from reprisals and will receive official awards or commendations in some measure proportionate to the inevitable risks they will have incurred for their careers when they reported wrongful or inappropriate conduct. No doubt this task of encouraging and protecting, sometimes rewarding, whistle blowers will be difficult. Even the most powerful commander cannot guarantee that the person who reports wrongful or inappropriate conduct may not suffer, in one way or another, more than the accused. Moreover, it is certain that many commanders will resist this mandate to encourage reporting of wrongful and inappropriate conduct. Such reporters are bearers of evil tidings for the commander who, by definition, may be seen as responsible to some extent for the failures in his command to meet just-war and limited-war standards. At the very least, the commander must account for these failures and show that he has taken appropriate measures to prevent recurrence and to punish those guilty. These duties, while unavoidable, are unpleasant for the commander who is attempting to project an image of the leader of a well-disciplined, efficient command effectively and properly pursuing its mission.

Few U.S. generals have achieved the merited reputation for military excellence and personal integrity of General Matthew B. Ridgway. His thoughts on the duty to question the policies of high

superiors are worth recording here. The context is the discussion
of General MacArthur's Olympian style of directing warfare rather
than of any conduct violative of law and morality. But the issue is
that of resistance to official policy when that policy is open to criticism—whether on military grounds, as in this instance, or on moral
or legal grounds. Ridgway writes:

> A more subtle result of the Inchon triumph was the de-
> velopment of an almost superstitious regard for General
> MacArthur's infallibility. Even his superiors, it seemed,
> began to doubt if they should question any of MacArthur's
> decisions and as a result he was deprived of the advantage
> of forthright and informed criticism, such as every com-
> mander should have—particularly when he is trying to
> "run a war" from 700 miles away. A good many military
> leaders have recognized that it takes a special kind of
> moral courage (rarer I think than physical courage) to
> stand up to your military superior and tell him you think
> his plan is wrong. That is the time, as General George
> C. Marshall used to say, when you "lay your commis-
> sion on the line." But every military leader, from the
> lowest to the highest, owes it to the men whose lives
> are at his disposal to speak out clearly when he feels
> that a serious mistake is about to be made.[56]

Thus, command responsibility requires the commander to go
against his own grain in order to encourage those in his command to
go against their grain, both parties combining their efforts to overcome their natural propensities in order to combat immoral, illegal,
and inappropriate conduct that will strip their pursuit of a mission of
honor and may very well mean the failure of the mission itself. A
truly heroic effort is required throughout the chain of command from
the commander in chief to the lowest enlisted man. The highest civilian and military commanders must persuade the key commanders
throughout the chain of command that they have a moral and legal
duty, as well as a professional necessity, to ensure observance of
the law of war and rules of engagement within their jurisdictions. To
that end, they must be persuaded that it is both their duty and in their
vital interest to encourage and protect those in their command who
bring them evidence of wrongdoing and inappropriate behavior that
must be prevented, repressed, and punished by any truly responsible
commander.

This prescription is not lightly given. I am aware that a commander is burdened with so many tasks that it is hard to consider
something like enforcement of the law of war and rules of engagement

as equal in importance to the accomplishment of the main military missions and the assurance of the security and welfare of his command. Yet the point of this book is that missions accomplished and commands protected without due regard for morality, law, and policy are barren military exercises that promote neither justice nor legitimate political advantage.

For the moral belligerent, the price of using the military instrument in observance of the moral/legal principles of just war and the guidelines of limited war. It is the responsible commander who must bear the main burden of paying that price. To that end, he must overcome some of the most prominent psychological and sociological patterns of military behavior to produce an instrument that he controls and uses in a manner responsive to the moral, legal, and policy prescriptions of his military and political superiors. If a nation's armed forces do not have such responsible commanders at the head of controlled, responsive commands, the nation does not have the kind of military instrument that can wage just and limited war. If this is the case, its recourse to war is morally and politically irresponsible ab initio. Since nations exist in a world where recourse to war is a necessary option, a nation whose values require that such recourse be consonant with the prescriptions and guidelines of just and limited war has no alternative to the development of a military force responsive to the enlightened leadership of responsible commanders who, in turn, make compliance with just-war/limited-war standards their highest priority. This is not fanciful idealism but the most quintessential realism.

14

THE CONDUCT OF JUST AND LIMITED WAR: STATE OF THE QUESTION

This book has addressed the problems of just and limited war from perspectives of Christian realism. It has been assumed that, in view of man's imperfect nature and history, war is a perennial fact of human life. Accordingly, it is necessary and just to prepare for the eventuality of war when efforts to avoid it have failed. The preparation for war of the just and prudent person requires the formulation of moral presumptions and broad policy guidelines that should inform his decisions concerning recourse to war and its conduct.

Even in the nuclear age, the best available foundation for the formulation of prescriptions and guidelines governing the use of the military instrument of foreign policy remains the traditional just-war doctrine. But, in our time it has become increasingly clear that the prescriptions of the just-war doctrine must be translated into political/military policy guidelines. If just-war doctrine is to be more than a curiosity salvaged from the history of ideas, its injunctions must be related to the practical world of statesmen and soldiers, as well as individual citizens confronting the personal dilemmas that war brings.

This book is an effort to begin the process of joining just-war doctrine, reiterated in the light of contemporary political/military realities, to limited-war doctrine and policies as they have emerged in the modern era. Just war cannot be initiated unless there is reason to believe that the just belligerent can make a controlled, limited use of the military instrument. There can be no just war without limited-war policies and capabilities. To be sure, all limited wars are not necessarily just, but in their limited character they may qualify for acceptance as just wars, something an unlimited war can never do, whatever the justice of the cause.

THE FUNCTION OF JUST-WAR
DOCTRINE TODAY

The first task of the just-war analyst today is not to recite once more, perhaps with more erudition, the history of just-war doctrines. It is important to study the sources of the tradition and learn from them. However, it is a hard fact that much of the traditional just-war writing addresses political/military contexts far removed from those of our present war and peace decisions. Moreover, the past record of serious application of just-war prescriptions, even in the days before modern total war, is not encouraging.

Accordingly, the first task of the just-war analyst today is to pose the hard questions that are the essence of the just-war doctrine in terms of contemporary issues of recourse to and conduct of war. It has been the position of this book that this can and should be done across the spectrum of conflict confronting the modern world.

At this point there must be a clear understanding of the function of just-war doctrine. The essence of just-war doctrine is the formulation of conditions that individuals and societies must apply in conscience to their decisions concerning war. There has been much discussion in this book of international law, and every effort has been made to integrate positive international legal prescriptions into the broad framework of just-war doctrine. However, in the final analysis it is clear that these legal obligations are either moral obligations or they are not very meaningful. Recent and potential enemies of the United States are not known for their scrupulous adherence to international law. Moreover, legal obligation alone will not, finally, determine the conduct of even so law-abiding a state as the United States. The reason that just-war/international-law prescriptions will be taken seriously and will be more or less observed will be because of the consciences of the belligerents (for example, the collective conscience of the belligerents and the individual consciences of the key decision makers).

It should be recalled that even the preambles to international conventions on war refer to "the rule of the principles of the law of nations, as they result from the usages established among civilized peoples, from the laws of humanity, and from the dictates of the public conscience."[1] It is the public conscience that makes the positive law of war whatever it has become, and it is to the public conscience, as well as the individual consciences of decision makers and citizens, that the just-war doctrine addresses itself.

Accordingly, it will not do to reject just-war prescriptions on the grounds that they are self-imposed, one-sided restrictions not observed by enemies. This may very well be true at times, but the individual and the society that wants to live with its own conscience must impose upon itself and accept such restrictions regardless of the behavior of others.

Since it is believed that the United States and its people, to whom this book is primarily addressed, respect their obligations in conscience to initiate and wage only just wars, I have written this book in the belief that it will provide some practical assistance to them in defining just wars in practice. In this connection, a word should be said about the dangers of using just-war doctrine as a vehicle for uncritical justification of U.S. policy. It will have been noted that the just-war assessments of the last three U.S. wars in Chapters 4 and 5 concluded that they essentially met just-war conditions. As regards the Vietnam War this is a minority view among legal analysts and moralists. It is also a minority view among politicians, media pundits, and other interpreters of public morality. This was vividly demonstrated during the 1980 presidential campaign when Ronald Reagan was both condemned and ridiculed for giving his opinion that the Vietnam War was a noble cause. It is, of course, instructive to record that this "blunder" did not seem to have lost him too many votes.

Nevertheless, it is true that if one were a politician or a public figure courting approval and avoiding "no-win" issues, one would not volunteer praise for U.S. intervention in Vietnam, a lost and widely condemned war. Indeed, it may even prove unfortunate that this book, which aspires to focus attention on issues of just and limited war to a degree hitherto unachieved, may seem to some to fall short of its own standards by failing to join in the conventional wisdom that the Vietnam War was illegal and immoral, as well as a political/military mistake.

There are two answers in terms of just-war and limited-war criteria for this objection to the treatment of Vietnam in Chapters 5 and 11. The first is that moral issues are and should be resolved on the basis of individual moral judgment, not on the basis of social pressure. An author undertaking a serious application of moral criteria to a controversial war would lack both moral and scholarly integrity if he tilted or slanted his analyses and conclusions in the direction of prevailing opinion, scholarly or popular.

Second, issues such as the moral character of a war do not lend themselves to what the military would call "school solutions." The empirical and normative judgments requisite to a conclusion as to the moral and legal permissibility of a war are complex and often flawed by reason of imperfect knowledge. Reasonable people can agree on the criteria for judgment and disagree on the interpretation and application of the criteria. Since I expect to reach an audience somewhat larger than that which agrees with me on Vietnam, I hope that those seriously concerned with the moral evaluation of past, present, and future wars will be interested in the approach followed even if they disagree with the results.

My own positions on controversial issues and the problems thereby created underscore a more general problem. That is the difficulty of avoiding two extremes in moral judgment about war. One extreme is the uncritical acceptance of all belligerent acts of one's own side. The other is the wholesale condemnation of all belligerent acts by one's own side.

With regard to the first extreme, John Yoder has challenged just-war analysts to demonstrate instances wherein their prescriptions have some bite in them, where they really cost the belligerent something in the way of military utility. With regard to the second extreme, Paul Ramsey has pointed out that the just-war doctrine was not intended and should not be the vehicle for the systematic denial of the existence of any just wars.[2]

There is no easy resolution of either of these objections, that just-war analysts are either unduly permissive or unreasonably harsh in their assessments. The line of resolution for the problem, however, is clear. Just-war analysis is not an exercise in propaganda or public relations, a debate, or even a trial at law. Just-war analysis goes to the conscience of the individual and the public conscience of the society confronting war. Slogans, debating points, and nice legal arguments do not resolve the questions of conscience. Nor, indeed, do the prescriptions of just-war doctrine resolve the questions of conscience. They simply aid the individual or society in formulating the questions that must be asked about war, and which the individual or society must finally answer.

THE CONTENT OF JUST-WAR DOCTRINE

Of the traditional conditions of just war, the first, competent authority, is the most neglected. It is generally ticked off in perfunctory fashion with the explanation that its importance was historical (for example, before the clear emergence of sovereign states with compétence de guerre, it was necessary to distinguish public from private war). An effort has been made in this book to call attention to two important modern aspects of competent authority. One is the question of the constitutional authority of an executive within a country such as the United States to commit the nation to war. Quite possibly, an action that was unconstitutional might be immoral in that it was a violation of the condition of competent authority.

In the aftermath of the 1973 War Powers Resolution and its accompanying post-factum chorus of recriminations about abuse of executive authority, the confused state of the question in the United States remains more confused—and more in need of serious reflection—than ever. Immediately related to the issue of competent authority is that of declaration of war as a just-war condition. I did not include declaration of war as a just-war requirement because diplomatic-legal declarations of war have become something between redundant formalities and practical impossibilities in a world where war is usually declared by striking first.

The essential point is that the decision to engage in war or take actions predictably leading to war is, in modern times, overwhelmingly in the hands of the executive. No amount of legal tinkering in the manner of the 1973 War Powers Resolution can change that fact. Indeed, this is recognized in U.S. presidential elections when the propensity of a candidate to get us into war is widely discussed.

My own assessment is that the performances of Truman in the Korean War and Johnson in the Vietnam War were constitutionally valid and morally justified. In the case of Vietnam, however, the war demonstrated a point reiterated in this book, namely, that the decision to engage in war is not the end of the just-war calculus. The just belligerent must reassess the cause, the means, and the prospects of success at critical junctures in the war to see whether it still meets just-war conditions. In so doing, it would certainly be prudent as well as constitutionally and politically necessary for the president to share his view of revised just-war calculations with the Congress and the people in order to obtain their agreement and support.

The second issue of competent authority arises in a revolutionary/counterinsurgency war. Here the dilemmas seem intractable. It is clear that revolutions do not usually break out unless there is a situation so bad as to invite revolution. The question is, Who has the right to speak for the revolution, to initiate or terminate the revolution, to determine the strategies and tactics of revolutionary war? In practice, the answer seems to be purely pragmatic. Whoever can mount revolutionary activity on a significant and sustained basis has competent authority and claims the right to speak for the people and their revolution.

As observed in Chapters 7 and 8, revolutionary power tends to derive primarily from the ability to subvert, tear down, or destroy the incumbent regime and/or existing social system. There is little question of legitimacy involved. The effective practice of revolutionary warfare, often in the form of extensive terrorism, may have little relation to the desires of the people or to their grievances.

On the counterinsurgent side, competent authority to conduct counterrevolutionary war is presumed to reside with the incumbent regime, subject to whatever constitutional limitations exist. The issue of competent authority is raised at the point where revolutionary resistance is so successful and/or regime counterinsurgency measures are so unsuccessful that the regime appears to lack both the political/military base and the legal-moral legitimacy to warrant its continuation of a counterinsurgency war. This is also a point of controversy regarding its competence to invite external assistance.

This is a more difficult standard of competent authority than that applied to the revolutionaries. The regime must govern adequately as well as fight, whereas the revolutionary forces need only disrupt governmental functions and fight a revolutionary war sufficiently sustained and effective to wear down the regime and the patience of the population.

I do not have a satisfactory solution for this problem. For the moment it appears that the best approach is roughly that of the 1977 Geneva Protocol II. Following that approach, one would judge revolutionary competent authority (belligerent status under international law) mainly on the basis of indications of military success plus such political success (for example, control of areas of the country) as might be manifested.[3] Meanwhile, I would recognize the regime's competent authority to wage counterinsurgency war unless the regime was so clearly tyrannical and lacking in popular support or acceptance as to forfeit its rights (for example, Idi Amin's regime in Uganda, admittedly an extreme case).

I am not at all sure how much order can be brought to this difficult subject. Perhaps, after much more intense analysis, we would still be limited to the working proposition that as long as a belligerent in a revolutionary/counterinsurgency war could maintain a continuing, significant war effort, it should be considered as having competent authority to authorize and order belligerent operations.

The consideration of the central condition of just war, just cause, has uncovered a major gap in the treatment of the subject in contemporary literature. It is impossible to discuss the component elements of just cause (for example, exhaustion of peaceful remedies, proportionality of the just cause to the effects of the proposed means, probability of success) without a thorough analysis of the just cause itself. Yet few writers in the just-war tradition seriously address this central issue.

The classical writers are of little help. Their just causes concern injuries and wrongs reflective of the historical period in which they wrote. However, just cause in our time has often involved the nature of the social system under which men live, whether as victims of some form of Gulag society or as citizens of societies that, no matter how imperfect or even repressive, are open to the possibility of change leading to tolerable respect for fundamental human dignity.

After a long period of wishful thinking about the convergence of the free and communist worlds, the "softening" of communist societies, and the prospects of semipermanent, institutionalized deténte, it is time to confront the fact that the main just cause in the world today is the defense of a people against the imposition of irreversible communist totalitarianism. There are other, somewhat similar, just causes to be considered. Where aggression would lead not only to the subjugation, but quite possibly to the genocidal extermination or degradation, of a people (for example, in a radical Arab victory over Israel, or possibly in an Indian victory over Pakistan), similar content would be given to the just cause of defense.

The problem in the literature and in the social teaching of the churches is that this fundamental fact of survival of a society as just cause is ignored or downplayed. Both legal and moral prescriptions concerning recourse to war are addressed to anonymous states irrespective of their characteristics and, ironically, irrespective of their justice. While it is proper, as international law has done under U.S. leadership, to avoid just-war claims with respect to the rights and duties of belligerents under the jus in bello, there is no way that a responsible just-war analysis of just cause can avoid the character of the societies in conflict and the implications for human rights and dignity if one side subjugates the other.

Of the just-war authorities cited in this book, only two have really acknowledged the problem. Ramsey takes it as given that societies should be protected if at all possible from communist aggression and domination.[4] Father Murray elaborates on the nature of communist states and communist imperialism, this analysis being the basis from which he makes his statement that there is a moral imperative to find the limited-war means to resist communist aggression.[5] However, most of the just-war literature concentrates on the means, generally the nuclear means, of defense. This is understandable, given the awesome character of modern means of warfare, but one cannot construct a just-war analysis of just cause without first stating clearly the stakes of such terrible risks and sacrifices. If there is one aspect of just-war doctrine that needs improvement, it is this element of just cause to defend a people from irreversible communist or other totalitarian tyranny, an issue that runs the spectrum of conflict from nuclear to conventional to revolutionary/counterinsurgency war.

The other aspects of just cause may be quickly recapitulated. Just cause in a revolutionary war, from the standpoint of the revolutionaries, is a subject that is generally ignored in the contemporary literature except by communists and radicals whose speculations generally go unchallenged. This is an area that needs attention along with the major issue of just cause in wars with communist or other totalitarian belligerents raised above.

The present international-law approach to revolutionary war is essentially one of self-determination by a Darwinian process of armed conflict. Whatever side prevails is legitimate, is the "self" that has been "determined." The great concern is to exclude foreign intervention in this Darwinian trial by ordeal. What moral and political theory exists at present regarding the right of revolution and its limits, if any, is all on the side of Marxist revolutionaries. There seems to be no substantial discussion of the right of revolution in Marxist societies against Marxist governments. This abdication of the field of revolutionary theory by non-Marxist theorists should be remedied. It is ridiculous that the right of revolution, even for Christians, should be conceived of mainly in Marxist terms when the spirit of resistance to communist tyranny is alive in Afghanistan and Poland and struggling to stay alive in many other communist countries. The need for a modern just-war/just-revolution doctrine is great.

The question of the exhaustion of peaceful remedies is also related to the fundamental issue of the stakes in a conflict. If the stakes are control of the social system, it is difficult to negotiate the differences between the parties, as Kissinger's experience with the Vietnamese Communists demonstrated. Here again, those writing from the perspectives of the past underestimate the problem. Many modern wars are not fought over disputes, they are fought for total control of societies. In such cases, a peaceful alternative to just war is surrender, however termed (for example, coalition governments that become communist after some interval).

The point was made in Chapter 2 that belligerents should be open to peaceful alternatives to continued hostilities (for example, the United Nations in the Korean War, the United States in the Vietnam War), but that peaceful alternatives are as likely to follow as to precede effective use of the military instrument. This point is developed in the discussions of fight-and-negotiate strategies in limited war.

In this connection, special care has been taken in this book to examine the state of positive international law with respect to recourse to armed coercion and intervention. It can be seen from this examination that the legal theorists have had to struggle to maintain a regime that essentially limits permissible armed coercion to some sort of individual or collective self-defense under UN Charter Article 51. This struggle continues in a world where there is no collective security, little effective machinery for the settlement of disputes, and a kind of revolutionary "wild card" that runs throughout the interactions of the international system.

These efforts to salvage the international-law jus ad bellum are deserving of support, but they may not succeed. Given community tolerance of communist and Third World violations of Article 2(4) (for example, by the Soviet Union in Afghanistan, India in the Bangladesh War, Iraq in Iran), one wonders how much longer the United

States, Westerners, and responsible Third World peoples will continue to take seriously the supposed legal prohibition against the threat or use of force in international relations. Whether there is a continued effort to observe Article 2(4) or a return to a 1914 Hobbesian state of nature, the need for a just-war jus ad bellum, holding out more criteria than the international-law, no-first-use-of-force standard, will be critically needed.

If the legal straitjacket of the UN jus ad bellum is in danger of giving way with respect to international conflict, it is even more vulnerable in the area of mixed civil-international wars, a major source of contemporary conflicts. The prevalence of indirect aggression in the form of decisive intervention on behalf of revolutionaries has been encouraging a concomitant growth of counterinsurgency counterinterventions, justified as collective self-defense, as in the U.S. intervention in Vietnam. The task of sorting out claims and counterclaims as to who intervened first at some critical level in a civil war becomes increasingly difficult.

This subject is in a chaotic state because both of the supposed controlling principles of international law are widely violated. First recourse to armed coercion in violation of UN Article 2(4) is not uncommon. Intervention in every form, military and nonmilitary, is as commonplace as the regularity with which states, particularly communist and Third World states, reaffirm the principle of nonintervention.

In these circumstances, a country like the United States may not feel compelled to wait until a civil war has been infused with the effects, perhaps irremediable, of indirect aggression/intervention by another party before it engages in counterintervention, justified as collective self-defense. The unhappy flirtation with the regional peace-keeping rationale of the 1965 Dominican intervention indicates that the collective self-defense justification will often be inappropriate in cases where a state asserts both vital interests and a moral right to assist a people in a civil war but is unable to point to any external indirect aggression/intervention sufficient to engender collective self-defense justifications. I am not here arguing in support of the anti-communist pretensions of the U.S.-OAS intervention in the Dominican civil war but merely pointing out that a determination to prevent a communist victory in a civil war, which might be much more credible in another war than it was in the Dominican Republic in 1965, might well tempt a state to engage in an intervention it held to be just even though it was not legal under the present international-law jus ad bellum.

As the discussion of the Vietnam War in Chapters 5 and 11 brought out, the question of probability of success has emerged increasingly as a subject that needs more serious attention in just-war analyses. Most discussions state that there must be an initial finding of probability of success, plus a probability that the good effects sought will exceed the anticipated evil effects, if a war is to be just. What is not usually emphasized is the point that, as a war goes on, an initial estimate of probability of success and of proportionality of evil to good effects may be substantially altered by the course of the conflict. It is incumbent on the just belligerent to monitor developments with a view to recurring reexaminations of the probability of success and the proportionality of the war to the just cause.

Finally, the elusive but important condition of right intention has been explored. It was seen to relate closely to limited-war concepts of limited objectives and to treating war as an instrument of politics and justice (not as a vendetta based on hatred), all with the view of creating the basis for just and lasting peace. That these noble phrases can be translated into practical terms has been amply illustrated in the salutory consequences of U. S. and Allied occupation policies in Germany and Japan after World War II.

With respect to the jus in bello portion of just-war doctrine, the first point that has been emphasized in this book is the close relationship between its requirements and those of the jus ad bellum. The jus in bello provides two general prescriptions, a prohibition of the malum in se crime of genocide and a substantial body of detailed rules developed in modern international law. The two general prescriptions, the principles of proportion and discrimination, have received unequal treatment at the hands of moral and legal analysts. The principle of proportion requires that the means of war be proportionate to their military ends. That is a prescription that is easily laid down but difficult to interpret and apply in practice. The principle of discrimination, on the other hand, has the sound of something more definite; namely, there must be no direct intentional attacks on noncombatants or nonmilitary targets. The principle of discrimination, long established as the heart of the just-war jus in bello, has suffered as a corresponding principle of positive international law because of the widespread violations of the principle in modern wars, most notably in the case of aerial bombardment of population centers.

Nevertheless, because of its more definite character, the principle of discrimination has attracted most of the attention of modern just-war writers, whereas the principle of proportion has usually been treated more briefly and generally. It may be that the comparative neglect of the principle of proportion has in part been due to the impression that it is too vague and permissive to produce genuine, meaningful limitations on belligerent conduct. Similar concepts in the law (for example, due process of law, the standard of reasonableness in tort law) are equally vague, but we find it necessary and possible to give them content by a process of successive and comparative interpretations of their meaning in individual cases.

In any event, the analyses in this study demonstrated that the principle of proportion requires serious and continuing attention, since it is both an inescapable component of the jus in bello and a vital link with its counterpart, the principle of proportion in the jus ad bellum condition of just cause. In this regard there is an issue of the referent of proportionality. As a general proposition, proportionality in the jus ad bellum should be judged in terms of the political/military, strategic ends of the war (raison d'état) and should involve a comprehensive calculation of the qualitative and quantitative effects of the war in the light of those ends. Generally speaking, the referent of jus in bello proportionality is the specific military end to which a military action is addressed (raison de guerre). Manifestly, however, there is a continuum of political/military ends to which military actions make a contribution. Sometimes, as in the case of the atomic bombing of Hiroshima and Nagasaki, the highest political/military ends may be achieved by discrete military actions. In such cases, the measure of proportionality is not calculated solely in terms of military objectives destroyed balanced against civilian casualties and damage but in terms of ending the war altogether and thereby avoiding massive military and civilian casualties and widespread destruction. Likewise, in the case of the Linebacker II bombing of North Vietnam, the referent of proportionality is the political goal of compelling the Communists to return to peace negotiations even though concomitant military effects are obtained by the destruction of communication, transportation, and military facilities.

However, in the case of strategic bombing of Germany in World War II, there is widespread agreement that the area-bombing raids wrought damage disproportionate to their contribution to the war effort, either in political or military terms. There is also broad agreement that the use of firepower by U.S./ARVN forces in Vietnam was disproportionate in terms of legitimate military necessity. Moreover, abuse of firepower was at odds with the political ends of the war in terms of protecting South Vietnamese society under the rule of the Saigon government.

Discussion of the relationship between the jus ad bellum level of the calculus of proportionality in terms of the highest political/military stakes of the war (raison d'état) and the jus in bello calculus of proportionality of military means to military ends (raison de guerre) raises again the issue of misuse of just-war categories in order to justify belligerent behavior. Tucker has pointed out that one can justify any means if the ends are stretched sufficiently.[6] This is a real problem, but it cannot be permitted to vitiate the importance of the principle of proportion. As remarked at the beginning of this chapter, the function of just-war analysis is to guide the conscience of the individual or society that is looking for moral guidance. If the individual or society is inclined to cheat and to seek spurious justifications, no principles or prescriptions will be safe from abuse. As Tucker demonstrates, the much more definite principle of discrimination has been twisted and explained in so many ways that its apparent dominant position in the law of war has been questioned. [7] The problem is not with the principle of proportion or with the principle of discrimination. The problem of abuse will remain the problem of dishonest or hypocritical individuals or nations that misuse these principles.

Even among those who honestly attempt to understand and abide by the principle of discrimination, however, there is serious disagreement. One has only to survey these disagreements to come to the central point. That is that a literal application of the principle of discrimination is incompatible with the conduct of modern war at all levels. In nuclear war, conventional war, and revolutionary/counterinsurgency unconventional war it becomes necessary to use means that by any fair interpretation involve the direct intentional attacking of noncombatants and nonmilitary targets. After all quibbles about the definition of a noncombatant and a nonmilitary target have been resolved, with the widest possible inclusion of persons and targets in the category of fair targets, there are still significant numbers of clear noncombatants and nonmilitary targets that will inevitably be attacked routinely as part of the process of carrying the war to the enemy. This is true of nuclear strikes, conventional bombing, combat operations on land, as well as typical measures of revolutionary/counterinsurgency warfare. Understandable concentration on the upper range of nuclear destruction has obscured the point that the problem of potential violation of the principle of discrimination is unavoidable at all levels of modern conduct.

One answer to this problem is pacifism. The arguments for this position have not been addressed in this book. The position is not wanting in advocates. [8] Manifestly, however, a pacifist stance is not desired by most citizens of the states that have the responsibility of protecting their freedom and possibly the freedom of others.

The other answer to the problem of reconciling the principle of discrimination and the realities of modern war is to adopt some form of the principle of double effect. This route has its difficulties, for the principle tends to become lost in arcane and unconvincing debates. It seems preferable for the ordinary person to eschew these debates (particularly their agonizing over intent) and acknowledge that modern acts of war will frequently have two effects. One effect is the preferred effect of injuring the enemy's military forces, facilities, lines of communication, and war industries. The other, often inescapable and predictable effect is reluctantly accepted. This involves the death and destruction of noncombatants and nonmilitary targets, so-called collateral damage.

What emerges from this approach is, interestingly enough, a further exercise in the assessment of proportionality. For the issue in cases where this simplified version of the principle of double effect is applied is not the intention, or preference, of the attacking party but the predictable amount of collateral damage to noncombatants and nonmilitary targets. This becomes a question of proportion. There is no doubt, for example, that the area bombing of German cities, culminating in the destruction of Dresden, was aimed in part at military targets. But the intended military targets were in fact incidental to the other intended targets—whole metropolitan areas. In such attacks the relation of counterforce to countervalue targeting was reversed. The intention was overwhelmingly to destroy the cities, not simply to attack military targets. In these circumstances the principle of discrimination as amended by the principle of double effect cannot be stretched to accommodate the Allied aerial attacks. The reason is not that one or a few noncombatants or nonmilitary targets were directly and intentionally attacked, but that massive numbers of such persons and targets were attacked. Thus, the principle of discrimination, even very loosely interpreted, was violated. Additionally, these attacks, whether judged in relation to military objectives or even to the strategic objectives of the war, were also disproportionate.

By contrast, the much-condemned "Christmas bombing" (Linebacker II) of North Vietnam was quite discriminate. The intention was to attack significant military targets, and they were destroyed by extraordinarily accurate bombing carried out in the face of the heaviest and most sophisticated air defenses of the century. Nevertheless, noncombatant casualties occurred, and hospitals and other nonmilitary, indeed, protected targets were hit. That this would happen was, again, predictable. But it was also predictable that the degree to which collateral damage would result from the Linebacker II raids would be proportionate to the specific military results obtained by counterforce attacks (raison de guerre) and to the political results of compelling the North Vietnamese to resume peace negotiations (raison d'état).

When one turns to nuclear deterrence and war, the difficulties of respecting the principle of discrimination, even as amended by the principle of double effect, reach a critical dimension. Clearly, a major, strategic nuclear exchange targeted on cities would involve the direct, intentional killing and destruction of noncombatants and nonmilitary targets beyond any possible justification as collateral damage under double-effect reasoning. Yet, it is the threat of such attacks that is the essence of mutual assured destruction (MAD), a source of comparative peace and stability in the world.

This grim state of affairs has produced an ironic situation among those who are morally concerned over the implications of strategic nuclear deterrence but have not joined the pacifist camp. The doves who would avoid war at all costs are advocates of minimal deterrence, which means, in effect, threatening the worst, most unthinkable kind of immoral, countervalue attacks on enemy cities in the belief and/or hope that the threat would never have to be carried out, since the awesome threat would not be challenged. The hawks, more inclined to risk limited war to avoid the either/or decision of carrying out the MAD threat of trading cities in a nuclear holocaust or surrendering, seek countervalue deterrent policies that could conceivably be carried out if deterrence failed (for example, the 1974 Schlesinger strategy). Thus, the doves would threaten clearly immoral war in the hope that the deterrent would work and the threat would never have to be carried out, while the hawks would threaten counterforce war in the hope that it would be a sufficient deterrent but in the belief that a morally acceptable, "fight-the-war" capability should be sought. [9]

Since I believe that no deterrent will long be effective unless it is based on a credible "fight-the-war" capability and the will to use it if necessary, I espouse the Schlesinger position in this matter. Nevertheless, it is clear that all concerned in the debate are subject to the course of military technology and the options it produces or precludes as well as on the unpredictable vagaries of perceptions and attitudes in the decision-making processes of the nuclear powers.

If the United States has the capability to inflict unacceptable damage on the USSR through counterforce attacks only, then we are in a fortunate situation wherein both the deterrent threat and the "fight-the-war" capability are potentially consonant with just-war/limited-war standards. There remains, to be sure, the everpresent specter of escalation to sustained strategic countervalue exchanges once any nuclear weapons have been used. There is also a major question of the extent of collateral damage in the event of major counterforce attacks. But at least it is possible to imagine a just and limited counterforce nuclear war.

Such an option, of course, depends on the state of military technology and on the willingness of belligerents to draw and hold the line between strategic counterforce and countervalue nuclear war. This is an issue that then works its way down the escalatory ladder through theater nuclear war to battlefield tactical nuclear war, as discussed in Chapter 6. At every level, a key issue is the willingness of belligerents to recognize and sustain nuclear thresholds.

Thus, the state of the question of nuclear deterrence, war, and morality is, after over 35 years, more complex than ever. There never has been a time since the early 1950s when prospects for détente, significant arms-control measures, avoidance of dangerous superpower confrontations, and local wars subject to expansion and escalation were less promising. It is a time, in brief, when the question of the morality of nuclear deterrence and war cannot be shunted aside in favor of some more positive subject. The alternatives to confronting the nuclear question have been tried and, to varying degrees, failed, and the moment when the confrontation can no longer be avoided is here.

At present, there are basically four moral positions on strategic nuclear deterrence and war. First, one can trust in MAD and, if that deterrent fails, engage in a suicidal and immoral countervalue war. Second, one can trust in MAD and, if the bluff is called, surrender. Third, one can mount a counterforce alternative to MAD and use it if necessary. If counterforce war is insufficient to stop aggression and/or strategic nuclear attack, use of strategic countervalue means would be the last resort, or a belated surrender would be indicated. Fourth, one can oppose even the maintenance of a strategic countervalue capability on the grounds that it is both unusable and immoral, as well as being too dangerous to maintain. This, too, would mean surrender. Theoretically this approach might envisage maintenance of only a counterforce deterrent upon which all hopes would be rested. Whether this is presently a realistic option is questionable, but it could be a goal that might prove achievable over time.

The upshot is that, if deterrence fails and one is obliged to engage in strategic nuclear countervalue exchanges, chances of survival are slim. If counterforce suffices, chances of survival are somewhat questionable, but they exist. If there is an unwillingness to engage in the suicidal and immoral acts of strategic countervalue nuclear war or the dangerous conduct of strategic counterforce war, then surrender looms as the alternative; however, it may be camouflaged. There have been brave words throughout the nuclear age from nuclear and other pacifists about nonviolent resistance in the case of surrender and occupation by totalitarian tyrants. Failure to find an acceptable nuclear deterrent will provide the opportunity to try out this approach in practice.

My own choice is the third, counterforce deterrent position. It involves both the imaginative development of counterforce policies and capabilities sufficient to inflict unacceptable damage on an aggressor and the stiffening of the will to fight for freedom of the United States and its allies. Counterforce nuclear war is not as bad as countervalue nuclear war, either in practical or moral terms, but it is bad enough. It would require a very determined people with outstanding leaders to survive a counterforce nuclear war and keep it limited to counterforce.

Returning to the principle of discrimination, if that principle is understood as interpreted here, namely, as the use of means that do not cause disproportionate loss of life and destruction to noncombatants and nonmilitary targets, credible deterrence based on a morally permissible "fight-the-war" policy and capability is possible.

The foregoing discussion has focused on strategic nuclear deterrence of strategic nuclear attacks on the United States. There are other issues of just-war limits on nuclear war that are but briefly contemplated in this book and require more extensive examination in just-war analyses. These are the problems of limited nuclear war, usually broken down into limited battlefield tactical nuclear war and theater nuclear war. These issues have been raised in Chapter 6. The first problem, of course, is that the limited nuclear-war issues are integrally bound up in the strategic-war issues. The inadequacies, for example of NATO's limited-war defenses, conventional and nuclear, arise both from the justified fear of the Western Europeans that such a limited defense of their countries would destroy them and from a reluctance to sustain the costs of efficacious limited-war defenses. Accordingly, there is a disposition in Western Europe to rely ultimately on U.S. strategic nuclear deterrence as the main defense of NATO. If strategic nuclear deterrence is difficult to think through convincingly in practical and moral terms insofar as protection of the United States from strategic nuclear attack is concerned, it is immeasurably more difficult to conceive and justify strategic nuclear countervalue war in defense of NATO. This problem becomes more acute in an era of Soviet strategic nuclear parity and possible superiority.

A just-war approach would insist that all chances of limited-war defense of NATO be explored before throwing defense of Western Europe into the kind of desperate strategic deterrence posture (either carry out the threat in a nuclear countervalue holocaust or surrender) that presently looms with respect to deterrence of strategic nuclear attack on the United States. But it is clear that a just-war defense of NATO with limited nuclear means, whether battlefield tactical or theater, is not easily accomplished. Major problems of reconciling such means used in such a heavily populated area with the principles of proportion and discrimination arise. But even these problems are not foremost, since one first must think through such questions as whether these nuclear thresholds are realistic, whether they will be observed by the aggressor, and whether such a limited nuclear defense would actually be more effective than a conventional defense, since the attacking force might profit as much if not more from nuclear war than the defenders. Underlying the whole discussion is the issue of escalation to strategic nuclear war once recourse to any nuclear weapons has been had.

Behind the intimidating issue of reconciling the just-war principles of proportion and discrimination with nuclear war in its several forms is that of applying those principles in a conventional war fought

in heavily populated areas, as in NATO. The destructive effects of
modern conventional weapons demonstrated in Vietnam, unfortunately
sometimes in populated areas, and in the Yom Kippur War, where
more typical exchanges of sophisticated weapons systems were fortunately carried out for the most part in open desert areas, alert us
to the difficulties of holding to just-war standards in conventional war.
At least here, however, there is some possibility of choice among
strategic and tactical options. These require the preliminary planning and mobilization for limited war as well as the disciplined control of the military instrument discussed in Chapter 13.

Last, and often overlooked in contemporary discussions of just
war are the issues of proportionality and discrimination in revolution-
ary/counterinsurgency war. As Chapters 7 and 8 demonstrate, it
may well be the case that success in revolutionary wars requires
means that are clearly indiscriminate and whose proportionality is
only legitimized by appeals to distant utopian goals. On the counterinsurgent side, both morality and prudence require greater discrimination and respect for proportionality defined in a more modest and
traditional sense than that invoked by the rebels.

Much more serious study would be required before strategies
and tactics could be suggested for revolutionaries that would conform
to the just-war standards of proportion and discrimination. This is
a work that needs to be done. There is more expert opinion on enlightened self-interest options for counterinsurgents, as suggested
in Chapter 8. These options need to be pursued notwithstanding the
provocations of the revolutionaries and their enjoyment of what
amounts to a double standard of conduct in revolutionary/counterin-
surgency warfare.

It is necessary only to reiterate the next component in the just-
war jus in bello, the judgment that genocide is malum in se. The
problem is to penetrate cynical and false allegations of genocide, as
in the Vietnam War, and apply this concept only in the sad cases
where a people are exterminated or destroyed as such. When this
is the case, there is a serious question whether the general moral
and legal presumptions against recourse to armed coercion in the
form of military intervention should not be overridden. Practically,
there seems to be no rush on the part of nations to volunteer such
humanitarian intervention, as observed in Chapter 7.

It has been observed in Chapter 6 that international law has not
registered many successful efforts to declare weapons or means of
warfare mala prohibita. The principal exception to this conclusion
is the outlawing of chemical and biological warfare (CW). However,
even in this case, the vulnerability of the existing bans is marked.
The prohibition of CW is basically a no-first-use prescription, which
might not survive use by an ally of a party to a conflict, much less an

immediate opponent. The troublesome issue of the inclusion or not of the nonlethal gas/herbicide means used by the United States in Vietnam in the CW ban raises the question of holding the threshold of a means not necessarily reprehensible or unreasonable in all of its manifestations but that may be subject to abuse if the Pandora's box of its use is once opened. The ominous CW preparations and policies of the USSR make necessary a capability and readiness to reply in kind to Warsaw Pact first use of chemical means, but initiation of their use would appear to be illegal and of questionable military utility.

Otherwise, this study has not pursued the debates concerning weapons alleged to cause superfluous suffering (for example, napalm, cluster bombs, the M-16 rifle). When the Geneva debates on weapons and the international conventions they produce have been reviewed, it will probably be seen that the arguments against these weapons have not proved to be nearly as persuasive as they appeared to some when first interjected into the more general criticism of the conduct of the Vietnam War.

Chapters 3 and 8 dealt with the problems of protecting prisoners of war (PWs) and civilians in modern war. Several problems have emerged. The most critical is the refusal of communist belligerents to apply the 1949 Geneva PW Convention and to accept the ICRC as the neutral international agency competent to monitor compliance with the PW regime. In the absence of such ICRC involvement in the appointment of a protecting power, communist belligerents have tortured and mistreated PWs, in part to coerce them into making statements or taking actions against their own side, a source of communist propaganda. Related to this is the distinct trend of communist and some other contemporary belligerents (for example, Syria in the 1973 Yom Kippur War) to use PWs as bargaining chips. When a belligerent is asked to give up a substantive political quid pro quo simply to obtain the lists of its military personnel held as PWs by the enemy, the international law of war is being violated in one of its most fundamental areas.

Chapter 8 considered the special problems of the jus in bello in revolutionary/counterinsurgency war. It was concluded that a double standard exists for revolutionaries and counterrevolutionaries. This standard arises in part out of the genuine limitations of many revolutionary forces and in part from calculated defiance of international law and morality. The problems of applying the law of war protecting PWs and civilians under military occupation in revolutionary/ counterinsurgency war were also seen to be exacerbated by the civil-war character of most of these conflicts. In such wars, both sides claim the allegiance of the people and tend to deny them the protection of the international law of war.

All of these considerations lead to the need for review of the functions and limitations of reprisals as a means of sanctioning the jus in bello. It was seen in Chapters 3 and 8 that many obvious forms of reprisal are prohibited by conventional law. Moreover, there is a great uncertainty as to the prospects for effective use of reprisals as a sanction for the law—as distinguished from their use as a means of and justification for dismantling the law, as in the case of the law of war and neutrality at sea in World War I and the law of aerial bombardment in World War II.

While it would not be prudent to relinquish altogether the right of reprisal, it seems clear that this right is not a promising source of sanctions for the law of war. Reciprocity is desirable for a law-abiding belligerent but is often denied by lawless opponents. The basic sanction for the law of war is the enlightened self-interest of the belligerent and a commitment to fundamental human values. The moral and law-abiding belligerent must try to maximize the coincidence of legitimate military necessity and the requirements of a just war. When there is a conflict between military utility and just-war standards, the standards must prevail. Otherwise the belligerent is reduced to the position of the discredited German Kriegsraison theory that necessity knows no law.

In summary, modern just-war doctrine, into which contemporary international law may be incorporated, provides a comprehensive body of prescriptions governing recourse to armed coercion (jus ad bellum) and the conduct of war (jus in bello). With the important exception of revolutionary/counterinsurgency war, this body of moral and legal prescriptions provides substantially adequate, basic moral-legal guidance on the great issues of initiating and conducting war. The problems of application are great, but, in intellectual, moral, and practical terms, they are no greater than those of other moral problem areas. What is needed is not an open-ended search for more and more specific prescriptions but an in-depth effort to make practical sense of the large body of moral-legal prescriptions now available to those who would understand and observe just-war standards.

There remains the final question of the relative importance and relation of the various just-war conditions in the just-war judgmental process. As suggested in Chapter 2, there is much to be said for requiring compliance with all of the conditions, they being, after all, the requirements for overcoming a basic presumption against war that informs the just-war tradition. This means that not only the conditions of the jus ad bellum must be met but that the war that was initiated in conformity with those conditions must be conducted as required by the jus in bello, especially in the matter of observing the basic principles of proportion and discrimination.

On the other hand, the application of the just-war categories to three contemporary U.S. wars brings out the fact that compliance with just-war conditions may be mixed. There may be an unquestioned just cause but questionable practices violative of proportion and discrimination, as in the Allied war effort in World War II. There may be a controversial just cause but a conduct of the war that is in many respects superior to that in World War II, as in the U.S. intervention in Vietnam. The issue is not one of justifying or excusing behavior in violation of just-war standards but whether such behavior may vitiate the generally valid claim of a belligerent to be fighting a just war. The best answer seems to be that the judgment must be made case by case, with all of the just-war conditions being treated very seriously. However, it does seem that, if there is one element in the just-war calculus that is most important, it is that of just cause, without which there is no occasion to contemplate the other conditions. A truly just cause, as with those opposed to Hitler's genocidal tyranny in World War II, may cover lapses such as area bombing in the sense that the immoral behavior does not render the whole war unjust. The immoral behavior, however, remains immoral and a delinquency for which the just belligerent is morally responsible.

LIMITED WAR—MAKING JUST WAR POSSIBLE

Limited war makes possible compliance with just-war conditions. Limited-war policies and capabilities are essential to the estimates of proportionality that the just belligerent must make when initiating and continuing a war. Limited-war practices are indispensable in the conduct of a war in accordance with just-war standards. Limited-war policies make possible the termination of a conflict on some terms other than unconditional surrender, perhaps secured at disproportionate costs.

The first guideline of limited war, political primacy, means that the war will not become an end in itself with its own independent logic compelling events in pursuit of military victory. Political primacy means that the choice of military options may be made in terms of appropriateness to the realization of the political objectives of the war.

A controlled military instrument, used wisely in the service of a nation's policies, may permit the civilian leaders to keep the focus on the achievement of the just cause and to avoid military temptations, as in the case of Truman's rejection of MacArthur's agenda for a wider conflict in Asia. To be sure, war is still a risky, unpredictable business, and the military instrument is often unresponsive to the nuances of policy. There is, moreover, the matter of winning sufficiently to achieve the limited-war objectives. The point is well expressed by

Osgood in terms of the tensions in limited war between the "limiters" and the "winners."[10] Political primacy does not automatically assure either wise or effective use of the military instrument, but it is the first precondition of just war.

Limited objectives likewise conform to just-war requirements. Limited objectives mean rejection of open-ended crusades that may engender total-war policies on both sides. The influence of unconditional surrender as a goal in World War II is all too clearly reflected in the Allied violations of proportion and discrimination in aerial bombardments. A just war has limited objectives, sufficient to warrant recourse to war but not extending beyond what is necessary to accomplish the just cause. Here again, modern limited-war concepts serve just-war imperatives well.

Just war requires proportion in the overall relation between the ends and means of the war. Limited war requires economy of force, the limiting of military assets and effort to what is genuinely necessary to take an objective. As the examination of the limited wars in Korea, Vietnam, and the Middle East revealed, the normative principle of proportion and the political/military principle of economy of force are not identical. Proportion enjoins a principled limitation of means; economy of force requires a prudential limitation of means. Sometimes the principled and prudential limitations may coincide or converge. Then just-war and limited-war concepts are mutually supporting sources of guidance for the conduct of war.

Sometimes, however, the two principles may diverge. Concern for proportionality would incline the belligerent to the low side of estimates for requirements of success, whereas a strictly military calculation of economy of force might induce the belligerent to make sure that enough force was employed to take the objective. Somewhere in the continuing debate about the pace, level, and form of U.S. escalatory policies in Vietnam, there is a question about the relationship between concern for proportionality and concern for economy of force in light of the principle of the objective. In broadest terms, U.S. policies were generally proportionate, whereas a military understanding of the principle of economy of force and of the objective might have led to a more decisive application of military assets at critical junctures.

The quotations from U.S. service publications in Chapter 9 indicate differences (for example, between the army and air force) in the definition of economy of force and its relation to the just-war principle of proportion.[11] This is a subject deserving of further study and reflection. But it is already clear that serious concern with economy of force, as demanded by limited-war policies, is a precondition of achievement of proportionality in the just-war sense.

The idea that even bitter enemies must communicate with each other and must finally temper their arbitrament at arms by some kind of rules of conflict is of the essence both in just-war doctrine and modern limited-war policy and practice. To be sure, the reviews of limited wars in Korea, Vietnam, and the Middle East indicated the vagaries of Schelling's coercive diplomacy and bargaining within a conflict. General Westmoreland's impatience with unwarranted faith in "signals" between enemies is understandable. [12] Nevertheless, in the wars discussed, there was direct communication between the belligerents regarding termination of the conflict that mitigated the dangers of expansion and escalation, and there was a "fight-and-negotiate" approach that, whatever its cruelties, was superior to a "fight-to-the-death-for-unconditional-surrender" approach.

The suggested rules of conflict offered in these analyses were neither homogeneous in character nor universally applicable. These limited-war guidelines are a rough list of recurring rules or characteristics of limited war, particularly as waged by the United States. Nevertheless, in contrast to those writers who would restrict the concept of limited war to nuclear powers using less than their total military capabilities, [13] I would hold to the idea that limited war is a universal requirement for states aspiring to protect their vital interests through just wars. Adjustments can be made in application of the limited-war guidelines suggested, according to the capabilities and situation of the individual belligerent.

In the wars discussed, superpower confrontation was carefully avoided in Korea and Vietnam. There was a brief but dangerous superpower confrontation in the Yom Kippur War. This is a good example of the abiding truth of the nuclear age that virtually any armed conflict may expand and escalate to nuclear confrontations and wars. This means that in the just-war calculus of proportionality of ends and means and probability of success, the contingency of nuclear superpower intervention in the conflict and confrontation is a central and limiting consideration.

It should be clear that superpower confrontation need not always be contrary to the values of just and limited war. As in the case of the 1973 Middle East war, such confrontations, properly handled, may have salutory effects (in this case, the exclusion of the USSR from further opportunities to make trouble in that part of the Middle East). Nevertheless, it is prudent to hold such confrontations to a minimum as well as to attempt to limit them, wherever possible, to situations where it is not likely that the USSR would emerge from the crisis with greater power and prestige.

No serious temptation to use nuclear weapons was registered in the limited-war studies with the exception of the nuclear threat against the People's Republic of China, which seems to have moved them to desist from their obstructionist policies at Panmunjom. Should another limited war break out, for example, in the NATO area or in vital parts of the Middle East, the deficiencies in conventional capabilities of the United States and its allies might make nuclear war the only alternative to retreat or surrender. This is an issue I have treated at the end of the list of limited-war guidelines under the requirement for flexible response.

Geographic confinement of conflicts is a well-established hallmark of limited war. It has the advantage of restricting the geographic scope of a conflict while serving as a highly visible symbol of the determination of belligerents to keep the war limited. However, limited-war geographic constraints are not unchallengeable ends in themselves. Circumstances may justify changed policies regarding geographic limits, as well may have been the case when Nixon sent U.S.-ARVN forces into Cambodia in 1970. The lesson of that venture is not so much one of the error of violating a self-imposed geographic limit that had long been violated and exploited by the enemy but of insuring the probability of a success proportionate to the political risks taken in exceeding the established limit.

The literature on limited war has generally ignored the fact that practitioners of such wars, especially the United States, are concerned to legitimize their actions through invocation of legal and moral justifications and by marshaling the support of other states in a collective enterprise. The dangers of confusing the ad hoc collection of more or less willing allies with a mandate from the international community are always present in these endeavors. The United States, it appears, has never forgotten the advantages of moral rectitude endowed by the "united nations" coalition of World War II and the UN peace-keeping mandate of the Korean War. The Dominican U.S.-OAS intervention, the tragicomic details of which have only been alluded to in this work, was a caricature of the U.S. thirst for legal warrant and collective character to cloak an action that was essentially unilateral.[14] The whimsical and futile references to the Southeast Asian Treaty Organization (SEATO) in the Vietnam War provide other examples of this tendency.

There is, to be sure, some merit in the proposition that a war endorsed by an international organization and/or based on a solid international legal rationale is more likely to be handled as a just and limited war than one avowedly based on raw national interests irrespective of the limitations of the law. It may also be true that a coalition of allied belligerents is more circumspect in its policies than a single belligerent acting as it pleases, and that this circumspection is conducive to just and limited war.

All this is plausible but not inevitable. The Arab states, for example, have amply demonstrated that a coalition of states invoking legal and moral mandates can wage wars that are neither just nor successful. I would recommend a somewhat different emphasis in the matter of legal justification for just and limited war. I would insist on a clear and honest legal justification for the action, as was indeed the case of the U.S. position in Korea and Vietnam, namely, collective self-defense against aggression and counterintervention under Article 51. Such a case is necessary for the just-war condition of just cause and for the limited-war guideline of limited objectives. Having made the case, I would hold to it as indeed the United States did in the Korean War (except for the brief interlude of unification of Korea, in itself a reasonable goal if practically achievable) and in the Vietnam War where there was no wavering from the goal of defending South Vietnam without any question of liberating North Vietnam. If others can be induced to join an essentially just and legal U.S. war, so much the better.

I am skeptical, however, of the idea that the solicitation of international organization mandates and/or allies somehow strengthens the legal-moral case for resort to war. In terms of domestic and international public opinion, such mandates and allies may add to the credibility of the just belligerent, but I think that a good case is a good case whether it is made by one state, an international organization, or a coalition of states. (All of this discussion assumes that there is no prospect of bona fide UN enforcement action under Chapter 7 of the UN Charter.)

The wars reviewed here show the importance of limited mobilization for a Great Power in imposing imminent restrictions on military capabilities and, thereby, on the scope, character, and intensity of the war. The Yom Kippur War, on the other hand, demonstrates the fact that wars fought by smaller powers may require total mobilization but still conform in essential respects to the guidelines of limited war.

Restraint in the use of the psychological instrument of policy, the government's public relations and propaganda operations, is not always emphasized explicitly in the limited-war literature. However, what might be called the pre-limited-war literature, the books critiquing total war after World War II (for example, by Liddell Hart, General Fuller, Baldwin, and Aron), all emphasized the deleterious effects of wartime propaganda on home-front attitudes, international public opinion, and the consequent total-war policies pursued by governments.[15] Governments that had whipped up a war spirit then found themselves encouraged to pursue the most exaggerated total-war measures and would have found it difficult to explain conspicuous restraints in policy in the atmosphere that they themselves had created.

The problem of restraint with the psychological instrument, demonstrated by the U.S. experience in Korea and Vietnam, has been that if a war spirit is not evoked, necessary support for the war may be lacking. In the case of the Vietnam War a virulent antiwar spirit was diligently whipped up by a broad spectrum of opponents of the war. There was no serious competitive effort by the U.S. government. Obviously, the merits of the case are beyond the issue of the comparative effectiveness of propaganda. But the problem of restraining the war spirit while maintaining popular support for a war is a serious one. In the wake of the Vietnam War, it is questionable whether a country like the United States can employ the psychological instrument with sufficient effectiveness to obtain and hold the support of the country and of essential foreign opinion without unleashing an uncritical and dangerous war spirit incompatible with the balanced, disciplined policies required by just and limited war.

It is much easier to explain a total-war crusade against evil personified than a limited war for limited objectives conducted under strict moral, legal, and policy restraints. This is especially the case if the limited war is prolonged and not clearly successful. If, as some suggest, the task is near hopeless in a democracy such as the United States, where popular opinions and pressures make a difference, it may be that the only wars that can be fought would be more akin to the total wars of this century than to the limited wars of Korea and Vietnam.

This is a critical variable in the just-war calculus. It is not for nothing that Gelb termed the American people the essential domino[16] and that post-Vietnam critiques incline to the judgment that the Vietnam War was finally lost in Washington. It is idle to contemplate embarking on a just and limited war that is technically feasible but practically impossible because of insufficient assurances of sustained public support.

The Yom Kippur War, on the other hand, shows a maturing of the Egyptian government and people and a willingness on the part of at least one state with a past record of wild, unrestrained (and sometimes counterproductive) use of the psychological instrument to conform its international propaganda to objectives consonant with just and limited war. The Israelis, too, in 1973 learned some lessons about the need for accurate and restrained public information policies.

Fight-and-negotiate strategies are typical of limited wars. This is all to the good in that it is an improvement over total-war goals and means. Moreover, the willingness to negotiate while fighting confirms both the limited-war principle of political primacy and the just-war principles of exhaustion of peaceful remedies and right intention.

The problem, of course, is to proportion and coordinate the fighting and the negotiations. The United States has found this difficult. Indeed, an important issue between just-war prescriptions and limited-war guidelines emerges from consideration of fight-and-negotiate strategies. The just-war imperative to seek peaceful resolution of the conflict, which I apply during the course of the war as well as before it, might incline a belligerent to put an emphasis on "going the last mile for peace," as Lyndon Johnson gave the appearance of doing. This, however, is not the way one engages in fight-and-negotiate relations with a determined communist enemy. The lesson might have been learned in the Korean War when Truman cut off the initiative of the UN forces in the expectation of serious and satisfactory negotiations that were very long in coming.

One can and must keep up adequate military pressure while pursuing negotiations in good faith. That is the nature of fight-and-negotiate strategies, as demonstrated, for example, by the Communist offensives in Korea in the spring of 1953 and in Vietnam in the spring of 1972. The lesson was finally learned by the United States and put into practice with the Christmas 1972 Linebacker II attacks on North Vietnam that brought the Communists back to serious negotiations. In the Yom Kippur War, too, the relation of the battlefield situation to the parties' willingness to negotiate reasonably was marked, as described in Chapter 12. All three wars show that military success can produce leverage in negotiations and that evidence of unwillingness to back up diplomacy with adequate force leads to stalling or demands for capitulation. If a war is just and limited, it deserves competent conduct in the fight-and-negotiate phases. It would be tragic to concede hard-won battlefield gains in a just war because of poorly conducted negotiations and an unwillingness to pursue the "fight" as well as the "negotiate" element in fight-and-negotiate situations.

Little attention has been given by limited-war theorists to the role of international organizations and/or ad hoc third parties in keeping wars limited and assisting in their termination. In the limited wars considered here, the roles of international commissions (Korea, Vietnam) and the UN (Yom Kippur) were of mixed importance, Vietnam being the least affected by an international presence. Unquestionably, however, international organizations or ad hoc, third-party intermediaries can help separate belligerents, monitor truces, assist in resolving practical dilemmas (such as the PW repatriation issue in Korea or the relief of the Egyptian Third Army in the Yom Kippur War), all of which may keep limited wars limited and contribute to the discouragement of their resumption. In this connection it should also be recalled that the United States served such a function, far surpassing the UN in the scope of its mediation activities, in and after the Yom Kippur War.

The last of the principal limited-war guidelines is the imperative requirement for flexible-response policies and capabilities. This imperative goes back to the 1950s reactions against undue reliance on massive retaliation. The need for flexible response is even greater in the 1980s when the Soviets have strategic parity or perhaps superiority and when credible threats of aggression abound.

It is obviously pointless to prescribe the just and limited use of the military instrument if the instrument at hand is inadequate for and inappropriate to the tasks of such wars. All of this sounds reasonable enough, perhaps, but flexible response has its determined critics. First, from the time of the "more-bang-for-the-buck" policies of the Eisenhower administration, the expense of maintaining flexible-response forces has been decried. In today's world of inflationary costs affecting both the payment and pensioning of military personnel and the purchase and maintenance of military hardware, flexible response is a very expensive goal that can probably be achieved only at the expense of some other important public responsibilities.

Second, it is argued that the more flexible the flexible-response capability, the more likely it is that there will be a response, that is to say, a war. Those who would avoid war at all costs like to narrow the military options down to the fewest and least likely. One need not be a dove to see the element of plausibility in this concern.

Eisenhower lacked flexible response and did very little intervening. (The 1958 excursion in Lebanon was a modest, noncombat affair that highlighted the inadequacies of U.S. flexible-response capabilities.) Kennedy and Johnson developed flexible response and produced the U.S. intervention in Vietnam that was escalated simultaneously with the intervention of over 20,000 elite combat troops in the Dominican Republic. It is certainly true that one way to stay out of wars is to lack the capability to engage in them, and, conversely, that one way to get into wars is to possess the capability to wage them.

It is believed, however, that even a power as well endowed with a flexible-response capability as the United States was in 1965 goes to war reluctantly and for reasons that are considered just and proportionate to the risks involved. In any event, the nature of the international system today does not allow for a return to isolationism under the MAD balance of terror. As limited-war theorists and practitioners have been pointing out since the 1950s, a power such as the United States predictably faces a continuing succession of challenges to its vital interests and to world peace and order. It cannot meet them with strategic nuclear threats. A power such as the United States must have a range of flexible-response capabilities sufficient to meet at least the main foreseeable military contingencies. Moreover, all states, depending on their situation, require flexible-response policies and capabilities if they contemplate any possibility of involvement in war.

This is, indeed, expensive as well as having major social consequences. For example, in the United States it is increasingly difficult to maintain a serious flexible-response capability, including a ready reserve, without a draft. It is also somewhat risky to develop flexible-response capabilities, since it is true that the temptations to intervene militarily increase with a flexible-response posture. (I have immodestly termed this truth O'Brien's Law, namely, "mission rises to meet capability.")

However, the failure to establish flexible-response policies and capabilities in time is a cardinal violation of limited-war doctrine. There obviously can be no limited war without appropriate limited-war policies and capabilities. Moreover, failure to make provision for flexible response is an abdication of the option of fighting a just war if war becomes necessary, despite fervent hopes that the unusable deterrent will deter it.

As the discussion of the Vietnam War illustrated, flexible response is not only a matter of military policies and capabilities. In more cases than not, foreseeable conflicts will require major civil affairs resources. Thus, for example, if the United States is at all likely to have to intervene in the Middle East, it is essential that provision be made in time for civil affairs activities in support of military forces. This involves at least two major components. First, there must be a centralized civil affairs organization within the U.S. government so that civil affairs activities, military and civilian, are not carried out in an uncoordinated, competitive, sometimes contradictory fashion. Such an organization must reconcile the "hard-line/soft-line" strategies discussed in Chapters 5, 8, and 11, whether the conflict be one of revolutionary/counterinsurgency war, conventional war, or nuclear war. It is clear that military flexible response without adequate civil affairs policy direction is in danger of being a wasted response.

Operationally, civil affairs flexible response requires teams of active, dedicated people, in or out of uniform, but under a single command (as in the Civil Operations and Revolutionary [Rural] Development Support [CORDS] program in Vietnam), who have a functional command of the local languages, some background and/or serious preparation for working in the area, and the practical skills requisite for the most difficult of political/military tasks, intervention in the lives of a foreign people victimized by war.

Unless flexible-response policies and capabilities are planned and made realities, there can be little possibility of just and limited war. This leads us to our last major concern in this book, the modes and channels through which just-war and limited-war policies become realities.

JUST AND LIMITED WAR IN PRACTICE

The enduring contribution of the Nuremberg Trial was not the negative point that war criminals should be punished but the positive assertion that it is men, working in governments and military forces, who make the decisions and take the actions attributed to states. Thus, it is men who have the opportunity to do right as well as wrong. Just-war prescriptions and limited-war guidelines must be taken seriously and acted on by the men and women within the processes of national security planning and programs and the conduct of military operations if the issues raised in this book are to be addressed.

Much of the moral and legal literature on war emphasizes the prohibitory effect of moral and legal rules regarding war. A good bit of this literature looks to the prevention, repression, and punishment of violations of just-war and international-law prescriptions. Comparable discussions exist concerning the enforcement of rules of engagement in limited war. The necessary functions of sanctioning just-war prescriptions and limited war guidelines has been discussed in Chapter 13. However, by far the more important sources of proper conduct in war are the plans, strategies, orders, missions, force compositions, and weapons systems development decisions that determine the nature of wars.

As repeatedly demonstrated in World War II, Korea, Vietnam, and the Yom Kippur War, military forces usually fight the kind of war for which they have been prepared. They tend to emphasize what they do well and avoid what they do poorly. If they have been trained and equipped to fight proportionate and discriminate counterforce war, they will probably do so. If they only have the training and capability to fight with disproportionate and indiscriminate means and methods, that is what they will employ when war comes.

The best time to affect the conduct of a war is in advance of the event. International lawyers and diplomats can draft conventions, Judge Advocate General (JAG) officers can give training in the law of war and advice to commanders, moralists can enjoin just-war behavior, and limited-war theorists can lay down guidelines for "rational actor" monoliths, but the decisions made as to the nature, composition, and missions of a military force, often well in advance of commitment to combat, are in large measure determinative of the course of a war.

Thus, as one considers the modes and channels of limitation of war, one starts with the highest political and military decision makers who determine the broad outlines of future conflicts. The proponents of just and limited war, then, must adopt a "forward strategy" of addressing their prescriptions and guidelines to those at the top of the political/military hierarchy. The process is outlined in Chapter 13.

However, even if extraordinary successes are registered in bringing just-war and limited-war values into the highest national security decision processes, there remains the unending task of implementing these enlightened policies. Here the hope of those committed to moral and rational defense policies is command control and discipline—central features of a good military system. The words military instrument of foreign policy come easily to the lips of the student of foreign and defense policy, but it takes strong commanders throughout a disciplined chain of command to make a military organization into such an instrument.

Among the issues raised in the discussion of this subject in Chapter 13, one in particular is controversial and important. This is the insistence on the role of the commander as a catalyst for responsible reaction to and, if necessary, dissent from strategic and tactical policies when they seem to depart from the objectives of the war. Nothing is more clear than the fact that modern war is characterized by uncertainty and danger to an extent that is extraordinary even by the historic standards of man's experience with war. It would be astonishing if official policies were not sometimes wrong; inconsistent with just-war/limited-war objectives, prescriptions, and guidelines; and in need of constructive criticism.

The discussion in Chapter 13 contended that it is too much to expect a great deal of this constructive criticism to come spontaneously from subordinates if they are likely to be severely rebuked or punished within the system for their audacity. It is a vital command function to solicit responsible criticism, consider it, act on it if necessary, and protect or even reward the critics. It should be added that while this is a matter of greatest concern within the military, where the requirement for disciplined obedience is greatest, the same prescription applies to the civilian component of the national security establishment. What is required of every military commander must, a fortiori, be required of the president, our commander in chief.

To be sure, the effect of such solicited criticism must still depend on the wisdom and vision of responsible commanders throughout the chain of command and the civilian leaders who set the political/military policies of grand strategy. Every person in the chain of command has his appropriate responsibility for respecting and enforcing the standards of just and limited war, but the heart of the matter of putting those standards into practice is the leadership and responsibility of key commanders, their civilian superiors, and, above all, the president.

After Vietnam, the Calley case, and the recriminations about the conduct of the Vietnam War, there was a disposition to lay the blame for the deficiencies of the U.S. war effort in Vietnam on the very nature of the military establishment. The truth is just the opposite.

That the Vietnam War, as well as the other U.S. wars here discussed, was as just and limited as it was is a tribute to the U.S. military establishment. That the Yom Kippur War was fought in consonance with just-war and limited-war standards is a reason for satisfaction on the part of Egyptian and Israeli commanders. Without the characteristics of the military establishment, namely, command responsibility and disciplined obedience throughout the chain of command, there is no controlled military instrument for enlightened civilian leaders to employ; there is no just and limited war.

The hope, then, for restraint in waging war and for a military instrument that makes the initiation of just and limited war a moral and politically responsible action remains with the military establishment of a nation and with its civilian national security organization under wise presidential leadership. Decision makers and advisers throughout these channels of control in the military instrument must be imbued with the standards of just and limited war. The modes for the implementation of these standards range from policy decisions and directives to rules of engagement to reiterations and interpretations of international law. Even when these standards are honored and vigorously applied throughout the system, the risks of catastrophic and immoral behavior, endemic in war, will remain. But the hope of those who would still defend a just cause with limited means is in the responsibility and discipline of the armed forces and their responsiveness to wise civilian leadership.

During the Vietnam War it was said that the U.S. armed forces and their problems were but a "mirror image of society." Although sometimes exaggerated, there is much truth in this theme. Ultimately, responsible commanders cannot exact disciplined responses from troops encouraged by society to defy authority and scorn the virtues that are necessary for a soldier. Moreover, if the people at home indulge in extremes, either of bellicism or appeasement, there are limits to the ability of the most enlightened civilian and military leaders to hold the armed forces firm on the course of just and limited war when war becomes necessary.

The doubts expressed in this book and in many others concerning the ability of a democracy to fight a just and limited war can only be resolved by the intelligence, courage, and moral stamina of a people confronting the uncertainties and dangers of modern war. In confronting those challenges, the people must recognize that their military establishment is not an alien or sinister force at odds with the political and moral values of the country but the representative and defender of those values. This, at least, has been the experience of the United States and it is from U.S. perspective that this book has been written.

The national security establishment and the people must unite in an understanding of their relationship of mutual trust and dependence. Both the key leaders and commanders in the national security system, as well as the people they represent, must understand the true relationships between politics, war, morality, and law, the understanding of which is essential to a commitment to the policies of just and limited war. When there exists such an understanding in the government, the armed forces, and the nation, there can be a commitment sufficient to withstand the frustrations of such wars. Ultimately, moral-legal prescriptions and political/military guidelines have to be interpreted and acted on by people. Moral men and women in government, in the armed forces, in the citizenry of the nation make possible a policy of just and limited war—and only just and limited war. Even in the nuclear age, man still has the option of defending himself, his society, and the rights of free people.

NOTES

NOTES TO CHAPTER 1

1. "Gaudium et Spes, the Pastoral Constitution on the Church in the Modern World," after surveying the characteristics of modern total war in the nuclear age, states that "all these considerations compel us to undertake an evaluation of war with an entirely new attitude." Walter M. Abbott, ed., "Gaudium et Spes, the Pastoral Constitution on the Church in the Modern World," in The Documents of Vatican II (New York: Guild/America/Association, 1966), p. 293.

Pope John XXIII took a similar position in Pacem in Terris, for example, in his insistence that "the fundamental principle on which our present peace depends must be replaced by another, which declares that the true and solid peace of nations consists not in equality of arms but in mutual trust alone." See Pope John XXIII, "Peace on Earth (Pacem in Terris)," Encyclical Letter (Washington, D.C.: National Catholic Welfare Conference, 1963), p. 27.

2. In his address to the UN General Assembly on October 4, 1965, Pope Paul VI observed that

> there is no need for a long talk to proclaim the main purpose of your Institution. It is enough to recall that the blood of millions, countless unheard-of-sufferings, useless massacres and frightening ruins have sanctioned the agreement that unites you with an oath that ought to change the future history of the world: never again war, never again war. It is peace, peace that has to guide the destiny of the nations of all mankind!

This well-remembered plea was followed by an exhortation to let "the arms fall from your hands." What is not always remembered was the following sad admission of the Pope:

> So long as man remains the weak, changeable and even wicked being that he so often shows himself to be, defensive arms will, alas, be necessary. But your courage and good qualities urge you on to a study of means that can guarantee the security of international life without any recourse to arms.

Pope Paul VI, "Address to the UN Assembly, October 4, 1965," in The Pope Speaks 11 (Washington, D.C.: TPS, 1966): 54-55.

It is the position of this book that man's perennial weakness and wickedness persist, that war persists as a fact of life, and that, pending the discovery of "means that can guarantee the security of international life without any recourse to arms," there is a need for just and limited war to meet the demands of the human condition as the Pope himself characterizes it.

The approach to just war taken in this book is supported by a recent analysis of contemporary Catholic official teaching on war. Bishop John J. O'Connor, In Defense of Life (Boston: St. Paul Editions, 1981).

3. For an authoritative and insightful discussion of the conflict in Clausewitz's thought between the concept of pure war with its own essence and logic and war as an instrument of politics, see H. Rothfels, "Clausewitz," in Makers of Modern Strategy, ed. Edward Mead Earle (Princeton, N.J.: Princeton University Press, 1943), pp. 93-113.

4. On the evolution of just-war doctrine, see Sydney D. Bailey, Prohibitions and Restraints in War (London: Oxford University Press, 1972); Roland H. Bainton, Christian Attitudes toward War and Peace (New York: Abingdon, 1960); James F. Childress, "Just-War Theories," Theological Studies 39 (1978): 427-44; idem, "Just-War Criteria," in War or Peace: The Search for New Answers, ed. Thomas A. Shannon (Maryknoll, N.Y.: Orbis, 1980); Yves de la Brière, Le droit de juste guerre (Paris: Pedone, 1933); James E. Dougherty and Robert L. Pfaltzgraff, Jr., Contending Theories of International Relations (Philadelphia: J. B. Lippincott, 1971), pp. 150-54, 167-71; John Eppstein, The Catholic Tradition of the Law of Nations (Washington, D.C.: Carnegie Endowment for International Peace/ Catholic Association for International Peace, 1935); Richard Shelly Hartigan, "Noncombatant Immunity: Reflections on Its Origins and Present Status," Review of Politics 29 (1966): 204-20; idem, "St. Augustine on War and Killing: The Problem of the Innocent," Journal of the History of Ideas 27 (1966): 195-204; J. Bryan Hehir, "The Just-War Ethic and Catholic Theology: Dynamics of Change and Continuity," in War or Peace: The Search for New Answers, ed. Thomas A. Shannon, pp. 15-39; James T. Johnson, Ideology, Reason and Limitation of War (Princeton, N.J.: Princeton University Press, 1975); idem, Just-War Tradition and the Restraint of War: A Moral and Historical Inquiry (Princeton, N.J.: Princeton University Press, forthcoming); idem, "Morality and Force in Statecraft: Paul Ramsey and the Just-War Tradition," in Love and Society: Essays in the Ethics of Paul Ramsey, ed. James T. Johnson and David Smith (Missoula, Mont.: American Academy of Religion/ Scholars Press, 1974), pp. 93-114; R. A. McCormick, New Catholic Encyclopedia, 1967, s.v. "War, Morality of"; Joseph C. Mc-

Kenna, "Ethics and War: A Catholic View," American Political
Science Review 54 (1960): 647-58; L. L. McReavy, Peace and War
in Catholic Doctrine (Oxford: Catholic Social Guild, 1963); Johannes Messner, Social Ethics, trans. J. J. Doherty, rev. ed. (St.
Louis: Herder, 1965), pp. 510-15, 665-69; John Courtney Murray,
Morality and Modern War (New York: Church Peace Union, 1959)—
also published as "Theology and Modern War," in Theological Studies
20 (1959): 40-61; in Morality and Modern Warfare, ed. William J.
Nagle (Baltimore: Helicon, 1960), pp. 69-91; in John Courtney Murray, We Hold These Truths (New York: Sheed & Ward, 1960), pp. 249-
73; and in The Moral Dilemmas of Nuclear Weapons, Essays from
Worldview, ed. William Clancy (New York: Council on Religion and
International Affairs, 1961), pp. 7-16—Nagle, ed., Morality and Modern Warfare; Ernest Nys, Le droit de la guerre et les précurseurs de
Grotius (Brussels: Librairie Européene, 1882); William O'Brien,
Nuclear War, Deterrence and Morality (Westminster, Md.: Newman,
1967); idem, War and/or Survival (Garden City, N.Y.: Doubleday,
1969); Ralph B. Potter, The Moral Logic of War (Philadelphia: United
Presbyterian Church, n.d.); idem, War and Moral Discourse (Rich-
mond, Va.: John Knox, 1969); Paul Ramsey, War and the Christian
Conscience: How Shall Modern War Be Conducted Justly? (Durham,
N.C.: Duke University Press, 1961); idem, The Just War: Force and
Political Responsibility (New York: Charles Scribner's Sons, 1968);
Robert Regout, La doctrine de la guerre juste de saint Augustin à nos
jours d'après les théologiens et les juristes canoniques (Paris: Pedone,
1935); Walter Stein, ed., Nuclear Weapons and Christian Conscience
(London: Merlin Press, 1961); Joan B. Tooke, The Just War in Aqui-
nas and Grotius (London: SPCK, 1965); Alfred Vanderpol, La doctrine
scolastique du droit de guerre (Paris: Pedone, 1919); LeRoy Walters,
"Five Classic Just-War Theories: A Study in the Thought of Thomas
Aquinas, Vitoria, Suarez, Gentili, and Grotius" (Ph.D. diss., Yale
University, 1971); and idem, "Historical Application of the Just War
Theory: Four Case Studies in Normative Ethics," in Love and So-
ciety: Essays in the Ethics of Paul Ramsey, ed. James T. Johnson
and David Smith (Missoula, Mont.: American Academy of Religion/
Scholars Press, 1974), pp. 115-38.

5. Protestant moralists have been in the forefront of contemporary just-war studies and debates. Clearly the leading figure has
been Paul Ramsey, whose principal works are War and the Christian
Conscience and The Just War. Johnson and Smith, Love and Society,
a festschrift volume honoring Ramsey, includes chapters on Ramsey's
contribution to "War and Political Ethics" by James T. Johnson, Le-
Roy Walters, David Little, and William O'Brien in pt. 2, pp. 91-184.

James T. Johnson's Ideology, Reason and Limitation of War
and Just War Tradition and Restraint of War are particularly useful

for their scholarly analyses of the evolution of just-war doctrine in concert with jus gentium to produce modern positive international law.

Other important contributions to just-war thought by contemporary Protestant scholars include John C. Bennett's chapter, "The Ethics of Force in the Nuclear Age," in his Foreign Policy in Christian Perspective (New York: Charles Scribner's Sons, 1966), pp. 102-26; Roger Shinn, Wars and Rumours of War (Nashville: Abingdon, 1972); Potter, The Moral Logic of War and War and Moral Discourse; Theodore Weber, Modern War and the Pursuit of Peace (New York: Council on Religion and International Affairs, 1968); Childress, "Just-War Criteria; and idem, "Just-War Theories."

6. The complementary relationship of the jus naturale and the jus gentium is admirably developed in Heinrich A. Rommen, The Natural Law, A Study in Legal and Social History and Philosophy, trans. R. Hanley (St. Louis: Herder, 1947).

7. No authority has so clearly brought out the jus gentium element in just-war doctrine, particularly in the jus in bello, as Johnson in Ideology, Reason and Limitation of War.

8. Incorporation of positive international law into contemporary just-war doctrine is notable; for example, in Eppstein's The Catholic Tradition, reflecting interwar developments in international law and organization. Recognition of the UN era is reflected in the social teaching on war and peace of Pope Pius XII and all his successors as well as in the Pastoral Constitution on the Church in the Modern World of Vatican II. See Father Murray's interpretation of just-war jus ad bellum in the teaching of Pope Pius XII in Murray, "Theology and Modern War," pp. 75-79. Tucker comments on this development in Robert E. Osgood and Robert W. Tucker, Force, Order and Justice (Baltimore: Johns Hopkins University Press, 1967), pp. 291-94.

9. See Ramsey, The Just War.

10. Murray, "Theology and Modern War," p. 82.

11. See E. H. Carr, International Relations between the Two World Wars (London: Macmillan, 1947); Hans A. Morgenthau, Politics among Nations (New York: Knopf, 1948); Kenneth W. Thompson, Political Realism and the Crisis of World Politics (Princeton, N.J.: Princeton University Press, 1960); Reinhold Niebuhr, Christianity and Power Politics (New York: Charles Scribner's Sons, 1940); and Ernest W. Lefever, Ethics and United States Foreign Policy (New York: Meridian, 1957).

12. A serious attempt is made to study the application both of just-war jus ad bellum and jus in bello doctrine in the periods of its development in LeRoy Walters's Ph.D. dissertation, "Five Classic Just War Theories," and in his chapter, "Historical Application of the Just-War Theory," pp. 115-38. There are interesting examples of application of just-war doctrine in Johnson's Ideology, Reason and

Limitation of War. Maurice H. Keen's The Laws of War in the Late Middle Ages (Toronto: University of Toronto Press, 1965) is a useful study of jus in bello practices.

There are no comprehensive just-war treatises on World Wars I and II, the Korean War, the Vietnam War, and the major Middle East wars. Review of bibliographies such as those found in Nagle, Morality and Modern Warfare, pp. 151-68; O'Brien, Nuclear War, Deterrence and Morality, pp. 111-20; and Potter, War and Moral Discourse, pp. 87-123, will demonstrate that applied discussions of just war since 1945 focus mainly on nuclear war and deterrence. Michael Walzer has developed his own just-war approach, which he applies selectively to problems of contemporary war and nuclear deterrence in Just and Unjust Wars (New York: Basic, 1977).

13. The most important works on limited war, reflecting the Korean experience and the problems of NATO defense, are cited in Chapter 9, n. 19.

14. A sample of the literature on revolutionary war and counterinsurgency is cited in Chapter 7, n. 3.

NOTES TO CHAPTER 2

1. This survey of the development of just-war doctrine owes much to the scholarship and clear analyses of James T. Johnson's Ideology, Reason and Limitation of War (Princeton, N.J.: Princeton University Press, 1975).

2. See the citation of Father Murray's article in Chapter 1, n. 4.

3. See Father Murray's discussion in "Theology and Modern War," in Morality and Modern Warfare, ed. William J. Nagle (Baltimore: Helicon, 1960), pp. 75-77.

4. John Bassett Moore begins his treatment of belligerent measures with a section entitled "Permissible Violence." This section consists of a definition and discussion of military necessity and elaboration of related questions of belligerent conduct, all quoted from Francis Lieber's "Instructions for the Government of the Armies of the United States in the Field," General Orders No. 100, April 24, 1863. See Green Haywood Hackworth, Digest of International Law, vol. 6 (Washington, D.C.: U.S. Government Printing Office, 1943), pp. 175-79.

Charles Cheney Hyde begins his treatment of belligerent measures and instrumentalities with a section entitled "Permissible Violence Generally, Military Necessity," based in part on Lieber's code and in part on the United States Army Field Manual on the Rules of Land Warfare of 1940. See Charles Cheney Hyde, International Law, Chiefly as Interpreted and Applied by the United States (Boston: Little, Brown, 1945-47), 3: 1801-02.

Note that the term <u>permissible violence</u> described relates only to the conduct of war, to the <u>jus in bello</u>. However, Myres S. Mc-Dougal and Florentino P. Feliciano employ the terms <u>permissible coercion</u> and <u>impermissible coercion</u> to characterize recourse to armed force, <u>jus ad bellum</u>, as well as retaining the usage with regard to means, <u>jus in bello</u>. See Myres S. McDougal and Florentino P. Feliciano, <u>Law and Minimum World Public Order</u> (New Haven, Conn.: Yale University Press, 1961).

In the present successor series to the Moore and Hackworth <u>Digests of International Law</u> the term <u>permissible violence</u> is not employed. See Marjorie M. Whiteman, <u>Digest of International Law</u>, vol. 10 (Washington, D.C.: U.S. Government Printing Office, 1968-73), wherein, under "Armed Conflict," there is a section, "Conduct of Hostilities," no. 9, "Basic Norms," pp. 298-317.

5. See n. 4 above.

6. There is a growing pacifist element in the Catholic church that includes bishops and clerical as well as lay organizations devoted to peace. Similar trends are no doubt to be found in the other Christian churches that have not been traditionally and/or doctrinally committed to pacifism. However, I discern no official Catholic retreat from the acceptance of defensive war as just war in papal statements or in the Pastoral Constitution on the Church in the Modern World of Vatican II. I develop this point in William V. O'Brien, <u>War and/or Survival</u> (Garden City, N.Y.: Doubleday, 1969), pp. 17-40. See the concise treatment of the older Christian traditions of just war and of pacifism and their contemporary manifestations in James E. Dougherty and Robert L. Pfaltzgraff, Jr., <u>Contending Theories of International Relations</u> (Philadelphia: J. B. Lippincott, 1971), pp. 150-59, 167-71.

7. See, for example, Majid Khadduri, <u>The Law of War and Peace in Islam</u> (Baltimore: Johns Hopkins University Press, 1955). The development of the positive law <u>jus ad bellum</u> is traced in Joachim von Elbe, "The Evolution of the Concept of the Just War in International Law," <u>American Journal of International Law</u> 33 (1939): 665-88; Josef L. Kunz, "Bellum Justum and Bellum Legale: Editorial Comment," <u>American Journal of International Law</u> 45 (1951): 528-34.

8. On the presumption against killing and the arguments to overcome this presumption, see St. Thomas Aquinas, <u>Summa theologica, secunda secundae</u> 40 (Art. 1), in Alfred Vanderpol, <u>La doctrine scolastique du droit de guerre</u> (Paris: Pedone, 1919), pp. 308-12; and Francisco de Vitoria, <u>De jure belli</u> in Vanderpol, <u>La doctrine scolastique</u>, pp. 326-29. Subsequent references to the works of Vitoria and Francisco Suarez will be given in the French translations of Vanderpol. See Francisco Suarez, <u>De bello</u>, section entitled "La guerre est-elle un mal en soi?" in Vanderpol, <u>La doctrine</u>

scolastique. For a synthetic summary of the Scholastic treatment of the presumption against war, see ibid., pp. 15-27.

The best contemporary treatment of this subject is that of James F. Childress, "Just-War Criteria," in War or Peace: The Search for New Answers, ed. Thomas A. Shannon (Maryknoll, N.Y.: Orbis, 1980), pp. 41-45; or idem, "Just-War Theories," Theological Studies 39 (1978): 428-35.

9. St. Thomas Aquinas, Summa theologica, secunda secundae, No. 15, Q. 40 (Art. 1) in A. P. D'Entrèves, ed., Aquinas, Selected Political Writings, trans. J. G. Dawson (Oxford, England: Blackwell, 1948), p. 159; see the French version in Vanderpol, La doctrine scolastique, pp. 309-10. See Vitoria, De jure belli, in Vanderpol, La doctrine scolastique, pp. 329-33; Suarez, De bello, in Vanderpol, La doctrine scolastique, pp. 367-72; Vanderpol's analysis of competent authority in La doctrine scolastique, pp. 76-84; and Childress, "Just-War Criteria," p. 46.

10. See Chapter 5, pp. 91-92.

11. For a skeptical Catholic view of revolution, see Johannes Messner, Social Ethics, trans. J. J. Doherty, rev. ed. (St. Louis: Herder, 1965), pp. 723-24. Rommen elaborates on the Thomistic concept of the popular right of resistance against tyrannical government but argues that the development of modern institutions limiting governmental power has reduced the occasions for invocations of this right. Unhappily, this proved to be an excessively optimistic view of twentieth century trends. He cites Leo XIII's strictures to the Irish in the 1880s to seek legal rather than violent means to redress their grievances, a point of view that was also to be overtaken by events in Ireland (continuing to the present conflict in Northern Ireland). See Heinrich A. Rommen, The State in Catholic Thought (St. Louis: Herder, 1945), pp. 473-76. See St. Thomas Aquinas, "The Right to Resist Tyrannical Government," Summa theologica, secunda secundae, Q. 42 (Art. 2), in D'Entrèves, Aquinas, p. 161.

In Populorum progressio, paragraph 30 of the encyclical, entitled "Temptation to Violence," Pope Paul VI observes that, when men are denied their rights, the necessities of life, and any share in the determination of their destinies, "recourse to violence as a means to right these wrongs to human dignity is a grave temptation." The Pope then continues in paragraph 31, "Revolution," with the following:

We know, however, that a revolutionary uprising—save where there is manifest, long-standing tyranny which would do great damage to fundamental personal rights and dangerous harm to the common good of the country—produces new injustices, throws more elements out of balance, and brings on new disasters. A great evil should not be fought against at the cost of great misery.

"On the Development of Peoples" (Washington, D.C.: United States Catholic Conference, March 26, 1967), pp. 22-23.
Pope Paul specifically warned against guerrilla warfare in his encyclical "Mense mai," in The Pope Speaks 10 (1965): 222.

12. St. Thomas Aquinas, Summa theologica, secunda secundae, Q. 40 (Art. 1) in D'Entrèves, Aquinas, p. 159. See the French version in Vanderpol, La doctrine scolastique, p. 310. On just cause, see Vitoria, De jure belli, in Vanderpol, La doctrine scolastique, pp. 333-35; Suarez, De bello in Vanderpol, La doctrine scolastique, pp. 377-96; Vanderpol's summary of Scholastic thought on just cause, La doctrine scolastique, pp. 59-71; Childress, "Just-War Criteria," p. 46; and idem, "Just-War Theories," p. 436.

13. Childress, "Just-War Criteria," p. 46.

14. Ibid.

15. A rare exception to the general tendency to avoid the "red-or-dead" issue in evaluating just cause is provided in the work of Father Murray whose writing on modern defense is based on his estimate of the nature of the communist threat to peace and justice. See, for example, Chapter 10, "Doctrine and Policy in Communist Imperialism," in John Courtney Murray, We Hold These Truths (New York: Sheed and Ward, 1960), pp. 221-47.

16. See Suarez, De bello, in Vanderpol, La doctrine scolastique, pp. 365-66 and Vanderpol's summary in La doctrine scolastique, pp. 29-32.

17. See Suarez, De bello, in Vanderpol, La doctrine scolastique, pp. 366-67 and Vanderpol's analysis in La doctrine scolastique, pp. 32-47. Father Murray interprets the teaching of Pope Pius XII as precluding traditional self-help by recourse to armed coercion in "Theology and Modern War," pp. 75-76.

18. On the abandonment of the claim to the right to wage wars of vindictive justice, see Father Murray's comments in "Theology and Modern War," p. 76.

19. Article 2(4) of the UN Charter provides that "all members shall refrain in their international relations from the threat or use of force against the territorial integrity or political independence of any state, or in any other manner inconsistent with the Purposes of the United Nations." This is generally intepreted as a relinquishment of the traditional sovereign compétence de guerre, prohibiting not only the initiation of war but of self-help measures of armed coercion termed measures short of war in traditional international law.
Article 42 of the charter provides for armed coercion if non-military means employed by the United Nations at the direction of the

Security Council have failed to restore peace. This is the basis for
UN "enforcement action" under Chapter 7 of the charter. Article
51, at the end of Chapter 7, reserves the right of individual and collective self-defense.

> Nothing in the present Charter shall impair the inherent
> right of individual or collective self-defense if an armed
> attack occurs against a Member of the United Nations,
> until the Security Council has taken measures to maintain
> international peace and security. Measures taken by Mem-
> bers in the exercise of this right of self-defense shall be
> immediately reported to the Security Council and shall not
> in any way affect the authority and responsibility of the Se-
> curity Council under the present Charter to take at any time
> such action as it deems necessary in order to maintain or
> restore international peace and security.

On contemporary international-law jus ad bellum, see D. W.
Bowett, Self-Defence in International Law (Manchester, England:
Manchester University Press, 1958); Ian Brownlie, International
Law and the Use of Force by States (Oxford, England: Clarendon
Press, 1963); McDougal and Feliciano, Law and Minimum World
Public Order, especially chaps. 3 and 4, pp. 121-383; Hans Kelsen,
Principles of International Law, ed. Robert W. Tucker, 2d rev. ed.
(New York: Holt, Rinehart and Winston, 1966), pp. 22-87; J. L.
Brierly, Law of Nations, ed. Sir Humphrey Waldock, 6th ed. (Oxford,
England: Oxford University Press, 1963), pp. 397-432; Louis Henkin,
How Nations Behave, 2d ed. (New York: Council on Foreign Rela-
tions/Columbia University Press, 1979), pp. 135-64, 250-312.

20. The issue of "humanitarian intervention" remains controversial. The term is often used to describe armed intervention to
protect a state's nationals and other aliens from clear and present
danger (for example, the 1964 intervention by Belgian paratroopers
delivered in U.S. aircraft in Stanleyville, Congo, to rescue Belgian
nationals and other endangered aliens). See Richard B. Lillich,
"Forcible Self-Help by States to Protect Human Rights," Iowa Law
Review 53 (1967): 325, 338-40. It is not uncommon to include aliens
of other states in an intervention to protect one's own nationals. The
issue, however, is more complicated in the case of intervention to
protect a people from its own government, a case for which I prefer
to reserve the term humanitarian intervention. See William V.
O'Brien, U.S. Military Intervention: Law and Morality, Washington
Papers, no. 68 (Beverly Hills, Calif.: Sage/Center for Strategic
and International Studies, Georgetown University, 1979), pp. 22-23,
30-36.

21. Some of the principal sources of the arguments in favor of humanitarian intervention to save a people from its own government are Lillich, "Forcible Self-Help," pp. 325-51; idem, "Intervention to Protect Human Rights," McGill Law Journal 15 (1969): 205-19; idem, "Humanitarian Intervention: A Reply to Ian Brownlie and a Plea for Constructive Alternatives," in Law and Civil War in the Modern World, ed. John Norton Moore (Baltimore: Johns Hopkins University Press, 1974), pp. 229-51; International Law Association, "The International Protection of Human Rights by General International Law," in Report of the 54th Conference, The Hague, 1970, pp. 633-41; and Myres S. McDougal and W. Michael Reisman, "Rhodesia and the United Nations: The Lawfulness of International Concern," American Journal of International Law 62 (1968): 1-19.

Professor McDougal has changed his view that recourse to armed coercion as self-help is limited to self-defense, as he held in McDougal and Feliciano, Law and Minimum World Public Order. He now holds that

> in the absence of collective machinery to protect against attack and deprivation, I would suggest that the principle of major purposes requires an interpretation [of Articles 2(4) and 51 of the UN Charter] which would honor self-help against prior unlawfulness. The principle of subsequent conduct certainly confirms this. Many states of the world have used force in situations short of the requirements of self-defense to protect national interests.

Myres S. McDougal, "Authority to Use Force on the High Seas," Naval War College Review 20 (1967): 29.

Arguments rejecting self-help in the form of humanitarian intervention are made in Ian Brownlie, "Humanitarian Intervention," in Law and Civil War in the Modern World, ed. John Norton Moore (Baltimore: Johns Hopkins University Press, 1974), pp. 218-27; Derek W. Bowett, "The Interrelation of Theories of Intervention and Self-Defense," in Law and Civil War in the Modern World, ed. John Norton Moore (Baltimore: Johns Hopkins University Press, 1974), pp. 38-50, particularly pp. 44-46; and Thomas M. Franck and Nigel S. Rodley, "After Bangladesh: The Law of Humanitarian Intervention by Military Force," American Journal of International Law 62 (1973): 275-305.

22. See Michael Walzer, Just and Unjust Wars (New York: Basic, 1977), pp. 101-8; Henry Kissinger, White House Years (Boston: Little, Brown, 1979), pp. 842-918; Franck and Rodley, "After Bangladesh," pp. 275-305.

23. For an excellent overall analysis of the relation between self-help and self-defense under the contemporary UN jus ad bellum,

see Tucker's treatment in Kelsen, International Law, pp. 84-87.
Claude notes that the revival of ideological just causes and just-war
thinking, particularly in UN resolutions endorsing wars of national
liberation in pursuit of self-determination, represents a reversal
of the contemporary trend in international law and organization to
subordinate claims of justice to the need to avoid disastrous international conflicts. See Inis L. Claude, "Just Wars: Doctrines and
Institutions," Political Science Quarterly 95 (1980): 95-96.

24. On the implications of the failure of collective security for
the UN jus ad bellum, see Julius Stone, Aggression and World Order
(Berkeley: University of California Press, 1958), particularly pp.
92-103; and idem, Legal Controls of International Conflict, 2d ed.
(New York: Rinehart, 1959), p. 246. Tucker considers this viewpoint in a comprehensive critique of the restrictive and permissive
interpretations of self-defense in Kelsen, International Law, pp.
64-87. He addresses the issue of reversion to the customary
right of self-defense in the absence of effective collective security.

25. This interpretation of the jus ad bellum would not be accepted
by those supporting the continued permissibility of self-help measures
of armed coercion beyond the right of self-defense, particularly with
respect to humanitarian intervention. See the authorities cited for
this position in n. 21 above.

26. On reprisals in the contemporary legal jus ad bellum, see
C. H. M. Waldock, "Use of Force in International Law," in Académie
de droit international de la Haye, recueil des cours 81 (1952): pt. 2,
455-61; Brownlie, International Law, pp. 219-24; Bowett, Self-Defence, pp. 13-14; L. Oppenheim, International Law, ed. H. Lauterpacht, 7th ed. (London: Longmans, Green, 1952), 2: 143-44;
Richard Falk, "The Beirut Raid and the International Law of Reprisal," American Journal of International Law 63 (1969): 415-43; Yehuda Blum, "The Beirut Raid and the International Double Standard:
A Reply to Professor Falk," American Journal of International Law
64 (1970): 73-105; William V. O'Brien, The Law of Limited International Conflict (Washington, D.C.: Georgetown University, 1965),
pp. 23-32, 35-38; and Nicholas Greenwood Onuf, Reprisals: Rituals,
Rules, Rationales, Center of International Studies, Woodrow Wilson
School of Public and International Affairs, Research Monograph no.
42 (Princeton, N.J.: Princeton University Press, 1974).

27. Waldock states, "Armed reprisals to obtain satisfaction
for an injury or any armed intervention as an instrument of national
policy otherwise than for self-defense is illegal under the Charter.
. . . Thus the only question is, what is the scope of the exception of
self-defense." In "Use of Force," p. 493. See Bowett, Self-Defence,
pp. 13-14, and his citations in notes 1-6 on p. 13 and note 1 on p. 14.

For arguments on the continued legitimacy of armed reprisals, see Stone, Aggression and World Order, pp. 92-103.

28. I deal with the Israeli case for anticipatory self-defense in the 1967 June War in William V. O'Brien, "International Law and the Outbreak of War in the Middle East, 1967," Orbis 11 (1967): 692-723. See Walzer, Just and Unjust Wars, pp. 80-85; and Kelsen, International Law, pp. 70-73.

29. The Scholastic emphasis in explaining just cause is on remedying a grave injustice (for example, by punishing the guilty party, by repressing the wrongful behavior, by forcing the guilty to make reparation). See the discussions of St. Thomas, Vitoria, and Suarez, as well as Vanderpol's summary analysis in the references in n. 12 above.

Not surprisingly, the most modern, Suarez, begins to reflect the rationale of defense of the state and its vital interests, while centering his discussion on grave violations of rights as the essence of just cause.

> Première Conclusion: Aucune guerre ne peut être juste si elle n'a pas une cause légitime et nécessaire . . . et cette cause juste et suffisante, c'est une grave violation du droit, accomplie, et ne pouvant être vengée ou réparée d'une autre manière. . . .
>
> 1. Une première raison, c'est que, si la guerre est permise pour la défense et la conservation des Etats, elle est d'autre part en opposition avec le bien du genre humanin, à raison des morts et des ruines qu'elle entraîne: si donc cette cause légitime cesse d'exister, la guerre cesse par là d'être juste. [Original emphasis]

Suarez, De bello, in Vanderpol, La doctrine scolastique, p. 378.

Vanderpol sums up the doctrine with "il faut une cause grave et proportionnée aux maux qui résultent de la guerre. Il serait tout à fair contraire à la raison de provoquer des désastres à l'occasion d'une légerè injure" (original emphasis), La doctrine scolastique, p. 62.

Vanderpol's formulation reflects the emphasis in the thought of Vitoria and Suarez, as well as other Scholastics to whom he refers, on the point that the cause must be sufficiently grave to warrant the evils of war. The caution is against pursuing an insufficiently grave cause and the evils of war seem to be generalized. There is no discussion of the situation where the cause is very grave, but the evils of a particular form of war or of a particular war would be too likely to cause more evil than the failure to fight for the just cause, a dilemma we often confront in the nuclear age. See William V. O'Brien, Nuclear War, Deterrence and Morality (Westminster, Md.: Newman, 1967), pp. 41-43.

30. Yves de la Brière emphasizes that the decision to engage in war must be in accord with prudence as well as justice. He rejects the notion that there should be certitude of success, this being impossible. But he insists on "une probabilité, si solide et si sérieuse qu'on la suppose, selon la loi des choses humaines dans la vie morale et sociale" (original emphasis) in Le droit de juste guerre (Paris: Pedone, 1933), p. 77. Father McKenna emphasizes that "a reasonable hope of success" does not mean "certitude" in "Ethics and War: A Catholic View," American Political Science Review 54 (1960): 651.

31. John Courtney Murray, "Theology and Modern War," in Morality and Modern Warfare, ed. William J. Nagle (Baltimore: Helicon, 1960), p. 80.

32. Ibid.

33. Robert E. Osgood and Robert W. Tucker, Force, Order and Justice (Baltimore: Johns Hopkins University Press, 1967), pp. 300-1. The argument is pursued relentlessly in Tucker's note 67 on pp. 301-2.

34. Murray, "Theology and Modern War," p. 80.

35. Father McKenna states that "a nation defending itself against attack, however, may more readily take its chances on fighting, as Finland did in 1939, than a nation on the offensive. In extreme cases the moral value of national martyrdom may compensate for the material destruction of unsuccessful war, as with Belgium in 1914." In "Ethics and War," p. 651.

36. I am indebted to my mentor, the late Professor Ernst H. Feilchenfeld, for the concept of the "clean center," an impartial and professional international civil service. See Ernst H. Feilchenfeld, The Next Step (Oxford, England: Basil Blackwell, 1938).

37. St. Thomas Aquinas, Summa theologica, secunda secundae, no. 15, Q. 40 (Art. 1), in D'Entrèves, Aquinas, pp. 159, 161. See Vanderpol, La doctrine scolastique, pp. 85-88. Vanderpol laments the fact that Vitoria and Suarez do not retain this condition as formulated by St. Thomas (for example, Suarez replaces right intention with "manière convenable de faire la guerre"). But he contends that the Thomistic concept of right intention informs the work of all of the principal Scholastic writers. Ibid., pp. 253-54. See de la Brière, Le droit de juste guerre, pp. 73-77; McKenna, "Ethics and War," p. 652; and Childress, "Just-War Criteria," pp. 48-49.

38. Vanderpol, La doctrine scolastique, p. 85.

39. Ibid., p. 88. See Childress's analysis of this aspect of right intention that rightly recalls the reflection of this concept in Francis Lieber's 1863 military code of conduct for the Union Army cited in n. 4 above. See "Just-War Criteria," pp. 48-49.

40. See Vanderpol, La doctrine scolastique, p. 88; McKenna, "Ethics and War," p. 652; and Childress, "Just-War Criteria," p. 48.

41. See the thoughtful analysis of the order, weight, and function of (just-war) criteria by Childress in "Just-War Criteria," pp. 50-54, wherein some of the alternative views on the function of the just-war conditions are discussed. Childress recalls Ramsey's position in War and the Christian Conscience, How Shall Modern War Be Conducted Justly (Durham, N.C.: Duke University Press, 1961), pp. 15, 28, 31-32, that justum bellum should be called "justified war" rather than "just war." The distinction is developed by Childress in n. 37 on pp. 57-58 of the same work. The term justified war would seem to correspond somewhat to the term permissible violence employed by U.S. international law authorities, cited in n. 4 above.

NOTES TO CHAPTER 3

1. Hague Convention IV Respecting the Laws and Customs of War on Land, October 18, 1907 (36 Stat. 2277, Treaty Series No. 539) [hereinafter cited 1907 Hague Convention IV].
2. Geneva Protocol Additional to the Geneva Conventions of 12 August 1949 and Relating to the Protection of Victims of International Armed Conflicts (Protocol I), December 12, 1977 (UN Doc. A/32/144 [1977]) [hereinafter cited as 1977 Geneva Protocol I].
3. Both in the just-war and modern international-law literature the treatment of proportionality in belligerent conduct tends to center on the jus ad bellum/raison d'état question of the political objectives of the war rather than on the discrete military objectives to which military means should be proportionate. An example of the latter usage is found in Article 51(5b) of the 1977 Geneva Protocol I, which includes among "types of attacks to be considered as indiscriminate" "an attack which may be expected to cause incidental loss of civilian life, injury to civilians, damage to civilian objects, or a combination thereof, which would be excessive in relation to the concrete and direct military advantage anticipated." On the tendency to relate proportionality to political objectives, see, for example, Suarez, De bello in Alfred Vanderpol, La doctrine scolastique du droit de guerre (Paris: Pedone, 1919), pp. 399-400; Yves de la Brière, Le droit de juste guerre (Paris: Pedone, 1933), pp. 98-100; and R. A. McCormick, New Catholic Encyclopedia, 1967, s.v. "War, Morality of."
See Tucker's critical analysis of the principle of proportion as a moral limitation on war in Robert E. Osgood and Robert W. Tucker, Force, Order and Justice (Baltimore: Johns Hopkins University Press, 1967), pp. 198, 202-3, 233-34, 237-40, 300-1, 314.
The most extensive analysis of the principle of proportion as a limit on the conduct of war in the international-law literature is Myres

McDougal and Florentino P. Feliciano, Law and Minimum World Public Order (New Haven, Conn.: Yale University Press, 1961), pp. 33-36, 524-30. I have discussed the subject in "The Meaning of 'Military Necessity' in International Law," World Polity 1 (1957): 142-49, and in "Legitimate Military Necessity in Nuclear War," World Polity 2 (1960): 49-52. Earlier analyses by international lawyers of the complex relation of the jus in bello principle of proportion to political ends may be found in Max Huber, "Die Kriegsrechtlichen Verträger und die Kriegsraison," Zeitschrift für Völkerrecht und Bundesstaatsrecht 7 (1913): 351-74 and Paul Weiden, "Necessity in International Law," Transactions of the Grotius Society 24 (1939): 113.

4. The position that all German belligerent acts were crimes per se because they served the illegal ends of aggression was advanced by one of the French prosecutors at Nuremberg, M. de Menthon. See Nuremberg International Military Tribunal, Trial of the Major War Criminals before the International Military Tribunal, Nuremberg, 14 November 1945-1 October 1946 (Nuremberg: 1947-49), 5: 387-88. This argument was implicitly rejected by the Judgment of the Tribunal, which does not mention it. See O'Brien, "The Meaning of 'Military Necessity,'" pp. 142-48.

A U.S. military tribunal explicitly rejected the de Menthon argument in United States v. List, Nuremberg Military Tribunals, Trials of War Criminals (Washington, D.C.: U.S. Government Printing Office, 1949-51), 11: 1247. See McDougal and Feliciano, Law and Minimum World Public Order, pp. 531-34.

5. Compare McDougal and Feliciano, Law and Minimum World Public Order, pp. 524-30, with my treatment in "The Meaning of 'Military Necessity,'" pp. 148-49; and in "Legitimate Military Necessity," pp. 53-57.

6. See McDougal and Feliciano, Law and Minimum World Public Order, pp. 523-30.

7. I am indebted to my teacher and friend the late Professor Ernst H. Feilchenfeld for the concept of the "reasonable commander." See the development of the doctrine of command responsibility in Chapter 13.

8. See U.S. v. List, pp. 1244-53.

9. See the reports of the several appeals of the Calley court-martial conviction and their rejection after review of the facts and law as collected in Joseph Goldstein, Burke Marshall, and Jack Schwartz, eds., The My Lai Massacre and Its Cover-up: Beyond the Reach of Law? (New York: Free Press, 1976), pp. 475-534.

10. Just-war expressions of the principle of discrimination may be found in the writings of the late Scholastics (for example, Vitoria, De jure belli, and Suarez, De bello) in Vanderpol, La doctrine sco-

lastique, pp. 346-49 and 405-9, respectively. Vanderpol limits his discussion of discrimination to quotations from Vitoria's treatment cited above. Ibid., pp. 151-52.

For some contemporary Catholic views on the principle of discrimination in modern just-war doctrine, see John C. Ford, "The Morality of Obliteration Bombing," Theological Studies 5 (1944): 261-309; idem, "The Hydrogen Bombing of Cities," in Morality and Modern Warfare, ed. William J. Nagle (Baltimore: Helicon, 1960), pp. 98-103; John R. Connery, "Morality of Nuclear Armament," in Morality and Modern Warfare, ed. William J. Nagle (Baltimore: Helicon, 1960), pp. 92-97; Joseph G. McKenna, "Ethics and War: A Catholic View," American Political Science Review 54 (1960): 656-58; McCormick, New Catholic Encyclopedia 14: 805; William V. O'Brien, Nuclear War, Deterrence and Morality (Westminster, Md.: Newman, 1967), pp 25-27, 30-31, 80-87; J. Bryan Hehir, "The Just-War Ethic and Catholic Theology, Dynamics of Change and Continuity," in War or Peace: The Search for New Answers, ed. Thomas A. Shannon (Maryknoll, N.Y.: Orbis, 1980), pp. 30-32; and Sydney D. Bailey, Prohibitions and Restraints in War (London: Oxford University Press, 1972), pp. 12-16.

The most comprehensive application of the principle of discrimination to contemporary moral dilemmas of war is found in the work of Paul Ramsey in War and the Christian Conscience and The Just War. See the critiques of Ramsey's treatment of discrimination in James T. Johnson, "Morality and Force in Statecraft, Paul Ramsey and the Just-War Tradition," in Love and Society: Essays in the Ethics of Paul Ramsey, ed. James T. Johnson and David Smith (Missoula, Mont.: American Academy of Religion/Scholars Press, 1974), pp. 102-5, 108-11; and William V. O'Brien, "Morality and War: The Contribution of Paul Ramsey," in Love and Society: Essays in the Ethics of Paul Ramsey, ed. James T. Johnson and David Smith (Missoula, Mont.: American Academy of Religion/Scholars Press, 1974), pp. 163-76, 180. See also James F. Childress's treatments of discrimination in "Just-War Criteria" in War or Peace: The Search for New Answers, ed. Thomas A. Shannon (Maryknoll, N.Y.: Orbis, 1980), pp. 49-50; and "Just-War Theories," Theological Studies 39 (1978): 440.

Tucker demonstrates the inadequacies of efforts to reconcile the moral principle of discrimination with the necessities of modern war and deterrence in Osgood and Tucker, Force, Order and Justice, pp. 290-322. Michael Walzer develops a concept of the "war convention" grounded in the distinction between combatants and noncombatants across a wide spectrum of contemporary wartime situations in Just and Unjust Wars (New York: Basic Books, 1977), pp. 136-37, 144-96, 269-83. Among the commentaries of international-law publicists, the following are representative: L. Oppenheim, International Law, ed. H. Lauterpacht, 7th ed. (London: Longmans, Green, 1952), 2: 349-50; Georg Schwarzenberger, The Legality of Nuclear Weapons

(London: Stevens, 1958), pp. 18-22; Julius Stone, Legal Controls of International Conflict (New York: Rinehart, 1959), pp. 548, 601-2, 625-31; McDougal and Feliciano, Law and Minimum World Public Order, pp. 76, 78-80, 573, 580-87; Hans Kelsen, Principles of International Law, ed. Robert W. Tucker, 2d ed. rev. (New York: Holt, Rinehart and Winston, 1966), pp. 112-24; Lester Nurick, "The Distinction between Combatants and Noncombatants in the Law of War," American Journal of International Law 39 (1945): 680-97.

11. See R. S. Hartigan, "Noncombatant Immunity: Reflections on Its Origins and Present Status," Review of Politics 29 (1966): 204-20; James T. Johnson, Ideology, Reason and Limitation of War (Princeton, N. J.: Princeton University Press, 1975), pp. 43-44, 69-73, 196-203; and Paul Ramsey, War and the Christian Conscience: How Shall Modern War Be Conducted Justly? (Durham, N. C.: Duke University Press, 1961), pp. 34-59.

12. On the historical and philosophical foundations of the positive law protecting noncombatant immunity, see William Edward Hall, A Treatise on International Law, ed. A. Pearce Higgens, 8th ed. (Oxford: Clarendon Press, 1924), pp. 84-91 (particularly p. 86); Oppenheim, International Law, 2: 204-7; and Paul Guggenheim, Traité de droit international public (Geneva: Librairie de l'Université, 1954), 2: 331-32. See particularly the incisive analysis of Geoffrey Best, Humanity in Warfare (New York: Columbia University Press, 1980), pp. 53-59, 63-67.

13. Among the works reflecting the absolutist view of the principle of discrimination, see Ford, "The Morality of Obliteration Bombing"; idem, "The Hydrogen Bombing of Cities"; Ramsey, War and the Christian Conscience; and idem, The Just War: Force and Political Responsibility (New York: Charles Scribner's Sons, 1968). Tucker claims that the just-war doctrine gave "the principle of noncombatant immunity an absolute and unconditional character," in Osgood and Tucker, Force, Order and Justice, p. 309 (generally pp. 306-22).

Father Hehir provides an insightful discussion of this issue, pointing out recent trends in Catholic theology regarding "direct" and "indirect" killing. He states that "the essence of the revisionist effort is to recast the moral calculus for decision making in conflict situations. The principle [sic] move is to devalue the role of direct v. indirect intentionality and to place at the center of the calculus the concept of proportionate reason." See "The Just-War Ethic," p. 31.

14. See, for example, the pacifist views in Walter Stein, ed., Nuclear Weapons and Christian Conscience (London: Merlin, 1961); and Shannon, War or Peace?

15. For an impressive array of efforts to come to grips with the issues of noncombatant immunity, double effect, collateral damage, and the question of proportionality of "unintended" collateral damage in

cases of attacks on military targets, see Ramsey, The Just War, pp. 153-64, 266-67, 285-366.

16. See Tucker's critique of Ramsey in Osgood and Tucker, Force, Order and Justice, pp. 310-19. In "Morality and War," pp. 163-90, I elaborate on my conclusion that Ramsey's absolute version of the principle of discrimination is not persuasive either as a normative position or as a practical guideline.

17. For examples of papal and conciliar pronouncements deploring or condemning modern warfare without explicit reference to the principle of discrimination, see, for example, Pope Pius XII, "Address to Delegates of the Eighth Congress of the World Medical Association, Rome, September 30, 1954," in Pattern for Peace: Catholic Statements on International Order, ed. Harry W. Flannery (Westminster, Md.: Newman, 1962), pp. 236-37; Pope John XXIII, "Peace on Earth (Pacem in Terris)," Arts. 111, 126-29, in Encyclical Letter (Washington, D.C.: National Catholic Welfare Conference), pp. 26-27, 29-30; Pope Paul VI, "Remarks before Recitation of the Angelus, August 8, 1965," in The Pope Speaks 10 (1965): 358, 406; Walter M. Abbott, "Gaudium et Spes, The Pastoral Constitution on the Church in the Modern World," in Documents of Vatican II, ed. by Walter M. Abbott (New York: Guild/America/Association, 1966), no. 80, p. 293. The papal statements are quoted and analyzed in O'Brien, Nuclear War, Deterrence and Morality, pp. 46-55; the Vatican II statement is quoted and analyzed in idem, War and/or Survival (Garden City, N.Y.: Doubleday, 1969), pp. 24-25.

18. See Osgood and Tucker, Force, Order and Justice, pp. 307-9, 313.

19. McCormick, "Morality of War," p. 805.

20. On the issue of indirect killing of innocents in war see Vitoria, De jure belli, and Suarez, De bello, in Vanderpol, La doctrine scolastique, pp. 347-48 and 407-9, respectively.

21. Walzer, Just and Unjust Wars, p. 155. Walzer's principal discussion of double effect is on pp. 151-59.

22. See Tucker's observations on intention in Osgood and Tucker, Force, Order and Justice, pp. 311-13.

23. The need to evaluate the proportion between the intended effects and the accidental effects of a means of war is acknowledged, for example, by Vitoria, De jure belli, and Suarez, De bello, in Vanderpol, La doctrine scolastique, pp. 347-48 and 405, respectively, and by McKenna, "Ethics and War," p. 657.

Tucker views the criterion of proportionality as inherently flawed by the open-ended propensities of the principle of necessity whereby men justify their behavior subject to little or no serious restraints (for example, Osgood and Tucker, Force, Order and Justice, pp. 233-38, 266-84, 289-90, 300-1, 319).

Ramsey manifests his view of the principle of proportion by according it a secondary place in his analyses of jus in bello, which turn almost wholly on the principle of discrimination. However, he, too, acknowledges the proportionality element in introducing a double-effect argument in the application of the principle of discrimination (for example, The Just War, pp. 154-55, 347-56, 430-31).

For the latest theological revisions of the concepts of direct and indirect intentionality and the principle of double effect, see Hehir, "The Just-War Ethic," pp. 31-32, citing Richard A. Mc-Cormick and Paul Ramsey, Doing Evil to Achieve Good (Chicago: Loyola University Press, 1978).

24. The low state of the principle of discrimination in international law after World War II is illustrated by Lauterpacht's following statement.

> (I)t is in (the) prohibition, which is a clear rule of law, of intentional terrorization—or destruction—of the civilian population as an avowed or obvious object of attack that lies the last vestige of the claim that war can be legally regulated at all. Without that irreducible principle of restraint there is no limit to the license and depravity of force. . . . It is clear that admission of a right to resort to the creation of terror among the civilian population as being a legitimate object per se would inevitably mean the actual and formal end of the law of warfare. For that reason, so long as the assumption is allowed to subsist that there is a law of the war, the prohibition of the weapon of terror not incidental to lawful operations must be regarded as an absolute rule of law.

H. Lauterpacht, "The Problem of the Revision of the Law of War," British Year Book of International Law 29 (1952): 360-69. McDougal and Feliciano comment in Law and Minimum World Public Order, pp. 79-80: "The essentially modest character of this 'absolute rule' needs no underlining." See the analysis of the collapse of the principle of discrimination before the assault of British/American bombing policies in Best, Humanity in Warfare, pp. 276-85. See, generally, Burrus M. Carnahan, "The Law of Air Bombardment in Its Historical Context," Air Force Law Review 17 (1975): 39-60.

25. See Chapter 7, pp. 360-63. For 1977 Geneva Protocol II see Protocol Additional to the Geneva Conventions of 12 August 1949 and Relating to the Protection of Victims of Non-international Armed Conflicts. (Protocol II), December 12, 1977 (UN Doc. A/32/144 [1977]), in International Legal Materials 16 (1977): 1442.

26. U.S., Department of the Air Force, International Law—The Conduct of Armed Conflict and Air Operations, 19 November 1976,

AFP 110-31 (Washington, D.C.: Department of the Air Force, 1976) [hereafter cited as AFP 110-31].

27. Ibid., 1-6 (pages in AFP 110-31 are designated by chapter and page, that is, 1-6 is chapter 1, p. 6).

28. Ibid., 5-1.

29. Ibid., 5-4-5.

30. Ibid., 5-5.

31. Ibid.

32. Ibid., 5-6.

33. Ibid., 5-7-12.

34. Ibid., 5-11.

35. Ibid.

36. Ibid., 5-12.

37. The Charter of the International Military Tribunal is annexed to the Agreement for the Establishment of an International Military Tribunal, U.S., Department of State, Trial of War Criminals 13, Department of State Publication no. 2420 (1945). The crimes defined by the charter are quoted in the Nuremberg International Military Tribunal, Trial of Major War Criminals, Judgment, 22: 414.

38. Raphael Lemkin, Axis Rule in Occupied Europe (Washington, D.C.: Carnegie Endowment for International Peace, 1944); idem, "Genocide as a Crime under International Law," American Journal of International Law 41 (1947): 145-51.

39. Nuremberg International Military Tribunal, Trial of Major War Criminals, Judgment, 22: 411-589.

40. Res. No. 260 (III) A, UN GAOR 3d sess. (I), Resolutions, p. 174; UN Doc. No. A/810; U.S., Department of State Bulletin No. 3416 (1946); American Journal of International Law Supplement (1951): 7-9.

41. The Netherlands Government, Documents Relating to the Program of the First Hague Peace Conference (1921), p. 25; American Journal of International Law Supplement (1907): 95-96.

42. On the interpretation of the concept of weapons causing superfluous suffering, see U.S., Department of the Army, The Law of Land Warfare, July 1956, FM 27-10 (Washington, D.C.: Department of the Army, 1956), no. 34, p. 18 [hereafter cited as FM 27-10]; and AFP 110-31, 6-2. See, generally, M. W. Royse, Aerial Bombardment (New York: Vinal, 1928).

The Vietnam debates raised questions as to whether use of napalm (see Chapter 5, n. 17), the M-16 rifle, and cluster bombs violated the prohibition against means causing superfluous suffering as well as the principle of discrimination in cases where napalm and cluster bombs were used in areas with a significant noncombatant population. The upshot of years of negotiations at Geneva on this subject is the 1980 Convention on Prohibitions or Restrictions on the Use of Certain Conventional Weapons, Which May Be Deemed To Be Excessively Injurious or To Have Indiscriminate Effects. U.S. negotiators prefer to refer to it as the 1980 Conventional Weapons Treaty. The convention was signed October 10, 1980. International Legal Materials 19 (1980): 1524-35.

The 1980 Geneva Conventional Weapons Treaty does not prohibit use of napalm, rifles such as the M-16, or cluster bombs against combatants. All of these means are increasingly recognized as weapons that are accepted in the practice of states. The 1980 Conventional Weapons Treaty lays down restrictions on the use of mines, booby-traps, and other devices, particularly as they present dangers to noncombatants (Protocol II) and restrictions on the use of incendiary weapons (Protocol III), where, again, the effort is made to limit or prohibit their use in populated areas where there is a perceived threat of collateral damage. Contrary to the thrust of the original initiatives at Geneva after the Vietnam War, none of these weapons is condemned as such.

43. See the Geneva Protocol for the Prohibition of the Use in War of Asphyxiating, Poisonous, or Other Gases, and of Bacteriological Methods of Warfare, 17 June 1925, 26 UST 571; T.I.A.S. 8061; 94 LNTS 65 (1975).

I summarize the development of the law on chemical warfare up to the Vietnam War in William V. O'Brien, "Biological/Chemical Warfare and the International Law of War," Georgetown Law Journal 51 (1962): 1-63. See generally Ann Van Wynen Thomas and A. J. Thomas, Jr., Legal Limits on the Use of Chemical and Biological Weapons (Dallas: Southern Methodist University Press, 1970).

44. On the no-first-use character of the Geneva Gas Protocol regime, see O'Brien, "Biological/Chemical Warfare," pp. 29-32 and Thomas and Thomas, Legal Limits, pp. 77-90.

On Soviet policy regarding use of chemical warfare, see John Erickson, "The Soviet Union's Growing Arsenal of Chemical Warfare," Strategic Review 7 (1979): 63-71; Amoretta M. Hoeber and Joseph D. Douglass, Jr., "The Neglected Threat of Chemical Warfare," International Security 3 (1978): 55-82; Charles H. Bay, "The Other Gas Crisis—Chemical Weapons," Parameters 9 (1979): pt. 1, 70-80; pt. 2, 65-78; Stockholm International Peace Research Institute, The Problem of Chemical and Biological Warfare (New York: Humanities Press, 1973), pp. 160-84.

45. The U.S. reservation to the 1925 Geneva Gas Protocol states "that the said Protocol shall cease to be binding on the Government of the United States with respect to the use in war of asphyxiating, poisonous or other gases, and of all analogous liquids, materials, or devices, in regard to any enemy State if such State or any of its allies fails to respect the prohibitions laid down in the Protocol." 26 UST 571; T.I.A.S. 8061; 94 LNTS 65 (1975). See AFP 110-31, 6-9.

46. See Gerald R. Ford, "Renunciation of Certain Uses in War of Chemical Herbicides and Riot Control Agents," Federal Register 40 (April 10, 1975). See AFP 110-31, 6-10.

47. 26 UST 571; TIAS 8062.

48. AFP 110-31, 6-4.

49. For GWS see 6 UST 3114; T.I.A.S. 3362; 75 UNTS 31 (1956). For GWS-SEA see 6 UST 3217; T.I.A.S. 3363; 75 UNTS 85 (1956). For GPW see 6 UST 3316; T.I.A.S. 3364; 75 UNTS 135 (1956). For GC see 6 UST 3516; T.I.A.S. 3365; 75 UNTS 287 (1956).

50. A definitive work on the law concerning prisoners of war is Howard S. Levie, Prisoners of War in Armed Conflict, International Law Studies, vol. 59 (Newport, R.I.: U.S. Naval War College, 1978). This volume is best used in conjunction with Levie's Documents on Prisoners of War, International Law Studies, vol. 60 (Newport, R.I.: U.S. Naval War College, 1979). See McDougal and Feliciano, Law and Minimum World Public Order, pp. 86-89, 542-55, 561, 574-77; FM 27-10, chap. 3, pp. 25-82; and AFP 110-31, 13-1-8.

51. On belligerent occupation, see Ernst H. Feilchenfeld, The International Economic Law of Belligerent Occupation (Washington, D.C.: Carnegie Endowment for International Peace, 1942); Gerhard von Glahn, The Occupation of Enemy Territory (Minneapolis: University of Minnesota Press, 1957); Stone, Legal Controls, pp. 723-32; McDougal and Feliciano, Law and Minimum World Public Order, pp. 732-832; FM 27-10, chaps. 5 and 6, pp. 98-164; and AFP 110-31, 14-1-7.

52. AFP 110-31, 1-5-6.

53. Ibid., 1-6.

54. The following authorities use such terms as permits, justifies, and authorizes with respect to the principle of military necessity as a positive source of "permissible violence": Francis Lieber in U.S., War Department, "Instructions for the Government of Armies of the United States in the Field, General Orders 100," Article 14. Reproduced in U.S. Naval War College, International Law Discussions, 1903 (Washington, D.C.: U.S. Government Printing Office, 1904), p. 118; John Bassett Moore, A Digest of International Law (Washington, D.C.: U.S. Government Printing Office, 1906), 7: 177; FM 27-10, p. 3; Robert W. Tucker, The Law of War and Neutrality at Sea, International Law Studies, vol. 50 (Newport, R.I.: U.S. Naval War College, 1955), p. 33; N. C. H. Dunbar, "Military Necessity in War Crimes Trials," British Year Book of International Law 29 (1952): 443-44; and McDougal and Feliciano, Law and Minimum World Public Order, pp. 72-76. For a view opposing the presumption that there is a positive principle of military necessity, see Lauterpacht, "The Problem of the Revision of the Law of War," pp. 361, 364. I summarize the literature in "Legitimate Military Necessity," pp. 38-48.

55. On the test of true utility in military necessity, see O'Brien, "The Meaning of 'Military Necessity,'" pp. 141-42; idem, "Legitimate Military Necessity," pp. 48-56; and McDougal and Feliciano, Law and Minimum World Public Order, pp. 35-36, 74-76.

56. See Chapter 9, pp. 225-28.

57. In relating the positive laws of war to military necessity, the United States has taken the position that these laws were drafted with relevant military necessities in mind and that, in accepting them in conventions, the states conceded, waived, or discounted any further claims to invoke rights of military necessity. FM 27-10, p. 4.

58. AFP 110-31, 1-6.

59. Ibid.

60. This is my definition of military necessity based on "The Meaning of 'Military Necessity,'" pp. 109-76, and then modified in "Legitimate Military Necessity," pp. 35-120, particularly in pp. 48-68.

61. U.S. v. Ohlendorf, Nuremberg Military Tribunals, Trials of War Criminals (Washington, D.C.: U.S. Government Printing Office, 1950), 4: 493.

62. AFP 110-31, 10-4-5. See generally Fritz Kalshoven, Belligerent Reprisals (Leiden, Netherlands: Sijthoff, 1971).

63. AFP 110-31, 10-5, emphasizes the risks and negative aspects of reprisals. See the description of the blockade and war-zone measures and countermeasures of the British and Germans and their allies in World War I in A. Pearce Higgins and C. John Colombos, The International Law of the Sea (London: Longmans, Green, 1945), pp. 535-53; Stone, Legal Controls, pp. 500-3, 508-10; Tucker, Law of War and Neutrality at Sea, pp. 184-90; and Best, Humanity in Warfare, pp. 244-58, 261-62.

On the claims and/or spurious rationales of reprisal as justification for countervalue bombing by both the British and the Germans in World War II, see Stone, Legal Controls, pp. 625-27; and Best, Humanity in Warfare, pp. 276-77.

64. FM 27-10, no. 497, p. 177.

65. AFP 110-31, 10-3.

66. There are specific conventional law prohibitions against reprisals designed to protect prisoners of war (1949 GPW, Art. 13); the wounded and sick, medical personnel, buildings and equipment (1949 GWS, Art. 46); the shipwrecked (GWS-SEA, Art. 47); and objects indispensable to the survival of the civilian population (1977 Geneva Protocol I, Art. 54[4]). The jus in bello for both international and noninternational conflicts also bans reprisals related to collective penalties, all measures of intimidation or terrorism directed at civilians, pillage, and the taking of hostages (1977 Geneva Protocol I, Art. 51[6]; 1977 Geneva Protocol II, Arts. 4, 13[2]). Finally, ci-

vilians under the enemy's control not previously protected from reprisals now are protected by Art. 51(6) of Protocol I.
    67. AFP 110-31, 10-5.

NOTES TO CHAPTER 4

    1. On the effects of the unconditional-surrender policy, see
J. F. C. Fuller, The Second World War (New York: Duell, Sloan &
Pearce, 1949), pp. 259, 265, 355, 364; B. H. Liddell Hart, The
Revolution in Warfare (New Haven, Conn.: Yale University Press,
1947), pp. 94-95; idem, Defense of the West (New York: William
Morrow, 1959), pp. 53-57; Hanson W. Baldwin, Great Mistakes of
the War (New York: Harper, 1949), pp. 15, 22; Anne Armstrong,
Unconditional Surrender: The Impact of the Casablanca Policy in
World War II (New Brunswick, N.J.: Rutgers University Press,
1961); and Kent Roberts Greenfield, American Strategy in World War
II: A Reconsideration (Baltimore: Johns Hopkins University Press,
1963), pp. 4, 9-10, 78.
    2. For the U.S. justification for the atomic bombing of Japan,
see Harry S. Truman, Memoirs (Garden City, N.Y.: Doubleday,
1955), 1: 415-23; and Henry L. Stimson and McGeorge Bundy, On Ac-
tive Service in Peace and War (New York: Harper, 1947), pp. 612-33.
    On the Hiroshima and Nagasaki decisions, see Michael Amrine,
The Great Decision (New York: Putnam's, 1959); Herbert Feis,
Japan Subdued, the Atomic Bomb and the End of the War in the Pacific
(Princeton, N.J.: Princeton University Press, 1961); Robert Batch-
helder, The Irreversible Decision (New York: Macmillan, 1965); Len
Giovannitti and Fred Freed, The Decision to Drop the Bomb (New
York: Coward-McCann, 1965); John Hersey, Hiroshima (New York:
Bantam, 1946); U.S., Strategic Bombing Survey, Summary Report
(Pacific War), July 1, 1946 (Washington, D.C.: U.S. Government
Printing Office, 1946); and idem, Japan's Struggle to End the War
(Washington, D.C.: U.S. Government Printing Office, 1946).
    3. On the rationales for U.S./British bombing policies in
World War II, see Sir Charles Webster and Noble Frankland, The
Strategic Air Offensive against Germany, 1939-1945 (London: Her
Majesty's Stationery Office, 1961), particularly 2: 12, and 4: 128-
29, 168, 323-24, 345; Max Hastings, Bomber Command (New York:
Dial, 1979), p. 170; Anthony Verrier, The Bomber Offensive (New
York: Macmillan, 1966), pp. 326-29; Greenfield, American Strategy,
pp. 88, 113, 115-16; David Irving, The Destruction of Dresden (New
York: Holt, Rinehart and Winston, 1963), pp. 33, 35-37, 91; Geoffrey
Best, Humanity in Warfare (New York: Columbia University Press,
1980), pp. 271-85; Wesley Frank Craven and James Lee Cate, eds.,

The Army Air Forces in World War II (Chicago: University of Chicago Press, 1948-58), 2: 274-307, 715-55.

4. See U.S., Strategic Bombing Survey, Overall Report (European War), September 30, 1945 (Washington, D.C.: U.S. Government Printing Office, 1945); idem, Summary Report (Pacific War); and Greenfield, American Strategy, pp. 120-21.

5. On the British attitude of bombing Germany, see the authorities cited in n. 3 above. The U.S. position favoring counterforce over countervalue bombing strategies is reflected, for example, in Ira C. Eaker's introduction to Irving, The Destruction of Dresden, pp. 5-8, and in Irving's account on p. 150. See U.S., Department of the Air Force, International Law—The Conduct of Armed Conflict and Air Operations, 19 November 1976, AFP 110-31 (Washington, D.C.: Department of the Air Force, 1976), p. 5-5 [hereafter cited as AFP 110-31]; and Greenfield, American Strategy, pp. 115-16.

6. For accounts of the multiphase, joint RAF/USAF raids on German metropolitan areas, see Irving, The Destruction of Dresden, pp. 94-95, 148-58; Webster and Frankland, Strategic Air Offensive, vol. 3; and Craven and Cate, Army Air Forces, vol. 3.

7. On fire-storm bombing, see Irving, The Destruction of Dresden, pp. 42-44, 46-47, 134-41.

8. See John C. Ford, "The Morality of Obliteration Bombing," Theological Studies 5 (1944): 261-309.

9. The UN War Crimes Commission stated that

> no record of trials in which allegations were made of the illegal conduct of aerial warfare had been brought to the notice of the United States War Crimes Commission, and since the indiscriminate bombing of allied cities by the German Air Force was not made the subject of a charge against any of the major German war criminals, the judgment of the Nuremberg International Military Tribunal did not contain any ruling as to the limits of legal air warfare.

Law Reports of Trials of War Criminals (London: His Majesty's Stationery Office, 1947-49), 15: 110; see AFP 110-31, 5-6.

10. See Chapter 3, n. 24.

11. See Truman, Memoirs, 1: 415-23; and Stimson and Bundy, On Active Service in Peace and War, pp. 612-33.

12. See the discussion of the concept of "superfluous suffering" in Chapter 3, p. 59.

13. See Georg Schwarzenberger, The Legality of Nuclear Weapons (London: Stevens, 1958), pp. 26-36, for a rare and generally unpersuasive effort to deal with nuclear weapons on the basis of the law governing poisonous and chemical means. I discuss this issue in

"Legitimate Military Necessity in Nuclear War," World Polity 2 (1960): 88-94.

14. On the U.S./UN goals in the Korean War, see Truman, Memoirs, 2: 333-34. See Tucker's critique of the change in the U.S./UN war aims in Korea in Robert W. Tucker, The Just War (Baltimore: Johns Hopkins University Press, 1960), pp. 60-63. See generally David Rees, Korea: The Limited War (New York: St. Martin's Press, 1964), pp. 28-31 and Glenn D. Paige, The Korean Decision (New York: Free Press, 1968).

NOTES TO CHAPTER 5

1. Guenter Lewy, America in Vietnam (New York: Oxford University Press, 1978).
2. For a cross section of opinion on the constitutional aspects of the Vietnam War, see Richard A. Falk, ed., The Vietnam War and International Law, 4 vols. (Princeton, N.J.: Princeton University Press, 1969-76), 2: 379-84, and 3: 163-489. See Anthony A. D'Amato and Robert M. O'Neill, The Judiciary and Vietnam (New York: St. Martin's Press, 1972).

Under the War Powers Resolution of 1973 the president must do the following:

1. Consult with Congress before introducing U.S. armed forces into "hostilities or into situations where imminent involvement in hostilities is clearly indicated by the circumstances."
2. Report within 48 hours to Congress, in cases where U.S. forces are introduced into hostilities or situations where combat is imminent, in the absence of a declaration of war, regarding the circumstances, constitutional authority, and "estimated scope and duration of the hostilities or involvement."
3. Terminate any commitment of U.S. forces to combat or imminent combat situations, where there is no declaration of war, within 60 days, unless Congress either extends the 60-day period or grants a formal request from the president for an additional, final, 30 days, based on "unavoidable military necessity respecting the safety of United States Armed forces," Pub. I, No. 93-148, 87 Stat. 555 (1973).

The system of congressional control established by the 1973 resolution gives the Congress a negative veto over the president's power to use the military instrument (for example, by failing to extend periods of legal U.S. commitment of forces the Congress could ipso facto force termination of the U.S. commitment. It is probable that this resolution will be declared unconstitutional if invoked and taken to the courts. It denies the president powers as commander in chief and sole agent for the conduct of foreign policy, developed over 200 years, such as the right to protect U.S. nationals abroad. Its ambiguities and complications were in part revealed during the Carter administration's abortive effort to rescue the U.S. hostages in Iran in April 1980, at which time no one seriously invoked the resolution despite Carter's failure to consult the Congress in advance.

See President Nixon's veto message of October 24, 1973, "War Powers Veto Text," Congressional Quarterly 31 (October 27, 1973): 2855-56; Statutory Comments, "The War Powers Resolution: Statutory Limitation on the Commander-in-Chief," Harvard Journal on Legislation 11 (1974): 181-204.

3. For the U.S. position on the legal permissibility of the Vietnam War, see U.S., Department of State, Legality of United States Participation in the Defense of Viet-Nam, Memorandum of Legal Adviser of Department of State, March 4, 1966, Department of State Bulletin 54 (1966): 474-89. Reprinted in American Journal of International Law 60 (1966): 565-85.

For a cross section of opinion on the legality of the U.S. intervention in Vietnam under international law, see Falk, The Vietnam War and International Law, 1: 163-522; 2: 89-270; and 3: 23-147. See also Louis Henkin, How Nations Behave (New York: Council on Foreign Relations/Columbia University Press, 1979), pp. 303-12.

4. The origin of the domino theory per se is in President Eisenhower's statement at an April 7, 1954, press conference. See U.S., President, Public Papers of the Presidents of the United States: Dwight D. Eisenhower, 1954 (Washington, D.C.: Government Printing Office, 1960), p. 383. On the long-term validity of the issues raised by the domino theory, see Lewy, America in Vietnam, pp. 426-29. Osgood comments on the abstractness of the argument that failure to resist communist aggression in Vietnam would weaken the defenses of other Southeast Asian countries and other regions of the world. Robert E. Osgood, Limited War Revisited (Boulder, Colo.: Westview, 1979), p. 34.

Leslie H. Gelb and Richard K. Betts, The Irony of Vietnam: The System Worked (Washington, D.C.: Brookings Institution, 1979), trace the origins of the domino theory in the Truman administration (p. 49), its statement by Eisenhower (p. 59), its continuing influence on the Kennedy administration (p. 79), and its role in the Johnson administration policies (p. 106) despite challenges from the Central Intelligence Agency in 1964 (p. 229). See also their summary treatment of the subject (pp. 197-200, 366).

5. As Lewy, America in Vietnam, p. 427, points out, the extensive defense of South Vietnam by the United States probably

bought time for other countries in Southeast Asia "to improve their own political and social institutions and thus left them in a stronger position to resist external and internal communist pressures."

6. Washington's faulty estimate of the situation in Vietnam and the time and assets necessary to deal with it are discussed in Osgood, Limited War Revisited, pp. 35-36; Lewy, America in Vietnam, pp. 432-33; and Gelb and Betts, The Irony of Vietnam, generally and especially pp. 125-28 and 302-10.

7. Kissinger emphasizes repeatedly the unacceptability to the United States of various communist proposals for coalition governments in South Vietnam that would have had the effect of overthrowing the Thieu regime and opening the way to the familiar fate of coalition governments, including strong communist elements eager to seize power. See, for example, Henry Kissinger, White House Years (Boston: Little, Brown, 1979), pp. 259, 269-71, 976-79, 982, 1019, 1028-32, 1044, 1172, 1318-19, 1332, 1336-37, 1342, 1344-45, and 1353.

Kissinger's account demonstrates that domestic U.S. opposition to the war so removed and limited U.S. military options that the Nixon administration had no alternative to terminating U.S. involvement in the least time and under the best terms possible. The terms of the 1973 Paris Peace Agreement seemed to be better than could have been expected. But the implied sanction of U.S. enforcement of the agreement fell victim to Nixon's decline and fall because of Watergate.

8. On U.S. peace efforts in the Vietnam War, see Lyndon Baines Johnson, The Vantage Point (New York: Holt, Rinehart & Winston, 1971), pp. 233-41, 249-57, 266-69, and 493-531; Allan E. Goodman, The Lost Peace (Stanford, Calif.: Hoover Institution Press, 1978); Chester Cooper, The Lost Crusade (New York: Dodd, Meade, 1970), pp. 284-468; and Gelb and Betts, The Irony of Vietnam, pp. 162-67.

9. On U.S. and ARVN overuse of firepower, see Lewy, America in Vietnam, pp. 58-60, 95-105, 181, 230-33, 269, 446-48; and Osgood, Limited War Revisited, pp. 41-42.

10. On communist tactics drawing fire on civilians, see Lewy, America in Vietnam, pp. 52-55, 58-60, 232.

11. Free-fire and specified strike zones are discussed by Lewy, ibid., pp. 79, 105-7, 150, 226, 229-30, 326. See W. R. Peers, The My Lai Inquiry (New York: Norton, 1979), p. 29; General Peers's report in Joseph Goldstein, Burke Marshall, and Jack Schwartz, eds., The My Lai Massacre and Its Cover-up: Beyond the Reach of Law (New York: Free Press, 1976), p. 212; and Robert E. Jordan III, "Counterinsurgency, Tactics and Law, 2," in Law and Responsibility in Warfare, The Vietnam Experience, ed. Peter D. Trooboff (Chapel Hill: University of North Carolina Press, 1975), pp. 60-61.

12. On the institution of body counts in Vietnam, see Lewy, America in Vietnam, pp. 63, 78-82, 137, 143, 241, 315, 328, 450, and 452; Douglas Kinnard, The War Managers (Hanover, N.H.: University Press of New England, 1977), pp. 72-75; Peers, Mylai Inquiry, p. 30; and Robert W. Tucker, "Weapons of Warfare, 13" in Law and Responsibility in Warfare: The Vietnam Experience, ed. Peter D. Trooboff (Chapel Hill: University of North Carolina Press, 1975), p. 171.

13. See Lewy, America in Vietnam, pp. 233-37, on MACV directives acknowledging and seeking to remedy practices involving disproportionate and indiscriminate use of firepower. See also Peers, Mylai Inquiry, p. 29, and General Peers's report in Goldstein, Marshall, and Schwartz, The My Lai Massacre, pp. 211-13.

14. On the bad effects of the body-count mentality when carried to extremes, see Lewy, America in Vietnam, p. 452 and Kinnard, The War Managers, pp. 72-75.

15. For critiques of the search-and-destroy strategy and tactics in Vietnam, see Lewy, America in Vietnam, pp. 50-63, 86, 119; Kinnard, The War Managers, pp. 39-46; Henry Kissinger, "The Vietnam Negotiations," Foreign Affairs 47 (1969): 212; Sir Robert Thompson, No Exit from Vietnam (New York: David McKay, 1970), p. 135; Alain C. Enthoven and Wayne K. Smith, How Much Is Enough? The Defense Program 1961-1969 (New York: Harper & Row, 1971), pp. 295-300; and Peers, Mylai Inquiry, pp. 29-30.

16. On alternative strategies in Vietnam emphasizing effective civil affairs programs supported by combat security operations, see Lewy, America in Vietnam, pp. 85-90, 116-19, 123-26, 134-39, 190-95, 437-41; Kinnard, The War Managers, pp. 99-108; William Colby and Peter Forbath, Honorable Men (New York: Simon & Schuster, 1978), pp. 248-88.

O'Connor emphasizes the context in which U.S.-South Vietnamese combat and civil affairs operations were conducted, namely, one of systematic terrorism and coercion carried out by the Communist forces. Positive policies of nation building are extremely difficult to pursue successfully in such a context of fear and intimidation. See John J. O'Connor, A Chaplain Looks at Vietnam (Cleveland: World, 1968), pp. 199-214.

17. On the use of napalm in Vietnam, see Lewy, America in Vietnam, pp. 58-59, 70, 246-48, 306; Howard S. Levie, "Weapons of Warfare, 12," in Law and Responsibility in Warfare: The Vietnam Experience, ed. Peter D. Trooboff (Chapel Hill: University of North Carolina Press, 1975), pp. 156-58; Tucker, "Weapons of Warfare, 13," pp. 164-65; George H. Aldrich, "Comments," in Law and Responsibility in Warfare: The Vietnam Experience, ed. Peter D. Trooboff (Chapel Hill: University of North Carolina Press, 1975),

p. 174; William V. O'Brien, War and/or Survival (Garden City, N.Y.: Doubleday, 1969), pp. 238-42.

18. On the legal status of CW, see generally, Ann Van Wynen Thomas and A. J. Thomas, Jr., Legal Limits on the Use of Chemical and Biological Weapons (Dallas: Southern Methodist University Press, 1970); William V. O'Brien, "Biological/Chemical Warfare and the International Law of War," Georgetown Law Journal 51 (1962): 1-63; and Wil D. Verwey, Riot Control Agents and Herbicides in War (Leiden, Netherlands: A. W. Sijthoff, 1977), pp. 207-304.

19. The use in Vietnam of nonlethal gas, often domestically used for riot control, is discussed in Lewy, America in Vietnam, pp. 248-57; Thomas and Thomas, Legal Limits, pp. 148-50; Levie, "Weapons of Warfare, 12," pp. 153-56; Tucker, "Weapons of Warfare, 13," pp. 165-68; Aldrich, "Comments," pp. 174-75; and Verwey, Riot Control Agents, pp. 3-11 and 50-65, in a detailed and critical assessment.

20. Claims of lethal effects of U.S. chemical means in Vietnam are made in Anthony A. D'Amato, Harvel L. Gould, and Larry D. Woods, "War Crimes and Vietnam: The 'Nuremberg Defense' and the Military Service Resister," California Law Review 57 (1969): 1093-95.

After a thorough survey of the issue, Lewy, America in Vietnam, pp. 252-53, concludes that there is little evidence of fatalities from U.S. use of nonlethal gas in Vietnam. For a contrast, see Verwey, Riot Control Agents, pp. 41-43, 66.

21. For the U.S. position on nonlethal gas, see President Gerald R. Ford's "Renunciation of Certain Uses in War of Chemical Herbicides and Riot Control Agents," Federal Register 40 (April 10, 1975), and an interpretation in U.S., Department of the Air Force, International Law—The Conduct of Armed Conflict and Air Operations, 19 November 1976, AFP 110-31 (Washington, D.C.: Department of the Air Force, 1976), p. 6-5 [hereafter cited as AFP 110-31]. Meyrowitz concludes that it is impossible to state with certainty whether the U.S. incapacitating agents or irritants were illegal "in the current state of positive law." Henri Meyrowitz, "The Law of War in the Vietnamese Conflict," in The Vietnam War in International Law, ed. Richard A. Falk, 4 vols. (Princeton, N.J.: Princeton University Press, 1969-76), 2: 557.

22. On U.S. use of herbicides in Vietnam, see Lewy, America in Vietnam, pp. 257-66; Meyrowitz, "The Law of War," pp. 558-59; Verwey, Riot Control Agents, pp. 73-154.

23. On the legality of the U.S. use of herbicides in Vietnam, see generally Lewy, America in Vietnam, pp. 261-62, 265-66; Thomas and Thomas, Legal Limits, pp. 150-51, 169; Levie, "Weapons of Warfare, 12," pp. 158-60; Tucker, "Weapons of Warfare, 13," pp. 168-69; Meyrowitz, "The Law of War," pp. 558-59; and Bernard Brungs, "The Status of Biological Warfare in International Law," Military Law Review 24 (1964): 47-95.

For a view critical of U.S. use of herbicides, see Richard A. Falk, "Methods and Means of Warfare 1," in Law and Responsibility in Warfare: The Vietnam Experience, ed. Peter D. Trooboff (Chapel Hill: University of North Carolina Press, 1975), pp. 45-47. On the charge of ecocide, see L. C. Johnstone, "Ecocide and the Geneva Protocol," Foreign Affairs 49 (1970-71): 711. See also Verwey's critical view of U.S. policies, Riot Control Agents, pp. 75-203. Other critical evaluations are Arthur H. Westing, "Proscription of Ecocide: Arms Control and the Environment," in The Vietnam War and International Law, ed. Richard A. Falk, 4 vols. (Princeton, N.J.: Princeton University Press, 1969-76), 4: 283-86; and Richard A. Falk, "Environmental Warfare and Ecocide," in The Vietnam War and International Law, ed. Richard A. Falk, 4 vols. (Princeton, N.J.: Princeton University Press, 1969-76), 4: 287-303.

24. On prohibitions against ecological destruction in Classical antiquity, see Coleman Phillipson, The International Law and Custom of Ancient Greece and Rome (London: Macmillan, 1911), 2: 209.

25. AFP 110-31, 6-5. See also Chapter 3.

26. The U.S. and South Vietnamese acknowledgment of the applicability of the 1949 PW Geneva Conventions to the Vietnam War and their practice regarding PWs are discussed in Howard S. Levie, Prisoners of War in Armed Conflict, International Law Studies, vol. 59 (Newport, R.I.: U.S. Naval War College, 1978), pp. 30, 57, 74, 100; David P. Forsythe, Humanitarian Politics: The International Committee of the Red Cross (Baltimore: Johns Hopkins University Press, 1977), pp. 152-56, 158-62; and Howard S. Levie, "Maltreatment of Prisoners of War in Vietnam," in The Vietnam War and International Law, ed. Richard A. Falk, 4 vols. (Princeton, N.J.: Princeton University Press, 1969-76), 2: 361-63, 375-80.

On communist positions and practice regarding PWs in Vietnam, see Levie, Prisoners of War, pp. 16-17, 30, 37-38, 137, 145, 148-49, 153, 157, 172, 350, 366, 382, 398, 408, 410, 417; idem, "Maltreatment," pp. 361-66, 380-96; Forsythe, Humanitarian Politics, pp. 156-58, 163-64; and Lewy, America in Vietnam, pp. 332-42.

27. See Forsythe, Humanitarian Politics, pp. 158-62, on the different and ill-defined categories of detainees ranging from PWs to political prisoners to regular prisoners held by South Vietnam during the war. On the Chieu Hoi program, whereby detained Vietcong PWs and suspects "rallied" to the government of South Vietnam, see Lewy, America in Vietnam, pp. 91-92, 173; and Levie, Prisoners of War, p. 80.

28. Charges of torture and mistreatment of Communist PWs by U.S. and, more often, ARVN forces are discussed in Levie, "Maltreatment," 2: 376, 378-80; Lawrence C. Petrowski, "Law and the Conduct of the Vietnam War," in The Vietnam War and International

Law, ed. Richard A. Falk (Princeton, N.J.: Princeton University Press, 1969-76), 2: 512-13; Meyrowitz, "The Law of War," p. 561; Lewy, America in Vietnam, pp. 287-88, 328-29; and Levie, Prisoners of War, pp. 28, 100, 318.

29. See Lewy's assessment of torture and other atrocities committed by U.S. troops in the light of the Peers Inquiry Report and other U.S. official investigations and court-martial records in America in Vietnam, pp. 329-31.

30. On charges of mistreatment of civilians by U.S. and ARVN troops, see Meyrowitz, "The Law of War," 2: 568-70. Lewy, America in Vietnam, pp. 317-21, shows the difficulties in verifying and assessing these charges.

31. Lewy, America in Vietnam, pp. 324-31, provides an authoritative summary of the U.S. court-martial record with respect to charges of atrocities committed against civilians in Vietnam.

32. Charges of illegal and inhumane behavior in the forcible transfer of the South Vietnamese population by the South Vietnamese authorities, ARVN, and the U.S. forces are made in Meyrowitz, "The Law of War," pp. 568-71. Lewy discusses the causes of population displacement and policies of forced relocation in America in Vietnam, pp. 25, 65, 107-14, 152, 226-30. See Cooper, The Lost Crusade, pp. 157-58; and Douglas Pike, War, Peace and the Viet Cong (Cambridge, Mass.: MIT Press, 1969), pp. 99-102.

33. The legal aspects of forced relocation are discussed in Meyrowitz, "The Law of War," pp. 568-71; Lewy, America in Vietnam, pp. 227-30; and O'Brien, "The Law of War, Command Responsibility and Vietnam," pp. 56-58.

34. The inadequacies of South Vietnamese relocation/refugee camps and the consequent shifts in combat strategies and tactics, as well as of relocation policies, necessitated by these inadequacies, are discussed in Lewy, America in Vietnam, pp. 65, 70, 108, 110-12, 118, 140, 151-52, 228-30.

35. On the treatment of civilian detainees by the South Vietnamese government and the critical attitude toward South Vietnamese policies of the ICRC, see Forsythe, Humanitarian Politics, pp. 158-62. For an evaluation of the South Vietnamese record with regard to civilian detainees, on which my account relies, see Lewy, America in Vietnam, pp. 285-99.

36. On the mixed political-military goals of the bombing of North Vietnam, see Neil Sheehan, Hedrick Smith, E. W. Kenworthy, and Fox Butterfield, eds., The Pentagon Papers, as Published by the New York Times (New York: Bantam, 1971), pp. 543-48, 552-53, 573-85; Johnson, The Vantage Point, pp. 120-21, 124-37, 233-41, 245, 366-69, 372-80, 387; Cooper, The Lost Crusade, pp. 258-62; Enthoven and Smith, How Much is Enough?, pp. 303-6; Kissinger,

White House Years, pp. 1109-23; Hamilton de Saussure and Robert Glasser, "Methods and Means of Warfare 9," in Law and Responsibility in Warfare: The Vietnam Experience, ed. Peter D. Trooboff (Chapel Hill: University of North Carolina Press, 1975), pp. 120-23; Lewy, America in Vietnam, pp. 31-47, 197, 374-417; and Gelb and Betts, The Irony of Vietnam, pp. 249-50.

37. The military results of the bombing of North Vietnam are discussed in Sheehan et al., The Pentagon Papers, pp. 502-9, 543, 550-53, 569-73; Johnson, The Vantage Point, pp. 240-41; Lewy, America in Vietnam, pp. 389-96; Enthoven and Smith, How Much Is Enough?, pp. 303-6; and Gelb and Betts, The Irony of Vietnam, pp. 140, 147-49, 167-70.

Lewy discusses the general immunity of points of entry for resupply of North Vietnam in America in Vietnam, pp. 392-94.

For a critical account of the bombing of North Vietnam, see Raphael Littauer and Norman Uphoff, eds., The Air War in Indochina (Boston: Beacon, 1972), generally and with conclusions, pp. 182-93. Another critical analysis centers on the flaws in the Washington decision-making process. See James Clay Thompson, Rolling Thunder: Understanding Policy and Program Failure (Chapel Hill: University of North Carolina Press, 1980), pp. 35-72 (Chapter 3, "Rolling Thunder Fails").

38. On the effects of bombing on nonmilitary and/or protected targets and on noncombatants, see the critical views of Forsythe, Humanitarian Politics, pp. 162-63 and Littauer and Uphoff, The Air War in Indochina, pp. 45-49.

For an evaluation supporting my analysis, see Lewy, America in Vietnam, pp. 396-406, 412-17.

39. On the "secret" bombing of Laos, see Kissinger, White House Years, pp. 448-57, 998.

40. Lewy discusses the Lavelle Affair in America in Vietnam, pp. 407-10.

NOTES TO CHAPTER 6

1. On nuclear deterrence, see generally Raymond Aron, The Great Debate: Theories of Nuclear Strategy, trans. Ernst Pawel (Garden City, N.Y.: Doubleday, 1965); Philip Green, Deadly Logic: The Theory of Nuclear Deterrence (Columbus: Ohio State University Press, 1966); Herman Kahn, On Thermonuclear War (Princeton, N.J.: Princeton University Press, 1960); idem, Thinking about the Unthinkable (New York: Horizon Press, 1962); Roger Speed, Strategic Deterrence in the 1980s (Stanford, Calif.: Hoover Institution, 1979): Paul Nitze, "The Relationship of Strategic and Theater Nuclear

Forces," International Security 2 (1977): 122-32; Patrick M. Morgan, Deterrence: A Conceptual Analysis (Beverly Hills, Calif.: Sage, 1977); and Donald M. Snow, "Current Nuclear Deterrence Thinking: An Overview and Review," International Studies Quarterly 23 (1979): 445-86.

2. Discussions of the nuclear decision process are rare, speculative, and pessimistic about how existing arrangements will work among the Western democracies. See Jeffrey Record and Thomas I. Anderson, U.S. Nuclear Weapons in Europe: Issues and Alternatives (Washington, D.C.: Brookings Institution, 1974), p. 30; Alton Frye, "Nuclear Weapons in Europe: No Exit from Ambivalence," Survival 22 (1980): 98-106; Fred Charles Iklé, "NATO's 'First Nuclear Use': A Deepening Trap?" Strategic Review 8 (1980): 18-23; Paul Bracken, "Collateral Damage and Theatre Warfare," Survival 22 (1980): 203-7; and Colin Gray, "NATO Strategy and the 'Neutron Bomb,'" Policy Review 7 (1979): 7-11.

A particularly helpful discussion is provided by G. Philip Hughes of the National Security and International Affairs Division of the Congressional Budget Office. His explanation warrants extensive quotation.

> Assuming that NATO theater nuclear weapons were effectively dispersed, a determination would have to be made as to what circumstances might necessitate the use of these weapons. The decision to employ theater nuclear weapons can only be made by the National Command Authority (NCA), in consultation with the NATO allies if time permits. There appear to be no particular circumstances which constitute a necessary or sufficient condition for their use without NCA authorization. However, it is possible to identify some conditions or criteria that might make a decision to employ theater nuclear weapons more likely, such as when:

> —the Warsaw Pact had initiated the use of nuclear weapons;
> —an unaccepatably large amount of NATO territory had been lost, perhaps with further losses imminent;
> —a significant portion of NATO's nuclear assets had been, or were in danger of being destroyed, so as to seriously erode the potential effectiveness of a nuclear response;
> —NATO defensive positions were in imminent danger of being breached by a Warsaw Pact offensive and reserves were unavailable or inadequate to contain the attack.

> These situations are only hypothetical and illustrative, however, and the NCA would not be constrained to use nuclear weapons in these or any other situations.

The actual employment of theater nuclear weapons has traditionally been divided into two types: selective use and general nuclear response (citing U.S. Security Issues in Europe: Burden Sharing and Offset, MBFR, and Nuclear Weapons, A Staff Report prepared for the use of the Sub-committee on U.S. Security Agreements and Commitments Abroad of the Senate Committee on Foreign Relations, 93 Cong., 1 sess., December 2, 1973, p. 21).

The current concept of selective use involves the pre-planning of "packages" of nuclear weapons for use against advancing Warsaw Pact troops or selected rear area targets of immediate military significance.

U.S., Congress, Congressional Budget Office, Planning U.S. General Purpose Forces: The Theater Nuclear Forces (Washington, D.C.: Government Printing Office, 1977), pp. 17-19. See the pessimistic view of a Belgian general in Robert Close, Europe without Defense? Forty-eight Hours That Could Change the Face of the World (New York: Pergamon, 1979), especially pp. 190-91.

3. The burden of contemporary Catholic teaching on nuclear war and deterrence is that the nuclear balance of terror is a "treacherous trap," a predicament that engenders a moral imperative for the nuclear powers to move out of the present state of affairs through arms control. See William V. O'Brien, War and/or Survival (Garden City, N.Y.: Doubleday, 1969), pp. 25-26, 29, 131. The U.S. record of working for arms control is reflected in United States Arms Control and Disarmament Agency, Arms Control and Disarmament Agreements, Texts and Histories of Negotiations (Washington, D.C.: United States Arms Control and Disarmament Agency, 1980).

4. For the debate over interpretation of the right of self-defense, see J. L. Brierly, The Law of Nations, ed. Sir Humphrey Waldock, 6th ed. (Oxford, England: Oxford University Press, 1963), pp. 397-432; and Hans Kelsen, Principles of International Law, ed. Robert W. Tucker, 2d rev. ed. (New York: Holt, Rinehart and Winston, 1966), pp. 62, 64-87.

5. See John Bassett Moore, A Digest of International Law, 8 vols. vols. (Washington, D.C.: U.S. Government Printing Office, 1966), 2: 412.

6. See William V. O'Brien, "International Law and the Outbreak of War in the Middle East, 1967," Orbis 11 (1967): 692-723.

7. On U.S. deterrence policies aiming at selective strategic counterforce retaliation, see Robert E. Osgood, Limited War Revisited (Boulder, Colo.: Westview, 1979), pp. 56-66. The central document is Secretary of Defense James R. Schlesinger's 1974 Report of the Secretary of Defense to the Congress on the FY 1975 Budget and FY 1975-1979 Defense Program (Washington, D.C.: U.S.

Government Printing Office, March 4, 1974). See Laurence Martin, "Limited Nuclear War," in Restraints on War: Studies in the Limitation of Armed Conflict, ed. Michael Howard (Oxford, England: Oxford University Press, 1979), pp. 115-20; and Lynn Etheridge Davis, "Limited Nuclear Options: Deterrence and the New American Doctrine," Adelphi Papers, no. 121 (London, International Institute for Strategic Studies, 1975-76).

The Schlesinger counterforce strategy and its ethical implications are debated in Robert A. Gessert and J. Bryan Hehir, The New Nuclear Debate (New York: Council on Religion and International Affairs, 1976). The debate has been revived after the leaking to the press in August 1980 of President Carter's Presidential Directive No. 59. It was reported that the P.D. 59 strategy emphasized counterforce attacks, including attacks on Soviet command and control centers, with "precise, limited nuclear strikes." See Robert A. Gessert, "P.D. 59: The Better Way," Worldview 23 (1980): 7-9; and J. Bryan Hehir, "P.D. 59: New Issue in an Old Argument," Worldview 23 (1980): 10-12. For an interesting collection of essays centered on counterforce deterrence and strategy in their ethical and policy aspects, see Harold P. Ford and Francis X. Winters, eds., Ethics and Nuclear Strategy (Maryknoll, N.Y.: Orbis, 1977).

8. There is no consistent usage with respect to the terms tactical nuclear and theater nuclear weapons. For examples of current usage of these terms, see Record and Anderson, U.S. Nuclear Weapons in Europe; Nitze, "The Relationship of Strategic and Theater Forces"; Frye, "Nuclear Weapons in Europe"; Iklé, "NATO's 'First Nuclear Use'"; Bracken, "Collateral Damage"; Gray, "NATO Strategy"; and U.S., Congress, Congressional Budget Office, Planning U.S. General Purpose Forces.

9. For a summary of the composition of NATO theater nuclear forces and indications as to their use, see the discussion of the Congressional Budget Office in U.S., Congress, Congressional Budget Office, Planning U.S. General Purpose Forces, pp. 8-20. See the discussions of the possible effects of use of theater nuclear weapons on the NATO areas defended and on attacking forces in the authorities cited in notes 2 and 8 above.

10. See Michael Walzer, Just and Unjust Wars (New York: Basic, 1977); p. 155. Walzer discusses deterrence as "an immoral response" to "the threat of an immoral attack." Ibid., pp. 269-74.

11. On the proportionality of a deterrent threat sufficient to the task of deterrence, see Paul Ramsey, The Just War, Force and Political Responsibility (New York: Charles Scribner's Sons, 1968), pp. 302-7.

12. See above, pp. 49-55.

13. For Ramsey's approach to profiting by the unthinkable potentialities of nuclear deterrence forces without intending to use them

in immoral, indiscriminate, countervalue "fight-the-war" strategies, see Ramsey, The Just War, pp. 253-58. Ramsey disavows this approach in "A Political Ethics Context for Strategic Thinking," in Strategic Thinking and Its Moral Significance, ed. Morton A. Kaplan, (Chicago: University of Chicago Center for Policy Study, 1973), p. 142.

14. Note that Ramsey consistently seeks evidence of a counterforce deterrent (counterforce implying substantial but permissible collateral damage) sufficient to the task of deterring strategic countervalue aggression, as in The Just War, pp. 252-53, 257-58. On U.S. efforts to develop counterforce policies and capabilities, see n. 7 above.

15. See John Courtney Murray, "Theology and Modern War," in Morality and Modern Warfare, ed. William J. Nagle (Baltimore: Helicon, 1960), pp. 87-91; and Thomas E. Murray, Nuclear Policy for War and Peace (New York: World, 1960).

16. For examples of the tendency to treat nuclear war as a malum in se category, see Pope John XXIII, "Peace on Earth (Pacem in terris)," in Encyclical Letter (Washington, D.C.: National Catholic Welfare Conference, 1963), arts. 109-13; Vatican II, Pastoral Constitution on the Church in the Modern World, art. 80. Likewise, the condemnation of "nuclear and thermonuclear weapons" in UN General Assembly Resolution 1653 (XV), adopted November 24, 1961, with the United States, the United Kingdom, France, Australia, Canada, China, and Italy among the negative votes, falls against the whole category of such weapons. See UN G.A.O.R. (1961) 807.

17. Proliferation of nuclear capabilities has been threatening increasingly, with India now a nuclear power, Israel generally thought to have had nuclear weapons for some time, and such states as Iraq and Pakistan said to be moving toward nuclear capabilities.

18. See Thomas C. Schelling, Arms and Influence (New Haven, Conn.: Yale University Press, 1966).

19. For discussions of Soviet rejection of the concept of tacit rules of conflict for nuclear powers, see Osgood, Limited War Revisited, pp. 22-24, 31-32, 58. In this connection, Osgood cites Richard G. Head, "Technology and the Military Balance," Foreign Affairs 56 (1978): 544-63; Benjamin S. Lambeth, "Selective Nuclear Operations and Soviet Strategy," in Beyond Nuclear Deterrence, ed. Johan J. Holst and Uwe Nerlich (New York: Crane, Russak, 1977); and Fritz Ermarth, "Contrasts in American and Soviet Strategic Thought," International Security 3 (1978): 138-55.

20. See Chapter 4 on the rationales for World War II bombing.

21. The continued relevance of the principle of discrimination and the technical feasibility of discriminating aerial bombing is affirmed in U.S., Department of the Air Force, International Law—The Conduct of Armed Conflict and Air Operations, 19 November 1976, AFP 110-31 (Washington, D.C.: Department of the Air Force, 1976), 5-6-14 [hereafter cited as AFP 110-31]. See Chapter 3.

22. On naval blockades in World War I, see A. C. Bell, The Blockade of Germany (London: Her Majesty's Stationary Office, 1961); James W. Gantenbein, The Doctrine of Continuous Voyage (Portland, Ore.: Keystone Press, 1929); Louis Guichard, The Naval Blockade, 1914-1918, trans. Christopher R. Tierney (New York: D. Appleton, 1930); Maurice Parmlee, Blockade and Sea Power (New York: Crowell, 1924); Robert W. Tucker, The Law of War and Neutrality at Sea, International Law Studies, vol. 50 (Newport, R.I.: U.S. Naval War College, 1955), pp. 296-317; and Walzer, Just and Unjust Wars, pp. 172-75.

23. See the discussion of starvation as a method of warfare in Chapter 8.

24. Conventional-law provisions requiring and/or facilitating emergency relief to noncombatant victims of blockades are found in Article 23 of the 1949 Geneva Civilians Convention, Article 70 of 1977 Geneva Protocol I, and Article 18 of 1977 Geneva Protocol II. See the discussion of starvation as a method of revolutionary/counterinsurgency warfare in Chapter 8.

25. On German scorched-earth strategies in World War I, see James Wilford Garner, International Law and the World War, 2 vols. (London: Longmans, Green, 1926), 1: 315-16, 319-20, 323.

26. On Rendulic's use of scorched-earth strategy, see U.S. v. List, Nuremberg Military Tribunal, Trial of War Criminals, 15 vols. (Washington, D.C.: U.S. Government Printing Office, 1949-51), 11: 770, 1124-25, 1296-97. Von Manstein's use of scorched-earth strategies in his retreats after the Stalingrad collapse is described in Erich von Manstein, Lost Victories, trans. Anthony G. Powell (Chicago: Henry Regnery, 1958), chaps. 16-22; R. T. Paget, Manstein (London: Collins, 1951), pp. 49-53, 102-4, 175-77; and B. H. Liddell Hart, The German Generals Talk (New York: William Morrow, 1948), pp. 63-67.

In U.S. v. von Leeb the U.S. military tribunal dealt with several charges involving scorched-earth policies by various German commands on the Soviet front and concluded the following:

> The devastation prohibited by the Hague Rules and the usages
> of war is that not warranted by military necessity. This
> rule is clear enough but the factual determination as to
> what constitutes military necessity is difficult. Defendants
> in this case were in many instances in retreat under arduous
> conditions wherein their commands were in serious danger
> of being cut off. Under such circumstances, a commander
> must necessarily make quick decisions to meet the particular
> situation of his command. A great deal of latitude must
> be accorded to him under such circumstances. What con-
> stitutes devastation beyond military necessity in these

situations requires detailed proof of an operational and
tactical nature. We do not feel that in this case the proof
is ample to establish the guilt of any defendant herein on
this charge.

Nuremberg Military Tribunal, Trials of War Criminals, 10, 11.
The passage quoted is at 11: 541.

In the Gerardmer case a French military tribunal condemned
as violative of the 1907 Hague Convention IV, Art. 23(g) a scorched-
earth strategy applied by the German forces defending the Vosges
Mountains front in September 1944. Tribunal militaire permanent
de Paris, Dossiers des pièces de la procédure suivie contre Balck,
Hermann; Weise, Henri; Petersen, Eric; Schiel, Othon E.—Jugement
No. 119/2745 de 19 janvier 1950. I discuss this case in "Military
Necessity: The Development of the Concept of Military Necessity
and Its Interpretation in the Modern Law of War" (Ph.D. diss.,
Georgetown University, 1953), pp. 556-71.

27. See Nuremberg International Military Tribunal, Trial of
Major War Criminals, Judgment.

28. See U.S. v. List, Nuremberg Military Tribunal, Trials of
War Criminals, 11: 1296.

29. General Hermann Ramcke, whose forces defended Brest in
August and September 1944 with such effectiveness that several U.S.
divisions were tied up in taking it, raised the defense that his tactical measures of destroying parts of the city were required by urgent
military necessity whereas no condemnation was made of Allied
bombing of Brest during the war. Tribunal militaire permanent de
Paris, Dossiers des pièces de la procédure suivie contre le Général
Ramke, Hermann et autres—Jugement No. 189/4176 de 21 Mars 1951.

I discuss the Ramcke case in O'Brien, "Military Necessity"
(Ph.D. diss.), pp. 572-88.

30. On Soviet doctrine and practice with regard to CW, see the
authorities cited in Chapter 3, n. 44.

31. On reprisals, see above, pp. 67-70.

32. See AFP 110-31, 6-4 and 6-9 n. 9; Ann Van Wynen Thomas
and A. J. Thomas, Jr., Legal Limits on the Use of Chemical and
Biological Weapons (Dallas: Southern Methodist University Press,
(1970), pp. 246-50, are extremely wary of any conclusion either as
to the legal status or the prospects of use of biological or chemical
warfare.

33. See Howard S. Levie, Prisoners of War in Armed Conflict,
International Law Studies, vol. 59 (Newport, R.I.: U.S. Naval War
College, 1978), pp. 145-58.

34. On Communist refusal to obey the PW regime in the Korean
War, see Howard S. Levie, "Maltreatment of Prisoners of War in

Vietnam," in The Vietnam War and International Law, ed. Richard
A. Falk, 4 vols. (Princeton, N.J.: Princeton University Press,
1969-76), 2: 364; Levie, Prisoners of War, pp. 30, 172, 177-78, 312,
349-50; and David P. Forsythe, Humanitarian Politics: The International Committee of the Red Cross (Baltimore: Johns Hopkins University Press, 1977), pp. 134-36.

35. On Communist failure to comply with the PW regime in the
Vietnam War, see Levie, "Maltreatment," pp. 364-69, 380-84, 386-
90; and Forsythe, Humanitarian Politics, pp. 155-56.

36. On Syrian policies regarding identification and exchange of
Israeli PWs after the 1973 Yom Kippur War, see Levie, Prisoners
of War, p. 31, n. 116.

37. Levie discusses communist reeducation and propaganda
programs in ibid., pp. 141-42.

38. See above, p. 68.

39. Note that in cases where only one side in a conflict permitted
ICRC inspections, the ICRC has been firm in its objections to questionable behavior by the cooperating party (for example, the United
States and South Vietnam in the Vietnam War). See Forsythe, Humanitarian Politics, pp. 152-65.

40. On the use of Communist PWs in the Korean War as instruments of continuing coercion through planned disruptive activities in
PW camps, see Levie, Prisoners of War, pp. 316-17 (particularly
n. 8 and authorities therein cited).

41. See Levie's treatment of measures for controlling and
punishing PWs who break their hors-de-combat status and otherwise
violate their obligations under the PW regime in ibid., chap. 5, pp.
315-42.

NOTES TO CHAPTER 7

1. For analyses of contemporary revolutionary/counterinsur-
gency warfare that include the element of external assistance to rebels
by communist states and organizations, see generally Richard L.
Clutterbuck, The Long, Long War: Counterinsurgency in Malaya and
Vietnam (New York: Praeger, 1966); David Galula, Counterinsurgency
Warfare: Theory and Practice (New York: Praeger, 1964); Sir
Robert Thompson, Defeating Communist Insurgency: The Lessons of
Malaya and Vietnam (New York: Praeger, 1966); and idem, Revolu-
tionary War in World Strategy, 1945-1969 (New York: Taplinger,
1970).

2. Walter Laqueur, Guerrilla: A Historical and Critical
Study (Boston: Little, Brown, 1976).

3. Laqueur's historical study of guerrilla war places modern revolutionary war in perspective. Ibid., pp. 278-409. See generally Clutterbuck, Long, Long War; Harry Eckstein, ed., Internal War: Problems and Approaches (New York: Free Press, 1964); Bernard Fall, Street without Joy: Indochina at War, 1946-54 (Harrisburg, Pa.: Stackpole, 1961); idem, The Two Vietnams (New York: Praeger, 1963); Galula, Counterinsurgency Warfare; Samuel B. Griffith, ed. and trans., Mao Tse-tung on Guerrilla Warfare (New York: Praeger, 1961); Otto Heilbrun, Partisan Warfare (New York: Praeger, 1962); Chalmers Johnson, Revolutionary Change (Boston: Little, Brown, 1966); Bard E. O'Neill, William R. Heaton, and Donald J. Alberts, eds., Insurgency in the Modern World (Boulder, Colo.: Westview, 1980); Franklin M. Osanka, Modern Guerrilla Warfare (New York: Free Press, 1960); Peter Paret, French Revolutionary Warfare from Indo-China to Algeria (New York: Praeger, 1964); Peter Paret and John W. Shy, Guerrillas in the 1960s (New York: Praeger, 1965); Harries-Clichy Peterson, ed., Che Guevara on Guerrilla Warfare (New York: Praeger, 1961); Douglas Pike, Viet Cong (Cambridge, Mass.: MIT Press, 1966); idem, War, Peace and the Vietcong (Cambridge, Mass.: MIT Press, 1969); Andrew M. Scott, ed., Insurgency (Chapel Hill: University of North Carolina Press, 1970); Thompson, Defeating Communist Insurgency; idem, Revolutionary War; and Roger Trinquier, Modern Warfare, trans. Daniel Lee (New York: Praeger, 1964).

4. For an evaluation of counterinsurgent theory in the light of the historical evolution of guerrilla and revolutionary warfare, see U.S., Department of the Army, Operations against Irregular Forces, FM 31-15 (Washington, D.C.: Department of the Army, 1961); Galula, Counterinsurgency Warfare; John J. McCuen, The Art of Counter-Revolutionary War: The Strategy of Counter-Insurgency (Harrisburg, Pa.: Stackpole, 1966); Osanka, Modern Guerrilla Warfare; Julian Paget, Counterinsurgency Operations (New York: Walker, 1967); John S. Pustay, Counter-insurgency Warfare (New York: Free Press, 1965); Scott, Insurgency; George Tanham, Communist Revolutionary Warfare: The Vietminh in Indochina (New York: Praeger, 1961); idem, War without Guns (New York: Praeger, 1966); Thompson, Defeating Communist Insurgency; idem, Revolutionary War; Trinquier, Modern Warfare; Bernard Fall, "The Theory and Practice of Insurgency and Counterinsurgency," Naval War College Review 17 (1965): 21-38; and George Tanham and Dennis J. Duncanson, "Some Dilemmas of Counterinsurgency," Foreign Affairs 48 (1969): 113-22.

For a retrospective view of counterinsurgency theory and practice, see Douglas S. Blaufarb, The Counterinsurgency Era: U.S. Doctrine and Performance (New York: Free Press, 1977).

5. See generally Griffith, Mao Tse-tung on Guerrilla Warfare.

6. However, with respect to Protocol II on noninternational conflicts, the report of the U.S. delegation to the Geneva Diplomatic Conference that produced the 1977 Geneva Protocols comments that:

> Given the easy availability of "outs" under Article 1, the Protocol nevertheless accomplishes much in developing the law—which is really more a matter of human rights than of the laws of war. In particular, Article 4 on funda-mental guarantees, Article 5 on persons whose liberty has been restricted, and Article 6 on guarantees during penal prosecutions provide an important safety net of basic pro-tection for all victims of civil wars. [Emphasis added]

U.S., Department of State, Report of the United States Delegation to the Diplomatic Conference on the Reaffirmation and Development of International Humanitarian Law Applicable in Armed Conflicts (Washington, D.C., September 8, 1977), p. 33 (submitted to the secretary of state by George H. Aldrich, chairman of the delegation, and hereafter cited as the Aldrich Report).

7. See Griffith, Mao Tse-tung on Guerrilla Warfare, p. 114; Laqueur, Guerrilla, pp. 378-79; and Thompson, Revolutionary War, p. 3.

8. See generally Griffith, Mao Tse-tung on Guerrilla Warfare; Laqueur, Guerrilla; and Thompson, Revolutionary War.

9. See Galula, Counterinsurgency Warfare, pp. 44-58; Griffith, Mao Tse-tung on Guerrilla Warfare, pp. 20-22; Laqueur, Guerrilla, pp. 254, 377-78; Pike, Viet Cong, pp. 36-40; Tanham, War without Guns, p. 12; Thompson, Revolutionary War, pp. 4-11.

10. On nation building and counterinsurgency, see Walt W. Rostow, "Countering Guerrilla Attack," in The Vietnam War and In-ternational Law, ed. Richard A. Falk, 4 vols. (Princeton, N.J.: Princeton University Press, 1969-76), 1: 127-34; and Tanham, War without Guns.

11. Michael Walzer, Just and Unjust Wars (New York: Basic, 1977), pp. 98-101.

12. On intervention and counterintervention in civil or internal wars, see generally John Norton Moore, "Intervention: A Mono-chromatic Term for a Polychromatic Reality," in The Vietnam War and International Law, ed. Richard A. Falk, 4 vols. (Princeton, N.J.: Princeton University Press, 1969-76), 2: 1061-88; Tom J. Farer, "Harnessing Rogue Elephants: A Short Discourse on Intervention in Civil Strife," in The Vietnam War and International Law, ed. Richard A. Falk, 4 vols. (Princeton, N.J.: Princeton University Press, 1969-76), 2: 1089-1115.

13. An exception to the legal presumption against armed intervention against an incumbent regime may arise from Article 1(4) of 1977 Geneva Protocol I, which gives belligerent status to national liberation movements engaged in wars of national liberation against "colonial" and "racist" regimes and "alien" occupants. If this becomes accepted international law (which is by no means certain insofar as countries like the United States are concerned), it might provide a warrant for armed intervention on behalf of such national liberation movements. See below, p. 162.

14. On recognition of belligerency, see Marjorie M. Whiteman, Digest of International Law, 15 vols. (Washington, D.C.: U.S. Government Printing Office, 1968-73), 2: 486-523.

15. Common Article 3 of the four 1949 Geneva Conventions provides for the following:

> In the case of armed conflict not of an international character occurring in the territory of one of the High Contracting Parties, each Party to the conflict shall be bound to apply, as a minimum, the following provisions:
> (1) Persons taking no active part in the hostilities, including members of the armed forces who have laid down their arms and those placed hors de combat by sickness, wounds, detention, or any other cause, shall in all circumstances be treated humanely, without any adverse distinction founded on race, colour, religion or faith, sex, birth or wealth, or any other similar criteria.
> To this end, the following acts are and shall remain prohibited at any time and in any place whatsoever with respect to the above-mentioned persons:
> (a) violence to life and person, in particular murder of all kinds, mutilation, cruel treatment and torture;
> (b) taking of hostages;
> (c) outrages upon personal dignity, in particular humiliating and degrading treatment;
> (d) the passing of sentences and the carrying out of executions without previous judgments pronounced by a regularly constituted court, affording all the judicial guarantees which are recognized as indispensable by civilized peoples.
> (2) The wounded and sick shall be collected and cared for.
> An impartial humanitarian body, such as the International Committee of the Red Cross, may offer its services to the Parties to the conflict.
> The Parties to the conflict should further endeavour to bring into force, by means of special agreements, all or part of the other provisions of the present Convention.

The application of the preceding provisions shall not
affect the legal status of the Parties to the conflict.

For a thorough analysis of Article 3, see Richard R. Baxter,
"Ius in Bello Interno: The Present and Future Law," in Law and
Civil War in the Modern World, ed. John Norton Moore (Baltimore:
Johns Hopkins University Press, 1974), pp. 518-36.

A valuable summary of the practice of civil war belligerents
regarding acceptance of the application of Article 3 is offered in
David P. Forsythe, "Legal Management of Internal War: The 1977
Protocol on Non-international Armed Conflicts," American Journal
of International Law 72 (1978): 272, 273-77.

16. Compare the requirements for belligerent status of 1977
Geneva Protocol II with the traditional requirements of 1907 Hague
Convention IV, Article 1, and 1949 Geneva PW Convention, Article 4,
for belligerent status.

17. On Article 1(4) of 1977 Geneva Protocol I, see G. I. A. D.
Draper, "Wars of National Liberation and Criminal Responsibility,"
in Restraints on War: Studies in the Limitation of Armed Conflict, ed.
Michael Howard (Oxford: Oxford University Press, 1979), pp. 146-51.
On the effects of ideological just causes on the contemporary international-law jus ad bellum, see Inis L. Claude, "Just Wars: Doctrines
and Institutions," Political Science Quarterly 95 (1980): 95-96.

18. Rommen's formulation of the "popular right to resist" is
that of active resistance against a tyrant who acts against the common
good. Rommen says that "popular uprising is then not sedition, but
lawful defense of the body politic's inalienable right to the realization of the common good." Heinrich A. Rommen, The State in Catholic Thought (St. Louis: Herder, 1945), p. 474. See generally ibid.,
pp. 473-76 and Johannes Messner, Social Ethics, trans. J. J.
Doherty (St. Louis: Herder, 1965), pp. 596-601.

19. For a typical example of the wary attitude of modern Scholastic natural-law treatments of revolution, see Messner's treatment, ibid., pp. 596-601.

20. On contemporary revolutionary theory and practice wherein
justification in terms of ends is implicit, see Carl Leiden and Karl
M. Schmitt, The Politics of Violence: Revolution in the Modern
World (Englewood Cliffs, N.J.: Prentice-Hall, 1968); Hannah
Arendt, On Revolution (New York: Viking, 1965); and Johnson,
Revolutionary Change.

The most explicit treatment of the question of jus ad bellum
proportionality in revolutionary war is that of Richard J. Neuhaus.
His brief but insightful effort seems to be unique in the recent literature. See Peter L. Berger and Richard J. Neuhaus, Movement and
Revolution (Garden City, N.Y.: Doubleday, 1970), pp. 209-14. See

also the thoughtful treatment of Christian approaches to revolution in chapter 6, "Justifiable Revolution," of Paul Ramsey's War and the Christian Conscience: How Shall Modern War Be Conducted Justly? (Durham, N.C.: Duke University Press, 1961), pp. 114-33.

21. On the reluctance of the Catholic Church to discuss revolutionary war, see Chapter 2, n. 11 above.

For an example of liberation theology and its position on revolution in Latin America, see Gustavo Gutierrez, A Theology of Liberation, trans. and ed. Sister Caridad Inda and John Eagleson (Maryknoll, N.Y.: Orbis, 1971). A useful survey of liberation theology and its views on revolution is found in Alfredo Fierro, The Militant Gospel: A Critical Introduction to Political Theologies, trans. John Drury (Maryknoll, N.Y.: Orbis, 1975), pp. 193-207.

22. See James N. Rosenau, "The Concept of Intervention," Journal of International Affairs 22 (1968): 165-76; idem, "Intervention as a Scientific Concept and Postscript," in The Vietnam War in International Law, ed. Richard A. Falk, 4 vols. (Princeton, N.J.: Princeton University Press, 1969-76), 2: 979-1015. A representative sample of the tortured and inconclusive literature on intervention, particularly as it bears on military intervention in mixed international/civil wars, is conveniently available in Richard A. Falk, ed., The Vietnam War and International Law, 4 vols. (Princeton, N.J.: Princeton University Press, 1969-76), 1: 17-159; 2: 979-1116, 1162-75. One of the most perceptive of this collection of reprinted articles and new contributions by leading international-law publicists is Moore, "Intervention." See also R. J. Vincent, Nonintervention and International Order (Princeton, N.J.: Princeton University Press, 1974).

23. See Rosenau, "The Concept of Intervention," pp. 167-71; idem, "Intervention as a Scientific Concept," pp. 997-1003.

24. On the historical evolution and rationale of the principle of nonintervention, see Ann Van Wynen Thomas and A. J. Thomas, Jr., Non-Intervention: The Law and Its Import in the Americas (Dallas: Southern Methodist University Press, 1956).

25. On Vattel, the principle of sovereign equality, and its consequences, see J. L. Brierly, Law of Nations, ed. Sir Humphrey Waldock, 6th ed. (Oxford: Oxford University Press, 1963), pp. 36-40, 131-33. See Albert de Lapradelle's introduction to E. de Vattel, The Law of Nations or the Principles of Natural Law Applied to the Conduct and to the Affairs of Nations and of Sovereigns, trans. Charles G. Fenwick, 3 vols. (Washington, D.C.: Carnegie Institution, 1916), 3: vii-xiii.

26. The contemporary international law on the principle of self-determination is discussed in Louis Henkin, How Nations Behave, 2d ed. (New York: Council on Foreign Relations/Columbia University Press, 1979), pp. 16, 115, 126, 134, 144, 176-78, 182, 195, 198, 203-6, 232.

The principle of self-determination is reaffirmed, inter alia, in the UN Declaration on the Granting of Independence to Colonial Countries and Peoples Adopted by the General Assembly, 14 December 1960 in Resolution 1514 (XIV) and in Articles 1 in both of the UN International Covenants on Human Rights annexed to G. A. Res. 2200 (XXI), reprinted in American Journal of International Law 61 (1967): 861.

For discussions of the principle of self-determination with particular reference to the issue of intervention in civil wars, see Moore, "Intervention," pp. 1067-69; and Farer, "Harnessing Rogue Elephants," pp. 1095-1102.

27. For an unusual instance of a publicist challenging the presumption that the nonintervention norm is always the highest value in international relations, see Rosenau, "Intervention as a Scientific Concept," pp. 982-84.

28. "A statement is 'normative-ambiguous' when its terms make indiscriminate reference to the events to which decision makers respond, to the policies which are assumed to guide and justify decision and to the decisions ('legal consequences') themselves." Myres S. McDougal and Florentino P. Feliciano, Law and Minimum World Public Order (New Haven, Conn.: Yale University Press, 1961), p. 5.

See the discussion of normative ambiguity of the term intervention in the sense of reference "both to operative facts and purported legal consequences," in Moore, "Intervention," p. 1062; William T. Burke, "The Legal Regulation of Minor International Coercion: A Framework of Inquiry," in Essays on Intervention, ed. Roland J. Stanger (Columbus: Ohio State University Press, 1964), pp. 87-88.

29. 1. No State has the right to intervene, directly or indirectly, for any reason whatever, in the internal or external affairs of any other State. Consequently, armed intervention and all other forms of interference or attempted threats against the personality of the State or against its political, economic and cultural elements, are condemned.

UN General Assembly Resolution 2131 (XX), adopted December 21, 1965. Reprinted in American Journal of International Law 60 (1966): 662. See comparable provisions in The Charter of the Organization of American States (1948), Articles 15-17, T.I.A.S. no. 2361.

30. Grounds for intervention are discussed in John Bassett Moore, A Digest of International Law, 8 vols. (Washington, D.C.: U.S. Government Printing Office, 1906), 6: 2-11; Thomas and Thomas, Non-Intervention, pp. 74-78, 79-97, 123-41, 215-40; and Henkin, How Nations Behave, pp. 156-61.

31. For critical views on intervention by invitation from regimes that are weak and/or challenged by civil war, see Walzer, Just and Unjust Wars, pp. 98-101.

32. For an extended, authoritative discussion of the presumption against intervention in civil wars, particularly where there is no antecedent intervention on the other side, see Wolfgang Friedmann, The Changing Structure of International Law (New York: Columbia University Press, 1964), pp. 262-74. See Moore, "Intervention," p. 1065; and Farer, "Harnessing Rogue Elephants," pp. 1098-1102.

33. On the presumption of sovereign equality and the corollary of nonintervention, see Thomas and Thomas, Non-Intervention, p. 5; and Friedmann, Changing Structure, pp. 264-65.

34. See Walzer, Just and Unjust Wars, pp. 98-101.

35. The British and French have intervened with troops to quell civil disturbances and mutinies in their former colonial dependencies in Africa on the invitation of incumbent governments. While I have been unable to locate bases in specific treaty undertakings for these interventions (reflecting the sensitivity of newly independent states), such interventions obviously reflect ongoing relationships of an intimacy much greater than that, for example, between the United States and the barely established rightist Dominican government, which invited U.S. intervention in the 1965 civil war.

Article IV of the Panama Canal Treaty of September 7, 1977, entered into force October 1, 1979, contains a pledge from both the United States and Panama to protect and defend the canal. This is elaborated on in an Agreement in Implementation of Article IV of the Panama Canal Treaty, effected by an Exchange of Notes at Panama, October 1, 1979, and entered into force October 1, 1979.

36. Humanitarian intervention in the sense of protecting the lives of one's nationals and other aliens from imminent danger is discussed in Whiteman, Digest of International Law, 5: 475-76, wherein the 1964 joint Belgian-U.S. intervention in Stanleyville during the Congo civil war is described. See generally Thomas and Thomas, Non-Intervention, pp. 303-58; and Moore, "Intervention," p. 1078.

37. See the discussion of humanitarian intervention in Chapter 2 and the literature cited in notes 20 and 21 of that chapter.

38. On counterintervention, see Henkin, How Nations Behave, pp. 156-61; and Friedmann, Changing Structure, pp. 262-74.

39. I compare the Dominican and Vietnamese cases of U.S. intervention by invitation in U.S. Military Intervention: Law and Morality, Washington Papers, no. 68 (Beverly Hills, Calif.: Sage/Center for Strategic and International Studies, Georgetown University, 1979). On the Dominican civil war and U.S. intervention, see Piero Gleijeses, The Dominican Crisis: The 1965 Constitutionalist Revolt and American Intervention, trans. Lawrence Lipson (Baltimore: Johns Hopkins University Press, 1978).

NOTES TO CHAPTER 8

1. On the inadequacies of 1977 Geneva Protocol II arising from the unwillingness of many Third World and other states to accord greater law-of-war protection to possible revolutionary forces in their own countries, see U.S., Department of State, Report of the United States Delegation to the Diplomatic Conference on the Reaffirmation and Development of International Humanitarian Law Applicable in Armed Conflicts (Washington, D.C., September 8, 1977), pp. 27-28 (submitted to the Secretary of State by George A. Aldrich, chairman of the delegation, and hereafter cited as the Aldrich Report); and G. I. A. D. Draper, "Wars of National Liberation and Criminal Responsibility," in Restraints on War: Studies in the Limitation of Armed Conflict, ed. Michael Howard (Oxford: Oxford University Press, 1979), pp. 148, 159.

2. Much of the counterinsurgent doctrine developed by French practitioners and theorists, while recognizing the need for positive programs of persuasion and reform as auxiliary strategies, is extremely hard-line in its prescriptions, for example, Roger Trinquier, Modern Warfare, trans. Daniel Lee (New York: Praeger, 1964), p. 105. Paret, discussing the French counterinsurgent policies in Algeria, observed that

> to the obvious query whether an attack on political, economic, and social motives of the insurrection might not prove a government's most effective strategy, the doctrine has an unequivocal and negative answer: it would be dangerous to confuse the will of an organization that sets off the struggle, and pursues it, with the internal contradictions and inequities of society. The former is the real, the latter only the pretended cause. . . . That the mass of the people may be dissatisfied and wish for change is not denied; but it is argued that the revolutionary elite fights either because it is committed to a particular ideology or for personal power.

Peter Paret, French Revolutionary Warfare from Indo-China to Algeria (New York: Praeger, 1964), p. 22. Paret also noted that reforms are regarded as "a useful auxiliary to pacification—but as no more than that" (pp. 22-23). See David Galula, Counterinsurgency Warfare: Theory and Practice (New York: Praeger, 1964), p. 79. George Tanham has been a leading and authoritative spokesman for the soft-line emphasis on positive development and reform programs. See War without Guns (New York: Praeger, 1966). Galula concludes that the essence of counterinsurgent warfare "can be summed up in a single sentence: Build (or rebuild) a political machine from the population upward." Counterinsurgency Warfare, p. 136.

Hence, Galula considers the problem ultimately political and not amenable to purely military solutions.

3. On the practices of the Algerian National Liberation Front and the French in the Algerian revolution, see Arnold Fraleigh, "The Algerian Revolution as a Case Study in International Law," in The International Law of Civil War, ed. Richard A. Falk (Baltimore: Johns Hopkins University Press, 1971), pp. 179-243. On Vietcong practice in the Vietnam War, see Douglas Pike, Viet Cong (Cambridge, Mass.: MIT Press, 1966), pp. 247-49.

4. On these revolutionary strategies and tactics see Galula, Counterinsurgency Warfare, pp. 44-58; Samuel B. Griffith, ed. and trans., Mao Tse-tung on Guerrilla Warfare (New York: Praeger, 1961), pp. 20-22; Walter Laqueur, Guerrilla: A Historical and Critical Study (Boston: Little, Brown, 1976), pp. 254, 377-78; Pike, Viet Cong, pp. 36-40; Tanham, War without Guns, p. 12; and Sir Robert Thompson, Revolutionary War in World Strategy 1945-1969 (New York: Taplinger, 1970), pp. 4-11.

5. Aldrich Report, pp. 27-28. See Article 51 of Protocol II for an effort to define "indiscriminate attacks."

6. Support for policies of proportionate and discriminate use of military means in conjunction with positive development programs is found in the writings of Peter Paret and John W. Shy, Guerrillas in the 1960s (New York: Praeger, 1965), pp. 40-49; Tanham, War without Guns; and Sir Robert Thompson, Defeating Communist Insurgency: The Lessons of Malaya and Vietnam (New York: Praeger, 1966), pp. 51-55.

7. See the insightful analysis of Jean Jacques Servan-Schreiber, Lieutenant in Algeria, trans. Ronald Matthews (New York: Knopf, 1957), pp. 70-72, 97-162; and Tanham, War without Guns, pp. 8, 120.

8. For an example of the confused and improper use of the term genocide in connection with the Vietnam War, see "Biafra, Bengal, and Beyond: International Responsibility and Genocidal Conflict," in American Society of International Law Proceedings, 1972, pp. 89, 97-100, 106.

9. Paul Ramsey is one of the rare moralists to address revolutionary/counterinsurgency war with the same seriousness that he has applied to the issues of nuclear war and deterrence. See pt. 5, "Vietnam and Insurgency Warfare," in Paul Ramsey, The Just War: Force and Political Responsibility (New York: Charles Scribner's Sons, 1968), pp. 427-536. I develop this subject in chap. 7, "Revolutionary War and Intervention," in William V. O'Brien, War and/or Survival (Garden City, N.Y.: Doubleday, 1969), pp. 185-215.

10. The four conditions for belligerent status are set in 1907 Hague Convention IV, Art. 1 and 1949 Geneva PW Convention, Art. 4.

11. Aldrich Report, Appendix C.

12. See Falk's introduction to The International Law of Civil War (Baltimore: Johns Hopkins University Press, 1971), in which he recognizes that the approach of states to civil war in another country is generally prudential and political, with little concern for legal concepts, conditions, or prescriptions (pp. 4-5, 14). See Rosalyn Higgins, "International Law and Civil Conflict," in The International Regulation of Civil War, ed. Evan Luard (New York: New York University Press, 1972), pp. 169-86.

13. The interpretation of Article 1 of 1977 Geneva Protocol II, as well as predictions about its application, is both complex and elusive. See Forsythe's discussion in "Legal Management of Internal War: The 1977 Protocol on Noninternational Armed Conflicts," American Journal of International Law 72 (1978): 272-95. Forsythe observes that

> there is the question of the relation between Common Article 3 and the Protocol. The ICRC, and a large number of states, believe that the scope of Common Article 3 is broader than that of the Protocol. From this perspective, there are two general types of internal war, legally speaking, a Protocol II situation and a Common Article 3 situation, the scope of the latter being wider. Nevertheless, some delegates expressed the personal view that the two instruments would in the future be taken as coterminous. They thought state practice would effectively redefine Common Article 3 "upwards," giving the article the same material application as the Protocol. [P. 286]

14. Article 43 of 1977 Geneva Protocol I defined the armed forces of a party to a conflict. Article 44 of the Protocol details the rights of combatants to be treated as prisoners of war.

15. See Howard S. Levie, "Maltreatment of Prisoners of War in Vietnam," in The Vietnam War and International Law, ed. Richard A. Falk, 4 vols. (Princeton, N.J.: Princeton University Press, 1969-76), 2: 363-66, 380-96.

16. See Falk, The International Law of Civil War, p. 8.

17. Article 5 of the Universal Declaration of Human Rights provides that "no one shall be subjected to torture or to cruel, inhuman or degrading treatment or punishment." G.A. Res. 217A, 3 UN GAOR, Resolutions 71, 73, UN Doc. A/810 (1948), reprinted in American Journal of International Law Supplement 43 (1949): 127, 128.

For an enumeration of international conventions and UN resolutions on torture see Comité International des Experts sur la Torture, "La prévention et la suppression de la torture/The Prevention and Suppression of Torture," in Revue international de droit pénal, 1977, pp. 67-69 [hereafter cited as "Prévention et suppression de la torture"].

18. On the prevalence of torture in revolutionary/counterinsurgency warfare, see Paret, French Revolutionary Warfare; Trinquier,

Modern Warfare, pp. 21, 23; Fraleigh, "The Algerian Revolution,"
p. 293; Levie, "Maltreatment," 2: 378-80, 396; and Lawrence C.
Petrowski, "Law and Conduct of the Vietnam War," in The Vietnam
War and International Law, ed. Richard A. Falk, 4 vols. (Princeton,
N.J.: Princeton University Press, 1969-76), 2: 439, 513.

The most common purpose of both mistreatment and torture in
communist belligerent practice is to "reeducate" the captives to a
view sympathetic to that of the captors. A belligerent also may force
PWs and detainees to collaborate in imposing the captor's will throughout the camps. The Communists in the Korean War mistreated PWs
in this manner. See David Rees, Korea: The Limited War (New York:
St. Martin's Press, 1964), pp. 328-46; Eugene Kinkaid, In Every
War but One (New York: Norton, 1959); W. L. White, The Captives
of Korea: Their Treatment of Our Prisoners and Our Treatment of
Theirs (New York: Scribner's, 1957); Jeremiah A. Denton, Jr.,
and Ed Brandt, When Hell Was in Session (New York: Reader's
Digest Press/Crowell, 1976); John A. Dramesi, Code of Honor (New
York: Norton, 1975); and James N. Rowe, Five Years to Freedom
(Boston: Little, Brown, 1971).

19. Prévention et suppression de la torture, p. 267.
20. O'Brien, War and/or Survival, pp. 225-29.
21. In Ireland v. United Kingdom, the European Court of Human
Rights decided in a judgment of January 18, 1978, that there is a difference between "inhuman and degrading treatment" and "torture."
Both practices are prohibited by Article 3 of the European Convention
for the Protection of Human Rights and Fundamental Freedoms, 213
UNTS 222, 224 (1955). The court found that such techniques as
wall-standing, hooding, subjection to noise, deprivation of sleep,
and deprivation of food and drink during the interrogation of detainees
in Northern Ireland by British Security Services constituted "inhuman
and degrading treatment" in the sense of Article 3 of the Convention,
but not "torture." In the course of the litigation the British government promised the court that these practices would not be repeated.
See International Legal Materials 17 (1978): 680.
22. See Chapter 6, pp. 150-53.
23. On hostages, see generally Bernard Joseph Brungs, "Hostages, Prisoner Reprisals, and Collective Penalties: The Development of the International Law of War with Respect to Collective and
Vicarious Punishment" (Ph.D. diss., Georgetown University, 1968).
24. U.S. v. List, 11: 759-1319.
25. Ibid., pp. 1248-53.
26. See Forsythe, "Legal Management," p. 293.
27. On the place of terror in revolutionary/counterinsurgency
warfare, see the authorities cited in n. 9 above. See also Falk, The
International Law of Civil War, p. 8; Forsythe, "Legal Management,"

p. 293; Howard J. Taubenfeld, "The Applicability of the Laws of War in Civil War," in Law and Civil War in the Modern World, ed. John Norton Moore (Baltimore: Johns Hopkins University Press, 1974), pp. 516-17.

28. The Charter of the International Military Tribunal included the charge of "ill-treatment, or deportation to slave labor or for any other purpose of civilian population of or on occupied territory" within the category of "war crimes." Nuremberg International Military Tribunal, Trial of Major War Criminals, 22: 414.

29. The conduct of troops and police in the field may undo even the wisest governmental policies and propaganda. See Paret and Shy, Guerrillas in the 1960s, p. 47. Overcoming pillage and troop misbehavior was a major achievement in the Philippine counterinsurgency effort against the Huks. See Frances Lucille Starner, Magsaysay and the Philippine Peasantry: The Agrarian Impact on Philippine Politics, 1953-1956 (Berkeley: University of California Press, 1961).

30. See Forsythe, "Legal Management," pp. 291-93.

31. Hyde states that

> a belligerent commander may lawfully lay seige to a place controlled by the enemy and endeavor by a process of isolation to cause its surrender. The propriety of attempting to reduce it by starvation is not questioned. Hence the cutting off of every source of sustenance from without is deemed legitimate. It is said that if the commander of a besieged place expels the non-combatants, in order to lessen the number of those who consume his stock of provisions, it is lawful, though an extreme measure, to drive them back, so as to hasten surrender.

Charles Cheney Hyde, International Law, Chiefly as Interpreted and Applied by the United States, 3 vols. (Boston: Little, Brown, 1945-47), 3: 1802-3.

For a thoughtful analysis of a subject long avoided by international lawyers and moralists, see Michael Walzer, Just and Unjust Wars (New York: Basic, 1977), pp. 160-75.

32. It appears that responsibility for the deaths of perhaps 2 million people from starvation in Biafra is shared by both revolutionaries and counterinsurgents, and perhaps by third-party states and international organizations. Nigeria's successful counterinsurgent campaign resulted in substantial measure from the effects of massive starvation. See David P. Forsythe, Humanitarian Politics: The International Committee of the Red Cross (Baltimore: Johns Hopkins University Press, 1977), pp. 184-96; John L. Stremlau, The

International Politics of the Nigerian Civil War (Princeton, N.J.: Princeton University Press, 1977), pp. 238-52, 334-39, 376; and Anthony Kirk-Greene, Crisis and Conflict in Nigeria: A Documentary Sourcebook (London: Oxford University Press, 1971), pp. 55-58, 71, 81, 94, 117-19, 141.

33. On U.S. destruction of crops through the use of herbicides, see Ann Van Wynen Thomas and A. J. Thomas, Jr., Legal Limits on the Use of Chemical and Biological Weapons (Dallas: Southern Methodist University Press, 1970), p. 150; Henri Meyrowitz, "The Law of War in the Vietnamese Conflict," in The Vietnam War and International Law, ed. Richard A. Falk, 4 vols. (Princeton, N.J.: Princeton University Press, 1969-76), 2: 558-59; and Guenter Lewy, America in Vietnam (New York: Oxford University Press, 1978), pp. 257-66.

34. On the role of population displacements in counterinsurgency warfare, see Richard L. Clutterbuck, The Long, Long War: Counterinsurgency in Malaya and Vietnam (New York: Praeger, 1966), pp. 57, 60-68, 87, 89, 179; Paret, French Revolutionary Warfare, pp. 24, 124; Paret and Shy, Guerrillas in the 1960s, pp. 46-47; and Thompson, Defeating Communist Insurgency, pp. 116-17, 121-40.

35. See Chapter 5.

36. See Chapter 3.

37. See Chapter 3.

38. Taubenfeld summarizes the dilemmas as follows:

> Difficulties are clear; rebels are faced by a dilemma. Will they lose if they fight "conventionally," if they are obliged to give up terror, subversion, and secrecy? Yet governments certainly will not observe rules that their opponents ignore. Would a waiver of trials and executions give a free hand to rebels? How does one distinguish a guerrilla from an ordinary bandit? The difficulties as well as the challenge to legal scholars to develop acceptable rules are clear. Even with broader, clearer, more generally known rules, there is no certainty that governments and their internal opponents will, short of the availability of an external policing authority, inevitably be persuaded to abide by restraints in what they consider to be life-and-death issues. Yet the clearer and more universally acknowledged are the constraints, the greater will be the pressure on particular governments and rebels alike to conform.

Taubenfeld, "Applicability of the Laws of War," p. 517.

Baxter, a major figure in the U.S. delegation at Geneva and in the study and development of the law of war generally, was skeptical and conservative in appraising the prospects for an effective Protocol II when he wrote the following in 1974:

> In the light of the widespread noncompliance with the exist-
> ing Geneva Conventions of 1949, one must cautiously ask
> whether the new protocol will simply be a number of new
> provisions adding to the existing bulk of the law or an ef-
> fective instrument for the protection of human rights and
> for the amelioration of the conditions of what is often the
> most savage form of warfare—domestic armed conflict
> within the borders of a state. The new protocol will in the
> end be effective only if states wish to make it so.

Richard R. Baxter, "Ius in Bello Interno: The Present and Future Law," in Law and Civil War in the Modern World, ed. John Norton Moore (Baltimore: Johns Hopkins University Press, 1974), p. 536. See the cautiously hopeful appraisal of Forsythe, "Legal Management," pp. 293-95.

NOTES TO CHAPTER 9

1. Raymond Aron, The Century of Total War (Garden City, N.Y.: Doubleday, 1954), pp. 27-28.
2. See Hans A. Morgenthau, Politics among Nations (New York: Knopf, 1948), and other realist literature cited in Chapter 1, n. 11.
3. For an influential expression of the realist view of politics and force, see Osgood's chapter 1 in Robert E. Osgood and Robert W. Tucker, Force, Order and Justice (Baltimore: Johns Hopkins University Press, 1967), pp. 3-40.
4. See Morgenthau, Politics among Nations; Reinhold Niebuhr, Christianity and Power Politics (New York: Charles Scribner's Sons, 1940); Kenneth W. Thompson, Political Realism and the Crisis of World Politics (Princeton, N.J.: Princeton University Press, 1960); and Ernest W. Lefever, Ethics and United States Foreign Policy (New York: Meridian, 1957).
5. The academic and "think tank" world of national security studies is well demonstrated in the issues and sources summarized in Alden Williams and David W. Tarr, eds., Modules in Security Studies (Lawrence: University Press of Kansas, 1974). See Osgood and Tucker, Force, Order and Justice, pp. 128-37.
6. On containment and its assumptions about the continuing communist threat, see Robert E. Osgood, "The Reappraisal of Limited War," Adelphi Papers, Monograph Studies no. 54 (London: International Institute for Strategic Studies, 1969), pp. 43-45.

7. Thus, I do not share the perspectives of revisionist studies of U.S.-Soviet relations such as William Appleman Williams, The Tragedy of American Diplomacy (New York: Dell, 1962); D. F. Fleming, The Cold War and Its Origins (Garden City, N.Y.: Doubleday, 1961); and Gabriel Kolko, The Politics of War: The World and United States Foreign Policy, 1943-1945 (New York: Random House, 1968).

For critiques of this literature, see Robert W. Tucker, The Radical Left and American Foreign Policy (Baltimore: Johns Hopkins University Press, 1971); Robert James Maddox, The New Left and the Origins of the Cold War (Princeton, N.J.: Princeton University Press, 1973); and Stephen P. Gibert, Soviet Images of America (New York: Crane, Russak, 1977), pp. 16-17.

8. On the domino theory, see Chapter 5, n. 4. Osgood discusses the underlying assumptions about reactions to the Munich aggression/appeasement syndrome in "The Reappraisal of Limited War," pp. 52-53.

9. Some influential views on the evolution of NATO and its policies may be found in Robert E. Osgood, NATO: The Entangling Alliance (Chicago: University of Chicago Press, 1959); Henry A. Kissinger, The Troubled Partnership: A Reappraisal of the Atlantic Alliance (New York: McGraw-Hill, 1965); and André Beaufre, NATO and Europe, trans. Joseph Green (New York: Knopf, 1966).

Despite the official adoption in 1967 of "flexible response" as NATO's strategic policy, growing concern over the obvious high level of destruction entailed either in a conventional or limited nuclear defense of Europe has, in fact, led to an increased reliance on the U.S. strategic deterrent and resistance to any suggestion that it be "decoupled" from NATO's limited defense forces. My point about the original relation between the defense of NATO and the development of limited-war capabilities and policies seems to have lost much if not all of its validity by sometime in the late 1960s. It is at present highly questionable whether a limited-war defense of NATO is possible or even desired by the Europeans. See the useful discussion of this subject in Laurence Martin, "Limited Nuclear War," in Restraints on War: Studies in the Limitation of Armed Conflict, ed. Michael Howard (Oxford, England: Oxford University Press, 1979), pp. 102-21.

10. Michael Walzer, Just and Unjust Wars (New York: Basic, 1977), pp. 32-33.

11. For some of the principal critiques of modern total-war concepts, practices, and mentalities, see Robert Endicott Osgood, Limited War (Chicago: University of Chicago Press, 1957), pp. 3-45; Bernard Brodie, Strategy in the Missile Age (Princeton, N.J.: Princeton University Press, 1959), p. 307; Robert W. Tucker, The Just War (Baltimore: Johns Hopkins University Press, 1960), pp. 21-29; and Henry A. Kissinger, Nuclear Weapons and Foreign Policy (New York: Harper, 1957), pp. 4-5, 86-95. The most fundamental

military critique of total war remains that of B. H. Liddell Hart in Strategy, 2d ed. (New York: Signet, 1967); and idem, The Revolution in Warfare (New Haven, Conn.: Yale University Press, 1947).

12. Some typical reactions against massive retaliation as the principal free-world deterrence and defense posture against the spectrum of possible aggressors are found in Osgood, Limited War, pp. 1, 4-8; Kissinger, Nuclear Weapons, pp. 11-13; and Brodie, Strategy in the Missile Age, pp. 305-9; and Seymour J. Deitchman, Limited War and American Defense Policy (Cambridge, Mass.: MIT Press, 1964), pp. 1-9.

13. On the emerging relationship of strategic deterrence and limited war, see Kissinger, Nuclear Weapons, pp. 201-2.

14. The influence of the Korean War on limited-war theory is authoritatively examined in Osgood, Limited War, pp. 163-233; and idem, Limited War Revisited (Boulder, Colo.: Westview, 1979), p. 6.

15. See MacArthur's views discussed in Chapter 10, below, pp. 239-41.

16. See Matthew B. Ridgway, Soldier: The Memoirs of Matthew B. Ridgway (New York: Harper, 1956); Maxwell D. Taylor, The Uncertain Trumpet (New York: Harper, 1959); and James M. Gavin, War and Peace in the Space Age (New York: Harper, 1958).

17. On the emergence of counterinsurgency as a leading form of limited war, see Osgood, Limited War Revisited, pp. 7, 24-27. For a representative sample of the counterinsurgency literature, see Chapter 6, n. 1-4. Robert McClintock includes "wars of national liberation" and "civil wars" in his definition of limited war in The Meaning of Limited War (Boston: Houghton Mifflin, 1967), pp. 5-12.

18. See John Courtney Murray, "Theology and Modern War," in Morality and Modern Warfare, ed. William J. Nagle (Baltimore: Helicon, 1960), pp. 69-91, and in the other versions and reprintings cited in Chapter 1, n. 4. Father Murray's assumptions about the communist threat that form the basis for his just-war/limited-war writings are found in his contribution to Foreign Policy and the Free Society (New York: Oceana, 1958), pp. 21-49. A revised version is reproduced as "Doctrine and Policy in Communist Imperialism, the Problem of Security and Risk," in We Hold These Truths, ed. John Courtney Murray (New York: Sheed and Ward, 1960), pp. 221-47.

See Paul Ramsey, War and the Christian Conscience: How Shall Modern War Be Conducted Justly? (Durham, N.C.: Duke University Press, 1961); idem, The Just War: Force and Political Responsibility (New York: Charles Scribner's Sons, 1968); Thomas E. Murray, Nuclear Policy for War and Peace (New York: World, 1960); William V. O'Brien, "Legitimate Military Necessity in Nuclear War," World Polity 2 (1960): 35-120; and idem, "Nuclear Warfare and the Law of Nations," in Morality and Modern Warfare, ed. William J. Nagle (Baltimore: Helicon, 1960), pp. 126-49.

19. The discussion of limited-war guidelines is based on the following cross section of the literature: Osgood, Limited War; idem, Limited War Revisited; Osgood and Tucker, Force, Order and Justice; Kissinger, Nuclear Weapons; Brodie, Strategy in the Missile Age; idem, War and Politics (New York: Macmillan, 1973); Morton H. Halperin, Limited War in the Nuclear Age (New York: John Wiley & Sons, 1963); Deitchman, Limited War; John C. Garnett, "Limited 'Conventional' War in the Nuclear Age," in Restraints on War: Studies in the Limitation of Armed Conflict, ed. Michael Howard (Oxford, England: Oxford University Press, 1979), pp. 79-102; and McClintock, The Meaning of Limited War.

20. The primacy of politics over the military instrument and of political over military decision makers is stressed in Osgood, Limited War, pp. 13-18, 23-24; idem, Limited War Revisited, pp. 2-3, 9-11; Osgood and Tucker, Force, Order and Justice, pp. 70-78, 190-91; Kissinger, Nuclear Weapons, pp. 139-41; Deitchman, Limited War; and McClintock, The Meaning of Limited War, pp. 1, 5.

21. On limited ends as a critical component of limited war, see Osgood, Limited War, pp. 24, 237-41; idem, Limited War Revisited, p. 3; Kissinger, Nuclear Weapons, pp. 140-41, 169; Deitchman, Limited War, p. 14; Brodie, Strategy in the Missile Age, pp. 312-13; and McClintock, The Meaning of Limited War, pp. 1, 4.

22. The principle of economy of force is examined in light of its treatment in past U.S. Army publications in William V. Murry, "Clausewitz and Limited Nuclear War," Military Review, 1975, pp. 15-28. It should be noted that Murry's article is based on the then existing field manual, FM 100-5, Operations of Armed Forces in the Field (Washington, D.C.: Department of the Army, 1968). Subsequently the Department of the Army issued FM 110-5, Operations (Washington, D.C.: Department of the Army, July 1, 1976). The 1976 FM 110-5 does not discuss the principles of war in the fashion of the preceding version of the manual. It is assumed here that the principles discussed by Murry remain valid as a basis for the discussions of use of the military instrument.

23. Osgood, Limited War, p. 18.

24. Myres S. McDougal and Florentino P. Feliciano, Law and Minimum World Public Order (New Haven, Conn.: Yale University Press, 1961), p. 36, referring in this connection to my "Legitimate Military Necessity," pp. 55-57. See generally the excellent discussion of McDougal and Feliciano, Law and Minimum World Public Order, pp. 33-36.

25. U.S., Department of the Air Force, International Law—The Conduct of Armed Conflict and Air Operations, 19 November 1976, AFP 110-31 (Washington, D.C.: Department of the Air Force, 1976), 1-6 [hereafter cited as AFP 110-31].

26. Ibid., 5-8, 5-10, 5-11.

27. U.S., Department of the Army, The Army, FM 110-1 (Washington, D.C.: Department of the Army, September 29, 1978), p. 15.

28. FM 100-5 (1968), 5-5, 5-6.

LTC Ed Burke, one of my graduate students, has brought to my attention the treatment of economy of force in the U.S. Army Infantry School in 1964, just before the escalation of the Vietnam War. Officers at the school were taught the following:

> a. Economy of force is the measured allocation of combat power to the primary task as well as secondary tasks. It connotes the application of force necessary to accomplish the mission and not the application of as little force as possible. To concentrate superior force in the main effort, minimum necessary force may be used elsewhere. This requires a careful evaluation, particularly where secondary efforts contribute heavily to the main effort. [Emphasis added]

United States Army Infantry School, Tactical Operations Handbook (Fort Benning, Ga.: U.S. Army Infantry School, September 1964), pp. 1-101.

29. See notes 25 and 26 above.

30. U.S., Department of the Air Force, Functions and Basic Doctrine of the United States Air Force, 14 February 1979, AFM 1-1 (Washington, D.C.: Department of the Air Force, 1979), 5-5.

31. Michael Howard, "Temperamenta Belli: Can War Be Controlled?" in Restraints on War: Studies in the Limitation of Armed Conflict, ed. Michael Howard (Oxford, England: Oxford University Press, 1979).

32. On the concept of voluntary rules of conflict in limited war, see Osgood, Limited War, pp. 241-43, 248-50; Kissinger, Nuclear Weapons, pp. 140-41; Brodie, Strategy in the Missile Age, pp. 309-12; Deitchman, Limited War, p. 14.

33. On interbelligerent communication and bargaining, see generally Thomas C. Schelling, The Strategy of Conflict (New York: Oxford University Press, 1963); idem, Arms and Influence (New Haven, Conn.: Yale University Press, 1966); and Halperin, Limited War in the Nuclear Age, pp. 30-35.

34. On self-imposed, unilateral rules of conflict, sometimes arising from considerations other than a principled determination to limit a war, see Halperin's comments in Limited War in the Nuclear Age, pp. 15, 31, 55-56. The proposition that war should be limited by voluntary guidelines and thresholds to prevent escalation to total war, conventional or nuclear, is discussed in Osgood, Limited War, pp. 241-43, 248-50.

35. Avoidance of superpower confrontation as a ground rule of limited war is discussed in Halperin, Limited War in the Nuclear Age, pp. 36-37 and Brodie, War and Politics, pp. 406-7, 425-26, 428.

Some of the most authoritative commentaries reserve the term limited war for wars in which the nuclear superpowers are directly or indirectly involved, consigning wars in which they are not involved to the category of local wars. See Brodie, Strategy in the Missile Age, pp. 309-10; Osgood, "The Reappraisal of Limited War," p. 41; Garnett, "Limited 'Conventional' War," pp. 80-82; and Osgood, Limited War Revisited, pp. 3, 7, 13-24.

I prefer to apply the term limited war across the board to all wars. Where a guideline such as avoidance of superpower confrontation is irrelevant, it can be discarded without prejudice to the remaining principal components of the limited-war concept and any particular limited-war guidelines that are appropriate.

36. Proposals for either the exclusion of nuclear weapons altogether or for some limited nuclear war threshold are offered in Kissinger's chapter, "The Problems of Limited Nuclear War," in Nuclear Weapons, pp. 174-202; Osgood, Limited War, pp. 251-59; Brodie, Strategy in the Missile Age, pp. 310-11, 321-27; idem, War and Politics, pp. 375-432; Deitchman, Limited War, pp. 43-52; and McClintock, The Meaning of Limited War, p. 4.

37. On the problems of maintaining nuclear thresholds, see Halperin, Limited War in the Nuclear Age, pp. 58-75; and Martin, "Limited Nuclear War," pp. 103-22. See Chapter 6. Note that there may be rules of conflict regarding conventional weapons and targets. See Halperin, Limited War in the Nuclear Age, pp. 28, 35-36.

38. Geographic limits in war are discussed in Osgood, Limited War, pp. 243-48; Kissinger, Nuclear Weapons, p. 139; Halperin, Limited War in the Nuclear Age, pp. 28, 34-37; and Brodie, War and Politics, pp. 66-68. Schelling puts priority on confinement of conflict outside the homelands of the major adversaries as an "ultimate threshold" in Arms and Influence, p. 159.

39. The United States converted the Korean War into a UN peace-keeping operation with numerous UN members as cobelligerents to varying degrees. See Chapters 4 and 10.

The Cuban Missile Crisis and the 1965 Dominican intervention were held out as Organization of American States (OAS) enforcement actions in which many Latin American states participated. On the efforts to collectivize the Vietnam War, see Chapter 11. Curiously, this recurring feature of limited war, so important in practice, is not mentioned in the principal works consulted on the subject.

40. Limited mobilization and its impact on economy of force are discussed in Osgood, Limited War, pp. 241-43; Brodie, Strategy in the Missile Age, pp. 310-11; and Halperin, Limited War in the Nuclear Age, pp. 6-7.

41. On restraint in the use of the psychological instrument, see Osgood, Limited War, pp. 92, 279-84; Kissinger, Nuclear Weapons, pp. 167-72; and Halperin, Limited War in the Nuclear Age, pp. 24-25.

42. See Brodie's comments on fight-and-negotiate strategies in War and Politics, pp. 91-106. See generally Schelling, The Strategy of Conflict; and idem, Arms and Influence.

43. The use of international organizations and ad hoc international bodies was conspicuous in the Korean War. See Chapters 4 and 10. Such use was considerably curtailed in the Vietnam War. See Chapter 11. However, international organizations have played an important role in Middle East and other limited wars (for example, the Yom Kippur War). See Chapter 12.

Once again, as in the case of the frequent efforts to collectivize limited wars, the standard limited-war literature has not recognized the importance of international organizations in keeping wars limited and in war termination. The exception is McClintock, a retired foreign service officer, who observes that "another characteristic of twentieth-century limited war is the fact that international organization has played an important role, either in settling these armed conflicts or as serving as a useful palliative and sally port for belligerents in need of saving face." McClintock, The Meaning of Limited War, p. 201.

44. The importance of flexible response capabilities and policies in limited war is stressed in Osgood, Limited War, pp. 235-37, 249-50; Kissinger, Nuclear Weapons, pp. 155-67; Deitchman, Limited War; and Brodie, Strategy in the Missile Age, pp. 331-42, 396.

NOTES TO CHAPTER 10

1. The concept of "local wars" is discussed in Morton H. Halperin, Limited War in the Nuclear Age (New York: John Wiley & Sons, 1963), pp. 1-3; and Robert Endicott Osgood, Limited War Revisited (Boulder, Colo.: Westview, 1979), pp. 3-11.

2. The precedental role of the Korean War is emphasized in Robert Endicott Osgood, Limited War (Chicago: University of Chicago Press, 1957), pp. 163-93; and Halperin, Limited War in the Nuclear Age, pp. 19-57.

3. On the Great Debate over Truman's relief of MacArthur and the ends and means of the U.S. policies in Korea, see Osgood, Limited War, pp. 173-78; U.S., Congress, Joint Senate Committee on Armed Services and Foreign Relations, Hearings, Military Situation in the Far East, 82d Cong., 1st sess., 1951 [hereafter cited as MacArthur Hearings]; David Rees, Korea: The Limited War (New York: St. Martin's Press, 1964), pp. 196-229, 264-85; Matthew B. Ridgway, The Korean War (Garden City, N.Y.: Doubleday, 1967), pp. 141-83.

4. See Osgood's account of MacArthur's rejection of political primacy in time of war in Limited War, p. 177.

5. For the JCS's perspectives on the Korean War and the controversies with MacArthur, see J. Lawton Collins, War in Peacetime (Boston: Houghton Mifflin, 1969).

6. On the concern to avoid war with the Soviet Union during the Korean War, see Harry S. Truman, Memoirs, 2 vols. (Garden City, N.Y.: Doubleday, 1955), 2: 333-34; and Osgood, Limited War, p. 169.

7. The avoidance of expansion of the Korean War into China is discussed in Osgood, Limited War, p. 175. He quotes General Bradley's famous dictum that such an expansion, "would involve us in the wrong war, at the wrong place, at the wrong time, and with the wrong enemy," citing the MacArthur Hearings, n. 3, pp. 731-32.

8. The influence of the U.S. concern that the Korean War might have been a communist feint requiring preparedness for an attack in Europe or elsewhere is evaluated in Halperin, Limited War in the Nuclear Age, pp. 44-45, 57; and Osgood, Limited War, pp. 169-70.

9. On political support for MacArthur and criticism of Korean-style limited war, see Osgood's assessment in Limited War, pp. 189-93; and Halperin, Limited War in the Nuclear Age, pp. 46-47.

10. For accounts of the contrast between MacArthur's protestations of subordination and loyalty and his independent and rebellious conduct see Rees, Korea, pp. 66-76, 116-22, 160-61, 174-77, 184, 188-89, 205-13; and Collins, War in Peacetime, pp. 268-87.

11. For discussion of the complications of political-military decision making arising from the collective character of the UN force in Korea, see Osgood, Limited War, pp. 170, 186-87; Rees, Korea, pp. 32-35; Halperin, Limited War in the Nuclear Age, p. 48 (regarding possible use of nuclear weapons); and Adam Ulam, The Rivals: America and Russia since World War II (New York: Viking, 1971), pp. 184-85.

12. On the discontinuation of major UN-force military pressure after November 1951 and the consequent political stalemate, see Rees, Korea, pp. 297-308; Bernard Brodie, Strategy in the Missile Age (Princeton, N.J.: Princeton University Press, 1959), p. 318; and Henry A. Kissinger, Nuclear Weapons and Foreign Policy (New York: Harper, 1957), pp. 50-51.

13. The original goals of the United States and the United Nations are authoritatively expressed in Truman, Memoirs, 2: 333-34. See the authorities cited in Chapter 4, n. 14; Osgood, Limited War, pp. 165-66; and Halperin, Limited War in the Nuclear Age, pp. 39-42.

14. The expansion of U.S./UN war aims to include liberation of North Korea and consequent unification of all of Korea is described in Osgood, Limited War, pp. 171-73; and Rees, Korea, pp. 98-104, 107-9.

15. The final objective was to hold a defensible line near or above the 38th parallel. See Osgood, Limited War, p. 173; and Rees, Korea, p. 257.

16. The interrelation between limited ends and limited available military assets in the Korean War is stressed in Osgood, Limited War, p. 170; and Halperin, Limited War in the Nuclear Age, p. 43.

17. The unsuccessful efforts of the U.S./UN side to reassure the PRC that a drive to the Yalu was not intended to threaten China and of the Red Chinese to convey their view of such a drive as a casus belli are discussed in Osgood, Limited War, pp. 171-72; Halperin, Limited War in the Nuclear Age, pp. 50-53; Allen S. Whiting, China Crosses the Yalu: The Decision to Enter the Korean War (New York: Macmillan, 1960), pp. 151-52, 159; Schelling, Arms and Influence, pp. 54-55; and Ulam, The Rivals, pp. 178-82.

18. The U.S./UN abstention from attacks across the Yalu and general Communist abstention from bombing of targets in South Korea are discussed in Halperin, Limited War in the Nuclear Age, pp. 53-55; Schelling, Arms and Influence, pp. 31, 129-30, 134-35; and Robert McClintock, The Meaning of Limited War (Boston: Houghton Mifflin, 1967), p. 48.

19. Target policies regarding the Suiho Dam hydroelectric complex are summarized in Rees, Korea, pp. 378-79; and Halperin, Limited War in the Nuclear Age, p. 53.

20. On U.S. abstention from bombing targets near the Soviet border, see Rees, Korea, pp. 366, 380; and Halperin, Limited War in the Nuclear Age, p. 53.

21. The still uncertain nature of the relationship between the Soviet and North Korean war policies is examined in Whiting, China Crosses the Yalu, p. 37; Halperin, Limited War in the Nuclear Age, pp. 10, 40-41; McClintock, The Meaning of Limited War, p. 35; and Ulam, The Rivals, pp. 170-73.

22. Truman's intentions and policies regarding avoidance of superpower confrontation in the Korean War are described in his Memoirs, 2: 333-34, 369.

23. The reasons for the nonuse of nuclear weapons in the Korean War are explained in Brodie, Strategy in the Missile Age, pp. 319-21, 410-11; and Halperin, Limited War in the Nuclear Age, pp. 47-50. The main reason, according to General Ridgway, was that their use would have been immoral. See Ridgway, The Korean War, pp. 76, 247.

24. This account of the role of nuclear threats in the termination of the Korean War is based on Dwight D. Eisenhower, Mandate for Change, 1953-1956 (Garden City, N.Y.: Doubleday, 1963), p. 181; Harold C. Hinton, Communist China in World Politics (New York: Houghton Mifflin, 1966), p. 222; and Rees, Korea, pp. 416-20.

25. For an account of the Declaration of Sixteen pledging defense of South Korea, see Rees, Korea, p. 436.

26. The geographic limitation of the Korean War is emphasized in Osgood, Limited War, pp. 174-76; Halperin, Limited War in the Nuclear Age, pp. 31, 56, 129-31, 134-35, 137-38, 155; and McClintock, The Meaning of Limited War, pp. 48-49.

27. On the international-law and UN aspects of the Korean War, see Myres S. McDougal and Florentino P. Feliciano, Law and Minimum World Public Order (New Haven, Conn.: Yale University Press, 1961), pp. 18, 20, 204-5, 255-56; Julius Stone, Legal Controls of International Conflict (New York: Rinehart, 1959), pp. 231-37; Hans Kelsen, Principles of International Law, ed. Robert W. Tucker, 2d rev. ed. (New York: Holt, Rinehart and Winston, 1966), pp. 42 (n. 34), 46-47 (n. 36), 55 (n. 45), 90; and Leland M. Goodrich, Korea: A Study of U.S. Policy in the United Nations (New York: Council on Foreign Relations, 1956).

28. The domestic constraints on U.S. mobilization in the Korean War are analyzed in Osgood, Limited War, pp. 189-93; and Halperin, Limited War in the Nuclear Age, pp. 45-47.

29. The difficulties of sustaining support for the U.S./UN "police action" in Korea are outlined in Osgood, Limited War, pp. 189-93; Halperin, Limited War in the Nuclear Age, pp. 45-47; and Rees, Korea, pp. 398-99. Ironically, the Red Chinese used the Korean War years as a period of intense and vehement propaganda against the United States and the West. See Rees, Korea, pp. 306-9.

30. The fighting in Korea from November 1951 to July 1953 is described by Rees, Korea, pp. 301-3, 408-14; and Robert Leckie, Conflict: The History of the Korean War, 1950-1953 (New York: Putnam's Sons, 1962), pp. 314-400. For a sample of the nature of the fighting during the fight-and-negotiate period, see S. L. A. Marshall, Pork Chop Hill (New York: William Morrow, 1956). See General Ridgway's characterization of the fighting in The Korean War, pp. 195-96, 203, 217-20, 222-25.

31. The difficulties engendered by Communist use of PWs as continuing instruments of policy are described in Rees, Korea, pp. 322-24; and Ridgway, The Korean War, pp. 205-16.

32. See Chapter 3.

33. See Chapter 3.

34. The tortured path of negotiations over the fate of Communist PWs in UN hands is described in Rees, Korea, pp. 311-27, 414-20; and C. Turner Joy, Negotiating while Fighting: The Diary of Admiral C. Turner Joy at the Korean Armistice Conference, ed. Allan E. Goodman (Stanford, Calif.: Hoover Institution Press, 1978).

35. On alleged nuclear threats against the PRC, see n. 24 above.

36. This account is based on Rees, Korea, pp. 416-25.

37. For typical reflections on the lesson of the Korean War that flexible response capabilities are needed to deter and fight limited wars, see Osgood, Limited War, pp. 248-84; Kissinger, Nuclear Weapons, pp. 27-28, 44, 54-61, 135-36, 144-45; and Halperin, Limited War in the Nuclear Age, pp. 113-31.

NOTES TO CHAPTER 11

1. See Chapter 5.
2. On the political emphasis in target selection for bombing North Vietnam, see Guenter Lewy, America in Vietnam (New York: Oxford University Press, 1978), pp. 377-96. See generally the sources cited in Chapter 5, n. 36.

Osgood analyzes "incremental expansion of the war" in terms of "the theory of limited war, which called for the restricted, flexible, controlled, proportionate use of force in order to persuade the adversary to terminate the war," in Robert E. Osgood, Limited War Revisited (Boulder, Colo.: Westview, 1979), p. 43.

3. Retrospective pessimism regarding the possibilities for victory in Vietnam is expressed, for example, in Lewy, America in Vietnam, pp. 430-41; Osgood, Limited War Revisited, pp. 37-48; and Leslie H. Gelb and Richard K. Betts, The Irony of Vietnam: The System Worked (Washington, D.C.: Brookings Institution, 1979).

4. The military advantages seized by the Communists during bombing pauses are described in Lyndon Baines Johnson, The Vantage Point (New York: Holt, Rinehart and Winston, 1971), pp. 235-36, 239-40, 381-82; and Lewy, America in Vietnam, pp. 338-89.

5. See President Johnson's account of events after his March 31, 1968, speech in Vantage Point, pp. 493-531; and Kissinger's recapitulation of these events in Henry A. Kissinger, White House Years (Boston: Little, Brown, 1979), p. 237.

6. See William C. Westmoreland's criticism of the loss of military opportunities after Tet in A Soldier Reports (Garden City, N.Y.: Doubleday, 1976), pp. 332-34, 410.

7. U.S. policy regarding limitation of the war to South Vietnam is discussed in Johnson, Vantage Point, pp. 125, 257; Morton H. Halperin, "The Lessons Nixon Learned," in The Vietnam Legacy, ed. Anthony Lake (New York: New York University Press, 1976), pp. 411-12.

8. Johnson's resolution to avoid war with the Soviet Union and the PRC is emphasized in Johnson, Vantage Point, pp. 125, 131, 369; Osgood, Limited War Revisited, pp. 43, 46; Lewy, America in Vietnam, pp. 392-94; and Gelb and Betts, The Irony of Vietnam, pp. 136-37, 264-65, 269-70. However, Kissinger explains Nixon's willingness

to risk injury to Soviet ships in attacks on Haiphong in April 1972 in White House Years, pp. 1121-22.

9. On U.S. policies toward Cambodia and Laos during the Nixon administration, see Kissinger's account in White House Years, pp. 239-54. These policies are severely criticized in William Shawcross, Sideshow: Kissinger, Nixon and the Destruction of Cambodia (New York: Simon and Schuster, 1979).

10. See the discussion of U.S. legal arguments in Chapter 5. On the issue of the credibility of U.S. commitments, see Johnson, Vantage Point, pp. 147-48; Gelb and Betts, The Irony of Vietnam, pp. 106, 187-90, (on the domino theory) 197-200; David M. Abshire, "Lessons of Vietnam: Proportionality and Credibility," in The Vietnam Legacy, ed. Anthony Lake (New York: New York University Press, 1976), pp. 147-48.

11. In retrospect, the generous allocation of military assets to the Vietnam War had a negative effect on the maintenance and development of the U.S. strategic deterrence forces inadequately camouflaged by SALT I and on NATO defenses, which fell further behind Warsaw Pact capabilities. See John M. Collins, American and Soviet Military Trends since the Cuban Missile Crisis (Washington, D.C.: The Center for Strategic and International Studies, Georgetown University, 1978), pp. 174, 337-40.

12. Morton H. Halperin emphasizes that the Korean War was a spontaneous limited war fought without a preconceived limited-war theory in Limited War in the Nuclear Age (New York: John Wiley & Sons, 1963), p. 44.

13. Thomas C. Schelling's Strategy of Conflict (New York: Oxford University Press, 1963) and Arms and Influence (New Haven, Conn.: Yale University Press, 1966) coincided with the increased U.S. involvement in Vietnam, and it may be assumed that these and similar works were well known to many of the "conflict managers" of the Kennedy and Johnson administrations.

14. On the Tonkin Gulf incidents, see Johnson, Vantage Point, pp. 112-18, 120; Lewy, America in Vietnam, pp. 32-36; and Gelb and Betts, The Irony of Vietnam, pp. 100-4.

The Communist attacks on U.S. bases and personnel at Pleiku and elsewhere are described in Johnson, Vantage Point, pp. 124-25, 129; Lewy, America in Vietnam, p. 38; and Gelb and Betts, The Irony of Vietnam, pp. 105, 117-18.

15. U.S. planning for escalatory moves, particularly bombing North Vietnam, prior to the February 1965 Communist attacks is described in Johnson, Vantage Point, p. 128; Lewy, America in Vietnam, pp. 29-31; and Gelb and Betts, The Irony of Vietnam, pp. 99-100, 105, 109-12, 116. Gelb and Betts comment: "Months later, when the United States began bombing North Vietnam in retaliation

for a Vietcong attack on American installations at Pleiku, McGeorge
Bundy would acknowledge the extent to which the incident served as
a pretext for escalation by saying, 'Pleikus are streetcars'; such incidents could be relied on to happen regularly, offering opportunities
to implement decisions already contemplated." The Irony of Vietnam,
p. 105.

    16. On the decision at the outset of the 1965 U.S. escalation to
follow a policy of "sustained reprisals," as recommended by Mc-
George Bundy and civilian officials, rather than an "intensive program
of attacks from the outset," as favored by the Joint Chiefs, see Johnson, Vantage Point, pp. 127-28, 132. On the first bombing pause
(May 12, 1965), see ibid., pp. 136-37, 233. On subsequent pauses
and debates thereon, see ibid, pp. 233-41, 266-69, 365-69, 372-
78, 397-415. For a summary of bombing pauses over North Vietnam
see ibid., p. 578. See Lewy, America in Vietnam, p. 376; and Gelb
and Betts, The Irony of Vietnam, pp. 139-40, 153, 156, 164, 169-70,
177.

    For General Westmoreland's perspectives on the bombing in
terms of "graduated response," see A Soldier Reports, pp. 112-18.
Westmoreland has some caustic words about bombing pauses, while
expressing skepticism about the extent to which strategic bombing of
North Vietnam could make a decisive difference, ibid., pp. 120,
214, 312, 318, 357, 359, 360, 384-85. Summing up his attitude
toward bombing as coercive diplomacy, Westmoreland says, "It was
all a matter of signals, said the clever civilian theorists in Washington. We won't bomb the SAM sites, which signals the North Vietnamese not to use them. Had it not been so serious, it would have
been amusing." Ibid., p. 120. He was referring, presumably, to
approaches such as Schelling's discussion of implicit and explicit political bargaining in Arms and Influence, pp. 141-51. For President
Johnson's summary reflections on his political-military decisions,
see Vantage Point, p. 531.

    17. On U.S. abstention from attacks on vital North Vietnamese
supply areas near the PRC, see Lewy, America in Vietnam, pp. 392-
94.

    President Johnson mentions decisions in the spring of 1967 that
rejected recommendations to mine Haiphong Harbor and led to curtailment of the bombing of Haiphong and other areas important to North
Vietnamese resupply. However, he emphasizes the costs of such attacks rather than the danger of extending the war. See Vantage Point,
p. 367. Gelb and Betts recall that, "There were other instances after 1966 when bombing and diplomacy seemed disjointed. One was
when Alexsei Kosygin's visit to the United Nations in June 1967 coincided with a U.S. raid on Haiphong that damaged the Soviet ship
Turkestan." See The Irony of Vietnam, pp. 153-54. See generally
ibid., pp. 158, 168, 218.

On the limitation of the U.S. naval blockade operations in South Vietnamese waters, see D. P. O'Connell, "Limited War at Sea since 1945," in Restraints on War: Studies in the Limitation of Armed Conflict, ed. Michael Howard (Oxford, England: Oxford University Press, 1979), pp. 127-29.

18. For the circumstances of the mining of Haiphong in May 1972, see Elmo R. Zumwalt, Jr., On Watch: A Memoir (New York: Quadrangle/New York Times Book Co., 1976), pp. 384-89; and Kissinger, White House Years, pp. 1165-1201.

19. Westmoreland, A Soldier Reports, p. 338. See Osgood, Limited War Revisited, p. 45.

20. For assessments of the Cambodian incursion, see the official view of Kissinger, White House Years, pp. 484-520. See the critical view of Shawcross, Sideshow, pp. 128-76.

21. See Chapters 2, 4, and 5.

22. See William V. O'Brien, U.S. Military Intervention: Law and Morality, Washington Papers, no. 68 (Beverly Hills, Calif.: Sage/Center for Strategic and International Studies, Georgetown University, 1979), pp. 51-56.

23. The role of allied forces supplementing the ARVN/U.S. effort is described in Johnson, Vantage Point, p. 246; Westmoreland, A Soldier Reports, pp. 132-34; and Gelb and Betts, The Irony of Vietnam, pp. 161-62.

24. The complex story of the media's role in the Vietnam War is still incomplete. It is widely agreed that this role was critical, if not decisive, and that the efforts of the media coverage were overwhelmingly negative insofar as understanding and support of the war were concerned. See generally, Lewy, America in Vietnam, pp. 321-23, 433-34. A highly instructive account is given of the 1968 Tet Offensive and its effects on U.S. public opinion and politics, critically affected by media coverage, in Don Oberdorfer, Tet! (Garden City, N.Y.: Doubleday, 1971). The most comprehensive analysis of the role of the media in the Vietnam War is Peter Braestrup, Big Story, How the American Press and Television Reported and Interpreted the Crisis of Tet 1968 in Vietnam and Washington, 2 vols. (Boulder, Colo.: Westview/Freedom House, 1977).

See also Ernest W. Lefever, TV and National Defense: An Analysis of CBS News, 1972-73 (Boston, Va.: The Institute for American Strategy, 1974), pp. 99-131; and David Halberstam, The Powers That Be (New York: Dell, 1979), pp. 616-23, 626-31, 639-51, 656-717, 733-45, 756-65, 789-807. These books, written from quite opposite perspectives, provide useful information and insights concerning the role of the media in the Vietnam War.

25. The frustrations of the Johnson administration's efforts to establish the bases for negotiated settlement of the Vietnam War are

described in Johnson, Vantage Point, pp. 233-41, 249-57, 266-69, 493-531; Chester Cooper, The Lost Crusade (New York: Dodd, Meade, 1970), pp. 284-468; Allan E. Goodman, The Lost Peace (Stanford, Calif.: Hoover Institution Press, 1978), pp. 23-73; and Gelb and Betts, The Irony of Vietnam, pp. 162-67.

26. The decline of U.S. involvement in Vietnam under Nixon and the constraints under which Kissinger tried to negotiate peace before complete U.S. unilateral withdrawal and Communist military ascendancy reduced the options to surrender are described in Kissinger, White House Years, pp. 226-311, 433-521, 968-1048, 1097-1123, 1165-1201, 1301-59, 1360-94, 1395-1470, 1471-76; and Goodman, The Lost Peace, pp. 100-80.

27. The relationship between the defeat of the 1972 Communist spring offensive and their attitude in negotiations is demonstrated in Kissinger, White House Years, pp. 1303, 1305-19; Goodman, The Lost Peace, pp. 121, 143-44; and Lewy, America in Vietnam, pp. 410-15.

28. On Linebacker II and its effects on negotiations, see Kissinger, White House Years, pp. 1448-50, 1452-61; Lewy, America in Vietnam, pp. 410-15; Osgood, Limited War Revisited, p. 45; and Goodman, The Lost Peace, pp. 158-63.

The operation is described in James R. McCarthy and George B. Allison, Linebacker II: A View from the Rock, ed. Robert E. Rayfield, USAF Southeast Asia Monograph Series, vol. 6, monograph 8 (Maxwell AFB, Ala.: Air Power Research Institute, 1979).

29. The collapse of the 1973 Paris Agreement and of the efforts of the International Commission for Control and Supervision (ICCS) to monitor and enforce it is described in Goodman, The Lost Peace, pp. 173-80; and Lewy, America in Vietnam, pp. 202-15.

30. Reflections on alternative emphases in Vietnam on local security and positive civil affairs programs are found in Lewy, America in Vietnam, pp. 437-40; and Osgood, Limited War Revisited, pp. 39-43.

31. Critiques of the U.S./South Vietnamese efforts at revolutionary development are to be found in Lewy, America in Vietnam, pp. 437-40; William Colby and Peter Forbath, Honorable Men (New York: Simon & Schuster, 1978), pp. 285-88; and Robert W. Komer, Bureaucracy Does Its Thing: Institutional Constraints on U.S.-GVN Performance in Vietnam (Santa Monica, Calif.: RAND, 1973).

NOTES TO CHAPTER 12

1. See Walter Laqueur, Confrontation: The Middle East and World Politics (New York: Bantam, 1974), pp. 102-3; Howard M.

Sachar, A History of Israel (New York: Knopf, 1976), p. 754; Chaim
Herzog, The War of Atonement, October 1973 (Boston: Little, Brown,
1975), pp. 452–54; Insight Team of the London Sunday Times, The
Yom Kippur War (Garden City, N.Y.: Doubleday, 1974), pp. 119–
23 [hereafter cited as London Sunday Times]; Zeev Schiff, October
Earthquake: Yom Kippur 1973, trans. Louis Williams (Tel Aviv:
University Publishing Projects, 1974), pp. 40, 42, 99–100; Marvin
Kalb and Bernard Kalb, Kissinger (New York: Dell, 1974), pp. 519–
21; Nadav Safran, Israel the Embattled Ally (Cambridge, Mass.:
Harvard University Press, 1978), p. 285.

    2. See Sachar, A History of Israel, pp. 777–78; Herzog, The
War of Atonement, pp. 227, 238, 241; London Sunday Times, pp.
231–37, 243–46, 324–26; and Schiff, October Earthquake, pp. 215, 220–
21, 237–39, 247, 249–50, 272–75, 282–84. Safran, Israel, pp. 307–8,
discusses Sharon's initiatives and clashes with military superiors.
On the controverted efforts to capture Suez City after the collapse of
the first ceasefire, see Sachar, A History of Israel, p. 781; Herzog,
The War of Atonement, pp. 249–50; Schiff, October Earthquake, p.
288; Laqueur, Confrontation, p. 113; and Safran, Israel, p. 310. On
Kissinger's objections to postceasefire "land grabs," see London
Sunday Times, p. 401.

    3. On Egypt's goals see Anwar el Sadat, In Search of Identity
(New York: Harper & Row, 1978), p. 244; Mohamed Heikal, The
Road to Ramadan (New York: Quadrangle/New York Times Book Co.,
1975); Hassan El Badri, Taha El Magdoub, and Mohammed Dia El
Din Zohdy, The Ramadan War, 1973 (New York: Hippocrene Books,
1974), pp. 15–27; Lawrence L. Whetten, The Canal War: Four-Power
Conflict in the Middle East (Cambridge, Mass.: MIT Press, 1974),
pp. 233–37; Laqueur, Confrontation, pp. 104, 127, 187; Sachar, A
History of Israel, pp. 748, 750; Herzog, The War of Atonement,
pp. 25, 27, 37, 233; London Sunday Times, pp. 62, 88–89; Schiff,
October Earthquake, p. 7; and Safran, Israel, pp. 279–80, 479.

    4. The limited character of Egypt's goals is a recurring theme
both in Sadat's In Search of Identity and Heikal's The Road to Ramadan. See Sachar, A History of Israel, p. 748; London Sunday Times,
p. 302; Laqueur, Confrontation, pp. 123, 196; and Herzog, The War
of Atonement, p. 75.

    5. Israel's goals are authoritatively expressed by Herzog in
The War of Atonement, pp. 128–29.

    6. See ibid., pp. 251–52; Schiff, October Earthquake, p. 248;
and Safran, Israel, p. 309.

    7. Sachar, A History of Israel, p. 765. See Laqueur, Con-
frontation, pp. 123–24.

    8. On the Soviet presence in and assistance to Egypt, see
Sachar, A History of Israel, pp. 747, 749; and Laqueur, Confronta-

tion, pp. 21-22. On the Soviet presence in and assistance to Syria, see Sachar, A History of Israel, p. 74. See generally Galia Golan, Yom Kippur and After: The Soviet Union and the Middle East Crisis (Cambridge: At the University Press, 1977); Yaacov Ro'i, From Encroachment to Involvement: A Documentary Study of Soviet Policy in the Middle East (New York: Wiley, 1974); and idem, ed., The Limits to Power: Soviet Policy in the Middle East (New York: St. Martin's, 1979).

9. See Laqueur, Confrontation, pp. 81-83, 85, 190-93; Sachar, A History of Israel, p. 768; and Kalb and Kalb, Kissinger, pp. 528, 531.

10. See Laqueur, Confrontation, p. 85; Sachar, A History of Israel, p. 768; London Sunday Times, pp. 276-77; and Kalb and Kalb, Kissinger, pp. 513-23.

11. On the alerting of Soviet airborne divisions for Middle East service, see Laqueur, Confrontation, p. 200; London Sunday Times, pp. 409-10; Kalb and Kalb, Kissinger, pp. 532, 535; Elmo R. Zumwalt, Jr., On Watch: A Memoir (New York: Quadrangle/New York Times Book , 1976), p. 439; and John L. Scherer, "Soviet and American Behavior during the Yom Kippur War," World Affairs 141 (1978): 14-15.

12. On the Soviet fleet buildup in the Mediterranean, see Zumwalt, On Watch, pp. 439, 446-48; and the London Sunday Times, p. 409.

13. On Kosygin's initiative in Egypt, see Sachar, A History of Israel, pp. 778-79; and the London Sunday Times, pp. 410, 417-18.

14. On Soviet threats and Kissinger's hurried trip to Moscow, see Sachar, A History of Israel, pp. 779-80; London Sunday Times, pp. 372-74, 377-79; and Kalb and Kalb, Kissinger, pp. 543-49.

15. Soviet charges of Israeli violations of the first ceasefire and threats of intervention are described in Laqueur, Confrontation, p. 198; Sachar, A History of Israel, pp. 781-83; and Safran, Israel, pp. 492-93.

16. Quoted from Sachar, A History of Israel, p. 783. See Laqueur, Confrontation, pp. 200-1; London Sunday Times, pp. 404-7; Zumwalt, On Watch, p. 445; and Safran, Israel, pp. 493-94.

17. On U.S. failure to condemn the Egyptian attack and general diplomatic posture; see Sachar, A History of Israel, pp. 767, 769; and Laqueur, Confrontation, pp. 166-67.

18. U.S. responses to Israeli appeals for wartime aid are described in Sachar, A History of Israel, pp. 769-70; Safran, Israel, pp. 481-83; and Kalb and Kalb, Kissinger, pp. 524-40.

19. The U.S. alert is described in Laqueur, Confrontation, p. 199; Sachar, A History of Israel, pp. 783-84; London Sunday Times, pp. 407-15; Zumwalt, On Watch, p. 443; Kalb and Kalb, Kissinger, pp. 554-55; and Safran, Israel, p. 494.

On Soviet alerts and deployment of air- and sealifts, see Kalb and Kalb, Kissinger, pp. 551-52; London Sunday Times, pp. 409-10; and Zumwalt, On Watch, pp. 439, 447.

Concern over possible Soviet introduction of nuclear weapons into Egypt, apparently developed after the U.S. alert decision, is discussed in Kalb and Kalb, Kissinger, p. 557; London Sunday Times, pp. 411-13; Safran, Israel, pp. 494-95; and Whetten, The Canal War, pp. 292-93.

20. On U.S. marshaling of forces during the alert as a signal to the Soviet Union, see Zumwalt, On Watch, p. 446; Sachar, A History of Israel, p. 784; and Kalb and Kalb, Kissinger, p. 555.

21. On the possibilities of Soviet direct military intervention had the second ceasefire not held, see Laqueur, Confrontation, pp. 201-3; Kalb and Kalb, Kissinger, pp. 561-63; Zumwalt, On Watch, p. 448; London Sunday Times, pp. 417-19; Scherer, "Soviet and American Behavior," pp. 3-19.

22. In his account of the 1973 war, Safran discusses, in context of the bitter dispute over U.S. failure to respond promptly to Israel's urgent pleas for resupply, Israel's nuclear capability. Safran states that

> Kissinger, along with a few people at the top government echelons, had long known that Israel possessed a very short nuclear option which it held as a weapon of last resort, but he had not dwelt much on the issue because of the remoteness of the contingency that would make it relevant. Suddenly, on October 12, 1973, the scenario of an Israel feeling on the verge of destruction resorting in despair to nuclear weapons, hitherto so hypothetical, assumed a grim actuality. The secretary of state, whose policy had been inspired by the desire to preserve détente and by fear of the chaotic consequences of a total Israeli victory, did not need much pondering to imagine the catastrophic consequences of Israel's taking this road.

See Israel, p. 483.

Safran also reports that

> Meir herself confessed shortly after the war that there was a moment in the course of it when she, too, had feared that Israel might be overwhelmed and destroyed. It is most probable that the time in question was late on October 8th, and it is perfectly plausible to assume (as Time magazine reported years later) that preparations to turn the nuclear option of Israel into usable nuclear weapons were initiated at that time.

Ibid., pp. 488-89. On possible Israeli nuclear deterrence, see Steven J. Rosen, "A Stable System of Mutual Deterrence in the Arab-Israeli Conflict," American Political Science Review 71 (1977): 1367-83.

23. On the Egyptian claims, see generally Sadat, In Search of Identity; Heikal, The Road to Ramadan; and El Badri, El Magdoub, and El Din Zohdy, The Ramadan War.

Supporters of the Egyptian position tended to adopt the formulation of French Foreign Minister Michel Jobert: "Can you call it unexpected aggression for someone to try to repossess his own land?" ("Est-ce que tenter remettre les pieds chez soi constitue forcément une aggression imprévue?") Quoted in Laqueur, Confrontation, p. 176.

24. See William V. O'Brien, "International Law and the Outbreak of War in the Middle East, 1967," Orbis 11 (1967): 692-723.

25. On the Arab oil weapon, see Laqueur, Confrontation, pp. 223-52; London Sunday Times, pp. 477-81; Kalb and Kalb, Kissinger, p. 547; and Safran, Israel, pp. 506, 508-10, 512, 514-16, 519, 529, 534, 589.

J. B. Kelly is of the opinion that the Arab oil weapon was as much a manifestation of the desire for selfish gain and for general political advantage vis-à-vis the developed states as it was a principled use of Arab oil power to advance the Arab cause against Israel and its supporters. See J. B. Kelly, Arabia, the Gulf and the West (New York: Basic, 1980), pp. 379-457.

26. See O'Brien, "International Law," pp. 714, 717-19, 721-23.

27. On Israeli public information policies, see Laqueur, Confrontation, p. 119; London Sunday Times, p. 217; and Sachar, A History of Israel, p. 764.

28. On the constraints on Israeli strategy resulting from the imminence of superpower and other external intervention, see Laqueur, Confrontation, pp. 112-13; and Schiff, October Earthquake, pp. 206-7.

29. On Egypt's early military success and lack of interest in negotiations, see Sachar, A History of Israel, pp. 767-68; and Safran, Israel, pp. 301-479.

30. The influence of an impending ceasefire on Israeli military policies is noted by General Herzog, The War of Atonement, p. 245.

31. On U.S. warnings to Israel not to press on to Damascus, see Sachar, A History of Israel, p. 771.

32. Kosygin's role in pressing for a ceasefire is described in the London Sunday Times, pp. 367-69; Sachar, A History of Israel, pp. 778-79; and Safran, Israel, pp. 484-85.

33. On the relationship between the Moscow Agreement and the battlefield situation, see Sachar, A History of Israel, p. 780.

34. The fate of the Egyptian Third Army is discussed in Herzog, The War of Atonement, p. 247; Sachar, A History of Israel, p. 781; London Sunday Times, pp. 391-98, 428-40; Schiff, October Earthquake, pp. 286-87; and Edgar O'Ballance, No Victor, No Vanquished: The Yom Kippur War (San Rafael, Calif.: Presido, 1978), pp. 258-64.

35. The last days of the fighting are described in Sachar, A History of Israel, pp. 781-82, 784-85; London Sunday Times, pp. 394-98, 428-31; Schiff, October Earthquake, p. 288; and O'Ballance, No Victor, No Vanquished, pp. 258-64.

36. Versions of how the first ceasefire was broken and by whom vary. The London Sunday Times states that, "Both sides claimed that the other started it. The most extended version of how it happened was provided by Israel at a subsequent UN meeting." The Sunday Times then quotes the explanation of Yosef Tekoah, after which the following is observed:

> Allocation of responsibility for renewed fighting was less clear to war correspondents in the area. It was certainly true that the Egyptian soldiers—particularly those of the Second Army in the north, unaware of the magnitude of their comrades' plight to the south—were as furious as the Israelis over the cease-fire. (One brigadier in the Second Army reportedly had to threaten to mortar any of his own troops who did not cease fighting.) So sporadic Egyptian shooting after the truce was predictable, but the UN resolution . . . called not only for a halt to all firing but also for the termination of "all military activity." There was scant evidence of Israel terminating its buildup of men, supplies, ammunition, and armor in the bulge west of the canal.

London Sunday Times, pp. 392, 394.

O'Ballance's version is the following:

> While the Egyptians seemed determined to honor the cease-fire (for example, the Cairo International Airport was briefly opened again), the Israelis, on the contrary, rushed troops across their three bridges throughout the night of the twenty-second/twenty-third. It seemed they had no intention of observing the cease-fire but were set upon exploiting their position on the west bank. . . .
>
> The fact that the Israelis broke the cease-fire and went on to encircle the Egyptian Third Army led the Soviet Union to think the United States had deliberately outwitted it.

No Victor, No Vanquished, pp. 256-58.

Sachar claims that "Egyptian commando and infantry teams on the east bank's southern sector ignored the cease-fire and shortly before midnight of October 22-23 struck repeatedly at Israeli tank laagers in a frenzied effort to open a corridor to the Third Army. At once, Gonen ordered Adan and Magen to continue their drive southward, and to tighten the noose." See A History of Israel, p. 781.

Safran says that Kissinger was informed by Israeli Ambassador Dinitz that the Egyptians had broken the ceasefire. "Kissinger then checked with his own intelligence sources, and these confirmed the Israeli story but added that the Israeli forces took advantage of the Egyptian violations to carry out offensive operations designed to encircle the Third Army." See Israel, pp. 492-93.

El Badri, El Magdoub, and El Din Zohdy claim that the Israeli forces were in a precarious position on the west side of the canal and that they violated the ceasefire both to protect themselves and to gain more territory for bargaining. See The Ramadan War, pp. 115-22. Whetten sees the Israelis as determined to maximize their positions of strength for the coming negotiations in The Canal War, pp. 290-91.

37. Laqueur describes the atmosphere in the United Nations, one which Israeli diplomats were to compare with that of a "lynching party." See Confrontation, pp. 164-66. See Sachar's comments on the changing attitude of the UN majority toward Israel in A History of Israel, p. 812.

38. See Sachar, A History of Israel, pp. 780-83.

39. The Kilometer 101 talks are described in the London Sunday Times, pp. 433-34, 448-49, 472-73; Sachar, A History of Israel, pp. 785, 792, 794; Kalb and Kalb, Kissinger, pp. 583-85; and Safran, Israel, pp. 513, 518.

40. On the December 1973 Geneva Conference, see Sachar, A History of Israel, pp. 792-94; London Sunday Times, pp. 482-86; and Safran, Israel, pp. 520-21.

41. This account and the quotation is from Sachar, A History of Israel, pp. 794-96. See Safran, Israel, pp. 521-27.

42. See Sachar, A History of Israel, pp. 795-96.

43. On the Second Sinai Agreement, see Safran, Israel, pp. 553-60; and Sachar, A History of Israel, pp. 820-25.

44. See Safran, Israel, pp. 556-67; and Sachar, A History of Israel, pp. 820-21.

45. On the U.S. contribution to the Second Sinai Agreement, see Safran, Israel, pp. 557-60; and Sachar, A History of Israel, pp. 821-22. The overall U.S. policy and contribution with regard to the Yom Kippur War is discussed in Bernard Reich, The Quest for Peace: United States-Israeli Relations and the Arab-Israeli Conflict (New Brunswick, N.J.: Transaction, 1977), pp. 241-94; and William B. Quandt, Decade of Decisions (Berkeley: University of California Press, 1977), pp. 165-252.

NOTES TO CHAPTER 13

1. On individual and command responsibility, see William H. Parks, "Command Responsibility for War Crimes," Military Law Review 62 (1973): 1-104; William V. O'Brien, "The Law of War, Command Responsibility and Vietnam," Georgetown Law Journal 60 (1972): 605-64; U.S., Department of the Army, The Law of Land Warfare, July 1956, FM 27-10 (Washington, D.C.: Department of the Army, 1956), pp. 180-83 [hereafter cited as FM 27-10]; U.S., Department of the Air Force, International Law—The Conduct of Armed Conflict and Air Operations, 19 November 1976, AFP 110-31 (Washington, D.C.: Department of the Air Force, 1976), 15-2-6 [hereafter cited as AFP 110-31]; idem, Commander's Handbook on the Law of Armed Conflict, AFP 110-34 (Washington, D.C.: Department of the Air Force, July 25, 1980), 8-1 [hereafter cited as AFP 110-34].

See the following that focus on Vietnam controversies of individual and command responsibility but have general application: Telford Taylor, Nuremberg and Vietnam: An American Tragedy (Chicago: Quadrangle, 1970); Waldemar A. Solf, "A Response to Telford Taylor's 'Nuremberg and Vietnam: An American Tragedy,'" in The Vietnam War and International Law, ed. Richard A. Falk, 4 vols. (Princeton, N.J.: Princeton University Press, 1969-76), 4: 421-46; Tom J. Farer, Robert G. Gard, Jr., and Telford Taylor, "Vietnam and the Nuremberg Principles: A Colloquy on War Crimes," in The Vietnam War and International Law, ed. Richard A. Falk, 4 vols. (Princeton, N.J.: Princeton University Press, 1969-76), 4: 363-420.

2. See the literature on strategic bombing in World War II in Chapter 4, n. 3.

3. On RAF policy in the fall of 1942, see the memorandum from the assistant chief of the air staff on October 12, 1942, quoted in Max Hastings, Bomber Command (New York: Dial, 1979), p. 170.

4. The Casablanca directive is quoted in Sir Charles Webster and Noble Frankland, The Strategic Air Offensive against Germany, 1939-1945, 4 vols. (London: Her Majesty's Stationery Office, 1961), 2: 12. See David Irving, The Destruction of Dresden (New York: Holt, Rinehart and Winston, 1971), pp. 36-37.

5. On the fire bombing of German cities, see generally Irving's account in The Destruction of Dresden, pp. 42-53.

6. This account of the development and approval of Westmoreland's search-and-destroy strategy is based on Guenter Lewy, America in Vietnam (New York: Oxford University Press, 1978), pp. 42-56. See chapter 8, "Evolution of Strategy," in William C. Westmoreland's A Soldier Reports (Garden City, N.Y.: Doubleday, 1976), pp. 144-61; and Leslie H. Gelb and Richard K. Betts, The Irony of Vietnam: The System Worked (Washington, D.C.: Brookings Institution, 1979), pp. 133-35.

7. Lewy, America in Vietnam, p. 51.

8. See Chapters 5 and 11.

9. On guidelines for MacArthur's mission in North Korea, see David Rees, Korea: The Limited War (New York: St. Martin's Press, 1964), pp. 98-104, 107-9, 128-31.

10. The mission of the UN forces after the second crossing of the 38th parallel is discussed in ibid., pp. 257-59.

11. On the relationship between Westmoreland's forces and his strategy, see his summary reflections in A Soldier Reports, pp. 350-57, 414-16. See Lyndon Baines Johnson, The Vantage Point (New York: Holt, Rinehart and Winston, 1971), pp. 369-70; David M. Abshire, "Lessons of Vietnam: Proportionality and Credibility," in The Vietnam Legacy, ed. Anthony Lake (New York: New York University Press, 1976), p. 398. The issue of force levels is integrally related to that of overuse of firepower under the concept "expend shells not men." See Lewy, America in Vietnam, p. 96; and William Hays Parks, "The Law of War Adviser," JAG Journal 31 (1980): 48-49.

12. The difficulties of successful defense of NATO are discussed in a vast literature. The following are some typical assessments: Stewart W. B. Menhaul, "The Shifting Theater Nuclear Balance in Europe," Strategic Review 6 (1978): 34-45; Steven L. Canby, "Rethinking the NATO Military Problem," International Security Studies Program Working Papers no. 3 (Washington, D.C.: Wilson Center, June 20, 1979); idem, "The Alliance and Europe: Part IV, Military Doctrine and Technology," Adelphi Papers no. 109 (London: International Institute for Strategic Studies, 1975); Colin S. Gray, "NATO Strategy and the 'Neutron Bomb,'" Policy Review 7 (1979): 7-11; and Robert Lucas Fischer, "Defending the Central Front: The Balance of Forces," Adelphi Papers no. 127 (London: International Institute for Strategic Studies, 1976).

See the authoritative and sobering view by Henry A. Kissinger, in "The Future of NATO," Washington Quarterly 2 (1979): 3-17.

13. The close control by the White House of U.S. bombing of North Vietnam is described by Lyndon Baines Johnson in The Vantage Point, pp. 127-32, 136-37, 240-41, 366-69; Chester Cooper, The Lost Crusade (New York: Dodd, Meade, 1970), p. 262; and Lewy, America in Vietnam, pp. 374-79. This control from Washington is criticized by General Westmoreland in A Soldier Reports, pp. 119-21. See Gelb and Betts, The Irony of Vietnam, pp. 137-239.

14. Alternatives to Westmoreland's strategy are discussed in Lewy, America in Vietnam, pp. 438-44.

15. A recent Air Force pamphlet explains the relationship of rules of engagement to the law of war.

1-2. Relation to Rules of Engagement. The law of armed conflict is not the same thing as "rules of engagement." These rules of engagement are guidelines that the United States imposes on its own military forces, while the law of armed conflict is binding on all nations and their armed forces. (More accurately, customary international law is binding on all nations; international law created by treaty is only binding on nations party to the treaty.) The United States government can, by its own action, change its rules of engagement. International law, on the other hand, can usually be changed only by an international agreement. The law of armed conflict is an important influence in drafting the rules of engagement, but it is not the only influence. In their final form, rules of engagement usually reflect political and diplomatic as well as legal factors. The rules of engagement will, then, often restrict operations far beyond the requirements of the law of armed conflict. The distinction between the law of armed conflict and the rules of engagement should always be kept in mind.

AFP 110-31, 1-1.
     A good example of the nature of the rules of engagement is provided in the case of General John D. Lavelle, who was dismissed as commander of the 7th Air Force during the Vietnam War "because of irregularities in the conduct of his responsibilities," specifically, for violating the rules of engagement governing bombing of North Vietnam north of the DMZ and for a coverup that included filing of false reports. See Lewy, America in Vietnam, pp. 407-9; and Hamilton de Saussure and Robert Glasser, "Methods and Means of Warfare 9," in Law and Responsibility in Warfare: The Vietnam Experience, ed. Peter D. Trooboff (Chapel Hill: University of North Carolina Press, 1975), p. 121.
     Senator Barry Goldwater inserted in the Congressional Record what Secretary of Defense Schlesinger termed "substantial portions" of the U.S. rules of engagement contained in MACV Directive 525-13 of May 1971. See U.S., Congress, Congressional Record, vol. 121, no. 88, June 6, 1975.
     16. The Peers Commission Report, reproduced in Joseph Goldstein, Burke Marshall, and Jack Schwartz, eds., The My Lai Massacre and Its Cover-up: Beyond the Reach of Law? (New York: Free Press, 1976), pp. 211-12 [hereafter cited as the Peers Report]. The editors of this volume admit in an inserted note that the Peers Report was the work of General William R. Peers and not of a "commission."

17. The strategy of substituting heightened firepower for adequate deployment of manpower is discussed in Lewy, America in Vietnam, pp. 52, 96, 99, 269. See n. 11 above.

18. See the discussion of Linebacker II in Chapter 11.

19. James R. McCarthy and George B. Allison, Linebacker II: A View from the Rock, ed. Robert E. Rayfield, USAF Southeast Asia Monograph Series, vol. 6, monograph 8 (Maxwell AFB, Ala.: Air Power Research Institute, 1979), pp. 46-47. Further elaboration of the rules of engagement during Linebacker II is provided in ibid., pp. 61, 67-68, 77, 80, 136. The close monitoring and supervision of Linebacker II by 8th AF, SAC, and the JCS is emphasized in ibid., pp. 41, 85-86, 96-100, 107.

Linebacker II is discussed in "Air Warfare—Christmas 1972," in Law and Responsibility in Warfare: The Vietnam Experience, ed. Peter D. Trooboff (Chapel Hill: University of North Carolina Press, 1975), pp. 119-49, with papers by Hamilton de Saussure and Robert Glasser and comments by Townsend Hoopes, Norman R. Thorpe, and James R. Miles.

Kissinger recalls that in the media in the United States and throughout the world, "the moral indignation [over the Christmas bombing] rose with each day. The proposition that the United States government was deliberately slaughtering civilians in a purposeless campaign of terror went unchallenged." He also gives samples of the condemnations of the bombing by political opponents of the war and of the Nixon administration in White House Years (Boston: Little, Brown, 1979), pp. 1453-54.

To this day the Christmas bombing seems to be remembered as a war crime, somehow related to the impeachment of President Nixon that never was completed. The facts sustain the view that Linebacker II was a model of just and limited conduct of war. It was directly related to the purpose of inducing a recalcitrant enemy to conclude a peace agreement to which it had committed itself, using means that were in fact discriminate and proportionate, employed at considerable risk and cost to the attacking airmen.

20. Peers Report in Goldstein, Marshall, and Schwartz, The My Lai Massacre, p. 211. See Lewy, America in Vietnam, p. 366.

21. Lewy details the increased efforts of the U.S. armed forces to improve law-of-war training during and after the Vietnam War in America in Vietnam, pp. 366-69. An extremely comprehensive and authoritative view of current efforts of the U.S. armed forces to train their personnel in the law of war and to maintain law-of-war advisers in key places is provided in Parks, "The Law of War Adviser." Parks describes the present process of "Review of Legality of Weapons under International Law," ibid., p. 10.

22. Directives regarding the reporting, prevention, repression, and punishment of war crimes are laid down in U.S., Department of the Army, Subject Schedule 27-1 (Washington, D.C.: 1970), pp. 1, 2, 4, 11.

Air Force personnel are given guidelines on this subject in AFP 110-31, 15-2-6; and AFP 110-34, 8-1.

23. U.S. concern for world opinion during the Vietnam War is reflected in President Johnson's close control over the bombing of North Vietnam, described in Vantage Point, pp. 127-32, 136-37, 240-41, 366-69.

24. See, for example, Stockholm International Peace Research Institute, Incendiary Weapons (Cambridge, Mass.: MIT Press, 1975).

25. On failure of communist belligerents to respect the role of the ICRC, see Howard S. Levie, "Maltreatment of Prisoners of War in Vietnam," in The Vietnam War and International Law, ed. Richard A. Falk, 4 vols. (Princeton, N.J.: Princeton University Press, 1969-76), 1: 364-66; and David P. Forsythe, Humanitarian Politics: The International Committee of the Red Cross (Baltimore: Johns Hopkins University Press, 1977), pp. 43, 134-35, 154-59, 165.

26. For a prominent example of domestic U.S. charges of U.S. violations of the law of war in Vietnam, see Clergy and Laymen Concerned about Vietnam, In the Name of America (Annandale, Va.: Turnpike Press, 1968).

27. On Communist bacteriological-warfare charges during the Korean War, see Rees, Korea, pp. 307, 352-63; Ann Van Wynen Thomas and A. J. Thomas, Jr., Legal Limits on the Use of Chemical and Biological Weapons (Dallas: Southern Methodist University Press, 1970), pp. 156, 165-67; and William V. O'Brien, "Biological/Chemical Warfare and the International Law of War," Georgetown Law Journal 51 (1962): 56-57, 61-62.

28. Lewy, America in Vietnam, pp. 224, 311-21.

29. See, for example, ibid., p. 236.

30. For a comprehensive analysis of the functions of the JCS, including their relations with CINCs, see John G. Kester, "The Future of the Joint Chiefs of Staff," AEI Foreign Policy and Defense Review (Washington, D.C.: American Enterprise Institution for Public Policy Research, 1980), 2: 2-36.

31. U.S. presidents have employed different systems of control. Except for Eisenhower, none has consistently used the National Security Council as the highest source of guidance and the locus of highest decisions. National security assistants have had varying degrees of influence with Kissinger having become, in effect, a partner with President Nixon in the decision process. As Kissinger himself has remarked, a president will choose the system and the personnel,

as well as the definition of relationships, that suits his style, regardless of formal titles and structures. On the U.S. national security decision process, see Keith C. Clark and Laurence J. Legere, eds., The President and the Management of National Security (New York: Praeger, 1966); I. M. Destler, Presidents, Bureaucrats and Foreign Policy (Princeton, N.J.: Princeton University Press, 1974); Henry F. Graff, The Tuesday Cabinet: Deliberation and Decision on Peace and War under Lyndon B. Johnson (Englewood Cliffs, N.J.: Prentice-Hall, 1970); John P. Leacacos, "Kissinger's Apparat," Foreign Policy 5 (1971-72): 2-7; and Kissinger, White House Years, pp. 38-48. The evolution of the national security decision process from Truman to Carter is summarized concisely, with helpful references to the main literature, in Charles W. Kegley, Jr., and Eugene R. Wittkopf, American Foreign Policy: Pattern and Process (New York: St. Martin's Press, 1979), pp. 248-61, 264-65.

32. The NATO command structure is explained in North Atlantic Treaty Organization, NATO Handbook (Brussels: NATO Information Service, 1980). On the complexities and uncertainties of the NATO decision processes, see the authorities cited in Chapter 6, n. 2.

33. In the Dominican intervention, the OAS Inter-American Peace Force was commanded by a Brazilian, General Hugo Manasco Alvim. U.S. General Bruce Palmer, the second in command of the IAPF and commander in chief of the U.S. forces that overwhelmingly predominated, was the effective commander of the U.S. force. See Piero Gleijeses, The Dominican Crisis: The 1965 Constitutionalist Revolt and American Intervention, trans. Lawrence Lipson (Baltimore: Johns Hopkins University Press, 1978), pp. 261-62.

34. For an authoritative and concise account of the My Lai massacre and cover-up, see W. R. Peers, Mylai Inquiry (New York: Norton, 1979).

35. The Nuremberg Judgment declared the Gestapo, S.D., S.S., and the Leadership Corps of the Nazi Party to be criminal organizations while finding that the S.A., Reich Cabinet, and General Staff and High Command were not criminal organizations. Nuremberg International Military Tribunal, Trial of Major War Criminals before the International Military Tribunal, Nuremberg, 14 November 1945—1 October 1946, 42 vols. (Nuremberg, 1947-49), 12: 493-523.

36. On international responsibility, see Charles Cheney Hyde, International Law, Chiefly as Interpreted and Applied by the United States, 3 vols. (Boston: Little, Brown, 1945-47), 2: 871-79, 909, 917; and Marjorie M. Whiteman, Digest of International Law, 15 vols. (Washington, D.C.: U.S. Government Printing Office, 1968-73), 8: 697-706.

37. Hyde distinguishes by chapter "Claims Arising from Acts Primarily Attributable to the Authorities of a State" and "Claims Arising from Tortious Acts Not Attributable to the State." International Law 2: 924-52; and Whiteman, Digest of International Law 8: 807-37.

38. See Hyde, International Law 2: 937-41.

Article 1 of 1907 Hague Convention IV provides that "the Contracting Powers shall issue instructions to their armed land forces which shall be in conformity with the Regulations respecting the Laws and Customs of War on Land, annexed to the present Convention." Article 3 of the Hague Convention states: "A belligerent party which violates the provisions of the said Regulations shall, if the case demands, be liable to pay compensation. It shall be responsible for all acts committed by persons forming part of its armed forces." All four 1949 Geneva conventions provide that the texts of the respective conventions must be disseminated and that instructions be given to ensure compliance.

1977 Geneva Protocol I provides in Part V, Section 2, Articles 85-91 for repression of breaches of this Protocol, failure to act, duty of commanders, mutual assistance in criminal matters, cooperation, and an international fact-finding commission and responsibility. 1977 Geneva Protocol II has no such provisions.

39. On international responsibility in revolutionary or other extraordinary circumstances, see Whiteman, Digest of International Law 8: 819-35.

40. On individual responsibility in U.S. military law see FM 27-10, p. 182; AFP 110-31, 15-3-6; and AFP 110-34, 8-1.

41. The U.S. armed forces have made major efforts to provide adequate training in the law of war as required by international law and traditional U.S. policies. See Parks, "The Law of War Adviser," pp. 8-9, 24-28, 51-52. See Peter Karsten's Law, Soldiers and Combat (Westport, Conn.: Greenwood Press, 1978), which contributes to the task of bringing the laws of war down to the realities of military life and discusses education in the laws of war.

A noteworthy example of the concern of the U.S. armed forces for improving understanding of the political-military as well as the legal-moral requirements of just and limited war is to be found in a volume prepared by Air Force Academy professors. See Malham M. Wakin, ed., War, Morality and the Military Profession (Boulder, Colo.: Westview, 1979).

42. In re Yamashita 327 U.S. 1 (1945).

43. U.S. v. von Leeb, Nuremberg Military Tribunals, Trials of War Criminals, 11: 759.

44. United Nations, War Crimes Commission, Law Reports of Trials of War Criminals, 15 vols. (London: His Majesty's Stationery Office, 1947-49), 4: 34.

45. On the interpretation of command responsibility in the Yamashita case, see Parks, "Command Responsibility," pp. 37-38; O'Brien, "The Law of War," pp. 627-28; Leonard B. Boudin, "Individual Responsibility in Warfare 19," in Law and Responsibility

in Warfare: The Vietnam Experience, ed. Peter D. Trooboff (Chapel Hill: University of North Carolina Press, 1975), pp. 212-13; and comments of Farer, Gard, and Taylor, "Vietnam and the Nuremberg Principles," pp. 217-30.

46. The absolute liability approach to command responsibility was put forward by the prosecution in the von Leeb case but rejected by the Court. Nuremberg Military Tribunals, Trials of War Criminals, 11: 544-45. See Parks, "Command Responsibility," pp. 40-41; and O'Brien, "The Law of War," p. 627.

Army Subject Schedule 27-1 states:

> The legal responsibility for the commission of war crimes frequently can be placed on the military commander as well as his subordinate who may have actually committed the crime. Since a commander is responsible for the actions of those he commands, he can be held as a guilty party if his troops commit crimes pursuant to his command, or if he knew the acts were going to be committed even though he did not order them. The commander is also responsible if he should have known, through reports or by other means, that those under his command are about to commit or have committed war crimes, and he fails to take reasonable steps to prevent such crimes or to punish those guilty of a violation. As a minimum, such a commander is guilty of dereliction of duty.

Subject Schedule 27-1, p. 10.

47. U.S. v. von Leeb, Nuremberg Military Tribunals, Trials of War Criminals, 11: 510, 555.

48. See Parks, "Command Responsibility," pp. 41-58.

49. U.S. v. List, Nuremberg Military Tribunals, Trials of War Criminals, 11: 1259-60. See Parks, "Command Responsibility," pp. 59-60.

50. O'Brien, "The Law of War," pp. 629; and Parks, "Command Responsibility," pp. 90-101.

51. U.S. v. List, Nuremberg Military Tribunals, Trials of War Criminals, 11: 770, 1295-97.

52. FM 27-10, p. 178.

53. Ibid., p. 182.

54. The Court of Military Appeals in the Calley case summarizes the offenses for which he was found guilty:

> First Lieutenant Calley stands convicted of the premeditated murder of 22 infants, children, and old men, and of assault with intent to murder a child of about 2 years of age. All the killings and the assault took place on March 16, 1968 in the area of the village of My Lai in the Republic of Vietnam.

United States v. Calley, 22 U.S.C.M.A. 534; 48 C.M.R. 19 (1973), reproduced in Goldstein, Marshall, and Schwartz, The My Lai Massacre, p. 520.

In the case of Captain Ernest L. Medina, Calley's company commander, there would appear to have been a clear instance of command responsibility for commission of war crimes by troops under his immediate command and supervision. However, the charge to the jury in his military trial led the jury not to consider his command responsibility in the sense that the concept was applied in war-crimes trials. Judge Col. Kenneth Howard told the jury that, "It is finally the prosecution's contention that since as a commander the accused, after actual awareness, had a duty to interfere, he may be held personally responsible because his unlawful inaction was the proximate cause of unlawful homicide by his men." United States v. Medina, C.M. 427162 (1971), reproduced in Goldstein, Marshall, and Schwartz, The My Lai Massacre, p. 466.

Judge Howard continued, "Contrary to the theory of the prosecution, the defense alleges that Captain Medina never became aware of the misconduct of his men until too late and immediately upon suspecting that his orders were being misunderstood and improper acts occurring, he ordered his men to cease fire." Ibid.

The judge's charge then concluded the following:

Considering the theories of the two parties and the general statements of legal principles pertaining to military law and customs and the law of war, you are now advised that the following is an exposition of the elements of the offense of involuntary manslaughter, an offense alleged to be in violation of Article 119 of the Uniform Code of Military Justice.

In order to find the accused guilty of this offense, you must be satisfied by legal and competent evidence beyond reasonable doubt, of the following four elements of that offense:

1. That an unknown number of unidentified Vietnamese persons not less than 100, are dead;

2. That their deaths resulted from the omission of the accused in failing to exercise control over subordinates subject to his command after having gained knowledge that his subordinates were killing non-combatants [in the Mylai massacre] . . .;

3. That this omission constituted culpable negligence; and

4. That the killing of the unknown number of unidentified Vietnamese persons, not less than 100, by subordinates of the accused and under his command was unlawful.

You are again advised that the killing of a human being
is unlawful when done without legal justification.

Ibid., p. 468.

Medina was acquitted on September 22, 1971, of the charges
against him. This case demonstrates the critical gap between the
law-of-war standard of command responsibility enjoined by the war-
crimes cases and U.S. Army Subject Schedule 27-1 and the U.C.M.J.
standard of guilt with respect to crimes under U.S. military law.
Medina was a commander who testified at his trial that he lost control of his company. This loss of control was not of the nature of
that of a general like Yamashita or von Leeb. He was a company
commander in a tactical situation. His troops slaughtered civilians
in an undefended hamlet. Medina clearly bore command responsibility for the actions of his men. If the proceedings under the
U.C.M.J. could not bring him to justice, there exists a serious de-
ficiency in the ability of the United States to punish commanders
whose troops commit war crimes. See O'Brien, "The Law of War,"
p. 664.

On the disposition of other charges relating to the My Lai massacre, including the censure, demotion, and other punishments of
the commander of the American Division at the time of the massacre,
Major General Samuel W. Koster, see Peers, Mylai Inquiry, pp. 221-
28. See Boudin's comments on the Medina case in "Individual Responsibility," p. 213.

55. No federal penal provision exists to allow trial in federal
courts of discharged military personnel charged with war crimes.
None of the present possibilities for trial of such persons is promising. Military commissions, authorized by Article 1(8) of the Constitution are ad hoc tribunals whose occasional use in the Civil War and
World War II was not very satisfactory. Such tribunals, moreover,
might not survive constitutional scrutiny if convictions of former
military personnel by them were reviewed by the courts. Courts-
martial proceedings are heavily constrained by the decisions in Reid
v. Covert, 354 U.S. 1 (1957); Kinsella v. Singleton, 361 U.S. 324
(1960); Grisham v. Hogan, 361 U.S. 278 (1960); McElroy v. Guiagliardo, 361 U.S. 281 (1960); and O'Callahan v. Parker, 395, U.S. 258
(1969). Transfer of jurisdiction from military courts-martial tribunals to U.S. District Courts has been opposed on grounds of lack
of jurisdiction and the practical grounds that the Justice Department
was unprepared to take on the additional workload.

Attempts to solve the problems by legislation have so far produced no results. The problems, moreover, are not solved simply
by legislation providing for jurisdiction over present and/or former
military personnel. The problems of obtaining the presence of the

accused, of critical witnesses, and of evidence are monumental. See
Jordan J. Paust, "After My Lai: The Case for War Crimes Juris-
diction over Civilians in Federal District Courts," in The Vietnam
War and International Law, ed. Richard A. Falk, 4 vols. (Princeton,
N.J.: Princeton University Press, 1969-76), 4: 447-75.

56. Matthew B. Ridgway, The Korean War (Garden City, N.Y.:
Doubleday, 1967), p. 42.

NOTES TO CHAPTER 14

1. Preamble to 1907 Hague Convention IV.

2. John Howard Yoder's position was expressed in his remarks
in an "Evening Dialogue" on the subject "Can Contemporary Armed
Conflict Be Just?" at the Woodrow Wilson Center of the Smithsonian
Institution, Washington, D.C., October 5, 1978. Yoder's views are
discussed in James F. Childress, "Just-War Criteria," in War or
Peace: The Search for New Answers, ed. Thomas A. Shannon (Maryknoll, N.Y.: Orbis, 1980), p. 52, and p. 58, n. 38.

Paul Ramsey, The Just War: Force and Political Responsibility
(New York: Charles Scribner's Sons, 1968), discussed the just conduct of counterinsurgency war and the need to come to grips with the
problems of fighting such a war on the terms that have been set by
the insurgents in a manner that is both just and gives some hope of
success. He stated the following:

> It is therefore the shape of insurgency warfare that defines
> the contours of the legitimate combatant destruction with
> its associated civil damage that it may be just to exact in
> order to oppose it, subject to the limits of proportionately
> lesser evil. The only way to avoid this conclusion is to
> suppose that the just-war theory is a device for abolishing
> war by a (false) definition of discrimination and insuring
> perpetual peace by a shiboleth. [Emphasis added]

Ibid., p. 436. In another chapter Ramsey decries "a legalist-pacifist
version of the just-war doctrine, as if the purpose of this teaching
was to bring peace by discrediting, one by one, all wars." He replies,
"Instead, the just-war doctrine is intended to indicate to political de-
cision-makers how, within tolerable moral limits, they are to defend
and preserve politically embodied justice in this world." Ibid., p.
482.

3. See Chapter 8.

4. See Ramsey, The Just War, pp. 448-49. I discuss this aspect of Ramsey's thought in "Morality and War: The Contribution of

Paul Ramsey," in Love and Society: Essays in the Ethics of Paul Ramsey, ed. James T. Johnson and David Smith (Missoula, Mont.: American Academy of Religion/Scholars Press, 1974), pp. 176-77.

5. See John Courtney Murray, We Hold These Truths (New York: Sheed and Ward, 1960), pp. 221-47.

6. See Tucker's discussion of proportion in Robert E. Osgood and Robert W. Tucker, Force, Order and Justice (Baltimore: Johns Hopkins University Press, 1967), pp. 300-1. See Chapter 2, above.

7. See Tucker's discussion of the interpretations of the principle of discrimination in Osgood and Tucker, Force, Order and Justice, pp. 302-22.

8. See Chapter 3, n. 14.

9. For an excellent example of the two positions on nuclear deterrence and war here outlined, see Robert A. Gessert and J. Bryan Hehir, The New Nuclear Debate (New York: Council on Religion and International Affairs, 1976).

10. See Robert Endicott Osgood, Limited War Revisited (Boulder, Colo.: Westview, 1979), p. 9.

11. See Chapter 9.

12. See William C. Westmoreland, A Soldier Reports (Garden City, N.Y.: Doubleday, 1976), p. 120, quoted in Chapter 9, n. 16.

13. See Chapter 9, n. 35.

14. See William V. O'Brien, U.S. Military Intervention: Law and Morality, The Washington Papers, no. 68 (Beverly Hills, Calif.: Sage/Center for Strategic and International Studies, Georgetown University, 1979), pp. 39-61.

15. See B. H. Liddell Hart, The Revolution in Warfare (New Haven, Conn.: Yale University Press, 1947); J. F. C. Fuller, The Second World War (New York: Duell, Sloan & Pearce, 1949); Hanson W. Baldwin, Great Mistakes of the War (New York: Harper, 1949); and Raymond Aron, The Century of Total War (Garden City, N.Y.: Doubleday, 1954).

16. See Leslie H. Gelb, "The Essential Domino: American Politics and Vietnam," Foreign Affairs 50 (1972): 459-75.

BIBLIOGRAPHY

BOOKS

Amrine, Michael. The Great Decision. New York: Putnam's, 1959.

Arendt, Hannah. On Revolution. New York: Viking, 1965.

Armstrong, Anne. Unconditional Surrender: The Impact of the Casablanca Policy in World War II. New Brunswick, N.J.: Rutgers University Press, 1961.

Aron, Raymond. The Century of Total War. Garden City, N.Y.: Doubleday, 1954.

_____. The Great Debate: Theories of Nuclear Strategy. Translated by Ernest Pawel. Garden City, N.Y.: Doubleday, 1965.

Bailey, Sydney D. Prohibitions and Restraints in War. London: Oxford University Press, 1972.

Bainton, Roland H. Christian Attitudes toward War and Peace. New York: Abingdon, 1960.

Baldwin, Hanson W. Great Mistakes of the War. New York: Harper, 1949.

Batchhelder, Robert. The Irreversible Decision. New York: Macmillan, 1965.

Beaufre, Andre. NATO and Europe. Translated by Joseph Green. New York: Knopf, 1966.

Bell, A. C. The Blockade of Germany. London: Her Majesty's Stationary Office, 1961.

Bennett, John C. Foreign Policy in Christian Perspective. New York: Charles Scribner's Sons, 1966.

Berger, Peter L., and Richard J. Neuhaus. Movement and Revolution. Garden City, N.Y.: Doubleday, 1970.

Best, Geoffrey. Humanity in Warfare. New York: Columbia University Press, 1980.

Blaufarb, Douglas S. The Counterinsurgency Era: U.S. Doctrine and Performance. New York: Free Press, 1977.

Bowett, D. W. Self-Defence in International Law. Manchester: Manchester University Press, 1958.

Braestrup, Peter. Big Story: How the American Press and Television Reported and Interpreted the Crisis of Tet 1968 in Vietnam and Washington. 2 vols. Boulder, Colo.: Westview/Freedom House, 1977.

Brierly, J. L. Law of Nations. Edited by Sir Humphrey Waldock. Oxford: Oxford University Press, 1963.

Brodie, Bernard. Strategy in the Missile Age. Princeton, N.J.: Princeton University Press, 1959.

_____. War and Politics. New York: Macmillan, 1973.

Brownlie, Ian. International Law and the Use of Force by States. Oxford: Clarendon Press, 1963.

Carr, E. H. International Relations between the Two World Wars. London: Macmillan, 1947.

Clark, Keith C., and Laurence J. Legere, eds. The President and the Management of National Security. New York: Praeger, 1966.

Clergy and Laymen Concerned about Vietnam. In the Name of America. Annandale, Va.: Turnpike Press, 1968.

Close, Robert. Europe without Defense? Forty-eight Hours That Could Change the Face of the World. New York: Pergamon, 1979.

Clutterbuck, Richard L. The Long, Long War: Counterinsurgency in Malaya and Vietnam. New York: Praeger, 1966.

Colby, William, and Peter Forbath. Honorable Men. New York: Simon & Schuster, 1978.

Collins, J. Lawton. War in Peacetime. Boston: Houghton Mifflin, 1969.

Collins, John M. American and Soviet Military Trends since the Cuban Missile Crisis. Washington, D.C.: The Center for Strategic and International Studies, Georgetown University, 1978.

Cooper, Chester. The Lost Crusade. New York: Dodd, Meade, 1970.

Craven, Wesley Frank, and James Lee Cate, eds. The Army Air Forces in World War II. 7 vols. Chicago: University of Chicago Press, 1948-58.

D'Amato, Anthony A., and Robert M. O'Neill. The Judiciary and Vietnam. New York: St. Martin's Press, 1972.

Deitchman, Seymour J. Limited War and American Defense Policy. Cambridge, Mass.: MIT Press, 1964.

de la Brière, Yves. Le droit de juste guerre. Paris: Pedone, 1933.

Denton, Jeremiah A., and Ed Brandt. When Hell Was in Session. New York: Reader's Digest Press/Crowell, 1976.

D'Entrèves, A. P., ed. Aquinas: Selected Political Writings. Translated by J. G. Dawson. Oxford: Blackwell, 1948.

Destler, I. M. Presidents, Bureaucrats and Foreign Policy. Princeton, N.J.: Princeton University Press, 1974.

de Vattel, E. The Law of Nations or the Principles of Natural Law Applied to the Conduct and to the Affairs of Nations and of Sovereigns. Translated by Charles G. Fenwick. 3 vols. Washington, D.C.: Carnegie Institution, 1916.

Dougherty, James E., and Robert L. Pfaltzgraff, Jr. Contending Theories of International Relations. Philadelphia: J. B. Lippincott, 1971.

Dramesi, John A. Code of Honor. New York: Norton, 1975.

Earle, Edward Mead, ed. Makers of Modern Strategy. Princeton, N.J.: Princeton University Press, 1943.

Eckstein, Harry, ed. Internal War: Problems and Approaches. New York: Free Press, 1964.

Eisenhower, Dwight D. Mandate for Change, 1953-1956. Garden
City, N.Y.: Doubleday, 1963.

El Badri, Hassan, Taha El Magdoub, and Mohammed Dia El Din Zohdy.
The Ramadan War, 1973. New York: Hippocrene Books, 1974.

Enthoven, Alain C., and Wayne K. Smith. How Much Is Enough?
The Defense Program 1961-1969. New York: Haper & Row,
1971.

Eppstein, John. The Catholic Tradition of the Law of Nations. Washington, D.C.: Carnegie Endowment for International Peace/
Catholic Association for International Peace, 1935.

Falk, Richard A., ed. The International Law of Civil War. Baltimore: Johns Hopkins University Press, 1971.

_____. The Vietnam War and International Law. 4 vols. Princeton,
N.J.: Princeton University Press, 1969-76.

Fall, Bernard. Street without Joy: Indo-China at War, 1946-1954.
Harrisburg, Pa.: Stackpole, 1961.

_____. The Two Viet-Nams. New York: Praeger, 1963.

Feilchenfeld, Ernst H. The International Law of Belligerent Occupation. Washington, D.C.: Carnegie Endownment for International Peace, 1942.

_____. The Next Step. Oxford: Basil Blackwell, 1938.

Feis, Herbert. Japan Subdued: The Atomic Bomb and the End of
the War in the Pacific. Princeton, N.J.: Princeton University
Press, 1961.

Fierro, Alfredo. The Militant Gospel: A Critical Introduction to
Political Theologies. Translated by John Drury. Maryknoll,
N.Y.: Orbis, 1975.

Flannery, Harry, ed. Pattern for Peace: Catholic Statements on
International Order. Westminister, Md.: Newman, 1962.

Fleming, D. F. The Cold War and Its Origins. 2 vols. Garden
City, N.Y.: Doubleday, 1961.

Ford, Harold P., and Francis X. Winters, eds. Ethics and Nuclear Strategy. Maryknoll, N.Y.: Orbis, 1977.

Forsythe, David P. Humanitarian Politics: The International Committee of the Red Cross. Baltimore: Johns Hopkins University Press, 1977.

Friedmann, Wolfgang. The Changing Structure of International Law. New York: Columbia University Press, 1964.

Fuller, J. F. C. The Second World War. New York: Duell, Sloan & Pearce, 1949.

Fund for the Republic. Foreign Policy and the Free Society. New York: Oceana, 1958.

Galula, David. Counterinsurgency Warfare: Theory and Practice. New York: Praeger, 1964.

Gantenbein, James W. The Doctrine of Continuous Voyage. Portland, Oreg.: Keystone Press, 1929.

Garner, James Wilford. International Law and the World War. 2 vols. London: Longmans, Green, 1926.

Gavin, James M. War and Peace in the Space Age. New York: Harper, 1958.

Gelb, Leslie H., and Richard K. Betts. The Irony of Vietnam: The System Worked. Washington, D.C.: Brookings Institution, 1979.

Gessert, Robert A., and J. Bryan Hehir. The New Nuclear Debate. New York: Council on Religion and International Affairs, 1976.

Gibert, Stephen P. Soviet Images of America. New York: Crane, Russak, 1977.

Giovannitti, Len, and Fred Freed. The Decision to Drop the Bomb. New York: Coward-McCann, 1965.

Gleijeses, Piero. The Dominican Crisis: The 1965 Constitutionalist Revolt and American Intervention. Translated by Lawrence Lipson. Baltimore: Johns Hopkins University Press, 1978.

Golan, Galia. Yom Kippur and After: The Soviet Union and the Middle East Crisis. Cambridge: At the University Press, 1977.

Goldstein, Joseph, Burke Marshall, and Jack Schwartz, eds. The My Lai Massacre and Its Cover-up: Beyond the Reach of Law? New York: Free Press, 1976.

Goodman, Allan E. The Lost Peace. Stanford, Calif.: Hoover Institution Press, 1978.

Goodrich, Leland M. Korea: A Study of U.S. Policy in the United Nations. New York: Council on Foreign Relations, 1956.

Graff, Henry F. The Tuesday Cabinet: Deliberation and Decision on Peace and War under Lyndon B. Johnson. Englewood Cliffs, N.J.: Prentice-Hall, 1970.

Green, Philip. Deadly Logic: The Theory of Nuclear Deterrence. Columbus: Ohio State University Press, 1960.

Greenfield, Kent Roberts. American Strategy in World War II: A Reconsideration. Baltimore: Johns Hopkins University Press, 1963.

Griffith, Samuel B., ed. and trans. Mao Tse-tung on Guerrilla Warfare. New York: Praeger, 1961.

Guichard, Louis. The Naval Blockade, 1914-1918. Translated by Christopher R. Tierney. New York: D. Appleton, 1930.

Guggenheim, Paul. Traité de droit international public. 2 vols. Geneva: Librairie de l'Université, 1954.

Gutierrez, Gustavo. A Theology of Liberation. Edited and translated by Sister Caridad Inda and John Eagleson. Maryknoll, N.Y.: Orbis, 1971.

Hackworth, Green Haywood. Digest of International Law. 8 vols. Washington, D.C.: U.S. Government Printing Office, 1943.

Halberstam, David. The Powers That Be. New York: Dell, 1979.

Hall, William Edward. A Treatise of International Law. Edited by A. Pearce Higgins. 8th ed. Oxford: Clarendon Press, 1924.

Halperin, Morton H. Limited War in the Nuclear Age. New York: John Wiley & Sons, 1963.

Hastings, Max. Bomber Command. New York: Dial, 1979.

Heikal, Mohamed. The Road to Ramadan. New York: Quadrangle/ New York Times, 1975.

Heilbrun, Otto. Partisan Warfare. New York: Praeger, 1962.

Henkin, Louis. How Nations Behave. 2d ed. New York: Council on Foreign Relations/Columbia University Press, 1979.

Hersey, John. Hiroshima. New York: Bantam, 1946.

Herzog, Chaim. The War of Atonement, October 1973. Boston: Little, Brown, 1975.

Higgins, A. Pearce, and C. John Colombos. The International Law of the Sea. London: Longmans, Green, 1945.

Hinton, Harold C. Communist China in World Politics. New York: Houghton Mifflin, 1966.

Holst, Johan J., and Uwe Nerlich. Beyond Nuclear Deterrence. New York: Crane, Russak, 1977.

Howard, Michael., ed. Restraints on War. Oxford: Oxford University Press, 1979.

Hyde, Charles Cheney. International Law, Chiefly as Interpreted and Applied by the United States. 3 vols. Boston: Little, Brown, 1945-47.

Insight Team of the London Sunday Times. The Yom Kippur War. Garden City, N.Y.: Doubleday, 1974.

Irving, David. The Destruction of Dresden. New York: Holt, Rinehart and Winston, 1963.

Johnson, Chalmers. Revolutionary Change. Boston: Little, Brown, 1966.

Johnson, James T. Ideology, Reason and Limitation of War. Princeton, N.J.: Princeton University Press, 1975.

_____. Just War Tradition and the Restraint of War: A Moral and Historical Inquiry. Princeton, N.J.: Princeton University Press, 1981.

Johnson, James T., and David Smith, eds. Love and Society: Essays in the Ethics of Paul Ramsey. Missoula, Mont.: American Academy of Religion/Scholars Press, 1974.

Johnson, Lyndon Baines. The Vantage Point. New York: Holt, Rinehart and Winston, 1971.

Joy, C. Turner. Negotiating while Fighting: The Diary of Admiral C. Turner Joy at the Korean Armistice Conference. Edited by Allan E. Goodman. Stanford, Calif.: Hoover Institution Press, 1978.

Kahn, Herman. On Thermonuclear War. Princeton, N.J.: Princeton University Press, 1960.

_____. Thinking about the Unthinkable. New York: Horizon, 1962.

Kalb, Marvin, and Bernard Kalb. Kissinger. New York: Dell, 1974.

Kalshoven, Fritz. Belligerent Reprisals. Leiden: Sijthoff, 1971.

Kaplan, Morton A., ed. Strategic Thinking and Its Moral Significance. Chicago: University of Chicago Center for Policy Study, 1973.

Karsten, Peter. Law, Soldiers and Combat. Westport, Conn.: Greenwood Press, 1978.

Keen, Maurice H. The Laws of War in the Late Middle Ages. Toronto: University of Toronto Press, 1965.

Kegley, Charles W., Jr., and Eugene R. Wittkopf. American Foreign Policy: Pattern and Process. New York: St. Martin's Press, 1979.

Kelly, J. B. Arabia, the Gulf and the West. New York: Basic, 1980.

Kelsen, Hans. Principles of International Law. Edited by Robert W. Tucker. 2d rev. ed. New York: Holt, Rinehart and Winston, 1966.

Khadduri, Majid. The Law of War and Peace in Islam. Baltimore: Johns Hopkins University Press, 1955.

Kinkaid, Eugene. In Every War but One. New York: Norton, 1959.

Kinnard, Douglas. The War Managers. Hanover, N.H.: University Press of New England, 1977.

Kirk-Greene, Anthony. Crisis and Conflict in Nigeria: A Documentary Sourcebook. London: Oxford University Press, 1971.

Kissinger, Henry A. Nuclear Weapons and Foreign Policy. New York: Harper, 1957.

_____. The Troubled Partnership: A Reappraisal of the Atlantic Alliance. New York: McGraw-Hill, 1965.

_____. White House Years. Boston: Little, Brown, 1979.

Kolko, Gabriel. The Politics of War: The World and United States Foreign Policy, 1943-1945. New York: Random House, 1968.

Komer, Robert W. Bureaucracy Does Its Thing: Institutional Constraints on U.S.-GVN Performance in Vietnam. Santa Monica, Calif.: RAND, 1973.

Lake, Anthony, ed. The Legacy of Vietnam. New York: New York University Press, 1976.

Laqueur, Walter. Confrontation: The Middle East and World Politics. New York: Bantam, 1974.

_____. Guerrilla: A Historical and Critical Study. Boston: Little, Brown, 1976.

Leckie, Robert. Conflict: The History of the Korean War, 1950-1953. New York: Putnam's Sons, 1962.

Lefever, Ernest W. Ethics and United States Foreign Policy. New York: Meridian, 1957.

_____. TV and National Defense: An Analysis of CBS News, 1972-1973. Boston, Va.: Institute for American Strategy, 1974.

Leiden, Carl, and Karl M. Schmitt. The Politics of Violence: Revolution in the Modern World. Englewood Cliffs, N.J.: Prentice-Hall, 1968.

Lemkin, Raphael. Axis Rule in Occupied Europe. Washington, D.C.: Carnegie Endowment for International Peace, 1944.

Levie, Howard S. Documents on Prisoners of War. International Law Studies, vol. 60. Newport, R.I.: U.S. Naval War College, 1979.

_____. Prisoners of War in International Armed Conflict. International Law Studies, vol. 59. Newport, R.I.: U.S. Naval War College, 1978.

Lewy, Guenter. America in Vietnam. New York: Oxford University Press, 1978.

Liddell Hart, B. H. Defense of the West. New York: William Morrow, 1959.

_____. The German Generals Talk. New York: William Morrow, 1948.

_____. The Revolution in Warfare. New Haven, Conn.: Yale University Press, 1947.

_____. Strategy. 2d rev. ed. New York: Signet, 1967.

Littauer, Raphael, and Norman Uphoff, eds. The Air War in Indochina. Rev. ed. Boston: Beacon, 1972.

Luard, Evan, ed. The International Regulation of Civil War. New York: New York University Press, 1972.

McCarthy, James R., and George B. Allison. Linebacker II: A View from the Rock. Edited by Robert E. Rayfield. USAF Southeast Asia Monograph Series, vol. 6, monograph 8. Maxwell AFB, Ala.: Air Power Research Institute, 1979.

McClintock, Robert. The Meaning of Limited War. Boston: Houghton Mifflin, 1967.

McCormick, Richard A., and Paul Ramsey. Doing Good to Achieve Evil. Chicago: Loyola University Press, 1978.

McCuen, John J. The Art of Counter-Revolutionary War: The Strategy of Counterinsurgency. Harrisburg, Pa.: Stackpole, 1966.

McDougal, Myres S., and Florentino P. Feliciano. Law and Minimum World Public Order. New Haven, Conn.: Yale University Press, 1961.

McReavy, L. L. Peace and War in Catholic Doctrine. Oxford: Catholic Social Guild, 1963.

Maddox, Robert James. The New Left and the Origins of the Cold War. Princeton, N.J.: Princeton University Press, 1973.

Marshall, S. L. A. Pork Chop Hill. New York: Morrow, 1956.

Messner, Johannes. Social Ethics. Translated by J. J. Doherty. Rev. ed. St. Louis: Herder, 1965.

Moore, John Bassett. A Digest of International Law. 8 vols. Washington, D.C.: U.S. Government Printing Office, 1906.

Moore, John Norton, ed. The Arab-Israeli Conflict. 3 vols. Princeton, N.J.: Princeton University Press, 1974.

_____. Law and Civil War in the Modern World. Baltimore: Johns Hopkins University Press, 1974.

Morgan, Patrick M. Deterrence: A Conceptual Analysis. Beverly Hills, Calif.: Sage, 1977.

Morgenthau, Hans A. Politics among Nations. New York: Knopf, 1948.

Murray, John Courtney. Morality and War. New York: Church Peace Union, 1959.

_____. We Hold These Truths. New York: Sheed and Ward, 1960.

Murray, Thomas E. Nuclear Policy for War and Peace. New York: World, 1960.

Nagle, William J., ed. Morality and Modern Warfare. Baltimore: Helicon, 1960.

Niebuhr, Reinhold. Christianity and Power Politics. New York: Charles Scribner's Sons, 1940.

Nys, Ernest. Le droit de la guerre et les précurseurs de Grotius. Brussels: Librairie Européene, 1882.

O'Ballance, Edgar. No Victor, No Vanquished: The Yom Kippur War. San Rafael, Calif.: Presido, 1978.

Oberdorfer, Don. Tet! Garden City, N.Y.: Doubleday, 1971.

O'Brien, William V. The Law of Limited International Conflict. Washington, D.C.: Georgetown University, 1965.

_____. Nuclear War, Deterrence and Morality. Westminister, Md. and New York: Newman, 1967.

_____. U.S. Military Intervention: Law and Morality. Washington Papers, no. 68. Beverly Hills, Calif.: Sage/Center for Strategic and International Studies, Georgetown University, 1979.

_____. War and/or Survival. Garden City, N.Y.: Doubleday, 1969.

O'Connor, John J. A Chaplain Looks at Vietnam. Cleveland and New York: World, 1968.

_____. In Defense of Life. Boston: St. Paul Editions, 1981.

O'Neill, Bard E., William R. Heaton, and Donald J. Alberts, eds. Insurgency in the Modern World. Boulder, Colo.: Westview, 1980.

Onuf, Nicholas Greenwood. Reprisals: Rituals, Rules, Rationales. Center of International Studies, Woodrow Wilson School of Public and International Affairs Research Monograph no. 42. Princeton, N.J.: Princeton University Press, 1974.

Oppenheim, L. International Law. Edited by H. Lauterpacht. 7th ed. 2 vols. London: Longmans, Green, 1952.

Osanka, Franklin M. Modern Guerrilla Warfare. New York: Free Press, 1960.

Osgood, Robert Endicott. Limited War. Chicago: University of Chicago Press, 1957.

_____. Limited War Revisited. Boulder, Colo.: Westview, 1979.

_____. NATO: The Entangling Alliance. Chicago: University of Chicago Press. 1959.

Osgood, Robert E., and Robert W. Tucker. Force, Order and Justice. Baltimore: Johns Hopkins University Press, 1967.

Paget, Julian. Counterinsurgency Operations. New York: Walker, 1967.

Paget, R. T. Manstein. London: Collins, 1951.

Paige, Glenn D. The Korean Decision. New York: Free Press, 1968.

Paret, Peter. French Revolutionary Warfare from Indo-China to Algeria. New York: Praeger, 1964.

Paret, Peter, and John W. Shy. Guerrillas in the 1960's. Rev. ed. New York: Praeger, 1965.

Parmlee, Maurice. Blockade and Sea Power. New York: Crowell, 1924.

Peers, W. R. The Mylai Inquiry. New York: Norton, 1979.

Peterson, Harries-Clichy, ed. Che Guevara on Guerrilla Warfare. New York: Praeger, 1961.

Phillipson, Coleman. The International Law and Custom of Ancient Greece and Rome. 2 vols. London: Macmillan, 1911.

Pike, Douglas. Viet Cong. Cambridge, Mass.: MIT Press, 1966.

_____. War, Peace and the Viet Cong. Cambridge, Mass.: MIT Press, 1969.

Potter, Ralph B. The Moral Logic of War. Philadelphia: United Presbyterian Church, n.d.

_____. War and Moral Discourse. Richmond, Va.: John Knox, 1969.

Pustay, John S. Counter-insurgency Warfare. New York: Free Press, 1965.

Quandt, William B. Decade of Decisions. Berkeley and Los Angeles: University of California Press, 1977.

Ramsey, Paul. The Just War: Force and Political Responsibility. New York: Charles Scribner's Sons, 1968.

_____. War and the Christian Conscience: How Shall Modern War Be Conducted Justly? Durham, N. C.: Duke University Press, 1961.

Record, Jeffrey, and Thomas I. Anderson. U.S. Nuclear Weapons in Europe: Issues and Alternatives. Washington, D. C.: Brookings Institution, 1974.

Rees, David. Korea: The Limited War. New York: St. Martin's Press, 1964.

Regout, Robert. La doctrine de la guerre just de saint Augustin à nos jours d'après les théologiens et les juristes canoniques. Paris: Pedone, 1935.

Reich, Bernard. The Quest for Peace: United States-Israeli Relations and the Arab-Israeli Conflict. New Brunswick, N. J.: Transaction, 1977.

Ridgway, Matthew B. The Korean War. Garden City, N. Y.: Doubleday, 1967.

_____. Soldier: The Memoirs of Matthew B. Ridgway. New York: Harper, 1956.

Ro'i, Yaacov, ed. From Encroachment to Involvement: A Documentary Study of Soviet Policy in the Middle East. New York: Wiley, 1974.

Ro'i, Yaacov, ed. The Limits to Power: Soviet Policy in the Middle East. New York: St. Martin's Press, 1979.

Rommen, Heinrich A. The Natural Law: A Study in Legal and Social History and Philosophy. Translated by R. Hanley. St. Louis: Herder, 1947.

_____. The State in Catholic Thought. St. Louis: Herder, 1945.

Rowe, James N. Five Years to Freedom. Boston: Little, Brown, 1971.

Royse, M. W. Aerial Bombardment. New York: Vinal, 1928.

Sachar, Howard M. A History of Israel. New York: Knopf, 1976.

Sadat, Anwar el. In Search of Identity. New York: Harper & Row, 1978.

Safran, Nadav. Israel the Embattled Ally. Cambridge, Mass.: Harvard University Press, Belknap Press, 1978.

Schandler, Herbert Y. The Unmaking of a President: Lyndon Johnson and Vietnam. Princeton, N.J.: Princeton University Press, 1977.

Schelling, Thomas C. The Strategy of Conflict. New York: Oxford University Press, 1963.

_____. Arms and Influence. New Haven, Conn.: Yale University Press, 1966.

Schiff, Zeev. October Earthquake: Yom Kippur 1973. Translated by Louis Williams. Tel Aviv: University Publishing Projects, 1974.

Schwarzenberger, Georg. The Legality of Nuclear Weapons. London: Stevens, 1958.

Scott, Andrew M., ed. Insurgency. Chapel Hill: University of North Carolina Press, 1970.

Servan-Schreiber, Jean Jacques. Lieutenant in Algeria. Translated by Ronald Matthews. New York: Knopf, 1957.

Shannon, Thomas A., ed. War or Peace: The Search for New Answers. Maryknoll, N.Y.: Orbis, 1980.

Shawcross, William. Sideshow: Kissinger, Nixon and the Destruction of Cambodia. New York: Simon and Schuster, 1979.

Sheehan, Neil, Hedrick Smith, E. W. Kenworthy, and Fox Butterfield, eds. The Pentagon Papers, as Published by the New York Times. New York: Bantam, 1971.

Shinn, Roger. Wars and Rumors of War. Nashville: Abingdon, 1972.

Spanier, John. The Truman-MacArthur Controversy. Cambridge, Mass.: Belknap Press, 1959.

Speed, Roger. Strategic Deterrence in the 1980's. Stanford, Calif.: Hoover Institution, 1979.

Stanger, Roland J., ed. Essays on Intervention. Columbus: Ohio State University Press, 1964.

Starner, Frances Lucille. Magsaysay and the Philippine Peasantry: The Agrarian Impact on Philippine Politics, 1953-1956. Berkeley and Los Angeles: University of California Press, 1961.

Stein, Walter, ed. Nuclear Weapons and Christian Conscience. London: Merlin, 1961.

Stimson, Henry L., and McGeorge Bundy. On Active Service in Peace and War. New York: Harper, 1947.

Stockholm International Peace Research Institute. Incendiary Weapons. Cambridge, Mass.: MIT Press, 1975.

_____. The Problem of Chemical and Biological Warfare. New York: Humanities Press, 1973.

Stone, Julius. Aggression and World Order. Berkeley and Los Angeles: University of California Press, 1958.

_____. Legal Controls of International Conflict. 2d ed. New York: Rinehart, 1959.

Stremlau, John L. The International Politics of the Nigerian Civil War. Princeton, N.J.: Princeton University Press, 1977.

Tanham, George. Communist Revolutionary Warfare: The Vietminh in Indo-China. New York: Praeger, 1961.

_____. War without Guns. New York: Praeger, 1966.

Taylor, Maxwell D. The Uncertain Trumpet. New York: Harper, 1959.

Taylor, Telford. Nuremberg and Vietnam: An American Tragedy. Chicago: Quadrangle, 1970.

Thomas, Ann Van Wynnen, and A. J. Thomas, Jr. Legal Limits on the Use of Chemical and Biological Weapons. Dallas: Southern Methodist University Press, 1970.

_____. Non-Intervention: The Law and Its Import in the Americas. Dallas: Southern Methodist University Press, 1956.

Thompson, James Clay. Rolling Thunder: Understanding Policy and Program Failure. Chapel Hill: University of North Carolina Press, 1980.

Thompson, Kenneth W. Political Realism and the Crisis of World Politics. Princeton, N.J.: Princeton University Press, 1960.

Thompson, Sir Robert. Defeating Communist Insurgency: The Lessons of Malaya and Vietnam. New York: Praeger, 1966.

_____. No Exit from Vietnam. New York: David McKay, 1970.

_____. Revolutionary War in World Strategy, 1945–1969. New York: Taplinger, 1970.

Tooke, Joan B. The Just War in Aquinas and Grotius. London: SPCK, 1965.

Trinquier, Roger. Modern Warfare. Translated by Daniel Lee. New York: Praeger, 1964.

Trooboff, Peter D., ed. Law and Responsibility in Warfare: The Vietnam Experience. Chapel Hill: University of North Carolina Press, 1975.

Truman, Harry S. Memoirs. 2 vols. Garden City, N.Y.: Doubleday, 1955.

Tucker, Robert W. The Just War. Baltimore: Johns Hopkins University Press, 1960.

_____. The Law of War and Neutrality at Sea. International Law Studies, vol. 50. Newport, R.I.: U.S. Naval War College, 1955.

_____. The Radical Left and American Foreign Policy. Baltimore: Johns Hopkins University Press, 1971.

Ulam, Adam. The Rivals: America and Russia since World War II. New York: Viking, 1971.

Vanderpol, Alfred. La doctrine scolastique du droit de guerre. Paris: Pedone, 1919.

Verrier, Anthony. The Bomber Offensive. New York: Macmillan, 1966.

Verwey, Wil D. Riot Control Agents and Herbicides in War. Leiden: A. W. Sijthoff, 1977.

Vincent, R. J. Nonintervention and International Order. Princeton, N.J.: Princeton University Press, 1974.

von Glahn, Gerhard. The Occupation of Enemy Territory. Minneapolis: University of Minnesota Press, 1957.

von Manstein, Erich. Lost Victories. Translated by Anthony G. Powell. Chicago: Henry Regnery, 1958.

Wakin, Malham M., ed. War, Morality and the Military Profession. Boulder, Colo.: Westview, 1979.

Walzer, Michael. Just and Unjust Wars. New York: Basic, 1977.

Wasserstrom, Richard A., ed. War and Morality. Belmont, Calif.: Wadsworth, 1970.

Weber, Theodore. Modern War and the Pursuit of Peace. New York: Council on Religion and International Affairs, 1968.

Webster, Sir Charles, and Noble Frankland. The Strategic Air Offensive against Germany, 1939-1945. 4 vols. London: Her Majesty's Stationery Office, 1961.

Westmoreland, William C. A Soldier Reports. Garden City, N.Y.: Doubleday, 1976.

Whetten, Lawrence I. The Canal War: Four-Power Conflict in the Middle East. Cambridge, Mass.: MIT Press, 1974.

White, W. L. The Captives of Korea: Their Treatment of Our Prisoners and Our Treatment of Theirs. New York: Scribner's, 1957.

Whiteman, Marjorie M. Digest of International Law. 15 vols. Washington, D.C.: U.S. Government Printing Office, 1968-73.

Whiting, Allen S. China Crosses the Yalu: The Decision to Enter the Korean War. New York: Macmillan, 1960.

Williams, Alden, and David W. Tarr, eds. Modules in Security Studies. Lawrence: University Press of Kansas, 1974.

Williams, William Appleman. The Tragedy of American Diplomacy. Rev. ed. New York: Dell, 1962.

Zumwalt, Elmo R., Jr. On Watch: A Memoir. New York: New York Times, Quadrangle, 1976.

CHAPTERS IN A FULL-LENGTH
WORK AND JOURNAL ARTICLES

Abbott, Walter M. "Gaudium et Spes, The Pastoral Constitution on the Church in the Modern World." In The Documents of Vatican II, edited by Walter M. Abbott, pp. 199-308. New York: Guild/America/Association, 1966.

Abshire, David M. "Lessons of Vietnam: Proportionality and Credibility." In The Vietnam Legacy, edited by Anthony Lake, pp. 392-410. New York: New York University Press, 1976.

Aldrich, George H. "Comments." In Law and Responsibility in Warfare: The Vietnam Experience, edited by Peter D. Trooboff, pp. 173-75. Chapel Hill: University of North Carolina Press, 1975.

American Society of International Law. "Panel: Biafra, Bengal, and Beyond: International Responsibility and Genocidal Conflict." In American Society of International Law Proceedings, 1972, pp. 89-108.

Baxter, Richard R. "Ius in Bello Interno: The Present and Future Law." In Law and Civil War in the Modern World, edited by John Norton Moore, pp. 518-36. Baltimore: Johns Hopkins University Press, 1974.

Bay, Charles H. "The Other Gas Crisis—Chemical Weapons." Parameters 9 (1979): pt. 1, 70-80; pt. 2, 65-78.

Blum, Yehuda. "The Beirut Raid and the International Double Standard: A Reply to Professor Falk." American Journal of International Law 64 (1970): 73-105.

Boudin, Leonard B. "Individual Responsibility in Warfare 19." In Law and Responsibility in Warfare: The Vietnam Experience, edited by Peter D. Trooboff, pp. 211-16. Chapel Hill: University of North Carolina Press, 1975.

Bowett, Derek W. "The Interrelation of Theories of Intervention and Self-defense." In Law and Civil War in the Modern World, edited by John Norton Moore, pp. 38-50. Baltimore: Johns Hopkins University Press, 1974.

Bracken Paul. "Collateral Damage and Theatre Warfare." Survival 22 (1980): 203-7.

Brownlie, Ian. "Humanitarian Intervention." In Law and Civil War in the Modern World, edited by John Norton Moore, pp. 218-27. Baltimore: Johns Hopkins University Press, 1974.

Brungs, Bernard. "The Status of Biological Warfare in International Law." Military Law Review 24 (1964): 47-95.

Burke, William T. "The Legal Regulation of Minor International Coercion: A Framework of Inquiry." In Essays on Intervention, edited by Roland J. Stanger, pp. 87-125. Columbus: Ohio State University Press, 1964.

Canby, Steven L. "The Alliance and Europe: Part IV, Military Doctrine and Technology." Adelphi Papers, Monographic Studies no. 109. London: International Institute for Strategic Studies, 1975.

_____. "Rethinking the NATO Military Problem." International Security Studies Program, Working Papers no. 3. Washington, D.C.: Wilson Center, June 20, 1979.

Carnahan, Burrus M. "The Law of Air Bombardment in Its Historical Context." Air Force Law Review 17(1975): 39-60.

Childress, James F. "Just-War Theories." Theological Studies 39 (1978): 427-45.

_____. "Just-War Criteria." In War or Peace: The Search for New Answers, edited by Thomas A. Shannon, pp. 40-58. Maryknoll, N.Y.: Orbis, 1980.

Claude, Inis L. "Just Wars: Doctrines and Institutions." Political Science Quarterly 95 (1980): 83-96.

Comité International des Experts sur la Torture. "La prévention et la suppression de la torture/The Prevention and Suppression of Torture." In Revue international de droit pénal, 1977, pp. 24-114, 267-310.

Connery, John R. "Morality of Nuclear Armament." In Morality and Modern Warfare, edited by William J. Nagle, pp. 92-97. Baltimore: Helicon, 1960.

D'Amato, Anthony A., Harvel L. Gould, and Larry D. Woods. "War Crimes and Vietnam: The 'Nuremberg Defense' and the Military Service Resister." California Law Review 57 (1969): 1093-1110.

Davis, Lynn Etheridge. "Limited Nuclear Options: Deterrence and the New American Doctrine." Adelphi Papers, Monographic Studies no. 121. London: International Institute for Strategic Studies, 1975-76.

De Saussure, Hamilton, and Robert Glasser. "Methods and Means of Warfare 9." In Law and Responsibility in Warfare: The Vietnam Experience, edited by Peter D. Trooboff, pp. 119-39. Chapel Hill: University of North Carolina Press, 1975.

Draper, G. I. A. D. "Wars of National Liberation and Criminal Responsibility." In Restraints on War: Studies in the Limitation of Armed Conflict, edited by Michael Howard, pp. 135-62. Oxford: Oxford University Press, 1979.

Dunbar, N. C. H. "Military Necessity in War Crimes Trials." British Year Book of International Law 29 (1952): 442-54.

Erickson, John. "The Soviet Union's Growing Arsenal of Chemical Warfare." Strategic Review 7 (1979): 63-71.

Ermarth, Fritz. "Contrasts in American and Soviet Strategic Thought." International Security 3 (1978): 138-55.

Falk, Richard. "The Beirut Raid and the International Law of Reprisal." American Journal of International Law 63 (1969): 415-43.

_____. "Environmental Warfare and Ecocide." In The Vietnam War and International Law, edited by Richard A. Falk. 4 vols. Princeton, N.J.: Princeton University Press, 1969-76, 4: 287-303.

_____. "Methods and Means of Warfare 1." In Law and Responsibility in Warfare: The Vietnam Experience, edited by Peter D. Trooboff, pp. 37-53. Chapel Hill: University of North Carolina Press, 1975.

Fall, Bernard. "The Theory and Practice of Insurgency and Counter-insurgency." Naval War College Review 17 (1965): 21-38.

Farer, Tom J. "Harnessing Rogue Elephants: A Short Discourse on Intervention in Civil Strife." In The Vietnam War and International Law, edited by Richard A. Falk. 4 vols. Princeton, N.J.: Princeton University Press, 1969-76, 2: 1089-1115.

Farer, Tom J., Robert G. Gard, Jr., and Telford Taylor. "Vietnam and the Nuremberg Principles: A Colloquy on War Crimes." In The Vietnam War and International Law, edited by Richard A. Falk. 4 vols. Princeton, N.J.: Princeton University Press, 1969-76, 4: 363-420.

Fischer, Robert Lucas. "Defending the Central Front: The Balance of Forces." Adelphi Papers, Monographic Studies no. 127. London: The International Institute for Strategic Studies, 1976.

Ford, John C. "The Hydrogen Bombing of Cities." In Morality and Modern Warfare, edited by William J. Nagle, pp. 98-103. Baltimore: Helicon, 1960.

_____. "The Morality of Obliteration Bombing." Theological Studies 5 (1944): 261-309.

Forsythe, David P. "Legal Management of Internal War: The 1977 Protocol on Non-International Armed Conflicts." American Journal of International Law 72 (1978): 272-95.

Fraleigh, Arnold. "The Algerian Revolution as a Case Study in International Law." In The International Law of Civil War, edited by Richard A. Falk, pp. 179-243. Baltimore: Johns Hopkins University Press, 1971.

Franck, Thomas M., and Nigel S. Rodley. "After Bangladesh: The Law of Humanitarian Intervention by Military Force." American Journal of International Law 62 (1973): 275-305.

Frye, Alton. "Nuclear Weapons in Europe: No Exit from Ambivalence." Survival 22 (1980): 98-106.

Garnett, John C. "Limited 'Conventional' War in the Nuclear Age." In Restraints on War: Studies in the Limitation of Armed Conflict, edited by Michael Howard, pp. 79-102. Oxford: Oxford University Press, 1979.

Gelb, Leslie H. "The Essential Domino: American Politics and Vietnam." Foreign Affairs 50 (1972): 459-75.

Gessert, Robert A. "P.D. 59: The Better Way." Worldview 23 (1980): 7-9.

Gray, Colin S. "NATO Strategy and the 'Neutron Bomb.'" Policy Review 7 (1979): 7-11.

Halperin, Morton H. "The Lessons Nixon Learned." In The Vietnam Legacy, edited by Anthony Lake, pp. 411-28. New York: New York University Press, 1976.

Hartigan, Richard Shelly. "Non-Combatant Immunity: Reflections on Its Origins and Present Status." Review of Politics 29 (1966): 204-20.

_____. "Saint Augustine on War and Killing: The Problem of the Innocent." Journal of the History of Ideas 27 (1966): 195-204.

Head, Richard G. "Technology and the Military Balance." Foreign Affairs 56 (1978): 544-63.

Hehir, J. Bryan. "The Just-War Ethic and Catholic Theology: Dynamics of Change and Continuity." In War or Peace: The Search for New Answers, edited by Thomas A. Shannon, pp. 15-39. Maryknoll, N.Y.: Orbis, 1980.

_____. "P. D. 59: New Issue in an Old Argument." Worldview 23 (1980): 10-12.

Higgins, Rosalyn. "International Law and Civil Conflict." In The International Regulation of Civil War, edited by Evan Luard, pp. 169-86. New York: New York University Press, 1972.

Hoeber, Amoretta M., and Joseph D. Douglass, Jr. "The Neglected Threat of Chemical Warfare." International Security 3 (1978): 55-82.

Howard, Michael. "Temperamenta Belli: Can War Be Controlled?" In Restraints on War: Studies in the Limitation of Armed Conflict, edited by Michael Howard, pp. 1-55. Oxford: Oxford University Press, 1979.

Huber, Max. "Die Kriegsrechtlichen Verträge und die Kriegsraison." Zeitschrift für Völkerrecht und Bundesstaatsrecht 7 (1913): 351-74.

Iklé, Fred Charles. "NATO's 'First Nuclear Use': A Deepening Trap?" Strategic Review 8 (1980): 18-23.

International Law Association. "The International Protection of Human Rights by General International Law." In Report of the 54th Conference, The Hague, 1970, pp. 633-41.

Johnson, James T. "Morality and Force in Statecraft: Paul Ramsey and the Just War Tradition." In Love and Society: Essays in the Ethics of Paul Ramsey, edited by James T. Johnson and David Smith, pp. 93-114. Missoula, Mont.: American Academy of Religion/Scholars Press, 1974.

Johnstone, L. C. "Ecocide and the Geneva Protocol." Foreign Affairs 49 (1970-71): 711-20.

Jordan, Robert E., III. "Counterinsurgency, Tactics and Law, 2." In Law and Responsibility in Warfare: The Vietnam Experience, edited by Peter D. Trooboff, pp. 60-61. Chapel Hill: University of North Carolina Press, 1975.

Kester, John G. "The Future of the Joint Chiefs of Staff." In AEI Foreign Policy and Defense Review, Washington, D.C.: American Enterprise Institution for Public Policy Research, 1980, 2: 2-36.

Kissinger, Henry. "The Future of NATO." Washington Quarterly 2 (1979): 3-17.

_____. "The Vietnam Negotiations." Foreign Affairs 47 (1969): 211-34.

Kunz, Josef L. "Bellum Justum and Bellum Legale: Editorial Comment." American Journal of International Law 45 (1951): 528-34.

Lambeth, Benjamin S. "Selective Nuclear Operations and Soviet Strategy." In Beyond Nuclear Deterrence, edited by Johan J. Holst and Uwe Nerlich, pp. 79-104. New York: Crane, Russak, 1977.

Lauterpacht, H. "The Problem of the Revision of the Law of War." British Year Book of International Law 29 (1952): 361.

Leacacos, John P. "Kissinger's Apparat." Foreign Policy 5 (1971-72): 2-7.

Lemkin, Raphael. "Genocide as a Crime under International Law." American Journal of International Law 41 (1947): 145-51.

Levie, Howard S. "Maltreatment of Prisoners of War in Vietnam." In The Vietnam War and International Law, edited by Richard A. Falk. 4 vols. Princeton, N.J.: Princeton University Press, 1969-76, 2: 361-97.

_____. "Weapons of Warfare, 12." In Law and Responsibility in Warfare: The Vietnam Experience, edited by Peter D. Trooboff, pp. 153-60. Chapel Hill: University of North Carolina Press, 1975.

Lillich, Richard B. "Forcible Self-Help by States to Protect Human Rights." Iowa Law Review 53 (1967): 325-51.

_____. "Humanitarian Intervention: A Reply to Ian Brownlie and a Plea for Constructive Alternatives." In Law and Civil War in the Modern World, edited by John Norton Moore, pp. 229-51. Baltimore: Johns Hopkins University Press, 1974.

_____. "Intervention to Protect Human Rights." McGill Law Journal 15 (1969): 205-19.

McCormick, R. A. "Morality of War." New Catholic Encyclopedia, 14 vols. New York: McGraw-Hill, 1967, 14: 802-7.

McDougal, Myres S. "Authority to Use Force on the High Seas." Naval War College Review 20 (1967): 19-31.

McDougal, Myres S., and W. Michael Reisman. "Rhodesia and the United Nations: The Lawfulness of International Concern." American Journal of International Law 62 (1968): 1-19.

McKenna, Joseph C. "Ethics and War: A Catholic View." American Political Science Review 54 (1960): 647-58.

Martin, Laurence. "Limited Nuclear War." In Restraints on War: Studies in the Limitation of Armed Conflict, edited by Michael Howard, pp. 102-21. Oxford: Oxford University Press, 1979.

Menhaul, Stewart W. B. "The Shifting Theater Nuclear Balance in Europe." Strategic Review 6 (1978): 34-45.

Meyrowitz, Henri. "The Law of War in the Vietnamese Conflict."
In The Vietnam War and International Law, edited by Richard
A. Falk. 4 vols. Princeton, N.J.: Princeton University
Press, 1969-76, 2: 516-71.

Moore, John Norton. "Intervention: A Monochromatic Term for a
Polychromatic Reality." In The Vietnam War and International
Law, edited by Richard A. Falk. 4 vols. Princeton, N.J.:
Princeton University Press, 1969-76, 2: 1061-88.

Murray, John Courtney. "Theology and Modern War." Theological
Studies 20 (1959): 40-61.

_____. "Theology and Modern War." In Morality and Modern War-
fare, edited by William J. Nagle, pp. 69-91. Baltimore: Helicon, 1960.

_____. "Theology and Modern War." In The Moral Dilemmas of
Nuclear Weapons: Essays from Worldview, edited by William
Clancy, pp. 7-16. New York: Council on Religion and Interna-
tional Affairs, 1961.

_____. "The Uses of a Doctrine on the Use of Force: Was as a Moral
Problem." In We Hold These Truths, edited by John Courtney
Murray, pp. 249-73. New York: Sheed and Ward, 1960.

Murry, William V. "Clausewitz and Limited Nuclear War." Military
Review 55 (1975): 15-28.

Nitze, Paul. "The Relationship of Strategic and Theater Forces."
International Security 2 (1977): 122-32.

Nurick, Lester. "The Distinction between Combatants and Noncombatants in the Law of War." American Journal of International
Law 39 (1945): 680-97.

O'Brien, William V. "Biological/Chemical Warfare and the International Law of War." Georgetown Law Journal 51 (1962): 1-63.

_____. "International Law and the Outbreak of War in the Middle East,
1967." Orbis 11 (1967): 692-723.

_____. "The Law of War: Command Responsibility and Vietnam."
Georgetown Law Journal 60 (1972): 605-64.

_____. "Legitimate Military Necessity in Nuclear War." World Polity 2 (1960): 35-120.

_____. "The Meaning of 'Military Necessity' in International Law." World Polity 1 (1957): 109-76.

_____. "Morality and War: The Contribution of Paul Ramsey." In Love and Society: Essays in the Ethics of Paul Ramsey, edited by James T. Johnson and David Smith, pp. 163-84. Missoula, Mont.: American Academy of Religion/Scholars Press, 1974.

O'Connell, D. P. "Limited War at Sea since 1945." In Restraints on War: Studies in the Limitation of Armed Conflict, edited by Michael Howard, pp. 123-34. Oxford: Oxford University Press, 1979.

Osgood, Robert E. "The Reappraisal of Limited War." Adelphi Papers, Monographic Studies no. 54. London: International Institute for Strategic Studies, 1969, pp. 41-54.

Parks, William Hays. "Command Responsibility for War Crimes." Military Law Review 62 (1973): 1-104.

_____. "The Law of War Adviser." JAG Journal 31 (1980): 1-52.

Paust, Jordan J. "After My Lai: The Case for War Crimes Jurisdiction over Civilians in Federal District Courts." In The Vietnam War and International Law, edited by Richard A. Falk. 4 vols. Princeton, N.J.: Princeton University Press, 1969-76, 4: 447-75.

Petrowski, Lawrence C. "Law and the Conduct of the Vietnam War." In The Vietnam War and International Law, edited by Richard A. Falk. 4 vols. Princeton, N.J.: Princeton University Press, 1969-76, 2: 439-515.

Pope John XXIII. "Peace on Earth (Pacem in Terris)." In Encyclical Letter. Washington, D.C.: National Catholic Welfare Conference, 1963.

Pope Paul VI. "Address to the UN Assembly, October 4, 1965." The Pope Speaks 11 (1966): 54-55.

_____. "Mense Mai." The Pope Speaks 10 (1965): 220-24.

_____. "On the Development of Peoples." Washington, D.C.: United States Catholic Conference, March 26, 1967.

_____. "Remarks before Recitation of the Angelus, August 8, 1965." The Pope Speaks 10 (1965): 358, 406.

Pope Pius XII. "Address to Delegates of the Eighth Congress of the World Medical Association, Rome, September 30, 1954." In Pattern for Peace: Catholic Statements on International Order, edited by Harry W. Flannery, pp. 236-37. Westminster, Md.: Newman, 1962.

Ramsey, Paul. "A Political Ethics Context for Strategic Thinking." In Strategic Thinking and Its Moral Significance, edited by Morton A. Kaplan, pp. 101-47. Chicago: University of Chicago Center for Policy Study, 1973.

Rosen, Steven J. "A Stable System of Mutual Deterrence in the Arab-Israeli Conflict." American Political Science Review 71 (1977): 1367-83.

Rosenau, James N. "The Concept of Intervention." Journal of International Affairs 22 (1968): 165-76.

_____. "Intervention as a Scientific Concept and Postscript." In The Vietnam War and International Law, edited by Richard A. Falk. 4 vols. Princeton, N.J.: Princeton University Press, 1969-76, 2: 979-1015.

Rostow, Walt W. "Countering Guerrilla Attack." In The Vietnam War and International Law, edited by Richard A. Falk. 4 vols. Princeton, N.J.: Princeton University Press, 1969-76, 1: 127-34.

Rothfels, H. "Clausewitz." In Makers of Modern Strategy, edited by Edward Meade Earle, pp. 93-113. Princeton, N.J.: Princeton University Press, 1943.

Scherer, John L. "Soviet and American Behavior during the Yom Kippur War." World Affairs 141 (1978): 2-23.

Snow, Donald M. "Current Nuclear Deterrence Thinking: An Overview and Review." International Studies Quarterly 23 (1979): 445-86.

Solf, Waldemar A. "A Response to Telford Taylor's 'Nuremberg and Vietnam: An American Tragedy'." In The Vietnam War and International Law, edited by Richard A. Falk. 4 vols. Princeton, N.J.: Princeton University Press, 1969–76, 4: 421–46.

Statutory Comments. "The War Powers Resolution: Statutory Limitation on the Commander-in-Chief." Harvard Journal on Legislation 11 (1974): 181–204.

Tanham, George, and Dennis J. Duncanson. "Some Dilemmas of Counterinsurgency." Foreign Affairs 48 (1969): 113–22.

Taubenfeld, Howard J. "The Applicability of the Laws of War in Civil War." In Law and Civil War in the Modern World, edited by John Norton Moore, pp. 499–517. Baltimore: Johns Hopkins University Press, 1974.

Tucker, Robert W. "Weapons of Warfare, 13." In Law and Responsibility in Warfare: The Vietnam Experience, edited by Peter D. Trooboff, pp. 161–72. Chapel Hill: University of North Carolina Press, 1975.

von Elbe, Joachim. "The Evolution of the Concept of the Just War in International Law." American Journal of International Law 33 (1939): 665–88.

Waldock, C. H. M. "Use of Force in International Law." In Académie de droit international de la Haye, recueil des cours 81 (1952): pt. 2, 455–514.

Walters, LeRoy. "Historical Application of the Just War Theory: Four Case Studies in Normative Ethics." In Love and Society: Essays in the Ethics of Paul Ramsey, edited by James T. Johnson and David Smith, pp. 115–38. Missoula, Mont.: American Academy of Religion/Scholars Press, 1974.

Weiden, Paul. "Necessity in International Law." Transactions of the Grotius Society 24 (1939): 113.

Westing, Arthur H. "Proscription of Ecocide: Arms Control and the Environment." In The Vietnam War and International Law, edited by Richard A. Falk. 4 vols. Princeton, N.J.: Princeton University Press, 1969–76, 4: 283–86.

PUBLIC DOCUMENTS

Ford, Gerald R. "Renunciation of Certain Uses in War of Chemical Herbicides and Riot Control Agents." Federal Register, vol. 40 (April 10, 1975).

The Netherlands Government. Documents Relating to the Program of the First Hague Peace Conference. 1921.

Nixon, Richard M. "War Powers Veto Text." Congressional Quarterly 31 (October 27, 1973): 2855-56.

North Atlantic Treaty Organization. NATO Handbook. Brussels: NATO Information Service, 1980.

United Nations, War Crimes Commission. Law Reports of Trials of War Criminals. 15 vols. London: His Majesty's Stationery Office, 1947-49.

U.S., Arms Control and Disarmament Agency. Arms Control and Disarmament Agreements—Texts and Histories of Negotiations. Washington, D.C.: Arms Control and Disarmament Agency, 1980.

U.S., Army Infantry School. Tactical Operations Handbook. Fort Benning, Ga., 1964.

U.S., Congress, Congressional Budget Office. Planning U.S. General-Purpose Forces: The Theater Nuclear Forces. Washington, D.C.: Government Printing Office, 1977.

U.S., Congress, Senate, Joint Committee on Armed Services and Foreign Relations. Hearings, Military Situation in the Far East. 82d Cong., 1st sess., 1951.

U.S., Department of the Air Force. Commander's Handbook on the Law of Armed Conflict, AFP 110-34. Washington, D.C.: Department of the Air Force, July 25, 1980.

_____. Functions and Basic Doctrine of the United States Air Force, 14 February 1979, AFM 1-1. Washington, D.C.: Department of the Air Force, 1979.

_____. International Law—The Conduct of Armed Conflict and Air Operations, 19 November 1976, AFP 110-31. Washington, D.C.: Department of the Air Force, 1976.

U.S., Department of the Army. The Army, FM 100-1. Washington, D.C.: Department of the Army, September 29, 1978.

_____. The Law of Land Warfare, July 1956, FM 27-10. Washington, D.C.: Department of the Army, 1956.

_____. Operations, FM 110-5. Washington, D.C.: Department of the Army, July 1, 1976.

_____. Operations against Irregular Forces, FM 31-15. Washington, D.C.: Department of the Army, 1961.

_____. Operations of Armed Forces in the Field, FM 100-5. Washington, D.C.: Department of the Army, September 1968.

_____. Subject Schedule 27-1. Washington, D.C.: Department of the Army, 1970.

U.S., Department of State. "Legality of United States Participation in the Defense of Viet-Nam." (Memorandum of legal adviser of Department of State, March 4, 1966). Department of State Bulletin 54 (1966): 474-89. Reprinted in American Journal of International Law 60 (1966): 565-85.

_____. Report of the United States Delegation to the Diplomatic Conference on the Reaffirmation and Development of International Humanitarian Law Applicable in Armed Conflicts. Washington, D.C., September 8, 1977.

_____. Trial of War Criminals 13. Department of State Publication no. 2420, 1945.

U.S., Naval War College. International Law Discussions, 1903. Washington, D.C.: Government Printing Office, 1904.

U.S., President. Public Papers of the Presidents of the United States: Dwight D. Eisenhower, 1954. Washington, D.C.: Government Printing Office, 1960.

U.S., Secretary of Defense. Report of the Secretary of Defense to the Congress on the FY 1975 Budget and FY 1975-1979 Defense Program. Washington, D.C.: Government Printing Office, March 4, 1974.

U.S., Strategic Bombing Survey. Japan's Struggle to End the War. Washington, D.C.: Government Printing Office, 1946.

_____. Overall Report (European War), September 30, 1945. Washington, D. C.: Government Printing Office, 1945.

_____. Summary Report (Pacific War), July 1, 1946. Washington, D. C.: Government Printing Office, 1946.

INTERNATIONAL AGREEMENTS

Charter of the Organization of American States. T. I. A. S. no. 2361. 1948.

European Convention for the Protection of Human Rights and Fundamental Freedoms. 213 UNTS 222. 1955.

Geneva Convention for the Amelioration of the Condition of the Wounded and Sick in Armed Forces in the Field, 12 August 1949. 6 UST 3114, T. I. A. S. 3362, 75 UNTS 31. 1956.

Geneva Convention for the Amelioration of the Condition of the Wounded, Sick and Shipwrecked Members of Armed Forces at Sea, 12 August 1949. 6 UST 3217, T. I. A. S. 3363, 75 UNTS 85. 1956.

Geneva Convention on Prohibitions or Restrictions on the Use of Certain Conventional Weapons Which May Be Deemed To Be Excessively Injurious or To Have Indiscriminate Effects. October 10, 1980.

Geneva Convention on the Prohibition of the Development, Production, and Stockpiling of Bacteriological (Biological) and Toxin Weapons and on Their Destruction, April 10, 1972. 26 UST 57, T. I. A. S. 8062.

Geneva Convention Relative to the Protection of Civilian Persons in Time of War, 12 August 1949. 6 UST 3516, T. I. A. S. 3365, 75 UNTS 287. 1956.

Geneva Convention Relative to the Treatment of Prisoners of War, 12 August 1949. 6 UST 3316, T. I. A. S. 3364, 75 UNTS 135. 1956.

Geneva Protocol Additional to the Geneva Conventions of 12 August 1949 and Relating to the Protection of Victims of International Armed Conflicts (Protocol I), December 12, 1977. UN Doc. A/32/144, (1977) International Legal Materials 16 (1977): 1391-1441.

Geneva Protocol Additional to the Geneva Conventions of 12 August 1949 and Relating to the Protection of Victims of Non-International Armed Conflicts (Protocol II), December 12, 1977. UN Doc. A/32/144 (1977). International Legal Materials 16 (1977): 1442-49.

Geneva Protocol for the Prohibition of the Use in War of Asphyxiating, Poisonous, or Other Gases, and of Bacteriological Methods of Warfare, 17 June 1925. 26 UST 571, T.I.A.S. 8061, 94 LNTS 65. 1975.

Hague Convention IV Respecting the Laws and Customs of War on Land, October 18, 1907. 36 Stat. 2277, Treaty Series no. 539.

CASES

European Court of Human Rights. Ireland v. United Kingdom. Judgment of January 18, 1978. International Legal Materials 17 (1978): 680.

Grisham v. Hogan. 361 U.S. 278. 1960.

Kinsella v. Singleton. 361 U.S. 324. 1960.

McElroy v. Guiagliardo. 361 U.S. 281. 1960.

Nuremberg International Military Tribunal. Trial of the Major War Criminals before the International Military Tribunal, Nuremberg, 14 November 1945-1 October 1946. 42 vols. Nuremberg, 1947-49.

O'Callahan v. Parker. 395 U.S. 258. 1969.

Reid v. Covert. 354 U.S. 1. 1957.

Tribunal militaire permanent de Paris, Dossiers des pièces de la procédure contre Black, Hermann; Weise, Henri; Petersen, Erich; Schiel, Othon E.—Jugement No. 119/2745 de 19 janvier 1950.

Tribunal militaire permanent de Paris, Dossiers des pièces de la procédure suivie contre le Général Ramke, Hermann et autres—Jugement No. 189/4176 de 21 Mars 1951.

United Nations, War Crimes Commission. Law Reports of Trials of War Criminals, 15 vols. London: His Majesty's Stationery Office, 1947-49.

United States v. Calley, 22 U.S.C.M.A. 534, 48 C.M.R. 19. 1973.

United States v. List. Nuremberg Military Tribunals, Trials of War Criminals, 15 vols. Washington, D.C.: U.S. Government Printing Office, 1949-51, 11: 757-1319.

United States v. Medina. C.M. 427162. 1971.

United States v. Ohlendorf. Nuremberg Military Tribunals, Trials of War Criminals. 15 vols. Washington, D.C.: U.S. Government Printing Office, 1950, 4: 3-596.

United States v. von Leeb. Nuremberg Military Tribunals, Trials of War Criminals, 15 vols. Washington, D.C.: U.S. Government Printing Office, 1949-51, 10; 11: 1-756.

UNPUBLISHED THESES

Brungs, Bernard Joseph. "Hostages, Prisoner Reprisals, and Collective Penalties: The Development of the International Law with Respect to Collective and Vicarious Punishment." Ph.D. dissertation, Georgetown University, 1968.

O'Brien, William V. "Military Necessity: The Development of the Concept of Military Necessity and Its Interpretation in the Modern Law of War." Ph.D. dissertation, Georgetown University, 1953.

Walters, LeRoy. "Five Classic Just War Theories: A Study in the Thought of Thomas Aquinas, Vitoria, Suarez, Gentili and Grotius." Ph.D. dissertation, Yale University, 1971.

INDEX

Abd al-Ghani al-Gamzi, 281

Abrams, Creighton W., Jr., 258

Adan, Avraham "Bren," 287, 290

aerial bombardment (see bombing)

Afghanistan, 212, 336

aggression, 73, 88, 94, 143, 337; and nuclear deterrence, 128-32; in Vietnam War, 92-93, 260-61, 268

Aldrich, George H., 408 n

Allison, George B., 428 n

American Civil War, 14, 18, 48, 50, 156, 207

Aqaba, Gulf of, 133, 286, 288

Aquinas, Saint Thomas, 4, 13, 15, 17, 19-22, 33-35

Arab League, 286 (see also Yom Kippur War)

Aristotle, 21-22

arms control, 130, 139-40

Army of the Republic of Vietnam (ARVN), 95, 99, 264 (see also Vietnam War)

Aron, Raymond, 6, 207, 236, 352

Article 2(4) (see United Nations Charter)

Article 51 (see United Nations Charter)

ARVN (see Army of the Republic of Vietnam)

atomic bomb (see bombing, World War II atomic)

Augustine, Saint, 4, 13, 17, 33-35

el Badri, Hassan, 434 n

balance of power, 74-75

balance of terror, 138, 140, 257, 355 (see also mutual assured destruction)

Baldwin, Hanson W., 352

Baxter, Richard R., 404 n, 413-14 n

Beaufre, André, 415 n

belligerent status, 16, 19; in international law, 160-62, 185-87

Bennett, John C., 364 n

Best, Geoffrey, 377 n, 379 n, 383 n

Betts, Richard K., 387 n, 424-26 n, 428 n

Biafran Civil War, 23, 198

biological warfare, 60-61, 144, 150, 314, 345 (see also chemical warfare; means mala prohibita)

Blitz, 77, 81, 84 (see also bombing, World War II conventional)

blockades, 144, 147; and starvation, 109; and Vietnam War, 264-65; in World War I, 48-49, 146

body count (see casualty statistics)

bombing, 48, 195; in Korean War, 53, 90, 146; United States Air Force manual on, 53-54; in Vietnam War, 93, 146, 258-59, 263-66 [Christmas Linebacker II attacks in, 273, 311-12, 339; and discrimination, 53, 341; and modes of limitation, 308; of North Vietnam, 98, 119-26; of South Vietnam, 98-102; and World War II policy compared, 120-22]; World War II atomic, 208 [and proportion, 40-41, 75-76, 84-87, 339 (see also nuclear war)]; World War II conventional, 40, 69, 75, 84, 347

[British strategic policy of, 303-5; and discrimination, 339, 341; fire-storm, 82-83; and North Vietnam bombing compared, 120-22; objectives of, 79-81; and proportion, 77, 145-46; U.S. practices of, compared with British and German, 53]
Bowett, Derek W., 371n
Bradley, Omar N., 421n
Braestrup, Peter, 427n
Brezhnev, Leonid I., 282-83
brinksmanship, 7
Britain, and World War II, 72, 77, 81, 303-5
Brodie, Bernard, 6, 222, 420n, 422n
Brungs, Bernard Joseph, 411n
Burke, Ed, 418n

Calley case (see United States v. Calley)
Cambodia, 21, 212; and human rights violations, 23, 173; and Vietnam War expansion to, 93, 97, 230-31, 260, 267
Carnahan, Burrus M., 379n
Caroline case, 132
Carr, E. H., 6
Casablanca directive (1943), 304, 305
casualty statistics, 99-101 (see also noncombatants)
Catholic church (see Christian teaching on war)
channels of limitation, 9, 314-17, 324-28, 357-60
chemical warfare, 144, 150; international-law ban of, 149, 345-46; use of gas in, 59, 86, 105-7; in Vietnam War, 60, 98, 107-10, 123 (see also biological warfare; means mala prohibita)
Chiang Kai-shek, 89, 241, 250

Childress, James F., 23, 364n, 367n, 373-74n, 376n
China, People's Republic of, 21, 75, 88, 211-13; and Korean War, 89-90, 240, 242-44, 247-48; and Vietnam War, 122, 264-65
chivalric code, 13, 37, 43, 65-66
Christian teaching on war, 1-5, 15-16, 44-46, 139-40, 163 (see also morality)
Churchill, Winston, 74, 304
city busting (see bombing, World War II conventional)
civil war (see counterinsurgency; revolutionary war)
civilian supremacy, 223-24, 241
civilians (see noncombatants)
civilians convention, Geneva (1949) (see Geneva Convention Relative to the Protection of Civilian Persons in Time of War)
Clark, Mark, 247
Claude, Inis L., Jr., 371n
Clausewitz, Karl von, 3, 209
Close, Robert, 395n
Colby, William, 428n
collateral damage, 81-82, 100, 184, 340-41 (see also double effect; proportion)
collective security, 1, 22-23, 143, 209; and limited war, 213-15, 231, 235-36
collective self-defense (see self-defense, collective)
command responsibility, 9, 39-40, 67, 122, 302, 315-19, 358-59; principles of, 319-24; and reporting violations, 325-28
communication between belligerents: in Korean War, 244-45, 261-62; and limited-war guidelines, 228, 349-50; in Vietnam

War, 261-63; in Yom Kippur War, 280-81

communism, threats of, 21, 211-12, 252, 270

Communist Chinese (see China, People's Republic of)

competent authority, 16-18, 129, 142, 332-33; in Korean War, 87; and revolutionary/counterinsurgency war, 158-62, 333-34; in Vietnam War, 91, 97; in World War II, 72

conduct of war (see jus in bello; just-war doctrine)

containment, 88, 211-13, 270

conventional war, 17, 127; just-war limits on, 142-53

Cooper, Chester, 428n

counterforce warfare, 43, 47, 341; and nuclear war, 128, 135, 139, 343 (see also countervalue warfare)

counterinsurgency, 47, 111, 127, 147, 220; dilemmas of, 202-3; and jus ad bellum, 154-74, 333-34; and jus in bello, 175-203, 346; and Vietnam War, 275-76

countervalue warfare, 47-48, 280-81; and nuclear war, 128, 135, 137-38, 343-44; in World War II, 77-78, 80-81, 83, 303-5, 341 (see also counterforce warfare)

crimes against humanity (see genocide)

crop destruction, 60, 104, 108-9, 146-47, 198 (see also chemical warfare)

Cuba, 133, 174, 212-13, 229, 268

D'Amato, Anthony A., 390n

Declaration of Sixteen (1953), 247

defense (see collective security; self-defense)

defoliation, 108, 110, 115, 117 (see also chemical warfare; Vietnam War)

Deitchman, Seymour J., 222

de la Brière, Yves, 373-74n

Dinitz, Simcha, 290

discrimination: as absolute principle, 44-47; and atomic bombing, 85-87; and command responsibility, 320-21; and conventional war, 144-47; and grave offenses, 61-62; historical origins of, 42-43; in international law, 49-55; and just-war doctrine, 338-41; and nuclear war, 130, 137-41, 343-44; and proportion related, 42, 45, 47, 81-83, 85-86, 338-39, 340-41, 343-44; and revolutionary/counterinsurgency war, 179-82, 184, 345; and scorched-earth policy, 148-49; and terrorism, 195; United States Air Force manual on, 52-54; and Vietnam War, 100-1, 103-4, 108-10, 121-24, 311; and World War II, 79, 82-84, 304

Dobrynin, Anatoly F., 282

Dominican Republic civil war (1965), 174, 268, 337, 351, 355

domino theory, 21, 92, 212-13

double effect, 44, 46-47, 83, 340-41 (see also collateral damage; proportion)

Dougherty, James E., 366n

Douhet, Guilio, 80

Draper, G. I. A. D., 408n

Dresden, 82, 145, 304

Dulles, John Foster, 7, 238

Eaker, Ira C., 385n

ecocide, 108, 110 (see also chemical warfare; Vietnam War)

economy of force, 65, 228, 349; and Korean War, 243–44, 261; and proportion related, 225–27; in Vietnam War, 261, 311; in Yom Kippur War, 279–80

Egypt, 133; and Third Army, 281, 284, 292–93, 295, 354; and Yom Kippur War, 277–98

Eisenhower, Dwight D. , 212, 219, 247, 254, 355, 387n, 422n

Elbe, Joachim von, 366n

England (see Britain, and World War II)

Eppstein, John, 364n

escalation, 7, 119–20, 127–29, 134, 136–37, 262

Falk, Richard A. , 391n, 409–10n

fallout (see radioactivity)

Feilchenfeld, Ernst H. , 373n, 375n

Feliciano, Florentino P. , 366n, 375n, 379n, 406n, 417n

Fierro, Alfredo, 405n

fight-and-negotiate strategy: in Korean War, 247, 253–54; and limited-war guidelines, 232–33, 236, 253–54; in Vietnam War, 259, 271–73; in Yom Kippur War, 289–94

firepower use, 144–45, 200; excessive, in Vietnam War, 98–102, 115, 117, 122–23, 310–11, 339

fire-storm bombing (see bombing, World War II conventional)

First Sinai Agreement (1974), 295–97

flexible response: in Korean War, 256; and limited-war guidelines, 233–34, 237, 354–56; in Vietnam War, 275–76; in Yom Kippur War, 298

food denial (see starvation)

Forbath, Peter, 428n

Ford, Gerald R. , 60, 107, 110, 271, 297

Ford, Harold P. , 396n

Forsythe, David P. , 391–93n, 404n, 410n

Free World, 88–89, 210–11, 217–18, 243, 253, 261

Friedmann, Wolfgang, 407n

Fuller, J. F. C. , 352

Galula, David, 408n

gas protocol, Geneva (1925) (see Geneva Protocol for the Prohibition of the Use in War of Asphyxiating, Poisonous, or Other Gases, and of Bacteriological Methods of Warfare)

gas warfare (see chemical warfare)

Gavin, James M. , 6, 219

Gelb, Leslie H. , 387n, 424–26n, 428n

Geneva Accords (1954), 274

Geneva conference (1973), 295–96

Geneva Conference on the Reaffirmation and Development of International Humanitarian Law Applicable in Armed Conflicts (1974–77), 160

Geneva Convention for Amelioration of the Condition of the Wounded, Sick and Shipwrecked Members of Armed Forces at Sea (1949), 61

Geneva Convention for the Amelioration of the Condition of the Wounded and Sick in Armed Forces in the Field (1949), 61

Geneva Convention on Prohibitions or Restrictions on the Use of Certain Conventional Weapons, Which May Be Deemed To Be Excessively Injurious or To Have Indiscriminate Effects (1980), 380–81n

Geneva Convention on the Prohibition of the Development, Production, and Stockpiling of Bacteriological (Biological) and Toxin Weapons and on Their Destruction (1972), 60

Geneva Convention Relative to the Protection of Civilian Persons in Time of War (1949), 50, 61, 63, 117, 192, 198-99

Geneva Convention Relative to the Treatment of Prisoners of War (1949), 61, 63, 111, 113, 150-52, 346

Geneva conventions (1949), 37, 38, 175, 182-85, 189-90, 194-95, 201, 312

Geneva Protocol I (1977) (see Protocol Additional to Geneva Conventions of 12 August 1949 and Relating to the Protection of Victims of International Armed Conflicts)

Geneva Protocol II (1977) (see Protocol Additional to the Geneva Conventions of 12 August 1949 and Relating to the Protection of Victims of Non-International Armed Conflicts

Geneva Protocol for the Prohibition of the Use in War of Asphyxiating, Poisonous, or Other Gases, and of Bacteriological Methods of Warfare (1925), 59-60, 84, 86, 105-8

genocide, 22, 73-74, 77, 173, 320, 338, 345; in international law, 56-58; in revolutionary/counterinsurgency war, 181-82

Genocide Convention (1951), 57, 182

geographic limits of war: in Korean War, 247-48; and limited-war guidelines, 230-31, 235, 351; in Vietnam War, 267; in Yom Kippur War, 285

Gerardmer case, 399 n

Germany, 39, 41, 80 (see also bombing, World War II conventional; World War II)

Gessert, Robert A., 446 n

Goldstein, Joseph, 375 n

Goldwater, Barry M., 258, 437 n

Goodman, Allan E., 428 n

Gould, Harvel L., 390 n

grave offenses, 61-62

Great Britain (see Britain, and World War II)

guerrilla warfare, 156, 180, 185, 188 (see also counterinsurgency; revolutionary war; terrorism)

Hague Convention II (1899), 196

Hague Convention IV Respecting the Laws and Customs of War on Land (1907), 37, 59, 86, 175, 185; and bombing, 53; and limited-war concept, 38; and prisoners of war, 63; and scorched-earth policy, 147-48

Haiphong, 120-22, 263-65, 273

Halberstam, David, 427 n

Halperin, Morton H., 222, 228, 422 n, 425 n

Hanoi, 97, 120-22, 263, 265, 273, 311-12

Hehir, J. Bryan, 377 n, 379 n, 446 n

herbicides (see chemical warfare)

High Command case (see United States v. von Leeb)

Hinton, Harold C., 422 n

Hiroshima (see bombing, World War II atomic)

Hitler, Adolph, 29, 73-75, 224, 348

Ho Chi Minh, 264

Holocaust, 58 (see also genocide)

Hostage case (see United States v. List)

hostages, 193-94
Howard, Michael, 227
Huber, Max, 375 n
Hughes, G. Philip, 394 n
humanity principle, and jus in
    bello, 23, 37, 52, 65, 67, 151,
    314
Hussein I, 296
Hyde, Charles Cheney, 365-66 n,
    412 n, 440 n

ICC (see International Control
    Commission)
ICCS (see international Commis-
    sion for Control and Supervision)
ICRC (see International Commit-
    tee of the Red Cross)
idealism, political, 208-10
Inchon, 242, 244, 258, 306
Indochina wars, 8, 120, 188 (see
    also Vietnam War)
International Commission for Con-
    trol and Supervision (ICCS), 274
International Committee of the
    Red Cross (ICRC), 63, 111, 150-
    53, 233, 255, 281, 313-14, 346
International Control Commission
    (ICC), 274
International Court of Justice, 32-
    33, 313
international law: and armed coer-
    cion, 23-25, 174, 214, 260, 336-
    37; and belligerent status, 185-
    87; and civil war, 158-62, 201,
    202; development of, 4-5; failure
    of, 1; and grave offenses, 61-62;
    and herbicide use, 108; and inter-
    vention, 168-70; jus in bello,
    provisions in, 64-70; as mode of
    limitation, 309, 311-14; and non-
    combatant immunity, 43; and
    nuclear weapons, 140-41; and
    prisoners of war, 63-64, 111;
    and starvation, 197-98; of state
    responsibility, 317-19

intervention, 88-89, 158-59, 165,
    167-74, 336-37
Ireland v. United Kingdom, 411 n
Israel, 21, 26, 133, 144; and Yom
    Kippur War, 277-98

Japan, 78 (see also bombing,
    World War II atomic; bombing,
    World War II conventional; World
    War II)
Jobert, Michel, 432 n
John XXIII, 16
Johnson, James T., 363-65 n,
    376 n
Johnson, Lyndon B., 17, 87, 91-
    92, 97, 213, 259, 266, 269-71,
    305-6, 333, 354-55, 424 n, 426-
    28 n
Johnstone, L. C., 391 n
Joint Chiefs of Staff, 306, 307,
    315
Jordan, 20, 285, 296
Joy, C. Turner, 241, 423 n
jus ad bellum (permissible re-
    course to war), 9, 13; and com-
    petent authority, 16-19; and con-
    ventional war, 142-44; judgmen-
    tal process of applying, 35-36;
    and jus in bello relation, 78,
    338-39; and just cause, 19-33;
    and Korean War, 87-90; and
    nuclear war, 127-34; and revo-
    lutionary/counterinsurgency war,
    154-74; and right intention, 33-
    35; and Vietnam War, 91-98; and
    World War II, 72-78; and Yom
    Kippur War, 286 (see also com-
    petent authority; jus in bello;
    just cause; just-war doctrine;
    right intention)
jus gentium (law of nations), 4, 5,
    13, 15 (see also international
    law)
jus in bello (just conduct of war),
    9, 13, 102, 309; and civil war,

110-11, 113, 117; and conventional war, 144-53; and jus ad bellum related, 78, 338-89; and law-of-war related, 64-67; and morality of war, 35; and nuclear war, 134-41; principles and prescriptions of, 37-63; and prisoners of war, 63-64; and reprisals, 67-70, 347; and revolutionary/counterinsurgency war, 18, 175-203, 346; and Vietnam War, 98-126; and World War II, 78-87 (see also discrimination; jus ad bellum; just-war doctrine; proportion)

jus naturale (natural law), 4, 5, 13, 15, 56, 67

just cause, 16, 19-22, 348; in Korean War, 87-90, 98; and nuclear war, 129; and peaceful remedies, exhaustion of, 31-33; and revolutionary/counterinsurgency war, 162-66; and self-defense, 142-43; and survival of a society, 334-36; in Vietnam War, 92-97; in World War II, 73-76, 98

just-war doctrine, 6-10, 125, 221; content of, 332-48; and conventional war, 142-53; implementation of guidelines of, 301-28; and Korean War, 87-90; and nuclear war, 127-40; and public conscience, 330-32; theological sources of, 1-5, 13-15; and World War II, 71-87 (see also jus ad bellum; jus in bello)

Karsten, Peter, 441 n
Keen, Maurice H., 365 n
Kegley, Charles W., Jr., 440 n
Kelly, J. B., 432 n
Kelsen, Hans, 371 n
Kennedy, John F., 355

Kester, John G., 439 n
Khrushchev, Nikita S., 281
Kilometer 101 Agreement (1973), 289, 293, 296
Kim Il Sung, 245
Kissinger, Henry A., 6, 222, 272-73, 281-82, 290-91, 295-97, 336, 388 n, 415-16 n, 424-25 n, 427-28 n, 438 n
Komer, Robert W., 428 n
Korea, 20-21, 212; unification of, 88-89, 242, 244 (see also Korean War)
Korean War, 8, 144, 306-7; communication between belligerents in, 244-45; and economy of force, 243-44; fight-and-negotiate strategy in, 253-54; and flexible response, 256; geographic limits of, 247-48; and just-war doctrine, 87-90; legal justification of, 248-50; limited mobilization in, 250; limited objectives of, 242-43; as limited war, 218-19, 257; nuclear weapons abstention in, 246-67; as police action, 214-15; and political primacy, 239-42; prisoners of war in, 151, 153; and psychological instrument, 251-52; superpower confrontation in, avoidance of, 245-46; third-party mediation in, 254-55
Kosygin, Alexsei N., 290-91
Kunz, Josef L., 366 n

Laos, 93, 122, 260, 267
Laqueur, Walter, 154, 432 n, 434 n
Lauterpacht, H., 379 n
Lavelle, John D., 122
League of Nations, 22, 31, 73, 209, 213-15
Lefever, Ernest W., 6, 209, 427 n

legal justification of war: and
  Korean War, 248-50; and Vietnam War, 267-68; and Yom Kippur War, 286-87
LeMay, Curtis, 121
Lemkin, Raphael, 56
Leninism, 19, 154-56
Levie, Howard S. , 400 n
Lewy, Guenter, 91, 314, 387-93 n,
  424 n, 427-28 n
Liddell Hart, B. H. , 352, 416 n
limited objectives: in Korean
  War, 242-43; and limited-war
  guidelines, 224-25, 349; in Vietnam War, 260-61; in Yom Kippur
  War, 279
limited war, 37; channels of limitation in, 314-28; 357-60; and
  counterinsurgency rise, 220;
  dilemmas of, 238-39; guidelines
  for, 222-37; and Korean War,
  218-19, 238-56; legal justifications for, 351-52; modes of limitation in, 301-14; as nuclear war
  alternative, 217-18; rules of conduct in, 228-33; and Vietnam
  War, 257-76; and Yom Kippur
  War, 277-98 (see also limited-
  war theory)
limited-war theory, 1-10, 221-22;
  as reaction to total war, 215-17;
  sources of, 207-21 (see also limited war)
List case (see United States v.
  List)
Littauer, Raphael, 393 n
London Sunday Times, 433 n

MacArthur, Douglas, 88, 219,
  224, 239-43, 247-48, 258, 306-
  7, 327, 348
McCarthy, James R. , 428 n
McCormick, Richard A. , 46,
  362 n

McDougal, Myres S. , 169, 226,
  366 n, 370 n, 373-75 n, 378-79 n,
  406 n, 417 n
McGovern, George, 272
McNamara, Robert S. , 306
MACV (see Military Assistance
  Command, Vietnam)
MAD (see mutual assured destruc-
  tion)
el Magdoub, Taha, 434 n
Malik, Jacob, 283
Manstein, Erich von, 147, 398 n
Maoism, 154-56
Mao Tse-tung, 117, 264
Marshall, Burke, 375 n
Marshall, George C. , 327
Marshall, S. L. A. , 423 n
Martin, Laurence, 415 n
Marxism, 154-56, 336
means mala in se (prohibited
  means), 56-58, 67 (see also
  genocide)
means mala prohibita (prohibited
  means), 56, 59-62, 106, 140,
  182-201, 345-46
Medina case (see United States v.
  Medina)
Meir, Golda, 297
Messner, Johannes, 367 n
Meyrowitz, Henri, 392 n, 490 n
Middle East, 142, 144, 222 (see
  also Yom Kippur War)
Military Assistance Command,
  Vietnam (MACV), 100, 310-11
military necessity, 85, 148; and
  economy of force, 226-28; and
  jus in bello requirements, 37,
  64-65; legitimate, 46, 66-67;
  in revolutionary/counterinsur-
  gency war, 177-79, 202-3; and
  torture, 189-90 (see also proportion, in jus in bello)
mobilization, 49, 216, 250, 269,
  287; and limited-war guidelines,
  231-32, 236, 352

modes of limitation, 9, 303-8, 357-59

momentum theory, 212-13

Moore, John Bassett, 365 n

morality: and chemical warfare, 149-50; and command responsibility, 318-19, and discrimination, 42-46; and just war, 2-3, 5-6, 15, 38, 330, 340-41, 351-52, 357, 360; and means mala in se, 56; and nuclear war, 140, 342-43; and proportion, 28-31; and reprisals, 69-70; and right intention, 34-35 (see also Christian teaching on war)

Morgenthau, Hans A., 6, 209

Moscow agreement (1973), 291

Murray, John Courtney, 5, 6, 14, 28-31, 139, 335, 364-65 n, 368 n, 416 n

Murray, Thomas E., 6

mutual assured destruction (MAD), 138-39, 341-43, 355

My Lai massacre, 41, 115, 310, 317 (see also command responsibility; search-and-destroy missions; United States v. Calley)

Nagasaki (see bombing, World War II atomic)

napalm, 59, 98, 123, 104-5 (see also chemical warfare; Vietnam War)

Nasser, Gamal Abdel, 133, 294

National Security Council, 306

national security studies, 210

NATO (see North Atlantic Treaty Organization)

natural law, 4, 5, 13, 15, 56, 67

negotiations: in Korean War, 253-54; in Vietnam War, 271-74; in Yom Kippur War, 290-98 (see also fight-and-negotiate strategy; third-party mediation)

Neuhaus, Richard J., 404 n

Neutral Nations Repatriation Commission, 255

Niebuhr, Reinhold, 6, 209

Nixon, Richard M., 95, 97, 110, 122, 260, 267, 269, 271-73, 282-84, 297, 311, 351

noncombatants, 63, 123, 137, 182; and bombing, World War II, 81, 85; and chemical warfare, Vietnam War, 106-7; and discrimination principle, 42-55; and firepower use, Vietnam War, 98-101; protection of, history of, 48-49; repressive measures against, in Vietnam War, 115-18; and revolutionary/counterinsurgency war, 170, 180-81, 183-84, 188, 192-93, 195-97; and search-and-destroy missions, Vietnam War, 103-4; and scorched-earth policy, 148; and starvation, 109, 197-98 (see also discrimination)

nonintervention (see intervention)

nonmilitary targets, 42-43, 48-49, 81, 85 (see also noncombatants)

North Atlantic Treaty Organization (NATO), 8, 128, 308, 316; collective-defense concept of, 142-43; 214-15; and economy of force, Korean War, 243, 246; and limited-war defense of, 344-45; and nuclear war, 229-30, 284

nuclear deterrence (see nuclear war)

nuclear fallout (see radioactivity)

nuclear nonproliferation treaty, 141

nuclear war, 3, 7, 25, 343; and discrimination, 87, 341; and first-use, 131-32, 235; just-war limits on, 127-40, 342, 344; and Korean War, 243, 246-47;

limited war as alternative to,
217-18; and radioactivity, 85-86;
and rules of conflict, 141, 229-
30; and Vietnam War, 265-66;
and Yom Kippur War, 284
Nuremberg International Military
Tribunal (see Nuremberg trials)
Nuremberg trials, 39, 41, 56, 84,
148, 194, 317, 322-23, 356 (see
also war crimes trials)

OAS (see Organization of Ameri-
can States)
O'Ballance, Edgar O. , 433n
Oberdorfer, Don, 427n
O'Brien, William V. , 191, 356,
372n, 375-76n, 378n, 385-86n
O'Connell, D. P. , 427n
O'Connor, John J. , 362n, 389n
occupation, 63-64, 76-78
Ohlendorf case (see United States
v. Ohlendorf)
Organization of American States
(OAS), 170, 316, 337, 351
Osgood, Robert E. , 6, 222, 225,
227, 349, 387n, 414-16n, 424n,
428n

pacification, 103, 157
pacifism, 8, 44, 340
Panama, 179
Panama Canal treaties and agreements (1977-79), 172
Paret, Peter, 408n
Paris Peace Agreement (1973),
95-96, 273-74
Parks, William Hays, 323, 438n,
441n
Paul VI, 2
Paust, Jordan J. , 445n
peaceful remedies, exhaustion of,
74 336; in Korean War, 90; and
nuclear war, 130; in revolutionary war, 165-66; in Vietnam War,
96-98; in World War II, 76

peaceful settlement of disputes,
1, 31-33
Pearl Harbor, 72, 76-77
Peers, William R. , 310, 312
permissible recourse to war (see
jus ad bellum)
Pfaltzgraff, Robert L. , Jr. , 366n
Phillipson, Coleman, 391n
pillage, 196
Pius XII, 28, 31, 44
political primacy, 319; and Korean
War, 239-42; and limited war,
223-24, 348-49; and Vietnam
War, 257-60; and Yom Kippur
War, 278
popes (see John XXIII; Paul VI;
Pius XII)
population displacement: and
counterinsurgency, 199-201; international-law restrictions on,
62, 117, 183, 198-99; in Vietnam
War, 101, 104, 115-18, 200
Potter, Ralph B. , 364n
PRC (see China, People's Republic of)
preemptive strikes, 131-33 (see
also self-defense)
prisoners of war, 144, 150-53,
182-83, 255, 346; international-
law protection of, 63-64, 111,
150; in Korean War, 253-54; in
revolutionary/counterinsurgency
war, 184-89; Vietnam War treatment of, 98, 110-14, 123
prisoners-of-war convention, Geneva (1949) (see Geneva Convention Relative to the Treatment of
Prisoners of War)
probability of success, 27, 30-31,
337-38; in Korean War, 89-90;
in nuclear war, 129-30; in revo-
lutionary/counterinsurgency war,
165; in Vietnam War, 93-95, 97-
98; in World War II, 74, 76

prohibited means, 37, 55-56 (see also means mala in se; means mala prohibita)

propaganda (see psychological instrument)

proportion: in jus ad bellum, 27, 36 [and jus in bello related, 38-42, 84-85, 119, 339; and moral values, 28-30; and nuclear war, 25, 129-32; and revolutionary war, 163-65; and Vietnam War, 93-96; and World War II, 73-75]; in jus in bello, 37-42, 144, 147, 344-45 [and atomic bombing of Japan, 84-87; and bombing of North Vietnam, 119-20; and bombing, World War II, 79, 81-83, 145, 304; and command responsibility, 319-20; and discrimination related, 42, 45, 47, 81-83, 85-86, 338-39, 340-41, 343-44; and economy-of-force related, 225-27, 349; and jus ad bellum related, 38-42, 84-85, 119, 339; and just-war doctrine, 338-39, 341; and Korean War, 88-89; and limited-war guidelines, 227-58; and military necessity, 65; and nuclear war, 134-37, 139; and reasonableness norm, 41-42; and revolutionary/counterinsurgency war, 177-79, 345; and scorched-earth policy, 148; and superfluous suffering, 59; and torture, 190; and Vietnam War, 100-1, 103-4, 107, 108-10, 122-24, 261, 311]

Protocol Additional to Geneva Conventions of 12 August 1949 and Relating to the Protection of Victims of International Armed Conflicts (Protocol I, 1977), 37, 61-63, 162, 176, 182-83, 185-87; and civilian protection, 49-51, 183; and discrimination principle, 52, 54-55; and limited-war concept, 38; and reprisals, 69, 202; and starvation, 147, 197-98; and torture, 189-90

Protocol Additional to the Geneva Conventions of 12 August 1949 and Relating to the Protection of Victims of Non-International Armed Conflicts (Protocol II, 1977), 37, 62, 160-62, 175-76, 181-84, 189, 200, 201; and belligerent status, 185-87; and collective punishments, 192-93; and hostages, 194; and slavery, 196; and starvation, 51, 147, 197-98; and terrorism, 195; and torture, 190

psychological instrument: in Korean War, 251-52, 270; and limited-war guidelines, 232, 236-37, 352-53; in total war, 216; in Vietnam War, 270-71; in Yom Kippur War, 288-89

public opinion, 9, 10, 92-93, 97 (see also psychological instrument)

Quandt, William B., 435n

Rabin, Itzhak, 297

radioactivity, 84-86, 129, 134, 136-37 (see also bombing, World War II atomic; nuclear war)

RAF (see Royal Air Force)

raison d'état (strategic/political goal), 339; and nuclear war, 131, 134; and proportion, 27, 38, 42; and revolutionary war, 179; and Vietnam War, 119-20; and World War II, 73, 76, 84

raison de guerre (tactical/military goal), 339; and nuclear war, 134; and proportion, 39, 42; and Vietnam War, 119-20; and World War II, 76, 84

Ramcke, Hermann, 399n
Ramsey, Paul, 44-45, 138, 332,
  335, 363n, 376-79n, 396-97n,
  405n, 409n, 445-46n
Rayfield, Robert E., 428n
Reagan, Ronald W., 331
realism, political, 208-10
Rees, David, 423n
refugees (see population displacement)
Reich, Bernard, 434n
Rendulic, Lothar, 147-48, 323,
  398n
reprisals, 51, 115, 152, 347; in
  jus ad bellum, 24-27; in jus in
  bello, 67-69; in revolutionary/
  counterinsurgency war, 180,
  201-3
revolutionary war, 47, 111, 127,
  154-57, 175, 335-36, 346; and
  competent authority, 17-19, 158-
  62, 333-34; dilemmas of, 202-3;
  and discrimination, 179-81; and
  foreign intervention, 167-74;
  and genocide, 181-82; and just
  cause, 162-66; and means mala
  prohibita, 182-201; and proportion, 177-79; and reprisals,
  201-3
Rhee, Syngman, 90, 255
Ridgway, Matthew B., 219, 241,
  306, 326-27, 422-23n
right intention, 338; and conventional war, 144; in jus ad bellum,
  16, 33-35; in Korean War, 90;
  and nuclear war, 130-31; and
  revolutionary/counterinsurgency
  war, 166; in Vietnam War, 97-
  98; in World War II, 76-78, 304
Rommen, Heinrich A., 4, 364n,
  367n, 404n
Roosevelt, Franklin Delano, 72,
  74, 304
Rosenau, James N., 167, 169,
  172, 406n

Rousseau, Jean Jacques, 168
Rousseau-Portalis doctrine, 43,
  48
Royal Air Force (RAF), 81, 303-5
rules of conflict, 228-33, 235
rules of engagement, 309-12
Rusk, Dean, 97, 213, 270

Sachar, Howard M., 280, 434n
Sadat, Anwar el, 278, 282, 288,
  291, 294-97
Safran, Nadav, 431n, 434n
Saint Petersburg Declaration
  (1868), 59
sanctuaries, 230, 248, 267
San Francisco Conference (1945),
  209
Schelling, Thomas C., 141, 228,
  262, 350, 419n, 425n
Schlesinger, James R., 342,
  395-96n
Schwartz, Jack, 375n
Schwarzenberger, Georg, 385n
scorched-earth policy, 144, 147-
  49, 323
search-and-destroy missions, 93,
  98, 102-4, 115, 122-23, 200,
  305, 308 (see also Vietnam War)
SEATO (see Southeast Asia
  Treaty Organization)
Second Sinai Agreement (1975),
  295, 297
self-defense, 21-22, 24, 26, 45,
  143, 173; collective, 24, 337,
  352 [in Korean War, 88, 97,
  248-49; and limited war, 213-15;
  and NATO, 142-43; in Vietnam
  War, 93, 96, 267-68; in World
  War II, 73]; and just cause, 142-
  43; in nuclear war, 129-34; in
  revolutionary war, 159-60; in
  Six-Day War, 286; in United Nations Charter (Article 51), 23,
  25, 174, 336; in Vietnam War,
  92; in World War II, 72-73

Servan-Schreiber, Jean Jacques, 409 n
Sharon, Ariel "Arik," 278, 290
Shawcross, Hartley, 56
Shawcross, William, 425 n, 427 n
Sherman, William T. , 216
Shinn, Roger, 364 n
Sihanouk, Norodom, 260, 268
Sisco, Joseph J. , 295
Six-Day War, 26, 133, 142, 261, 281, 286
slavery, 196
Southeast Asia, 92-93, 212, 265, 270 (see also Vietnam War)
Southeast Asia Treaty Organization (SEATO), 268, 286, 351
Soviet Union, 20-21, 29, 88, 141, 211-13, 281, 350; and chemical warfare, 60, 149, 346; and Korean War, 89, 240, 245-46; and naval power, 222; as nuclear power, 128-29; and Vietnam War, 122, 264-65; and World War II, 74-75; and Yom Kippur War, 282-84, 290-95
starvation, 51, 62, 108-9, 146-47, 183, 197-98
Stimson, Henry L. , 85
Stone, Julius, 371-72 n, 383 n
strategic bombing (see bombing)
Suarez, Francisco, 372 n, 374 n, 378 n
Suez City, 292, 295
superfluous suffering principle, 85, 104-5
superpower confrontation, avoidance of, 229, 235; in Korean War, 240, 245-46; in Vietnam War, 260, 264-65; in Yom Kippur War, 281-84, 292, 294, 350
supply routes, interdiction of, 264-66
Syria, 21, 151, 277, 279-80, 282, 285-87, 290-91, 296, 346 (see also Yom Kippur War)

Tanham, George, 408 n
Taubenfeld, Howard J. , 413 n
Taylor, Maxwell D. , 219
terrorism, 17-19, 68, 161, 183, 194-95
Tet offensive, 94, 259
theology (see Christian teaching on war)
third-party mediation: in Korean War, 254-55; as limited-war guideline, 233, 236-37, 354; in Vietnam War, 271-74; in Yom Kippur War, 294-98
Third World, 21, 92, 175, 217, 222, 249, 286
Thomas, A. J. , Jr. , 399 n
Thomas, Ann Van Wynen, 399 n
Thompson, Kenneth W. , 6, 209
Tiran, Straits of, 261
Tonkin Gulf Resolution, 269
torture, 112-13, 152, 183, 189-92
Torture, Comité des Experts sur la, 190-91
total war, 3, 6-7, 43, 74, 80, 207-8, 216-17, 234
Treaty on the Non-Proliferation of Nuclear Weapons (1968), 141
Trenchard, Hugh, 303
Truman, Harry S. , 85, 211, 239-43, 246, 250, 307, 333, 348, 354
Tucker, Robert W. , 29-30, 44-45, 339-40, 364 n, 371 n, 373-74 n, 376-78 n, 386 n, 446 n

UN (see United Nations)
unconditional surrender, 74-78, 224, 349
United Kingdom (see Britain, and World War II)
United Nations, 31, 33; and collective security system, 213-15; and collective self-defense, Vietnam War, 268; declining role of, 336-37; formation of, 76, 78; and

Korean War, role in, 231, 242, 248-50, 255; and Middle East wars, role in, 133, 283, 291-92, 294-98; and Uniting for Peace Resolution (1950), 248, 268

United Nations Charter, 89, 92; Article 2(4) (use of armed force), 22, 159, 336-37; Article 51 (self-defense), 23, 25, 92, 97, 159, 336; intervention in Korea, basis for, 88; on self-determination, 168; as social contract, 24

United States: and channels of limitation, 314-15; and chemical warfare, 60, 105-8; containment policy of, 211-13; and international-law training requirement for military, 312-13; Korean War, and just-war doctrine of, 87-90; on mutual assured destruction (MAD), 138; as nuclear power, 128-29; and Panama Canal treaties and agreements, 172; and Strategic Bombing Surveys, 80; and United Nations, 78, 249; and Vietnam War, 98-126; and War Powers Resolution (1973), 92, 332-33; and World War II, just-war record in, 78-87; and Yom Kippur War, 283-84, 291, 293-98

United States Air Force, 151, 304-5; manuals of, 52-54, 60-61, 64-69, 81, 138, 226-27

United States Army, 219-20; manuals of, 67, 226-27

United States v. Calley, 9, 41, 324, 358

United States v. List, 41, 148, 194, 321-23

United States v. Medina, 324

United States v. Ohlendorf, 67, 68

United States v. von Leeb, 321, 322, 398-99 n

Uphoff, Norman, 393 n

USSR (see Soviet Union)

Vanderpol, Alfred, 372-76 n

Van Fleet, James, 241

Vatican II, 1-4, 44

Vattell, Emerich de, 168

Verwey, Wil D., 391 n

Vietcong, 58, 94-95, 99-100, 103, 111, 259 (see also Vietnam War)

Vietnam, 21, 212 (see also Vietnam War)

Vietnam War, 8, 9, 17, 60, 112, 141, 330; and bombing of North Vietnam, 119-26; communication between belligerents in, 261-63; and economy of force, 261; fight-and-negotiate strategy in, 271-73; firepower use in, 98-102, 144, 310-11; and flexible response; 275-76; and genocide charge, 58; and just cause, 92-97; legality of, 91-93, 267-68; limited mobilization in, 269; limited objectives of, 260-61; military directives of, 305-6, 308; nuclear weapons abstention in, 265-66; and Paris peace settlement (1973), 95-96; and political primacy, 257-60; population displacement in, 116-18; and prisoners of war, 110-14, 151; and psychological instrument, 270-71; search-and-destroy missions in, 102-4; superpower confrontation in, avoidance of, 264-65; third-party mediation in, 274

Vitoria, Francisco de, 378

von Leeb case (see United States v. von Leeb

Wakin, Malham M. 441 n

Waldheim, Kurt, 296

Waldock, C. H. M., 371n
Walters, LeRoy, 364-65n
Walzer, Michael, 23, 46-47, 137, 158, 216, 365n, 376-78n, 396n, 407n, 412n
war: approaches to, 1-3; declarations of, 18, 72, 129, 269, 333; moral judging of, 331-32
war crimes, 76-77, 102, 112-13, 324 (see also genocide; Nuremberg trials; war crimes trials)
war crimes trials, 39, 41, 57, 67, 84, 325; and command responsibility, 321-23; and scorched-earth policy, 147-48; and Vietnam War, 112-13, 116, 324 (see also Nuremberg trials)
War of Attrition, 281-82
War Powers Resolution (1973), 92, 332-33
Warsaw Pact, 128, 142, 308, 346
weapons treaty, Geneva (1980) (see Geneva Convention on Prohibitions or Restrictions on the Use of Certain Conventional Weapons, Which May Be Deemed To Be Excessively Injurious or To Have Indiscriminate Effects)
Weber, Theodore, 364n
Webster, Daniel, 132
Western Europe (see North Atlantic Treaty Organization)
Westmoreland, William C., 258-59, 266, 305-8, 350, 424n, 426n
Wheeler, Earle G., 266

Whetten, Lawrence L., 434n
Wilson, Woodrow, 209, 224
Winters, Francis X., 396n
Wittkopf, Eugene R., 440n
Woods, Larry D., 390n
World War I, 48-49, 69, 86, 144, 146-47, 207-9, 347
World War II, 9, 39, 49, 74, 147-48, 207, 216-17 (see also bombing, World War II)

Yalu River, 244-45, 248, 306-7
Yamashita, in re, 321-22
Yariv, Aharon, 281
Yoder, John, 332, 445n
Yom Kippur War, 142, 277; communication between belligerents in, 280-81; and economy of force, 279-80; fight-and-negotiate strategy in, 289-94; fire-power use in, 144-45; and flexible response, 298; geographic limits of, 285; legal justification of, 285-87; limited mobilization in, 287; limited objectives of, 279; nuclear weapons abstention in, 284; and political primacy, 278; and prisoners of war, 151; and psychological instrument, 288-89, 353; superpower confrontation in, limited, 281-84, 292, 294, 350; third-party mediation in, 294-98

Zohdy, Mohammed Dia El Din, 434n

ABOUT THE AUTHOR

William V. O'Brien is professor of government at Georgetown University, Washington, D.C. He has been on the faculty at Georgetown University since 1950. O'Brien was chairman of Georgetown's Institute of World Policy, 1956 to 1974, and chairman of the Department of Government from 1974 to 1977.

Professor O'Brien is the author of <u>War and/or Survival</u> (1969), <u>Nuclear War, Deterrence and Morality</u> (1967), and numerous other books and articles dealing with issues of international law and morality and national security questions.

Doctor O'Brien holds the degrees of B.S. (Foreign Service), M.S. (Foreign Service), and Ph.D. from Georgetown University.